Redefining Independent Learning With AI Agents

Momina Shaheen
https://orcid.org/0000-0001-9424-9787
University of Roehampton, UK

Jay Kumar Pandey
https://orcid.org/0000-0003-4086-5730
Shri Ramswaroop Memorial University, India

Faizan Ahmad
Department of Computer Science & Digital Technologies, University of East London, UK

Jawad Rasheed
https://orcid.org/0000-0003-3761-1641
IClean Energy Technologies Institute, Yıldız Technical University, Istanbul, Turkey

Maqbool Khan
https://orcid.org/0000-0001-7656-0184
American University of Bahrain, Bahrain

IGI Global
Scientific Publishing
Publishing Tomorrow's Research Today

Vice President of Editorial	Melissa Wagner
Director of Acquisitions	Mikaela Felty
Director of Book Development	Jocelynn Hessler
Production Manager	Mike Brehm
Cover Design	Jose Rosado

Published in the United States of America by
IGI Global Scientific Publishing
701 East Chocolate Avenue
Hershey, PA, 17033, USA
Tel: 717-533-8845 | Fax: 717-533-7115
Website: https://www.igi-global.com E-mail: cust@igi-global.com

Library of Congress Cataloging-in-Publication Data

Names: Shaheen, Momina, 1993- editor | Pandey, Jay Kumar, 1987- editor | Ahmad, Faizan, 1988- editor | Rasheed, Jawad, 1987- editor | Khan, Maqbool, 1982- editor
Title: Redefining independent learning with AI agents / Momina Shaheen, Jay Kumar Pandey, Faizan Ahmad, Jawad Rasheed, Maqbool Khan.
Description: Hershey, PA : IGI Global Scientific Publishing, [2027] | Includes bibliographical references and index. | Summary: "This book examines how AI agents are transforming independent learning by providing adaptive guidance, personalized feedback, and accessible support. Blending research, case studies, and practical models, it explores opportunities and challenges in creating intelligent, equitable, and meaningful learning experiences for autonomous learners of all ages"-- Provided by publisher.
Identifiers: LCCN 2026002361 (print) | LCCN 2026002362 (ebook) | ISBN 9798337372259 hardcover | ISBN 9798337372266 paperback | ISBN 9798337372273 ebook
Subjects: LCSH: Independent study | Artificial intelligence--Educational applications
Classification: LCC LB1049 .R43 2026 (print) | LCC LB1049 (ebook)
LC record available at https://lccn.loc.gov/2026002361
LC ebook record available at https://lccn.loc.gov/2026002362

British Cataloguing in Publication Data
A Cataloguing in Publication record for this book is available from the British Library.

Table of Contents

Detailed Table of Contents

act as cognitive prostheses and normative gatekeepers. Synthesising systems, activity-theoretical, and ecological perspectives, the chapter proposes typologies of AI mentors, pedagogy-first design principles, and governance matrices that foreground epistemic agency, capability expansion, and psychological wellbeing. It culminates in a global framework for scaffolded, inquiry-oriented, culturally sustaining, and autonomy-supportive AI mediation that is analytically rigorous, ethically reflexive, and operationally useful for educators, policy makers, technologists, and workforce professionals.

This chapter evaluates ways in which artificial intelligence (AI) agents are changing independent learning with regard to personalization, adaptive feedback, and learner autonomy. Constructivism, connectivism, and self-determination are referred to because they explain how cognitive, motivational, and engagement processes are mediated with the help of AI systems like chatbots, intelligent tutors, and adaptive learning platforms. Recent works and international case studies are harmonized to weigh the pros and cons of AI in education, including access democratization potential and bias, privacy, and automation over-reliance potential. Human-centered, transparent, and culturally responsive approaches are suggested with consideration of the ethical imbalance created by the excess of technological advancement. The chapter culminates with the stand, arguing education's future should be AI-augmented, not AI-dominated. Learning should be a partnership between people and AI systems, fostering a shared sense of creativity, empathy, and wisdom.

In order to provide readers with an overview of, and summarize, the content of the chapter, the purpose is stated as rethinking and exploring education in the age of Artificial Intelligence (AI) when considering from smartboards replacing chalkboards to what else? Against the background of redefining independent learning with AI agents, the chapter will e.g., discuss ethics, privacy, and governance in AI-powered education, as well as future research directions with regard to self-learning and AI companions.

This chapter argues that artificial intelligence (AI) offers a revolutionary opportunity to rethink outdated, standardised educational models as responsive, dynamic systems. Building on rethought pedagogy theories such as constructivism and cognitive learning, AI promises to enable the shift from static learning pathways to dynamic mapping and learning pathways. This chapter explores the development of AI-enhanced assessment and highlights how it has evolved from a summative process to an ongoing, more

This chapter examines how artificial intelligence (AI) is reshaping formative assessment in language education through a shift from retrospective feedback toward forward-oriented feedforward. Drawing on formative assessment, self-regulated learning, and feedback literacy research, it explores how AI-driven systems can generate timely, individualized guidance that supports learners in planning, monitoring, and revising their work across tasks. AI is situated within a sociocultural understanding of learning and conceptualized as a scaffold that operates alongside teachers rather than as a replacement for professional judgement. The chapter addresses pedagogical and ethical challenges related to automation, trust, equity, and algorithmic bias, with particular attention to language-specific concerns. Practical recommendations are presented for integrating AI within hybrid feedback models that preserve dialogue, strengthen feedback literacy, and sustain formative assessment as a genuinely developmental practice.

AI gamification, virtual reality, and immersive agents converge to transform independent learning by increasing motivation, personalization, and transfer of skills. Adaptive game mechanics use learner models and reinforcement signals to tailor challenges, feedback, and rewards that sustain engagement and scaffold mastery. VR situates practice in high-fidelity, embodied contexts that enhance spatial reasoning, situational judgment, and procedural fluency through deliberate practice and contextualized feedback. Immersive agents, conversational, multimodal tutors and peers provide coaching, prompts, and personalized remediation while modelling expert strategies and supporting metacognitive reflection. When designed with universal design principles, ethical data governance, and clear learning objectives, this triad supports autonomy, deep learning, and measurable outcomes for diverse independent learners.

The notion of gamification has emerged as a promising approach for reshaping educational environments. The integration of gamification with immersive technologies such as augmented reality (AR), virtual reality (VR) and mixed reality (MR) to develop an interactive and engaging platforms for learners. In recent years, artificial intelligence (AI) agents have been prevalent in learning environments that can bring several advantages including personalization, predictive modelling and real-time adaptability. On the other hand, these agents can possess risks including technical implementation, computational and performance, privacy and security. ethical and social presence. In education literature, very limited studies have explored AI-based benefits and challenges in gamified immersive learning environments.

However, none of the studies found in the literature discuss the current trends of the use of AI agents and their potential risks. This chapter presents the current trends along with potential risks and future directions in gamified immersive learning environments.

This chapter explores how Artificial Intelligence (AI) agents can transform education by advancing accessibility and inclusion for diverse learners. Moving beyond personalization, AI is positioned as a tool to remove systemic barriers and create equitable learning opportunities for students with disabilities, multilingual learners, and those in under-resourced contexts. The chapter examines how AI technologies—such as adaptive learning systems, intelligent tutoring agents, and assistive interfaces—can support individualized learning pathways aligned with Universal Design for Learning (UDL) principles. It also addresses ethical challenges, emphasizing data equity, bias prevention, and responsible AI design. Through theoretical synthesis and case-based analysis, the chapter provides actionable frameworks and design guidelines for educators, policymakers, and developers. Ultimately, it argues that inclusive AI design is essential to achieving the broader vision of independent, equitable, and human-centered learning for all.

Systemic barriers like inequal access to education, affordability, gender, geography, disability, and language diversity have contributed to the entrenchment of educational inequalities in the developing and least developed countries. Such obstacles deny the marginalised learners the opportunity to participate fully in the education. This chapter explains the role of ethically constructed, low-cost, and context-sensitive artificial intelligence to personalize the learning experience and inclusivity in education by addressing all these overlapping obstacles. Basing its arguments on case studies, empirical research and policy analysis, it states that inclusive AI, when chosen to be implemented with fairness and community engagement, can help to facilitate equitable and accessible education. The chapter recommends collaboration by multiple stakeholders to make AI-based solutions respect the educational justice, inclusivity, and equity of every learner.

Artificial Intelligence (AI) is fundamentally transforming educational institutions, shifting from a teaching tool to a strategic driver of institutional transformation. This paper explores how AI necessitates a thorough

Preface

INTRODUCTION

Education has always evolved in response to technological innovation, societal needs, and expanding understandings of how people learn. From printed textbooks to digital classrooms, each advancement has broadened opportunities for knowledge acquisition while reshaping the roles of educators and learners alike. Today, artificial intelligence (AI) represents the next major milestone in this evolution, offering unprecedented opportunities to transform independent learning into a more personalized, adaptive, and engaging experience. Rather than replacing the learner or diminishing the importance of human guidance, AI agents have the potential to become intelligent collaborators that empower individuals to take greater ownership of their educational journeys.

Redefining Independent Learning With AI Agents was conceived to explore this transformative moment in education. As editors, we recognized the growing need for a comprehensive resource that examines both the theoretical foundations and practical applications of AI-driven learning systems. While AI technologies continue to advance rapidly, their successful integration into education depends upon thoughtful implementation, ethical consideration, and a clear understanding of how intelligent agents can complement—not replace—the cognitive, creative, and social dimensions of learning. This volume brings together diverse perspectives from researchers, educators, practitioners, and innovators who collectively examine how AI agents are redefining the nature of self-directed education across formal, informal, and lifelong learning environments.

Throughout this book, contributors investigate the capabilities of AI-powered agents to deliver personalized instruction, adaptive feedback, intelligent tutoring, and learner-centered support. The chapters demonstrate how these technologies enable learners to progress at their own pace while developing critical thinking, problem-solving abilities, creativity, and self-regulation. Beyond simply providing information, AI agents are presented as dynamic learning companions capable of responding to individual needs, facilitating engagement, and supporting continuous knowledge development across diverse educational contexts.

At the same time, this volume acknowledges that the adoption of AI in education raises important questions regarding ethics, privacy, transparency, governance, equity, and accessibility. As AI systems become increasingly embedded within learning environments, educators, institutions, developers, and policymakers must carefully balance technological innovation with responsible implementation. Several chapters critically examine these challenges, offering valuable insights into designing trustworthy AI systems that respect learner autonomy, protect personal data, minimize bias, and promote equitable educational opportunities for individuals from diverse socioeconomic, linguistic, and cognitive backgrounds.

A defining strength of this collection lies in its interdisciplinary perspective. The contributing authors draw upon expertise spanning artificial intelligence, educational technology, learning sciences, computer science, instructional design, policy studies, psychology, and human-computer interaction. Their combined scholarship illustrates that the future of AI-enhanced education requires collaboration across disciplines to ensure that technological advancement remains firmly grounded in sound pedagogical principles and human-centered design.

This reference work also demonstrates the broad applicability of AI agents beyond traditional classrooms. Readers will encounter discussions of intelligent tutoring systems, curriculum development, teacher support tools, workforce training, professional development, lifelong learning, inclusive education, and emerging educational technologies. Real-world case studies, conceptual frameworks, implementation models, and empirical research provide practical guidance for educators seeking to integrate AI into teaching and learning while offering researchers valuable directions for future investigation.

The intended readership reflects the wide-reaching impact of AI on contemporary education. This volume will serve educators, instructors, students, academic researchers, educational technologists, software developers, corporate learning professionals, and institutional leaders seeking to understand the opportunities presented by intelligent learning systems. It will also benefit policymakers, educational administrators, nonprofit organizations, entrepreneurs, parents, and technology enthusiasts interested in shaping the future of equitable, accessible, and responsible AI-enabled education.

As editors, we hope this book encourages readers to move beyond viewing artificial intelligence merely as an instructional technology and instead consider its broader role as a catalyst for reimagining independent learning. The future of education is unlikely to be defined solely by increasingly sophisticated algorithms, but by meaningful partnerships between human learners and intelligent systems that foster curiosity, creativity, critical thinking, and lifelong learning. AI agents possess remarkable potential to personalize educational experiences, expand access to quality learning, and empower individuals to become more autonomous learners. Realizing that potential, however, requires thoughtful leadership, interdisciplinary collaboration, and a steadfast commitment to ensuring that technological innovation serves the needs of learners first.

We extend our sincere appreciation to the contributing authors for sharing their expertise and research, to the reviewers for their thoughtful evaluations that strengthened each chapter, and to the publishing team whose guidance and support made this volume possible. We also thank the educators, researchers, developers, and learners whose continued exploration of AI in education inspires the conversations presented throughout this book.

It is our hope that *Redefining Independent Learning With AI Agents* serves not only as a comprehensive scholarly resource but also as a catalyst for future research, innovation, and responsible practice. As AI continues to reshape educational ecosystems around the world, we invite readers to engage critically with the ideas presented here and to contribute to building learning environments where intelligent technologies enhance human potential, promote lifelong learning, and empower every learner to thrive in an increasingly interconnected world.

ORGANIZATION OF THE BOOK

The volume opens by establishing the theoretical foundations necessary for understanding AI-enabled independent learning. Chapter 1 reconsiders classical learning theories—including constructivism, socio-cultural theory, and connectivism—through the lens of AI-mediated education. By proposing a co-evolutionary learning model that positions AI as an ethically governed learning partner, the chapter offers a human-centered framework that redefines the relationships among learners, intelligent systems, and educators while emphasizing agency, responsibility, and sustainable educational transformation.

Building upon this theoretical foundation, Chapter 2 provides a comprehensive introduction to AI agents, examining their underlying architectures, instructional functions, and evolving roles as mentors, collaborators, and assessors. The chapter balances the transformative potential of AI-driven personalization and learner autonomy with thoughtful discussions of ethical concerns, bias, dependency, and the importance of maintaining meaningful collaboration between AI systems and human educators.

Continuing the exploration of learner autonomy, Chapter 3 examines independent learning through the perspective of distributed cognition and human-AI co-regulation. The chapter reframes autonomy as a collaborative process occurring within interconnected learning ecologies, proposing governance frameworks, AI mentor typologies, and pedagogy-first design principles that promote learner agency, psychological well-being, cultural responsiveness, and ethical AI integration.

Chapter 4 presents a critical review of emerging educational pathways shaped by AI agents, synthesizing contemporary research and international case studies to evaluate both the opportunities and limitations of AI-supported independent learning. Drawing upon constructivism, connectivism, and self-determination theory, the chapter argues for an educational future where AI enhances rather than replaces human creativity, empathy, and collaborative learning.

Expanding the discussion beyond current practice, Chapter 5 reflects on the broader evolution of education in the age of artificial intelligence. Beginning with the technological transformations that have already reshaped classrooms, the chapter considers future possibilities for AI companions, self-directed learning, ethical governance, and privacy, encouraging readers to envision the next stage of educational innovation.

Shifting from theory to instructional practice, Chapter 6 explores how artificial intelligence is revolutionizing curriculum design and assessment. The contributors demonstrate how AI enables dynamic, personalized learning pathways and continuous formative assessment while emphasizing the importance of educator preparation, ethical governance, and international best practices that support equitable and inclusive educational transformation.

The practical implementation of AI mentorship is further illustrated in Chapter 7, which introduces intelligent digital mentors designed to strengthen student autonomy through adaptive learning systems. By integrating learning analytics, conversational AI, and adaptive dashboards into a functional prototype, the chapter demonstrates how AI can provide contextual guidance, personalized feedback, and ongoing support while complementing the essential role of educators.

Chapter 8 extends the discussion of AI mentorship by emphasizing trust, reflection, and emotional intelligence within self-directed learning. Introducing the Trust-Reflection Framework, the chapter explores how AI mentors can encourage metacognition, support reflective practice, and foster lifelong learning through transparent, empathetic, and ethically grounded interactions that strengthen rather than diminish learner independence.

Focusing on language education, Chapter 9 examines the evolution of formative assessment from traditional feedback toward forward-looking feedforward supported by artificial intelligence. The chapter demonstrates how AI-generated guidance can strengthen self-regulated learning, feedback literacy, and continuous improvement while preserving the indispensable role of teachers within collaborative assessment processes.

The following two chapters investigate the growing influence of immersive technologies on independent learning. Chapter 10 explores how gamification, virtual reality, and AI-powered immersive agents create engaging educational experiences that personalize learning, enhance motivation, and facilitate meaningful skill development through adaptive feedback and experiential learning environments. Complementing this discussion, Chapter 11 surveys current trends in AI-supported gamified learning while critically examining implementation challenges, privacy concerns, computational limitations, ethical considerations, and future directions for immersive educational technologies.

Accessibility and educational equity become the central focus of the next section. Chapter 12 demonstrates how AI agents can remove barriers to learning by supporting students with diverse abilities, multilingual backgrounds, and varied educational needs. Grounded in Universal Design for Learning principles, the chapter offers practical frameworks for designing inclusive, equitable, and human-centered AI learning environments that expand educational opportunities for all learners.

Extending these discussions into global contexts, Chapter 13 examines the transformative potential of AI within developing and least-developed countries. The chapter addresses persistent educational inequalities related to affordability, geography, disability, language, and gender while presenting ethically designed, context-sensitive AI solutions that promote educational justice through collaboration among educators, policymakers, communities, and technology developers.

Broadening the perspective from individual learners to institutional systems, Chapter 14 explores how artificial intelligence is reshaping educational organizations themselves. The chapter presents AI as a catalyst for institutional transformation, examining the governance structures, leadership strategies, ethical frameworks, and organizational cultures necessary to build sustainable, learner-centered educational ecosystems supported by intelligent technologies.

Complementing this institutional perspective, Chapter 15 showcases the development of a web-based adaptive learning system powered by conversational AI. Through an innovative prototype that combines machine learning, real-time analytics, and natural language interaction, the chapter demonstrates how intelligent systems can personalize instruction, foster learner engagement, and strengthen collaboration between students, educators, and AI agents within practical educational settings.

Recognizing that technological advancement must be accompanied by responsible implementation, Chapter 16 addresses the ethical, legal, and governance considerations surrounding AI-powered education. The contributors examine issues including data privacy, algorithmic transparency, fairness, accountability, and regulatory compliance, emphasizing the importance of establishing trustworthy frameworks that protect learners while enabling responsible innovation.

The volume concludes with Chapter 17, which explores the future of trust and credential verification in AI-supported education through blockchain technologies. By integrating decentralized identities, verifiable credentials, and content provenance standards, the chapter proposes a comprehensive trust architecture that safeguards learner achievements, protects privacy, and ensures the authenticity of AI-assisted educational credentials in increasingly digital and autonomous learning environments.

Collectively, these chapters provide a comprehensive examination of how AI agents are redefining independent learning across theoretical, pedagogical, technological, ethical, institutional, and societal dimensions. Together, they present a balanced vision in which artificial intelligence serves as a trusted educational partner—empowering learners, supporting educators, promoting inclusion, and advancing lifelong learning while reinforcing the enduring importance of human judgment, ethical responsibility, and meaningful educational relationships.

CONCLUDING REMARKS

As editors, we believe that the contributions presented in this volume demonstrate that the future of independent learning is not defined solely by technological advancement, but by the thoughtful integration of artificial intelligence into learner-centered educational ecosystems. Across diverse theoretical perspectives, empirical investigations, technological innovations, and practical applications, the chapters collectively reveal that AI agents have the capacity to become far more than intelligent tools—they can serve as collaborative learning partners that empower individuals to develop autonomy, critical thinking, creativity, and lifelong learning habits. At the same time, the authors consistently remind us that these opportunities must be pursued with careful attention to ethics, transparency, inclusivity, privacy, and human agency.

One of the defining themes that emerges throughout this book is the importance of maintaining a human-centered approach to AI-enabled education. Whether examining adaptive learning systems, intelligent digital mentors, immersive learning environments, inclusive educational design, institutional transformation, or trustworthy credentialing, the contributors emphasize that meaningful learning continues to depend upon reflection, collaboration, empathy, and sound pedagogical practice. Artificial intelligence should not replace educators or diminish the value of human interaction; rather, it should enhance the educational experience by providing personalized support, expanding access to knowledge, and enabling learners to take greater ownership of their educational journeys.

The breadth of perspectives represented in this collection also illustrates that redefining independent learning requires collaboration across disciplines. Researchers, educators, instructional designers, software developers, institutional leaders, and policymakers each have critical roles to play in shaping AI technologies that are equitable, transparent, and responsive to the diverse needs of learners worldwide. As AI capabilities continue to evolve, so too must our educational frameworks, governance models, and ethical standards to ensure that innovation remains aligned with the broader goals of educational excellence and social responsibility.

We hope that this volume serves as both a scholarly reference and a source of inspiration for future research, dialogue, and innovation. The questions surrounding AI-powered education are far from settled, and many opportunities remain to explore how intelligent systems can further support personalized learning, accessibility, assessment, collaboration, and lifelong professional development. It is our aspiration that the ideas presented throughout these chapters will encourage readers to critically examine existing practices, embrace emerging possibilities, and contribute to the responsible evolution of AI-enhanced education.

Ultimately, *Redefining Independent Learning With AI Agents* envisions a future in which human intelligence and artificial intelligence work in partnership to create richer, more inclusive, and more meaningful learning experiences. By embracing innovation while preserving the enduring values of education, we can build learning environments that empower individuals not only to acquire knowledge, but also to think independently, adapt confidently, and continue learning throughout their lives. We invite readers to engage with the insights presented in this volume and to participate in shaping an educational future where technology amplifies human potential and lifelong learning becomes more accessible to all.

Momina Shaheen
University of Roehampton, UK

Jay Kumar Pandey
Shri Ramswaroop Memorial University, India

Faizan Ahmad
Cardiff Metropolitan University, UK

Jawad Rasheed
Istanbul Sabahattin Zaim University, Turkey

Maqbool Khan
American University of Bahrain, Bahrain

Chapter 1
Reimagining Learning Theories in the Age of AI Agents:
From Constructivism to Connectivism

Ratan Sarkar
http://orcid.org/0009-0008-5480-0165
Tezpur University, India

ABSTRACT

The increasing integration of Artificial Intelligence (AI) in education is reshaping learning processes and challenging traditional understandings of cognition and pedagogy. This conceptual chapter re-examines Constructivism, Socio-cultural Theory, and Connectivism within AI-mediated learning environments. It explores how AI extends key learning principles while raising concerns related to agency, authority, and ethics. Addressing gaps in existing theories, the chapter proposes a co-evolutionary learning model that frames learning as interaction among human intentionality, algorithmic responsiveness, and ethical mediation. The model positions AI as a pedagogically governed partner rather than an autonomous educator, offering a human-centered framework to guide sustainable and ethical educational transformation.

1. INTRODUCTION

1.1 Background of the Study

The contemporary educational landscape is undergoing a profound transformation driven by rapid advances in Artificial Intelligence (AI) (Young, 2024). Unlike earlier digital technologies that functioned primarily as supplementary instructional tools, AI agents are increasingly emerging as *epistemic partners* within learning processes (Tilepbergenovna, 2024). These intelligent systems—capable of adaptation, prediction, and interaction—are beginning to participate actively in the construction, mediation, and organization of knowledge. As a result, learning is no longer confined to human cognition alone but unfolds through continuous interaction between learners and algorithmically driven environments (Patel et al., 2025).

This transformation has significantly altered traditional pedagogical arrangements. Education is progressively shifting from teacher-centered models toward AI-mediated and learner-driven forms of

DOI: 10.4018/979-8-3373-7225-9.ch001

engagement, where individuals navigate personalized learning pathways supported by intelligent systems (Sholeh, 2025). AI-powered platforms now facilitate self-paced exploration, real-time feedback, and adaptive scaffolding, enabling learners to exercise greater autonomy over their learning trajectories. In such environments, independent learning is increasingly shaped by algorithmic guidance as much as by human instruction (Ahamed, 2025).

The proliferation of adaptive tutoring systems, generative AI applications, recommender engines, and learning analytics has further intensified this shift. These technologies dynamically respond to learner behavior, analyze performance patterns, and curate content in ways previously unimaginable (Yadav et al., 2025). While such developments promise enhanced personalization and accessibility, they simultaneously challenge existing assumptions about how learning occurs, who controls knowledge, and how pedagogical responsibility is distributed in AI-enriched contexts.

1.2 Problem Statement

Despite the rapid institutional adoption of AI in education, prevailing learning theories remain largely rooted in cognitive and social conditions that predate intelligent systems (Chen et al., 2020). Classical theories such as Constructivism and Socio-cultural Theory were developed within human-centered learning environments, where cognition, interaction, and mediation were assumed to be exclusively human processes (Popenici & Kerr, 2017). Consequently, these frameworks offer limited explanatory power when learning is increasingly shaped by algorithmic decision-making, automated feedback, and data-driven personalization.

Existing pedagogical models struggle to account for learning situations in which AI agents actively influence the sequencing of content, the pacing of instruction, and the nature of learner engagement (Holstein et al., 2020). The absence of theoretical clarity has resulted in a disconnect between technological innovation and pedagogical understanding, often leading to the uncritical adoption of AI tools based on efficiency rather than educational purpose (Mørch & Andersen, 2023).

This misalignment raises critical concerns: How should learning be understood when cognition is partially distributed across human and machine systems? What pedagogical principles should guide AI-mediated learning environments? Without coherent theoretical alignment between AI functionalities and human learning processes, educational practice risks becoming technologically sophisticated yet pedagogically superficial.

1.3 Conceptual Gap

A significant conceptual gap exists in current educational discourse regarding the theoretical positioning of AI within learning processes. Constructivist theory emphasizes active meaning-making and learner agency but remains largely silent on the role of algorithmic mediation in shaping cognition (Levin et al., 2025). While it provides a strong foundation for understanding experiential learning, it does not sufficiently address environments where learning interactions are continuously filtered, shaped, and optimized by intelligent systems (Tabor, 2025).

Similarly, Socio-cultural Theory foregrounds the importance of social interaction, cultural tools, and mediated learning (Gajdamaschko, 2015). However, its traditional formulations presume mediation through human actors or symbolic artifacts, offering limited conceptual guidance for understanding AI agents that simulate interaction, provide automated scaffolding, and dynamically redefine the Zone of Proximal Development (Elvis, 2025).

Connectivism, in contrast, acknowledges the networked nature of knowledge and the role of digital technologies in learning. Yet, it often lacks a robust ethical and pedagogical framework, offering limited insight into questions of power, agency, values, and educational purpose (Şahin, 2012). As a result, none of these theories independently provides a comprehensive explanation of learning in AI-mediated environments.

This fragmentation highlights the need for an integrated theoretical perspective capable of reconciling human cognition, socio-cultural mediation, and algorithmic intelligence within a unified pedagogical framework.

2. NEED AND SIGNIFICANCE OF THE STUDY

2.1 Need of the Study

The accelerating incorporation of Artificial Intelligence (AI) into educational systems has generated unprecedented opportunities for personalization, automation, and scalability in learning (Bouchareb & GHEDIR, 2024). However, this rapid institutional adoption has largely outpaced the development of robust theoretical frameworks capable of guiding pedagogical decision-making (Salloum et al., 2024). In many educational contexts, AI technologies are being implemented pragmatically—driven by innovation agendas, market forces, and efficiency imperatives—rather than by coherent educational theory. This disconnect has created an urgent need to critically examine the pedagogical assumptions underpinning AI-mediated learning environments (Lameras, 2022).

A prominent concern lies in the growing emphasis on efficiency, optimization, and personalization, often framed through data analytics and algorithmic recommendation systems (Tanaka, 2025). While such approaches promise improved learning outcomes, they risk reducing education to a technical process of performance management, thereby marginalizing deeper pedagogical values such as critical reflection, dialogue, and meaning-making (Selwyn, 2019). Without theoretical grounding, personalization may become procedural rather than pedagogical, shaping what learners consume without adequately supporting how they think, inquire, and construct understanding.

Furthermore, the absence of theory-driven frameworks for AI-integrated curriculum design presents a significant challenge. Current curricular models rarely articulate how learning objectives, content organization, assessment practices, and learner autonomy should be reconceptualized when AI agents actively mediate instruction (Anbumaheshwari et al., 2025). As a result, AI is frequently appended to existing curricula rather than meaningfully embedded within a reimagined learning ecology.

The need for this study is further intensified by the growing reliance on AI to support independent and self-directed learning. Learners increasingly depend on intelligent systems for guidance, feedback, and knowledge navigation, often outside formal instructional settings. In such contexts, AI agents assume quasi-pedagogical roles traditionally occupied by teachers or peers. Yet, theoretical clarity regarding how such mediation aligns with established learning principles remains insufficiently developed. Addressing this gap is essential to ensure that AI-supported independence fosters genuine learner agency rather than algorithmic dependence.

2.2 Significance of the Study

a) Theoretical Significance

The study holds substantial theoretical significance by re-examining foundational learning theories within the epistemic conditions of the AI era (Niemi, 2021). It contributes to contemporary educational discourse by repositioning Constructivism, Socio-cultural Theory, and Connectivism as dynamic rather than static paradigms, capable of evolving in response to technological transformation (Baek et al., 2024). By integrating these perspectives, the study advances a synthesized theoretical understanding that captures learning as simultaneously cognitive, social, and networked.

In doing so, the chapter bridges fragmented theoretical traditions and offers a cohesive framework for interpreting AI-mediated learning (Oleet & Yu, 2025). This theoretical alignment strengthens the conceptual foundations of AI in education, moving beyond techno-deterministic narratives toward pedagogically informed interpretations of human–machine interaction.

b) Pedagogical Significance

From a pedagogical standpoint, the study provides conceptual guidance for designing AI-aligned teaching–learning processes that remain grounded in educational purpose (Machajewski, 2024). By articulating how AI agents can function as mediating artifacts rather than authoritative instructors, the framework supports pedagogies that emphasize learner agency, inquiry, and reflective engagement (Uden & Ching, 2024).

The chapter assists educators in reconceptualizing their roles—from transmitters of knowledge to designers of learning environments in which human judgment and algorithmic support coexist. Such clarity is particularly valuable in contexts of blended, online, and independent learning, where AI increasingly shapes learner experience.

c) Policy and Ethical Significance

The study also carries significant policy and ethical implications. As educational institutions and governments formulate strategies for AI adoption, there is an urgent need for theoretically informed governance frameworks. This chapter provides a conceptual basis for responsible AI integration by foregrounding principles of human agency, transparency, equity, and inclusion.

By situating AI within humanistic and socio-cultural traditions, the study challenges purely managerial or market-oriented approaches to educational technology. It emphasizes that decisions about AI in education are not merely technical choices but normative ones that shape learners' identities, opportunities, and futures.

d) Research Significance

In terms of research contribution, the chapter offers a foundational theoretical platform for future empirical investigations. The proposed conceptual synthesis can inform qualitative, quantitative, and mixed-method studies examining AI-supported learning practices across diverse contexts.

Moreover, the interdisciplinary orientation of the study encourages dialogue among scholars in education, learning sciences, artificial intelligence, philosophy, and ethics. By clarifying conceptual relationships between learning theories and AI agents, the study helps structure future research agendas aimed at understanding the evolving nature of learning in intelligent educational environments.

3. OBJECTIVES

The objectives of the present work are as follows

1. To critically examine the intersections of Constructivism, Socio-cultural Theory, and Connectivism in the context of AI-mediated learning.
2. To analyze how AI agents embody or extend core principles of contemporary learning theories.
3. To propose a theoretical framework for aligning AI-driven education with humanistic and socio-cultural values.
4. To explore implications for curriculum design, pedagogy, and assessment in AI-augmented learning environments.
5. To identify ethical and philosophical considerations necessary for sustainable integration of AI in education.

4. REVIEW OF LITERATURE (ROL)

4.1 Learning Theories in Education

Learning theories have long provided the conceptual foundations for understanding how knowledge is constructed, mediated, and internalized (Shuell, 2001). Among these, Constructivism, Socio-cultural Theory, and Connectivism represent major paradigmatic shifts in educational thought, each emphasizing distinct yet complementary dimensions of learning (Ku et al., 2015).

Constructivism, primarily associated with the works of Jean Piaget and Jerome Bruner, conceptualizes learning as an active process in which learners construct meaning through interaction with their environment (Sharma & Bansal, 2017). Piaget's cognitive constructivism emphasizes developmental stages and internal cognitive restructuring, while Bruner foregrounds discovery learning and the spiral organization of knowledge (Hoidn, 2016). These perspectives underscore learner agency, prior knowledge, and experiential engagement as central to learning processes. However, constructivist theory was developed within human-centered cognitive environments and offers limited explanation for contexts in which algorithmic systems actively influence learning pathways, feedback mechanisms, and content sequencing (Grubaugh et al., 2023).

Socio-cultural theory, articulated by Lev Vygotsky, extends constructivist thought by situating learning within social, cultural, and historical contexts (O'Connell, 2018). Central concepts such as mediation, cultural tools, and the Zone of Proximal Development (ZPD) emphasize the role of interaction and guided participation in cognitive development (Kozulin, 2015). From this perspective, learning is not merely individual but socially constituted. While socio-cultural theory provides powerful insights into mediated learning, its traditional formulations presume mediation through human actors or symbolic tools, leaving open questions about how non-human agents—such as AI systems capable of adaptive interaction—fit within this framework (Säljö, 2023).

Connectivism, proposed by George Siemens and Stephen Downes, responds to the challenges posed by digital knowledge environments. It conceptualizes learning as the ability to form and traverse networks across human and non-human nodes (Khatibi & Fouladchang, 2015). Knowledge, within this framework, is fluid, distributed, and continuously evolving (Glassner & Back, 2020). Connectivism offers an important lens for understanding learning in technologically saturated environments; however, critics argue that it often lacks sufficient pedagogical depth and ethical orientation. While it explains how knowledge flows, it provides limited guidance regarding educational values, agency, and meaning-making (Khatibi & Fouladchang, 2015).

Together, these theories illuminate different dimensions of learning but remain insufficient in isolation for explaining AI-mediated educational contexts.

4.2 Artificial Intelligence in Education

Research on Artificial Intelligence in education has expanded rapidly, focusing primarily on technological applications and instructional efficiency (He, 2024). Intelligent tutoring systems represent one of the earliest and most extensively studied applications, designed to simulate individualized instruction through adaptive feedback and learner modeling (Abinaya et al., 2024). These systems aim to replicate aspects of human tutoring by diagnosing learner misconceptions and adjusting instructional strategies accordingly.

Adaptive learning technologies further extend this approach by employing machine learning algorithms to personalize content, pacing, and assessment (Gligorea et al., 2023). Such systems promise enhanced engagement and improved learning outcomes by tailoring instruction to individual learner profiles (Dash & Bhoi, 2024). Complementing these technologies, learning analytics has emerged as a powerful tool for monitoring learner behavior, predicting performance, and informing instructional decisions.

While this body of literature demonstrates the functional potential of AI, much of it remains technocentric, emphasizing effectiveness, optimization, and scalability. Comparatively less attention is devoted to examining how these technologies align with established learning theories or reshape pedagogical relationships (Dash & Bhoi, 2024). As a result, AI is often framed as a solution-driven innovation rather than as a phenomenon requiring theoretical reinterpretation.

4.3 AI and Independent Learning

A growing strand of literature highlights the role of AI in supporting independent and self-directed learning (Delello et al., 2024). AI-powered systems enable learners to access knowledge autonomously, receive instant feedback, and navigate learning resources without constant teacher intervention. Such affordances are particularly significant in online, blended, and lifelong learning contexts (Juan & Nagappan, 2025).

Research suggests that AI can enhance learner autonomy by offering personalized scaffolding and adaptive guidance (Umar & Purwanto, 2025). However, concerns have emerged regarding the nature of this autonomy. Algorithmic scaffolding may inadvertently shape learner choices, constrain epistemic exploration, or foster dependency on automated recommendations (Deckker et al., 2025). Thus, while AI appears to support independence, it simultaneously redefines the conditions under which autonomy is exercised.

This paradox underscores the need to distinguish between pedagogical autonomy and algorithmic control—an issue that remains insufficiently theorized within existing literature.

4.4 Human–AI Collaboration in Learning

Recent scholarship increasingly conceptualizes AI not as a replacement for human intelligence but as a collaborator within learning processes (Niemi, 2021). The notion of augmented intelligence emphasizes complementarity, wherein AI enhances human cognition rather than supplanting it (Kayyali, 2025). Within this perspective, AI agents function as cognitive partners that support inquiry, reflection, and problem-solving.

Studies on human–AI collaboration highlight the potential for dialogic interaction, co-regulation, and shared decision-making between learners and intelligent systems (Ouariach et al., 2025). However, empirical findings also reveal tensions related to authority, trust, and transparency. When AI systems generate content or feedback, learners may attribute epistemic authority to machines, thereby altering traditional pedagogical relationships (Pushparani et al., 2025).

These dynamics raise critical questions about the distribution of agency within learning environments and the role of educators in mediating human–AI interaction.

4.5 Ethical and Governance Perspectives

Ethical considerations have become central to debates surrounding AI in education. Concerns regarding algorithmic bias highlight the risk of reinforcing existing social inequalities through data-driven systems (Vasile, 2023). Similarly, the increasing datafication of education—through continuous monitoring and analytics—raises issues of privacy, surveillance, and learner consent (Singh & Thakur, 2024).

Governance frameworks emphasize the need for transparency, accountability, and explainability in educational AI systems (Chaudhry et al., 2022). Scholars argue that without ethical oversight, AI may shift educational priorities toward performativity and measurement, undermining holistic developmental goals (Shashwat & Pundhir, 2025). Equity and access concerns further complicate the landscape, particularly in contexts marked by digital divides and socio-economic disparity.

These ethical debates underscore that AI integration is not merely a technical challenge but a normative and political one.

4.6 Research Gaps Identified

A critical synthesis of the existing literature reveals several unresolved conceptual limitations in current scholarship on AI-mediated learning. Although substantial research has explored learning theories and technological innovation independently, much of this work remains theoretically fragmented (Zhang & Aslan, 2021). Studies often examine constructivist, socio-cultural, or connectivist perspectives in isolation, resulting in partial explanations that fail to capture the complexity of learning environments shaped simultaneously by human cognition, social mediation, and algorithmic processes (Istrate, 2024).

Moreover, there is a noticeable absence of comprehensive theoretical models capable of integrating Constructivism, Socio-cultural Theory, and Connectivism within a unified framework responsive to AI-driven educational contexts. While each theory offers valuable insights, their lack of conceptual alignment has limited the development of coherent pedagogical explanations for learning mediated by intelligent systems (Han, 2025). Consequently, AI is frequently positioned either as a neutral instructional tool or as an external technological enhancement, rather than as an active participant in learning processes (Mørch & Andersen, 2023).

Another significant gap lies in the limited conceptual clarity surrounding the pedagogical role of AI agents (Xu & Ouyang, 2021). Existing literature oscillates between viewing AI as a supportive resource, a mediating artifacts, or an autonomous instructional entity, without adequately theorizing the implications of these roles for learner agency, cognition, and teacher responsibility (PAWAR & Das, 2023). This ambiguity has contributed to inconsistent pedagogical interpretations and uneven educational practices.

Furthermore, ethical discussions related to AI—such as concerns about algorithmic bias, surveillance, datafication, and equity—are often addressed in parallel to learning theory rather than being theoretically integrated within pedagogical frameworks. As a result, ethical considerations remain peripheral, treated as regulatory or technical issues rather than as foundational elements of educational design (Mishara, 2024).

Collectively, these gaps point to the urgent need for a theoretically grounded and integrative framework capable of conceptualizing learning as a hybrid phenomenon—one shaped through the dynamic interplay of human cognition, socio-cultural mediation, and algorithmic intelligence (Tanaka, 2025). Addressing this theoretical absence constitutes the central focus of the present chapter, which seeks to reconceptualize learning theories for the emerging epistemic conditions of the AI era.

5. METHODOLOGY

5.1 Nature of the Study

The present study adopts a conceptual and theoretical research orientation. Rather than seeking to generate empirical data, the chapter aims to develop a coherent theoretical understanding of learning in AI-mediated educational environments. Conceptual research is particularly appropriate in contexts characterized by rapid technological change, where existing theoretical models struggle to explain emerging pedagogical phenomena (Holmberg, 2017). By focusing on theory development and reinterpretation, the study seeks to clarify foundational assumptions, redefine conceptual relationships, and propose an integrative framework capable of guiding future research and practice.

5.2 Research Design

An analytical–interpretive research design underpins the study. This design facilitates systematic examination of existing theoretical constructs and enables their reinterpretation in light of contemporary educational realities shaped by artificial intelligence. Through interpretive analysis, the study moves beyond description to critically interrogate how learning theories function, overlap, and diverge when applied to AI-driven learning contexts. Such a design supports reflective inquiry into meanings, assumptions, and epistemological positions embedded within both educational theory and technological discourse.

5.3 Methodological Approach

The methodological approach of the study is multi-dimensional, integrating critical, comparative, and philosophical modes of inquiry.

First, critical theory analysis is employed to examine power relations, agency, and ideological assumptions embedded in AI-mediated education. This perspective enables interrogation of how algorithmic systems may influence learner autonomy, reshape pedagogical authority, and reproduce or challenge existing educational inequalities.

Second, comparative theoretical synthesis is used to analyze key learning theories—Constructivism, Socio-cultural Theory, and Connectivism—by identifying their core principles and examining their relevance within AI-enriched environments. This comparative process allows for recognition of complementarities as well as conceptual tensions among the theories.

Third, philosophical interpretation supports deeper reflection on epistemological and ontological questions concerning knowledge, cognition, and mediation in human–AI interaction. This interpretive stance is essential for understanding learning not merely as a technical process but as a value-laden human endeavor.

Together, these approaches enable the development of an integrative theoretical perspective rather than a fragmented or technology-driven account.

5.4 Sources of Data

As a conceptual inquiry, the study draws upon secondary sources of scholarly knowledge. These include peer-reviewed journal articles in education, learning sciences, and educational technology; foundational theoretical texts associated with major learning theories; and contemporary scholarship addressing artificial intelligence in educational contexts. The selected literature reflects both classical theoretical traditions and recent critical perspectives, allowing for a balanced synthesis between enduring pedagogical principles and emerging technological realities.

5.5 Analytical Framework

The analytical framework guiding the study involves a systematic mapping of learning theory principles against key functionalities of AI systems used in education. Core theoretical constructs—such as active meaning-making, mediated learning, scaffolding, distributed cognition, and learner autonomy—are examined in relation to AI capabilities including personalization, adaptation, feedback generation, and data-driven recommendation.

Through this mapping process, the analysis identifies points of convergence, where AI practices align with established learning principles; divergence, where tensions or contradictions emerge; and theoretical gaps, where existing frameworks fail to adequately explain observed learning dynamics. This structured analysis forms the basis for proposing a synthesized theoretical model that conceptualizes learning as a co-evolutionary process shaped by human cognition, socio-cultural mediation, and algorithmic intelligence.

6. ANALYSIS AND RESULTS

6.1. Intersections of Constructivism, Socio-cultural Theory, and Connectivism in AI-mediated learning contexts

The emergence of Artificial Intelligence as an active component of educational environments necessitates a fundamental reconsideration of how learning theories conceptualize cognition, mediation, and knowledge formation (Niemi, 2021). Classical learning theories were developed under assumptions of human-centered cognition, where agency, interpretation, and interaction were exclusively human processes. AI-mediated learning environments disrupt these assumptions by introducing non-human agents capable of adaptation, feedback generation, and decision-making (Cukurova, 2024).

From a constructivist standpoint, learning is understood as an active and intentional process through which learners construct meaning based on experience and prior knowledge. In traditional contexts, this construction unfolds through interaction with content, tasks, and reflective engagement (McComas, 2013). However, in AI-supported environments, the learner's experience is increasingly shaped by algorithmic systems that curate content, adjust difficulty levels, and influence cognitive pathways. While this may enhance engagement and personalization, it also raises critical questions regarding the locus of agency in meaning-making (Ali, 2024). Constructivism emphasizes learner autonomy, yet algorithmic mediation subtly structures the conditions under which autonomy is exercised. Thus, knowledge construction becomes co-determined by human interpretation and machine-driven inference (Behnagh & Yasrebi, 2020).

Socio-cultural theory provides an essential lens for understanding this shift by foregrounding mediation as the central mechanism of learning. Vygotskian theory posits that cognitive development occurs through interaction with cultural tools and more knowledgeable others (Gebhard, 2008). In AI-mediated environments, intelligent systems increasingly function as mediating artifacts that scaffold learning, simulate dialogue, and offer adaptive guidance (Gibson et al., 2023). These systems reshape the Zone of Proximal Development by dynamically responding to learner performance. However, unlike human mediators, AI lacks intentional consciousness and moral judgment, raising concerns about the nature of guidance and the values embedded within algorithmic design (PAWAR & Das, 2023). This challenges traditional socio-cultural assumptions regarding dialogic interaction, reciprocity, and shared meaning-making.

Connectivism further expands the analytical frame by conceptualizing learning as distributed across networks of information, technologies, and social actors (Dogan, 2014). Within AI-driven environments, knowledge is no longer located solely within individuals but emerges through participation in complex digital ecosystems (Shang & Bai, 2024). AI systems operationalize connectivist principles by enabling rapid navigation across knowledge nodes, pattern recognition, and real-time synthesis (Alashwal, 2024). Yet, while connectivism accounts for the structural dynamics of learning networks, it offers limited guidance regarding epistemic responsibility, ethical agency, and pedagogical intention. Consequently, learning risks being reduced to connectivity without criticality (AlDahdouh et al., 2015).

When examined collectively, these theories reveal both complementarity and tension. Constructivism highlights meaning-making, socio-cultural theory emphasizes mediation and context, and connectivism explains networked knowledge flow. However, none independently addresses the epistemological implications of intelligent systems that participate actively in learning processes (Packer & Goicoechea, 2000). The intersection of these theories therefore exposes a theoretical rupture—one that demands integration rather than substitution.

The critical synthesis of learning theories within AI-mediated contexts yields several significant theoretical outcomes.

First, learning emerges as a form of hybrid cognition, wherein cognitive activity is distributed across human learners and algorithmic systems. Meaning is not produced solely within the individual mind, nor entirely within networks, but through continuous interaction between human intentionality and machine responsiveness (Scardamalia & Bereiter, 2014). This reconfiguration challenges dichotomous distinctions between subject and tool, suggesting a relational epistemology of learning.

Second, learning in AI-supported environments becomes simultaneously personal, social, and networked. It is personal through individualized pathways and adaptive feedback; social through mediated interaction and cultural framing; and networked through engagement with distributed knowledge infrastructures (Maghsudi et al., 2021). These dimensions operate concurrently rather than sequentially, producing a layered learning ecology.

Third, the analysis reveals that AI does not merely support existing pedagogical processes but actively reshapes the architecture of learning itself (Ouyang & Jiao, 2021). The learner's cognitive experience is influenced by algorithmic logic, data patterns, and system design, thereby redefining how knowledge is accessed, interpreted, and validated.

Finally, the results underscore the inadequacy of single-theory explanations in AI-mediated education. Learning in the AI era cannot be fully understood through constructivist, socio-cultural, or connectivist perspectives alone (Ouyang & Jiao, 2021). Instead, it necessitates an integrated theoretical orientation that recognizes learning as a co-evolutionary process shaped through interaction between human cognition, socio-cultural mediation, and algorithmic intelligence.

These findings establish the theoretical foundation for the subsequent objectives of the chapter, particularly the development of an integrative model that conceptualizes AI agents not as substitutes for pedagogy but as participants within ethically grounded learning ecosystems.

6.2 AI Agents as Extensions of Contemporary Learning Theory Principles

The increasing presence of AI agents in educational environments has transformed them from peripheral instructional aids into active participants within learning processes. To understand this transformation theoretically, it is essential to examine how AI agents extend—and in some cases reconfigure—the foundational principles of major learning theories.

From a constructivist perspective, learning occurs through active engagement, exploration, and scaffolding that supports learners in constructing meaning. Traditionally, scaffolding has been provided by teachers or peers who adjust guidance based on learners' evolving understanding (Kim & Baylor, 2006). In AI-mediated contexts, intelligent systems increasingly assume this scaffolding function through adaptive feedback, personalized task sequencing, and real-time error diagnosis (Buckreus & Ally, 2020). AI agents monitor learner behavior, identify misconceptions, and offer graduated support, thereby simulating instructional responsiveness. However, unlike human scaffolding, algorithmic support is driven by probabilistic inference rather than pedagogical judgment, raising critical questions regarding the depth, intentionality, and epistemic quality of such guidance (Weitekamp & Koedinger, 2023).

Viewed through a socio-cultural lens, AI agents can be conceptualized as mediating artifacts within the learning environment. Vygotsky emphasized that cognition develops through interaction with cultural tools that shape thinking processes (Uden & Ching, 2024). AI systems now function as advanced digital tools capable of structuring interaction, language use, and problem-solving pathways. By facilitating dialogue, prompting reflection, and modelling strategies, AI agents mediate learning in ways analogous to human tutors (Sarıdaş, 2025). Yet this mediation is fundamentally asymmetrical: while AI can simulate interaction, it does not participate in shared meaning-making grounded in lived social experience (Sarıdaş, 2025). This distinction exposes a theoretical tension between functional mediation and dialogic mediation.

Connectivist theory further illuminates the role of AI by positioning learning within networks of human and non-human nodes. Within this framework, AI agents operate as dynamic network participants that store, retrieve, filter, and recombine knowledge (Jho, 2024). Through recommender systems and generative capabilities, AI shapes learners' access to information and influences the formation of cognitive connections. However, the delegation of epistemic authority to algorithmic nodes introduces risks related to over-reliance, homogenization of knowledge, and diminished critical evaluation (Imran et al., 2024). Connectivism explains the structural logic of these networks but offers limited guidance regarding normative control and educational purpose.

Across these theoretical perspectives, AI agents emerge not merely as tools but as *functional extensions* of pedagogical processes. Yet this extension simultaneously amplifies and destabilizes foundational learning assumptions.

Table 1. Mechanism Mapping (Theory AI Extension Risk Design Response)

Learning theory principle	*AI agent extension mechanism*	*Key risk introduced*	*Pedagogical response (control point)*
Constructivist meaning-making	Adaptive prompts, feedback loops, generated examples	"Guided" learning becomes *steered* learning	Require learner justification + multiple solution paths
Cognitive conflict & inquiry	Socratic questioning, counterexamples, simulations	AI may avoid productive struggle (over-helping)	"Desirable difficulty" settings + fade scaffolds
Mediation (Vygotsky)	AI as cultural tool: language, representations, supports	Pseudo-dialogue without shared meaning/values	Human-designed discourse norms + teacher orchestration
ZPD	Dynamic difficulty adjustment, personalized scaffolding	ZPD becomes *algorithm-defined*, not socially negotiated	Mixed mediation: AI proposes, human validates/calibrates
Distributed cognition	Retrieval, synthesis, network routing	Epistemic outsourcing; shallow understanding	Reflection tasks + source tracing + learner knowledge mapping
Network navigation	Recommenders, learning path curation	Filter bubbles; narrowing of perspective	Diversity constraints + "show opposites" + user control

The critical analysis yields several significant theoretical outcomes.

First, AI agents can be understood as digital operationalization of learning theories. Constructivist scaffolding, socio-cultural mediation, and connectivist networking are no longer abstract pedagogical concepts but are enacted algorithmically through adaptive systems (Ouyang & Jiao, 2021). In this sense, AI translates theoretical principles into computational processes that shape learning in real time.

Second, the analysis reveals a transformation of the Zone of Proximal Development. In AI-mediated environments, the ZPD becomes dynamically adaptive rather than socially negotiated. Instead of being defined through interaction with a more knowledgeable other, learning potential is continuously recalculated through data-driven modelling of learner performance (Wang, 2024). This enables immediate personalization but simultaneously shifts developmental judgment from pedagogical insight to algorithmic prediction.

Third, the results indicate a redistribution of pedagogical authority. As AI agents assume functions traditionally associated with teachers—such as feedback provision, pacing, and task selection—the boundaries between instructional support and instructional control become blurred (Ren, 2025). This transformation underscores the necessity of retaining human oversight to ensure that learning remains dialogic, reflective, and value-oriented.

Overall, the findings suggest that AI agents do not replace learning theories but extend them into digital form, transforming theoretical principles into operational mechanisms. However, this extension is not neutral; it reshapes the epistemological and ethical conditions of learning. Consequently, AI agents must be understood not as autonomous educators but as mediating partners whose role must remain anchored within human-centered pedagogical frameworks.

6.3 Development of a Theoretical Alignment Model for AI-Mediated Learning

The preceding analysis demonstrates that learning in AI-mediated environments cannot be adequately explained through isolated theoretical lenses. The growing entanglement of human cognition and intelligent systems has produced a learning condition in which meaning-making emerges through continuous interaction between learners and algorithmic agents (Siemens et al., 2022). This condition demands a theoretical model capable of explaining not only *how* learning occurs, but *where agency resides* and *how responsibility is distributed* within human–AI interaction.

At the cognitive level, learning remains grounded in human intentionality—learners formulate goals, interpret experiences, and assign meaning to knowledge (Rink, 2012). However, AI systems simultaneously engage in algorithmic inference by analyzing learner behavior, predicting needs, and generating adaptive responses. These two forms of cognition operate according to fundamentally different logics: human cognition is reflective, contextual, and value-laden, whereas algorithmic cognition is probabilistic, data-driven, and optimization-oriented (Ifenthaler, 2025). Learning in AI-supported environments thus emerges at the intersection of these distinct epistemic processes.

Central to this interaction are feedback loops that connect learner action and system response. Each learner input becomes data for algorithmic interpretation, which in turn shapes subsequent learning conditions through recommendations, prompts, or adaptive sequencing (Ninaus & Sailer, 2022). Over time, these recursive feedback loops influence not only performance outcomes but also learning trajectories, patterns of engagement, and epistemic habits. While such responsiveness enhances personalization, it also introduces the risk of pedagogical opacity, wherein learners remain unaware of how algorithmic decisions shape their learning experiences (Mahmoudi-Dehaki & Nasr-Esfahani, 2025).

This dynamic interaction reveals that AI-mediated learning is neither fully learner-driven nor system-controlled. Instead, it is relational—emerging through continuous negotiation between human agency and machine responsiveness (Williams, 2025). However, without an explicit theoretical alignment, this negotiation risks drifting toward technological determinism, where algorithmic logic subtly governs educational processes (Salameh, 2024). Consequently, a mediating framework is required—one that integrates cognitive interaction with ethical oversight and pedagogical intention.

The analytical synthesis leads to the formulation of a *Co-evolutionary Learning Model*, which conceptualizes learning as a dynamic process shaped through reciprocal adaptation between human learners and AI agents, governed by ethical and pedagogical mediation.

1. Human Intentionality

At the core of the model lies human intentionality. Learning begins with the learner's purposes, values, curiosity, and reflective judgment. Unlike algorithmic processes, human intentionality is normative—it involves decisions about what is meaningful, worthwhile, and ethically acceptable (Hung, 2014). In the co-evolutionary model, learners and educators retain epistemic authority by defining learning goals, interpreting feedback, and exercising critical judgment over AI-generated outputs. This component ensures that learning remains a purposive human activity rather than a system-optimized process (Sharples, 2023).

2. Algorithmic Responsiveness

Surrounding human intentionality is algorithmic responsiveness. AI agents contribute by adapting instruction, generating feedback, identifying patterns, and supporting navigation across knowledge networks (August & Tsaima, 2021). Their role is not to determine learning outcomes but to respond intelligently to learner input. Algorithmic responsiveness enhances scalability, personalization, and immediacy, enabling learning environments to adjust continuously (Machajewski, 2024). However, within the proposed model, responsiveness is explicitly constrained: AI responds *to* human intention rather than replacing it.

3. Ethical Mediation

The third and governing dimension of the model is ethical mediation. This component functions as the regulatory layer that aligns technological capability with educational values. Ethical mediation ensures transparency, protects learner autonomy, mitigates bias, and preserves equity and inclusion (Barnes & Hutson, 2024). It also assigns responsibility to educators and institutions for overseeing AI design, deployment, and interpretation. Without this mediating layer, the interaction between cognition and computation risks becoming asymmetrical, privileging algorithmic efficiency over educational purpose.

Co-Evolutionary Learning Model for AI-Mediated Education

The Co-Evolutionary Learning Model for AI-Mediated Education (figure 1) views learning as a dynamic partnership between human learners and AI systems. It emphasizes that while AI provides adaptive support and personalization, human intentionality remains central in defining meaning, goals, and judgment. Guided by ethical mediation, the model ensures that AI enhances learning without undermining learner autonomy, positioning education as a human-centered and ethically governed learning ecosystem.

Figure 1. Co-evolutionary learning model for AI-mediated education

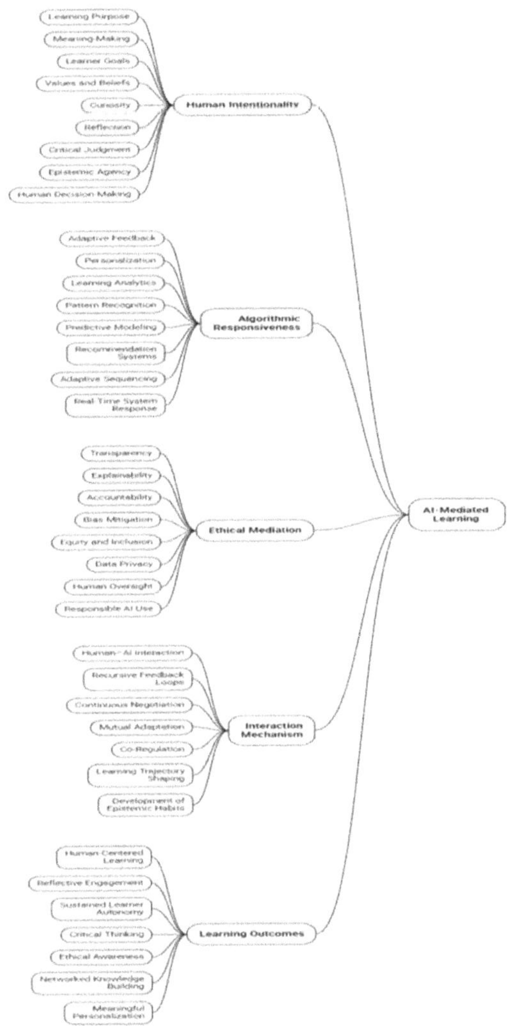

Together, these components form a co-evolutionary system:

- Human cognition evolves through interaction with adaptive AI support.
- AI systems evolve through continuous learning from human inputs.
- Ethical mediation stabilizes this relationship by anchoring it within humanistic and democratic values.

Learning, therefore, is not a unidirectional process of instruction but a reciprocal developmental relationship in which humans and intelligent systems mutually influence learning processes—while humans retain normative and moral authority (Riedl, 2019).

The Co-evolutionary Learning Model thus provides a theoretically grounded framework for aligning contemporary learning theories with AI-mediated education. It reconceptualizes AI agents not as autonomous instructors, but as responsive partners situated within pedagogically governed learning ecosystems (Patel et al., 2025). By integrating intentionality, responsiveness, and ethics, the model offers a comprehensive explanation of how learning can remain meaningful, reflective, and humane in the age of intelligent systems.

6. 4 Implications for Curriculum Design, Pedagogy, and Assessment in AI-augmented Learning Environments

The integration of AI agents into educational practice necessitates a fundamental rethinking of curriculum, pedagogy, and assessment. Traditional educational structures were designed for relatively stable knowledge systems and linear instructional models. In contrast, AI-mediated learning environments are dynamic, adaptive, and continuously evolving, requiring educational design to shift from fixed planning toward flexible learning ecologies (Ahamed, 2025).

From a curricular perspective, AI challenges the notion of curriculum as a predetermined sequence of content. Instead, curriculum increasingly functions as an adaptive learning ecology—a structured yet flexible environment that supports multiple learning pathways (Asrifan et al., 2024). Within such ecologies, AI systems assist learners in navigating content, identifying knowledge gaps, and connecting ideas across domains. However, this adaptability also introduces the risk of fragmentation and curricular incoherence if learning pathways are driven solely by algorithmic recommendation rather than pedagogical intent (Ahamed, 2025). Consequently, curriculum design must balance adaptability with coherence, ensuring that personalization serves educational meaning rather than mere efficiency.

Pedagogically, the presence of AI agents redefines the role of educators. As AI assumes routine instructional functions—such as content delivery, feedback generation, and progress monitoring—teachers increasingly assume roles as facilitators, designers, and orchestrators of learning experiences (Taufikin et al., 2024). Pedagogy thus shifts from direct transmission toward the cultivation of inquiry, dialogue, and reflection. In this model, AI supports learning processes, but pedagogical authority remains human. The educator's role becomes critical in framing questions, mediating interpretation, and ensuring that learning remains socially situated and ethically grounded (Dadhich et al., 2025).

Assessment practices are similarly transformed. AI enables continuous data collection and real-time analytics, making it possible to move beyond episodic, summative evaluation toward formative, data-informed, and reflective assessment (Saputra et al., 2024). Learning evidence can be generated through interaction patterns, problem-solving processes, and reflective engagement rather than final products alone (Agrawal et al., 2024). Nevertheless, overreliance on automated assessment risks reducing learning to measurable behaviors, neglecting interpretive judgment and qualitative understanding. Therefore, assessment must integrate algorithmic insight with human evaluation to preserve fairness, transparency, and developmental purpose.

The analysis yields several significant educational implications.

First, a conceptual shift emerges from content mastery to learning-to-learn. In AI-supported environments where information is readily accessible, the educational priority moves toward cultivating metacognition, critical thinking, ethical reasoning, and adaptive learning skills (Anbumaheshwari et al., 2025). Learners are increasingly required to evaluate information, interpret AI-generated outputs, and regulate their own learning processes. This repositioning aligns education with lifelong learning demands rather than short-term knowledge accumulation (Elstad, 2024).

Second, the results indicate that meaningful personalization is achievable without the erosion of learner agency, provided that AI operates within pedagogically governed frameworks. When learners retain control over goals, choices, and interpretation, personalization enhances engagement and autonomy (Salameh, 2024). Conversely, when personalization is imposed algorithmically without transparency, it risks narrowing intellectual exploration. The proposed framework demonstrates that personalization and agency are not oppositional but mutually reinforcing when guided by human judgment (Deckker et al., 2025).

Overall, the findings suggest that AI-augmented education demands systemic transformation rather than incremental adjustment. Curriculum must function as an adaptive ecology, pedagogy as intentional orchestration, and assessment as reflective interpretation. Together, these shifts support an educational model that leverages AI's capabilities while preserving the human values at the heart of learning.

6.5 Ethical and Philosophical Considerations Necessary for Sustainable Integration of AI in Education

The integration of Artificial Intelligence into educational environments raises profound ethical and philosophical concerns that extend beyond questions of technical efficiency or instructional effectiveness. At its core, education is a moral and social practice concerned with human development, identity formation, and democratic participation (Salloum, 2024). The increasing automation of pedagogical processes therefore necessitates careful scrutiny of how AI reshapes power, agency, and responsibility within learning systems (Mishara, 2024).

One of the most significant risks associated with AI-mediated education is the expansion of automation and surveillance. AI systems rely heavily on continuous data collection to generate personalized feedback, predictive analytics, and adaptive learning pathways (Leta & Vancea, 2023). While such data-driven processes promise improved responsiveness, they also normalize constant monitoring of learners' behaviors, interactions, and cognitive patterns (Mimoudi, 2024). This datafication of learning risks transforming educational spaces into sites of surveillance, where learners are persistently evaluated through metrics that may not capture the complexity of understanding, creativity, or emotional development (Shtayyat et al., 2025).

Closely related to this concern is the emergence of algorithmic authority. As AI systems generate recommendations, feedback, and evaluations, learners may increasingly attribute epistemic credibility to machine outputs (Pawar & Das, 2023). When algorithmic judgments are perceived as objective or neutral, they may override learners' critical reasoning and educators' professional judgment. This shift challenges foundational educational values by repositioning authority from dialogic human relationships to opaque computational systems.

The tension between algorithmic authority and learner autonomy is therefore central. Autonomy in education involves more than independent task completion; it requires the capacity to question, interpret, and make value-based decisions (Júnior et al., 2025). If AI systems subtly steer learning trajectories through predictive modelling and optimization logic, learner choice may become constrained in invisible ways. Such conditions risk producing compliance rather than critical consciousness, undermining the emancipatory purpose of education (Favero et al., 2025).

Philosophically, these concerns reveal a deeper issue: the misalignment between computational rationality and educational rationality. Algorithms operate through probabilistic optimization, whereas education operates through normative judgment (Li, 2024). Without explicit ethical mediation, there is a danger that educational goals will be redefined according to what is measurable, efficient, or predictable rather than what is meaningful, transformative, or socially just (Cabrera et al., 2024).

The ethical and philosophical analysis leads to two central conclusions.

First, the findings affirm the necessity of human-centered AI frameworks in education. Such frameworks recognize that while AI can support cognition, it cannot assume moral responsibility. Human actors—educators, institutions, and policymakers—must therefore retain authority over pedagogical decisions, learning goals, and evaluative judgments (Nguyen, 2023). AI should function as a supportive infrastructure rather than an autonomous decision-maker within educational systems.

Second, the analysis establishes that ethics must be foundational rather than supplementary to AI integration. Ethical considerations cannot be treated as post-implementation safeguards or regulatory add-ons (Azad & Kumar, 2024). Instead, values such as transparency, fairness, inclusivity, accountability, and learner dignity must inform the design, deployment, and evaluation of AI systems from the outset (Farooqi, 2025). When ethics is embedded structurally, AI becomes aligned with educational purpose; when ethics is appended reactively, technology risks reshaping education according to market or managerial logics (Mogoale et al., 2025).

Collectively, these results reinforce the argument that sustainable AI integration depends not on technological sophistication alone, but on philosophical clarity regarding what education is for and whom it serves. By grounding AI-mediated learning within humanistic and democratic values, education can harness technological innovation while preserving its commitment to autonomy, equity, and critical inquiry.

7. DISCUSSION

The findings of this chapter collectively suggest that learning in the age of Artificial Intelligence cannot be adequately conceptualized as either a purely human or a purely machine-driven process. Instead, learning emerges as a hybrid phenomenon shaped through continuous interaction between human cognition, socio-cultural mediation, and algorithmic systems. This transformation marks a decisive departure from traditional pedagogical assumptions and calls for a reconceptualization of learning theories within AI-mediated educational environments (Baek et al., 2024).

The analysis demonstrates that while Constructivism remains indispensable for understanding how learners actively construct meaning, it offers limited explanatory power in contexts where learning pathways are algorithmically shaped (Kucirkova, 2019). Constructivist theory foregrounds cognition and experience but does not fully account for the role of intelligent systems that curate content, guide inquiry, and influence epistemic choices. Meaning-making in AI-supported environments is therefore no longer solely learner-driven; it is co-shaped through algorithmic mediation (Marais et al., 2024).

Conversely, Connectivism provides a compelling explanation for the networked nature of contemporary knowledge. It captures how learning unfolds across distributed digital systems and emphasizes the importance of navigating information-rich environments (Jung, 2019). However, connectivist theory remains largely silent on questions of value, agency, and educational purpose. While it explains *how* knowledge flows, it does not sufficiently address *why* certain knowledge should matter, nor who should govern learning decisions within technologically mediated networks (Khatibi & Fouladchang, 2015).

Socio-cultural theory occupies a crucial mediating position within this theoretical landscape. Its emphasis on mediation, dialogue, and cultural tools offers a normative framework through which AI can be pedagogically situated (Liu, 2025). By interpreting AI agents as mediating artifacts rather than autonomous instructors, socio-cultural theory enables the preservation of learning as a relational and value-laden process. It is within this theoretical space that ethical considerations become pedagogically meaningful rather than externally imposed (Sharples, 2023).

A central theme emerging from the discussion is that of human–AI co-evolution. Learning is not simply enhanced by AI, nor is it displaced by it; rather, human cognition and algorithmic systems evolve through reciprocal adaptation (Ouyang & Jiao, 2021). Learners adjust strategies in response to AI feedback, while AI systems recalibrate based on learner behavior. This mutual shaping process reinforces the necessity of pedagogical governance to ensure that co-evolution remains developmentally constructive rather than technologically deterministic (Lodge et al., 2024).

Equally significant is the need to preserve dialogic learning within AI-mediated environments (Sharples, 2023a). Dialogue—understood as reflective exchange, questioning, and interpretation—remains foundational to deep learning. While AI can simulate conversational interaction, it cannot replace dialogic meaning-making grounded in human subjectivity and social experience (Santamaría, 2025). The role of educators thus becomes essential in sustaining interpretive spaces where learners critically engage with AI-generated outputs rather than accepting them unreflectively.

The discussion also highlights the delicate balance between personalization and pedagogy. AI-enabled personalization offers unprecedented opportunities to support diverse learners, yet personalization driven solely by algorithmic optimization risks narrowing intellectual exploration and reinforcing cognitive conformity (Laak & Aru, 2024). Pedagogical intentionality must therefore frame personalization as a means to expand learning possibilities rather than restrict them. When governed by human judgment, personalization and learner agency can coexist productively.

Ultimately, the analysis reaffirms that education is not merely a technical enterprise but a moral and democratic practice. Decisions about AI integration inevitably shape learners' identities, opportunities, and ways of knowing (Mishara, 2024). Without explicit ethical grounding, AI risks redefining education in terms of efficiency, prediction, and control. By contrast, when embedded within human-centered and socio-cultural frameworks, AI can serve as a catalyst for reflective, inclusive, and transformative learning (Peddi & Manoharan, 2025).

Taken together, the discussion underscores the central argument of this chapter: learning theories must not be replaced in the AI era but reinterpreted, integrated, and ethically re-grounded. The proposed co-evolutionary learning model offers one such pathway—one that preserves human agency, recognizes technological affordances, and situates education firmly within its enduring commitment to autonomy, dialogue, and social responsibility.

8. IMPLICATIONS OF THE STUDY

The theoretical alignment model proposed in this chapter carries significant implications for educational practice, curriculum design, policy formation, and future research. By conceptualizing learning as a co-evolutionary process shaped through human intentionality, algorithmic responsiveness, and ethical mediation, the study offers guidance for stakeholders seeking to integrate AI into education without compromising pedagogical integrity or democratic values.

8.1 Implications for Educators

The findings suggest a fundamental reconfiguration of the teacher's role in AI-mediated learning environments. Rather than functioning primarily as transmitters of content, educators increasingly assume the role of designers of learning ecologies. This involves structuring meaningful learning experiences, framing inquiry, cultivating dialogue, and guiding learners in critically engaging with AI-generated outputs.

Within this framework, AI should function as a pedagogical assistant rather than an epistemic authority. While AI can support feedback, personalization, and resource navigation, educators remain responsible for interpreting learning data, contextualizing knowledge, and nurturing ethical and reflective thinking. Teachers thus serve as mediators between learners and intelligent systems, ensuring that technological support enhances understanding rather than replaces pedagogical judgment.

8.2 Implications for Curriculum Designers

For curriculum designers, the study emphasizes the necessity of theory-driven AI integration. AI should not be appended to existing curricula as an efficiency tool but embedded within curricular structures informed by learning theory (You, 2024). Curriculum design must articulate how AI supports meaning-making, mediation, and networked learning rather than merely accelerating content delivery (Santamaría, 2025).

The findings further underscore the importance of flexible and adaptive curricula capable of accommodating diverse learner pathways. Such curricula should allow personalization while maintaining conceptual coherence, ensuring that learners encounter essential ideas, values, and disciplinary ways of thinking (Souza et al., 2024). Adaptive design must therefore be guided by pedagogical intention rather than algorithmic optimization alone.

8.3 Implications for Policymakers

At the policy level, the study highlights the urgent need for comprehensive AI governance frameworks in education. Policymakers must recognize that AI adoption is not a neutral technical decision but a normative intervention with long-term implications for equity, agency, and access (Mahrishi et al., 2024).

Effective governance should prioritize transparency, explainability, data protection, and accountability. Policies must clarify responsibilities among institutions, educators, technology providers, and regulatory bodies, ensuring that algorithmic decision-making does not operate beyond democratic oversight (Sywelem & Mahklouf, 2024). By embedding ethical principles within policy design, educational systems can promote innovation while safeguarding learner rights and institutional trust.

8.4 Implications for Researchers

The proposed co-evolutionary learning model offers a conceptual foundation for future empirical inquiry. Researchers can use the framework to design studies examining how human intentionality, AI responsiveness, and ethical mediation interact across diverse educational contexts (Kayyali, 2024).

The study also points toward the value of mixed-method research approaches that combine learning analytics with qualitative investigation of learner experience, agency, and meaning-making. Such approaches can move beyond outcome-based evaluation to explore how learners interpret, negotiate, and respond to AI-mediated learning environments. In doing so, future research can contribute to a more nuanced and human-centered understanding of AI's educational impact (Ejjami, 2024).

9. FUTURE DIRECTIONS

While the present chapter offers a conceptual synthesis, it also opens several avenues for future inquiry.

- First, empirical validation of the proposed co-evolutionary learning model is required. Future studies may examine how human intentionality, algorithmic responsiveness, and ethical mediation interact in real classroom, online, and hybrid learning contexts.
- Second, longitudinal research is needed to explore the long-term implications of AI-supported independent and self-directed learning. Such studies could investigate how sustained engagement with AI agents influences learner autonomy, epistemic habits, motivation, and critical thinking over time.
- Finally, there is a pressing need for the development of ethical AI pedagogical standards that translate philosophical principles into actionable educational guidelines. Collaborative efforts among educators, researchers, technologists, and policymakers will be essential to ensure that AI integration remains aligned with educational values and social justice.

Together, these directions underscore the continuing responsibility of educational scholarship to guide AI innovation with theoretical clarity, ethical commitment, and human purpose.

10. CONCLUSION

This chapter set out to re-examine foundational learning theories in light of the expanding presence of Artificial Intelligence within contemporary educational environments. The analysis demonstrates that classical and contemporary learning theories—particularly Constructivism, Socio-cultural Theory, and Connectivism—remain profoundly relevant; however, their explanatory power depends on critical reinterpretation within AI-mediated contexts. When treated as static frameworks, these theories struggle to account for learning shaped by algorithmic mediation, adaptive feedback, and networked knowledge systems. When reimagined dynamically, however, they offer essential insights into cognition, mediation, and connectivity in the AI era.

The findings affirm that AI agents do not replace human cognition but extend it. Through personalization, pattern recognition, and adaptive support, AI systems enhance learners' capacity to explore, reflect, and connect knowledge. Yet cognition remains fundamentally human—anchored in intentionality, judgment, and ethical reasoning. The chapter therefore argues against narratives of technological substitution and instead advances a model of pedagogical partnership in which AI functions as a responsive collaborator rather than an autonomous authority.

Equally central to this argument is the recognition that education must remain ethical, dialogic, and emancipatory. Learning is not merely an information-processing activity but a relational and moral practice concerned with meaning, identity, and social responsibility. Without ethical mediation, AI risks redefining education in terms of efficiency, prediction, and control. When guided by human-centered values, however, AI can support more inclusive, reflective, and adaptive learning ecosystems.

The proposed Co-evolutionary Learning Model synthesizes these insights by conceptualizing learning as a reciprocal process shaped through human intentionality, algorithmic responsiveness, and ethical governance. This model positions human agency not at the periphery but at the core of AI-mediated education, ensuring that technological advancement serves pedagogical purpose rather than redefining it.

Ultimately, learning in the age of AI must be technologically advanced yet pedagogically grounded—innovative yet humane. The future of education lies not in human–machine substitution, but in thoughtful human–AI co-evolution, where intelligent systems amplify learning possibilities while remaining firmly anchored within democratic, dialogic, and humanistic traditions.

REFERENCES

Abinaya, S., Alphonse, A. S., Indira, K., & Lavanya, R. (2024). Intelligent tutoring systems. In *Advances in educational technologies and instructional design* (pp. 226–250). CRC Press. DOI: 10.1201/9781003469315-11

Agrawal, A., Bhadhouriya, S., Pandey, A. K., Bhadoriya, S., Shrivastava, D., Dubey, G., Dubey, M., Sengar, H., Shakywar, K., & Shrivastava, V. (2024). Transforming student assessment in higher education. In *Advances in educational technologies and instructional design* (pp. 363–386). IGI Global. DOI: 10.4018/979-8-3693-6170-2.ch013

Ahamed, F. I. (2025). The transformative role of artificial intelligence in modern education. *World Journal of Advanced Research and Reviews*, *26*(1), 3239–3247. DOI: 10.30574/wjarr.2025.26.1.1453

Alashwal, M. (2024). Empowering education through AI: Potential benefits and future implications for instructional pedagogy. *PUPIL International Journal of Teaching. Education and Learning*, *8*(2), 201–212. DOI: 10.20319/ictel.2024.201212

AlDahdouh, A. A., Osório, A. J., & Caires, S. (2015). Understanding knowledge networks, learning, and connectivism. *International Journal of Instructional Technology and Distance Learning*, *12*(10), 3–21. DOI: 10.5281/zenodo.46186

Ali, A. (2024). Implication of e-learning and AI: Individualized pedagogical perspectives. *Journal of Electrical Systems*, *20*(7s, 7S), 2510–2515. DOI: 10.52783/jes.4074

Anbumaheshwari, K., Jayalakshmi, J., & Pavunraj, D. (2025). AI-driven curriculum innovation for adaptive and learner-centric education. In *Advances in computational intelligence and robotics* (pp. 99–132). IGI Global. DOI: 10.4018/979-8-3373-1062-6.ch004

Asrifan, A., Susanto, A. K., Elpisah, E., Saodi, S., & Herlina, H. (2024). AI-driven curriculum design and course management. In *Advances in educational technologies and instructional design* (pp. 195–222). IGI Global. DOI: 10.4018/979-8-3373-1017-6.ch007

August, S. E., & Tsaima, A. (2021). Artificial intelligence and machine learning: An instructor's exoskeleton in the future of education. In *SpringerBriefs in statistics* (pp. 79–105). Springer., DOI: 10.1007/978-3-030-58948-6_5

Azad, Y., & Kumar, A. (2024). Ethics and artificial intelligence. In *Advances in web technologies and engineering* (pp. 228–268). IGI Global. DOI: 10.4018/979-8-3693-1762-4.ch012

Baek, E., Wilson, R. V., & Liu, C. (2024). Redefining learning in the digital age. In *Advances in educational technologies and instructional design* (pp. 119–152). IGI Global. DOI: 10.4018/979-8-3693-6130-6.ch006

Barnes, E., & Hutson, J. (2024). Navigating the ethical terrain of AI in higher education: Strategies for mitigating bias and promoting fairness. *Forum for Education Studies*, *2*(2), 1–29. DOI: 10.59400/fes.v2i2.1229

Behnagh, R. F., & Yasrebi, S. (2020). An examination of constructivist educational technologies: Key affordances and conditions. *British Journal of Educational Technology, 51*(6), 1907–1919. DOI: 10.1111/bjet.13036

Bouchareb, A., & Ghedir, H. (2024). Harnessing artificial intelligence for educational innovation: Enhancing learning outcomes and teaching practices. *African Transactions on Research in Education, 5*(3), 414–431. DOI: 10.70091/atras/AI.26

Buckreus, K., & Ally, M. (2020). "Smart" practices: Machine intelligence for transforming pedagogy and learning. In *Bridging human and machine: Future education with intelligence* (pp. 53–73). Springer. DOI: 10.1007/978-981-15-0618-5_4

Cabrera, U. O. I., Vilca, J. S., Oliva, E. G. C., García, K. R. S., Rojas, R. G., & Casaverde, M. H. (2024). *Artificial intelligence in the ethics of education.* Editorial Macro., DOI: 10.70288/emc.9789915970646

Chaudhry, M. A., Cukurova, M., & Luckin, R. (2022). A transparency index framework for AI in education. *arXiv.* /arXiv.2206.03220DOI: 10.1007/978-3-031-11647-6_33

Chen, X., Xie, H., Zou, D., & Hwang, G. J. (2020). Application and theory gaps during the rise of artificial intelligence in education. *Computers and Education: Artificial Intelligence, 1*, 100002. DOI: 10.1016/j.caeai.2020.100002

Cukurova, M. (2024). The interplay of learning, analytics, and artificial intelligence in education: A vision for hybrid intelligence. *British Journal of Educational Technology, 56*(2), 469–488. DOI: 10.1111/bjet.13514

Dadhich, A., Yadav, R., Yadav, M., Huzooree, G., & Dewasiri, N. J. (2025). Teacher–AI collaboration and the future of the educator's role. In *Advances in computational intelligence and robotics* (pp. 355–378). IGI Global. DOI: 10.4018/979-8-3693-8744-3.ch013

Dash, S., & Bhoi, C. (2024). Exploring the intersection of education and artificial intelligence: A comprehensive review. *International Journal of Multidisciplinary Approach Research and Science, 2*(2), 601–610. DOI: 10.59653/ijmars.v2i02.637

de Souza, A. P., Conceição, C. de J., Pancoto, M. A., Cecote, N. Q. B., Pedra, R. R., Oliveira, R. M. da S., Pinão, V. R. Z., & Gomes, W. T. (2024). Personalização da aprendizagem com inteligência artificial: Como a IA está transformando o ensino e o currículo. *Aracê, 6*(3), 5816–5831. DOI: 10.56238/arev6n3-092

Deckker, D., Sumanasekara, S., & Fakhrou, A. (2025). AI-powered personalised learning: Promise and pitfalls. *World Journal of Advanced Research and Reviews, 26*(3), 2081–2095. DOI: 10.30574/wjarr.2025.26.3.2425

Delello, J. A., Watters, J. B., & Garcia-Lopez, A. (2024). Artificial intelligence in education. In *Advances in business information systems and analytics* (pp. 1–26). IGI Global. DOI: 10.4018/979-8-3693-3003-6.ch001

Elvis, M. (2025). Reframing AI in education: A Vygotskian perspective on proximal development. *International Journal of Arts, Humanities &. Social Science, 6*(Special Issue), 7–13. DOI: 10.56734/ijahss.v6nSa2

Farooqi, S. A. (2025). Ethical framework for AI in education. In *Advances in computational intelligence and robotics* (pp. 153–188). IGI Global. DOI: 10.4018/979-8-3373-5550-4.ch007

Favero, L., Pérez-Ortiz, J., Käser, T., & Oliver, N. (2025). Do AI tutors empower or enslave learners? Toward a critical use of AI in education. *arXiv*. /arXiv.2507.06878DOI: 10.48550

Gajdamaschko, N. (2015). Vygotsky's sociocultural theory. In *International encyclopedia of the social & behavioral sciences* (pp. 329–334). Elsevier., DOI: 10.1016/B978-0-08-097086-8.23203-0

Gebhard, S. (2008). Vygotsky and the zone of proximal development. In *Encyclopedia of information communication technologies* (pp. 948–950). IGI Global., DOI: 10.4018/978-1-59904-881-9.ch148

Gibson, D., Kovanovic, V., Ifenthaler, D., Dexter, S., & Feng, S. (2023). Learning theories for artificial intelligence promoting learning processes. *British Journal of Educational Technology*, *54*(5), 1125–1146. DOI: 10.1111/bjet.13341

Glassner, A., & Back, S. (2020). Connectivism: Networks, knowledge, and learning. In *Exploring heutagogy in higher education* (pp. 45–63). Springer. DOI: 10.1007/978-981-15-4144-5_3

Gligorea, I., Cioca, M., Oancea, R., Gorski, A., Gorski, H., & Tudorache, P. (2023). Adaptive learning using artificial intelligence in e-learning: A literature review. *Education Sciences*, *13*(12), 1216. DOI: 10.3390/educsci13121216

Grubaugh, S., Levitt, G., & Deever, D. (2023). Harnessing AI to power constructivist learning: An evolution in educational methodologies. *EIKI Journal of Effective Teaching Methods*, *1*(3). Advance online publication. DOI: 10.59652/jetm.v1i3.43

Han, P.-C. (2025). Artificial intelligence in education. In *Advances in computational intelligence and robotics* (pp. 387–408). IGI Global. DOI: 10.4018/979-8-3373-5102-5.ch014

He, W. (2024). Application and development trends of artificial intelligence in education. *Journal of Education and Educational Research*, *10*(1), 157–160. DOI: 10.54097/bf5qzn92

Hoidn, S. (2016). Constructivist foundations and common design principles of student-centered learning environments. In *The pedagogy of higher education* (pp. 23–103). Palgrave Macmillan., DOI: 10.1057/978-1-349-94941-0_2

Holmberg, J. (2017). Applying a conceptual design framework to study teachers' use of educational technology. *Education and Information Technologies*, *22*(5), 2333–2349. DOI: 10.1007/s10639-016-9536-3

Holstein, K., Aleven, V., & Rummel, N. (2020). A conceptual framework for human–AI hybrid adaptivity in education. In *Lecture notes in computer science* (pp. 240–254). Springer. DOI: 10.1007/978-3-030-52237-7_20

Hung, W. (2014). Intrinsic and extrinsic intentional learning: The difference made by self-determination. *Australian Journal of Education*, *58*(1), 50–58. DOI: 10.1177/0004944113517832

Ifenthaler, D. (2025). Information processing re-visited: Reciprocal perspectives on artificial intelligence and human-centered systems. *AI-Enhanced Learning*, *1*(1), 229–243. DOI: 10.70725/465418kgasdx

Imran, M., Almusharraf, N., Abdellatif, M. S., & Abbasova, M. Y. (2024). Artificial intelligence in higher education: Enhancing learning systems and transforming educational paradigms. *International Journal of Interactive Mobile Technologies, 18*(18), 34–48. DOI: 10.3991/ijim.v18i18.49143

Istrate, O. (2024). AI agents in education: An early systematic review of emerging roles, potential, and limitations. *Revista de Pedagogie Digitală, 3*(1), 24–30. DOI: 10.61071/RPD.2496

Jho, H. (2024). Learning beyond boundaries: Addressing the transformative and challenging impacts of artificial intelligence on education. *Preprints*. DOI: 10.20944/preprints202408.1788.v1

Juan, H., & Nagappan, R. (2025). A comprehensive literature review on AI-enhanced autonomous learning mechanisms in vocational education. *Malaysian Journal of Social Sciences and Humanities, 10*(3), e002958. DOI: 10.47405/mjssh.v10i3.2958

Jung, I. (2019). Connectivism and networked learning. In *Springer briefs in education* (pp. 47–55). Springer., DOI: 10.1007/978-981-13-7740-2_6

Júnior, J. F. C., Lins, P. P. M., de Oliveira, A. P. S., Ruas, G. C. R., Neto, R. A. D. R., Moraes, L. S., de Barros, M. J., Martins, P. C. M., Lopes, L. C. L., Schimidt, M. Q., Giese, W., & Santos, I. B. D. (2025). Algorithms vs. autonomy: The risks of dependence on AI in the critical training of students. In *Seven Editora eBooks*. DOI: 10.56238/sevened2025.026-014

Kayyali, M. (2024). The future of AI in education. In *Advances in educational technologies and instructional design* (pp. 367–406). IGI Global. DOI: 10.4018/979-8-3693-7220-3.ch013

Kayyali, M. (2025). Generative AI and education. In *Advances in computational intelligence and robotics* (pp. 25–52). IGI Global. DOI: 10.4018/979-8-3693-8332-2.ch002

Khatibi, M., & Fouladchang, M. (2015). Connectivism: A review. *International Journal of Indian Psychology, 2*(4). Advance online publication. DOI: 10.25215/0204.049

Kim, Y., & Baylor, A. L. (2006). A social-cognitive framework for pedagogical agents as learning companions. *Educational Technology Research and Development, 54*(6), 569–596. DOI: 10.1007/s11423-006-0637-3

Kozulin, A. (2015). Vygotsky's theory of cognitive development. In *International encyclopedia of the social & behavioral sciences* (pp. 322–328). Elsevier., DOI: 10.1016/B978-0-08-097086-8.23094-8

Ku, K. Y., Phillipson, S., & Phillipson, S. N. (2015). Educational learning theory. In *International encyclopedia of the social & behavioral sciences* (pp. 238–245). Elsevier., DOI: 10.1016/B978-0-08-097086-8.92150-0

Kucirkova, N. (2019). The learning value of personalization in children's reading recommendation systems: What can we learn from constructionism? *International Journal of Mobile and Blended Learning, 11*(4), 1–15. DOI: 10.4018/IJMBL.2019100106

Laak, K., & Aru, J. (2024). AI and personalized learning: Bridging the gap with modern educational goals. *arXiv*. /arXiv.2404.02798DOI: 10.48550

Lameras, P. (2022). A vision of teaching and learning with AI. In *Proceedings of the 2022 IEEE Global Engineering Education Conference (EDUCON)* (pp. 1796–1803). IEEE. DOI: 10.1109/EDUCON52537.2022.9766718

Leta, F. M., & Vancea, D. P. C. (2023). Ethics in education: Exploring the ethical implications of artificial intelligence implementation. *Ovidius University Annals. Economic Sciences Series, 23*(1), 413–421. DOI: 10.61801/OUAESS.2023.1.54

Levin, I., Semenov, A., & Gorsky, M. (2025). Papert's vision realized: Constructionism and generative AI. In *Constructionism conference proceedings* (Vol. 8, pp. 419–426). DOI: 10.21240/constr/2025/36.X

Li, Z. (2024). The shadow of the algorithm: The ethical blind spot of artificial intelligence education. *Journal of Education. Humanities and Social Sciences, 26*, 1146–1152. DOI: 10.54097/pk0ajq60

Liu, X. (2025). Reconceptualizing foreign language learning through artificial intelligence within the framework of the zone of proximal development. *GBP Proceedings Series, 8*, 9–15. DOI: 10.70088/790gnb90

Lodge, J. M., De Barba, P., & Broadbent, J. (2024). Learning with generative artificial intelligence within a network of co-regulation. *Journal of University Teaching & Learning Practice, 20*(7). Advance online publication. DOI: 10.53761/1.20.7.02

Machajewski, S. (2024). *AI instructional framework*. Open Science Framework. DOI: 10.35542/osf.io/j8ct9

Maghsudi, S., Lan, A., Xu, J., & Van der Schaar, M. (2021). Personalized education in the artificial intelligence era: What to expect next. *IEEE Signal Processing Magazine, 38*(3), 37–50. DOI: 10.1109/MSP.2021.3055032

Mahmoudi-Dehaki, M., & Nasr-Esfahani, N. (2025). Enhancing engagement and equity in personalized learning through adaptive systems. In *IGI Global eBooks* (pp. 219–246). IGI Global., DOI: 10.4018/979-8-3373-0740-4.ch009

Mahrishi, M., Abbas, A., & Siddiqui, M. K. (2024). Global initiatives towards regulatory frameworks for artificial intelligence in higher education. *Digital Government: Research and Practice, 6*(2), 1–9. DOI: 10.1145/3672462

Marais, E., Marais-Botha, R., & Coertzen, F. (2024). Constructing an artificial intelligence higher education environment: Guidelines for the future. In *Helsinki University Press eBooks* (pp. 173–192). Helsinki University Press., DOI: 10.33134/HUP-25-9

McComas, W. F. (2013). Constructivist teaching practices. In *Science education research and practice in Europe* (p. 23). Sense Publishers., DOI: 10.1007/978-94-6209-497-0_20

Mimoudi, A. (2024). AI, personalized education, and challenges. In *Proceedings of the International Conference on AI Research* (Vol. 4, No. 1, pp. 271–280). DOI: 10.34190/icair.4.1.3133

Mishara, P. (2024). The ethical implications of AI in education: Privacy, bias, and accountability. *Journal of Informatics Education and Research, 4*(2). Advance online publication. DOI: 10.52783/jier.v4i2.1827

Mogoale, P., Pretorius, A., Mogase, R., & Segooa, M. (2025). Ethical considerations in artificial intelligence-driven environments for higher education. *South African Journal of Information Management*, *27*(1), a2007. Advance online publication. DOI: 10.4102/sajim.v27i1.2007

Mørch, A. I., & Andersen, R. (2023). Human-centred AI in education in the age of generative AI tools. In *CEUR Workshop Proceedings* (Vol. 3408). https://ceur-ws.org/Vol-3408/short-s2-08.pdf

Nguyen, N. D. (2023). Exploring the role of AI in education. *London Journal of Social Sciences*, *6*(6), 84–95. DOI: 10.31039/ljss.2023.6.108

Niemi, H. (2021). AI in learning. *Journal of Pacific Rim Psychology*, *15*, e34. DOI: 10.1177/18344909211038105

Ninaus, M., & Sailer, M. (2022). Closing the loop – The human role in artificial intelligence for education. *Frontiers in Psychology*, *13*, 956798. DOI: 10.3389/fpsyg.2022.956798 PMID: 36092115

O'Connell, C. (2018). Learning as a shared process: Vygotsky and the socio-cultural theories of learning. In *Vygotsky and sociocultural approaches to teaching and learning* (pp. 161–176). Routledge., DOI: 10.4324/9781315299358-10

Oleet, J. B., & Yu, C. (2025). AI and the future of education. In *Advances in computational intelligence and robotics* (pp. 407–440). IGI Global. DOI: 10.4018/979-8-3693-7873-1.ch015

Ouariach, S., Ouariach, F. Z., & Khaldi, M. (2025). Artificial intelligence as a harbinger of engagement and collaboration. In *Advances in educational technologies and instructional design* (pp. 147–180). IGI Global. DOI: 10.4018/979-8-3373-2262-9.ch006

Ouyang, F., & Jiao, P. (2021). Artificial intelligence in education: The three paradigms. *Computers & Education: Artificial Intelligence*, *2*, 100020. DOI: 10.1016/j.caeai.2021.100020

Packer, M. J., & Goicoechea, J. (2000). Sociocultural and constructivist theories of learning: Ontology, not just epistemology. *Educational Psychologist*, *35*(4), 227–241. DOI: 10.1207/S15326985EP3504_02

Patel, C., Suthar, F., & Patel, S. (2025). AI agents in education: Transforming learning through intelligent systems. *Preprints*. DOI: 10.20944/preprints202506.1870.v1

Pawar, M., & Rai, R. D. (2023). Ethical challenges of artificial intelligence in education: Achieving learner centricity with respect to learner autonomy. In *Proceedings of the International Conference on Computers in Education*. DOI: 10.58459/icce.2023.1437

Peddi, S., & Manoharan, G. (2025). Ethical guidelines for the thoughtful implementation of AI in higher education. *EthAIca*, *5*, 409. DOI: 10.56294/ai2026409

Popenici, S. A. D., & Kerr, S. (2017). Exploring the impact of artificial intelligence on teaching and learning in higher education. *Research and Practice in Technology Enhanced Learning*, *12*(1), 22. DOI: 10.1186/s41039-017-0062-8 PMID: 30595727

Pushparani, R. (2025). Review on collaboration intelligence in education. *International Research Journal on Advanced Engineering Hub*, *3*(9), 3606–3611. DOI: 10.47392/IRJAEH.2025.0526

Ren, X. (2025). Policy, pedagogy, and technological disruption: Teacher agency in AI-integrated educational ecosystems. *Business and Social Sciences Proceedings*, *2*, 31–37. DOI: 10.71222/azryt912

Riedl, M. O. (2019). Human-centered artificial intelligence and machine learning. *Human Behavior and Emerging Technologies*, *1*(1), 33–36. DOI: 10.1002/hbe2.117

Rink, J. E. (2012). Instruction from a learning perspective. In *Teaching physical education for learning* (pp. 157–176). Routledge., DOI: 10.4324/9780203487150-16

Şahin, M. (2012). Pros and cons of connectivism as a learning theory. *International Journal of Physical and Social Sciences*, *2*(4), 437–454.

Salameh, W. A. K.Waleed Abdullatif Khader Salameh. (2024). The dual role of AI in personalized learning: Enhancements and hindrances for diverse learners. *International Journal of Science and Research Archive*, *13*(2), 62–67. DOI: 10.30574/ijsra.2024.13.2.2057

Säljö, R. (2022). Learning from a sociocultural perspective. In *International encyclopedia of education* (pp. 36–43). Elsevier., DOI: 10.1016/B978-0-12-818630-5.14006-0

Salloum, S. A. (2024). AI perils in education: Exploring ethical concerns. In *Studies in big data* (pp. 669–675). Springer., DOI: 10.1007/978-3-031-52280-2_43

Salloum, S. A., Salloum, A., & Alfaisal, R. (2024). Objectives and obstacles of artificial intelligence in education. In *Studies in big data* (pp. 605–614). Springer., DOI: 10.1007/978-3-031-52280-2_38

Santamaría, J. S. (2025). *A pedagogical sense of artificial intelligence in education*. Open Science Framework. DOI: 10.31219/osf.io/z4bg6_v1

Saputra, I., Kurniawan, A., Yanita, M., Putri, E. Y., & Mahniza, M. (2024). The evolution of educational assessment: How artificial intelligence is shaping the trends and future of learning evaluation. *Indonesian Journal of Computer Science*, *13*(6). Advance online publication. DOI: 10.33022/ijcs.v13i6.4465

Sarıdaş, G. (2025). The use of artificial intelligence agents in education. *International Society That Learn Journal*, *2*(1). Advance online publication. DOI: 10.64782/istlj22286172

Scardamalia, M., & Bereiter, C. (2014). Smart technology for self-organizing processes. *Smart Learning Environments*, *1*(1), 1. Advance online publication. DOI: 10.1186/s40561-014-0001-8

Selwyn, N. (2019). What's the problem with learning analytics? *Journal of Learning Analytics*, *6*(3). Advance online publication. DOI: 10.18608/jla.2019.63.3

Sharma, M. S., & Bansal, D. (2017). Constructivism as paradigm for teaching and learning. *International Journal of Physical Education. Sports Health*, *4*, 209–212.

Sharples, M. (2023). Towards social generative AI for education: Theory, practices and ethics. *Learning. Research and Practice*, *9*(2), 159–167. DOI: 10.1080/23735082.2023.2261131

Sharples, M. (2023). *Towards social generative AI for education: Theory, practices and ethics*. arXiv. /arXiv.2306.10063DOI: 10.48550

Shashwat, K., & Pundhir, S. K. S. (2025). Artificial intelligence in education. In *IGI Global eBooks* (pp. 137–176). IGI Global., DOI: 10.4018/979-8-3693-9861-6.ch005

Sholeh, M. I. (2025). Educational transformation through artificial intelligence. In *Advances in computational intelligence and robotics* (pp. 25–40). IGI Global. DOI: 10.4018/979-8-3693-7260-9.ch002

Shtayyat, A., Gawanmeh, A., & Mashaleh, A. (2025). Risk analysis of AI integration in educational systems. In *Advances in computational intelligence and robotics* (pp. 401–428). IGI Global. DOI: 10.4018/979-8-3373-0832-6.ch017

Shuell, T. (2001). Learning theories and educational paradigms. In *International encyclopedia of the social & behavioral sciences* (pp. 8613–8620). Elsevier., DOI: 10.1016/B0-08-043076-7/02385-8

Siemens, G., Marmolejo-Ramos, F., Gabriel, F., Medeiros, K., Marrone, R., Joksimovic, S., & De Laat, M. (2022). Human and artificial cognition. *Computers & Education: Artificial Intelligence*, *3*, 100107. DOI: 10.1016/j.caeai.2022.100107

Singh, G., & Thakur, A. (2024). AI in education. In *Advances in computational intelligence and robotics* (pp. 18–38). IGI Global. DOI: 10.4018/979-8-3693-2964-1.ch002

Sywelem, M. M. G., & Mahklouf, A. M. E.-S. (2024). Ethical considerations in the integration of artificial intelligence in education: An overview. [CSIT]. *Computer Science and Information Technology*, *14*, 201–216. DOI: 10.5121/csit.2024.141201

Tabor, J. (2025). Cognitivism, constructivism, and the classroom. In *Advances in computational intelligence and robotics* (pp. 211–240). IGI Global. DOI: 10.4018/979-8-3373-6007-2.ch007

Tanaka, S. (2025). *Beyond the algorithm: Reimagining education in the age of AI personalization.* Open Science Framework. DOI: 10.31235/osf.io/rdvwg_v1

Taufikin, M. S. I., Supaat, S., Azifah, N., Nikmah, F., & Kuanr, J., & Parminder. (2024). The impact of AI on teacher roles and pedagogy in the 21st century classroom. In *2024 International Conference on Knowledge Engineering and Communication Systems (ICKECS)* (pp. 1–5). IEEE. DOI: 10.1109/ICKECS61492.2024.10617236

Tilepbergenovna, U. A. (2024). The role of artificial intelligence in education. *International Journal of Pedagogics*, *4*(10), 184–187. DOI: 10.37547/ijp/Volume04Issue10-32

Uden, L., & Ching, G. S. (2024). Activity theory-based ecosystem for artificial intelligence in education (AIED). *International Journal of Research Studies in Education*, *13*(5). Advance online publication. DOI: 10.5861/ijrse.2024.24000

Umar, U., & Purwanto, M. B. (2025). AI and decision assistance for enhancing self-directed learning. [English Teaching Journal]. *ETERNAL*, *16*(2), 457–465. DOI: 10.26877/eternal.v16i2.1524

. Vasile, C. (2023). Artificial intelligence in education: Transformative potentials and ethical considerations. *Journal of Educational Sciences & Psychology, 13*(75)(2), 1–2. DOI: 10.51865/JESP.2023.2.01

Wang, Y. (2024). Integration of AI technology and ZPD: Pinpointing the zone of student development to promote educational innovation and efficiency improvement. *Journal of Education. Humanities and Social Sciences*, *38*, 99–104. DOI: 10.54097/wws14m21

Weitekamp, D., & Koedinger, K. (2023). Computational models of learning: Deepening care and carefulness in AI in education. In *Communications in computer and information science* (pp. 13–25). Springer., DOI: 10.1007/978-3-031-36336-8_2

Williams, P. (2025). *Human–AI learning: Architecture of a human-agentic AI learning system. Preprints.* org. DOI: 10.20944/preprints202508.1351.v1

Xu, W., & Ouyang, F. (2021). A systematic review of AI role in the educational system based on a proposed conceptual framework. *Education and Information Technologies*, *27*(3), 4195–4223. DOI: 10.1007/s10639-021-10774-y

Yadav, R., Huzooree, G., Yadav, M., & Gangodawilage, D. S. K. (2025). Generative AI for personalized learning content creation. In *Advances in computational intelligence and robotics* (pp. 107–130). IGI Global. DOI: 10.4018/979-8-3693-8744-3.ch005

You, S. (2024). A qualitative case study on the implementation experience of curriculum using generative AI. *Korean Educational Research Association Journal*, *62*(4), 1–26. DOI: 10.30916/KERA.62.4.1

Young, J. (2024). The rise of artificial intelligence in education. *International Journal of Innovative Research and Development*, *13*(2). Advance online publication. DOI: 10.24940/ijird/2024/v13/i2/FEB24019

Zhang, K., & Aslan, A. B. (2021). AI technologies for education: Recent research and future directions. *Computers & Education: Artificial Intelligence*, *2*, 100025. DOI: 10.1016/j.caeai.2021.100025

Chapter 2
Understanding AI Agents:
Working Mechanisms, Instructional Roles, and Challenges for Self-learning

Rahul Kumar Ghosh
http://orcid.org/0000-0002-1814-2133
Brainware University, India

Hind Hammouch
http://orcid.org/0000-0002-5897-1649
Sidi Mohamed Ben Abdellah University, Morocco

Gourab Dutta
http://orcid.org/0000-0003-4493-6508
Brainware University, India

Sandip Chakraborty
http://orcid.org/0009-0000-1166-0846
Brainware University, India

ABSTRACT

AI agents in the realm of education are being viewed as independent beings with the ability to make decisions, change, and communicate, outdoing standard tools by taking the roles of mentors, peers, or assessors that customize the learning process. They display features such as independence, reactivity, and social presence, complying with different paradigms like reactive or hybrid agents, backed up by decision models and machine learning. At the same time, they undoubtedly provide incredibly self-driven and personalized learning experiences, they also serve as a warning that some bias, dependence, and ethical issues may come to the surface. According to the predictions, the next step for these agents will be to master emotional intelligence and establish a more solid relationship with human teachers so as to remain trustworthy and effective, thus giving birth to new educational ways.

DOI: 10.4018/979-8-3373-7225-9.ch002

1. INTRODUCTION

With AI growing swiftly in recent times, there has also been a significant technological shift in education, focusing on improvements in autonomous learning and self-management in learning processes. Such development of AI also gives rise to artificial intelligence agents, which the systems are in themselves capable of autonomous behavior, adapting and evolving. Unlike the traditional educational tools, based on discrete steps, AI agents on the other hand exist in a variable environment, consequently allowing individualized and contextual support.

The concept of self-directed learning where the learner is in charge of their own learning process, engages metacognitive processes and is able to self-regulate, calls for it to be adapted to the needs of all types of learners. The use of Artificial Intelligence technology particularly addresses this issue by incorporating teaching, guidance, and self-evaluation features, allowing educational activities to transcend the traditional classroom boundaries.

This chapter will show what AI agents are and how they operate in schools, discuss the underlying structures that are involved in AI-enabled learning, including their classroom roles in autodidactic processes, examine moral, technical and other issues, and suggest further steps including oversight measures, guided by governance indicators.

In this chapter, We are mainly considering researchers, educators, instructional designers, civil servants and businessmen interested in finding out about the place artificial intelligence agents take in self-directed learning.

2. BACKGROUND

The term AI agents can be defined as agents from the systems based on agents in the AI domain in which an agent is received as an entity that perceives the environment around it and attempts to influence and transform it so as to accomplish a certain task. In education, the early applications of AI were mostly centered around the rule-based ITS (Intelligent Tutor System) that used fixed or hard-coded rules to guide the student in the process of learning. These traditional rule-based systems are criticised for their inefficiency new AI approaches such as machine learning, reinforcement learning and natural language processing, and are also to the development of adaptive and interactive AI systems.

Educational settings have incorporated AI agents in teaching by using learning management systems; for example adaptive programs and conversational tutors. These AI based tutors make the learning instruction custom for each student by analyzing data and behavior and projecting future behaviors of the individual for enhanced learning.

3. RESEARCH APPROACH

This chapter uses a conceptual literature review and a structured methodology. To find recent research, we used Scopus indexed database of research papers and other peer-reviewed journals of the period between 2020 – 2025. The scope of the literature was centred in keywords such as "AI agents,", "intelligent tutoring systems,", "adaptive learning" and "educational AI." Selection of studies was made to determine how well they informed the development of AI-driven learning systems, teacher support tools or ethics. Having been selected, the literature was organized around conceptual framework, methods and new perspectives gathered from it.

4. CONCEPTUAL FOUNDATIONS OF AI AGENTS

The cornerstone of understanding learning technologies of this age involves rigorously defining an AI agent and differentiating it from the broader category of general AI systems. General AI (GAI) or Artificial General Intelligence (AGI) describes a theoretical mechanism that embodies characteristics similar to the cognitive abilities of humans, including the capacity to perform diverse tasks. Unlike General AI, the AI agent—specifically, a specialized, concrete software entity—is defined by its capacity to perceive its environment and the ability to act autonomously upon it earnestly in quest of specific, predefined goals (Serban et al., 2020). This functionality element is the core factor to consider in real terms; that is, it targets an agent to work for a specific goal within a specific context, such as teaching algebra or scheduling resources. Essentially, this stark difference means that the AI agent goes beyond conventional fixed protocols by being adaptive—in other words, the purpose of education transforms AI's spirit to act dynamically. The four core functional characteristics serve as the theory for the operational sketching, implementation, and classification of the AI agent: autonomy, reactivity, proactiveness, and sociality. Autonomy is probably the forerunner characteristic to highlight, holding a pivotal role due to the agent's self-control and ability to undertake tasks within the framework of being reactive, proactive, and social. It refers to the agent's ability to perform any task and process even in the immediate absence of control and guidance from a user to provide a design framework. Autonomy in education gives the agent control over complex and long-term learning paths for a student so that with some moment-to-moment instructional decisions—for example, deciding when to introduce a new topic, to give a clue, or to enforce the review cycle—points of reference may be internal representations of student knowledge states, curricular scopes, and agents' pedagogical strategies (Hutsalo et al., 2024). It is this independence that turns the agent into a real, intelligent tutor, lightening the cognitive load of human educators and providing reliable, continuous, one-on-one tutoring. The technical manifestation of autonomy is to make various decisions that are based on sophisticated decision-making models, which, in turn, may involve logical reasoning systems, heuristic search mechanisms, or utility functions that allow agents to choose the best strategies from their set of options, always benefiting their utility (e.g., maximizing the student's learning gain). Philosophically, autonomy for an agent means that it steps into the realm of pedagogical authority, which will need procedural guidance that delimits the extent of autonomous governance and is set to mandate compliance with human educational values. Complementing the autonomy would be reactivity, which essentially refers to the capacity to take into account the agent's surroundings, including any external stimulations that may be pertinent, and respond to them promptly. Reactivity is the main element that makes the agent more responsive, making it possible for fast feedback and dynamic adjustments within a learning system. The environment of an educational agent is made up of students' input (e.g., completing a task, clicking a link, or putting a video on pause), the variable passage of time applied to anyone (e.g., spending too long on one problem), or another kind of change at a system level. Concretely though, reactivity is driven by fast sensor-action loops, representing the perceptual component of the agent that monitors state changes in the continuous feedback mechanism. Thus, opportune responses prove to be instrumental when not just awaiting a particular form of feedback, possibly an instruction from the command-room screen, but when it instantly flags a syntax error line of text or an incorrect concept—marking it for the future in case of error identification. The instantaneous feedback loop creates a nearly perfect EC and reinforcement mechanism because it helps learners in real-time to correct their perceptions, stopping reinforcement of contradictions. The absence of quick reactive capability renders learning assistant agents of much lower pedagogical efficacy, as delayed feedback really loses the potency to steer the immediate cognitive process of the learner. Instead, the two major rules guiding the agent in exploiting its effectiveness are reactivity (short-term tactical responses) and autonomy (long-term strategy) that work together, thus offering an all-pervasive learning partner (Gourlay et al., 2021).

The conceptual framework is complete when a new aspect is added, such as social skills and proactiveness, which turn the AI Agent into an agent that takes actions for goals and becomes truly interactive, defining that relationship. A concept of learning is proactivity, which involves behaviors motivated by end goals in addition to knowing the score and taking the leap. Proactive behavior is the capacity of a motivational agent to do and make what is needed without needing someone else to say or do something to precipitate action. Instead of waiting for explicit commands or guides from the learner, the agents act according to their built-in models and the overriding goals of the student's learning, like a heuristic youth agency. Literally, proactivity depends on an agent keeping this highly detailed internal world's state model and planning part for future actions for a specific purpose: an AI agent operates by an internal state model and executive function to make future plans towards a fixed target goal. For instance, once a learner successfully mastered one module of algebra, a proactive agent doesn't await the next unit chosen by the student; it utilizes the student's performance data, and at the same time, the agent looks at the long-run structure of the curriculum; it tends to make a suggestion about reviewing some basic prerequisite material before the next, more complex unit instead of guiding that individual learner to whatever topic he or she feels would seem to be beneficial. This pre- and postdictive role is what most truly defines ITS and AL systems, ensuring learning maneuvers to processing efficiency and strategic optimization. A hallmark of distinguished agents is proactivity and need advanced reasoning to balance risk and reward of intervention—a series of actions may get in the learner's way while not intervening enough will counteract the foresight. Finally, the agent's social capabilities are considered to be its ability to interact and communicate with other agents or human users, expanding its role beyond mere isolated instruction (Wang et al., 2023). This quality is tremendously important, as learning is by nature a social activity. Social ability supports communication (by means of NLP), negotiation (in cooperative problem-solving cases), and collaboration (in agent collectives). It allows agents to mimic the interactions among their peers, thus making it possible for them to engage in problem-solving scenarios just like students do, and so they practice teamwork and communication skills in a secure, supervised environment. In addition, the art of manipulating these complex, multi-agent interactions involve the use of communication protocols and a common knowledge representation, which facilitates the attaining of the mutual understanding of the agents' goals. The theory of these four correlated attributes—autonomy, reactivity, proactivity, and social ability—comprises the whole framework necessary for both the classification and the design of the learning support agents that would eventually become the best companions of the learning process, offering flexibility and quality. The merging of those traits helps the AI agent not only to tutor but also to mature with the student on his development journey so that both become dynamic academic organisms whose basic processes have a direct reflection on the provided support, the guided interaction, and the flexible evaluation methods, all of which lie at the heart of the truly learner-directed and independent learning environment. The educational implications of these main traits are particularly noteworthy in the modern landscape, opening up the battle against stubborn educational problems, especially with respect to scale, personalization, and continuous engagement (Tariq, 2024).

The four conceptual traits mentioned all have a high educational value and can be utilized when teaching to a certain extent, possibly leading to mass education improvements. The virtual teacher AI system's internal features can be characterized in four ways those are - self-management, immediacy, anticipation, and social interaction—which in turn give rise to the educational benefits of the four main pillars, with the shift from conventional to more adaptive and independent learning being the major one (Zhao & Zhong, 2024).

4.1 Foundation for Personalized, Scaffolding Instruction (Autonomy & Proactivity in Action)

When combining Autonomy and Proactivity, the agent stands as the most advanced instrument for personalized, scaffolding instruction. Its autonomy makes it able to control the learning process and curriculum on its own; thus, it is an intelligent tutor that gives continuous and highly accurate but personalized one-to-one mentoring suitable to the pace, style, and knowledge gaps of the student. This trait deals with the main point of the conventional classroom, which was the inadequacy of a single human teacher in providing individual attention to 30 or more students at the same time. On the other hand, the agent's proactivity is the one that provides the support. While it also refers to the robot's independence of the learner, scaffolding involves executing temporary and tailor-made assistance to the learner to help them in a task they cannot handle alone, the level of support decreasing as the student learns. The model detects the area in which a person will have difficulty and guides the learner through a hint, a non-immediate question, or a resource recommendation that is adapted to his/her level of understanding before he/she gets overwhelmed or becomes unproductive in working out the solution. The support given gradually motivates the student to use his/her problem-solving techniques, thus building an essential autonomy and, at the same time, a deep involvement in the subject/field. The personalization aspect becomes apparent when the learner's scaffolding needs vary greatly: an intelligent student may receive very challenging conceptual tasks to get them out of their comfort zone and to think critically, while a less efficient student may be receiving more help in the form of clearer and step-by-step instructions. The independent agent ensures that the whole operation goes on, does not let the learner's mind be overloaded with tasks, and helps maintain the "productive struggle" element needed for robust study; hence, educators, who are no longer expected to give constant, individualized attention, are released from that burden. This is directly related to self-directed learning skills only gained through learning when one forces a student to be responsible for their own learning progress within a safety net of the AI (Del Rosario Navas Bonilla et al., 2025).

4.2 The Agent's Role in Continuous, Dynamic Formative Assessment

The ability of the agent to React is empowered by the Knowledge Representation and decision-making models supporting the internal process; in that sense, it is the unrivalled driving force behind continuous, dynamic formative assessment. Formative assessment—assessment for learning—is a process laid out to monitor student learning in order to provide continuous feedback to help teachers improve teaching activities and students improve their learning. The agent ensures it is in place and also provides immediate feedback (every single student answer is a data point) in real-time further than just the classroom drills. The immediate feedback not only allows for improved learning but also for the learners' self-correction of their own mistakes, and therefore, this strategy has been proved to lead to much better outcomes compared to delayed feedback. The agent's dynamism lies in the fact that the agent is able to renew its knowledge model of the student after each click, each answer, and/or each hesitation. This internal model is nothing but a constantly updated profile of the student, which does not just track the student's performance; it also provides reasons for failure, and thus, it concludes in the identification of the specific misconceptions or knowledge gaps (e.g., mixing two formulas, having difficulties with spatial reasoning). This diagnostic capability allows the agent not only to go beyond a simple right/wrong verdict but also to provide a very special remedy, such as, for instance, offering remedial resources that match the given error's root cause. This constant, detailed data collection paves the way for all other intelligent functions, as the agent's assessment role is regarded as the core mechanism that not only feeds but also validates its personalized guidance and strategic planning. Due to the agent's transformation of learning into an assessment process, it is required that the testing process moves from being a stressful, summative occasion into a learning activity that is low-stakes and integrated, increasing the time the students spend on the tasks that have learning actual value in them (Freitas, 2022).

4.3 The Agent's Function in Fostering Collaborative Learning and Socialization

The social skills of the agent surpass the original intended designs and also extend to the area of collaborative learning and socializing, two aspects that are very important for numerous individuals' lives. People learn most effectively when they do so in a social environment that is geared towards discussion, debate, and the expression of ideas. Artificial Intelligence (AI) can serve as classmates for students by forming agent collectives; this way the individual knowledge gap and the knowledge application in a social setting will be minimized. In the agent collectives, the agents are given different cognitive and social profiles (e.g., one agent may act as the "devil's advocate," another as the "resource finder," and a third as the "facilitator"). The human student interacts with those agents, participating in joint problem solving, negotiation, and division of labor. This is a successful method of teaching teamwork, communication, and conflict resolution in a predictable, replicable, anxiety-free environment and without the coordination issues of human peer groups. The collective of agents, therefore, is a community of co-learners that is more useful for learners who are studying at their own pace, who are far from their study group, and who are in need of human contact but cannot find it. Additionally, the agents in such a community can be programmed to provide the much-needed supportive interaction required by the students—such as stepping in to mediate conflicts or encouraging reserved students to speak up, which offloads the burden of teaching those skills from the human teacher. This feature is what changes the agent from a mere transmitter of knowledge into a collaborative educational aid; hence, the learner will not only learn better but also will develop the kind of social/interpersonal skills that are a must for both the academic and professional worlds. These skills are mostly ignored in the current way of "learning in silos" (Libertson, 2023).

4.4 The Agent as a Driver of Metacognitive Development and Self-Regulation

The educational synthesis of the prominent features of all four concepts can only be said to be taking place when the AI, as the agent, is perceived as a factor that arms the student with the ability to govern his cognitive development as well as self-regulation. Metacognition is being referred to as "thinking about one's thinking" most of the time and is the capability and readiness of the student to be able to plan their own learning, to monitor their own acquired knowledge, and to correct their mistakes; it is the best measure of the independent learner. The AI agent system, by virtue of its transparent actions, really externalizes the cognitive and planning processes that very effective students do internally. For example, the proactive agent not only suggests reviewing Chapter 2, citing reasons such as spending two minutes more than usual on the last three geometry problems, which indicates a lack of fluency with the area formula, but also helps the student understand the pattern behind recognizing when a review is needed. Similarly, the immediate feedback of the reactive agent on study habits (e.g., "You tried to rush through this complex problem in 15 seconds; consider slowing down") asks the student to monitor and adjust self-regulated strategies. The agent's autonomy in managing the long-term pathway forces the student to trust the system's strategic planning, releasing the student's cognitive energy to divert attention from the content to the curriculum's structure only. Similarly, by sharing its internal models of planning, monitoring, and diagnosing, the AI functions as an external cognitive framework for the learner, assisting in internalizing these essential skills. Through this synthesis, AI agents are being established not only as tools for doing tasks but also as profound pedagogical instruments for teaching the student how to learn with personalized support; hence, the reduced reliance on the technology and the birth of an independently empowered lifelong learner (Bhardwaj et al., 2025).

5. CATEGORIES OF AI AGENTS IN LEARNING ENVIRONMENTS

The sector of educational technology and the potential technological advancements basically shape the landscape. These AI agents come in different forms of configurations based on simple software development and the operational complexity in general. These changes are causing technology companies to be limited not only to software products but also to intelligent beings that are responsive and roam around the process of education. At the most elementary level, there are Reactive agents that are simply reactive and deal with the world in the way a machine would—primarily providing feedback for your questions. It is very basic and easy to feed these agents with the necessary content and set the right types of feedback. Since their initial model is the learner, you have them dedicate their efforts mainly towards finding mistakes—practicing like pair programming. Nonetheless, the no-mind behavior of such agents is getting very limiting, and so, if the learning scenario could do with some anticipation or advice of a psychological sort, then the Deliberative agent is brought in (Galvin, 2025). A deliberative agent possesses a detailed internal model of the environment, encompassing the student's ongoing development, the organization of the curriculum, and the final mastery goals. Through the help of this internal modeling capability, the agent is able to perform complex reasoning and planning operations; therefore, the main role of the agent in education is to plan study paths that are individualized. By applying logical reasoning and goal-oriented algorithms, deliberative agents can identify a student's weaknesses and predict their future learning requirements by aggregating the weaknesses detected across various sessions. In the end, the agent rearranges the learning modules, reading materials, and practice exercises sequence over weeks or months. This process leads to the creation of a personalized and strategic curriculum design. The student is no longer placed on a one-size-fits-all approach. The learning process is tailored to individual needs to ensure the optimal and efficient acquisition of advanced competencies. Reactive agents address the current phase of learning, in contrast to deliberative agents, who manage the entire learning pathway (Outay et al., 2024).

The most effective AI-powered modern educational systems often operate on hybrid agent architectures combining reactive and deliberative components and learning agents, thus introducing a new and improved dimension that surpasses the sole-mechanism methods. Hybrid agents are an intermediate solution in the architecture, working in the way that they have a reactive component to the swift and low-level responses and a deliberative component to the strategic and high-level planning. The fact that there are two is to their advantage in that they can be relied upon to work effectively in adaptive learning systems, where their main task is to help in real time and adjust the program for the long term at the same time. A student who is having a difficult time solving a geometry problem may be offered a quick reactive clue after the first attempt fails to avoid frustration. Also, the deliberative part of the prevailing hybrid agent sees the difficulty, modifying the student's underlying knowledge and deciding to reserve the entire week for a geometric proofs review module. (Outay et al., 2024). This equilibrium style of working ensures that the agent is at the right time and right place while, at the same time, is committedly engaged in becoming the expert in the field in the long run. Helping to stretch the adaptability, learning agents represent the category of agents that bring about the possibility of real self-improvement based on the record. These agents are special in their kind, as they employ Machine Learning (ML) algorithms to update themselves in accordance with the students' queries or concerns. In comparison with other categories of agents who follow predefined rule sets, learning agents change their inner parameters, models, and decision-making rules as per the stream of data coming from the student. Thus, as the student interacts more and more frequently and in different ways with the agent, the agent becomes increasingly better at predicting the next mistake of the student, choosing the most appropriate format for presenting the information to the student (e.g., video vs. text), and identifying the most effective scaffolding strategy over time. One example that can be given is that a learning agent might first utilize a general pedagogical rule to give harder problems after correct answers, but after some time, it learns through observations that a particular student's mood goes up when s/he is given an easier problem after a tough one is solved and, consequently, it decides to concentrate on this kind of technique. This process is emblematic of continuous evolution, and the learning agent becomes the key instrument for attaining fully personalized teaching, thus changing AI from a fixed entity to a completely adaptive and informed companion in the venture of the solitary learning path (Ion & Popescu, 2024).

6. MECHANISMS DRIVING AI AGENTS

The efficiency of AI agents in the learning settings where they work independently greatly relies on a complicated variety of tech mechanisms underpinning their perception, reasoning power, flexibility, and interaction. The very basic mechanisms are all about the agent handling data and deciding what to do with it, commencing with the practices of knowledge representation and decision-making models. Knowledge representation is when an agent takes information from the environment and structures it, i.e., stores it in such a way as to represent the world, holding such particular pieces of information as historical dates, mathematical theorems, instructional strategies, and the learner's continuous profile (mastery levels, learning style preferences) and using different contexts as a basis for providing learner guidance. The techniques employed can be anywhere from simple rule-based systems and semantic networks to complex ontologies and probabilistic graphical models, the latter of which are able to help the agent handle the human learning's inherent uncertainty. As an example, an agent might represent a student's knowledge as the probability of denoting its distribution over a set of concepts, i.e., its likelihood of mastery being less (Liu et al., 2024). Truly, the decision-making models are very closely knit with this representation, as these models are configured against the knowledge store to get the best action out of the available actions each moment. Agents utilize forms of logic, one of which is logical inference; they include planning algorithms (like Markov Decision Processes for sequence planning), and they may apply heuristic search algorithms to move in a space that is defined by all possible actions (e.g., selecting an action, asking students to review, proceeding to the next topic). A decision model, on the other hand, ensures the agent's actions are continuously in line with the defined pedagogical goals, such as learning gain maximization and student frustration minimization (Khodadad, 2023). This is how this particular mechanism enables the agent to change from a mere reactor to a thoughtful, goal-minded intervener, thus acting very effectively as the learner's intelligent planner. These models are so well built up that they enable the agent to do a number of things, such as interpreting very slight and hard-to-get cues from the learner's interaction and giving guidance that is not only accurate but also contextually right. A well-curated knowledge base and decision model have the ability to transition the agent with great ease from being a tutor, a collaborator, or an assessor depending on the immediate situation and educational need. The very essence of this mechanism is the major distinction between a really intelligent agent and a basic algorithm (Panait, & Luke, 2005).

Machine Learning (ML) models are the innovation alongside the static or pre-programmed decision models, which allow the agents to be adaptable. The provision of data and the agents also have the ability to adapt, and hence, if it were not for the machine learning where the agent becomes self-adjustable and personalizes its actions over time, the term "learning agent" could not be truly applied. The data comes in a continuous stream, and these algorithms give the agent the capability to learn from it. The data may be the output of learner interactions such as right or wrong answers, task completion time, clicks, etc. It also allows the modification of the agent's internal algorithms and models without the need for manual reprogramming. On the other hand, the learning algorithms are trained to be supervised by powerful and secure datasets of successes and failures to guide the student toward the next step, which is the best step in the performance metrics, especially for learning students (Hashim et al., 2020). Reinforcement learning (RL) is the area in which the agent becomes autonomous by performing trial and error processes that will have an outcome in the long term, such as the final assessment score or reducing time to ultimate success. Plus, it can be a little bit more understood when we say that a pattern of hinting is more effective for specific learners than for general ones, and an RL agent learns this. Additionally, NLP is central in conversational agents, as it enables human-like communication that is a must for deeper connection—the NLP pieces of software allow the agents to talk, interpret, and write like people. Assistants that answer questions and assist with the discussion, excluding unnecessary questions. Moreover, sentiment analysis, topic modelling, and natural language generation (NLG) methods, besides capturing the student's words, can be the agent's interpreters of the intent or emotional state of the student (thus paving the way to the development of emotionally intelligent agents). The adoption of ML with a wide range of suitable applications for personalization and NLP with a very strong direct application in communication creates a situation where the AI agent can effectively, flexibly, and adaptively carry on a conversation (chatting) or tutoring, therefore making the learning practice more of a human-to-human interaction. The agent's adaptability is the utmost factor making the self-directed learning a smooth process by providing the adaptive prompts in accordance with and modifying in real time the difficulty level of the activities (Strielkowski et al., 2024).

The data infrastructure and the interaction with learning management systems (LMS) are two major contributors toward the operation of an AI entity in an educational institution. Without the perfect symbiosis with the technological infrastructure of the organization, the AI would not find a place in the institution. One of the ways that an AI agent can gain access to the students' data and the academic calendar, for example, is through the LMS integration process (Alotaibi, 2024). This is normally achieved through the use of APIs and standardized protocols (e.g., LTI, Caliper, or xAPI) that would allow the agent to transmit and receive the authenticated data. Moreover, the integration of the API is necessary for the effectiveness of the agent to be sustained. It helps the agent by pulling out the information that is of standard or past course-giving activities and current activities of the student using different systems (logs) and putting it into the official system to create professional information that is visible to the administrator for tracking or generating reports. Additionally, the ethical and practical challenges of the system also require this connection (Zhao et al., 2023). Diverse as the education system may be, the main thing is that the LMS, which is a procurement of the organization, always provides the security standards that are necessary for data privacy and addressing surveillance issues in education. Batch data synchronization and the technical framework of the integration mechanics set the ground for balancing the agent and customizing it to the needs of the student while meeting the school's standardized system. The whole thing, from knowledge representation to machine learning and system integration, will eventually form an integrated and interrelated technical system. This very system is what makes a simple idea of an AI agent become real, flexible, and a great pedagogical tool that can support self-study in a wide range of educational settings, paving the way for the future human-AI co-agent model (Katsenou & Deliyannis, 2025).

7. PEDAGOGICAL ROLES OF AI AGENTS

Introducing AI agents in the field of educational technology is a game-changer. The role that is being played by these artificially intelligent agents represents a significant advancement in pedagogical effectiveness. Moreover, with their very own smart technology, they help their learners and their teachers as well. With AI integrated into all educational settings, it will serve as a guiding force that consistently remembers its area of expertise and offers help to those open to learning. One of the added benefits of these AI-driven intelligent tutoring systems is that AI agents augment and support teachers rather than replace them. How can one help with other things, such as giving the whole class the basics and then leaving this tutoring tool to deal with every other thing that the attention span of each student won't allow for? The AI-driven intelligent systems can help make the human teachers' presence in the classroom much lighter. This help is in the form of communicating with the students with diverse learning needs in class and making sure that they are getting what they need. The agent, who can wait and be accessible around the clock, also adds to its mentoring potential by guiding the student through difficult concepts and problem topics that require complex problem-solving skills. The AI tutor's tailored remediation ensures that the student is neither bored nor frustrated, as the material is always within the learner's Zone of Proximal Development. In reality, the AI tutor duplicates the advantages of the master-apprentice relationship, thus making the elite tutoring accessible to a huge population. The agent's central traits of being autonomous and proactive are the very reasons it is able to be a tutor that starts the conversation with the student and takes charge of the tutoring session without the need for a human mentor (V. Liu et al., 2025).

A second key aspect of the pedagogical process is the production of peer collaboration conditions through the use of agent collectives. The task of learning is naturally social, so collaborative problem-solving is an essential requirement in the acquisition of critical thinking, communication, and negotiation skills. AI agents with their social attributes can work together to mimic the dynamics of a study group or project team. The AI agents in these simulations might take on different roles (such as an expert, a skeptic, or a facilitator), questioning the student's answers, giving their point of view, or else supporting the student in solving a complex, multi-layered problem. By doing so, students can have a safe, repeatable place to perform teamwork without the burden or fear of making mistakes that are generally related to human peer groups. Besides that, an agent collective can be purposely configured to put certain learning obstacles or collaborative breakdowns in place, thus enabling the student to build up the required skills in conflict resolution and leadership as the agents assist in an invisible way by providing continuous scaffolding. This educational method is a must for those students who are taking distance learning or for places where it is difficult to form various human groups. The agents, by presenting a rich, interactive social layer, make sure that the detached learning does not become a lonely experience, and they cross the bridge from individual knowledge acquisition to collaborative professional or academic knowledge application. The agent collectives are designed using highly advanced decision-making models and communication protocols through the use of NLP (Dorri et al., 2018).

The final set of related functions—advancing from solo efforts by suggesting adaptive prompts to customizing, diagnosing, and achieving mastery through evaluation and performance tracking—are crucial in fostering full independence and metacognitive skills in the learner.

7.1 Scaffolding Self-Directed Learning with Adaptive Prompts

Scaffolding refers to the process of providing a learner with temporary support in order to help him or her master the task that he or she was not able to finish on his or her own and gradually taking away this support as the individual becomes more competent. This is where AI comes in, as it can very well provide adaptive hints that are exactly tailored to the learner's need at that very moment. Such an ability flows from the reactive nature of the agent along with its machine learning algorithms. For instance, if a learner is stuck on a problem, the agent may start with a very small hint (a memory of the formula they learned before) and then proceed to give a conceptual hint (a Socratic question that sets them on the right path of reasoning) and only as a last resort, give the solution step directly. This arranged help prompts students to try their own abilities to solve the problem before they are given more help, thereby fostering the critical autonomy and deep engagement with the material (Singer et al., 2000). The 'adaptive' property makes sure that the agent's hints are tailored to the individual; a highly capable learner might get only conceptual challenges, while a struggling learner might get more structural support. The focused intervention is a necessity for self-directed learning since it shields learners from information overload, helps to build self-regulation, and ensures the learner engages with the necessary cognitive effort. The agent thus takes the form of an invisible mentor, adjusting the cognitive load and providing a real-world and flexible context for the learning process. 'Productive struggling' is a term well known among educators that leads to 'deep learning' (Booth et al., 2023).

7.2 Continuous Assessment and Performance Monitoring

It is the function that serves as the main source of the agent's intelligence and its adaptability. Having a continuous assessment means that the agent, unlike with end-of-unit testing, can still progress. Every action taken by the learner, for example, a mouse click, the time in which a paragraph is read, the order in which the problems are tried, etc., is seen as a data point that the agent will/can use in the future to learn more about the learner's knowledge. This type of data-driven insight aids in building and preserving the agent's mental model, including its knowledge, decision-making mechanisms, and the machine learning algorithms that support the system. The agent has performance monitoring, which is the checking of the system's performance against these metrics, thus enabling it to identify and stop misconceptions and errors from happening. Also, the agent can predict future performance with high predictive accuracy under controlled conditions, subject to data quality and contextual variability. In other words, this is a diagnostic power that makes the other pedagogical functions possible: it is the driver for the adaptive prompts (scaffolding), it is the reason for the selection of the next topic (intelligent tutoring), and it provides the hard data for the simulation design (peer collaboration). In addition, the monitoring can be taken even further so that the student's learning behaviors, such as consistency in studying and strategies of asking for help, are being tracked, and as a result, the learner will receive valuable metacognitive feedback. The system offers detailed, real-time information that is usually merged with learning management systems (LMS) to provide educators and policymakers with a clearer insight into learner behavior. This facilitates more effective and efficient teaching, especially in large-scale programs where learners are not physically overseen (Pellas, 2024).

7.3 Integration and Ethical Implications of AI Agent Roles

The effectiveness in playing these roles is determined by the ability to work with learning management systems (LMS) that are integrated seamlessly with the very system platform for the deployment and data exchange. The teaching-based attractiveness of AI agents—acting as instructors, colleagues, or evaluators, for instance—goes with the amount of open data and the type of processing mechanisms they use (Ghosh et al., 2025b). Still, the high-quality aspect of these roles makes them thoughtful agents, which means negative impacts, on the other hand, are inevitable. Likewise, the learner being overly reliant on the scaffolding mechanism and slightly losing critical autonomy is among the undesirable outcomes. The possibility of the AI agent in the pedagogical context to play the role of the test center manager or learning process enhancer makes the learning process not only much more individual but also more attractive to the learner. The foundation of this depends on careful and beneficial design such that personalization does not happen at the expense of standardization and that technology does not take the place of the learner but rather supports their intellect and growth. It is anticipated that the future scenario will be one in which we move toward co-agency models where the human educator and the agent work together to get the maximum learning outcome, and the adoption of such models will be guided by well-defined policy and governance frameworks ensuring responsible deployment and usage (Zhang et al., 2025).

8. ETHICAL AND PRACTICAL CHALLENGES OF AI AGENTS IN INDEPENDENT LEARNING

The collaboration of AI agents and independent learning environments, although very beneficial from a pedagogical point of view, will lead to numerous ethical and practical obstacles to be dealt with not only by educators and technologists but also by legislators with equivalent expertise. The primary apprehension is the chance of unfairness in adaptive learning, which in essence will destroy the foundation of fair education. AI agents, particularly those that work on machine learning (ML) principles, take their cues from extensive collections of historical data on students' performance and interaction. It is a realistic possibility that the initial data used for training will be biased, which may cause the agents to pick up and even intensify the bias (Mökander, & Axente, 2021). If, for example, the training data sets expose that scholars from a particular socio-economic class traditionally presented weakly in some topic because of their limited opportunities, the agent through its adaptive pathway generation could very well lead all students from that group to the easier curriculum, the less demanding track, or even the less promising field of career, in spite of the student's high capability. This self-fulfilling prophecy signifies the past disadvantage to be integrated into the schooling life opportunities of the student. The issue is not only about the bias of the algorithm but also about data and systemic biases being utilized in the long run. To minimize it, the software engineers have to work with the stringent equality framework, which includes fairness among different groups and the metrics, as well as the adversarial debiasing methods, to continually regulate disparate outcomes for the different student groups (e.g., gender, race, disability status). Besides the above-mentioned point, the lack of access and the complex deep learning models that cannot be explained, the problem of "lack of transparency in the model" worsens the issue as it is not possible for the educators or the students to inspect the reason for the recommended adaptive pathway or find if any bias was accidentally introduced. The issue even extends to feedback loops giving students agent-centered pedagogical resources based on how they engaged, and student engagement being influenced by cultural background or internet connectivity, so the setting may punish students interacting through means hindered by external factors. That said, the remedy for bias inclines not only toward employing technical treatments but also, to a great extent, toward the moral obligation entailing making adaptive pathways that foster equity and inclusiveness rather than perpetuate separation and isolation, which demands continuous auditing and ethical review of the agent throughout its life cycle (Mökander & Axente, 2021).

Another major issue is the psychological and developmental effects on the student, which can be very dangerous, for example, in cases of over-reliance on the learner's side and the reduced autonomy to critically think. The AI agents' efficiency itself, especially in their ability to provide specific and continuous support and immediate feedback, can be harmful if not managed properly. If the teacher always gets the right support and guidance, he/she may just rely on it and not do the necessary hard work, which can lead to shallow learning and even a decline in the development of metacognitive skills. Metacognition, the state that allows one to choose the methods of learning and mark the level of understanding, as well as being able to self-correct errors, is the main feature of free learning (Ruangpattanakul, 2025). The student will be denied the opportunity to strengthen his/her self-regulation strategies and demonstrate the affective domain of learning if the agent is always present to give reminders or cues at the slightest sign of student error. The over-reliance difficulty is further intensified by personalized convenience being guised as simple: students may possibly take the easy way out subconsciously following the path of least resistance steered by the AI, rather than being sceptical about the curriculum, exploring side topics, or creating new methods of problem solving—the very conduct which is emphasized with advanced thinking and creative skills. In turn, this can be a decline in critical autonomy, that is, the student will be good at studying within the system's boundaries but will have a hard time when faced with unstructured, uncertain, or novel problems outside of the agent's domain. A possible solution to this would be to have agents to be developed with a specific policy of scaffolding withdrawal so that the situation tapers off in a programmed and measured manner, thereby making the learner take up the monitoring and planning activities themselves. In addition to this, the designing of the curriculum must encompass the presence of activities with a high degree of structuring that necessitate the student to go on without the assistance of the agent and apply his or her knowledge to a new environment while, in the process, he or she is testing for self-reliance. The challenge is a matter of fine adjustment: making full use of the agent's help to ensure that one learns while at the same time not interfering too much with the student's independence in order to make sure that s/he becomes self-sufficient. Not only does this build the foundation for the long-term success in academics and occupational arenas but it also ensures the essential reinforcement of a continuously evolving and dynamic system of intellectual capacity (Darling-Hammond et al., 2019).

The last difficult challenge is where technology, law, and institutional trust meet each other, particularly in reference to the problems of Data privacy and surveillance issues in education and the requirement of balancing personalization with standardization.

8.1 Data Privacy and Surveillance Concerns in Education

The capability of AI agents to adapt instruction according to the student's personal needs is directly related to their ability to evaluate continuously and keep track of performance, which will lead to the collection of a large amount of very sensitive, detailed student data. This data will consist not only of marks resulting from assessments and quizzes but also of behavioral biometrics too, such as keystroke dynamics, the time that the student takes per question, emotions inferred from conversational patterns, and even webcam-monitoring data in some supervision situations, which have all been incorporated into the collection process. The entire data gathering is thus seen to bring up big questions concerning both the privacy and the control that might not be restricted only to the academic arena but may spread to other areas like advertising, prediction of criminal activities, background checks for job seekers, and so on. The moral necessity is for the school or authority to take the required actions by putting in place the necessary security and de-identification measures, by being very compliant to the legal-ethical imperatives such as FERPA, GDPR, and COPPA, and by giving the students and their guardians full control and obvious understanding of their data (Ghosh et al., 2025a). The monitoring element involves very serious issues too: the constant and later through the minutest tracking knowledge can subtly drive the student to go along with what is expected rather than being really involved in the process of learning (what some call the "chilling effect"), thereby undermining the genuineness of the learning process that the AI agent is supposed to facilitate. Dealing with this problem means that data minimalism has to be adopted (only getting the data which is strictly necessary for the learning process) and purpose limitation—the data collected should only be used for achieving the educational goal, and nothing else (C. Wang, 2024).

8.2 Balancing Personalization with Standardization

The profound disagreement between artificially intelligent agents' empowering of personalized teaching methods and the request for uniformity in the educational system remains a significant practical and political issue. One of the main reasons for the absence of personalized education is the lack of differentiation among students in meeting the educational benchmarks and ensuring fairness in academic credits and laying the groundwork for all students to achieve academic credentials. However, the leading function of the AI agent is to come up with the best possible learning path for every student, which would, of course, lead to highly varying experiences, resource sequences, and even tempo of coverage. If two students obtain the same final grade but followed completely different adaptive pathways, how can the institution assert the equality of their educational experiences and the maintenance of their competencies is consistent? This problem needs the establishment of very intricate governance systems that will steer responsible adoption of the technology by the institutions. These governance systems will have to dictate the degree of personalization by identifying the learning outcomes that are irrefutable and thus have to be accomplished under standardized evidence and by freely adjusting different parts of the syllabus for algorithms only. The cure can be sought by pinpointing the personalization not on the path but on the definitive result (the competence demonstrated), thereby enforcing new forms of competency-based assessment that can accurately evaluate learning regardless of the teaching method used. (Açıkgöz & Babadoğan, 2021).

8.3 Policy and Institutional Oversight

In the end, these ethical and practical problems focus on the demand for the most efficient policy and governance frameworks possible, which would then contribute to the adoption of responsible AI. The progress in AI is so fast that it leaves the regulations far behind, and that is why developers chip in as the primary lawmakers. If we want AI agents to do good for the people, it is the responsibility of the learners, and not only of the developers, to critically understand and intervene in the above-listed AI principles. The public's interests should be served, and education, technology, and policy experts must work together to set the rules that will be used for checking bias, identifying and acting on data rights, demanding transparency, and determining the limits of AI autonomy in education. The goal is to make full use of the agent's ability to be extremely personalized and efficient while at the same time firmly but carefully protecting primary educational principles: fairness, critical autonomy, and privacy. If not properly and timely governed, the spread of AI agents would indeed raise the problem of the gap widening among learners, with the result that it would become impossible to meet the goals of individual learning development (Dobrescu et al., 2025).

9. SOLUTIONS AND RECOMMENDATIONS

If one is to the effective and ensuring intelligence systems are used appropriately and responsibly in autonomous learning settings, the best strategy to adopt would be one that incorporates aspects relating to technology, education and ethics. Such strategies has the following solutions and suggestions, that is that, recommendations on adjusting AI agent implementation, as to minimize risks to academic malpractice.

9.1 Adoption of Explainable AI (XAI)

One of the major concerns linked to artificial intelligence enhanced educational systems is the lack of explainability in mechanisms. Using Explainable Artificial Intelligence techniques can place confidence on computers and account for them as teachers or students will be able to know how AI is reasoning out what to recommend or adapt, or which test to conduct. Open algorithms make it possible for the stakeholders to screen out any case of discrepancy, touch the truth of the system outputs and correspond them to the pedagogical objectives.

9.2 Bias Detection and Auditing Frameworks

In order to lessen algorithmic bias, there needs to be a sustained monitoring by institutions of AI agents across many various learner groups. This will involve the combined application of equity indicators, occasional assessments of prejudice and the application of adversarial techniques top Decrease it, as well as the provision of enlarged adversarial debiasing. Furthermore, there is a need to caution against using training datasets which do not take a wider perspective in data sampling, leading to older patterns of learning disparities to resurface in the future.

9.3 Human-in-the-Loop (HITL) Systems

The usage of AI is convenient and reliable however it should be limited to supportive role (human assisted), especially in decision-making in risky conditions like education. Through the establishment of Human In The Loop (HITL) systems, the position of the teacher ensures that they observe the decisions that were previously made by the AI algorithm, evaluate and adjust them when necessary. With the help of all this, the integrity of the educational environment is preserved, and principals, for example, teachers, are given the possibility to include AI, running the risk of manipulating it with a view to protecting their livelihood.

9.4 Scaffold Withdrawal and Learner Autonomy Design

In order to steer clear of the complete dependence on AI systems, it is necessary to work on pedagogical methodologies that adaptive in nature, and gradually scale down the support as learners progress. For this reason, it is proposed that AI agents incorporate the dimension of fading in the design of their interactive user interfaces. This implies that it is encouraging that professional self-regulation is foreseen based on the advancement of learners' development through a certain type of instruction.

9.5 AI Literacy and Educator Training Programs

To effectively use AI agents, educators should possess a basic knowledge of AI terminologies, data concepts, and moral or ethical factors. Training the teachers in AI critical thinking skills to understand the generated information, recognize its limitations and responsibly incorporate the pedagogical recommendations given by AI changes the traditional edifices of learning. This change involves a reimagining of educators' roles from that of dictator to even tutors, analysts, as well as ethical assessors.

9.6 Data Governance and Privacy Protection Policies

It is no sterling truth that data governance frameworks are a prerequisite in connection with privacy and security matters around AI learning systems. Therefore, requires information systems be designed with data processing principles which observing such as data minimization, safe data storage and access control principles. Where applicable, institutions should adequately implement their data ETHICAL AND LEGAL considerations, including the General Data Protection Regulation in Europe (GDPR) and the Family Educational Rights and Privacy Act (FERPA) in the US. Nonetheless, instructive in the sense that the data usage goals of the learners should reflect understanding of the different levels of data, how they are stored and the relationship they have with the policies and the attitudes towards both the teacher and the other learners.

9.7 Standardization with Flexible Personalization

An educational institution should adapt to the use of competency-based approaches, where they should setup structured learning outcomes and flexible learning paths with a view to balancing personalization and institutional consistencies. Computerized adaptive test training can allow for individual adjustment of study without disproving any academic norms by making sure that the range of adaptive learning is targeted towards objectively stipulated achieved levels.

9.8 Continuous Evaluation and System Improvement

It is important to acknowledge the necessity for regular appraisals of AI systems regarding certain aspects that include their efficient functioning, fairness and alignment with teaching and learning aims. Also, there should be proper feedback mechanisms with the feedback from the teachers, learners and even developers in order to make changes in the algorithms so as to enhance user experience as well as meet the current objective of education. Surveillance activities provide means of accountability and assure that ethical standards have been maintained in designing pedagogically relevant AI applications.

9.9 Emerging Trends in AI Agents for Education

Recent tendencies in AI agents for education point towards efforts to develop systems providing non-verbal, emotional and speech data and analysis, emotionally intelligent tutoring, and language interpretation tools. More and more authors are proposing the use of models that allow AI and human beings to co-create, real-time feedback application, and system update. Apart from that, there is a higher tendency of regulation targeting the moral question of AI. These cover all aspects of technology deployment and even the governance of data.

10. FUTURE TRAJECTORIES OF AI AGENTS IN EDUCATION

As effective as they are at giving personal education and tests, AI agents of the current generation are nowhere near the first stages of educational technology. The field is quickly advancing forward, particularly in three major directions that are the design of emotionally intelligent and situation-aware agents, the definition of human-AI co-agency models in classrooms, and—crucially—the requirement of policy and governance frameworks for responsible adoption. The first path, which is the most radical, soars over the cognitive instruction and lands on the affective and environmental planes, which exert a tremendous amount of influence on learning. Emotionally intelligent and context-aware agents are designed to detect, interpret, and act on the emotional state, motivational levels, and physical surroundings of a learner. The current agents mostly just work with a student's cognition, or in other words, "what a student knows"; however, the future agents will not only recognize the student's feeling about what they know but also where and when they are learning (contextual state). Moreover, the development of emotional intelligence mainly requires technological innovations that are sufficiently complex, and one of the innovations is to make use of multimodal sensing in learning, like voice characteristics, facial expressions (using computer vision), text sentiment, and physiological data (heart rate, etc., from wearables, if ethically permissible). The agent would then use these data to determine the frequent emotional states, e.g., frustration, curiosity, boredom, or anxiety. To exemplify, the agent would not only give a conceptual hint (cognitive response) if it observes high frustration in the behavior and communications of the student, like repetitive, erratic mouse movements, slow response times, and negative sentiment in typed responses; it would do an emotional intervention, such as delivering an encouraging message, suggesting a short cognitive break, or subtly changing the difficulty of the problem to reduce the feeling of threat. The importance of this ability lies in the fact that emotional factors significantly impact learning performance: anxious students typically face difficulties in recalling facts, while curious students are more likely to keep going. Context-awareness broadens this level of intelligence by utilizing the real-life environmental factors as part of the teaching and learning process (De Souza Zanirato Maia et al., 2023). This indicates that the system will recognize the mobile device, background noise, late-night study routines, and changes in subjects being studied. A context-aware agent would change its teaching method—for instance, if the student is tired, it may present shorter, more dynamic presentations, or it may refer to a possible energy-hogging application that might be stopped—or adapt the pace and difficulty of the task to the student's/learner's energy and attention levels. Simultaneously, creating these agents requires addressing significant technical challenges in precisely annotating emotional data and guaranteeing that the emotional models are valid across different cultures, alongside ethical considerations such as respecting students' privacy while tracking their mental health. We are on the brink of introducing a very caring and personally tailored learning companion to education, which may be considered the utmost goal by instructors and school administrators.

Positioning human educators and electronic tutors as collaborating partners is the second revolutionary educational shift. Instead of treating AI agents as tools or automated tutors, co-agency shifts the focus to a new paradigm where both the human educator and the AI agent work together as a team, each of them utilizing their unique skills for the betterment of the learning environment. In the co-agency model, the AI agent acts as a super-assistant to the human teacher (Yambal & Waykar, 2025). The agent's role is to perform continuous, data-based evaluation and personalized adaptation as a result of cognitive evaluation; thus, it can simultaneously monitor the performance and the engagement of each one in the class. The human teacher's strength is getting along with people, making interesting lessons, doing group work, and developing ethics and society with a strong sense of ethics. Through co-agency, the AI agent continuously provides the human teacher with very detailed and real-time diagnostic reports: "Student A is not grasping concept X and needs an illustration," or "Everybody in the class except students B, C, and D has mastered this concept, and they can be involved in a project that requires higher skills." The teacher, by using this very precise and predictive data, significantly improves the quality of their in-class teaching, thereby shifting from general assessment to specific assistance to small groups, the modern version of the Socratic Method, and mentoring. Then the teacher has the liberty to devote his or her limited time to the students whom the agent has identified as needing human touch, motivation, or counseling for their complex and critical guidance. This same teamwork is also seen in the development of the curriculum; the teacher takes the agent's big data observations on curriculum effectiveness to perfect and redo lesson plans. Co-agency is crucial for the moral and legal implementation of AI because it guarantees that the teacher, who is the ultimate authority and humanistic guide, remains so, thereby lessening the risks of losing critical autonomy and becoming overly ministered. The shift to this model requires educators' extensive training and professional development, whereby their part changes from being providers of information to the interpreters of data, personal mentors, and the ones who capably use the AI-driven insights. This change requests the making of user-friendly dashboards and communication protocols that make it easy for the teacher's practical pedagogical decision-making and the AI's sophisticated models to communicate with each other, bringing out the desired outcomes. This approach is the best option for bringing about customized and tech-based learning at the same time building rich human connections between a learner and their tutor (Osher et al., 2018).

The successful and sustained deployment of these advanced agents hinges entirely on the third critical trajectory: the establishment of robust policy and governance frameworks for responsible adoption. Without clear legal, ethical, and institutional guidelines, the rapid proliferation of AI agents risks exacerbating social inequities, violating fundamental privacy rights, and undermining the core principles of education. This trajectory necessitates the creation of four distinct interlinked governance components.

10.1 Algorithmic Transparency and Auditability Mandates

Future integration of advanced AI agents into the fabric of learning and teaching—particularly in the case of self-reliant learning pathways—is creating a very serious demand for the so-called Algorithmic Transparency and Auditability Mandates. This mandate is seen as the main ethical and efficient mechanism by which any bias found in the continuous and individualized learning paths can be identified, and at the same time accountability can be maintained when high-stakes decisions are made. The very basic difficulty arises from the "black box" characteristics of the present-day machine learning models, which are the deep neural networks, specifically, where intricate, non-linear relationships among thousands of input features (student's data points) and the output (a grade, a pathway recommendation, or an intervention) are not comprehensible to the human mind. The lack of translucency, as with the opaque algorithm-driven agent that takes a decision that will fundamentally change a student's academic path—e.g., giving a lower mark, suggesting some remedial course track, or even the most problematic one, denying a student a place in a program in progress—will not allow the transparency of the system to be verified, and so the student, parent, or teacher will never be able to guarantee if the decision was fair, non-discriminatory, or pedagogically sound. The invisibility of the process puts at risk the fact that bias may be integrated into the educational system through automation. If the training data that the agent used to develop itself has typical disparities (e.g., some demographic groups have always fared poorly in the past, and this is attributed to unequal resource allocation), the algorithm will absorb and augment this unfairness thus creating and perpetuating adaptive paths that are self-fulfilling and exclusionary and also, as a result, reinforcing the same inequities that the educational system is intended to eliminate (Miglani, 2025).

Ensuring this would require policies to not just mention the agent's role but also to put in place a strong standard of explainable AI (XAI) and an obligatory auditing system. The developers need to comply with the XAI standard—a crucial requirement for them to provide a clear and understandable reason for a machine-made high-stakes judgment. Such an explanation could, for example, be the disclosure of the feature importance scores that had the most influence on a recommendation, leading to a human-like expression: "The system suggested Unit 3 to you as your last three quizzes showed 40% faster completion times than average, indicating a high COVID-19 or flu season prevalence." On the other hand, auditability is an even tougher requirement since it demands that not only the final model weights but also the whole data path starting from the dataset sources be clear to be inspected by the third-party auditors or the regulatory bodies. These audit conditions are to be seen in relation to the necessity of the developers to not only document and store but also make public the training datasets that they used. The purpose of the disclosure is to allow the auditors to not only verify data bias (e.g., lack of adequate representation of certain populations, cultural bias in content) and sample bias (e.g., data from schools with high achievers solely used) but also to check the methods of debiasing—i.e., the statistical and algorithmic methods used to eliminate unintended discrimination among the protected attributes. The policymakers should come up with simple, easily quantifiable, and indicative fairness measures (e.g., the agent has to be able to provide equalized odds or meet demographic parity), which should already be met by the time of deployment. The closest we can get to ensuring fairness and educational standards is by implementing auditability in practice, which ensures that the ways the agents assess the student's learning process are not only fair but also consistent with the established educational pedagogical norms, making AI not only more reliable but also less likely to interfere with established educational values (like student-centered learning, individualization of learning, etc.). This generation by regulation ensures that the AI systems are still bonded to human values and hence one can transform the black-box into a tool that educators can engage and understand, bringing back the humans' moral authority in the education process (Tanksley, 2024).

10.2 Data Sovereignty and Privacy Rights Legislation

The future effectiveness of AI agents is heavily reliant on the need to regularly assess and monitor performance, which will subsequently necessitate the gathering of very sensitive, detailed educational data. Apart from test scores, this data will encompass the biometry of behavior, cognitive metrics, and, to an increasing extent, inferred affects (like frustration or boredom inferred from eye tracking or conversational sentiment). This kind of private digital surveying leads to the immense data privacy and surveillance concerns in education; thus, a new legislative framework based on data sovereignty is required. Current privacy regulations like FERPA in the United States were designed for paper-based records and are now obsolete given the real-time, rapid-flow behavioral data utilized by adaptive artificial intelligence. Therefore, new legislation that focuses on educational technology is a must, where the main actor—the student—and their digital learning profile must be considered a new entity. The fundamental concept of data sovereignty is to secure students' and, if necessary, their parents' complete rights to own and manage their learning information (Agesilaou & Kyza, 2022). This sovereignty should encompass several essential rights: the entitlement to access all raw and processed data related to behavior and performance collected by the agent; the ability to contest the correctness or interpretation of this data, such as disputing a low confidence score; the right to correct any inaccuracies in their profile; and, possibly the most important, the right to delete their data after a specific duration or once their educational program ends. The power to delete data is the most fundamental of all, as otherwise, an extremely detailed, lifelong digital learning profile could be misused against the individual in future job, insurance, or other critical areas. The surveillance issue is also made worse by the fear of reusing the educational data for commercial or even non-educational surveillance purposes. The entities creating the educational AI usually depend on business models that are focused on data marketing, and they do this by means of data monetization, which can either be anonymous or, more dangerously, through focused marketing and predicting characteristics. Proper use of data must be a rule so that more data and more people are brought together for IT companies to conduct their research and business, and thus, data collection would be reduced to the least. Along with that should go the policy of data minimalism, where only the exact minimal amount that is necessary for the agents' stated pedagogical function will be collected, thereby reducing the privacy risk's "surface area." Furthermore, the shift in the law should also make it compulsory, for privacy by design, that AI systems be built with secure encryption and anonymization as core features by default rather than added later, ensuring security and anonymity by default from the start. By setting up precise legal and technical requirements for data sovereignty, the future of AI in education can be freed from the negative effects that could come through the collecting of bright micro-information, provided continuous assessment is, therefore, making learning better while not in any way infringing on the learner's innate right to privacy and control over their digital identity (Alier et al., 2021).

10.3 Standardization and Interoperability Protocols

The broad adoption of personalized AI agents cannot happen, at least not without some sort of obtrusive standardization, which somewhat contradicts the said radical personalization. Although personalization is the main and most important function of the AI agent, it is also seen as a very reliable way to the top by the people, and therefore they can't see the need for anything else to be done other than optimization of the learning process for the individual. To certify integrity and make student exchange between schools an easy and possible process without any compromises, an organized system (standardization) is a must. Just for example, if two students get a B+ in the 'College Physics' course, one of them might have studied from traditional and standardized materials, and the other one may have chosen a completely different, AI-optimized pathway that, according to the AI system, omitted certain redundant modules for the specific learner. Here the institution has to face the problem of comparing the two works and determining the equivalence of the educational experiences. This concerns the very essence of academic degrees and certificates. The only way this can be worked out is to have governance frameworks in place that establish technical interoperability protocols and focus on the outcome rather than the process of standardization. For interoperability to take place, a set of technical protocols must be defined (for example, xAPI, LTI, and Caliper), ensuring that different AI agents' and LMSs' data exchange is very smooth and to the same standard (Ruano et al., 2023). Such a requirement is sure to stop vendor lock-in, or the student being unable to take a break or change schools while keeping all of their learning progress in a system that belonged to a provider that would not share the system or the data. Truly, interoperability is the way to go in situations where a student's learning pathway is personalized, consistent, and efficiently understandable across different institutional contexts. The second strategy, besides the quality assurance through the technical interoperability system, is the policy that outlines the criteria and process for awarding credits and aims at outcome equivalence between the personalized and the standardized curriculum. This policy would need to establish solid linkages and transitions for grading from the current, time-based, seat-time-based model to the competency-based model. In this case, the standardization will not come from completion of specific courses or modules (the pathway or the how), but from the real attainment of certain minute skills and knowledge that can be verified by the student who has participated in an assessment based on the skills or outcomes (the outcome or the what). The AI agent's main function is to track module completion, but this will shift to proving the competence by providing that the actual completion was correct. The validation and verification of the competency-mapping model of the AI agent as well as of the tools for assessment through governance frameworks are the measures in place to confirm that they are all reliable, valid, and free of bias. Making interoperability a rule and setting up a policy system that relies on a competency-based approach will pull the educational system out of the struggle between individuality and standardization that would have otherwise caused AI agents to serve as optimal learners while the credibility and utility of academic credentials remained intact in the wider education community. This down-to-earth approach is the key to the realization of massive and successful adaptive education without the need to compromise the institutional values (Chergui et al., 2024).

10.4 Professional Ethics and Educator Training Standards

Future responsible AI agent adoption is mostly guaranteed once the human aspect is tackled via new teaching ethics and trainer instruction standards. The goal of a successful model in which AI and humans cooperate, and where the AI becomes almost like a second teacher, mainly depends on the human teacher's ability to comprehend, analyze, and, of course, ethically apply the generated data and the AI-based recommendations. This calls for a fairly large-scale change in teacher professional development that goes a step further than just acquiring the technical knowledge and skills of AI to having advanced literacy in AI. AI literacy in this regard is the obligatory training integrated with the following three focus areas: interpreting agent diagnostics (understanding the predictive probability behind an agent's recommendation, rather than just accepting it), recognizing algorithmic bias (finding out when an agent's adaptive pathway is putting a student at an unfair disadvantage), and ethically integrating AI insights in teaching practice (knowing when to intervene with human empathy versus when to follow the data). The governance system should guarantee that educators are not trained as mere machine operators but rather as the ultimate moral human controllers of the educational procedure (Omodan, 2025). By directly attacking the risks of learners becoming excessively dependent on technology and losing their critical independence, this regulation safeguards the teacher's pivotal role of catching and correcting any negative consequences. It is of paramount importance that governance elucidates the ethical boundaries of the teacher-agent relationship. Accordingly, policy should be crystal clear in affirming that the human educator is always the last resort with respect to moral and pedagogical decisions. The AI agent might be seen as a data-driven consultant, but its advice is not only to be accepted but also to be overruled in cases where the teacher's human judgment, emotional intelligence, or empathy suggests otherwise. This notion has to be upheld system-wise through legal and moral standards that protect teachers from being pressured by their schools to submit to an agent's directives. It is mandatory to revise the teacher certification requirements so that they include these panels on AI and data ethics. Also, there must be a set of rules of good conduct regarding the use of AI in education, through which the ethical aspects concerning data handling, students' information disclosure, and non-discrimination can be articulated clearly and deliberately observed. By implementing comprehensive training and clear ethical standards, policymakers have integrated the Human-AI business model into daily practice, allowing the technology to serve as a tool within personalized education while also protecting the fundamental human and relational aspects of the learning process.

11. CONCLUSION

The exploration that was previously conducted and which spanned the conceptual grounds, technical sides, pedagogical purposes, and ethical difficulties of AI agents reaffirms that grasping the phenomenon as a proper, changeable, and mainstay element is the key to being literate in the education landscape that the agents will be reshaping. We pointed out that AI agents are not just a regular type of software tool, but they are intellectual fellows characterized by autonomy, reactivity, proactivity, and social ability. AI agents are equipped with advanced capabilities that allow them to handle preparatory tasks, achieved through their sophisticated systems that employ machine learning and decision making models. These tools enable them to perform key educational functions, such as offering in-person assistance to learners, creating a simulated peer environment for collaborative learning, and continuously and adaptively monitoring and assessing student progress. Nevertheless, this strength is linked to, and is potentially compromised by, serious ethical and practical problems, such as the discrimination and unfair treatment of marginalized and minority populations through AI bias, the creation of student dependency on AI, and the creation of privacy hazards around sensitive student data. It is evident that without a comprehensive and carefully considered approach to these difficult problems, the field of humanistic education and its core goals like fairness and equality will be significantly affected.

It is expected that the future will be very difficult to achieve, and the three main stakeholders, educators, technologists, and policymakers, will have to cooperate closely in order to avoid the many threats along the way to complicated and interactive AI systems. From the teachers' point of view, the near future is going to be the period when they start to present themselves as educational consultants and not only deliver the content but also moderate ethically. This requires that they receive AI literacy training, which is the first in a series of steps that will make them able to interpret complex agent diagnostics, recognize and mitigate algorithmic bias, and, even more importantly, use AI insights strategically in practice. It's a long way, but they have to go through it, as only when they are equipped with such newly emerging competencies will teachers make AI a part of their ecosystem and not the whole of it. It is crucial for teachers to serve as the first human-AI co-partners, upholding their role as moral and educational authorities, resisting the influence of machines, and focusing on tasks that require human interaction, like supporting students' physical and social growth. The focus for developers should shift from optimization to prioritizing equity and trust above all else. The group designing the AI system must take extra measures to enable inspections and public audits and also provide Explainable AI (XAI) and verifiable de-biasing methods. Additionally, Parkland County should adhere to the principle of Privacy-by-Design in developing future systems, as this ensures individuals' data control rights and data minimization practices. The former is a theoretical requirement for the well-being of the learner to be put at the center of designs.

For policymakers, their topmost priority is to create an all-encompassing governance structure that can always adapt to technological advancements. This includes the passing of new laws to safeguard data privacy and define data ownership through constant reviews. Moreover, legislators should implement interoperability and standardization procedures so that lock-in can be avoided and personalized routes ultimately result in learning based on competencies that are as good as those obtained through traditional curricula. Through proactive control, the regulators of this powerful technology are making sure its widespread use brings about common good, protects the basic rights of students, and eliminates a situation in which the educational system divides into elite and underprivileged groups based on uninvestigated and prejudiced AI. The future of self-directed learning will not be a machine-dominated one, but a joint effort where the AI agent's rigorous analytical skills are fused in a responsible manner with the educator's wisdom, empathy, and ethical authority.

REFERENCES

. Açıkgöz, T., & Babadoğan, M. C. (2021). COMPETENCY-BASED EDUCATION: THEORY AND PRACTICE. *Psycho-Educational Research Reviews*. https://doi.org/DOI: 10.52963/PERR_Biruni_V10.N3.06

Agesilaou, A., & Kyza, E. A. (2022). Whose data are they? Elementary school students' conceptualization of data ownership and privacy of personal digital data. *International Journal of Child-Computer Interaction*, *33*, 100462. DOI: 10.1016/j.ijcci.2022.100462

Alier, M., Guerrero, M. J. C., Amo, D., Severance, C., & Fonseca, D. (2021). Privacy and E-Learning: A pending task. *Sustainability (Basel)*, *13*(16), 9206. DOI: 10.3390/su13169206

Alotaibi, N. S. (2024). The impact of AI and LMS integration on the future of higher Education: Opportunities, challenges, and strategies for transformation. *Sustainability (Basel)*, *16*(23), 10357. DOI: 10.3390/su162310357

Bhardwaj, V., Zhang, S., Tan, Y. Q., & Pandey, V. (2025). Redefining learning: Student-centered strategies for academic and personal growth. *Frontiers in Education*, *10*, 1518602. Advance online publication. DOI: 10.3389/feduc.2025.1518602

Booth, B. M., Bosch, N., & D'Mello, S. K. (2023). Engagement Detection and its Applications in Learning: A tutorial and selective review. *Proceedings of the IEEE*, *111*(10), 1398–1422. DOI: 10.1109/JPROC.2023.3309560

Chergui, M., Nagano, A., & Ammoumou, A. (2024). Toward an adaptive learning system by managing pedagogical knowledge in a smart way. *Multimedia Tools and Applications*, *84*(24), 27777–27793. DOI: 10.1007/s11042-024-20207-w

Darling-Hammond, L., Flook, L., Cook-Harvey, C., Barron, B., & Osher, D. (2019). Implications for educational practice of the science of learning and development. *Applied Developmental Science*, *24*(2), 97–140. DOI: 10.1080/10888691.2018.1537791

De Souza Zanirato Maia, J., Bueno, A. P. A., & Sato, J. R. (2023). Applications of Artificial intelligence models in educational analytics and decision making: A Systematic review. *WORLD (Oakland, Calif.)*, *4*(2), 288–313. DOI: 10.3390/world4020019

Del Rosario Navas Bonilla, C., Carrasco, L. M. V., Pupiales, J. C. G., & Noriega, D. E. M. (2025). The Future of Education: A Systematic Literature Review of Self-Directed Learning with AI. *Future Internet*, *17*(8), 366. DOI: 10.3390/fi17080366

Dobrescu, P., Durach, F., & Vladu, L. (2025). AI USE IN EDUCATION: INSIGHTS FOR THE MITIGATION OF RISKS. *INTED Proceedings*, *1*, 4124–4130. DOI: 10.21125/inted.2025.1045

Dorri, A., Kanhere, S. S., & Jurdak, R. (2018). Multi-agent systems: A survey. *IEEE Access : Practical Innovations, Open Solutions*, *6*, 28573–28593. DOI: 10.1109/ACCESS.2018.2831228

Freitas, K. (2022). Low-stakes writing in an active-learning classroom needs focus and feedback to be effective. *The Journal of Economic Education*, *54*(3), 243–255. DOI: 10.1080/00220485.2022.2075505

Galvin, B. (2025). The role of foresight in public policy: Lessons from deliberative democracy and perspectival realism. *European Journal of Futures Research, 13*(1), 1. Advance online publication. DOI: 10.1186/s40309-024-00246-0

Ghosh, R. K., Çela, E., Chakraborty, S., Gupta, B., Dutta, G., Chakraborty, S., & Roy, S. (2025a). Ethical artificial intelligence and machine learning in Self-Service technologies. In IGI Global eBooks (pp. 155–204). https://doi.org/DOI: 10.4018/979-8-3373-1295-8.ch007

Ghosh, R. K., Chakraborty, S., & Dutta, G. (2025b). AI in Enhancing Bilingual Proficiency. In Advances in computational intelligence and robotics book series (pp. 141–176). https://doi.org/DOI: 10.4018/979-8-3373-0275-1.ch005

Gourlay, L., Rodríguez-Illera, J. L., Barberà, E., Bali, M., Gachago, D., Pallitt, N., Jones, C., Bayne, S., Hansen, S. B., Hrastinski, S., Jaldemark, J., Themelis, C., Pischetola, M., Dirckinck-Holmfeld, L., Matthews, A., Gulson, K. N., Lee, K., Bligh, B., Thibaut, P., & Knox, J. (2021). Networked Learning in 2021: A Community Definition. *Postdigital Science and Education, 3*(2), 326–369. DOI: 10.1007/s42438-021-00222-y PMID: 40477233

Hashim, A. S., Awadh, W. A., & Hamoud, A. K. (2020). Student Performance Prediction Model based on Supervised Machine Learning Algorithms. *IOP Conference Series. Materials Science and Engineering, 928*(3), 032019. DOI: 10.1088/1757-899X/928/3/032019

. Hutsalo, L., Skliar, I., Abrosimov, A., Kharchenko, N., & Ordanovska, O. (2024). Strategies for developing critical thinking and problem-based learning in the modern educational environment. *Multidisciplinary Science Journal, 6*, 2024ss0209. https://doi.org/DOI: 10.31893/multiscience.2024ss0209

Ion, T., & Popescu, E. (2024). An innovative distance learning platform for mathematics education in secondary schools: Design, development and preliminary studies. *Education and Information Technologies, 30*(5), 5529–5560. DOI: 10.1007/s10639-024-13040-z

Katsenou, R., & Deliyannis, I. (2025). PROGRAMMING AS PLAY: A COLLABORATIVE AUTOETHNOGRAPHY ON AI LITERACY IN EDUCATION. *INTED Proceedings, 1*, 5661–5671. DOI: 10.21125/inted.2025.1448

Khodadad, D. (2023). Creating a supportive and effective learning environment for engineering students. [iJEP]. *International Journal of Engineering Pedagogy, 13*(8), 33–50. DOI: 10.3991/ijep.v13i8.41755

Libertson, F. (2023). Inner transitions in higher education in Sweden: Incorporating intra-personal skills in education for sustainable development. *International Journal of Sustainability in Higher Education, 24*(9), 213–230. DOI: 10.1108/IJSHE-12-2022-0395

Liu, H., Zhang, T., Li, F., Yu, M., & Yu, G. (2024). A probabilistic generative model for tracking multi-knowledge concept mastery probability. *Frontiers of Computer Science, 18*(3), 183602. Advance online publication. DOI: 10.1007/s11704-023-3008-x

Miglani, P. (2025, May 6). *Invisible Chains: caste, religious, nationalism, and the struggle for freedom to innovate in India*. https://openresearch.ocadu.ca/id/eprint/4722

Mökander, J., & Axente, M. (2021). Ethics-based auditing of automated decision-making systems: Intervention points and policy implications. *AI & Society*, *38*(1), 153–171. DOI: 10.1007/s00146-021-01286-x

Omodan, B. I. (2025). Redefining the role of supervisors in the era of artificial intelligence: Implications for hybrid postgraduate research governance. *Cogent Education*, *12*(1), 2536534. Advance online publication. DOI: 10.1080/2331186X.2025.2536534

Osher, D., Cantor, P., Berg, J., Steyer, L., & Rose, T. (2018). Drivers of human development: How relationships and context shape learning and development1. *Applied Developmental Science*, *24*(1), 6–36. DOI: 10.1080/10888691.2017.1398650

Outay, F., Jabeur, N., Bellalouna, F., & Hamzi, T. A. (2024). Multi-agent system-based framework for an intelligent management of competency building. *Smart Learning Environments*, *11*(1), 41. Advance online publication. DOI: 10.1186/s40561-024-00328-3

Panait, L., & Luke, S. (2005). Cooperative multi-agent learning: The state of the art. *Autonomous Agents and Multi-Agent Systems*, *11*(3), 387–434. DOI: 10.1007/s10458-005-2631-2

Pellas, N. (2024). Comparing quality and autonomous learning of teacher professional development programs in MOOCs and LMS. *Education and Information Technologies*, *30*(7), 9005–9039. DOI: 10.1007/s10639-024-13154-4

Ruangpattanakul, K. (2025). Enhancing English Writing Competence and Self-Correction Awareness through the RADAR Process in Argumentative Writing. *Journal of English Language and Linguistics*, *6*(2), 220–238. DOI: 10.62819/jel.2025.1171

Ruano, I., Estévez, E., Gámez, J., & Gómez, J. (2023). Standards for the integration of online laboratories with learning management systems. *IEEE Access : Practical Innovations, Open Solutions*, *11*, 125267–125290. DOI: 10.1109/ACCESS.2023.3330666

Serban, A., Poll, E., & Visser, J. (2020). A standard driven software architecture for fully autonomous vehicles. *Journal of Automotive Software Engineering*, *1*(1), 20. DOI: 10.2991/jase.d.200212.001

Singer, J., Marx, R. W., Krajcik, J., & Chambers, J. C. (2000). Constructing Extended inquiry Projects: Curriculum materials for science Education Reform. *Educational Psychologist*, *35*(3), 165–178. DOI: 10.1207/S15326985EP3503_3

Strielkowski, W., Grebennikova, V., Lisovskiy, A., Rakhimova, G., & Vasileva, T. (2024). AI-driven adaptive learning for sustainable educational transformation. *Sustainable Development (Bradford)*, *33*(2), 1921–1947. DOI: 10.1002/sd.3221

Tanksley, T. C. (2024). "We're changing the system with this one": Black students using critical race algorithmic literacies to subvert and survive AI-mediated racism in school. *English Teaching*, *23*(1), 36–56. DOI: 10.1108/ETPC-08-2023-0102

Tariq, M. U. (2024). Navigating the personalization pathway. In *Advances in educational technologies and instructional design book series* (pp. 265–291). https://doi.org/DOI: 10.4018/979-8-3693-3641-0.ch012

Wang, C. (2024). Using design thinking for interdisciplinary curriculum design and teaching: A case study in higher education. *Humanities & Social Sciences Communications*, *11*(1), 307. Advance online publication. DOI: 10.1057/s41599-024-02813-z

Wang, T., Zheng, P., Li, S., & Wang, L. (2023). Multimodal Human–Robot Interaction for Human-Centric Smart Manufacturing: A survey. *Advanced Intelligent Systems*, *6*(3), 2300359. Advance online publication. DOI: 10.1002/aisy.202300359

Yambal, S., & Waykar, Y. A. (2025). Future of education using adaptive AI, intelligent systems, and ethical challenges. In *Advances in educational technologies and instructional design book series* (pp. 171–202). https://doi.org/DOI: 10.4018/979-8-3693-6527-4.ch006

Zhang, S., Wang, H., & Yi, X. (2025). Exploring Collaboration Patterns and Strategies in Human-AI Co-creation through the Lens of Agency: A Scoping Review of the Top-tier HCI Literature. *Proceedings of the ACM on Human-Computer Interaction*, *9*(7), 1–43. DOI: 10.1145/3757594 PMID: 41869684

Zhao, Y., Zhao, M., & Shi, F. (2023). Integrating Moral Education and Educational Information Technology: A Strategic approach to enhance rural teacher training in Universities. *Journal of the Knowledge Economy*, *15*(3), 15053–15093. DOI: 10.1007/s13132-023-01693-z

Zhao, Y., & Zhong, R. (2024). Paradigm Shifts in Education: An Ecological analysis. *ECNU Review of Education*, *8*(1), 21–40. DOI: 10.1177/20965311241296162

Chapter 3
Distributed Cognition in AI-Mediated Learning Environments for Self-Directed Independent Learners:
Human-AI Co-Regulation in Learning Ecologies

Ashraf Alam
http://orcid.org/0000-0001-6178-1187
Department of Education, National Institute of Technology Calicut, Kozhikode, India

ABSTRACT

This chapter interrogates independent learning in AI-saturated ecologies through lenses of distributed cognition, self-directed and self-regulated learning, mentoring theory, and justice-oriented ethics. It reframes autonomy as relational, co-constructed within human-AI assemblages where AI mentors act as cognitive prostheses and normative gatekeepers. Synthesising systems, activity-theoretical, and ecological perspectives, the chapter proposes typologies of AI mentors, pedagogy-first design principles, and governance matrices that foreground epistemic agency, capability expansion, and psychological wellbeing. It culminates in a global framework for scaffolded, inquiry-oriented, culturally sustaining, and autonomy-supportive AI mediation that is analytically rigorous, ethically reflexive, and operationally useful for educators, policy makers, technologists, and workforce professionals.

1. INTRODUCTION

1.1 Situating Self-Directed Independent Learning in the Age of AI and Distributed Cognition

Independent learning has traversed a long trajectory from correspondence courses and programmed instruction to open schooling, digital platforms, and ubiquitous conversational agents, yet the underlying

DOI: 10.4018/979-8-3373-7225-9.ch003

aspiration has remained the cultivation of learners who can regulate their own cognitive, affective, and behavioral processes (Yellanki et al., 2025; Garg, 2025; Olujimi et al., 2025). Contemporary environments saturated with algorithmic mediation fundamentally reconfigure what it means to learn independently because learners now work within dense socio-technical assemblages of devices, platforms, knowledge repositories, and intelligent services. The construct of *distributed cognition* foregrounds this shift by locating cognitive activity across brains, artifacts, and environments rather than treating the individual mind as a sealed container (Dwivedi et al., 2025; Kanumolu et al., 2025; Hu et al., 2025). In AI-mediated ecologies, the notebook, the search engine, the learning management system, and the *large language model* together constitute a composite cognitive system in which offloading, external memory, and machine-generated inferences become routine. Self-directed independent learning therefore needs to be reconceptualised as an orchestration of human capacities and non-human affordances rather than as solitary study.

1.2 Human-AI Assemblage in Learning Ecologies

The traditional imaginary of the autonomous learner presupposes a subject who formulates goals, discovers resources, and evaluates progress through largely internal capacities, with occasional human mentoring (Sheelam & Komaragiri, 2025; Komaragiri, 2025; Biswas & Talukdar, 2025). In AI-mediated learning ecologies, the learner operates instead as a node within a *human-AI assemblage* that includes intelligent tutors, recommender systems, personal knowledge graphs, and analytic dashboards. These entities not only deliver content but also nudge attention, propose strategies, structure practice, and generate feedback that shapes metacognition and motivation (Kumar et al., 2025; Sharma & Chaturvedi, 2025; Sheelam, 2025). The learner's agency becomes relational, negotiated continuously with algorithmic agents that propose, prioritise, and sometimes pre-empt choices. *Self-regulated learning* cycles of forethought, performance, and reflection unfold in interaction with prompts, predictions, and automated summaries generated by AI mentors (Hughes et al., 2025; Cheung et al., 2025; Tiwari, 2025). Independent learning in this context is better described as *co-regulated* activity, where planning and monitoring are distributed, and where autonomy emerges from the capacity to manage, contest, and appropriate AI assistance rather than from isolation from technological guidance.

1.3 Conceptual Scope, Methodological Stance, and Exclusions

This chapter advances a conceptual-theoretical account of *distributed cognition* and *human-AI co-regulation* in independent learning and therefore does not report empirical datasets, statistical models, or design experiments. The narrative synthesises constructs from learning sciences, cognitive science, philosophy of mind, human-computer interaction, critical data studies, and educational ethics in order to articulate a coherent conceptual framework. AI mentors are treated as socio-technical ensembles that incorporate models, training corpora, interface conventions, data infrastructures, and institutional norms, rather than as abstract algorithms detached from context. The chapter does not prescribe a specific architecture, vendor ecosystem, or implementation protocol, and it does not compare performance metrics of particular systems. Instead it elaborates theoretical vocabularies, typologies, and design logics that can inform diverse implementations. Descriptive references to global trends in AI-mediated learning serve only as contextual scaffolds. The focus remains on constructs such as *self-directed learning*, *self-regulated learning*, *mentoring constellations*, *learning ecologies*, and *algorithmic governance*.

1.4 Central Questions, Arguments, and Conceptual Propositions

The analysis is organised around several interlocking conceptual questions that interrogate the nature of independence under conditions of pervasive AI mediation. One question concerns how *self-directed learning* and *self-regulated learning* must be reinterpreted once cognitive, metacognitive, and motivational processes are continuously scaffolded by AI mentors that plan schedules, anticipate difficulties, and generate just-in-time explanations. A second question addresses the status of *epistemic agency* when learners co-produce knowledge artefacts with generative models that supply candidate arguments, examples, and representations. A third question explores how *mentoring theory* and *coaching frameworks* can be extended to encompass algorithmic interlocutors that simulate empathy and expertise. The core argument is that independent learning should be reframed as a form of *distributed, justice-oriented co-agency*, where learners exercise authorship by orchestrating human and AI resources in ways that preserve autonomy, cultivate critical judgement, and respect ethical constraints. The chapter proposes conceptual models that make this orchestration analytically tractable and normatively assessable.

1.5 Audiences, Contributions, and Structure of the Chapter

The chapter is written for a heterogeneous readership that spans academics in education and cognitive science, policy makers concerned with responsible AI governance, workforce development professionals who design reskilling ecosystems, and digital learning technologists who architect AI-mediated platforms. For academic readers, the chapter offers an integrative framework that links *distributed cognition*, *learning ecologies*, *mentoring constellations*, and *ethical governance* into a single analytic scaffold. For practitioners and technologists, it distils this scaffold into design-relevant constructs such as AI mentor typologies, scaffolding logics, and co-regulation patterns that can be operationalised in product roadmaps and pedagogical guidelines. For policy makers, it articulates normative criteria for evaluating AI mentors in relation to autonomy, equity, and wellbeing. The chapter unfolds in six further sections that respectively develop theoretical foundations, conceptualise AI mentors as socio-technical entities, derive pedagogical design principles, situate AI mentors across diverse ecologies, elaborate ethics and governance frameworks, and synthesise these strands into forward-looking conclusions.

2. THEORETICAL FOUNDATIONS OF INDEPENDENT LEARNING, AGENCY, MENTORING, AND DISTRIBUTED COGNITION

2.1 Classical and Cognitive-Constructivist Accounts of Independent Learning

Classical learning paradigms configure independent learning as disciplined engagement with structured stimuli, yet their underlying ontologies of mind diverge in consequential ways. In a *behaviorist* frame, ostensibly solitary study becomes a sequence of discriminative stimuli, operant responses, and contingently delivered reinforcers that gradually sculpt performance repertoires (Acharya et al., 2025; Bapna et al., 2025; Hughes et al., 2025). Cognitive and information-processing accounts refigure this process as the construction and reorganisation of internal representations, where independent learners encode, store, and retrieve propositions, schemas, and mental models. Cognitive-constructivist views accentuate active meaning-making, with learners reorganising prior conceptions through cognitive conflict, elaboration, and self-explanation (Karunanayake, 2025; Goyal, 2025; Jaggavarapu, 2025). Across these traditions, instructional design, task structuring, and feedback channels remain latent scaffolds that script what appears to be autonomous work. In AI-mediated ecologies, these foundational constructs are instantiated in adaptive practice engines, automated feedback generators, and task-sequencing algorithms, which externalise reinforcement schedules and schema-building routines (Olujimi et al., 2025; Suura, 2024; Raza et al., 2025). Table 1 later in this section synthesises how such paradigms configure agency, guidance, and the role of intelligent technologies.

2.2 Self-Directed and Self-Regulated Learning as Architectures of Personal Governance

Self-directed learning and *self-regulated learning* articulate independent learning as a highly orchestrated system of internal governance rather than a romanticised state of isolation. In a self-directed orientation, the learner assumes responsibility for diagnostic appraisal of competence, formulation of proximal and distal goals, negotiation of resources, and evaluation of outcomes, effectively functioning as project manager of a personal learning enterprise (Paduraru et al., 2025; Pop et al., 2025; Viswanathan, 2025). Self-regulated learning specifies cyclical phases of forethought, performance, and self-reflection, each populated by micro-processes such as goal calibration, strategic planning, selective attention allocation, self-monitoring, and attributional reasoning. These constructs reveal independence as an intensive regulatory labour that coordinates motivation, cognition, and affect over time (Raza et al., 2025; Kumar et al., 2025; Satav, 2025). Within AI-mediated environments, planning dashboards, analytic visualisations, and conversational prompts can become co-regulatory actuators that support or override these cycles. Table 1 positions self-directed and self-regulated learning as paradigms in which AI mentors can function as meta-cognitive prostheses, augmenting but also potentially displacing the learner's own regulatory apparatus.

2.3 Motivation, Agency, and Epistemic Cognition as Engines of Independent Learning

Motivation and agency constructs supply the energetic and directional substrates that make independent learning sustainable rather than fragile. Within a *self-determination* lens, autonomy, competence, and relatedness operate as basic psychological nutriments that must be preserved even when AI mentors provide pervasive guidance (Mustafaraj, 2025; Ma & Wang, 2024; Huang, 2025). Expectancy-value and goal-orientation constructs explain how perceived task value, cost, and probability of success shape the intensity and persistence of self-initiated study. *Epistemic cognition* adds a meta-level dimension, foregrounding how learners construe knowledge as certain or tentative, simple or complex, authority-driven or evidence based, and how they justify claims in light of these epistemic beliefs (Cheung et al., 2025; Parikh, 2026; Wissuchek & Zschech, 2025). Independent learning in AI-mediated ecologies therefore hinges on whether AI mentors cultivate robust *epistemic agency* by inviting justification, counter-argument, and uncertainty recognition, or whether they tacitly reward acquiescent consumption of fluent, yet unexamined, outputs. Within Table 1, motivation and epistemic constructs appear as cross-cutting dimensions that modulate how different paradigms operationalise learner agency and configure AI support.

2.4 Sociocultural, Distributed, and Critical-Contextual Perspectives on Independence

Sociocultural and activity-theoretical perspectives dislodge the notion of independence from purely intrapsychic territory and relocate it within historically sedimented practices, symbol systems, and division-of-labour arrangements (AlZu'Bi et al., 2025; Artsın & Bozkurt, 2025; Koutra et al., 2025). In a *Vygotskian* and activity-system view, independent performance corresponds to internalised mastery of practices that were once scaffolded within a *zone of proximal development* through mediated interaction with more capable others and cultural artifacts. Communities-of-practice constructs depict independent learners as legitimate participants who appropriate shared repertoires, identities, and norms (Portugal et al., 2024; Raheem & Hossain, 2025; Widad, 2025). The lens of *distributed cognition* and the *extended mind* further radicalises this shift by treating notebooks, diagrams, search engines, and AI mentors as integral components of cognitive systems rather than peripheral aids. Critical-pedagogical and decolonial frames interrogate which knowledges, identities, and languages are privileged within these systems and which are systematically marginalised (Martin & Olszewska, 2025; Rusum & Anasuri, 2025; Xu et al., 2025). These convergent perspectives render independence a politically saturated, infrastructurally mediated achievement. Table 1 assembles these paradigms into a compact matrix that contrasts their ontologies of agency, patterns of mediation, and conceptual implications for AI mentors.

Table 1. Conceptual paradigms of independent learning and AI mediation

Theoretical Paradigm	Ontology of Learner Agency	Configuration of Guidance and Mediation	Construal of Technology and Artifacts	Implications for AI Mentors and Co-Regulation
Behaviorist Learning	Contingent responder shaped by reinforcement contingencies	External scheduling of stimuli, responses, and reinforcement cycles	Instrumental apparatus for stimulus delivery and response capture	AI tutor as programmable contingency manager that calibrates difficulty and reinforcement density
Cognitive-Constructivist Learning	Active information processor constructing and reorganising mental schemas	Structured tasks, explanations, and feedback that trigger assimilation and accommodation	Cognitive amplifier that presents representations, analogies, and elaborations	AI mentor as adaptive explainer that tailors representations and prompts elaborative processing
Self-Directed and Self-Regulated Learning	Metacognitively governed agent planning, monitoring, and evaluating learning trajectories	Internal and external regulation cycles coordinating goals, strategies, and reflections	Regulatory scaffold that visualises progress and suggests strategy repertoires	AI companion as co-regulatory orchestrator that supports goal calibration and strategic adaptation
Sociocultural and Activity Perspectives	Situated participant enacting roles within culturally scripted practices	Guided participation through tools, norms, and division-of-labour configurations	Mediational means that encode cultural histories and participation rules	AI mediator as practice-sensitive artefact that aligns prompts with communal norms and roles

continued on following page

Table 1. Continued

Theoretical Paradigm	Ontology of Learner Agency	Configuration of Guidance and Mediation	Construal of Technology and Artifacts	Implications for AI Mentors and Co-Regulation
Distributed Cognition and Extended Mind	Node within hybrid cognitive system spanning brains, bodies, and artifacts	Coordination of representational states across internal and external media	Constitutive substrate of cognitive processes and external memory fields	AI system as integral cognitive node that must be designed for transparent coupling and decoupling
Critical-Pedagogical and Mentoring Frameworks	Reflexive subject negotiating power, recognition, and identity	Dialogic, relational mentoring that foregrounds voice, agency, and justice	Arena in which epistemic authority and symbolic power are materialised	AI mentor as justice-oriented mediator that foregrounds marginalised knowledges and critical reflexivity

Table 1 renders visible how paradigms that appear commensurable at a superficial level in fact encode sharply different assumptions about where cognition resides, how guidance should operate, and what kinds of technological mediation are normatively desirable. The behaviorist row foregrounds the hazard that AI mentors might devolve into high-frequency reinforcement engines that narrow agency to compliance, whereas the distributed cognition and critical-pedagogical rows articulate more expansive understandings in which AI systems function as negotiable cognitive partners situated within contested sociopolitical terrains. For designers and policy makers, this comparative lens clarifies that choosing a design language for AI mentors is implicitly a choice among ontologies of agency and justice, not a merely technical optimisation problem.

2.5 Mentoring, Coaching, and Integrative Synthesis for Human-AI Co-Regulation

Mentoring and coaching constructs provide a relational grammar through which the preceding paradigms can be integrated into a coherent account of human-AI co-regulation. In a developmental mentoring frame, the mentor performs cognitive, socio-emotional, and identity work, modelling strategies, offering scaffolds, affirming potential selves, and selectively withdrawing support as competence consolidates (Tiwari, 2025; Pamisetty, 2024; Allam & Dempere, 2025). Coaching frameworks emphasise goal alignment, performance diagnostics, feedforward guidance, and reflective debriefing, all of which map naturally onto *self-regulated learning* cycles. When these constructs are transposed into AI-mediated environments, the AI mentor becomes part of a *mentoring constellation* that includes teachers, peers, family, and community actors, each contributing different modalities of guidance (Boskabadi et al., 2025; Hu et al., 2025; Pop et al., 2025). An integrative synthesis therefore conceptualises independent learning as the orchestrated outcome of interacting systems of reinforcement, cognition, regulation, sociocultural participation, distributed artifact use, and mentoring. In such a synthesis, human-AI co-regulation is evaluated by its capacity to enlarge the learner's zone of autonomous, critically reflective activity while remaining accountable to ethical, cultural, and epistemic constraints articulated across the paradigms summarised in Table 1.

3. AI MENTORS AS SOCIO-TECHNICAL ENTITIES IN DISTRIBUTED LEARNING ECOLOGIES

3.1 Quasi-Agentic Mentors

Within AI-mediated learning ecologies, the conceptual status of digital systems has migrated from inert instruments to quasi-agentic interlocutors that participate in pedagogical decision making. Classical tool metaphors treat software as passive extensions of human intention, while contemporary conversational agents exhibit interactional properties that simulate initiative, responsiveness, and attunement (Acharya et al., 2025; Sheelam, 2024; Chawla et al., 2024). This shift invites the vocabulary of *artificial sociality*, in which dialogic turn taking, personalised address, and contingent feedback generate a phenomenology of presence that resembles mentoring encounters. Learners interpret these systems through anthropomorphic schemas, attributing competence, care, and authority, even when the underlying processes remain probabilistic and opaque (Kshetri, 2025; Banerjie et al., 2025; Thorat, 2025). The resulting assemblage can be described as a *human-AI dyad* nested within broader institutional and infrastructural networks, where agency is co-constructed through reciprocal prompting, suggestion, and uptake (Portugal et al., 2024; Motamary, 2025; Borghoff et al., 2025). In such contexts, independent learning no longer occurs in isolation from technological mediation but unfolds within socio-technical circuits that configure how guidance, evaluation, and reflection are distributed.

3.2 Typological Cartography of AI Mentor Instantiations

The proliferation of AI-mediated supports has produced a heterogeneous landscape of mentoring configurations that differ in granularity, persistence, and institutional anchoring. Some systems operate as embedded micro-mentors that surface within productivity tools to offer contextual hints and micro-explanations, while others manifest as course-bound tutors aligned with specific curricula and assessment regimes. Cross-platform companions follow learners across devices and platforms, aggregating interaction traces into longitudinal profiles that inform adaptive scaffolding (Patel, 2024; Warrier, 2025; Gudipati, 2025). Domain-specific expert mentors leverage specialised corpora to simulate disciplinary reasoning, whereas institutional policy mentors translate regulations, academic integrity norms, and procedural rules into conversational guidance. Hybrid human-AI mentoring networks, in which automated feedback, peer commentary, and teacher interventions are orchestrated, further complicate this ecology (Neelu et al., 2025; Artsin & Bozkurt, 2026; Hosseini & Seilani, 2025). Table 2 synthesises this typological cartography by juxtaposing archetypes of AI mentors with their dominant pedagogical functions, temporal configurations, identity scripts, and conceptual vulnerabilities, thereby providing a compact lens through which designers and policy makers can appraise design choices.

3.3 Functional Affordances, Constraints, and Temporalities of AI Mentoring

The functional repertoire of AI mentors spans explanation, error diagnosis, strategy coaching, metacognitive prompting, affective support, and resource curation, yet these affordances are always entangled with constraints such as hallucinated content, latent bias, and limited situational awareness (Nicoletti & Appolloni, 2025; Kostopoulos et al., 2025; Jaradeh & Auer, 2025). In short-session contexts, AI mentors may deliver granular hints and clarifications that prevent frustration, while in longitudinal engagements they can co-construct study plans, track evolving competencies, and support identity narratives as learners traverse educational transitions. Temporal configuration therefore becomes a crucial design dimension, structuring how dependence, habit formation, and trust accumulate over repeated encounters (Porter et al., 2025; Bandi et al., 2025; Xu et al., 2025). Table 2 articulates how distinct mentor archetypes couple specific functional clusters with episodic, routine, or long-horizon temporalities, highlighting the ways in which design choices can amplify or attenuate risks such as over-reliance, surveillance, and attenuation of human relationships. By situating affordances within these temporal matrices, the table underscores that functionality cannot be evaluated in an atemporal vacuum.

Table 2. Typology of AI mentor configurations for independent learning

AI Mentor Archetype	Primary Pedagogical Functions	Temporal Configuration of Engagement	Dominant Identity Script and Relational Stance	Principal Conceptual Risks and Vulnerabilities
Embedded Micro-Mentor	Contextual hints, error signalling, just-in-time nudging	Brief, task-bound, highly fragmented interactions	Discreet assistant that quietly augments local performance	Fragmented dependence, invisibility of influence, attenuation of holistic reflection
Course-Bound Tutor	Curriculum alignment, stepwise guidance, assessment rehearsal	Term-length, module-specific, synchronised with course pacing	Authoritative instructor surrogate that enforces curricular logics	Reinforcement of narrow outcome metrics, erosion of pedagogical pluralism
Cross-Platform Companion	Longitudinal planning, study analytics, habit formation	Persistent, cross-context, life-course spanning support	Intimate confidant that tracks preferences and trajectories	Deep datafication, surveillance normalisation, difficulty of strategic disengagement
Domain-Specific Expert Mentor	Disciplinary reasoning, problem modelling, conceptual elaboration	Episodic yet recurrent, tied to disciplinary tasks	Specialist consultant that simulates expert cognition	Overestimation of epistemic reliability, masking of uncertainty and contestation
Institutional Policy Mentor	Rule interpretation, procedural navigation, integrity counselling	Intermittent, event-triggered, aligned with institutional events	Bureaucratic interpreter that translates rules into advice	Over-legitimisation of rigid norms, suppression of situated judgement
Hybrid Human-AI Mentoring Network	Orchestration of feedback, triage of cases, escalation to humans	Multi-layered, adaptive, responsive to complexity of needs	Collaborative mentor constellation that distributes labour	Governance opacity, ambiguous accountability, diffusion of responsibility

Table 2 makes explicit that AI mentors are never neutral computational utilities but crystallisations of particular institutional logics, temporal regimes, and relational imaginaries. Embedded micro-mentors exemplify minimalistic yet pervasive influence, cross-platform companions instantiate deeply intimate surveillance potentials, and hybrid mentoring networks foreground questions of accountability and role clarity. For architects of learning ecosystems, the typology illustrates that the same learner may be simultaneously addressed by multiple archetypes, each with different scripts of authority and care, thereby generating complex constellations of guidance that require coherent governance. The table also signals that responsible design must consider not only what tasks AI mentors perform but how those tasks are distributed across time and institutional space, and how learners can strategically modulate their engagement with these entities.

3.4 Architectures, Data Ecologies, and Socio-Material Networks

AI mentors operate within layered architectures that integrate *large language models*, retrieval systems, learner modelling modules, and analytics pipelines into composite cognitive infrastructures (Pandey, 2025; Huang, 2025; Murugesan, 2025). At the data layer, learning record stores, platform logs, and institutional databases feed into representational structures that encode trajectories of participation, success, and disengagement, forming the substrate for predictive inferences and personalised recommendations. At the interface layer, conversational front ends, dashboards, and notifications choreograph how learners perceive, query, and contest these inferences (Ali et al., 2024; Park & Kwon, 2024). These components do not exist in isolation but participate in *socio-material networks* that include timetables, syllabi, accreditation regimes, and funding structures. When interpreted through *actor-network* and *distributed cognition* lenses, AI mentors become actants that stabilise certain practices and destabilise others (Yadav, 2024; Jafari & Keykha, 2024; Wang et al., 2025). The heuristic categories in Table 2 can be mapped directly onto architectural configurations, highlighting how infrastructural choices influence not only efficiency and scalability but also legibility, contestability, and the possibility of human oversight.

3.5 Conceptual Identity Scripts and Role Repertoires for AI Mentors

Beyond functional taxonomies, AI mentors are animated by implicit identity scripts that govern how learners and institutions position them in everyday practice. Some configurations encourage a *companion* script, in which the system is framed as an always-available confidant that shares struggles and celebrates milestones, while others foreground a *coach* script that accentuates challenge, performance elevation, and disciplined feedback (Kong & Yang, 2024; Sağın et al., 2024; Mikeladze et al., 2024). Guardian scripts emphasise norm enforcement, risk detection, and compliance monitoring, whereas gatekeeper scripts tie access to advanced resources or opportunities to algorithmic judgements. These scripts are not merely rhetorical labels but performative devices that shape expectations, power asymmetries, and affective investments (Marengo et al., 2024; Celik et al., 2024; Sova et al., 2024). In heterogeneous learning ecologies, conflicting scripts may collide, for instance when a cross-platform companion with intimate access to behavioural traces is simultaneously configured as an institutional guardian of academic integrity (Nedungadi et al., 2024; Yang et al., 2024; Ma & Lei, 2024). A rigorous conceptualisation of human-AI co-regulation therefore requires explicit negotiation of these role repertoires, so that autonomy, trust, and justice are preserved across the mentoring constellation outlined throughout this section.

4. PEDAGOGICAL ALIGNMENT AND DESIGN PRINCIPLES FOR AI MENTORS

4.1 Pedagogical and Value Alignment as Foundational Design Imperatives

AI mentors that operate in independent learning ecologies must be explicitly configured as pedagogical instruments rather than generic optimisation engines, which requires that design choices be anchored in clearly articulated theories of learning, knowledge, and human development (Wu, 2024; Vistorte et al., 2024; Yang, 2024). A constructivist, inquiry-oriented orientation will favour designs in which the AI mentor elicits hypotheses, foregrounds conceptual conflict, and scaffolds sense-making, whereas a performance-oriented, drill-centric orientation will channel the system toward task decomposition and rapid feedback (Famaye et al., 2024; Al-Abdullatif, 2024; Thorat et al., 2024). Parallel commitments to *critical pedagogy* and *education for justice* require that AI-mediated interactions continuously interrogate whose knowledge is centred, which perspectives are omitted, and how power differentials are reproduced or mitigated (Adams & Thompson, 2025; Yuan & Liu, 2025; Shailendra et al., 2024). Value alignment therefore extends beyond superficial content filters to encompass deeper commitments to *autonomy-supportive* interactional patterns, dialogic respect, and epistemic humility. Subsequent sections in this chapter, particularly the synthesis in Table 3, translate these abstract orientations into granular design principles that can be operationalised by technologists and educators.

4.2 Scaffolded Support, Graduated Fading, and Metacognitive Orchestration

Pedagogically aligned AI mentors must operationalise *scaffolding* as a dynamic choreography of support rather than as a static provision of hints, which implies sensitivity to learner state, task complexity, and temporal trajectories. In early encounters, the system may provide high-contingency guidance that models strategy selection, decomposes problems, and externalises metacognitive routines such as planning and monitoring (Ma et al., 2024; Aguilar-Cruz & Salas-Pilco, 2025; Roshanaei, 2024). As competence consolidates, the same mentor should progressively withdraw direct guidance, shift toward reflective questioning, and prompt learners to generate their own criteria for success, thereby enacting the principle of *fading* that underpins durable internalisation (Bender, 2024; Mouta et al., 2024; Topaz et al., 2025). Metacognitive orchestration occurs when the AI mentor synchronises prompts about goals, strategies, and emotional regulation with meaningful junctures in the learning process instead of relying on uniform, time-based nudges (Fadlelmula & Qadhi, 2024; Storey & Wagner, 2024; Erduran & Levrini, 2024). These operations, when viewed through the integrated lens later codified in Table 3, reposition the mentor as a regulator of cognitive load, self-efficacy, and epistemic curiosity, rather than as a mere answer generator.

4.3 Dialogic, Inquiry-Oriented, and Epistemically Reflexive Interaction Designs

Design principles that privilege dialogic and inquiry-oriented engagements conceptualise AI mentors as partners in *knowledge building* rather than as oracle-like solutions providers. The conversational flows are structured so that the system responds to learner queries with counter-questions, requests for clarification, and invitations to generate conjectures, thereby enacting the spirit of *Socratic* and *inquiry-based* pedagogies (Singha & Singha, 2024; Merchán Sánchez-Jara et al., 2024; Williamson, 2024). Epistemic reflexivity is promoted when the mentor routinely surfaces alternative explanations, highlights uncertainty, and prompts evaluation of evidential strength, which positions the learner as an active *epistemic agent* rather than a consumer of monologic assertions (Gökçearslan et al., 2024; Ayanwale et al., 2024; Tassoti, 2024). These dialogic grammars demand careful calibration to avoid frustration, which is why a synthesised view of design principles, theoretical anchors, and learner dispositions, as presented in Table 3, becomes indispensable for balancing cognitive challenge with affective containment in independent learning contexts.

Table 3. Design principles for AI mentors and independent learning

Design Principle	Theoretical Anchors	Interactional Configuration	Learner Disposition Targets	Risks and Safeguarding Considerations
Scaffolded Contingent Support	*Scaffolding theory, zone of proximal development, cognitive load regulation*	Graduated hints, worked fragments, adaptive task decomposition	Strategic flexibility, tolerance of productive difficulty, error resilience	Over-scaffolding, learned helplessness, suppression of exploratory risk-taking
Fading and Autonomy Transfer	*Internalisation, self-regulated learning, autonomy-supportive motivation*	Progressive withdrawal of explicit guidance, transition to self-explanation	Self-initiated planning, monitoring, and evaluative judgement	Premature withdrawal, destabilised confidence, inequitable autonomy trajectories
Dialogic and Inquiry Orientation	*Dialogic teaching, inquiry learning, knowledge-building communities*	Question-rich exchanges, hypothesis generation, iterative refinement of ideas	Epistemic curiosity, argumentative sophistication, collaborative stance toward knowledge	Pseudo-dialogue that masks directive control, overload of questioning without consolidation
Epistemic and Metacognitive Prompting	*Epistemic cognition, metacognitive regulation, intellectual virtue ethics*	Prompts to justify, compare, and reflect on strategies and claims	Critical scrutiny, intellectual humility, reflective endorsement of beliefs	Ritualised compliance without genuine reflection, superficial rationalisation of AI outputs
Culturally and Linguistically Responsive Mediation	*Culturally sustaining pedagogy, translanguaging, capability-expansion frameworks*	Localised examples, multilingual affordances, identity-affirming narratives	Sense of belonging, narrative agency, cross-cultural hermeneutic competence	Reinscription of stereotypes, tokenistic localisation, erasure of minoritised epistemologies

Table 3 crystallises how abstract pedagogical and ethical commitments can be refracted into operational properties of AI mentor behaviour that are legible to designers and educators. Each row encodes a compact design script that links theoretical constructs to interactional grammars and to desired transformations in learner dispositions, while simultaneously flagging characteristic hazards that must be mitigated. For instance, scaffolded contingent support becomes pedagogically generative only when paired with deliberate fading and epistemic prompting, otherwise the interaction degrades into a sequence of dependency-inducing hints. Similarly, culturally responsive mediation requires attention not only to surface-level translation but to deeper questions of which epistemic traditions are afforded authority. By treating these rows as interdependent rather than modular options, practitioners can configure AI mentors as coherent pedagogical agents that reinforce, rather than fragment, independent learning capacities.

4.4 Culturally Sustaining, Linguistically Plural, and Inclusion-Oriented Design Logics

AI mentors embedded in global learning ecologies must be attentive to the semiotic, cultural, and linguistic heterogeneity of their users, which mandates design logics that are simultaneously *culturally sustaining*, linguistically plural, and inclusion oriented (Sanusi et al., 2024; Katsamakas et al., 2024; Pack & Maloney, 2024). A culturally sustaining orientation requires that examples, metaphors, and problem contexts draw from the lived realities and knowledge systems of diverse communities rather than imposing a single, ostensibly neutral canon (Ruiz-Rojas et al., 2024; Obenza et al., 2024; Khreisat et al., 2024). Linguistic plurality entails the capacity to recognise and work within translanguaging practices, where learners fluidly mobilise multiple languages and registers as cognitive resources (Gkintoni et al.,

2025; Ivanashko et al., 2024; Sanusi et al., 2024). Inclusion oriented design further demands alignment with *Universal Design for Learning* so that multiple representational modalities, response formats, and engagement pathways are available to learners with varied sensory, cognitive, and socio-emotional profiles (Lan, 2024; Li, 2025; Naixin et al., 2024). When mapped against the categories in Table 3, these design logics reveal that cultural and linguistic responsiveness is not an optional aesthetic embellishment but a central determinant of which learners can realistically actualise independent learning.

4.5 Human Oversight, Professional Judgement, and Practitioner Heuristics for Co-Regulation

Even the most sophisticated AI mentor must remain nested within a human-led pedagogical ecology in which educators exercise professional judgement, recalibrate design assumptions, and provide relational anchoring. Human oversight involves more than episodic monitoring of outputs; it includes critical interrogation of the implicit curricula encoded in prompts, default pathways, and recommendation algorithms, as well as deliberative alignment with institutional missions and community values (Liu et al., 2024; Alam & Mohanty, 2024; Karataş et al., 2025). Practitioner heuristics such as encouraging learners to articulate an initial plan before consulting the mentor, reviewing AI mediated learning logs together during supervision sessions, and periodically disabling automated hints to probe underlying competence, can operationalise co-regulation in practical settings (Sarwar & Ms Saima, 2024; Dai & Liu, 2024; Cheah et al., 2025). These heuristics resonate with the design principles in Table 3, particularly those concerning fading and epistemic prompting, by ensuring that AI support is periodically decoupled so that learners can rehearse self-governance (Musolin et al., 2024; Wang & Li, 2024; Lim, 2024). Through such arrangements, AI mentors become accountable collaborators within a broader mentoring constellation rather than de facto pedagogical sovereigns.

5. AI MENTORS ACROSS EDUCATIONAL ECOLOGIES AND LEARNER DIVERSITIES

5.1 Ecological and Life-Course Framing of Independent Learning

Independent learning unfolds within multilayered ecologies rather than within abstract cognitive vacuums, which makes an ecological and life-course framing indispensable for conceptualising AI mentors (Rane, 2024; Ezeoguine & Eteng-Uket, 2024; Ng et al., 2025). From the perspective of *ecological systems theory*, learners inhabit nested structures of micro-systems, such as families, classrooms, and peer groups, meso-systems that link these contexts, and macro-systems that encode cultural, economic, and regulatory regimes (Salloum, 2024; Baltezarević & Baltezarević, 2024; Opesemowo & Adekomaya, 2024). Across the life course, transitions from childhood to adolescence, from schooling to higher education, and from education to work generate inflection points where identities, goals, and temporal horizons are renegotiated (Opesemowo & Ndlovu, 2024; Saatchi et al., 2025; Kazanidis & Pellas, 2024). AI mentors enter these ecologies as novel actants that redistribute information flows, feedback loops, and normative expectations, sometimes amplifying existing affordances and sometimes compensating for structural deficits (Mahmoud & Sørensen, 2024; Karakose & Tülübas, 2024; Yue et al., 2024). Their influence therefore cannot be understood solely in terms of individual outcomes; it must be traced through shifts in relational patterns, institutional routines, and access to epistemic resources (Alam & Mohanty, 2023; Lye & Lim, 2024; Xia et al., 2024). Subsequent subsections, including the comparative synthesis in Table 4, map how these ecological layers condition both risks and possibilities for human-AI co-regulation.

5.2 Compulsory Schooling, Developmental Plasticity, and AI-Scaffolded Study

In compulsory schooling systems, AI mentors interact with learners who are undergoing intense neurocognitive and socio-emotional development, while also being subject to dense webs of adult supervision and high-stakes assessment. Theoretical frames from developmental psychology position these learners as agents with evolving capacities for abstract reasoning, moral judgement, and meta-cognition, yet also as vulnerable to suggestibility and extrinsic pressure (Grájeda et al., 2024; Dieterle et al., 2024; Jatileni et al., 2024). AI mentors that support homework, revision, and project work therefore operate within tightly scripted temporalities defined by timetables and examination calendars, and within regulatory regimes that emphasise safety, integrity, and age-appropriate exposure (Zhang et al., 2025; Joel Augustus et al., 2025; Abbasi et al., 2025). Properly configured mentors can externalise stepwise strategies, scaffold *executive functioning*, and provide emotionally attuned encouragement that buffers academic stress (Yang et al., 2024; Shamsuddinova et al., 2024; Storozhyk, 2024). Poorly configured systems, by contrast, may promote shortcut-seeking, attenuate deep processing, or normalise surveillance (Samala et al., 2025; Ozodakhon, 2024; Fullan et al., 2024). The cross-ecological comparison in Table 4 later in this section positions compulsory schooling as one archetype among several, highlighting how its characteristic constraints demand particularly stringent governance of AI-mediated mentoring.

5.3 Higher Education, Professional Formation, and AI-Mediated Literacies

Higher education environments position learners as emerging members of disciplinary communities who must appropriate specialised discourses, epistemic norms, and professional identities. Within this context, AI mentors often function as writing advisors, problem-solving assistants, and research companions that mediate access to complex symbolic artefacts such as proofs, models, and scholarly arguments (Tan et al., 2024; Franco D'Souza et al., 2024; Yadav & Shrawankar, 2025). Theoretical constructs of *academic literacies* and *disciplinary enculturation* depict this phase as one in which learners must negotiate tensions between reproduction of established canons and experimentation with new syntheses (Mah & Groß, 2024; Zarei et al., 2024; Fundi et al., 2024). AI mentors can facilitate this negotiation by modelling argumentative structures, explicating inferential moves, and prompting critical appraisal of competing frameworks (Zohuri & Mossavar-Rahmani, 2024; Al-Zahrani & Alasmari, 2024; Alam & Mohanty, 2022). They can also, if naively deployed, obscure the provenance of ideas, flatten contestation, and erode the cultivation of voice (Zhou et al., 2024; Fitrianto et al., 2024; Forero-Corba & Bennasar, 2024). Table 4 synthesises these dynamics across ecologies, positioning massified higher education alongside schooling, workplace, and community spaces, and contrasting their developmental features, independent learning challenges, preferred AI functions, and justice imperatives.

Table 4. Global learning ecologies and AI mentoring configurations

Learning Ecology Archetype	Dominant Developmental and Contextual Features	Core Independent Learning Challenges	Preferred AI Mentoring Functions	Equity and Justice Considerations
Compulsory Schooling Systems	Heightened neurocognitive plasticity, strong adult control, standardised curricula	Sustaining attention, internalising foundational schemas, managing assessment anxiety	Stepwise scaffolding, executive-function coaching, integrity-aware feedback	Protection from manipulation, safeguarding of minors, reduction of tracking and stratification
Massified Higher Education	Diverse cohorts, specialised discourses, credential-driven selection mechanisms	Mastering disciplinary literacies, integrating theory and practice, negotiating academic identity	Argumentation support, research navigation, conceptual modelling of complex systems	Mitigation of stratified access, preservation of authorship, resistance to epistemic homogenisation
Workplace and Lifelong Learning	Time-constrained adults, performance evaluation, volatile skills ecosystems	Balancing productivity and learning, transferring knowledge across roles, sustaining motivation	Just-in-time micro-learning, career-planning analytics, reflective debriefing of practice	Prevention of coercive upskilling, avoidance of exclusion through automated profiling
Marginalised and Low-Resource Settings	Infrastructural scarcity, intermittent connectivity, socio-economic precarity	Accessing quality materials, sustaining engagement amid hardship, bridging language divides	Offline-sympathetic tutoring, multimodal explanations, resilience-oriented encouragement	Correction of digital divides, protection from predatory data practices, amplification of local knowledges
Postcolonial Global South Contexts	Hybrid curricula, imported standards, contested language hierarchies	Reconciling local epistemologies with global benchmarks, navigating colonial residues	Bi-epistemic mediation, context-sensitive exemplification, translanguaging-friendly dialogue	Decolonisation of content, defence against epistemic dominance, valorisation of indigenous frameworks
Informal and Community-Based Spaces	Interest-driven participation, fluid roles, peer-led knowledge circulation	Structuring self-chosen projects, validating non-institutional expertise, sustaining communities	Project-scoping assistance, peer-connection brokering, recognition of community credentials	Prevention of platform enclosure, protection of community autonomy, visibility of grassroots innovation

Table 4 demonstrates that educational ecologies are not interchangeable canvases on which a single AI mentoring architecture can be inscribed. Each archetype exhibits a characteristic constellation of developmental trajectories, temporal regimes, and institutional logics that yield distinct independent learning challenges and corresponding mentoring needs. Compulsory schooling systems foreground protection and foundational schema building, whereas workplace and lifelong learning ecologies prioritise flexibility, transfer, and dignity amid economic volatility. Marginalised and postcolonial contexts foreground questions of infrastructural justice and epistemic sovereignty, and informal spaces centre community autonomy. For designers, funders, and regulators, the table underlines that equity-sensitive AI mentoring must be differentially articulated across these ecologies, with configurations of functionality, data practices, and governance tailored to their specific vulnerabilities and aspirations.

5.4 Adult, Workplace, and Lifelong Learning Ecologies with AI Companions

Adult learners in workplace and community settings confront independent learning tasks that are tightly coupled to livelihood, social recognition, and evolving family responsibilities. Theoretical constructs of *workplace learning* and *lifelong learning* emphasise situated participation in practice communities, tacit knowledge exchange, and identity renegotiation as workers move across roles and sectors (Annuš,

2024; Chen, 2024; Rahiman & Kodikal, 2024). AI mentors in these ecologies often manifest as coaching interfaces embedded within enterprise platforms, as recommendation engines for micro-credentials, or as personal learning companions that track reskilling trajectories over many years (Tzirides et al., 2024; Nikolopoulou, 2024; Weidener & Fischer, 2024). They can mitigate cognitive overload by curating resources, modelling complex procedures, and supporting reflective after-action reviews (Cordero et al., 2024; Wang et al., 2024; Alier et al., 2024). However, they also risk entrenching asymmetrical power if performance analytics and learning traces are harnessed for opaque managerial surveillance or coercive reskilling mandates (Afzaal et al., 2024; Rabiatu & Shehu, 2024; Lérias et al., 2024). The archetypes and justice considerations summarised in Table 4 signal that ethical deployment in adult contexts requires explicit separation between developmental mentoring functions and disciplinary control architectures.

5.5 Marginalised, Low-Resource, and Postcolonial Learning Contexts

Marginalised, low-resource, and postcolonial contexts expose most starkly the stakes of AI-mediated mentoring for global educational justice. Learners in such settings inhabit ecologies shaped by infrastructural fragility, linguistic hierarchies, and enduring patterns of exclusion that limit access to qualified teachers, diverse materials, and credentialing opportunities (Abuhassna et al., 2024; Alam, 2023a; Yılmaz, 2024). Theoretical frameworks of *capability expansion* and *decolonial pedagogy* cast independent learning here as a struggle to convert scarce resources into genuine freedoms to pursue valued knowledge trajectories, while resisting epistemic domination (Sasikala & Ravichandran, 2024; Amdan et al., 2024; Alqahtani & Wafula, 2025). AI mentors that are sensitised to intermittent connectivity and device sharing can provide offline-capable explanations, compressive representations, and low-bandwidth interactions that partially compensate for systemic deficits (Sana et al., 2024; Nguyen et al., 2024; Obidovna, 2024). More profoundly, they can function as *bi-epistemic mediators* that articulate connections between indigenous knowledges and dominant global frameworks without subsuming the former (Bulathwela et al., 2024; Amado-Salvatierra et al., 2024; Abulibdeh et al., 2024). As highlighted in Table 4, such configurations must be governed by stringent safeguards against extractive data practices and must be co-designed with communities to ensure that mentoring scripts align with local aspirations and normative horizons.

6. ETHICS, GOVERNANCE, AND EVALUATIVE FRAMEWORKS FOR AI-MENTORED INDEPENDENT LEARNING

6.1 Normative and Justice-Oriented Foundations for Evaluating AI Mentors

Ethical appraisal of AI mentors in independent learning ecologies requires explicit normative architectures rather than ad hoc intuitions about harm and benefit. Within a consequentialist register, design choices are judged by their aggregate effects on learning outcomes, wellbeing profiles, and long-term capability expansion, while deontological perspectives foreground duties of respect, noninstrumentalisation, and informational fiduciary responsibility toward learners (Suryanarayana et al., 2024; Özer, 2024; Galindo-Domínguez et al., 2024). Virtue-ethical frames highlight the cultivation of intellectual and moral excellences such as *prudence*, *courage*, and *intellectual humility* in both designers and users (Sharma et al., 2024; Robert et al., 2024; Bukar et al., 2024). *Care ethics* emphasises attentiveness to vulnerability, relational interdependence, and situated responsibility, particularly for minors and marginalised learners (Alam, 2023b; Zadorina et al., 2024; Iqbal et al., 2024). Capability oriented perspectives scrutinise whether AI mentors genuinely enlarge the substantive freedoms that individuals and communities enjoy in charting educational trajectories (Mouta et al., 2024; Davis et al., 2024). Across these frameworks, justice remains transversal, encompassing distributive allocation of benefits, recognitional respect for diverse identities, and procedural inclusion in governance (Choi et al., 2024; Al-Shorman et al., 2025; Stolpe & Hallström, 2024). Table 5 later in this section consolidates these normative strands into issue clusters and safeguarding priorities that can orient institutional decision making.

6.2 Datafication, Surveillance, and Epistemic Injustice in AI-Mentored Learning

AI mentors typically depend on intensive datafication of learner activity, whereby clicks, keystrokes, latency patterns, affective proxies, and interaction histories are transmuted into analyzable traces. From a critical data perspective, such processes reconfigure learners as iterable data subjects whose behaviours can be predicted, nudged, and monetised (Martin et al., 2024; Kong et al., 2025; Vieriu & Petrea, 2025). Surveillance logics emerge when continuous monitoring of study rhythms and content choices becomes normalised, often without commensurate capacities for contestation or refusal (Walter, 2024; Adeleye et al., 2024; Kumar et al., 2024). Algorithmic profiling can ossify expectations about ability, motivation, or risk, thereby shaping the menu of opportunities that a learner encounters, in some cases long after the original data were produced (Mustafa et al., 2024; Ng et al., 2024; Alwaqdani, 2025). Epistemic injustice concepts such as *testimonial injustice* and *hermeneutical injustice* illuminate how AI mentors may misrecognise certain learners as less credible, or fail to supply interpretive resources that make sense of their experiences (Sperling et al., 2024; Lin & Chen, 2024; Tashtoush et al., 2024). These dynamics show that data architectures are not neutral substrates but active sites of power that must be governed through robust ethical and legal constraints.

Table 5. Ethical and governance matrix for AI-mediated mentoring

Issue Cluster	Normative Focus	Relevant Theoretical Lenses	Evaluation Dimensions for Independent Learning	Key Safeguarding Priorities
Datafication and Surveillance	Legitimacy of tracking, proportionality of monitoring, informational self-determination	*Critical data studies, privacy ethics, informational fiduciary theory*	Sense of privacy, trust in systems, perceived control over personal traces	Data minimisation, transparent logging, meaningful consent, local data sovereignty
Algorithmic Bias and Epistemic Injustice	Fair recognition, non-discrimination, inclusivity of epistemic perspectives	*Fairness in machine learning, epistemic injustice theory, intersectionality*	Equitable access to support, non-stigmatizing feedback, recognition of diverse knowledges	Bias audits, counterfactual evaluation, participatory testing, redress mechanisms
Autonomy and Manipulative Design	Integrity of choice architecture, voluntariness of engagement, relational autonomy	*Autonomy theory, nudge ethics, persuasive technology critique*	Capacity for self-initiated learning, resistance to coercive nudging, reflective endorsement of goals	Constraints on dark patterns, transparency of recommendation logics, friction for high stakes choices

continued on following page

Table 5. Continued

Issue Cluster	Normative Focus	Relevant Theoretical Lenses	Evaluation Dimensions for Independent Learning	Key Safeguarding Priorities
Accountability and Transparency Regimes	Traceability of decisions, allocable responsibility, contestability of outcomes	*Governance theory, accountability frameworks, socio-technical systems analysis*	Ability to query rationale, clarity of escalation channels, institutional answerability	Explainable interaction summaries, multi-party oversight, enforceable liability allocations
Equity, Access, and Capability Expansion	Distributive justice, capability enhancement, infrastructural fairness	*Capability approach, distributive justice theory, infrastructural ethics*	Inclusive access to AI mentoring, reduction of structural learning gaps, empowerment of marginalised groups	Tiered access models, subsidised provision, offline-sympathetic designs, community co-design
Wellbeing and Psychological Safety	Protection from harm, support for flourishing, affective sustainability	*Wellbeing science, trauma-informed practice, care ethics*	Emotional safety, manageable workload, resilience, authenticity of learner identity	Safeguards against overuse, crisis escalation protocols, humane interaction pacing, stigma reduction

Table 5 demonstrates that ethical and governance concerns cannot be treated as peripheral add-ons but must be encoded directly into how AI mentors are specified, procured, and deployed. Each issue cluster integrates a normative emphasis, theoretical vocabulary, and concrete evaluation dimension, thereby enabling institutions to operationalise abstract principles through observable practices and learner experiences. For example, datafication and surveillance must be scrutinised not only in terms of cybersecurity but also regarding learners' phenomenology of privacy and control, while autonomy and manipulative design must be assessed through indicators of self-initiated learning and resistance to coercive nudges. The safeguarding column underscores that effective protection involves layered interventions, from architectural constraints and audit protocols to participatory oversight and community level deliberation. By embedding such matrices into policy instruments, institutions can move beyond compliance minimalism toward genuinely learner centred governance.

6.3 Autonomy, Dependence, Manipulation, and Psychosocial Wellbeing

Autonomy in AI-mentored independent learning should be understood as a relational and graded capacity to author one's learning trajectory in dialogue with human and technical others, rather than as complete disengagement from guidance. AI mentors can support this capacity when they scaffold *reflective endorsement* of goals, invite critical evaluation of their own suggestions, and make it easy for learners to disengage or override recommendations (Guo et al., 2024; Galindo-Domínguez et al., 2024; Alam, 2023c). They undermine autonomy when they employ attention capturing designs, obscure trade-offs, or instrumentalise learner data for third party interests (Linderoth et al., 2024; Almasri, 2024; Perkins et al., 2024). The distinction between supportive dependence and harmful dependency is crucial; periodically relying on an AI mentor as a cognitive prosthesis can be developmentally beneficial if learners are also encouraged to internalise strategies and test themselves without assistance (Guettala et al., 2024; Memarian & Doleck, 2024; Filgueiras, 2024). Psychosocial wellbeing enters when patterns of use influence anxiety, self-worth, and social connectedness (Bulut et al., 2024; Murdan & Halkhoree, 2024; Sămărescu et al., 2024). The autonomy related rows in Table 5 highlight that evaluation must therefore encompass affective and identity level indicators, not only behavioural metrics.

6.4 Accountability, Transparency, and Multilevel Governance Architectures

Accountability for AI-mentored learning practices is inherently distributed, since developers, platform operators, educational institutions, educators, and learners all participate in socio-technical assemblages that produce outcomes (Farooqi et al., 2024; Tang, 2024; Edwards-Fapohunda & Adediji, 2024). Robust governance architectures must therefore specify role differentiated responsibilities and escalation pathways, so that harms can be addressed without diffuse blame or abdication (Airaj, 2024; Ramirez & Esparrell, 2024; Alam, 2022). Transparency is a precondition of such accountability, yet it must be conceived broadly, encompassing not only technical explainability of outputs but also organisational clarity about purposes, data flows, and decision rights (Leong et al., 2024; Yim & Su, 2025; Sanusi et al., 2024). Multilevel governance involves alignment of institutional policies with regulatory frameworks and with transnational norms concerning educational rights and digital ethics (Cukurova, 2025; Lee et al., 2024; Tahir et al., 2024). Mechanisms such as impact assessments, independent audits, advisory councils with learner representation, and publicly accessible documentation can instantiate the accountability regime envisioned in Table 5. Without such scaffolds, even well-intentioned AI mentoring systems risk drifting toward opaque, unchallengeable infrastructures that subtly reshape pedagogy and power.

6.5 Evaluative Frameworks and Conceptual Agendas for Responsible Co-Regulation

Evaluation of AI-mentored independent learning must transcend narrow reliance on test scores or engagement statistics and instead adopt multidimensional frameworks aligned with the capability focused and justice-oriented constructs elaborated across this chapter. Such frameworks would interrogate whether learners exhibit increased *self-regulated learning* sophistication, stronger epistemic virtues, and more robust senses of agency and belonging, while also monitoring distributional patterns across social categories and geographies (Farahani & Ghasmi, 2024; Mao et al., 2024; Yim, 2024). They would combine learner self-reports, qualitative accounts of experience, and structural indicators such as access, reliability, and human support integration (Uygun, 2024; AlAli & Wardat, 2024; Selwyn, 2024). Conceptually, there is a continuing agenda to refine models of human-AI co-agency, to theorise long term identity effects of continuous mentoring, and to articulate criteria for legitimate refusal of AI mediation in education (Salloum et al., 2024; Díaz & Nussbaum, 2024; Ifenthaler et al., 2024). The evaluative dimensions and research prompts embedded in Table 5 offer a scaffold for such work, signalling that responsible co-regulation is an ongoing collective project rather than a one time design decision.

7. CONCLUSION

7.1 Synthesis of Conceptual Threads and Reframed Independence

The foregoing analysis has reconceptualised independent learning as a distributed, relational, and justice-oriented achievement that emerges within complex human-AI assemblages rather than as an isolated psychological state. The lenses of *self-directed learning*, *self-regulated learning*, *distributed cognition*, *activity theory*, and *mentoring frameworks* collectively reveal that planning, monitoring, and meaning-making are always scaffolded by artifacts, norms, and communities, which AI mentors now powerfully reconfigure. Across the typologies of AI mentor archetypes, pedagogical design matrices, ecological comparisons, and ethical governance schemas, a consistent image has surfaced of AI mentors as socio-technical actants that can either enlarge or truncate learners' zones of autonomous, critically reflective activity. Independence under these conditions is best understood as the learner's expanding capacity to orchestrate and contest human and non-human supports, to maintain epistemic agency in the face of fluent machine-generated suggestions, and to align personal trajectories with broader projects of collective flourishing and epistemic justice.

7.2 Normative Design and Governance Orientations for Human-AI Co-Regulation

A coherent normative orientation for AI-mentored independent learning must integrate pedagogical rigor, ethical safeguards, and ecological sensitivity into a single design and governance stance. Pedagogically, AI mentors should instantiate *constructivist*, *inquiry-based*, and *autonomy-supportive* principles through scaffolded assistance, deliberate fading, and epistemic prompting that cultivate self-regulatory and critical capacities rather than passive reliance. Ethically, they must embed commitments to privacy, fairness, capability expansion, and psychological wellbeing, operationalised through transparent data practices, bias sensitive architectures, and mechanisms for refusal or contestation. Ecologically, configurations must be tuned to the specific constraints and aspirations of compulsory schooling, higher education, workplace learning, and marginalised or postcolonial contexts, avoiding universalist templates. Human educators, institutional leaders, technologists, and learners themselves all carry differentiated responsibilities within this arrangement, and robust co-regulation arises only when AI mentors are explicitly positioned as accountable collaborators that augment, but never supplant, human pedagogical and moral judgement.

7.3 Future Theorising, Collective Responsibilities, and Closing Reflection

Future theorising on AI-mentored independent learning must deepen accounts of *human-AI co-agency*, refine criteria for legitimate dependence, and articulate models of educational justice that explicitly incorporate algorithmic infrastructures. Conceptual work is needed on the long-term identity effects of continuous mentoring by simulated interlocutors, on the phenomenology of authorship when cognitive labour is routinely hybrid, and on the right to unaugmented spaces for struggle, error, and solitude. These inquiries should be pursued through interdisciplinary coalitions that join learning sciences, philosophy, critical data studies, design research, and policy analysis, while remaining accountable to learners and communities who live with the consequences of design decisions. Ultimately, independent learning in AI-saturated ecologies must be safeguarded as a site where persons rehearse self-determination, solidarity, and epistemic humility. AI mentors can assist in this project only when they are treated as revisable instruments within democratic educational futures, not as inevitable horizons of human development.

REFERENCES

Abbasi, B. N., Wu, Y., & Luo, Z. (2025). Exploring the impact of artificial intelligence on curriculum development in global higher education institutions. *Education and Information Technologies*, *30*(1), 547–581. DOI: 10.1007/s10639-024-13113-z

Abuhassna, H., Awae, F., Adnan, M. A., Daud, M., & Almheiri, A. S. (2024). The information age for education via artificial intelligence and machine learning: A bibliometric and systematic literature analysis. *International Journal of Information and Education Technology (IJIET)*, *14*(5), 700–711. DOI: 10.18178/ijiet.2024.14.5.2095

Abulibdeh, A., Zaidan, E., & Abulibdeh, R. (2024). Navigating the confluence of artificial intelligence and education for sustainable development in the era of industry 4.0: Challenges, opportunities, and ethical dimensions. *Journal of Cleaner Production*, *437*, 140527. DOI: 10.1016/j.jclepro.2023.140527

Acharya, D. B., Kuppan, K., & Divya, B. (2025). Agentic ai: Autonomous intelligence for complex goals–a comprehensive survey. *IEEE Access : Practical Innovations, Open Solutions*, *13*, 18912–18936. DOI: 10.1109/ACCESS.2025.3532853

Adams, D., & Thompson, P. (2025). Transforming school leadership with artificial intelligence: Applications, implications, and future directions. *Leadership and Policy in Schools*, *24*(1), 77–89.

Adeleye, O. O., Eden, C. A., & Adeniyi, I. S. (2024). Innovative teaching methodologies in the era of artificial intelligence: A review of inclusive educational practices. *World Journal of Advanced Engineering Technology and Sciences, 11*(2), 069-079.

Afzaal, M., Shanshan, X., Yan, D., & Younas, M. (2024). Mapping artificial intelligence integration in education: a decade of innovation and impact (2013-2023)-a bibliometric analysis. *IEEE Access*.

Aguilar-Cruz, P. J., & Salas-Pilco, S. Z. (2025). Teachers' perceptions of artificial intelligence in Colombia: AI technological access, AI teacher professional development and AI ethical awareness. *Technology, Pedagogy and Education*, *34*(2), 219–238. DOI: 10.1080/1475939X.2025.2451865

Airaj, M. (2024). Ethical artificial intelligence for teaching-learning in higher education. *Education and Information Technologies*, *29*(13), 17145–17167. DOI: 10.1007/s10639-024-12545-x

Al-Abdullatif, A. M. (2024). Modeling teachers' acceptance of generative artificial intelligence use in higher education: The role of AI literacy, intelligent TPACK, and perceived trust. *Education Sciences*, *14*(11), 1209. DOI: 10.3390/educsci14111209

Al-Shorman, H. M., Saatchi, S. G., Alanaziand, T., Alzboon, M. S., Alka'awneh, S. M. N., Wahed, M. K. Y. A., & Al-Momani, A. A. M. (2025). Evaluating Artificial Intelligence Integration in Education Through Integrating TAM and S–O–R. In *Intelligence-Driven Circular Economy: Regeneration Towards Sustainability and Social Responsibility–Volume 1* (pp. 353–367). Springer Nature Switzerland. DOI: 10.1007/978-3-031-73899-9_28

Al-Zahrani, A. M., & Alasmari, T. M. (2024). Exploring the impact of artificial intelligence on higher education: The dynamics of ethical, social, and educational implications. *Humanities & Social Sciences Communications*, *11*(1), 1–12. DOI: 10.1057/s41599-024-03432-4

AlAli, R., & Wardat, Y. (2024). Opportunities and challenges of integrating generative artificial intelligence in education. *International Journal of Religion*, *5*(7), 784–793. DOI: 10.61707/8y29gv34

Alam, A. (2022). Impact of university's human resources practices on professors' occupational performance: empirical evidence from India's higher education sector. In *Inclusive businesses in developing economies: Converging people, profit, and corporate citizenship* (pp. 107–131). Springer International Publishing. DOI: 10.1007/978-3-031-12217-0_6

Alam, A. (2023a). Media multitasking with M-learning technology in real-time classroom learning: Analysing the dynamics in formal educational settings for the future of E-learning in India. In *2023 2nd International Conference on Smart Technologies and Systems for Next Generation Computing (ICSTSN)* (pp. 1-6). IEEE.

Alam, A. (2023b). The secret sauce of student success: Cracking the code by navigating the path to personalized learning with educational data mining. In *2023 2nd International Conference on Smart Technologies and Systems for Next Generation Computing (ICSTSN)* (pp. 1-8). IEEE.

Alam, A. (2023c). Intelligence unleashed: An argument for AI-enabled learning ecologies with real world examples of today and a peek into the future. In *International Conference on Innovations in Computer Science, Electronics & Electrical Engineering*-2022 (Vol. 2717, No. 1, p. 030001). AIP Publishing LLC. DOI: 10.1063/5.0129803

Alam, A., & Mohanty, A. (2022, December). Facial analytics or virtual avatars: competencies and design considerations for student-teacher interaction in AI-powered online education for effective classroom engagement. In *International Conference on Communication, Networks and Computing* (pp. 252-265). Cham: Springer Nature Switzerland.

Alam, A., & Mohanty, A. (2023, January). Learning on the move: a pedagogical framework for state-of-the-art mobile learning. In *International Conference on Data Management, Analytics & Innovation* (pp. 735-748). Singapore: Springer Nature Singapore. DOI: 10.1007/978-981-99-1414-2_52

Alam, A., & Mohanty, A. (2024). Integrated constructive robotics in education (ICRE) model: A paradigmatic framework for transformative learning in educational ecosystem. *Cogent Education*, *11*(1), 2324487. DOI: 10.1080/2331186X.2024.2324487

Ali, O., Murray, P. A., Momin, M., Dwivedi, Y. K., & Malik, T. (2024). The effects of artificial intelligence applications in educational settings: Challenges and strategies. *Technological Forecasting and Social Change*, *199*, 123076. DOI: 10.1016/j.techfore.2023.123076

Alier, M., Peñalvo, F. J. G., & Camba, J. D. (2024). Generative Artificial Intelligence in Education: From Deceptive to Disruptive. *International Journal of Interactive Multimedia and Artificial Intelligence*, *8*(5), 5–14. DOI: 10.9781/ijimai.2024.02.011

Allam, H., & Dempere, J. (2025). Agentic AI for IT and Beyond: A Qualitative Analysis of Capabilities, Challenges, and Governance. *The Artificial Intelligence Business Review*, *1*(1).

Almasri, F. (2024). Exploring the impact of artificial intelligence in teaching and learning of science: A systematic review of empirical research. *Research in Science Education*, *54*(5), 977–997. DOI: 10.1007/s11165-024-10176-3

Alqahtani, N., & Wafula, Z. (2025). Artificial intelligence integration: Pedagogical strategies and policies at leading universities. *Innovative Higher Education, 50*(2), 665–684. DOI: 10.1007/s10755-024-09749-x

Alwaqdani, M. (2025). Investigating teachers' perceptions of artificial intelligence tools in education: Potential and difficulties. *Education and Information Technologies, 30*(3), 2737–2755. DOI: 10.1007/s10639-024-12903-9

AlZu'Bi, S., Almiani, M., & Jararweh, Y. (2025, May). Agentic AI for Healthcare: Solutions to Intelligent Patient Care. In *2025 12th International Conference on Information Technology (ICIT)* (pp. 33-38). IEEE.

Amado-Salvatierra, H. R., Morales-Chan, M., Hernandez-Rizzardini, R., & Rosales, M. (2024, March). Exploring educators' perceptions: Artificial intelligence integration in higher education. In *2024 IEEE World Engineering Education Conference (EDUNINE)* (pp. 1-5). IEEE. DOI: 10.1109/EDUNINE60625.2024.10500578

Amdan, M. A. B., Janius, N., & Kasdiah, M. A. H. B. (2024). Concept paper: Efficiency of Artificial Intelligence (AI) tools for STEM education in Malaysia. *International Journal of Science and Research Archive, 12*(2), 553–559. DOI: 10.30574/ijsra.2024.12.2.1273

Annuš, N. (2024). Education in the age of artificial intelligence. *TEM Journal, 13*(1), 404–413. DOI: 10.18421/TEM131-42

Artsın, M., & Bozkurt, A. (2025). Charting new horizons: What agentic artificial intelligence (AI) promises in the educational landscape. In *EDULEARN25 Proceedings* (pp. 2019-2023). IATED.

Artsin, M., & Bozkurt, A. (2026). Dreams, Distortions, and Disruptions: Deconstructing the Educational Promises of Agentic AI. In *Rethinking Education and Agency in the Age of Human-Generative AI Interaction* (pp. 1-18). IGI Global Scientific Publishing.

Ayanwale, M. A., Adelana, O. P., Molefi, R. R., Adeeko, O., & Ishola, A. M. (2024). Examining artificial intelligence literacy among pre-service teachers for future classrooms. *Computers and Education Open, 6*, 100179. DOI: 10.1016/j.caeo.2024.100179

Baltezarević, R., & Baltezarević, I. (2024). Students' attitudes on the role of artificial intelligence (AI) in personalized learning. *International Journal of Cognitive Research in Science. Engineering and Education, 12*(2), 387–397.

Bandi, A., Kongari, B., Naguru, R., Pasnoor, S., & Vilipala, S. V. (2025). The rise of agentic ai: A review of definitions, frameworks, architectures, applications, evaluation metrics, and challenges. *Future Internet, 17*(9), 404. DOI: 10.3390/fi17090404

Banerjie, S., Zhu, Y., Freeman, I., Machado, J. V., Ahmed, A., Sarker, A., & Al-Garadi, M. (2025). Agentic AI in Healthcare: A Comprehensive Survey of Foundations, Taxonomy, and Applications. *Authorea Preprints*. DOI: 10.36227/techrxiv.176238073.31262603/v1

Bapna, R., Bapna, S., Kumar, P., Pamuru, V., Umyarov, A., & Yang, M. (2025). Agentic AI and Managers' Analytics Capabilities: An Exploration. *Available at SSRN* 5293722. DOI: 10.2139/ssrn.5293722

Bender, S. M. (2024). Awareness of artificial intelligence as an essential digital literacy: ChatGPT and Gen-AI in the classroom. *Changing English, 31*(2), 161–174. DOI: 10.1080/1358684X.2024.2309995

Biswas, A., & Talukdar, W. (2025). *Building Agentic AI Systems: Create intelligent, autonomous AI agents that can reason, plan, and adapt*. Packt Publishing Ltd.

Borghoff, U. M., Bottoni, P., & Pareschi, R. (2025). Human-artificial interaction in the age of agentic AI: A system-theoretical approach. *Frontiers in Human Dynamics*, *7*, 1579166. DOI: 10.3389/fhumd.2025.1579166

Boskabadi, M. R., Cao, Y., Khadem, B., Clements, W., Gerek, Z. N., Reuthe, E., & Mansouri, S. S. (2025). Industrial Agentic AI and generative modeling in complex systems. *Current Opinion in Chemical Engineering*, *48*, 101150. DOI: 10.1016/j.coche.2025.101150

Bukar, U. A., Sayeed, M. S., Razak, S. F. A., Yogarayan, S., & Sneesl, R. (2024). Decision-making framework for the utilization of generative artificial intelligence in education: A case study of ChatGPT. *IEEE Access : Practical Innovations, Open Solutions*, *12*, 95368–95389. DOI: 10.1109/ACCESS.2024.3425172

Bulathwela, S., Pérez-Ortiz, M., Holloway, C., Cukurova, M., & Shawe-Taylor, J. (2024). Artificial intelligence alone will not democratise education: On educational inequality, techno-solutionism and inclusive tools. *Sustainability (Basel)*, *16*(2), 781. DOI: 10.3390/su16020781

Bulut, O., Beiting-Parrish, M., Casabianca, J. M., Slater, S. C., Jiao, H., Song, D., . . . Morilova, P. (2024). The rise of artificial intelligence in educational measurement: Opportunities and ethical challenges. *arXiv preprint arXiv:2406.18900*.

Celik, I., Gedrimiene, E., Siklander, S., & Muukkonen, H. (2024). The affordances of artificial intelligence-based tools for supporting 21st-century skills: A systematic review of empirical research in higher education. *Australasian Journal of Educational Technology*, *40*(3), 19–38. DOI: 10.14742/ajet.9069

Chawla, C., Chatterjee, S., Gadadinni, S. S., Verma, P., & Banerjee, S. (2024). Agentic AI: The building blocks of sophisticated AI business applications. *Journal of AI. Robotics & Workplace Automation*, *3*(3), 1–15. DOI: 10.69554/XEHZ1946

Cheah, Y. H., Lu, J., & Kim, J. (2025). Integrating generative artificial intelligence in K-12 education: Examining teachers' preparedness, practices, and barriers. *Computers and Education: Artificial Intelligence*, *8*, 100363. DOI: 10.1016/j.caeai.2025.100363

Chen, H. (2024). The ethical challenges of educational artificial intelligence and coping measures: A discussion in the context of the 2024 World Digital Education Conference. *Science Insights Education Frontiers, 20*(2), 3263-3281.

Cheung, L. H., Wang, L., & Lei, D. (2025). Conversational, agentic AI-enhanced architectural design process: Three approaches to multimodal AI-enhanced early-stage performative design exploration. *Architectural Intelligence*, *4*(1), 1–25. DOI: 10.1007/s44223-025-00092-5

Choi, J. I., Yang, E., & Goo, E. H. (2024). The effects of an ethics education program on artificial intelligence among middle school students: Analysis of perception and attitude changes. *Applied Sciences (Basel, Switzerland)*, *14*(4), 1588. DOI: 10.3390/app14041588

Cordero, J., Torres-Zambrano, J., & Cordero-Castillo, A. (2024). Integration of generative artificial intelligence in higher education: Best practices. *Education Sciences*, *15*(1), 32. DOI: 10.3390/educsci15010032

Cukurova, M. (2025). The interplay of learning, analytics and artificial intelligence in education: A vision for hybrid intelligence. *British Journal of Educational Technology*, *56*(2), 469–488. DOI: 10.1111/bjet.13514

Dai, K., & Liu, Q. (2024). Leveraging artificial intelligence (AI) in English as a foreign language (EFL) classes: Challenges and opportunities in the spotlight. *Computers in Human Behavior, 159*, 108354. DOI: 10.1016/j.chb.2024.108354

Davis, C., Bush, T., & Wood, S. (2024). Artificial intelligence in education: Enhancing learning experiences through personalized adaptation. *International Journal of Cyber and IT Service Management*, *4*(1), 26–32. DOI: 10.34306/ijcitsm.v4i1.146

Díaz, B., & Nussbaum, M. (2024). Artificial intelligence for teaching and learning in schools: The need for pedagogical intelligence. *Computers & Education*, *217*, 105071. DOI: 10.1016/j.compedu.2024.105071

Dieterle, E., Dede, C., & Walker, M. (2024). The cyclical ethical effects of using artificial intelligence in education. *AI & Society*, *39*(2), 633–643. DOI: 10.1007/s00146-022-01497-w PMID: 36185064

Dwivedi, Y. K., Helal, M. Y. I., Elgendy, I. A., Albashrawi, M. A., Hughes, L., Shawosh, M., & Jeon, I. (2025). Artificial intelligence agents and agentic systems in hospitality and tourism: Challenges, opportunities and research agenda. *International Journal of Contemporary Hospitality Management*.

Edwards-Fapohunda, M. O., & Adediji, M. A. (2024). Sustainable development of distance learning in continuing adult education: The impact of artificial intelligence. *Iconic Research and Engineering Journals*, *8*(1), 113–114.

Erduran, S., & Levrini, O. (2024). The impact of artificial intelligence on scientific practices: An emergent area of research for science education. *International Journal of Science Education*, *46*(18), 1982–1989. DOI: 10.1080/09500693.2024.2306604

Ezeoguine, E. P., & Eteng-Uket, S. (2024). Artificial intelligence tools and higher education student's engagement. *Edukasiana: Jurnal Inovasi Pendidikan*, *3*(3), 300–312. DOI: 10.56916/ejip.v3i3.733

Fadlelmula, F. K., & Qadhi, S. M. (2024). A systematic review of research on artificial intelligence in higher education: Practice, gaps, and future directions in the GCC. *Journal of University Teaching & Learning Practice*, *21*(6), 146–173. DOI: 10.53761/pswgbw82

Famaye, T., Bailey, C. S., Adisa, I., & Irgens, G. A. (2024). What Makes ChatGPT Dangerous Is Also What Makes It Special": High-School Student Perspectives on the Integration or Ban of Artificial Intelligence in Educational Contexts. *International Journal of Technology in Education*, *7*(2), 174–199. DOI: 10.46328/ijte.651

Farahani, M. S., & Ghasmi, G. (2024, July). Artificial intelligence in education: A comprehensive study. In *Forum for Education Studies* (Vol. 2, No. 3, pp. 1379-1379). DOI: 10.59400/fes.v2i3.1379

Farooqi, M. T. K., Amanat, I., & Awan, S. M. (2024). Ethical considerations and challenges in the integration of artificial intelligence in education: A systematic review. *Journal of Excellence in Management Sciences*, *3*(4), 35–50. DOI: 10.69565/jems.v3i4.314

Filgueiras, F. (2024). Artificial intelligence and education governance. *Education, Citizenship and Social Justice*, *19*(3), 349–361. DOI: 10.1177/17461979231160674

Fitrianto, I., Setyawan, C. E., & Saleh, M. (2024). Utilizing Artificial Intelligence for Personalized Arabic Language Learning Plans. *International Journal of Post Axial: Futuristic Teaching and Learning*, 30-40.

Forero-Corba, W., & Bennasar, F. N. (2024). Techniques and applications of Machine Learning and Artificial Intelligence in education: a systematic review. *RIED-Revista Iberoamericana de Educación a Distancia, 27*(1).

Franco D'Souza, R., Mathew, M., Mishra, V., & Surapaneni, K. M. (2024). Twelve tips for addressing ethical concerns in the implementation of artificial intelligence in medical education. *Medical Education Online*, *29*(1), 2330250. DOI: 10.1080/10872981.2024.2330250 PMID: 38566608

Fullan, M., Azorín, C., Harris, A., & Jones, M. (2024). Artificial intelligence and school leadership: Challenges, opportunities and implications. *School Leadership & Management*, *44*(4), 339–346. DOI: 10.1080/13632434.2023.2246856

Fundi, M., Sanusi, I. T., Oyelere, S. S., & Ayere, M. (2024). Advancing AI education: Assessing Kenyan in-service teachers' preparedness for integrating artificial intelligence in competence-based curriculum. *Computers in Human Behavior Reports*, *14*, 100412. DOI: 10.1016/j.chbr.2024.100412

Galindo-Domínguez, H., Delgado, N., Campo, L., & Losada, D. (2024). Relationship between teachers' digital competence and attitudes towards artificial intelligence in education. *International Journal of Educational Research*, *126*, 102381. DOI: 10.1016/j.ijer.2024.102381

Galindo-Domínguez, H., Delgado, N., Losada, D., & Etxabe, J. M. (2024). An analysis of the use of artificial intelligence in education in Spain: The in-service teacher's perspective. *Journal of Digital Learning in Teacher Education*, *40*(1), 41–56. DOI: 10.1080/21532974.2023.2284726

Garg, V. (2025). Designing the Mind: How Agentic Frameworks Are Shaping the Future of AI Behavior. *Journal of Computer Science and Technology Studies*, *7*(5), 182–193. DOI: 10.32996/jcsts.2025.7.5.24

Gkintoni, E., Antonopoulou, H., Sortwell, A., & Halkiopoulos, C. (2025). Challenging cognitive load theory: The role of educational neuroscience and artificial intelligence in redefining learning efficacy. *Brain Sciences*, *15*(2), 203. DOI: 10.3390/brainsci15020203 PMID: 40002535

Gökçearslan, S., Tosun, C., & Erdemir, Z. G. (2024). Benefits, challenges, and methods of artificial intelligence (AI) chatbots in education: A systematic literature review. *International Journal of Technology in Education*, *7*(1), 19–39. DOI: 10.46328/ijte.600

Goyal, S. (2025). A Critical Review of Agentic AI: Core Technologies, Applications, Ethical Implications, and Future Research Directions. *Jurnal Masyarakat Informatika*, *16*(2), 268–283. DOI: 10.14710/jmasif.16.2.77084

Grájeda, A., Burgos, J., Córdova, P., & Sanjinés, A. (2024). Assessing student-perceived impact of using artificial intelligence tools: Construction of a synthetic index of application in higher education. *Cogent Education*, *11*(1), 2287917. DOI: 10.1080/2331186X.2023.2287917

Gudipati, M. R. (2025, November). Agentic AI: A Tool-Guided Approach to Achieving Precision in Engineering Numerical Operations. In *Abu Dhabi International Petroleum Exhibition and Conference* (p. D021S081R007). SPE. DOI: 10.2118/229446-MS

Guettala, M., Bourekkache, S., Kazar, O., & Harous, S. (2024). Generative artificial intelligence in education: Advancing adaptive and personalized learning. *Acta Informatica Pragensia*, *13*(3), 460–489. DOI: 10.18267/j.aip.235

Guo, S., Zheng, Y., & Zhai, X. (2024). Artificial intelligence in education research during 2013–2023: A review based on bibliometric analysis. *Education and Information Technologies*, *29*(13), 16387–16409. DOI: 10.1007/s10639-024-12491-8

Hosseini, S., & Seilani, H. (2025). The role of agentic ai in shaping a smart future: A systematic review. *Array (New York, N.Y.)*, *26*, 100399. DOI: 10.1016/j.array.2025.100399

Hu, C., Zhang, L., Lim, Y., Wadhwani, A., Peters, A., & Kang, D. (2025, July). REPRO-BENCH: Can Agentic AI Systems Assess the Reproducibility of Social Science Research? In *Findings of the Association for Computational Linguistics: ACL 2025* (pp. 23616-23626).

Huang, K. (2025). The Genesis and Evolution of AI Agents. In Agentic, A. I. (Ed.), *Theories and Practices* (pp. 1–22). Springer Nature Switzerland. DOI: 10.1007/978-3-031-90026-6_1

Hughes, L., Dwivedi, Y. K., Li, K., Appanderanda, M., Al-Bashrawi, M. A., & Chae, I. (2025). AI Agents and Agentic Systems: Redefining Global it Management. *Journal of Global Information Technology Management*, *28*(3), 1–11. DOI: 10.1080/1097198X.2025.2524286

Hughes, L., Dwivedi, Y. K., Malik, T., Shawosh, M., Albashrawi, M. A., Jeon, I., Dutot, V., Appanderanda, M., Crick, T., De', R., Fenwick, M., Gunaratnege, S. M., Jurcys, P., Kar, A. K., Kshetri, N., Li, K., Mutasa, S., Samothrakis, S., Wade, M., & Walton, P. (2025). AI agents and agentic systems: A multi-expert analysis. *Journal of Computer Information Systems*, *65*(4), 1–29. DOI: 10.1080/08874417.2025.2483832

Ifenthaler, D., Majumdar, R., Gorissen, P., Judge, M., Mishra, S., Raffaghelli, J., & Shimada, A. (2024). Artificial intelligence in education: Implications for policymakers, researchers, and practitioners. *Technology. Knowledge and Learning*, *29*(4), 1693–1710. DOI: 10.1007/s10758-024-09747-0

Iqbal, M., Khan, N. U., & Imran, M. (2024). The role of artificial intelligence (AI) in transforming educational practices: Opportunities, challenges, and implications. *Qlantic Journal of Social Sciences*, *5*(2), 348–359. DOI: 10.55737/qjss.349319430

Ivanashko, O., Kozak, A., Knysh, T., & Honchar, K. (2024). The role of artificial intelligence in shaping the future of education: Opportunities and challenges. *Futurity Education*, *4*(1), 126–146.

Jafari, F., & Keykha, A. (2024). Identifying the opportunities and challenges of artificial intelligence in higher education: A qualitative study. *Journal of Applied Research in Higher Education*, *16*(4), 1228–1245. DOI: 10.1108/JARHE-09-2023-0426

Jaggavarapu, M. K. R. (2025). The evolution of agentic ai: Architecture and workflows for autonomous systems. *Journal Of Multidisciplinary*, *5*(7), 418–427.

Jaradeh, M. Y., & Auer, S. (2025). Deep Research in the Era of Agentic AI: Requirements and Limitations for Scholarly Research. In *CEUR Workshop Proceedings* (Vol. 4065).

Jatileni, C. N., Sanusi, I. T., Olaleye, S. A., Ayanwale, M. A., Agbo, F. J., & Oyelere, P. B. (2024). Artificial intelligence in compulsory level of education: Perspectives from Namibian in-service teachers. *Education and Information Technologies*, *29*(10), 12569–12596. DOI: 10.1007/s10639-023-12341-z

Joel Augustus, D., Asiegbu Victor, I., & Obinna, E. (2025). Leveraging artificial intelligence (AI) for educational development in Nigeria: Examining the challenges and opportunities. *Journal of Social Sciences*, *2*(2).

Kanumolu, G., Urlana, A., Charaka, V. K., & Garlapati, B. M. (2025). Agent ideate: A framework for product idea generation from patents using agentic ai. In *Proceedings of the 2nd Workshop on Agent AI for Scenario Planning* (pp. 50-57).

Karakose, T., & Tülübas, T. (2024). School Leadership and Management in the Age of Artificial Intelligence (AI): Recent Developments and Future Prospects. *Educational Process: International Journal*, *13*(1), 7–14. DOI: 10.22521/edupij.2024.131.1

Karataş, F., Eriçok, B., & Tanrikulu, L. (2025). Reshaping curriculum adaptation in the age of artificial intelligence: Mapping teachers' AI-driven curriculum adaptation patterns. *British Educational Research Journal*, *51*(1), 154–180. DOI: 10.1002/berj.4068

Karunanayake, N. (2025). Next-generation agentic AI for transforming healthcare. *Informatics and Health*, *2*(2), 73–83. DOI: 10.1016/j.infoh.2025.03.001

Katsamakas, E., Pavlov, O. V., & Saklad, R. (2024). Artificial intelligence and the transformation of higher education institutions: A systems approach. *Sustainability (Basel)*, *16*(14), 6118. DOI: 10.3390/su16146118

Kazanidis, I., & Pellas, N. (2024). Harnessing generative artificial intelligence for digital literacy innovation: A comparative study between early childhood education and computer science undergraduates. *AI*, *5*(3), 1427–1445. DOI: 10.3390/ai5030068

Khreisat, M. N., Khilani, D., Rusho, M. A., Karkkulainen, E. A., Tabuena, A. C., & Uberas, A. D. (2024). Ethical implications of AI integration in educational decision making: Systematic review. *Educational Administration: Theory and Practice*, *30*(5), 8521–8527.

Komaragiri, V. B. (2025). Agentic AI for Autonomous Network Orchestration: A New Frontier in Telecommunications. *EKSPLORIUM-BULETIN PUSAT TEKNOLOGI BAHAN GALIAN NUKLIR*, *46*(1), 221–241.

Kong, S. C., Korte, S. M., Burton, S., Keskitalo, P., Turunen, T., Smith, D., Wang, L., Lee, J. C.-K., & Beaton, M. C. (2025). Artificial Intelligence (AI) literacy–an argument for AI literacy in education. *Innovations in Education and Teaching International*, *62*(2), 477–483. DOI: 10.1080/14703297.2024.2332744

Kong, S. C., & Yang, Y. (2024). A human-centered learning and teaching framework using generative artificial intelligence for self-regulated learning development through domain knowledge learning in K–12 settings. *IEEE Transactions on Learning Technologies*, *17*, 1562–1573. DOI: 10.1109/TLT.2024.3392830

Kostopoulos, G., Gkamas, V., Rigou, M., & Kotsiantis, S. (2025). Agentic AI in Education: State of the Art and Future Directions. *IEEE Access : Practical Innovations, Open Solutions*, *13*, 177467–177491. DOI: 10.1109/ACCESS.2025.3620473

Koutra, D., Huang, L., Kulkarni, A., Prioleau, T., Soh, B. W. Y., Wu, Q., . . . Zou, J. (2025). Towards Agentic AI for Science: Hypothesis Generation, Comprehension, Quantification, and Validation. In *ICLR 2025 Workshop Proposals*.

Kshetri, N. (2025). Revolutionizing Higher Education: The Impact of Artificial Intelligence Agents and Agentic Artificial Intelligence on Teaching and Operations. *IT Professional*, *27*(2), 12–16. DOI: 10.1109/MITP.2025.3550697

Kumar, P., Mazrouei, B. S. A., Fayyaz, M. F., Jan, S. A., & Maysari, J. A. (2025, November). Realizing the Need for Agentic AI for Subsurface Data and Workflows. In *Abu Dhabi International Petroleum Exhibition and Conference* (p. D021S069R003). SPE. DOI: 10.2118/229586-MS

Kumar, S., Rao, P., Singhania, S., Verma, S., & Kheterpal, M. (2024). Will artificial intelligence drive the advancements in higher education? A tri-phased exploration. *Technological Forecasting and Social Change*, *201*, 123258. DOI: 10.1016/j.techfore.2024.123258

Lan, Y. (2024). Through tensions to identity-based motivations: Exploring teacher professional identity in Artificial Intelligence-enhanced teacher training. *Teaching and Teacher Education*, *151*, 104736. DOI: 10.1016/j.tate.2024.104736

Lee, Y. J., Davis, R. O., & Ryu, J. (2024). Korean in-service teachers' perceptions of implementing artificial intelligence (AI) education for teaching in schools and their AI teacher training programs. *International Journal of Information and Education Technology (IJIET)*, *14*(2), 214–219. DOI: 10.18178/ijiet.2024.14.2.2042

Leong, W. Y., Leong, Y. Z., & San Leong, W. (2024, October). Artificial Intelligence in education. In *IET International Conference on Engineering Technologies and Applications (ICETA 2024)* (Vol. 2024, pp. 183-184). IET.

Lérias, E., Guerra, C., & Ferreira, P. (2024). Literacy in artificial intelligence as a challenge for teaching in higher education: A case study at portalegre polytechnic university. *Information (Basel)*, *15*(4), 205. DOI: 10.3390/info15040205

Li, M. (2025). Integrating artificial intelligence in primary mathematics education: Investigating internal and external influences on teacher adoption. *International Journal of Science and Mathematics Education*, *23*(5), 1283–1308. DOI: 10.1007/s10763-024-10515-w

Lim, E. M. (2024). Metaphor analysis on pre-service early childhood teachers' conception of AI (Artificial Intelligence) education for young children. *Thinking Skills and Creativity*, *51*, 101455. DOI: 10.1016/j.tsc.2023.101455

Lin, H., & Chen, Q. (2024). Artificial intelligence (AI)-integrated educational applications and college students' creativity and academic emotions: Students and teachers' perceptions and attitudes. *BMC Psychology*, *12*(1), 487. DOI: 10.1186/s40359-024-01979-0 PMID: 39285268

Linderoth, C., Hultén, M., & Stenliden, L. (2024). Competing visions of artificial intelligence in education—A heuristic analysis on sociotechnical imaginaries and problematizations in policy guidelines. *Policy Futures in Education, 22*(8), 1662–1678. DOI: 10.1177/14782103241228900

Liu, R., Zenke, C., Liu, C., Holmes, A., Thornton, P., & Malan, D. J. (2024, March). Teaching CS50 with AI: leveraging generative artificial intelligence in computer science education. In *Proceedings of the 55th ACM technical symposium on computer science education* V. 1 (pp. 750-756).

Lye, C. Y., & Lim, L. (2024). Generative artificial intelligence in tertiary education: Assessment redesign principles and considerations. *Education Sciences, 14*(6), 569. DOI: 10.3390/educsci14060569

Ma, D., Akram, H., & Chen, I. H. (2024). Artificial intelligence in higher education: A cross-cultural examination of students' behavioral intentions and attitudes. *International Review of Research in Open and Distance Learning, 25*(3), 134–157. DOI: 10.19173/irrodl.v25i3.7703

Ma, S., & Lei, L. (2024). The factors influencing teacher education students' willingness to adopt artificial intelligence technology for information-based teaching. *Asia Pacific Journal of Education, 44*(1), 94–111. DOI: 10.1080/02188791.2024.2305155

Ma, X., & Wang, J. (2024, October). WIP: Active Learning through Prompt Engineering and Agentic AI Simulation-A Pilot Project in Computer Networks Education. In *2024 IEEE Frontiers in Education Conference (FIE)* (pp. 1-5). IEEE.

Mah, D. K., & Groß, N. (2024). Artificial intelligence in higher education: Exploring faculty use, self-efficacy, distinct profiles, and professional development needs. *International Journal of Educational Technology in Higher Education, 21*(1), 58. DOI: 10.1186/s41239-024-00490-1

Mahmoud, C. F., & Sørensen, J. T. (2024). Artificial intelligence in personalized learning with a focus on current developments and future prospects. *Research and Advances in Education, 3*(8), 25–31. DOI: 10.56397/RAE.2024.08.04

Mao, J., Chen, B., & Liu, J. C. (2024). Generative artificial intelligence in education and its implications for assessment. *TechTrends, 68*(1), 58–66. DOI: 10.1007/s11528-023-00911-4

Marengo, A., Pagano, A., Pange, J., & Soomro, K. A. (2024). The educational value of artificial intelligence in higher education: A 10-year systematic literature review. *Interactive Technology and Smart Education, 21*(4), 625–644. DOI: 10.1108/ITSE-11-2023-0218

Martin, F., Zhuang, M., & Schaefer, D. (2024). Systematic review of research on artificial intelligence in K-12 education (2017–2022). *Computers and Education: Artificial Intelligence, 6*, 100195. DOI: 10.1016/j.caeai.2023.100195

Martin, G., & Olszewska, J. (2025). Automation Testing Framework for Reliable Autonomous Agentic AI. *2025 IEEE Engineering Reliable Autonomous Systems (ERAS)*, 1-8.

Memarian, B., & Doleck, T. (2024). Human-in-the-loop in artificial intelligence in education: A review and entity-relationship (ER) analysis. *Computers in Human Behavior: Artificial Humans, 2*(1), 100053. DOI: 10.1016/j.chbah.2024.100053

Merchán Sánchez-Jara, J. F., González Gutiérrez, S., Cruz Rodríguez, J., & Syroyid Syroyid, B. (2024). Artificial intelligence-assisted music education: A critical synthesis of challenges and opportunities. *Education Sciences*, *14*(11), 1171. DOI: 10.3390/educsci14111171

Mikeladze, T., Meijer, P. C., & Verhoeff, R. P. (2024). A comprehensive exploration of artificial intelligence competence frameworks for educators: A critical review. *European Journal of Education*, *59*(3), e12663. DOI: 10.1111/ejed.12663

Motamary, S. (2025). Empowering Retail Oss/Bss Platforms With Agentic Ai And Scalable Data Engineering. *Metallurgical and Materials Engineering*, 1361-1380.

Mouta, A., Pinto-Llorente, A. M., & Torrecilla-Sánchez, E. M. (2024). Uncovering blind spots in education ethics: Insights from a systematic literature review on artificial intelligence in education. *International Journal of Artificial Intelligence in Education*, *34*(3), 1166–1205. DOI: 10.1007/s40593-023-00384-9

Mouta, A., Torrecilla-Sánchez, E. M., & Pinto-Llorente, A. M. (2024). Design of a future scenarios toolkit for an ethical implementation of artificial intelligence in education. *Education and Information Technologies*, *29*(9), 10473–10498. DOI: 10.1007/s10639-023-12229-y

Murdan, A. P., & Halkhoree, R. (2024, June). Integration of Artificial Intelligence for educational excellence and innovation in higher education institutions. In *2024 1st International Conference on Smart Energy Systems and Artificial Intelligence (SESAI)* (pp. 1-6). IEEE. DOI: 10.1109/SESAI61023.2024.10599402

Murugesan, S. (2025). The rise of agentic AI: Implications, concerns, and the path forward. *IEEE Intelligent Systems*, *40*(2), 8–14. DOI: 10.1109/MIS.2025.3544940

Musolin, M. H., Ismail, M. H., Farhan, M., Rois, N., Ismail, A., Huda, M., & Rohim, M. A. (2024, February). Understanding of artificial intelligence for Islamic education support and service: insights from empirical literature review. In *International Congress on Information and Communication Technology* (pp. 27-43). Singapore: Springer Nature Singapore.

Mustafa, M. Y., Tlili, A., Lampropoulos, G., Huang, R., Jandrić, P., Zhao, J., Salha, S., Xu, L., Panda, S., Kinshuk, , López-Pernas, S., & Saqr, M. (2024). A systematic review of literature reviews on artificial intelligence in education (AIED): A roadmap to a future research agenda. *Smart Learning Environments*, *11*(1), 59. DOI: 10.1186/s40561-024-00350-5

Mustafaraj, E. (2025, May). Dreams in Hypertext: Berners-Lee, Agentic AI, and the Next Web Frontier. In *Companion Publication of the 17th ACM Web Science Conference 2025* (pp. 19-21).

Naixin, Z., Wai Yie, L., Tong, Z., & Changqing, W. (2024). Artificial Intelligence in Engineering Education: A Review of Pedagogical Innovations. *INTI JOURNAL*, *2024*(46), 1–10.

Nedungadi, P., Tang, K. Y., & Raman, R. (2024). The transformative power of generative artificial intelligence for achieving the sustainable development goal of quality education. *Sustainability (Basel)*, *16*(22), 9779. DOI: 10.3390/su16229779

Neelu, A., Pramod, J. P., & Lahari, A. (2025). Optimizing Networks Using AI and Machine Learning: The Role of Agentic AI in Transforming Network Management. In *The Power of Agentic AI: Redefining Human Life and Decision-Making: In Industry 6.0* (pp. 229–254). Springer Nature Switzerland. DOI: 10.1007/978-3-031-89424-4_16

Ng, D. T. K., Chan, E. K. C., & Lo, C. K. (2025). Opportunities, challenges and school strategies for integrating generative AI in education. *Computers and Education: Artificial Intelligence*, 100373.

Ng, D. T. K., Su, J., Leung, J. K. L., & Chu, S. K. W. (2024). Artificial intelligence (AI) literacy education in secondary schools: A review. *Interactive Learning Environments*, *32*(10), 6204–6224. DOI: 10.1080/10494820.2023.2255228

Nguyen, A., Kremantzis, M., Essien, A., Petrounias, I., & Hosseini, S. (2024). Enhancing student engagement through artificial intelligence (AI): Understanding the basics, opportunities, and challenges. *Journal of University Teaching & Learning Practice*, *21*(6), 1–13. DOI: 10.53761/caraaq92

Nicoletti, B., & Appolloni, A. (2025). A digital twin framework for enhancing human–agentic AI–machine collaboration. *Journal of Intelligent Manufacturing*, •••, 1–17.

Nikolopoulou, K. (2024). Generative artificial intelligence in higher education: Exploring ways of harnessing pedagogical practices with the assistance of ChatGPT. *International Journal of Changes in Education*, *1*(2), 103–111. DOI: 10.47852/bonviewIJCE42022489

Obenza, B. N., Salvahan, A., Rios, A. N., Solo, A., Alburo, R. A., & Gabila, R. J. (2024). University students' perception and use of ChatGPT: Generative artificial intelligence (AI) in higher education. *International Journal of Human-Computer Studies*, *5*(12), 5–18.

Obidovna, D. Z. (2024). The pedagogical-psychological aspects of artificial intelligence technologies in integrative education. *International Journal Of Literature And Languages*, *4*(03), 13–19. DOI: 10.37547/ijll/Volume04Issue03-03

Olujimi, P. A., Owolawi, P. A., Mogase, R. C., & Wyk, E. V. (2025). Agentic AI frameworks in SMMEs: A systematic literature review of ecosystemic interconnected agents. *AI*, *6*(6), 123. DOI: 10.3390/ai6060123

Opesemowo, O. A., & Ndlovu, M. (2024). Artificial intelligence in mathematics education: The good, the bad, and the ugly. *Journal of Pedagogical Research*, *8*(3), 333–346. DOI: 10.33902/JPR.202426428

Opesemowo, O. A. G., & Adekomaya, V. (2024). Harnessing artificial intelligence for advancing sustainable development goals in South Africa's higher education system: A qualitative study. *International Journal of Learning. Teaching and Educational Research*, *23*(3), 67–86. DOI: 10.26803/ijlter.23.3.4

Özer, M. (2024). Potential Benefits and Risks of Artificial Intelligence in Education. *Bartin University Journal of Faculty of Education, 13*(2).

Ozodakhon, K. (2024). The benefits and drawbacks of using artificial intelligence (ChatGPT) in education. *University Research Base*, 805-808.

Pack, A., & Maloney, J. (2024). Using artificial intelligence in TESOL: Some ethical and pedagogical considerations. *TESOL Quarterly*, *58*(2), 1007–1018. DOI: 10.1002/tesq.3320

Paduraru, C., Paduraru, M., & Stefanescu, A. (2025, June). Enhancing Game AI Behaviors with Large Language Models and Agentic AI. In *Proceedings of the 33rd ACM International Conference on the Foundations of Software Engineering* (pp. 286-296). DOI: 10.1145/3696630.3728553

Pamisetty, A. (2024). Application of agentic artificial intelligence in autonomous decision making across food supply chains. *Available at SSRN* 5231360.

Pandey, R. (2025). The Rise of Agentic AI: Redefining Human–Machine Collaboration. [IJARCST]. *International Journal of Advanced Research in Computer Science & Technology*, *8*(5), 12794–12801. DOI: 10.15662/IJARCST.2025.0805005

Parikh, N. A. (2026). Agentic AI in Product Management: A Co-Evolutionary Model. In *High Performance Leadership for Organizational Excellence: Innovation, Technology, and Resilience* (pp. 1-36). IGI Global Scientific Publishing.

Park, W., & Kwon, H. (2024). Implementing artificial intelligence education for middle school technology education in Republic of Korea. *International Journal of Technology and Design Education*, *34*(1), 109–135. DOI: 10.1007/s10798-023-09812-2 PMID: 36844448

Patel, K. (2024). Agentic AI for Self-Healing Production Lines: Autonomous Root Cause Analysis & Correction. *Journal of Information Systems Engineering & Management*, *9*, 124–135.

Perkins, M., Furze, L., Roe, J., & MacVaugh, J. (2024). The Artificial Intelligence Assessment Scale (AIAS): A framework for ethical integration of generative AI in educational assessment. *Journal of University Teaching & Learning Practice*, *21*(6), 49–66. DOI: 10.53761/q3azde36

Pop, M. V., Ton , G., Flonta, F. V., & Flore, M. (2025). Agentic AI in STEM Education: Enhancing Cognitive Flexibility and Workforce Readiness. *BRAIN. Broad Research in Artificial Intelligence and Neuroscience, 16*(1 Sup1), 239-249.

Porter, Z., Calinescu, R., Lim, E., Hodge, V., Ryan, P., Burton, S., Habli, I., Lawton, T., McDermid, J., Molloy, J., Monkhouse, H., Morgan, P., Noordhof, P., Paterson, C., Standen, I., & Zou, J. (2025). INSYTE: A classification framework for traditional to agentic AI systems. *ACM Transactions on Autonomous and Adaptive Systems*, *20*(3), 1–39. DOI: 10.1145/3760424

Portugal, I. D. S., Alencar, P., & Cowan, D. (2024, December). An agentic AI-based multi-agent framework for recommender systems. In *2024 IEEE International Conference on Big Data (BigData)* (pp. 5375-5382). IEEE. DOI: 10.1109/BigData62323.2024.10825765

Rabiatu, M. M., & Shehu, S. A. (2024). Adopting artificial intelligence (AI) in education: Challenges & possibilities. *Asian Journal of Advanced Research and Reports*, *18*(2), 106–111. DOI: 10.9734/ajarr/2024/v18i2608

Raheem, T., & Hossain, G. (2025, May). Agentic AI Systems: Opportunities, Challenges, and Trustworthiness. In *2025 IEEE International Conference on Electro Information Technology (eIT)* (pp. 618-624). IEEE. DOI: 10.1109/eIT64391.2025.11103638

Rahiman, H. U., & Kodikal, R. (2024). Revolutionizing education: Artificial intelligence empowered learning in higher education. *Cogent Education*, *11*(1), 2293431. DOI: 10.1080/2331186X.2023.2293431

Ramirez, E. A. B., & Esparrell, J. A. F. (2024). Artificial Intelligence (AI) in Education: Unlocking the Perfect Synergy for Learning. *Educational Process: International Journal, 13*(1), 35–51.

Rane, N. (2024). Enhancing the quality of teaching and learning through Gemini, ChatGPT, and similar generative Artificial Intelligence: Challenges, future prospects, and ethical considerations in education. *TESOL and Technology Studies*, *5*(1), 1–6. DOI: 10.48185/tts.v5i1.1000

Raza, S., Sapkota, R., Karkee, M., & Emmanouilidis, C. (2025). Responsible Agentic Reasoning and AI Agents: A Critical Survey: Proposal for Safe Agentic AI via Responsible Reasoning AI Agents (R2A2). *SuperIntelligence-Robotics-Safety & Alignment, 2*(6).

Robert, A., Potter, K., & Frank, L. (2024). The impact of artificial intelligence on students' learning experience. *Wiley Interdisciplinary Reviews: Computational Statistics*, *2*(01), 75–84.

Roshanaei, M. (2024). Towards best practices for mitigating artificial intelligence implicit bias in shaping diversity, inclusion and equity in higher education. *Education and Information Technologies*, *29*(14), 18959–18984. DOI: 10.1007/s10639-024-12605-2

Ruiz-Rojas, L. I., Salvador-Ullauri, L., & Acosta-Vargas, P. (2024). Collaborative working and critical thinking: Adoption of generative artificial intelligence tools in higher education. *Sustainability (Basel)*, *16*(13), 5367. DOI: 10.3390/su16135367

Rusum, G. P., & Anasuri, S. (2025). Agentic AI: Building Self-Directed Software Agents with Multimodal Reasoning. *American International Journal of Computer Science and Technology*, *7*(1), 1–14. DOI: 10.63282/3117-5481/AIJCST-V7I1P101

Saatchi, S. G., Wahed, M. K. Y. A., Alqaraleh, M. K. S., Al-Shorman, H. M., Alanazi, T., Alka'awneh, S. M. N., & Alzyoud, M. (2025). The influence of compatibility on the acceptance of artificial intelligence in Kuwaiti universities. In *Intelligence-Driven Circular Economy: Regeneration Towards Sustainability and Social Responsibility–Volume 1* (pp. 103–117). Springer Nature Switzerland. DOI: 10.1007/978-3-031-73899-9_9

Sağın, F. G., Özkaya, A. B., Tengiz, F., Geyik, Ö. G., & Geyik, C. (2024). Current evaluation and recommendations for the use of artificial intelligence tools in education. *Türk Biyokimya Dergisi*, *48*(6), 620–625. DOI: 10.1515/tjb-2023-0254

Salloum, S. A. (2024). AI perils in education: Exploring ethical concerns. *Artificial intelligence in education: The power and dangers of ChatGPT in the classroom*, 669-675.

Salloum, S. A., Salloum, A., & Alfaisal, R. (2024). Objectives and Obstacles of Artificial Intelligence in Education. *Artificial Intelligence in Education: The Power and Dangers of ChatGPT in the Classroom*, 605-614.

Samala, A. D., Rawas, S., Wang, T., Reed, J. M., Kim, J., Howard, N. J., & Ertz, M. (2025). Unveiling the landscape of generative artificial intelligence in education: A comprehensive taxonomy of applications, challenges, and future prospects. *Education and Information Technologies*, *30*(3), 3239–3278. DOI: 10.1007/s10639-024-12936-0

Sămărescu, N., Bumbac, R., Zamfiroiu, A., & Iorgulescu, M. C. (2024). Artificial intelligence in education: Next-gen teacher perspectives. *Amfiteatru Economic*, *26*(65), 145–161. DOI: 10.24818/EA/2024/65/145

Sana, E., Fitriani, A., Soetarno, D., & Yusuf, M. (2024). Analysis of user perceptions on interactive learning platforms based on artificial intelligence. *Journal of Computer Science and Technology Application*, *1*(1), 26–32. DOI: 10.33050/corisinta.v1i1.12

Sanusi, I. T., Agbo, F. J., Dada, O. A., Yunusa, A. A., Aruleba, K. D., Obaido, G., Olawumi, O., & Oyelere, S. S.Centre for Multidisciplinary Research and Innovation (CEMRI). (2024). Stakeholders' insights on artificial intelligence education: Perspectives of teachers, students, and policymakers. *Computers and Education Open*, *7*, 100212. DOI: 10.1016/j.caeo.2024.100212

Sanusi, I. T., Ayanwale, M. A., & Chiu, T. K. (2024). Investigating the moderating effects of social good and confidence on teachers' intention to prepare school students for artificial intelligence education. *Education and Information Technologies*, *29*(1), 273–295. DOI: 10.1007/s10639-023-12250-1

Sanusi, I. T., Ayanwale, M. A., & Tolorunleke, A. E. (2024). Investigating pre-service teachers' artificial intelligence perception from the perspective of planned behavior theory. *Computers and Education: Artificial Intelligence*, *6*, 100202. DOI: 10.1016/j.caeai.2024.100202

Sarwar, M. A., & Ms Saima, A. G. (2024). The role of artificial intelligence in shaping the future of education at higher secondary level. *Journal of Education and Social Studies*, *5*(1), 34–45. DOI: 10.52223/jess.2024.5104

Sasikala, P., & Ravichandran, R. (2024). Journal of Digital Learning and Education. *Journal of Digital Learning and Education*, *4*(2), 145–155. DOI: 10.52562/jdle.v4i2.1234

Satav, A. (2025). Enterprise API & Platform Strategy in the era of Agentic AI. *Journal of Computer Science and Technology Studies*, *7*(1), 380–385. DOI: 10.32996/jcsts.2025.7.1.28

Selwyn, N. (2024). On the limits of artificial intelligence (AI) in education. *Nordisk tidsskrift for pedagogikk og kritikk, 10*(1), 3-14.

Shailendra, S., Kadel, R., & Sharma, A. (2024). Framework for adoption of generative artificial intelligence (GenAI) in education. *IEEE Transactions on Education*, *67*(5), 777–785. DOI: 10.1109/TE.2024.3432101

Shamsuddinova, S., Heryani, P., & Naval, M. A. (2024). Evolution to revolution: Critical exploration of educators' perceptions of the impact of Artificial Intelligence (AI) on the teaching and learning process in the GCC region. *International Journal of Educational Research*, *125*, 102326. DOI: 10.1016/j.ijer.2024.102326

Sharma, A., & Chaturvedi, S. (2025). Agentic AI with Model Context Protocol. *ICT Systems and Sustainability: Proceedings of ICT4SD 2025, Volume 2, 2*, 433.

Sharma, S., Singh, G., Sharma, C. S., & Kapoor, S. (2024). Artificial intelligence in Indian higher education institutions: A quantitative study on adoption and perceptions. *International Journal of System Assurance Engineering and Management*, •••, 1–17. DOI: 10.1007/s13198-023-02193-8

Sheelam, G. K. (2024). Towards Autonomic Wireless Systems: Integrating Agentic AI with Advanced Semiconductor Technologies in Telecommunications. *American Online Journal of Science and Engineering (AOJSE), 2*(1).

Sheelam, G. K. (2025). Architecting Agentic AI for Real-Time Autonomous Edge Systems in Next-Gen Mobile Devices. *Advances in Consumer Research. Association for Consumer Research (U. S.)*, *2*(3).

Sheelam, G. K., & Komaragiri, V. B. (2025). Self-Adaptive Wireless Communication: Leveraging ML And Agentic AI In Smart Telecommunication Networks. *Metallurgical and Materials Engineering*, 1381-1401.

Singha, S., & Singha, R. (2024). The application of artificial intelligence in education: Opportunities and challenges. *Educational perspectives on digital technologies in modeling and management*, 282-292.

Sova, R., Tudor, C., Tartavulea, C. V., & Dieaconescu, R. I. (2024). Artificial intelligence tool adoption in higher education: A structural equation modeling approach to understanding impact factors among economics students. *Electronics (Basel)*, *13*(18), 3632. DOI: 10.3390/electronics13183632

Sperling, K., Stenberg, C. J., McGrath, C., Åkerfeldt, A., Heintz, F., & Stenliden, L. (2024). In search of artificial intelligence (AI) literacy in teacher education: A scoping review. *Computers and Education Open*, *6*, 100169. DOI: 10.1016/j.caeo.2024.100169

Stolpe, K., & Hallström, J. (2024). Artificial intelligence literacy for technology education. *Computers and Education Open*, *6*, 100159. DOI: 10.1016/j.caeo.2024.100159

Storey, V. A., & Wagner, A. (2024). Integrating artificial intelligence (ai) into adult education: Opportunities, challenges, and future directions. [IJAET]. *International Journal of Adult Education and Technology*, *15*(1), 1–15. DOI: 10.4018/IJAET.345921

Storozhyk, M. (2024). Philosophy of future: Analytical overview of interaction between education, science, and artificial intelligence in the context of contemporary challenges. *Futurity Philosophy*, *3*(1), 23–47.

Suryanarayana, K. S., Kandi, V. P., Pavani, G., Rao, A. S., Rout, S., & Krishna, T. S. R. (2024). Artificial intelligence enhanced digital learning for the sustainability of education management system. *The Journal of High Technology Management Research*, *35*(2), 100495. DOI: 10.1016/j.hitech.2024.100495

Suura, S. R. (2024). Agentic artificial intelligence systems for dynamic health management and real-time genomic data analysis. [EJAAI]. *European Journal of Analytics and Artificial Intelligence*, *2*(1).

Tahir, M., Hassan, F. D., & Shagoo, M. R. (2024). Role of artificial intelligence in education: A conceptual review. *World Journal of Advanced Research and Reviews*, *22*(1), 1469–1475. DOI: 10.30574/wjarr.2024.22.1.1217

Tan, X., Cheng, G., & Ling, M. H. (2024). Artificial intelligence in teaching and teacher professional development: A systematic review. *Computers and Education: Artificial Intelligence*, 100355.

Tang, K. H. D. (2024). Implications of artificial intelligence for teaching and learning. *Acta Pedagogia Asiana*, *3*(2), 65–79. DOI: 10.53623/apga.v3i2.404

Tashtoush, M. A., Wardat, Y., Ali, R. A., & Saleh, S. (2024). Artificial intelligence in education: Mathematics teachers' perspectives, practices and challenges. *Iraqi Journal for Computer Science and Mathematics*, *5*(1), 20. DOI: 10.52866/ijcsm.2024.05.01.004

Tassoti, S. (2024). Assessment of students use of generative artificial intelligence: Prompting strategies and prompt engineering in chemistry education. *Journal of Chemical Education*, *101*(6), 2475–2482. DOI: 10.1021/acs.jchemed.4c00212

Thorat, S. H. (2025). Agentic AI for Customer Service and Contact Center Solutions. *Journal of Computer Science and Technology Studies*, *7*(8), 444–451.

Thorat, V., Rao, P., Joshi, N., Talreja, P., & Shetty, A. R. (2024). Role of artificial intelligence (AI) in patient education and communication in dentistry. *Cureus*, *16*(5). Advance online publication. DOI: 10.7759/cureus.59799 PMID: 38846249

Tiwari, A. (2025). Beyond Automation: The Emergence of Agentic Urban AI. *Automation*, *6*(3), 29. DOI: 10.3390/automation6030029

Tiwari, A. (2025). Conceptualising the emergence of Agentic Urban AI: From automation to agency. *Urban Informatics*, *4*(1), 13. DOI: 10.1007/s44212-025-00079-7

Topaz, M., Peltonen, L. M., Michalowski, M., Stiglic, G., Ronquillo, C., Pruinelli, L., Song, J., O'Connor, S., Miyagawa, S., & Fukahori, H. (2025). The ChatGPT effect: Nursing education and generative artificial intelligence. *The Journal of Nursing Education*, *64*(6), e40–e43. DOI: 10.3928/01484834-20240126-01 PMID: 38302101

Tzirides, A. O. O., Zapata, G., Kastania, N. P., Saini, A. K., Castro, V., Ismael, S. A., You, Y., Santos, T. A., Searsmith, D., O'Brien, C., Cope, B., & Kalantzis, M. (2024). Combining human and artificial intelligence for enhanced AI literacy in higher education. *Computers and Education Open*, *6*, 100184. DOI: 10.1016/j.caeo.2024.100184

Uygun, D. (2024). Teachers' perspectives on artificial intelligence in education. *Advances in Mobile Learning Educational Research*, *4*(1), 931–939. DOI: 10.25082/AMLER.2024.01.005

Venkatesh, A. N., & Jayavardhan, G. V. (2025). Future of Work: Managing Ethical Challenges of Agentic AI and Super Intelligence in Organizations. *Advances in Consumer Research. Association for Consumer Research (U. S.)*, *2*, 5277–5284.

Vieriu, A. M., & Petrea, G. (2025). The impact of artificial intelligence (AI) on students' academic development. *Education Sciences*, *15*(3), 343. DOI: 10.3390/educsci15030343

Vistorte, A. O. R., Deroncele-Acosta, A., Ayala, J. L. M., Barrasa, A., López-Granero, C., & Martí-González, M. (2024). Integrating artificial intelligence to assess emotions in learning environments: A systematic literature review. *Frontiers in Psychology*, *15*, 1387089. DOI: 10.3389/fpsyg.2024.1387089 PMID: 38966729

Viswanathan, P. S. (2025). Agentic AI: A comprehensive framework for autonomous decision-making systems in artificial intelligence. *International Journal of Computer Engineering and Technology*, *16*(1), 862–880. DOI: 10.34218/IJCET_16_01_069

Walter, Y. (2024). Embracing the future of Artificial Intelligence in the classroom: The relevance of AI literacy, prompt engineering, and critical thinking in modern education. *International Journal of Educational Technology in Higher Education, 21*(1), 15. DOI: 10.1186/s41239-024-00448-3

Wang, C., Wang, H., Li, Y., Dai, J., Gu, X., & Yu, T. (2025). Factors influencing university students' behavioral intention to use generative artificial intelligence: Integrating the theory of planned behavior and AI literacy. *International Journal of Human-Computer Interaction, 41*(11), 6649–6671. DOI: 10.1080/10447318.2024.2383033

Wang, J., & Li, J. (2024). Artificial intelligence empowering public health education: Prospects and challenges. *Frontiers in Public Health, 12*, 1389026. DOI: 10.3389/fpubh.2024.1389026 PMID: 39022411

Wang, S., Wang, F., Zhu, Z., Wang, J., Tran, T., & Du, Z. (2024). Artificial intelligence in education: A systematic literature review. *Expert Systems with Applications, 252*, 124167. DOI: 10.1016/j.eswa.2024.124167

Warrier, A. (2025). Collaborative Agentic AI for Personalized Treatment Protocol Optimization: Autonomous Clinical Decision Networks. *International Journal of Emerging Trends in Computer Science and Information Technology*, 154-164.

Weidener, L., & Fischer, M. (2024). Artificial intelligence in medicine: Cross-sectional study among medical students on application, education, and ethical aspects. *JMIR Medical Education, 10*(1), e51247. DOI: 10.2196/51247 PMID: 38180787

Widad, J. (2025). The Evolution of Autonomy: From Reactive AI to Agentic AI. *The Power of Agentic AI: Redefining Human Life and Decision-Making: In Industry 6.0*, 1-9.

Williamson, B. (2024). The social life of AI in education. *International Journal of Artificial Intelligence in Education, 34*(1), 97–104. DOI: 10.1007/s40593-023-00342-5

Wissuchek, C., & Zschech, P. (2025, June). Challenges in Managing the Relationship Between Agentic AI Systems and Humans in Organizations. In *International Conference on Business Information Systems* (pp. 3-17). Cham: Springer Nature Switzerland. DOI: 10.1007/978-3-031-94193-1_1

Wu, X. Y. (2024). Artificial Intelligence in L2 learning: A meta-analysis of contextual, instructional, and social-emotional moderators. *System, 126*, 103498. DOI: 10.1016/j.system.2024.103498

Xia, Q., Weng, X., Ouyang, F., Lin, T. J., & Chiu, T. K. (2024). A scoping review on how generative artificial intelligence transforms assessment in higher education. *International Journal of Educational Technology in Higher Education, 21*(1), 40. DOI: 10.1186/s41239-024-00468-z

Xu, A., Du, M., Yu, T., Puvvadi, M., Yu, T., Guo, Y., & Gottschlich, J. G. (2025, August). Agentic AI for Enterprise: Emerging Applications and Real-world Challenges. In *Proceedings of the 31st ACM SIGKDD Conference on Knowledge Discovery and Data Mining* V. 2 (pp. 6300-6301). DOI: 10.1145/3711896.3737871

Yadav, S. (2024). Artificial Intelligence (AI) Integration in Higher Education: Navigating Opportunities and Ethical Frontiers in Education with Advanced Technologies. In *Impact of artificial intelligence on society* (pp. 43-59). Chapman and Hall/CRC.

Yadav, U., & Shrawankar, U. (2025). Artificial intelligence across industries: A comprehensive review with a focus on education. *AI applications and strategies in teacher education*, 275-320.

Yang, A. (2024). Challenges and opportunities for foreign language teachers in the era of artificial intelligence. *International Journal of Education and Humanities*, *4*(1), 39–50. DOI: 10.58557/(ijeh).v4i1.202

Yang, W., Hu, X., Yeter, I. H., Su, J., Yang, Y., & Lee, J. C. K. (2024). Artificial intelligence education for young children: A case study of technology-enhanced embodied learning. *Journal of Computer Assisted Learning*, *40*(2), 465–477. DOI: 10.1111/jcal.12892

Yang, Y., Chen, L., He, W., Sun, D., & Salas-Pilco, S. Z. (2024). Artificial intelligence for enhancing special education for K-12: A decade of trends, themes, and global insights (2013–2023). *International Journal of Artificial Intelligence in Education*, •••, 1–49.

Yellanki, S. K., Kummari, D. N., Sheelam, G. K., Kannan, S., & Chakilam, C. (2025). Synthetic Cognition Meets Data Deluge: Architecting Agentic AI Models for Self-Regulating Knowledge Graphs in Heterogeneous Data Warehousing. *Metallurgical and Materials Engineering*, *31*(4), 569–586. DOI: 10.63278/1487

Yılmaz, Ö. (2024). Personalised learning and artificial intelligence in science education: Current state and future perspectives. *Educational Technology Quarterly*, *2024*(3), 255–274. DOI: 10.55056/etq.744

Yim, I. H. Y. (2024). A critical review of teaching and learning artificial intelligence (AI) literacy: Developing an intelligence-based AI literacy framework for primary school education. *Computers and Education: Artificial Intelligence*, *7*, 100319. DOI: 10.1016/j.caeai.2024.100319

Yim, I. H. Y., & Su, J. (2025). Artificial intelligence (AI) learning tools in K-12 education: A scoping review. *Journal of Computers in Education*, *12*(1), 93–131.

Yuan, L., & Liu, X. (2025). The effect of artificial intelligence tools on EFL learners' engagement, enjoyment, and motivation. *Computers in Human Behavior*, *162*, 108474. DOI: 10.1016/j.chb.2024.108474

Yue, M., Jong, M. S. Y., & Ng, D. T. K. (2024). Understanding K–12 teachers' technological pedagogical content knowledge readiness and attitudes toward artificial intelligence education. *Education and Information Technologies*, *29*(15), 19505–19536. DOI: 10.1007/s10639-024-12621-2

Zadorina, O., Hurskaya, V., Sobolyeva, S., Grekova, L., & Vasylyuk-Zaitseva, S. (2024). The role of artificial intelligence in creation of future education: Possibilities and challenges. *Futurity Education*, *4*(2), 163–185.

Zarei, M., Mamaghani, H. E., Abbasi, A., & Hosseini, M. S. (2024). Application of artificial intelligence in medical education: A review of benefits, challenges, and solutions. *Medicina Clínica Práctica*, *7*(2), 100422. DOI: 10.1016/j.mcpsp.2023.100422

Zhang, H., Perry, A., & Lee, I. (2025). Developing and validating the artificial intelligence literacy concept inventory: An instrument to assess artificial intelligence literacy among middle school students. *International Journal of Artificial Intelligence in Education*, *35*(1), 398–438. DOI: 10.1007/s40593-024-00398-x

Zhou, X., Zhang, J., & Chan, C. (2024). Unveiling students' experiences and perceptions of artificial intelligence usage in higher education. *Journal of University Teaching & Learning Practice*, *21*(6), 126–145. DOI: 10.53761/xzjprb23

Zohuri, B., & Mossavar-Rahmani, F. (2024). Revolutionizing education: The dynamic synergy of personalized learning and artificial intelligence. *International Journal of Advanced Engineering and Management Research*, *9*(1), 143–153. DOI: 10.51505/ijaemr.2024.9111

Chapter 4
AI Agents and Independent Learning:
A Critical Review of Emerging Pathways in Education

Sovannaroth Chheang
http://orcid.org/0009-0007-3382-7169
Department of Education, Sovanna Elton Foreign Language School (SELS), Phnom Penh, Cambodia

Sovanna Huot
http://orcid.org/0009-0006-8335-442X
Department of Education, National Institute of Education (NIE), Phnom Penh, Cambodia

ABSTRACT

This chapter evaluates ways in which artificial intelligence (AI) agents are changing independent learning with regard to personalization, adaptive feedback, and learner autonomy. Constructivism, connectivism, and self-determination are referred to because they explain how cognitive, motivational, and engagement processes are mediated with the help of AI systems like chatbots, intelligent tutors, and adaptive learning platforms. Recent works and international case studies are harmonized to weigh the pros and cons of AI in education, including access democratization potential and bias, privacy, and automation over-reliance potential. Human-centered, transparent, and culturally responsive approaches are suggested with consideration of the ethical imbalance created by the excess of technological advancement. The chapter culminates with the stand, arguing education's future should be AI-augmented, not AI-dominated. Learning should be a partnership between people and AI systems, fostering a shared sense of creativity, empathy, and wisdom.

1. INTRODUCTION

As AI becomes integrated into routine learning activities, there are significant epistemological and technological changes in education. For more than thirty years, the history of educational technologies has progressed from non-interactive digital archives and computer-assisted educational methods to smart tutoring systems, adaptive learning systems, and software agents that engage in conversations

DOI: 10.4018/979-8-3373-7225-9.ch004

(Holmes et al., 2019; Luckin & Holmes, 2016). Such advances represent a more profound transformation in the production, mediation, and internalization of knowledge than simple alterations in instructional instruments. In this chapter, artificial intelligence agents are seen as more than just instructional aids. They are seen as operative agents in social and technical systems which change the way cognitive work, deliberative work, and educational work are done.

In the past, digital education concentrated on the delivery of content and access to resources, such as Khan Academy and online encyclopedias (Redecker, 2017). There has certainly been more than just a superficial change since the advent of advanced AI. Zawacki-Richter et al. (2019) describe how the more sophisticated AI of today, which incorporates machine learning, natural language processing (NLP), and other techniques from the realm of advanced neural networks, can 'read' a learner's activities and modify the learning materials on the fly. In contrast to previous generations of digital technology that was static, these systems analyze learning and modify behavior, infer learning needs and respond to cues constructively, thus engaging in a type of pedagogical reasoning that only other human teachers possessed. The development of large language models (LLMs), such as ChatGPT by OpenAI, Gemini by Google, and Claude by Anthropic, has now shifted the possibilities in educational practice (Huot & Loch, 2025b). These systems can converse, explain concepts, and provide feedback appropriate to the educational context (Kasneci et al., 2023). They can organize sparse educational resources, fix learners' misconceptions, and provide evaluative feedback through a cycle of learning and teaching, akin to the personalized mentorship of one-on-one tutoring (Zimmerman, 2018). Other learning platforms, such as Duolingo Max, Khanmigo, and Socratic by Google, instrument AI in continuously adjusting content and pacing to learner profiles through data-soaked algorithms (Baker & Inventado, 2014). These changes compel educational practitioners to rethink the core pedagogical principles of autonomy, self-regulation, and the machine-human learning nexus.

People and intelligent systems are networks. This network-related learning shifts learning paradigms. This impacts the role AI agents play. AI agents are not only instructional tools, designed to help humans learn, but also conscious partners in the learning and cognitive processes (Selwyn, 2019). This function of AI shifts the learning environment and blurs the age-old defined roles of the teacher, learner, and tool. This demands research to evaluate the promised potentials and possible threats of such a scenario. Amid the numerous defensible pedagogical claims surrounding the use of AI, there are equally defensible critiques. For example, Knox (2025) warns against the unreflective application of algorithmic systems, which may modify learning into something fully automated, data-centric, and devoid of critical engagement as the process becomes increasingly efficient. Likewise, Filgueiras (2024) points out that increasingly algorithmically mediated learning may erode educational agency as decisions that were traditionally made by teachers and learners are taken over by hidden, opaque systems of computation. The rapidly evolving AI agents, therefore, pose an ethical and philosophical question within educational theory: Can autonomy be retained within learning, accompanied by an algorithm? Answering this question requires going beyond what has been described as smart systems and looking at the way through which algorithmic systems change the current framework of educational independence, agency, and accountability.

Optimizing skepticism while blending calm is an objective. Thus, AI an educational vehicle and an intricate are considered participants in fluid human-machine systems. This chapter aims to: (1) integrate and assess existing studies to understand the extent to which AI agents have been integrated and the impacts on pedagogy in formal and informal educational contexts (K-12 and higher education, and lifelong learning); (2) analyze the extent to which AI agents facilitate or inhibit learner autonomy, self-regulation, and personalized learning, in light of constructivism, connectivism, and self-determination theories, and (3) explore the ethical, pedagogical, and policy dimensions of AI-supported autonomous learning, focusing on equity, transparency, and the human-centered design of pedagogy. Addressing these objectives aims to close an important research gap: the rapid growth of AI research in education raises the need to understand its relevance and impacts on autonomy, empowerment, and ethical dimensions, which are still in an incipient stage (Zawacki-Richter et al., 2019; Zimmerman, 2018).

2. CONCEPTUAL AND THEORETICAL FOUNDATIONS

Independent learning continues to be a fundamental aspect of educational philosophy, defining the transition from instructor-centered to learner-centered educational models. Essentially, independent learning describes the ability of a learner to take initiative, set goals, choose a plan, assess progress, and finally, evaluate the learning results (Candy, 1991; Knowles, 1975). As a learner engages in independent learning, the learner addresses the cognitive, metacognitive, and affective components. Unlike a passive learner, he/she is active in the learning process. In older educational models, independence took the form of self-directed learning (SDL). In this model, learners are trusted to make educational decisions and take overall control of learning (Knowles, 1975). In contrast, learning in the new digital and AI environments implies independence more profoundly. Agency in algorithmic systems is described as a learner's ability to navigate, negotiate, and resist (Filgueiras, 2024; Selwyn, 2019) in learning systems governed by Artificial Intelligence. When algorithmic systems are used in education, independence becomes a negotiated outcome in which learners engage in self-regulation and no passive engagement, but rather active engagement in self-regulation, self-contestation, and self-adjustment of the output of systems, which act as agents, but whose inner mechanisms are neither visible nor understandable by the learners.

Zimmerman (2000) describes a model of self-regulated learning (SRL) that helps track the development of independence from the user's internal processes. It describes the forethought (goal-setting and planning), performance (self-control and self-monitoring), and self-reflection (evaluation and adaptation) stages as a cyclical process. In digital environments, AI agents can perform various functions within each of these stages by providing feedback, scaffolding goal-setting, and visualizing goal progress. While AI can perform these functions and does so to a troubling degree, Luckin (2018) suggests that it might erode the one core piece of independence learning seeks to develop: metacognitive awareness. The independence users can be expected to construct should be routed as the ability to self-regulate learning in collaboration with digital tools, and not as isolation from instruction. This is also where the AI educational system most enables the exercise of agency as defined by Bandura (2001) as the capacity to act and reflect upon a given setting, which in this case is profoundly sociotechnical. The exercise of control by learners to decide on the learning path and to determine the process of learning influenced by the algorithms at work best illustrates agency in AI driven education. If AI delineates hurdles and prescribes subsequent steps, there is a possibility of implicit contract where the self and self-review and self-evaluation are reassigned, which means the learners will develop the ability to follow instructions but will not have the ability to formulate and assess their own plans.

Mediated self regulation is a developmental phenomenon as proposed by Paris and Paris (2003). Digital systems provide a diversity of mediation tools augmented reflection and adaptive learning system that situate these prompts in digital environments. AI agents can, for example, identify when learners are struggling and offer help in the form of tailored strategic recommendations, which mimic the functions of a tutor. Nevertheless, this kind of support triggers cognitive offloading, whether learners are assimilating self-regulatory skills or relying on co-existing cognitive resources (Clark & Chalmers, 1998). In this scenario, the ability to collaborate with intelligent systems without ceding control is a new kind of literacy with this level of independent learning. As Selwyn (2021) describes, this new literacy comprises algorithmic literacy, or the capacity to understand, interrogate, and scrutinize the workings of AI tools that facilitate learning. For this reason, current self-teaching practices require extensiveness of both mental self-sufficiency and a sophisticated engineering conceptualization of systemic control, with the technological mediation as the more dominant and focal element of the learning. The question of cognitive offloading arises: to what extent should design, control, and evaluation be reassigned to systems, and when does offloading design, control, and evaluation be reassigned frustrate the ultimate goal of education, which is the development of independent self-regulation.

AI is starting to be used in education in various, fully agentic ways, and is being integrated with other various technologies, pedagogical designs, and degrees of autonomy. These systems all shift the parameters of what constitutes teaching as opposed to what constitutes interaction and what defines a teacher as opposed to what defines a piece of technology. Conversational agents, or what most people call chatbots, are probably the most noticeable and easiest to use forms of education AI. These systems use AI and large language models to engage directly with learners in natural language, handling questions and providing feedback in a dialogue as well as tutoring in a simulated conversation (Kasneci et al., 2023). ChatGPT, Khanmigo, and Google's Socratic are some examples, and, as described, they can help learners scaffold questions and elaborate explanations and articulate a thoughtful analysis.

The pedagogical promise these systems hold is not only theoretical. Fryer and Carpenter (2006) demonstrated that social dialogue agents can motivate learners by simulating social presence, finishing dialogue, and sustaining an interaction, all of which are critical to online engagement. Mokmin et al. (2023) captured the more recent phenomenon of AI in education, stating that teacher-moderated, ChatGPT-integrated learning activities enhanced learners' comprehension and critical reasoning. Yet, when agents are positioned as authoritative answerers rather than dialogic agents, students can come to equate confident and fluent responses with correct answers, resulting in an epistemic dependence which may be difficult to overcome. The final point is that conversational agents are a risk in and of themselves. When students are taught to see AI as an epistemic authority that can address all inquiries rather than as a dialogic partner, these over-reliance issues can become problematic as AI can generate false responses (Huot & Tep, 2025; Kasneci et al., 2023).

ITSs are among the first examples of AI in the educational sector. These technologies function by attempting to model learners' cognitive processes and tailoring instruction to suit individual needs. Carnegie Learning's MATHia, ALEKS, and AutoTutor are examples of cognitive modeling systems that assess performance and offer personalized feedback and scaffolding. Graesser et al. (2012) explain the integration of domain and pedagogical knowledge, as well as a student model that attempts to function like a human tutor. They also points out that all tutoring systems enhance the learner's ability to understand concepts and solve problems. VanLehn (2011) observed that students using the ITS obtained much better results in post-test evaluation than those from classes where traditional methods of instruction were utilized. Nonetheless, a lack of transferability and flexibility remains a core design limitation within most Intelligent Tutoring Systems. Most of the systems function in pre-specified, narrow domains and discrete, rule-based problem-situations, making them poorly suited to open-ended, non-structured tasks and creative problem-solving (Roll & Wylie, 2016). Most current systems are hybridized to a limited extent with other AI components, most notably NLP and affective computing, to respond to not just student actions but also student emotions, which is considered to enhance system engagement D'Mello and Graesser (2015). These developments enhance the position of Intelligent Tutoring Systems in emotionally-responsive, adaptive teaching frameworks. The more systems can identify and respond to individual learners, the more it can be seen to reduce learning to a technical optimization problem, rather than a process of balancing uncertainty, disagreement, and moral concern.

Virtual learning companions (VLCs) represent a new frontier in human–AI interaction. These systems, either as an embodied agent or an avatar, aim to simulate the human interactions needed to sustain an individual's motivation and effort via social and emotional engagement (Deci & Ryan, 2008). Kim et al. (2024) found that the presence of an adaptive emotional agent in emotionally charged interactions is able to not only improve academic achievement, but the learner's self-efficacy as well. Empathy and resilience training are the educational adaptations of Replika and Woebot that were originally developed for mental health support. The emotional attachments, authenticity of the interactions, and data collection and privacy issues, Williamson (2021) should not go ignored, though. The emotionally responsive systems should have their design purpose and pedagogical potential balanced between engagement and the ethical and emotional concerns. This suggests the need for longitudinal studies on learners to understand the consequences of interacting with support systems, particularly digital affective agents and the risk of uncare in human terms. The four categories of AI agents illustrate the integration of cognitive, affective, and social intelligence in educational design. They transform learning into an exercise in co-agency, the partnership of human cognition and machine adaptivity.

Constructivism, which takes Piaget (1952) and Vygotsky (1978) as foundational theorists, asserts that learners, through engagement, experiences, and social interactions, build knowledge, which means knowledge is not passed down but constructed as learners add newly acquired information to what is already stored in their cognitive frameworks. Within constructivist learning, AI agents can perform as scaffolds. By adaptive questioning, feedback loops, and simulations, the AI agents (Luckin, 2018; Vygotsky, 1978) create different complexity ZPDs where learners perform scaffolded tasks that become progressively unscaffolded as the learners gain more skills. An example in this is the problem-solving strategy simulations in Integrated Teaching Systems (ITS), which are not directly instructive, but provide learners an opportunity to iteratively explore and learn, thus being constructivist. Yet, one must remember that constructivism encompasses more than the learning of a given concept; that is, the constructivism of Papert (1980) is learning through the act of creating. AI systems where learners design, code, or create content e.g., Scratch and generative AI platforms, exemplify this principle as they position learners as creators, as illustrated in **Figure 1**.

Figure 1.

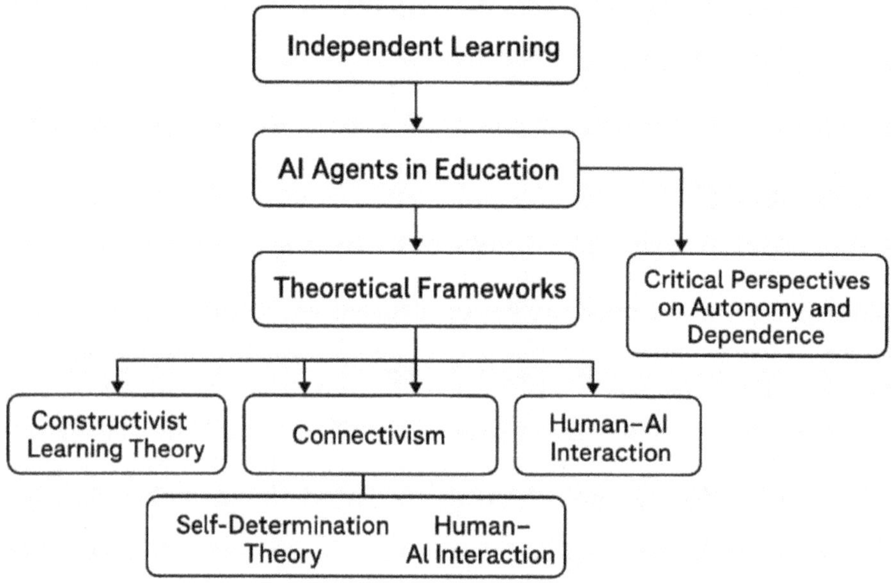

3. AI AGENTS IN PRACTICE: CURRENT APPLICATIONS

AI in education reshapes the differentiation and individualized instruction frameworks that have been the foundation for teaching for many years. Personalized learning shifted from a teacher's wish, intuition, and a little bit of assessed data, to adaptive learning technologies that capture real-time behavioral, knowledge, and emotional data about the learner (Holmes et al., 2019; Zawacki-Richter et al., 2019). Systems that adjust to learner data capture the shift to AI-driven real-time personalization, wherein instructional sequences, pacing, and modality are altered in real-time to suit the learner's readiness and preferences. There is a benefit of adaptation systems in terms of teaching activities, however, they may reduce the scope of the syllabus by providing a limited number of activities which may be considered as teaching to the learners the best way to complete the tasks, rather than providing challenging activities which may bring the learners to a state of confusion. This requires a pedagogical stance where the aim is to promote self-explanation and strategy selection rather than the invisible scripting of learners' approaches to problem solving.

Innovative platforms leading the way in this field include Knewton, Smart Sparrow, and MATHia by Carnegie Learning, all of which are incorporating learning analytics, machine learning, and cognitive modeling to provide personalized learning experiences. For instance, Knewton's adaptive engine captures and continuously evaluates learner feedback and implements adaptive scaffolding and enrichment, or alters the complexity of a learning task depending on the learner's capability (Baker & Inventado, 2014). These personalized technologies are built on Self-Determination Theory (Deci & Ryan, 2000) as well as constructivism, since learners get greater control over the pacing and the way each component is navigated (Luckin, 2018), fulfilling autonomy and intrinsic motivation (Deci & Ryan, 2008, 2012).

Beyond personalized learning, scholars emphasize personalization in learning. The learning technologies industry is now abuzz with the term personalization, especially in the context of adaptive algorithms and individualized learning experiences. Scholars point to the problem of algorithmic adaptivity, wherein learners become trapped within a narrow box and lose exposure to learning a range of perspectives (Knox, 2025). This has been termed automated differentiation by Williamson (2021), and it is not without its paradoxical disbenefits of equitable loss from its predictive power locking learners in a narrow range of content to consume. Hence, the personalization of learning experiences must scale balanced pedagogical exposure to prevent learners from being passive receivers of adaptive pathways. From the standpoint of justice, automated differentiation can be dangerous in that it can worsen the current state of equity in the education system, whereby learners in disadvantage socioeconomic circumstances are more likely to be entrenched in activities of a remedial nature, whilst the more fortunate learners are provided with an educational pathway of a more advanced and exploratory nature.

Khanmigo, created by Khan Academy in partnership with OpenAI, combines Chat AI with step-by-step instructions, walking students through the problem-solving processes while encouraging them to think about their own thinking processes. This seems to align with the constructionist principles as proposed by Papert (1980), in which learners digitally manipulate objects to grasp internalized abstract concepts. In the field of mathematics education, ALEKS and the MATHia software by Carnegie Learning are examples of intelligent tutoring systems that help learners develop their procedural fluency and deepen their understanding of concepts. The adaptive sequencing algorithms designed by these systems recognize and respond to learners' misconceptions through tailored instruction and scaffolding until the learners reach mastery (Graesser et al., 2012; Huot & Loch, 2025a).

Artificial Intelligence Agents as Learning Coaches. In Education and training, AI agents act as coaches for individualized, just-in-time learning. LinkedIn Learning, IBM Watson Education, and Coursera Career pathways provide personalized micro learning interventions using adaptive AI according to users' skills and the industry demand. According to Holmes et al. (2019), such systems facilitate continuous reskilling and upskilling needed to respond to the labor market's fluid and ever-changing demands. The use of AI and machine learning to automate analytics represents a significant improvement in educational practice assessments. The historical assessment burden has been tedious, subjective, and scale limited. As of right now, AI is able to automate formative and summative assessment feedback and provide personalized review and evaluations for students and teachers (Luckin & Holmes, 2016; Zimmerman, 2018).

AI literacy and adaptive learning are integrated into Finland's national education programs. The Elements of AI project exemplifies the democratization of AI. It offers accessible educational courses to the entire population and was created by Schiff (2022). Similarly, within the framework of the Smart Nation strategy, Singapore prioritizes AI within the context of lifelong learning and employs intelligent tutoring systems throughout the primary and secondary educational systems (Foong et al., 2024; Huot & Such, 2025).

In South Korea, during the Education 4.0 project, the Korea Education and Research Information Service (KERIS) incorporates adaptive materials in mathematics and language education into e-learning systems with AI tutors (Jeong, 2025). The reports on the improvements in learners' engagement and test results are testimony to the value of state funding on infrastructure and teacher training for sustainable system adoption.

Bottom-up innovation can be observed in places such as Kenya and Cambodia. Projects such as AI4D Africa and SmartStart Cambodia work on open-source AI technologies to provide culturally relevant resources in local dialects as a response to the lack of qualified teachers in the more rural parts of the world (UNESCO, 2021a). In Kenya, the Zuri chatbot offers support in literacy and numeracy through an SMS interface. In Cambodia, NGOs provide AI-assisted learning through inexpensive tablets that operate on offline data models. In these situations, the world is seen to be interconnected, as the global AI instruments available are compared with local tools for education (Marginson, 2010). Innovation does not always have to come from high-end technological resources. Local adaptations to low-end technological resources can still achieve innovation in teaching, as depicted in **Table 1**.

Table 1.

Application Area	Key AI Tools	Function	Theoretical Connection
Personalized Learning Pathways	Knewton, Coursera Adaptive Assessments, Carnegie Learning (MATHia)	Customizes pacing, difficulty, and content through real-time analytics to support learner autonomy.	Constructivism (Piaget, Vygotsky); Self-Determination Theory (Deci & Ryan)
Skill Development: Language Learning	Duolingo Max, ChatGPT, Babbel	Facilitates conversational practice and adaptive grammar feedback, promoting self-directed language acquisition.	Constructivism; Connectivism
Skill Development: STEM Education	Labster, ALEKS, Khanmigo	Provides simulation-based experiments, adaptive problem-solving, and mastery-based progression.	Constructionism (Papert); Self-Determination Theory
Professional and Lifelong Learning	LinkedIn Learning, IBM Watson Education, Coursera AI Pathways	Delivers personalized microlearning for workforce reskilling and reflective professional growth.	Adult Learning Theory (Knowles); Connectivism
Assessment and Feedback	Gradescope, Turnitin Draft Coach, ChatGPT-based Feedback	Automates formative/summative evaluation and generates personalized feedback loops.	Vygotsky's Zone of Proximal Development; Constructivist Assessment Theory
Global Case Studies	Elements of AI (Finland), Smart Nation (Singapore), AI4D Africa (Kenya)	Showcases contextual adaptation of AI agents across diverse cultural and infrastructural settings.	Glocal Theory (Marginson); Cultural-Historical Activity Theory

4. OPPORTUNITIES AND BENEFITS

Autonomy is fundamental to both independent learning and Self-Determination Theory (SDT) (Deci & Ryan, 2000). In educational settings, autonomy is understood as the ability learners have towards goal setting, self-initiated progress monitoring within a learning episode, and the selection of learning strategies to be employed within a learning episode. AI agents help learners achieve scaffolded independence, which is a state of controlled and purposeful independence (Luckin, 2018; Vygotsky, 1978).

AI-supported educational tools like Khanmigo, adaptive tutoring in Coursera, and learning assistants based on ChatGPT allow learners to control the demand and use of educational support while preserving decision-making control (Huot & Loch, 2025b). These systems are capable of helping the learners formulate learning goals, perform competency self-assessments, and receive adaptive prompts that maintain seamless engagement without coercing the learners to comply (Huot & Tep, 2025; Kasneci et al., 2023).

For instance, ChatGPT helps learners to explore self-assessment by requesting it to critique an essay or simulate a peer debate. In this instance, they exercise autonomy as they frame questions, interpret, and decide whether to abide by the generated critiques (Kasneci et al., 2023; Zimmerman, 2018). These engagements fall within constructivist learning theory and learning by doing, which is active engagement defined by the learner as an agent of meaning (Piaget, 1952). In this instance, AI is a partner in the knowledge construction process as it facilitates inquiry and reflection. In practice, this means that learning objectives should be made explicit, particularly when integrating AI. This would involve pointing out the boundaries of what learners can determine and what AI or other technologies can assist with, without compromising the desired learning outcomes. AI as a cognitive amplifier, Luckin (2018) refers to cognitive amplification in AI to the self-assurance, self-regulation, and metacognitive awareness that AI tools enable in learners. The ability to plan, track, and assess one's learning autonomously, Zimmerman (2000) relies on metacognitive regulation. AI technology can enhance insights into one's thinking processes' by offering real-time data, feedback, and analytic dashboards. For instance, learners using Smart Sparrow and MATHia by Carnegie Learning can access visualizations of their learning and use these aids to recalibrate their approaches to learning. Dashboards and visualizations can also mislead if learners lack the critical and statistical thinking needed to interpret them, emphasizing the need to use AI-based feedback to teach digitally about data and the importance of context, uncertainty, and bias.

Holmes et al. (2019) contend that data-driven AI feedback nurtures what they call 'autonomous accountability', the condition whereby learners self-regulate to escalate their performance. Nonetheless, Selwyn (2021) cautions that genuine autonomous learning must be human-centred. For instance, learners must acquire the ability to unpack and critique the algorithms that provide feedback. Thus, teaching algorithmic literacy is important to achieve true autonomy in AI-driven contexts. The best AI systems find a balance in pedagogical structure and flexibility. VanLehn (2011) defends the position of AI tutors, unlike static systems, on the basis that they simulate the exquisite contingent scaffolding of expert teachers. The phrases offering hints or questions at key moments and gradually fading describe how expert teachers help students gain competence. This is Vygotsky's (1978) zone of proximal development (ZPD), where AI scaffolding assists tasks that are just out of reach for learners to do independently.

Personalized learning is an educational goal that remains ideal due to the constraints of time and resources for all the people involved. With the advent of artificial intelligence, this educational goal is achievable on a much larger scale since it is capable of providing personalized pathways for millions of learners at the same time and on an ongoing basis through continuous feedback and predictive analytics (Holmes et al., 2019; Zawacki-Richter et al., 2019). AI-based personalized learning systems create and optimize feedback loops in which learner inputs, responses, and engagement patterns for different segments of a program are compared at a distance to dynamically change the learning interface, as seen in **Table 2**.

Table 2.

Area	Description	Key Examples	Benefits
Enhanced Learner Autonomy	AI facilitates goal-setting, self-assessment, and reflective learning through adaptive prompts and dashboards. Learners manage progress within guided independence.	Khanmigo, Coursera AI Tutors, ChatGPT Learning Assistant	Promotes self-regulation, metacognition, and agency while preserving human oversight.
Personalization at Scale	Adaptive systems analyse learner data to customize pacing, content, and modality in real time, creating individualized learning pathways.	Knewton, DreamBox Learning, ALEKS, Coursera, Adaptive Pathways	Enables equity through tailored instruction, improves retention, and optimizes learner engagement.
Accessibility and Inclusion	AI breaks barriers of geography, language, and disability through assistive tools such as speech recognition, translation, and adaptive interfaces.	AI4D Africa, Microsoft Immersive Reader, Google Live Caption, SmartStart Cambodia	Expands participation, supports diverse learners, and promotes equitable access in low-resource contexts.
Motivation and Engagement	AI maintains motivation through gamification, adaptive feedback, and conversational agents that foster socio-emotional engagement.	Duolingo, Quizizz AI, Labster, Replika, ChatGPT	Enhances intrinsic motivation, emotional resilience, and persistence in learning tasks.

5. CHALLENGES AND RISKS

The implementation of AI agents within educational contexts relies primarily on the availability of advanced digital infrastructure, high-quality datasets, and scalable, interoperable systems that can function within multiple learning environments. UNESCO (2021a) highlighted that more than 50 percent of sub-Saharan Africa schools, as well as some in Southeast Asia, lack reliable internet connectivity and digital tools, rendering the hope of integrating AI unrealistic. Due to the inequalities that exist in support systems, the concept of "AI-augmented autonomy" hides a reality in which only a few designed, well-resourced learners gain access to support systems designed to respond to their needs, while others receive inadequate, low-tech support. Even in digital-rich environments, inequitable access to lower quality devices and less bandwidth, as well as institutional readiness, contribute to the inequity.

Luckin (2018) and Selwyn (2021) warn that the integration of ignorant AI in automating the educational process neglects the essential educational components of teaching and learning. For the absence of explainable AI (XAI), students will be unable to interrogate the rationale of the system's feedback, and teachers will be unable to assess the computing judgments made. This ignorance runs against educational values and the importance of critical thinking that ought to be at the core of the process. Common approaches to resolving these issues include the design of interpretable models and algorithmic audit tools that allow users to see the reasoning behind a model's computation. However, as Holmes et al. (2019) explain, real transparency is much more than the preoccupation of the technology enthusiasts with the technical components of transparency along with the pedagogical know-how that situates educators in the position to be critical of the AI reasoning and its gaps, and thus be limited. Explainability in education has two functions: it enables inspection of system logic, and it equips teachers and learners with the tools to interrogate when and why that logic should be resisted or bypassed.

Zimmerman (2018) argues that the prevailing dominant design philosophies neglects bias as a socio-technical challenge, that inequitable power, influence, and values of the system's definers are inequity's determinants. These conceptualizations demonstrate a need for bias to be addressed through the design of sociotechnical systems. This is because design can provide the channels for the needed participatory processes that allow educators, students, and disenfranchised communities to construct the models. Recently, initiatives like UNESCO (2021b) AI Ethics in Education Toolkit and OECD (2019) AI Principles focus on fairness auditing and algorithmic accountability, envisioning equity as the AI system's designer intent. However, when AI systems function as intended, algorithmic accountability will still be a complex issue to tackle. Unresolved accountability puzzles will remain in education. For instance, when an AI tutor misguides a learner or misgrades a test, who is accountable: the tutor, the developer, the institution, or the teacher? Without appropriate governance, accountability dissipates.

Effective oversight of the ethical dimensions of AI necessitates a collaboration of the primary stakeholders: audit of the technology, oversight of the human elements, and application of legislation. Educators need more training to evaluate AI results meaningfully to guarantee that decisions made by algorithms are subordinate to the educator's discretion (Selwyn, 2021). According to Luckin and Holmes (2016), the aim of AI ethics need not be the achievement of perfection in AI, but rather, the achievement of a level of transparency in AI's defects that flows ethically within the bounds of human control. Beyond the ethical and technological aspects, AI also raises substantial pedagogical problems, which, in turn, clash with the humanistic aspects of education. The intelligent systems employed in education are likely to compromise the human aspects, such as collaboration, creativity, and critical thinking, as education tends to become a mere quantifiable process. AI systems are superb at recognizing patterns and solving problems, but they lack true understanding. Bender et al. (2021) liken large language models to stochastic parrots, systems that imitate comprehension by predicting language elements and providing a response without true comprehension. Learners who depend on AIs to generate explanations and essays may confuse comprehension with fluency. This resemblance to automated systems, as Carr (2020) describe the shallowing of the digital age, cognitive, automated systems discouraging reflection. Students may develop a form of epistemic passivity by accepting AI results as authoritative.

In response to these challenges, educators need to incorporate AI literacy into the curriculum, equipping learners with the skills to interrogate, authenticate, and interpret AI-generated outputs (Selwyn, 2021). AI should not be viewed as an epistemic authority, but as an epistemic partner, a heuristic in the inquiry process that encourages additional reasoning. Learning, as Bandura (2001) and Vygotsky (1978) assert, is a social process, and the production of knowledge arises from dialogue, interaction, and collaborative modeling. AI has no social interaction learning is designed for and can automate peer interaction and teacher scaffolding, but has no way of offering the empathic engagement and communal understanding that the social supportive framework of teaching and learning fosters.

Dron and Anderson (2014) and Knox (2025) warn that AI-mediated learning has the risk of "pedagogic isolation" where learners are likely to interact with algorithms than other human learners. Hybrid arrangements, therefore, must be assessed not only on learning outcomes, but on how they redistribute genuine opportunities for dialogue, dissent, and cooperative problem-solving. It is this isolation that undermines the very tenets of connectivist learning where knowledge is assumed to be constructed within the networks of people and technologies. Hybrid AI-augmented learning approaches, where teachers, peers, and AI support learning, provide a better balance. Luckin (2018) describes this as orchestrated learning in which AI takes care of the administrative and adaptive tasks and teachers are free to mentor, engage in dialogue, and attend to the ethical aspects of learning and teaching. The issue is not the rejection of automation as pedagogy, but the design of automation incorporates pedagogical ecologies in which human relationships and interactions are core. The automation of tasks in education can also cause automation bias, the unjustified over trust in the faulty results of algorithms (Crawford, 2021; Huot et al., 2025). Those learners that depend on AI technologies for content explanation and work corrections, risk the atrophy of essential skills necessary to independently reason, write, and solve problems. In higher education, the use of AI-based writing tools has been shown to lead to a decline in the effort students apply to the revision and critical editing processes (Huot & Tep, 2025; Kasneci et al., 2023). Dependency on AI tools in learning could gradually lead to a decline in self-efficacy, which runs counter to independent learning. Tasks designed to be 'AI-free' can help to counteract the dependency on AI, and make the effort to think more visible.

Inequality also has the dimension of language. AI systems assume English fluency and, therefore, other language speakers are unserved, or in some cases, entirely excluded. Bender et al. (2021), and Geyser (2025) describe this as an instance of linguistic bias, and as a form of epistemic injustice that elevates Western discourse, at the same time disregarding the indigenous and local voices. The need for developing localized AI systems has been well justified the need for an NLP ecosystem that is multilingual, and produces content that is contextually appropriate. SmartStart Cambodia and the Pan-African NLP Consortium are examples of inclusive AI innovations that consider language diversity as an educational asset, rather than a challenge. Finally, the inequity is also caused by the disparity in the amount of available data. Learners from the unrepresented parts of the world are less contributors of data, which background the AI systems, and results in flawed AI models that do not solve problems, and therefore, do not impact the daily lives of these learners. Uncorrected, AI will perpetuate the very exclusion it professes to solve. Decentralized data governance requires that different regions ethically exchange educational data while retaining sovereignty over their data to enable equitable AI. UNESCO (2021a) proposes federated learning models as a means of collaborative AI training across borders while ensuring that sensitive data remains decentralized. This affords the opportunity to simultaneously protect data and foster inclusivity.

6. PATHWAYS FOR THE FUTURE

Future learning ecosystems will rely on hybrid intelligence, the cooperation of teachers and AI (Holmes et al., 2019; Luckin, 2018). Instead of seeing AI as a replacement for human educators, hybrid systems, and cognitive AI as a pedagogical partner that can amplify and complement the human-designed learning experiences. The phenomenon is called data colonialism (Crawford, 2021). It is driven by AI, augmented intelligence systems which, alongside human AI educators, scale learning with precision, while offering the human touch, contextualization, and ethics. AI learning systems help educators identify learning patterns, provide individualized resources and feedback, and offer formative feedback (Selwyn, 2021; Zimmerman, 2018). Education combines the best of humanity with the worst of learning automation. The real question is, under what circumstances is hybrid intelligence compatible with education that is dem ocratic, inclusive, and critically engaged, as opposed to extending the reach of control and management?

This phenomenon has been described by Luckin (2018) as co-orchestration, the symbiotic construct whereby AI performs real-time analysis and execution of administrative tasks. This enables educators to concentrate their cognitive energies on creativity, ethics, and emotional considerations. In turn, teachers no longer just pass content; they become learning designers. teachers, using AI, customize support to different learner path ways. Research shows that hybrid education, automation and human instructor, achieves better results than education systems with only human educators or only automation. Intelligent tutoring systems, combined with teacher presence, provided greater learning compared to education with only AI or only human instruction (VanLehn, 2011). AI-supported education achieves better results, Zawacki-Richter et al. (2019) showed, when teachers do their own contextualization of AI findings and recommendations. Luckin (2018) has described AI in such educational settings as a cognitive amplifier, a tool that enhances intelligence without supplanting it. In the learning environment, AI tutors might offer real-time instructional feedback to the teacher while AI systems address autonomous reflection, social interaction, and moral reasoning. The uniqueness of hybrid education is the balance of autonomy and empathy, showing that education retains its humanistic elements, even with high levels of technological advancement, is particularly noteworthy.

Following the principles of human-centered design (HCD) focusing on equity, transparency, and overall well-being rather than prioritizing efficiency is fundamental to the success and sustainability of the adoption of AI in education. IEEE (2019), OECD (2019) and UNESCO (2021a) provide a human centered vision on the ethics of AI that emphasizes the need for technology to uphold human dignity and enable participation and engagement in democracy. AI systems that are governed by HCD principles must be transparent in their functioning and their outcomes. Both students and teachers should understand what the AI is doing and the rationale for those actions. Trust and the ability to contest, think critically about, and modify the AI outcomes are by gaining control over the system, resulting in what Shneiderman (2020) describes as the principal requirement and building block of explainability. In this context, learners must be able to challenge AI opinions on their work and learning paths, and that this is seen to be a natural part of responsible use and not a form of defiance. The educational trust in AI transparency will be critical to sustained use and will encourage informed decision-making in the context of possible over-reliance on the system. The European Commission's Ethics Guidelines for Trustworthy AI (2019) provides three foundational pillars for human-centered systems, which are: (1) lawful (rights and rules compliance), (2) ethical (fairness and beneficence), and (3) robust (social and technical sustainability). HCD principles must be applied to all AI in education, from personalized tutoring to adaptive testing.

Human centered design should include contextual factors as well. AI should account for users' cultural, language, and cognitive variances. As pointed by Geo-JaJa (2013) and Geyser (2025), the use of Western frameworks can lead to the insidious sustaining of epistemic hierarchies that sideline indigenous knowledge. Inclusive design implies that, rather than erasing cultural identity, technology should be developed in partnership with the teachers and learners, and with the community, who all, to some degree, must use the AI tools. This is possible through participatory design, which entails inclusive design. Involving educators in the iterative design process helps to ensure that the developed AI tools take into account local emphasis in the curriculum, educational ideology, and AI pedagogy aligned (Holmes et al., 2019). In a similar sense, involving learners in user testing and getting feedback makes them active participants in the design and development of their educational ecosystem. Such an ecosystem sees learners as collaborators and gives them a sense of agency, and in stark contrast to most educational contexts, where students are passive. These approaches also challenge traditional structures of dominance, placing teachers and learners as serious stakeholders, with their knowledge as part of the design, and not simply data that are exploited. Design thinking is an example of a problem-solving methodology that draws from the ideals of human-centered design. The process encapsulated in its steps, empathize, define, ideate, prototype, and test, mirrors the iterative process of ethical AI creation. Consider, for example, when an AI assessment system is to be designed. Designers are expected to empathize with students' experiences of test anxiety, define issues of fairness, and prototype feedback systems that counter ranking and promote growth. Ethical AI design in education, therefore, is an indication that AI use in teaching is not a technocratic exercise, but a reflective practice.

Consequently, Human Centered-AI reshapes the educational relationship with technology. Learners are no longer merely data points; they are active partners. Teachers are no longer just system operators; they are ethical curators of digital pedagogy. Sustained maturity of any technological innovation depends on the establishment of governance frameworks that foster accountability and incorporate justice and equity. As AI agents enter and permeate educational systems globally, ethical and legally binding policies on data governance, quality standards, and rights protection will all be necessary. Such policies are essential at the intergovernmental and institutional levels (OECD, 2019; UNESCO, 2021a). As of now, the most comprehensive global AI governance framework is the UNESCO (2021b) Recommendation on the Ethics of Artificial Intelligence and its accompanying implementation guidelines. It ensures equity of outcome through proportionality, safety, transparency, accountability and sustainability. It also requires that the employment of AI enhances the safeguarding of human rights as well as the rights to education and the protection of cultural diversity. The OECD AI Principles (2019) serve as the basis for national and institutional policy and reiterate similar principles and the need for human-centered values in conjunction with transparency and robustness. In education, these principles translate into the following practical imperatives: (1) transparency in data and algorithmic decision-making, (2) accountability through human presence and ethical audits, (3) equity in system design and outcome distribution, and (4) privacy through data governance and protection.

As education integrates intelligent systems, the primary focus should be on building educational ecologies, intelligent systems that incorporate ethics, empathy, and evidence into learning. Hybrid learning, human-centered design, ethical governance, and critical research should be viewed as interdependent components, as building the 'social' sustainable future entails the integration of all four. These components illustrate possible human-AI symbiosis, whereby technology enhances curiosity, compassion, and creativity rather than replacing these traits. AI should be viewed as an equal educational partner in the pursuit of collaborative learning, social equity, and collective prosperity, rather than the primary driver of future education systems.

7. CONCLUSION

Integrating artificial intelligence (AI) into education represents one of the greatest transformations in the history of learning and human development. In this chapter focused on how AI adaptive tutors and conversational companions perform independent learning, personalizing educational experiences, and transforming learner-teacher relationships. AI's transformative potential stems from the ability to process large amounts of data, discern cognitive patterns, and provide individualized feedback at a scale never seen before. Nevertheless, the transformative promise of AI should be greeted with a degree of caution, given the technological as well as the social and ethical issues that arise. The conclusions drawn from previous sections indicate the impact AI agents are likely to have on the automation of educational processes: Instead of automation, there is the augmentation of education. If designed ethically and used for the right purposes, AI has the potential to foster autonomy, creativity, and inclusion. It can enable users to learn in a manner that is constructivist, relevant, and self-paced. In contrast, unethically designed and deployed technology will worsen inequity, generate distrust, and commoditize human thinking.

Although AI facilitates the work involved in the mechanics of learning, the relational aspects of learning (e.g. education, caregiving, social work, and teaching), will always remain human. Teaching will always require the empathy of the teacher, the curiosity of the learner, and the purpose of the community. Therefore, AI should be viewed not as a terminal point, but as a medium for rehumanizing education, refocusing attention on the social, emotional, and ethical frameworks of learning that education automation cannot maintain. AI will, most likely, automate lower-level cognitive tasks and allow for the integration of more advanced theoretical constructs. AI-enriched learning settings can engender authentic autonomy, as described by the combination of learning theories. It is Constructivism, which posits that learners actively create knowledge, and Connectivism, which involves the nexuses of learning and people and technologies.

Lastly, SDT outlines the psychological needs of autonomy, competence, and relatedness, which are critical to motivation . Therefore, all three together propose, most emphatically, that AI should primarily support and not replace human learning. In practice, AI offers benefits, personalization, accessibility, and engagement, but these assets are always accompanied by risks: bias, dependency, and inequity. The next step will be to reconfigure AI from a technological disruptor to an ethical collaborator. This shift is about creating systems and policies where friction, when learners question, reject, or modify the outcome of AI, is seen as positive critical engagement instead of a failure to comply. The true measure of progress will not be the sophistication of the new algorithms, but the ability of AI systems to enlarge the learner's voice, honor diverse cultural traditions, and support the moral purpose of education.

The educational future that envision should include artificial intelligence, but should not be fully dominated by it, creating a future educational environment where human wisdom and machine intelligence work hand in hand in a balanced manner. This entails a rejection of both techno-utopian and techno-dystopian extremes, and the adoption of a hybrid intelligence paradigm where AI promotes reflection, personalization, and access within the educational environment. This way, the teacher and learners retain the creative and ethical control. Classrooms begin to transform into ecosystems of co-agency where students work with AI tutors, evaluate feedback, and co-construct knowledge with their classmates and digital peers. In education's impending future educators will have to employ knowledge orchestration as they will have to become inquiry facilitators, ethical guiding mentors, and interpreters of insights.

The sense of community in future education will be built around the collaborative and collective responsibilities of educators, learners, and policymakers. This means creating educational environments where human wisdom and machine intelligence work hand in hand, balanced. Facilitator of inquiry, ethical guider, and interpreter of insights are the educational objective roles of the knowledge orchestrator. The chapter offers a view of autonomy as co-constructed among human and machine actors. This view is based on placing AI agents in the intersecting frameworks of constructivism, connectivism, and self-determination theory. It argues against seeing autonomy as the absence of technology. The shared responsibility is the present, and the future to come. Achieving a future in which AI in education continues to prioritize human-centered objectives demands a partnership of educators, policymakers, technologists, and learners. Moving beyond basic technical understanding, this encounter necessitates a form of ethical comprehension centered on the values and power dynamics embedded within AI systems:

1. **For Educators:** Teachers need to be empowered to be co-designers of AI pedagogy, which calls for professional development to be calibrated toward pedagogical AI theory, where instructors understand the intricacies of algorithms, the constituent data, and the ways different algorithms impact learning. Reflective AI use must be taught alongside curiosity and skepticism so that instructors can uphold the pedagogy of AI.For
2. **Policymakers:** Governments are to implement policy and regulatory frameworks that respond to the baseline policy expectations of the UNESCO Recommendation on the Ethics of AI (2021b) and the OECD AI Principles (2019). AI in education policy must entail equity, accountability, and data sovereignty to ensure that educational AI is a public resource, not a tool for private exploitation.
3. **For Technologists and Developers:** AI systems must be based on the principles of human-centered design that include transparency, equity, inclusive, and be explainable. Ethical collaboration involves educators and learners from diverse backgrounds and cultures. Ethical design is not an afterthought; it must be a primary design principle.
4. **For Learners:** Students as AI systems users must be taught to interrogate the recommendations provided by algorithms, perform source critique, and understand the breach of ethics algorithms impose on intelligent systems. Ensuring that learners are not passive consumers of technology, "AI citizenship" promotes active participation in the design and development of technology.

In the chapter, the conceptual framework of autonomy as granted from AI technologies is advanced further as it relates to the duality of human and artificial intelligences as regarding their independence and interdependence. This signifies a move to think about autonomy beyond mere separation. AI is integrated into foundational learning theories, Constructivism, Connectivism, and Self-Determination Theory, to illustrate how technology can facilitate self-regulated learning if there are ethical design and oversight processes, and relevant, transparent instructions. The chapter makes a practical contribution by curating global exemplars of hybrid learning frameworks that are Akademeia and Minerva Schools' cognitive analytics, and Kiron's humanitarian AI for refugees. Here, institutions are positioned as innovators and inclusion as a safeguard to ensure AI enhances, not replaces, the educator.

From a policy standpoint, as this chapter discusses, governance and accountability are of utmost priority. In the absence of ethical oversight, AI becomes even more of a potential risk for deepening and broadening surveillance, bias, and inequity. This principle will guide the transformation of learning and teaching within digital environments. The combination of values advocated by UNESCO's The Ethics of AI and the IEEE's Ethically Aligned Design allows us to detail a draft opportunity to outline transparency and the part of a range of governance Frameworks that Protect and Institute the Safeguards of the learner's rights and agency. To this end, it argues that education's principal aim should transition from the mere acquisition of knowledge to the mastery of wise, discerning, empathetic, and actionable citizenship in complexity. In this regard, AI should not be viewed as the final terminus of human teaching, but rather as the means to realign attention on the more relational, ethical, and creative dimensions of learning, which lie beyond the capabilities of the machine.

In the end, the extent to which AI will affect education will not be a function of the sophistication of the algorithms, but rather of the capacity of AI-in-education tools to humanize learning. The real benchmark of sophistication is whether AI technologies in education enable societies to develop empathy, critical awareness, and intercultural respect. This chapter concludes with an education system visionary AI that mirrors human intelligence, allowing learners to interact with machines to rediscover, not escape, humanity, and where the digital and ethical realms form two sides of the same coin.

REFERENCES

Baker, R. S., & Inventado, P. S. (2014). Educational data mining and learning analytics. In Larusson, J. A., & White, B. (Eds.), *Learning Analytics* (Vol. 7, pp. 61–75)., DOI: 10.1007/978-1-4614-3305-7_4

Bandura, A. (2001). Social cognitive theory: An agentic perspective. *Annual Review of Psychology, 52*(1), 1–26. DOI: 10.1146/annurev.psych.52.1.1 PMID: 11148297

Bender, E. M., Gebru, T., McMillan-Major, A., & Shmitchell, S. (2021). On the dangers of stochastic parrots: Can language models be too big? In Irani, L., Kannan, S., Mitchell, M., & Robinson, D. (Eds.), *Proceedings of the 2021 ACM conference on fairness, accountability, and transparency* (pp. 610–623). Association for Computing Machinery, New York, NY, United States. DOI: 10.1145/3442188.3445922

Candy, P. C. (1991). *Self-direction for lifelong learning. A comprehensive guide to theory and practice.* ERIC.

Carr, N. (2020). *The shallows: What the Internet is doing to our brains.* WW Norton & Company.

Clark, A., & Chalmers, D. (1998). The extended mind. *analysis, 58*(1), 7–19. https://www.jstor.org/stable/3328150

Crawford, K. (2021). *Atlas of AI: Power, politics, and the planetary costs of artificial intelligence.* Yale University Press.

D'Mello, S., & Graesser, A. (2015). Feeling, thinking, and computing with affect-aware learning. In Calvo, R., D'Mello, S., Gratch, J., & Kappas, A. (Eds.), *The Oxford handbook of affective computing* (pp. 419–434). Oxford University Press., DOI: 10.1093/oxfordhb/9780199942237.013.032

Deci, E. L., & Ryan, R. M. (2000). The" what" and" why" of goal pursuits: Human needs and the self-determination of behavior. *Psychological Inquiry, 11*(4), 227–268. DOI: 10.1207/S15327965PLI1104_01

Deci, E. L., & Ryan, R. M. (2008). Facilitating optimal motivation and psychological well-being across life's domains. *Canadian Psychology, 49*(1), 14–23. DOI: 10.1037/0708-5591.49.1.14

Deci, E. L., & Ryan, R. M. (2012). Self-determination theory. In Paul, A. M. V. L., Kruglanski, A. W., & Higgins, E. T. (Eds.), *Handbook of theories of social psychology* (Vol. 1, pp. 416–436). SAGE. DOI: 10.4135/9781446249215.n21

Dron, J., & Anderson, T. (2014). *Teaching crowds: Learning and social media.* Athabasca University Press.

Ethics Guidelines for Trustworthy AI. (2019). *High-level expert group on artificial intelligence.* European Commission. https://digital-strategy.ec.europa.eu/en/library/ethics-guidelines-trustworthy-ai

Filgueiras, F. (2024). Artificial intelligence and education governance. *Education, Citizenship and Social Justice, 19*(3), 349–361. DOI: 10.1177/17461979231160674

Foong, Y. P., Pidani, R., Sithira Vadivel, V., & Dongyue, Y. (2024). Singapore smart nation: Journey into a new digital landscape for higher education. In Kwok, A. O. J., & Teh, P.-L. (Eds.), *Emerging technologies in business: innovation strategies for competitive advantage* (pp. 281–304). Springer., DOI: 10.1007/978-981-97-2211-2_13

Fryer, L., & Carpenter, R. (2006). Bots as language learning tools. *Language Learning & Technology, 10*(3), 8–14. DOI: 10.64152/10125/44068

Geo-JaJa, M. A. (2013). Education localization for optimizing globalization's opportunities and challenges in Africa. In S. Majhanovich & M. A. Geo-JaJa (Eds.), *Economics, aid and education: Implications for development* (pp. 159–181). Sense Publishers, Rotterdam. DOI: 10.1007/978-94-6209-365-2_11

Geyser, H. (2025). Decoloniality, digital-coloniality and computer programming education. *ACM Transactions on Computing Education, 24*(4), 1–30. DOI: 10.1145/3702332

Graesser, A. C., Conley, M. W., & Olney, A. (2012). Intelligent tutoring systems. In Harris, K. R., Graham, S., Urdan, T., Bus, A. G., Major, S., & Swanson, H. L. (Eds.), APA educational psychology handbook: Vol. 3. *Application to learning and teaching* (pp. 451–473). American Psychological Association., DOI: 10.1037/13275-018

Holmes, W., Bialik, M., & Fadel, C. (2019). *Artificial intelligence in education promises and implications for teaching and learning*. Center for Curriculum Redesign.

Huot, S., & Loch, S. (2025a). Digital practices in Cambodian EFL classrooms: Teacher narratives from remote learning. In K. Khette & Tayade (Eds.), *Proceeding of one day national conference on English language, literature, cultural studies and media studies* (Vol. 2, pp. 19–31). Centre for Learning, Research and Development, Savda, Maharashtra. DOI: 10.5281/zenodo.16921807

Huot, S., & Loch, S. (2025b). From rote to reflective: Integrating ChatGPT to transform learning outcomes in Cambodian education. *International Journal of Language and Literary Studies, 7*(4), 1–15. DOI: 10.36892/ijlls.v7i4.2188

Huot, S., Loch, S., Nget, R., & Em, S. (2025). Exploring multiliteracies in the digital era: A framework for 21st-century learning. [CJESS]. *Cambodian Journal of Educational and Social Sciences, 2*(1), 7–27. DOI: 10.69496/cjess.v2i1.50

Huot, S., & Such, C. (2025). Leveraging social media for language learning: Opportunities and challenges. [JEILT]. *Journal of Education Innovation and Language Teaching, 1*(2), 10–29. DOI: 10.63381/jeilt.v1i2.56

Huot, S., & Tep, P. (2025). Advancing ChatGPT for pedagogical innovation in Cambodia: Insight from global evidence and local implications. *The Context: Journal of English Studies, 12*(4), 115–135. DOI: 10.5281/zenodo.15806972

IEEE. (2019). *Ethically aligned design: A vision for prioritizing human well-being with autonomous and intelligent systems.* IEEE Global Initiative on Ethics of Autonomous and Intelligent Systems. https://standards.ieee.org/wp-content/uploads/import/documents/other/ead1e.pdf

Jeong, H. (2025). From curriculum to strategy: Tracing shifts in AI Education policy in South Korea through keyword and topic analysis. *Asia Pacific Journal of Education*, •••, 1–30. DOI: 10.1080/02188791.2025.2580988

Kasneci, E., Seßler, K., Küchemann, S., Bannert, M., Dementieva, D., Fischer, F., Gasser, U., Groh, G., Günnemann, S., Hüllermeier, E., Krusche, S., Kutyniok, G., Michaeli, T., Nerdel, C., Pfeffer, J., Poquet, O., Sailer, M., Schmidt, A., Seidel, T., & Kasneci, G. (2023). ChatGPT for good? On opportunities and challenges of large language models for education. *Learning and Individual Differences*, *103*, 1–9. DOI: 10.1016/j.lindif.2023.102274

Kim, H., Han, B., Kim, J., Lubis, M. F. S., Kim, G. J., & Hwang, J.-I. (2024). Engaged and affective virtual agents: Their impact on social presence, trustworthiness, and decision-making in the group discussion. In Mueller, F. F., Kyburz, P., Williamson, J. R., Sas, C., Wilson, M. L., Dugas, P. T., & Shklovski, I. (Eds.), *Proceedings of the 2024 CHI conference on human factors in computing systems* (pp. 1–17). Association for Computing Machinery, New York, NY, United States. DOI: 10.1145/3613904.3642917

Knowles, M. S. (1975). *Self-directed learning* (Vol. 291). Association Press New York.

Knox, J. (2025). Educational development in the postdigital era. In Peters, M. A., Green, B. J., Kamenarac, O., Jandrić, P., & Besley, T. (Eds.), *The geopolitics of postdigital educational development* (pp. 21–40). Springer., DOI: 10.1007/978-3-031-99378-7_2

Luckin, R. (2018). *Machine learning and human intelligence. The future of education for the 21st century*. UCL institute of education press.

Luckin, R., & Holmes, W. (2016). *Intelligence unleashed: An argument for AI in education*. Pearson. https://www.pearson.com/content/dam/corporate/glob

Marginson, S. (2010). Higher education in the global knowledge economy. *Procedia: Social and Behavioral Sciences*, *2*(5), 6962–6980. DOI: 10.1016/j.sbspro.2010.05.049

OECD. (2019). *OECD Principles on Artificial Intelligence*. Paris: Organisation for Economic Co-operation and Development. https://oecd.ai/en/ai-principles

Papert, S. (1980). *Mindstorms: Children, computers, and powerful ideas*. Basic Books., DOI: 10.5555/1095592.C1104753

Paris, S. G., & Paris, A. H. (2003). Classroom applications of research on self-regulated learning. In Good, T. L., & Levin, J. R. (Eds.), *Educational Psychology* (pp. 89–101). Routledge., DOI: 10.4324/9781410608130

Piaget, J. (1952). *The origins of intelligence in children*. International Universities Press. DOI: 10.1037/11494-000

Redecker, C. (2017). *European framework for the digital competence of educators: DigCompEdu*. Publications Office of the European Union. https://joint-research-centre.ec.europa.eu/system/files/2018-11/digcompeduorg-en-2018-11_a4new.pdf

Roll, I., & Wylie, R. (2016). Evolution and revolution in artificial intelligence in education. *International Journal of Artificial Intelligence in Education*, *26*(2), 582–599. DOI: 10.1007/s40593-016-0110-3

Schiff, D. (2022). Education for AI, not AI for education: The role of education and ethics in national AI policy strategies. *International Journal of Artificial Intelligence in Education*, *32*(3), 527–563. DOI: 10.1007/s40593-021-00270-2

Selwyn, N. (2019). *Should robots replace teachers?: AI and the future of education*. John Wiley & Sons.

Selwyn, N. (2021). *Education and technology: Key issues and debates*. Bloomsbury Publishing.

UNESCO. (2021a). *AI and education: Guidance for policy-makers*. UNESCO. https://unesdoc.unesco.org/ark:/48223/pf0000376709

UNESCO. (2021b). *Recommendation on the ethics of artificial intelligence*. Paris: UNESCO. https://unesdoc.unesco.org/ark:/48223/pf0000381137

VanLehn, K. (2011). The relative effectiveness of human tutoring, intelligent tutoring systems, and other tutoring systems. *Educational Psychologist*, *46*(4), 197–221. DOI: 10.1080/00461520.2011.611369

Vygotsky, L. S. (1978). *Mind in society: The development of higher psychological processes*. Harvard University Press.

Williamson, T. (2021). *The philosophy of philosophy*. John Wiley & Sons.

Zawacki-Richter, O., Marín, V. I., Bond, M., & Gouverneur, F. (2019). Systematic review of research on artificial intelligence applications in higher education–where are the educators? *International Journal of Educational Technology in Higher Education*, *16*(1), 1–27. DOI: 10.1186/s41239-019-0171-0

Zimmerman, B. J. (2000). Attaining self-regulation: A social cognitive perspective. In Boekaerts, M., Pintrich, P. R., & Zeidner, M. (Eds.), *Handbook of self-regulation* (pp. 13–39). Elsevier., DOI: 10.1016/B978-012109890-2/50031-7

Zimmerman, M. (2018). *Teaching AI: Exploring new frontiers for learning*. ASCD.

KEY TERMS AND DEFINITIONS

AI Agents: Educators have begun implementing educational AI Agents, partly or fully automated systems that can sense, reason, and act in the fields of learning and education. Technologies, such as chatbots, intelligent tutoring systems, virtual learning assistants, and other forms of personalized learning systems, are educational AI Agents. AI Agents in education can help self-paced, self-directed education by personalizing the instruction, providing automated feedback, and adjusting the learning tempo. Ethical design and implementation of AI Agents must consider the potential consequences of over-reliance, bias, and loss of agency by using AI as an adjunct to, rather than a substitute for, personal teaching.

Digital Pedagogy: describes the merging of pedagogy and technology. In this case, the merging of pedagogy and technology focuses on the theoretical and ethical dimensions. A digital pedagogical approach seeks the construction of technology-enabled learning ecosystems, encouraging active, equitable and collaborative learning. When applying pedagogical theories to the teaching of AI the role of the teacher moves away from being a content teacher to a learning facilitator who combines data with human empathy and culture.

Educational Innovations: When educational innovations occur, there are intentional alterations made to the structures of teaching and learning, and also to other activities of educational institutions. Innovations in education seek to ensure participation and efficacy, and to achieve and address equity and imbalance. In innovations in education, the use of technology as the change agent. However, innovations in education are of little benefit if the change is not towards the renewal of pedagogy. With innovative technologies, particularly with the use of AI, innovations in education aim to increase accommodation and personalization of education. In educational innovations, it is not the emphasis on the new technology of education that is of most importance, but the establishment of flexible and inclusive lifelong education systems that allow learners to thrive in dynamic and complex technologically transformed environments.

Ethical AI: describes automated systems as human controlled and unbiased, and responsive to the learner. Within a classroom, Ethical AI will prioritize human agency, and quickly, combat discrimination. Several frameworks promote Ethical AI. UNESCO AI Ethics Recommendations (2021b), and the IEEE's Ethically Aligned Design (2019). Ethical AI shifts the technological education paradigm from being surveillance oriented to being human and socially aware.

Human-Centered Design: In focusing on the people involved, what tends to get overshadowed within the Human-Centered Design approach is the human values and experience as relating to the human inf0ormation technology systems, and in the case of the educational AI, the HCD approach is reshaped to focus on transparency and explainable AI as well as culture contextualization. This enables educational AI systems to incorporate the ethical pluralism and the pedagogical diversity of the educational technology AI systems stakeholders (educators, buyers, and learners). With empathy and inclusivity as the focus of human-centered design, the educational technology AI systems designed in human-centered design seek to shift the focus of the discourse on AI to one that supports the human and goes beyond to uplift the human.

Independent Learning: Autonomous learning as a construct describes the ability of the learner to self-initiate, self-manage, and self-reflect on the processes and outcomes of learning, without the necessity of an educator's continuous and direct involvement. This stems from theories of self-directed learning (Knowles, 1975) and self-regulated learning (Zimmerman, 2000). In the context of AI, autonomy also includes digital agency, the learner's ability to control, tailor, and give feedback within the bounds of the automated system. Autonomous learning describes the combination of self-regulation and a particular technological competence that bestows the learner the capability for self-directed learning.

Chapter 5
Redefining, Rethinking, and Exploring Education in the Age of e-Learning With Artificial Intelligence:
From Smartboards Replacing Chalkboards to . . . ?

Regina Mosima Tefo
http://orcid.org/0000-0002-5116-8554
University of South Africa, South Africa

Leila Goosen
http://orcid.org/0000-0003-4948-2699
University of South Africa, South Africa

ABSTRACT

In order to provide readers with an overview of, and summarize, the content of the chapter, the purpose is stated as rethinking and exploring education in the age of Artificial Intelligence (AI) when considering from smartboards replacing chalkboards to what else? Against the background of redefining independent learning with AI agents, the chapter will e.g., discuss ethics, privacy, and governance in AI-powered education, as well as future research directions with regard to self-learning and AI companions.

INTRODUCTION

This section will describe the general perspective of the chapter and end by specifically stating the objectives.

DOI: 10.4018/979-8-3373-7225-9.ch005

Redefining Independent Learning with Artificial Intelligence Agents

Rethinking Education in the Age of Artificial Intelligence

Theory and applications at the *frontiers in intelligent computing* presenting an integration of the Internet of Things (IoT) into educational environment during Covid-19 pandemic (Dhal, Samantaray, & Satapathy, 2022) show how the education landscape had experienced a historic shift. From traditional chalkboards in schools in Gauteng province, South Africa being "replaced with smartboard technologies for Grades 10–12" (Tefo & Goosen, 2024a, p. 289), to digital platforms and repositories taking the place of libraries (Mehboob, Kamran, & Ain, 2024), the impact of such media on modern education means that the way in which people learn had improved continually. Now, we are on the cusp of an even broader transformation, one fueled by artificial intelligence (AI). With this period of exponential technological growth, the conventional notion of solo learning is being redefined, not as a one-person activity, but as an interactive partnership between students and smart digital guides. As part of this book, Redefining Independent Learning with AI Agents, the chapter will investigate the ways in which AI-powered agents are transforming independent learning. These agents are more than mere information-retrieval tools but adaptive companions with the ability to facilitate, encourage, and customize the learning process. These allow learners to access information effortlessly, get customized feedback, and develop critical thinking at their own pace shattering the constraints of time, place, and standardized education. Based on research findings, case studies, and pragmatic models, this book and the chapter explore the potential and challenges of infusing AI into independent learning. It shows how learners of every generation can leverage the capability of AI agents to develop autonomy, imagination, and lifelong learning behaviors in a constantly evolving world. As one proceeds, a question holding one in place is:

- How can AI assist one not just to learn more effectively but also more meaningfully?

The following chapter tries to respond, presenting a vision of education in which autonomy is augmented, and not displaced, by the wisdom of machines.

Redefining, Rethinking and Exploring Education in the Age of e-Learning with Artificial Intelligence: From Smartboards Replacing Chalkboards to ... ?

"Against the background of *transdisciplinary approaches to learning outcomes in higher education*, the purpose of" the latest chapter by Tefo and Goosen (2024b, p. 327) was "exploring transdisciplinary approaches to teaching Physical Sciences (PS) in selected schools of Gauteng province, South Africa with regard to a pedagogy of using smartboard technologies."

Fostering pedagogical innovation through effective smartboard instruction, the "purpose of the study reported on in" an earlier chapter by Tefo and Goosen (2024a, p. 287) was "exploring the pedagogy with regard to the teaching, learning, and assessment of grade 12 Physical Sciences using" smart board "technologies in schools selected from one of the districts in the city of Tshwane".

The performance of South African learners in Mathematics and Physical Sciences from Grades 8 through 12 has lagged the global average (Tefo & Goosen, 2024a). The concern is not only in SA but globally. The decline in scientific achievement in Nigeria is a significant issue, and is caused by many factors, including lack laboratory and educational materials (Olojo, Akinwumi, & Olofin, 2022). The scientific terminology, the teacher's incapacity, and the students' disapproval of "learning science as a subject" all contribute the underperformance of Physical Sciences (Tefo, 2021, p. 1). The quality of science education has influenced students' ability to become qualified individuals' post-graduation, which is due to insufficient educational resources and teacher proficiency (Jammeh, Karegeya, & Ladage, 2022).

The purpose of Physical Sciences "is to make learners aware of their environment and to equip learners with investigating skills relating to physical and chemical phenomena, for example, lightning and solubility" (Department of Basic Education, 2011, p. 8). Physical Sciences as a subject consists of Chemistry and Physics.

Current difficulties impacting the quality of scientific education include pedagogical techniques (Bayram-Jacobs, et al., 2019) and insufficient content understanding (Tal, Herscovitz, & Dori, 2021; Usak, Ozden, & Eilks, 2011). It is therefore essential that stakeholders collaborate to address the challenges that impede the successful integration of Information and Communications Technology (ICT) in secondary schools, including a lack of resources, training, time, support, curriculum alignment, and pedagogical change (Msafiri, Kangwa, & Cai, 2023). Additionally, the development of curriculum has entirely changed and improved by digital technology, which enables educators to develop lessons that are adaptive to different environments and adaptable in their content (Faridi & Shaheen, 2024). Chigamba (2021) added that it is regrettable that technology in schools in South Africa is not used effectively to benefit both teachers and pupils due to a lack of seriousness in the training of both parties.

The abstract nature of Physical Sciences as a subject influences the underachievement of learners locally and globally (Ogegbo & Ramnarain, 2022). This abstract nature may be one of the reasons learners are not doing well in science subjects, as discussed in chapter two. The principles of chemistry are difficult to comprehend, particularly through traditional methods. Therefore, an alternative strategy, such as the integration of smartboards, is necessary to facilitate active and ensure learning for students (Jammeh et al., 2022).

In the same breath, the literature review aims to explore the pedagogy for teaching Physical Sciences using the smart board to ensure teaching and learning through the successful assessment of learners. Firstly, literature will address the benefits of the smart board in teaching and learning Physical Sciences, the pedagogy of teaching Physical Sciences using the smart boards, and the digital technologies within the smart board that are used to assess Physical Sciences.

Recommended Topics

From the recommended topics suggested for the book, this chapter will address:

- Introduction: Rethinking Education in the Age of AI
- Gamification, Augmented Reality (AR)/ Virtual Reality (VR), and Immersive Learning Agents
- AI for Accessible and Inclusive Education
- Ethics, Privacy, and Governance in AI-Powered Education
- The Future of Self-Learning and AI Companions

Target Audience

In line with the primary target audience proposed for this book, that of the chapter include e.g.,

1. Educators and teachers seeking to understand and integrate AI agents into classrooms for enhanced teaching, personalized instruction, and curriculum design.
2. Students and lifelong learners interested in leveraging AI-powered tools, intelligent tutors, and self-learning systems to build knowledge and skills independently.
3. Academic researchers and scholars exploring the theoretical foundations, methodologies, and future research directions related to AI-driven education and learning sciences.
4. Educational Technology (EdTech) innovators and developers building AI-based platforms, tools, and applications aimed at transforming educational experiences.
5. Policymakers and education leaders designing frameworks, policies, and governance models to responsibly adopt AI in schools, universities, and professional training ecosystems.
6. Corporate trainers, as well as learning and development professionals applying AI for reskilling, workforce training, and professional development in dynamic industries.

Secondary target audience:

1. Parents and guardians, who wish to understand how AI agents can support their children's learning journeys and supplement traditional education.
2. Non-Governmental Organizations (NGOs) and social enterprises working to expand access to quality education in underserved communities through technology-driven initiatives.
3. Start-ups and entrepreneurs exploring opportunities to design innovative AI-driven educational platforms and personalized learning solutions.
4. Technology enthusiasts and general readers curious about the evolving relationship between AI and human learning, and its societal implications.
5. Policy advocates and think tanks interested in the ethical, legal, and social dimensions of AI adoption in global education systems.
6. Futurists and innovators seeking insights into the long-term role of AI in shaping self-learning, lifelong education, and human–AI collaboration.

Objectives

In line with the goal of this book, the purpose of this chapter includes to illustrate how AI agents can reimagine education and self-learning fundamentally by providing adaptive, personalized, and scalable solutions. As part of the book, this chapter aims to shine a spotlight on the role of AI in designing intelligent learning environments that encourage critical thinking, creativity, inclusivity, and lifelong learning, by:

1. Providing an extensive overview of AI agents, their design, and their possible uses in formal and informal education.
2. Depicting the evolution of teaching and learning frameworks with adaptive, personalized, and learner-focused methodologies fueled by AI.
3. Demonstrating real-world applications where AI agents augment self-learning, teacher assistance, curriculum design, and learner engagement.
4. Advocating for accessibility and inclusion by highlighting how AI facilitates bridging educational disparities among varied socioeconomic, linguistic, and cognitive profiles.

5. Analyzing critically ethical, privacy, and governance concerns related to AI in education to foster responsible and transparent adoption.
6. Predicting future research directions and emerging trends related to the potential of AI as an active collaborator in human learning, making it possible for autonomous learners and intelligent lifelong learning environments to emerge.

BACKGROUND

This section will provide broad definitions and discussions of the topic on Rethinking and Exploring Education in the Age of Artificial Intelligence when considering From Smartboards Replacing Chalkboards to … ? and incorporate the views of others (in the form of a literature review) into the discussion to support, refute, or demonstrate the authors' position on the topic.

"The process of sequence labeling (POS) by assigning syntactic tags to words in" a given context is "an important role in various" Natural Language Processing (NLP) "applications. The core motive of" the chapter by Raza, et al. (2025, p. 23) as part of a book on *Innovations in Optimization and Machine Learning* was employing NLP techniques for the development of a voting-based POS tagger in the Urdu language.

Ethics, Privacy, and Governance in Artificial Intelligence-Powered Education

With regard to the ethics of AI in education, the *AI* and *society* journal article by Luckin (2023a) discussed self-regulation, autonomy, and the human factor.

The study reported on by Khurana, Gawshinde and Shaheen (2025, p. 461) as part of a book on *Strategic Blueprints for AI-Driven Marketing in the Digital Era* explored "the intersection of neuromarketing and ethical consumption in the realm of sustainable finance, with a specific focus on socially responsible investing."

An earlier chapter by Uunona and Goosen (2023) was leveraging ethical standards in artificial intelligence technologies as a guideline for responsible teaching and learning applications, as well as leveraging ethics in artificial intelligence technologies and applications as part of e-learning management systems in Namibia (Uunona & Goosen, 2024). More recent chapter were leveraging ethics for supporting students' artificial intelligence skills development in a book on *supporting personalized learning and students' skill development with AI* (Uunona & Goosen, 2025a), as well as navigating ethical consideration of artificial intelligence and the metaverse in scientific research (Uunona & Goosen, 2025b).

A chapter by Webb, Luckin and Ecoff (2023) on ethical principles for the development and application of artificial intelligence in K-12 education appeared in an *International Handbook on Education Development in the Asia-Pacific*.

"To drive ethical design for AI agents" and humans, as well as untangling the marketing of artificial intelligence in learning environments, Pedersen and Duin (2022, p. 10) argued "that learners in learning contexts need to be included as partners in decision-making systems".

Although Luckin (2023b) agreed that AI could profoundly disrupt education, it was also pointed out that maybe was not a bad thing. An Organization for Economic Co-operation and Development (*OECD) Education Working Paper* by Luckin, Holmes, Griffiths and Forcier (2023) on AI and education provided guidance for policy makers, while although "teachers understand enough about AI to buy tools that will be useful and appropriate to their context, to use AI", a book on *AI for school teachers* by Luckin, George and Cukurova (2022) had already laid out why the latter authors thought it was "critical for teachers to understand AI." An earlier book by Luckin, Holmes, Griffiths and Forcier (2016) provided *an argument for AI in education*.

As AI is being implemented more and more, an *applied sciences* journal article provided a systematic review towards "insight into how AI is being applied to" and for student assessment (González-Calatayud, Prendes-Espinosa, & Roig-Vila, 2021, p. 1).

The increasing availability of artificial intelligence "and related tools and technologies" had "made it possible to use AI in various domains of life. The field of education is also witnessing" such an increase and the *world journal* article on *advanced research and reviews* by Tahir, Hassan and Shagoo (2024, p. 1469) offered a conceptual review of the role of artificial intelligence in education.

"Numerous decision-making situations are faced in education where" artificial intelligence "may be prevalent as a" new decision-making support tool of disruption in educational performance assessment (Halagatti, et al., 2023).

In line with the fourth secondary target audience mentioned in the INTRODUCTION, artificial intelligence had "significantly transformed teaching and learning, facilitating a shift from teacher-centered to student-centered education." The review journal article by Tang (2024, p. 65) outlined the broad implications of artificial intelligence for teaching and learning.

Artificial Intelligence for Accessible and Inclusive Education

Ansu-Kyeremeh and Goosen (2022) were exploring the socio-economic facets of online inclusive education in Ghana with regard to the effects of technological advancements in academia, while the OECD (2023) discussed opportunities, as well as providing guidelines and guardrails for effective and equitable use of AI in education.

A *journal* article on *educational studies* by Dlamini (2022) presented a multi-level analysis of in-service teachers' technological knowledge competencies towards digital equity in schools.

Gamification, Augmented Reality/Virtual Reality and Immersive Learning Agents

The introduction of games in teaching and learning increases interaction with learners and motivates them to participate in activities. Game-based learning is considered a pedagogical approach with great use in cognitive processes, where teachers can take a deeper look at computer games and recreate the learning content that adds to the learners' prior knowledge and their previous learning experiences (Triantafyllou & Sapounidis, 2023). These games are free to use in classrooms or offices. These games, amongst others, include jeopardy, Who Wants to Be a Millionaire, Kahoot, Pictionary and Memory Match. Twenty-two smart board applications are used for business, teaching, and learning. From Ben Q Instashare to Educreations Whiteboard applications, teachers can install them on their smart boards to enhance teaching. Nancy, Parimala and Livingston (2020) also agreed that Kahoot! is a game-learning app installed on a smart board and uses quizzes to review students' knowledge using formative assessment, or as a break from traditional classroom activities. Most apps are free, but the teacher or school can buy updated ones. They are compatible with Androids, iPhones, and MacBooks, to name a few.

Using artificial agents with deep learning in the trust game was explored in the study reported on by Wu, Wu, Chen and Hua (2023, p. 7236) in a *management science* journal article, which offered "evidence that AI agents can", "purely from an interactive trial-and-error learning process", constitute a first step towards building socially intelligent AI systems.

Yang, Li and Lee (2025, p. 1) used "AI agents within the Project Approach in early childhood education (ECE) to enhance children's creative learning". The latter *Computers and Education: Artificial Intelligence* journal article conceptualized "how AI agents can be specifically tailored" for early learning.

The research reported on in an *applied sciences* journal article by Xia, Shin and Lee (2024, p. 3) sought "to determine the specific adaptive learning capabilities required by AI agents in the Metaverse. It" focused "on understanding how these agents process and respond" as part of the Adaptive Learning Model for AI Agents (ALMAA) framework.

Apart from a "learning framework for developing AI agents", one of the chapters also introduced deep *reinforcement learning*. In the book regarding *Hands-On Intelligent Agents with OpenAI Gym*, Palanisamy (2018) trained "an AI agent using reinforcement learning to drive".

Information and Communications Technologies in Education

As technologies advance, the South African national Department of Education (2004), through its policy on using ICTs for teaching and learning, must adapt and initiate the effective use of smart board technologies in South African schools. The purpose of the *professional development framework for digital learning* (Department of Basic Education (DBE), 2017, p. 9) is to "ensure competent educators who use ICTs to enhance teaching and learning and leaders and support staff who can facilitate the development of educator digital learning competencies".

Smart boards were introduced to Gauteng in schools in 2015, when the pass rate in 2014 was 30% in Physical Sciences. Fast forward, and the pass rate in Physical Sciences, on average, had increased by 4.9%, with 35% of learners reaching the 60% threshold (Department of Basic Education, 2024).

Learners today are born into, and are maturing in, a digitally sophisticated environment. They arrive at school armed with cell phones, iPods, and laptops and arrange playdates and excursions using text messages and emails, establish connections with others on social networking platforms, maintain personal web pages, and use blogging and tweeting to attain status (Min & Siegel, 2011). Hence, Dlamini (2022) proposed that to enhance the quality of education, it is imperative to provide educators with opportunities for professional development in digital skills as teaching and learning paradigms transition to a multimodal approach.

European countries and the United States of America (USA) have integrated ICTs into their curriculum, but the challenge is pedagogical techniques for effective integration (Çapuk, 2015). In most Sub-Saharan African countries, such as Uganda, Ghana and Ethiopia, teachers have been trained to use ICT in teaching and learning. But teachers experienced some challenges, including a lack of skills in integrating technology with pedagogy and content to improve teaching and learning methodologies in their subjects (Agyei, 2021).

Kennedy and Cronjé (2023) stated that teachers are empowered to use ICT after being pushed into technology globally and in South Africa. Conversely, teachers have adapted to it slowly post-COVID-19. Schools should transform into enabling environments where teachers can use ICT innovatively in their classes. ICT training is inadequate, and the integration and innovative use of digital devices for teaching and learning are also ineffective.

Teachers' Information and Communications Technology Skills

Teachers' confidence in technology education remains a significant determinant affecting their attitudes towards technology usage in class (Goosen & Koekemoer, 2011). Notably, it is not only the attitude and confidence of teachers but also the behavioral control and subjective norms to use ICT in classrooms (Moosa & Ramnarain, 2023; Rahimi & Tafazoli, 2022). Behavioral control refers to teachers' perceptions of their ability to integrate ICT resources into their teaching. Subjective norms refer to teachers' views regarding implementing ICT in their classes. In the same breath, teachers are not receptive, perhaps due to their ability to use technologies compared to their learners, who are digital natives and understand technology better than teachers do (Jie & Sunze, 2023). The latter authors were investigating pedagogical challenges related to using mobile technologies for English teaching in *interactive learning environments*.

Arek-Bawa and Reddy (2022) asked whether digital curricular transformation was deepening divides or building bridges? Academics at universities should therefore review their curriculum to digitize education qualifications to assist in developing their student teachers and graduates in the use of technology for accessing, content and creation of knowledge in fourth Industrial Revolution 4.0 (4IR) classrooms. Adequate training assists teachers in being digitally competent. In their analysis and comparison of international digital competence frameworks for education, Mattar, Santos and Cuque (2022) showed that the training will help teachers use digital technologies confidently and responsibly during teaching and learning. In addition, Teane (2024) suggests that online competencies should commence with teachers at training institutions before being integrated into school education.

In the context of *e-learning and digital media,* teachers' perspectives and viewpoints regarding the ingestion and integration of ICTs for pedagogy in Indian private schools are crucial (Kundu & Bej, 2021). Tefo and Goosen (2024a) agreed that employing a smart board as an ICT tool for learning necessitates various teaching techniques to ensure effective learning. It does not rely only on teachers' digital or teaching abilities but also on content knowledge as presented by Technology Pedagogy and Content Knowledge (TPACK) (Tefo & Goosen, 2024b).

The Smartboard

Information and communication technology devices include computers, cell phone gadgets, digital media tools, and smart boards. Khairnar (2015) was of the opinion that technologies serve as justification for the objectives of content results and had integrated perfectly into the classroom curriculum.

A smartboard (SB) consists of an interactive touch-sensitive board connected to a projector and a computer with electronic pens for writing or using a finger to operate (Al-Faki & Khamis, 2014).

Benefits of the Smartboard

Smart boards captivate learners' interest and attention via visual and auditory stimulation, render the subject matter tangible, offer substantial learning content, simplify, and enhance the learning experience, "increase student participation in the classroom", minimize distractions, and streamline lesson delivery for educators (Akar, 2020, p. 267).

Fu (2013) asserted that the smart board, an ICT tool, enhances teaching and learning by stimulating engagement, motivation, collaboration, knowledge development, and research and management competencies.

Smart gadgets and web tools, such as digital books, slides, graphic images, audios, videos, smart boards, and other electronic reference tools, are utilized in computational Internet of Things to ensure a well-structured, well-understood, and smoother class than a class that lacks such mechanisms (Dhal, et al., 2022).

Aktas and Aydin (2016) emphasized that using smart boards enhances learners' understanding of science and technology subjects and reinforces their acquired knowledge. These authors, furthermore, mention the noticeable increase in participation during the lessons.

Tenzin, Tendar and Zagmo (2022, p. 76) stated that using ICTs "can make its abstract and complex ideas easier to understand." Learners can comprehend abstract and complex concepts when the Physical Sciences abstract concept is demonstrated or presented. The demonstration methodology is a pedagogical approach adopted as a visual aid for clarifying the application of scientific ideas, hence boosting the learning and understanding of abstract topics (Lestari, Supahar, Paidi, Suwarjo, & Herianto, 2023). It enables learners and teachers to participate in the lesson and clarify concepts. The teacher can explain using the videos on the smart board. For example, teachers can download a video from an open online resource to demonstrate or present any challenging concept on the smart board. Instead of imagining it, the learner can see the actual concept.

It is, however, crucial to remember that since technology is a tool for delivering teaching and learning, pedagogy is crucial in determining the technology employed (Fedorov, 2021).

Pedagogy, Instructional Techniques and/or Teaching Methods for Physical Sciences Using the Smartboard

Scholars such as Amiruddin, Fiskia Rera, Takbir, Wirawan and Muhammad (2023), Baharuddin and Setialaskana (2023), as well as Joshi (2021), had explored and presented structural equation model approaches to the pedagogy-andragogy continuum with peeragogy, heutagogy, and cybergogy as contributions to promote self-regulated learning.

Pedagogy for the Smartboard

Molotsi (2014, p. 34) added that when preparing for "a technology-integrated lesson, the choice of pedagogy depends on" the technological tool.

MAIN FOCUS OF THE CHAPTER

Issues, Problems

This section will present the authors' perspectives on the issues, problems, etc., as these relate to theme of the book on Redefining Independent Learning with AI Agents and arguments supporting the authors' position on Rethinking and Exploring Education in the Age of Artificial Intelligence when considering From Smartboards Replacing Chalkboards to … ? It will also compare and contrast with what had been, or is currently being, done as it relates to the specific topic of the chapter and the main theme of the book.

In a book on the *Issues and Challenges in Science Education Research*, the chapter by Yung (2012) presented *issues and challenges* in school-based assessment of science practical work, while the chapter by Paige and Lloyd (2012) discussed pedagogical practices and science learning with a focus on educating for sustainability for pre-service primary and middle years educators.

"Considering the increasing importance of Artificial Intelligence in Education (AIEd) and the absence of a comprehensive review on" this, the research reported on by Chen, Xie, Zou and Hwang (2020, p. 1) aimed to conduct such a review on application and theory gaps during the rise of artificial intelligence in education.

A *journal* article on *educational technology and innovation* by Zhao (2024, p. 39) indicates that "AI tools are increasingly used in education, impacting teaching and learning across various disciplines. However, previous review articles and empirical studies" had not systematically reviewed AI-assisted assessment in higher education.

Another *journal* article on *research and development* by Noothigattu, et al. (2019, p. 1) aimed to develop techniques that allow for AI "agents to not only maximize their reward" but also for teaching these agents ethical values using *reinforcement* learning and policy orchestration by "learning to learn a set of unspecified constraints from demonstrations and *reinforcement learning*".

Challenges Related to Artificial Intelligence

The study reported on in an emerging technology trends journal article by Celik, Dindar, Muukkonen and Järvelä (2022, p. 616) provided a systematic review "of research on teachers' use of artificial intelligence … applications and machine learning methods to analyze teachers' data." The analysis by the latter authors showed the promises and challenges of artificial intelligence for teachers.

Although the integration and rise of artificial intelligence in educational measurement had "transformed assessment methods, allowing for automated scoring, swift content analysis, and" brought many more opportunities, the journal article by Bulut, et al. (2024, p. 1) also pointed to ethical challenges in this regard.

Efforts had "been made to include artificial intelligence" in teaching and learning. Nevertheless, according to the *Iraqi Journal for Computer Science and Mathematics* article by Tashtoush, Wardat, Ali and Saleh (2024, p. 60) "the successful deployment of new instructional" technologies depends on mathematics teachers' perspectives, practices and challenges.

Challenges Related to Smartboards

A journal article by Tigere and Netshitangani (2022, p. 20024) described infrastructure challenges in "township and rural secondary schools in" KwaZulu-Natal province, South Africa as perceived by school management teams related to "information and communication technology integration."

Apart from its benefits, the smart board has some challenges. Switching it on can take time before it can be ready for use, it may distract learners' attention. Training for teachers that do not have the teaching and digital knowledge as required by TPACK. This may lead to teachers being stressed when integrating this technology into their lessons (Depietro-Covey, 2023). Technology and Content Knowledge, as well as technology and pedagogy are still a challenge for most teachers.

Technical issues that teachers cannot handle due to lack of technical skills is a concern (Obaid, 2022). As part of *research papers in language teaching* and *learning* regarding interactive whiteboards in English as a Foreign Language (EFL) from teachers' and students' perspective, Giannikas (2021) added that when it comes to creating an atmosphere in the classroom that encourages students to actively participate and connect with one another, it can be challenging to effectively manage and combine the use of technology and pedagogy. This includes the smart board as the technology under study. Teachers were also concerned about the time spent during lesson preparations to when using the Interactive Whiteboard or smart board (Gadbois & Haverstock, 2009).

The Interactivity of the Smartboard

An exploration of the interactivity of the smartboard is presented next (Ramsden, 2019).

Visual Learning

Complex concepts can be represented visually, aiding in comprehension. Teachers can illustrate ideas using diagrams, videos, and animations that can be manipulated in real-time. Smart boards can showcase diagrams, animations, and videos, making learning more accessible (Ndwandwe, Ramaligela, & Mtshali, 2024). In terms of the *impact of interactive smartboards on learning achievement in Senegalese primary schools*, pictures/images also enabled a concrete representation of concepts, hence enhancing pupil comprehension and understanding of concepts much faster and improving "lesson pacing", which helps to "cover curriculum faster" (Lehrer, Mawoyo, & Mbaye, 2017, p. 36).

Collaboration

Students can collaborate on the smart board, facilitating peer interaction. Students' perspectives on the impact of smart boards on their learning in secondary schools in Botswana showed that they demonstrated significant interaction during lessons through collaborative learning activities, both in small groups and at the class level, when using interactive smart boards (Tsayang, Batane, & Majuta, 2020).

Group activities become more engaging as students can communicate their concepts and responses on the board. According to Zenda (2024), active learning, which includes collaboration and communication between learners, is missing in schools. Can the smart board improve on collaboration? The interactivity of the smart board supports collaboration, and the videos and animations on the board motivate learners to engage in activities together. The touching activity of the board makes the collaborative interaction easier.

Instant Feedback

Artificial intelligence can facilitate the automation of the assessment process, save time for teachers, and provide instant feedback to learners regarding their work (Khlaif, Salha, & Kouraichi, 2021). Quizzes and polls installed in the smart boards can be adapted and used as teaching strategies to engage learners (Nuci, Tahir, Wang, & Imran, 2021). The clicking devices or tablets distributed by the Department of Education can be used for immediate feedback to students. In addition, learners could critique each other's work during the problem-solving process can be further enhanced by the IWB's large screen (Bourbour, 2023). Real time responses during interactions renders learning authentic especially for those using the board 100% of their time (Handley, 2023). As presented earlier, teachers in Gauteng use the smart boards 100% since the chalkboards have been replaced by the boards (Mzekandaba, 2016). Instant feedback is possible and can benefit the learners if the teachers are using it.

Owan, Abang, Idika, Etta, and Bassey (2023), exploring the potential of artificial intelligence tools in educational measurement and assessment, emphasized that teachers can utilize gamification techniques such as Classcraft, Kahoot! and Quizlet to enhance learners' engagement, facilitate learning, and deliver immediate feedback on performance. Gaming applications ('apps') that teachers can download on the smart board also assist with instant feedback to learners. Game-based learning enables teachers to reimagine education by integrating the processes of knowing, doing, being, and valuing, which are considered essential for authentic learning methodology for acquiring knowledge (Paige & Lloyd, 2012).

Accessibility

Gauteng schools have access to Smart boards since they replaced chalkboards in 2015. Teachers can integrate various multimedia resources, catering to different learning styles and making content more *accessible* to all learners from different categories (Gbordzekpor, Kwakye, & Aggrey, 2023). Learners with different kinds of learning needs can benefit from technology, which is also crucial for children who struggle academically, and teachers can support them with a variety of technology and smart classroom management (Kambala & Mathe, 2022). Different learning styles, such as gaming or tactile, can accommodate learners with learning difficulties. Zenda (2024, p. 415) added that "gamified apps can be used to teach physics principles through problem-solving". For example, learners who are a bit slow can use recording after school to catch up or for revision. Visual learners can rely on videos and colorful charts, which make learning fun. The smart boards have installed videos and colorful pens that learners and teachers can use to attract learners and enhance participation.

Nevertheless, the interactivity of the whiteboards depends on the objectives of the lesson, methodology and the utilization for the board (Bílý & Miština, 2023). This means selection of topic to be taught, learners' capabilities, the duration of lesson and resources to facilitate teaching and learning. Lesson planning is important and gives direction for the teachers to achieve the lesson objective. Irrespective of the resources, teachers need to plan for lessons.

Assessment

Informal assessment is carried out through daily activities, from class observations, demonstrations, to classroom interactions. Informal assessment is a daily monitoring of learners' progress in developing a knowledge base together with the related skills and safe attitudes needed in practical subjects (Department of Basic Education, 2011).

This type of assessment can be utilized as a screening procedure and to ascertain whether learners are eligible for remedial services and supports or special education (Spinelli, 2008). Learners should be assessed with at least two problem-solving exercises frequently through homework and/or classwork.

An *Asian Social Science* journal article by Nair, et al. (2014) explored teachers' knowledge and issues in the implementation of school-based assessment in a case of schools in Terengganu, a traditional region of northeastern West Malaysia.

According to Mehboob, et al. (2024, p. 419), some teachers indicated that they prefer the smart board over chalkboards because as it transformed their teaching especially during assessment. One teacher was quoted as saying "I can pull up interactive exercises and allow students to take part in the lesson in real-time, which wasn't possible with traditional blackboards".

Formal assessment, according to Department of Basic Education (2011), are tasks that are recorded and marked by the teacher for the purpose of progression and certification. It is "assessment of learning" whereas informal "assessment for learning" (Department of Basic Education, 2014, p. 3). Formal assessments are moderated to ensure that appropriate standards are maintained and ensures quality assurance. Formative/ formal assessment which develops inquiry competency in science learners, is a method that is highly prioritized in educational policies of several countries globally (Staberg, Febri, Gjøvik, Sikko, & Pepin, 2023).

Practical Tasks

A *journal* article on *curriculum studies research* by Tsakeni (2023) discussed primary preservice science teachers' perceptions of *practical* work in remote learning environments.

Teachers need a Physical Sciences laboratory to do practical work. Laboratory environments give skills in manipulation, organization, experimentation, and interpretation, and learners acquire practical experiences. The students can implement theoretical knowledge in practice. According to Preetha, Venkataraman, Hariharan and Prabavathy (2022, p. 243), "integrating practical laboratory-based learning bridged the gap between theory and practice".

Rahayu and Makmur (2024) stated that internet connectivity and access to digital resources facilitate access to e-books, educational videos, and interactive simulations. Simulation can be used for practical work. Figures 1 and 2 are examples of simulations used to teach electricity in a science class using a Smart board (SMART Technologies ULC, 2025).

Figure 1. Example of simulations used to teach electricity in a science class using a smartboard (SMART Technologies ULC, 2025)

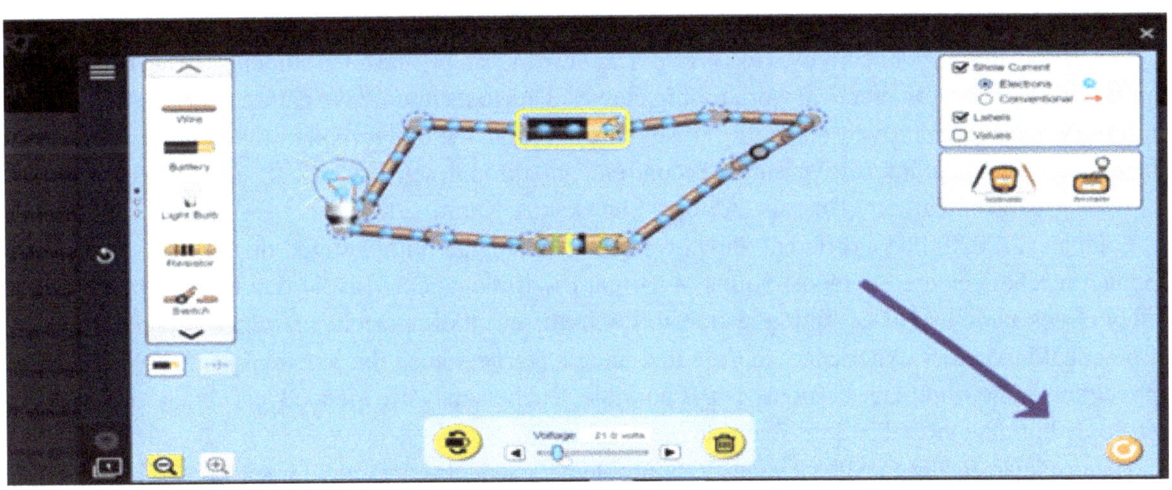

Figure 2. Example of simulations used to teach electricity in a science class using a smartboard (SMART Technologies ULC, 2025)

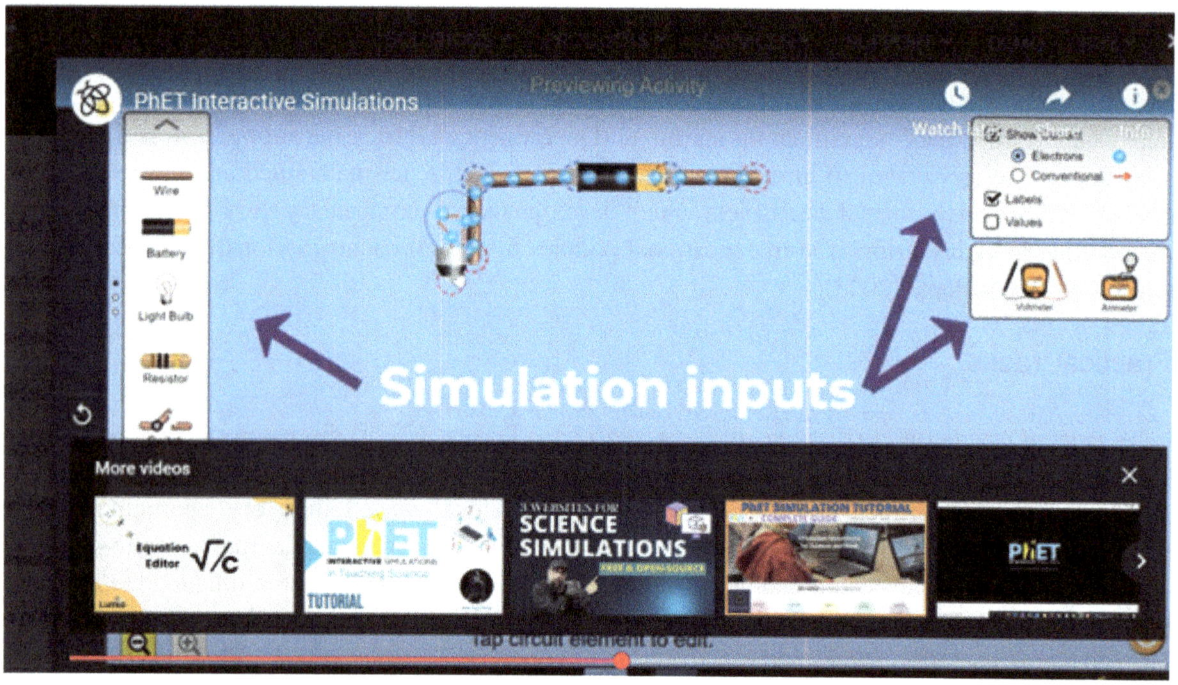

The software installed allows learners to work as a group or as individuals to present an electricity connection. This collaboration allows multiple students to interact with the board, encouraging teamwork and collaborative problem-solving (Mateer, 2020). The interactivity and touch sensitivity of the board allows learners to move the apparatus around the board while doing the practical work. Teachers can also evaluate learners on the work they present. Learners can collectively write a practical report for their assessment. This saves time when unpacking and packing the appliances used in the physical sciences laboratories.

Due to its internet connectivity, videos of practical work can be played to students, rather than taking two days to do hands-on practical work for big classes. Due to its interactive nature, learners can engage with the video collaboratively and collect results. In addition, the integration of the smart board has enabled the fulfilment of interactive learning requirements (through sensory, visual, and aural dimensions) for large groups of learners (Hussein, Ahmed, Shawkat, & Kamil, 2022).

Gudyanga (2020) had a different view or concern. The latter author stated that teachers frequently conduct teacher-centered demonstrations or virtual experiments exclusively due to uncertainty about safety issues and a fear of accepting responsibility in the event of an accident, which deprives learners of practical laboratory experience. In the same breath, learners need the practical work experience for application at the workplace or industries. If possible, teachers may use blended learning where learners can apply both the virtual and the hand-on practical work.

Historic investigation involves identifying problems, conducting practical work to confirm or refute assumptions, and analyzing and discussing results with peers. It seeks to inspire learners, overcome their fear towards scientific subjects, and provide knowledge more engagingly (Chekour, Laafou, &

Janati-Idrissi, 2018). The discovery of penicillin by the scientist Alexander Fleming in 1928 (Gaynes, 2017) can be used as a research assignment to encourage learners to be observant and curious about the world around them. In addition, it assists learners in realizing that science is not only in class but also around them.

SOLUTIONS AND RECOMMENDATIONS

This section will discuss possible solutions and recommendations in dealing with the issues or problems presented in the preceding section.

Possible Solutions

In line with one of the secondary target audiences established for the book (start-ups and entrepreneurs), this chapter is exploring opportunities to design innovative AI-driven educational platforms and *personalized learning* solutions.

Klinck-Van der Merwe and Goosen (2024) suggested a framework for online learning analytics in K-12 classrooms as a precursor for *personalized learning* as emergent practices in schools, while the more recent chapter by the latter authors (Klinck-van der Merwe & Goosen, 2025) made recommendations regarding artificial intelligence algorithms as a precursor for *personalized learning* and education in terms of real-world applications of innovation.

A similar context appeared in the chapter by Tandon and Shaheen (2024, p. 429) as part of a book on *Maintaining a sustainable world in the nexus of environmental science and AI*, which explored the integration of AI-driven innovations and technologies for "promoting environmental sustainability across various sectors" focusing on e.g., agriculture, energy, and transportation.

Possible solutions for challenges with regard to integrating ICTs into rural South African schools were discussed by Amedzo and Dzansi (2014, p. 341) in an *international journal* article on *science education*. The influence of ICTs "in schools cannot be overemphasized as its utility is changing the way students learn, teachers teach, and support staff work."

Problem-solving skills, as explained in a previous chapter (Tefo & Goosen, 2024a), can assist in developing learners' ability to identify problems and solve them using the smart board. For example, the teachers can expand the lesson and add a component of inquiry through an assignment for learners solve the electricity challenge in South Africa from the same electricity lesson. The learners can use the internet connectivity of the smart board to collect data, analyze it and come up with possible solutions to the electricity problems.

Most countries, including e.g., Sri Lanka and Pakistan, had successfully integrated ICTs into education. However, a chapter on the identification of facilitators and barriers of ICT usage in the education sector of Pakistan presented a systematic literature review in a book providing *ICT solutions for improving smart communities in Asia*. One of the common challenges is not basic training but training specifically in the integration of "digital media" into teaching and learning (Adnan, Shaikh, Afzaal, Ali, & Ponnusamy, 2021, p. 41). In South Africa, the integration of ICT has grown not only in the education curriculum but in all arears including workplaces and social life (Triantafyllou & Sapounidis, 2023).

Recommendations

Science teachers' academic qualification and their pedagogical practices enhance learners' performance in a specific field of study (Assem, Nartey, Appiah, & Aidoo, 2023). The latter authors made recommendations related to teachers, who lack the relevant science qualifications should attend in-service training on the content knowledge for the subject. This is in line with the TPACK theory as presented by Mishra and Koehler (2006) on pedagogical content knowledge.

An informal assessment is designed to assist students in recognizing their learning challenges and receiving constructive feedback from the teacher, which can assist them in identifying their weaknesses and receiving recommendations for improvement (Tumanggor & Supahar, 2020). Learners can make corrections during the learning process daily. It will help them do better during the formal assessment. Informal assessment is an everyday activity that involves the monitoring of learners' progress through informal classroom interactions, discussions, hands-on experiments, learner-teacher discussions, and observations (Department of Basic Education, 2011).

FUTURE RESEARCH DIRECTIONS

This section will discuss future and emerging trends, as well as provide insight about the future of the theme of the book on Redefining Independent Learning with AI Agents from the perspective of the chapter focus on Rethinking and Exploring Education in the Age of Artificial Intelligence when considering From Smartboards Replacing Chalkboards to … ? The viability of a paradigm, model, implementation issues of proposed programs, etc., may be included in this section. If appropriate, the section will suggest future research opportunities within the domain of the topic.

In line with one of the primary target audiences established for the book (academic researchers and scholars), this chapter is exploring the theoretical foundations, methodologies, and future research directions related to AI-driven education and learning sciences.

The Future of Self-Learning and Artificial Intelligence Companions

The digital changes the world is going "through are thrilling, jarring, full of opportunity and, at the same time, terrifying." The United Nations Educational, Scientific and Cultural Organization (UNESCO, 2023a, p. 1) therefore issued a report on generative AI and the future of education.

A survey by UNESCO (2023b) indicated that less than 10% of schools and universities have formal guidance on AI. It was therefore necessary to provide *guidance for generative AI in education and research* (UNESCO, 2023c) by e.g., showing *how generative AI is reshaping education in Asia-Pacific* (UNESCO, 2023d) and suggesting draft AI competency frameworks for teachers and for school students (UNESCO, 2024).

In terms of the future of building controls (Petrus, 2019), "SMITHGROUP-AI would be an independent, multifunctional *reinforcement learning* software agent responsible for the monitoring and control of all agents that control all building systems", "and all agents and coordinators will share knowledge to continuously improve their predictions through *reinforcement learning*."

According to an *AI magazine* article by Ponnusamy, et al. (2022, p. 44), feedback-based self-learning in large-scale conversational AI agents provided a seamless experience and engaged "more with the AI agents."

As part of a book on *Machine and Deep Learning Techniques for Emotion Detection*, a chapter on advancements in facial expression recognition using machine and deep learning techniques (Singh, Pandey, Rai, & Saxena, 2024, p. 149) indicated that in "the field of computer vision, facial expression recognition is" one of the prominent emerging trends in the "field that looks at visual face data to try and understand human emotions."

Distributed cryptographic ledger (commonly known as blockchain) "is a decentralized, intermediary-free platform that deals with imperfections present in the existing monetary system" (Qureshi, Khan, Jabeen, & Shah, 2025). A chapter by the latter authors was exploring blockchain transaction patterns using graph-based visualization in a book on *cybersecurity, cybercrimes, and smart emerging* trends related to *technologies.*

Teachers can explore several ICT pedagogies to enhance the teaching and learning of Physical Sciences. Pedagogies, teaching techniques or methods have evolved frequently due to socio-economic reasons. This includes using technology to enhance teaching and learning locally and globally. COVID-19 and emerging technology trends have forced teaching and learning to use pedagogy, andragogy, and cyber approaches (Amiruddin, et al., 2023). Pedagogy is the instructional technique or method teachers use to ensure learning takes place. According to Joshi (2021, p. 1), pedagogy answers the following questions:

- What is it that learners should learn?
- "How will the teacher help them to learn?"
- How "does the teacher know they have learned?"

Current practices and future research directions related to artificial intelligence in mathematics education were described as part of a systematic review presented by Awang, Yusop and Danaee (2025, p. 1) in an *international electronic journal* article. "Mastering mathematics is often challenging for many students; however, the rise of artificial intelligence … offers numerous advantages, including" e.g., enhanced data analysis.

Another systematic literature review on the opportunities, challenges, and future research recommendations related to artificial intelligence in education by Chiu, Xia, Zhou, Chai and Cheng (2023, p. 1) indicated that applications "of artificial intelligence in education" represent emerging trends "and are new to researchers and practitioners alike", which reviews "of the relevant literature have not examined".

The Use of Smartboard Technologies for the Assessment of Physical Sciences

Assessment is a method of gathering factual, qualitative, and quantitative data to monitor learners' development, assisting in the planning of future approaches to learning (Mohan, 2023). In a classroom, assessments measure how well learners performed across different tasks and contexts.

Emerging trends and practices in basic education related to formative and summative assessment were discussed by Mogboh and Okoye (2019, p. 44) in a *journal* article on *education and practice.* "Nonetheless, improved integration of formative and summative assessment", as well as "professional development, and further research and development" are needed. According to Mogboh and Okoye (2019), assessment offers a basis for setting educational goals and tracking and communicating learners' progress to determine the extent of learning that has occurred. Assessment task must be guided by the objectives that the teachers want to achieve to ensure learning occurs.

The continuous nature of school-based assessment (SBA) makes it a vital component of all teaching and learning strategies, as it provides learners with exposure to a variety of learning activities (Dube-Xaba, 2024). Based on the experiences of tourism learners, the conference paper by the latter author also indicated that SBA as a driver of self-regulated learning. This assessment is used by teachers throughout the academic year.

School-based assessment is implemented globally in countries and regions such as Malaysia (Fook & Sidhu, 2011; Nair, et al., 2014), Nigeria (Mkpae & Obowu-Adutchay, 2017), Asia and South Africa, where it constitutes 25% of the year end assessment in grades 10-12 (Department of Basic Education, 2011). SBA encompasses informal, formative, and formal (summative) assessment tasks that are established and evaluated by teachers (Dube-Xaba, 2024). Claassen (2025) proved that there is positive correlation between SBA and National Curriculum Statement results for Mathematics. Learners' performance has improved since the implementation of SBA.

First, with big classes, SBA can be time consuming. According to Wadesango (2021), it is possible for logical concerns, such as maintaining an attendance register, assessment, and providing frequent and detailed feedback, may become overwhelming very quickly. Many teachers may employ unproductive teaching methods, such as relying exclusively on lectures, to address these logical concerns.

In a journal article on school-based assessment among English as a Second Language (ESL) teachers in Malaysian secondary schools, Fook and Sidhu (2011) added that several individuals cited time constraints, the pressure to finish the syllabus, a heavy teaching burden, and administrative responsibilities as obstacles to utilizing SBA results to improve student learning. However, given the smartness of the smart boards, teachers may overcome such challenges. The study will reveal if the smart board can assist with SBA for big classes without hindering accurate and beneficial feedback to learners and parents.

Learning specific content or knowledge can be measured through the assessment of learners using different assessment tasks. Traditional curriculum objectives and assessment methods prioritize learners' competence in subject matter (Paige & Lloyd, 2012). Given the expanding accessibility of data and the advancing complexity of machine learning computer programs, artificial intelligence possesses the capacity to transform the techniques of learning, instruction, and evaluation of learners' advancement (Owan, et al., 2023).

The assessment of Physical Sciences is guided by the Department of Basic Education (2011, p. 143). According to the policy, assessment "is a process that measures individual learners' attainment of knowledge (content, concepts and skills) in a subject by collecting, analyzing and interpreting the data and information obtained from this process". The policy guides that learners must be assessed formally and informally.

Paige and Lloyd (2016, p. 269) discussed the use of future studies/scenarios as a pedagogical approach for science education. The latter authors defined future scenarios as "aimed at developing foresight skills" and assist in integrating learning by connecting it to their present lives and possible futures". They further explained that the building of future scenarios enhances learning, aids students in decision-making, and serves as an effective pedagogical approach to scientific education.

A practical example is global warming, which scientists have predicted and taught from grade 11 (Department of Basic Education, 2011). Learners can learn to predict the future through research and critical thinking. Learners can still argue whether what was predicted long ago about global warming was true. In addition to critical thinking, the learners can use research skills to validate global warming.

The teacher can allow learners to engage with the smart board to search more about global warming if the world is going through it, or if there is more to come. The teacher can probe further about solving the problem scientifically.

Similarly, Mellado-Moreno, Sánchez-Antolín and Blanco-García (2021, p. 172) presented "more publications on formative and summative assessment, in" a journal article on emerging trends in formative and summative student assessment in Web of Sciences. In the latter article "on formative and summative assessment," Mellado-Moreno, et al. (2021, p. 175) concluded that formative dominated summative assessment.

CONCLUSION

This last section will provide discussion of the overall coverage of the chapter and concluding remarks.

The literature outlined the benefits of ICTs and the smart board in teaching and learning. The pedagogy includes teaching techniques and assessment strategies using the smart board to enhance learners' productivity and improvement in Physical Sciences performance. Scholars have researched and presented different results on the integration of technology in the teaching and learning of science to improve learner performance. However, Physical Sciences results are still below average. Luo, Tan, He and Wu (2023) identified a gap on the usefulness of the seewo interactive whiteboard (IWB) for ESL teaching, citing the need to explore its qualitative impact.

Reducing the abstract nature of chemistry specifically and Physical Sciences more broadly may present a challenge to the successful progression of leaners through the FET band (Igboanugo, Egolum, & Igboegwu, 2021). The smartness of the smart board as presented above may assist in improving on the results of the Physical Sciences subject. Different apps or software are available withing the smart boards whereas another's available on-line for the benefit of both teachers and learners.

The researcher needs to explore the pedagogy or pedagogies that Physical Sciences teachers employ to teach content and assess the learners for a maximum output. Other pedagogies that can be intersected for teaching and learning of Physical Sciences are pedagogy and cybergogy. Literature has indicated different smart board features and apps that the teachers can employ to improve on the teaching practices or pedagogies and learning of Physical Sciences. Technology training is adequate. However, the challenge of pedagogical skills still exists. Training at higher academic institutions should include pedagogical skills for integrating technology in teaching and learning.

The study will explore these pedagogies or classroom practices including assessment strategies. In addition, the learning strategies presented in a previous chapter (Tefo & Goosen, 2024a) will be explored, as these may lead to learners' high performance for Physical Sciences using the smart board features available. This will include both the formative and summative assessment as outlined in the Physical Sciences curriculum.

REFERENCES

Adnan, K., Shaikh, F. B., Afzaal, R., Ali, A. B., & Ponnusamy, V. (2021). Identification of facilitators and barriers of ICT usage in the education sector of Pakistan: a systematic literature review. In *ICT Solutions for Improving Smart Communities in Asia* (pp. 27–53). IGI Global. DOI: 10.4018/978-1-7998-7114-9.ch002

Agyei, D. D. (2021). Integrating ICT into schools in Sub-Saharan Africa: From teachers' capacity building to classroom implementation. *Education and Information Technologies*, *26*(1), 125–144. DOI: 10.1007/s10639-020-10253-w

Akar, H. (2020). The Effect of Smart Board Use on Academic Achievement: A Meta-Analytical and Thematic Study. *International Journal of Education in Mathematics. Science and Technology*, *8*(3), 261–273.

Aktas, S., & Ayden, A. (2016). The effect of the smart board usage in science and technology lessons. *Eurasian Journal of Educational Research*, *64*(64), 125–138. DOI: 10.14689/ejer.2016.64.7

Al-Faki, I. M., & Khamis, A. H. (2014). Difficulties facing teachers in using interactive whiteboards in their classes. *American International Journal of Social Science*, *3*(2), 136–158.

Amedzo, K., & Dzansi, D. Y. (2014). Integrating ICT into rural South African schools: Possible solutions for challenges. *International Journal of Science Education*, *6*(2), 341–348.

Amiruddin, A., Fiskia Rera, B., Takbir, T., Wirawan, S., & Muhammad, H. (2023). Pedagogy-Andragogy Continuum with Cybergogy to Promote Self-Regulated Learning: A Structural Equation Model Approach. *European Journal of Educational Research*, *12*(2), 811–824. DOI: 10.12973/eu-jer.12.2.811

Ansu-Kyeremeh, E. K., & Goosen, L. (2022). Exploring the Socioeconomic Facet of Online Inclusive Education in Ghana: The Effects of Technological Advancement in Academia. In Garcia, M. (Ed.), *Socioeconomic Inclusion During an Era of Online Education* (pp. 47–66). IGI Global., DOI: 10.4018/978-1-6684-4364-4.ch003

Arek-Bawa, O., & Reddy, S. (2022). Digital curricular transformation and fourth industrial revolution 4.0 (4IR): Deepening divides or building bridges. *E-Journal of Humanities. Arts and Social Sciences*, *7*, 308–326.

Assem, H. D., Nartey, L., Appiah, E., & Aidoo, J. K. (2023). A review of students' academic performance in physics: Attitude, instructional methods, misconceptions and teachers qualification. *European Journal of Education and Pedagogy*, *4*(1), 84–92. DOI: 10.24018/ejedu.2023.4.1.551

Awang, L. A., Yusop, F. D., & Danaee, M. (2025). Current practices and future direction of artificial intelligence in mathematics education: A systematic review. *International Electronic Journal of Mathematics Education*, *20*(2), em0823. Advance online publication. DOI: 10.29333/iejme/16006

Baharuddin, F. R., & Setialaksana, W. (2023). Andragogy, Peeragogy, Heutagogy and Cybergogy Contribution on SelfRegulated Learning: A Structural Equation Model Approach. *International Journal of Instruction*, *16*(3), 551–572. DOI: 10.29333/iji.2023.16330a

Bayram-Jacobs, D., Henze, I., Evagorou, M., Shwartz, Y., Aschim, E. L., Alcaraz-Dominguez, S., Barajas, M., & Dagan, E. (2019). Science teachers' pedagogical content knowledge development during enactment of socioscientific curriculum materials. *Journal of Research in Science Teaching*, *56*(9), 1207–1233. DOI: 10.1002/tea.21550

Bilý, J., & Miština, J. (2023). Using an interactive whiteboard to increase the effectiveness of teaching at secondary schools. *Resource*, •••, 38–49. DOI: 10.53349/resource.2023.is1.a1189

Bourbour, M. (2023). Using digital technology in early education teaching: Learning from teachers' teaching practice with interactive whiteboard. *International Journal of Early Years Education*, *31*(1), 269–286. DOI: 10.1080/09669760.2020.1848523

Bulut, O., Beiting-Parrish, M., Casabianca, J. M., Slater, S. C., Jiao, H., Song, D., & Morilova, P. (2024). The Rise of Artificial Intelligence in Educational Measurement: Opportunities and Ethical Challenges. *Chinese/English Journal of Educational Measurement and Evaluation*, *5*(3). Advance online publication. DOI: 10.59863/MIQL7785

Çapuk, S. (2015). ICT Integration models into middle and high school curriculum in the USA. *Procedia: Social and Behavioral Sciences*, *191*, 1218–1224. DOI: 10.1016/j.sbspro.2015.04.409

Celik, I., Dindar, M., Muukkonen, H., & Järvelä, S. (2022). The promises and challenges of artificial intelligence for teachers: A systematic review of research. *TechTrends*, *66*(4), 616–630. DOI: 10.1007/s11528-022-00715-y

Chekour, M., Laafou, M., & Janati-Idrissi, R. (2018). What are the adequate pedagogical approaches for teaching scientific disciplines? Physics as a case study. *Journal of Educational and Social Research*, *8*(2), 141–148. DOI: 10.2478/jesr-2018-0025

Chen, X., Xie, H., Zou, D., & Hwang, G. J. (2020). Application and theory gaps during the rise of artificial intelligence in education. *Computers and Education: Artificial Intelligence*, *1*, 100002. Advance online publication. DOI: 10.1016/j.caeai.2020.100002

Chigamba, T. (2021). Exploring the pedagogical value of using Smartboards and Tablets in high school physical science classrooms. (Project: MEd course work). University of the Witwatersrand.

Chiu, T. K., Xia, Q., Zhou, X., Chai, C. S., & Cheng, M. (2023). Systematic literature review on opportunities, challenges, and future research recommendations of artificial intelligence in education. *Computers and Education: Artificial Intelligence*, *4*, 100118. Advance online publication. DOI: 10.1016/j.caeai.2022.100118

Claassen, J. (2025). *Assessing the Relationship Between School-Based Assessment and Matric Performance in Mathematics: A Quantitative Analysis of Poor Schools in Limpopo*. Stellenbosch University. Retrieved from https://resep.sun.ac.za/wp-content/uploads/2024/12/WP04_25-Assessing-the-relationship-between-school-based-assessment-and-matric-performance-Janke-Claasen.pdf

Department of Basic Education. (2011). *Curriculum and Assessment Policy Statement Physical Sciences Further Education and Training Phase Grades 10-12*. Government Printing Works.

Department of Basic Education. (2014). *Physical Sciences School-based assessment exemplars- CAPS Grade 12 Teacher Guide.* Retrieved from https://www.education.gov.za/SchoolBasedAssessment Tasks2014/tabid/611/Default.aspx

Department of Basic Education. (2024). *Naional Senior Certificate School Subject Report.* Retrieved from https://www.ecexams.co.za/2024_NSC_Exam_Results/2024 NSC School Subject Report.pdf

Department of Basic Education (DBE). (2017). *Professional development framework for digital learning*. DBE.

Department of Education. (2004, September 2). White Paper on e-Education: Transforming Learning and Teaching through Information and Communication Technologies (ICTs). *Government Gazette* (26734), pp. 3 - 46.

Depietro-Covey, K. E. (2023). *Northeast Pennsylvania Teachers' Self-Reported Adoption of Technology Integration: A Qualitative Comparative Case Study. (DEd thesis).* Northcentral University.

Dhal, S., Samantaray, S., & Satapathy, S. C. (2022, February). From chalk boards to smart boards: An integration of IoT into educational environment during Covid-19 pandemic. *Intelligent Data Engineering and Analytics: Proceedings of the 9th International Conference on Frontiers in Intelligent Computing: Theory and Applications (FICTA 2021)* (pp. 301-309). Singapore: Springer Nature.

Dlamini, R. (2022). Digital equity in schools: A multilevel analysis of in-service teachers' technological knowledge competencies. *Journal of Educational Studies*, *21*(2), 40–60.

Dube-Xaba, Z. (2024). School-Based Assessment as a Driver of Self-Regulated Learning: Experiences of Tourism Learners. *40th AAEA Conference Proceedings*, (pp. 46-60). DOI: 10.38140/obp2-2024-04

Faridi, B., & Shaheen, S. S. (2024). From chalkboards to digital boards: The evolution of educational apps in India through digital transformation. *International Journal of Multidisciplinary Trends*, *6*(9), 42–52. DOI: 10.22271/multi.2024.v6.i9a.481

Fedorov, V. A. (2021). SCIENTIFIC INFORMATION ABOUT THE INTERNATIONAL SCIENTIFIC-PRACTICAL CONFERENCE «Linguistic picture of the world under the conditions of multilingualism and multiculturalism: Translational, linguistic and didactic aspects». *Scientific Journal Modern Linguistic and Methodical-and-Didactic Researches*, (1), 94–95. DOI: 10.36622/MLMDR.2021.32.1.010

Fook, C. Y., & Sidhu, G. K. (2011). School based assessment among ESL teachers in Malaysian secondary schools. *Journal of the Malaysian Education Dean's Council*, *9*, 75–87.

Fu, J. S. (2013). Complexity of ICT in education: A critical literature review and its implications. *International Journal of Education and Development using ICT, 9*(1), 112-125.

Gadbois, S., & Haverstock, N. (2009). Using SMART Board Technology to Teach Grade 6 Science: Teachers' Experiences with and Perceptions of Its Use. In *Manitoba Education Research Network (MERN) Research Forum on Science, Mathematics, Technology, Teaching and Learning.* Winnipeg, Manitoba.

Gaynes, R. (2017). The discovery of penicillin—New insights after more than 75 years of clinical use. *Emerging Infectious Diseases*, *23*(5), 849–853. https://pmc.ncbi.nlm.nih.gov/articles/PMC5403050/. DOI: 10.3201/eid2305.161556

Gbordzekpor, S. H., Kwakye, D. O., & Aggrey, J. (2023). Multimedia Resources Available in Senior High Schools and Mathematics Teachers' Perceived Ability to use them in Teaching Due to their Gender. *Journal of Education and Teaching Methods*, *2*(1), 23–43. DOI: 10.58425/jetm.v2i1.118

Giannikas, C. N. (2021). Interactive whiteboards in EFL from the Teachers' and students' perspective. *Research Papers in Language Teaching & Learning*, *11*(1), 203–219.

González-Calatayud, V., Prendes-Espinosa, P., & Roig-Vila, R. (2021). Artificial intelligence for student assessment: A systematic review. *Applied Sciences (Basel, Switzerland)*, *11*(12), 5467. Advance online publication. DOI: 10.3390/app11125467

Goosen, L., & Koekemoer, A. (2011). Pre-Service Teachers' Attitudes Towards Effective Teaching And Meaningful Learning In Technology Education. In Mogari, D., Mji, A., & Ogbonnaya, U. I. (Eds.), *Proceedings of the ISTE International Conference* (pp. 382–394). Unisa Press., Retrieved from http://uir.unisa.ac.za/bitstream/handle/10500/22467/L.%20Goosen%20&%20%20A.%20Koekemoer.pdf?seque

Gudyanga, R. (2020). Probing physical sciences teachers' chemical laboratory safety awareness in some South African high schools. *African Journal of Research in Mathematics. Science and Technology Education*, *24*(3), 423–434.

Halagatti, M., Gadag, S., Mahantshetti, S., Hiremath, C. V., Tharkude, D., & Banakar, V. (2023). Artificial intelligence: the new tool of disruption in educational performance assessment. In *Smart analytics, artificial intelligence and sustainable performance management in a global digitalised economy* (Vol. 110, pp. 261–287). Emerald Publishing Limited., Retrieved from https://www.emerald.com/books/edited-volume/15334/chapter-abstract/86524842/Artificial-Intelligence-The-New-Tool-of-Disruption?redirectedFrom=fulltext DOI: 10.1108/S1569-37592023000110A014

Handley, H. (2023). Best practices for using online interactive whiteboards. *The journal of applied instructional design, 12*(4), 57-73.

Hussein, H. A., Ahmed, A. M., Shawkat, S. A., & Kamil, R. A. (2022, November). The effect of using smart board technology on the educational process in the colleges of education in terms of features and challenges. *AIP Conference Proceedings. 2394.* AIP Publishing LLC. DOI: 10.1063/5.0122282

Igboanugo, B. I., Egolum, E. O., & Igboegwu, E. N. (2021, November). Reducing The Abstract Nature Of Chemistry Through Science-Technology-Society Instructional Approach. *South Africa International Conference on Education Proceedings* (pp. 57-64). African Academic Research Forum.

Jammeh, A. L., Karegeya, C., & Ladage, S. (2022). The Smartboard in Chemistry Classrooms: What is Its Effect on Chemistry Teaching and Learning in Selected Topics in Grade 11? *International Journal of Learning. Teaching and Educational Research*, *21*(9), 217–231.

Jie, Z., & Sunze, Y. (2023). Investigating pedagogical challenges of mobile technology to English teaching. *Interactive Learning Environments*, *31*(5), 2767–2779. DOI: 10.1080/10494820.2021.1903933

Joshi, A. (2021). Understanding '5 Gogy': Pedagogy, Andragogy, Peeragogy, Heutagogy, and Cybergogy. *Cummins College Digest of Engineering Education*(2). Retrieved from https://cumminscollege.org/wp-content/uploads/2023/04/2.-CCDEE_Issue-2-2021.pdf#page=7

Kambala, Y. J., & Mathe, R. (2022). Importance of smart classroom: A study. *Journal of Multidisciplinary Research, 2*(1), 25–35. DOI: 10.37022/tjmdr.v1i2.280

Kennedy, I., & Cronjé, J. (2023). The dynamics of access to ICT and technology practices of secondary school teachers. *Electronic Journal of e-Learning, 21*(3), 200–210. DOI: 10.34190/ejel.21.3.2999

Khairnar, C. M. (2015). Advance pedagogy: Innovative methods of teaching and learning. *International Journal of Information and Education Technology (IJIET), 5*(11), 869–872. DOI: 10.7763/IJIET.2015.V5.629

Khlaif, Z. N., Salha, S., & Kouraichi, B. (2021). Emergency remote learning during COVID-19 crisis: Students' engagement. *Education and Information Technologies, 26*(6), 7033–7055. DOI: 10.1007/s10639-021-10566-4

Khurana, A., Gawshinde, S., & Shaheen, M. (2025). The Intersection of Neuromarketing and Ethical Consumerism in Sustainable Finance. In *Strategic Blueprints for AI-Driven Marketing in the Digital Era* (pp. 461–494). IGI Global Scientific Publishing. DOI: 10.4018/979-8-3373-3897-2.ch014

Klinck-Van der Merwe, R., & Goosen, L. (2024). A Framework for Online Learning Analytics in K-12 Classrooms as a Precursor for Personalized Learning: Emergent Practices in Schools. In *Emergent Practices of Learning Analytics in K-12 Classrooms* (pp. 115–141). IGI Global., DOI: 10.4018/979-8-3693-0066-4.ch0067

Klinck-van der Merwe, R., & Goosen, L. (2025). Artificial Intelligence Algorithms as a Precursor for Personalized Learning and Education: Real-World Applications of Innovation. In Mallik, S., Mathivanan, S., Sangeetha, S., & Soufiene, B. (Eds.), *Real-World Applications of AI Innovation* (pp. 175–198). IGI Global Scientific Publishing., DOI: 10.4018/979-8-3693-4252-7.ch009

Kundu, A., & Bej, T. (2021). Ingestion and integration of ICTs for pedagogy in Indian private schools. *E-Learning and Digital Media, 18*(2), 163–184. DOI: 10.1177/2042753020957493

Lehrer, K., Mawoyo, M., & Mbaye, S. (2017). *The impacts of interactive smartboards on learning achievement in Senegalese primary schools, 3ie Grantee Final Report.* New Delhi: International Initiative for Impact Evaluation (3ie). Retrieved from https://www.3ieimpact.org/sites/default/files/2019-01/GFR-PW2.14-NEPAD-Senegal-e-school.pdf

Lestari, D. P., Supahar, , Paidi, , Suwarjo, , & Herianto, . (2023). Effect of science virtual laboratory combination with demonstration methods on lower-secondary school students' scientific literacy ability in a science course. *Education and Information Technologies, 28*(12), 16153–16175. DOI: 10.1007/s10639-023-11857-8

Luckin, R. (2023a). The ethics of AI in education: Self-regulation, autonomy, and the human factor. *AI & Society, 38*(2), 211–228.

Luckin, R. (2023b, July 14). Yes, AI could profoundly disrupt education. But maybe that's not a bad thing. *The Guardian.* Retrieved from https://www.theguardian.com/commentisfree/2023/jul/14/ai-artificial-intelligence-disrupt-education-creativity-critical-thinking

Luckin, R., George, K., & Cukurova, M. (2022). *AI for school teachers* (2nd ed.). CRC Press. DOI: 10.1201/9781003193173

Luckin, R., Holmes, W., Griffiths, M., & Forcier, L. B. (2016). *Intelligence unleashed: An argument for AI in education*. Pearson Education.

Luckin, R., Holmes, W., Griffiths, M., & Forcier, L. B. (2023). *AI and education: Guidance for policy makers (No. 253). OECD Education Working Papers*. UNESCO.

Luo, Z., Tan, X., He, M., & Wu, X. (2023). The seewo interactive whiteboard (IWB) for ESL teaching: How useful it is? *Heliyon*, *9*(10), e20424. Advance online publication. DOI: 10.1016/j.heliyon.2023.e20424

Mateer, S. (2020). *The Effects of Graphic Novels on the Affective Domain in Elementary Boys: A Case Study of a 4th Grade Boys Book Club*. (DEd dissertation). Indiana University of Pennsylvania.

Mattar, J., Santos, C. C., & Cuque, L. M. (2022). Analysis and comparison of international digital competence frameworks for education. *Education Sciences*, *12*(12), 932. Advance online publication. DOI: 10.3390/educsci12120932

Mehboob, K., Kamran, F., & Ain, Q. U. (2024). From chalkboards to digital platforms: The impact of media on modern education. *Gomal University Journal of Research*, *40*(4), 411–424. DOI: 10.51380/gujr-40-04-02

Mellado-Moreno, P. C., Sánchez-Antolín, P., & Blanco-García, M. (2021). Trends in formative and summative student assessment in Web of Sciences. *Alteridad*, *16*(2), 166–179.

Min, K., & Siegel, C. (2011). Integration of SMART board technology and effective teaching. *Imanager's Journal on School Educational Technology*, *7*(1), 38–47. DOI: 10.26634/jsch.7.1.1518

Mishra, P., & Koehler, M. J. (2006). Technology pedagogical content knowledge: A framework for teacher knowledge. *Teachers College Record*, *108*(6), 1017–1054. DOI: 10.1111/j.1467-9620.2006.00684.x

Mkpae, S. G., & Obowu-Adutchay, V. (2017). School-based assessment: Benefit and teachers' perception in Nigerian secondary schools. *International Journal of Education and Evaluation*, *3*(2), 19–27.

Mogboh, V. E., & Okoye, A. C. (2019). Formative and summative assessment: Trends and practices in basic education. *Journal of Education and Practice*, *10*(27), 39–45.

Mohan, R. (2023). *Measurement, evaluation and assessment in education*. PHI Learning Pvt. Ltd.

Molotsi, A. R. (2014, November). *Secondary-school teachers' information communication technology competencies in classroom practices*. Pretoria: University of South Africa. Retrieved from http://hdl.handle.net/10500/18586

Moosa, S., & Ramnarain, U. (2023, July). The impact of an empowerment evaluation professional development program on physical sciences teachers' attitudes, beliefs and behavioral intentions to integrate ICT into their science lessons. *Frontiers in Education*, *8*, 1159373. Advance online publication. DOI: 10.3389/feduc.2023.1159373

Msafiri, M. M., Kangwa, D., & Cai, L. (2023). A systematic literature review of ICT integration in secondary education: What works, what does not, and what next? *Discover Education*, *2*(44), 44. Advance online publication. DOI: 10.1007/s44217-023-00070-x

Mzekandaba, S. (2016, July 14). *Gauteng gets more tech into classrooms*. Retrieved November 22, 2022, from ITWeb: https://www.itweb.co.za/content/okYbe97XVlRqAWpG

Nair, G. K., Setia, R., Samad, N. Z., Zahri, R. N., Luqman, A., Vadeveloo, T., & Ngah, H. C. (2014). Teachers' knowledge and issues in the implementation of school-based assessment: A case of schools in Terengganu. *Asian Social Science*, *10*(3), 186–194.

Nancy, W., Parimala, A., & Livingston, L. M. (2020). Advanced teaching pedagogy as innovative approach in modern education system. *Procedia Computer Science*, *172*, 382–388. DOI: 10.1016/j.procs.2020.05.059

Ndwandwe, K. P., Ramaligela, S. M., & Mtshali, T. I. (2024). The effectiveness of smartboards in enhancing technology teachers' creativity. *African Perspectives of Research in Teaching and Learning*, *8*(1), 1-9. Retrieved from https://search.proquest.com/openview/23f638fecb3234a7a0c6df7f7ee5a357/1?pq-origsite=gscholar&cbl=5126680

Noothigattu, R., Bouneffouf, D., Mattei, N., Chandra, R., Madan, P., Varshney, K. R., Campbell, M., Singh, M., & Rossi, F. (2019). Teaching AI agents ethical values using reinforcement learning and policy orchestration. *IBM Journal of Research and Development*, *63*(4/5), 2:1–2:9. https://www.cs.cmu.edu/~rnoothig/papers/policy_orchestration.pdf. DOI: 10.1147/JRD.2019.2940428

Nuci, K. P., Tahir, R., Wang, A. I., & Imran, A. S. (2021). Game-based digital quiz as a tool for improving students' engagement and learning in online lectures. *IEEE Access : Practical Innovations, Open Solutions*, *9*, 91220–91234. DOI: 10.1109/ACCESS.2021.3088583

Obaid, S. (2022). The effect of smart board on students' engagement in English. *International Journal of Research in Social Sciences & Humanities*, *12*(3), 52–64. DOI: 10.37648/ijrssh.v12i03.004

Ogegbo, A. A., & Ramnarain, U. (2022, August 6). Teaching and learning Physics using interactive simulation: A guided inquiry practice. *South African Journal of Education*, *42*(1), 1997. Advance online publication. DOI: 10.15700/saje.v42n1a1997

Olojo, O. J., Akinwumi, I. O., & Olofin, S. O. (2022). Comparative analysis of secondary school students' performance in science subjects in Ekiti State, Nigeria. *Brock Journal of Education*, *10*(3), 73–84. DOI: 10.37745/bje.2013/vol10no3pp.73-84

Organisation for Economic Co-operation and Development (OECD). (2023). Opportunities, Guidelines and Guardrails for Effective and Equitable Use of AI in Education. In *OECD Digital Education Outlook 2023: Towards an Effective Digital Education Ecosystem*. OECD Publishing., DOI: 10.1787/2b39e98b-

Owan, V. J., Abang, K. B., Idika, D. O., Etta, E. O., & Bassey, B. A. (2023). Exploring the potential of artificial intelligence tools in educational measurement and assessment. *Eurasia Journal of Mathematics, Science and Technology Education*, *19*(8), em2307. Advance online publication. DOI: 10.29333/ejmste/13428

Paige, K., & Lloyd, D. (2012). Pedagogical Practices and Science Learning with a Focus on Educating for Sustainability for Pre-service Primary and Middle Years Educators. In Tan, K., & Kim, M. (Eds.), *Issues and Challenges in Science Education Research* (pp. 191–207). Springer., DOI: 10.1007/978-94-007-3980-2_13

Paige, K., & Lloyd, D. (2016). Use of future scenarios as a pedagogical approach for science teacher education. *Research in Science Education, 46*(2), 263–285. DOI: 10.1007/s11165-015-9505-7

Palanisamy, P. (2018). *Hands-On Intelligent Agents with OpenAI Gym: Your guide to developing AI agents using deep reinforcement learning.* Packt Publishing Ltd. Retrieved from https://dl.acm.org/doi/abs/10.5555/3285236

Pedersen, I., & Duin, A. (2022). AI agents, humans and untangling the marketing of artificial intelligence in learning environments. *55th Annual Hawaii International Conference on System Sciences (HICSS)* (pp. 4-13). IEEE Computer Society. DOI: 10.24251/HICSS.2022.002

Petrus, I. (2019). SMITHGROUP-AI: THE FUTURE OF BUILDING CONTROLS: SMITHGROUP-AI would be an independent, multifunctional reinforcement learning software agent responsible for the monitoring and control of all agents that control all building systems. *Engineered Systems, 36*(4), 32-36. Retrieved from https://go.gale.com/ps/i.do?id=GALE%7CA584177473&sid=googleScholar&v=2.1&it=r&linkaccess=abs&issn=08919976&p=AONE&sw=w

Ponnusamy, P., Ghias, A., Yi, Y., Yao, B., Guo, C., & Sarikaya, R. (2022). Feedback-based self-learning in large-scale conversational ai agents. *AI Magazine, 42*(4), 43–56. DOI: 10.1609/aimag.v42i4.15102

Preetha, B., Venkataraman, G., Hariharan, G. N., & Prabavathy, V. R. (2022). The "Every Child A Scientist" program: Using digital technologies to enhance science learning among middle grade students from corporation schools in Chennai. *CSI Transactions on ICT, 10*(3), 237–244. DOI: 10.1007/s40012-022-00368-5

Qureshi, F., Khan, M., Jabeen, S., & Shah, S. (2025). Exploring blockchain transaction patterns using graph-based visualization. In *Cybersecurity, Cybercrimes, and Smart Emerging Technologies* (pp. 155-166). CRC Press. Retrieved from https://www.taylorfrancis.com/chapters/edit/10.1201/9781003614197-16/exploring-blockchain-transaction-patterns-using-graph-based-visualization-fahad-qureshi-maqbool-khan-saima-jabeen-sajid-shah

Rahayu, M. A., & Makmur, A. (2024). The effectiveness of using smartboard interactive toward learning innovation in schools. *JIV-Jurnal Ilmiah Visi, 19*(1), 23–31. DOI: 10.21009/JIV.1901.3

Rahimi, A. R., & Tafazoli, D. (2022). The role of university teachers' 21st-century digital competence in their attitudes toward ICT integration in higher education: Extending the theory of planned behavior. *The JALT CALL Journal, 18*(2), 238–263. DOI: 10.29140/jaltcall.v18n2.632

Ramsden, P. (2019). *Successful Teaching and Learning in Grade 10 - 12 Subjects.* Department of Basic Education. Retrieved from https://www.eccurriculum.co.za/Circulars/2022-Circulars/04%20FET%20%20Successful%20Teaching%20and%20Learning%20Framework-2019%20FINAL%20DOCUMENT.pdf

Raza, A., Ahmed, U., Saleem, K., Sarwar, M., Shaheen, M., & Farooq, M. S. (2025). Employing Natural Language Processing Techniques for the Development of a Voting-Based POS Tagger in the Urdu Language. In *Innovations in Optimization and Machine Learning* (pp. 23–46). IGI Global Scientific Publishing. DOI: 10.4018/979-8-3693-5231-1.ch002

Singh, S., Pandey, J. K., Rai, M., & Saxena, A. K. (2024). Advancements in Facial Expression Recognition Using Machine and Deep Learning Techniques. In *Machine and Deep Learning Techniques for Emotion Detection* (pp. 149–166). IGI Global. DOI: 10.4018/979-8-3693-4143-8.ch007

SMART Technologies ULC. (2025). *SMART Support*. Retrieved from How can we help you?: https://support.smarttech.com/

Spinelli, C. G. (2008). Introduction: The benefits, uses, and practical application of informal assessment procedures. *Reading & Writing Quarterly*, *24*(1), 1–6. DOI: 10.1080/10573560701753005

Staberg, R. L., Febri, M. I., Gjøvik, Ø., Sikko, S. A., & Pepin, B. (2023). Science teachers' interactions with resources for formative assessment purposes. *Educational Assessment, Evaluation and Accountability*, *35*(1), 5–35. DOI: 10.1007/s11092-022-09401-2

Tahir, M., Hassan, F. D., & Shagoo, M. R. (2024). Role of artificial intelligence in education: A conceptual review. *World Journal of Advanced Research and Reviews*, *22*(1), 1469–1475. DOI: 10.30574/wjarr.2024.22.1.1217

Tal, M., Herscovitz, O., & Dori, Y. J. (2021). Assessing teachers' knowledge: Incorporating context-based learning in chemistry. *Chemistry Education Research and Practice*, *22*(4), 1003–1019. DOI: 10.1039/D0RP00359J

Tandon, N., & Shaheen, M. (2024). AI-driven innovations for environmental sustainability across sectors. In *Maintaining a sustainable world in the nexus of environmental science and AI* (pp. 429–454). IGI Global. DOI: 10.4018/979-8-3693-6336-2.ch017

Tang, K. H. (2024). Implications of artificial intelligence for teaching and learning. *Acta Pedagogia Asiana*, *3*(2), 65–79. DOI: 10.53623/apga.v3i2.404

Tashtoush, M. A., Wardat, Y., Ali, R. A., & Saleh, S. (2024). Artificial intelligence in education: Mathematics teachers' perspectives, practices and challenges. *Iraqi Journal for Computer Science and Mathematics*, *5*(1). Advance online publication. DOI: 10.52866/ijcsm.2024.05.01.004

Teane, F. M. (2024). Technological literacy and its influence on teachers' adoption of a blended learning approach. *Reading & Writing-Journal of the Reading Association of South Africa, 15*(1). Retrieved from https://hdl.handle.net/10520/ejc-reading_v15_n1_a426

Tefo, R. M. (2021). *The influence of smartboards on the teaching and learning of grade 12 Physical Sciences in Tshwane District*. University of South Africa.

Tefo, R. M., & Goosen, L. (2024a). Fostering Pedagogical Innovation Through the Effective Smartboard Instruction of Physical Sciences: Technologies in Gauteng Schools, South Africa. In Khaldi, M. (Ed.), *Fostering Pedagogical Innovation Through Effective Instructional Design* (pp. 287–307). IGI Global., DOI: 10.4018/979-8-3693-1206-3.ch013

Tefo, R. M., & Goosen, L. (2024b). Exploring Transdisciplinary Approaches to Teaching Physical Sciences in Gauteng, South Africa: The Pedagogy of Using Smartboard Technologies. In R. Kumar, E. Ong, S. Anggoro, & T. Toh (Eds.), *Transdisciplinary Approaches to Learning Outcomes in Higher Education* (pp. 327-346). IGI Global. DOI: 10.4018/979-8-3693-3699-1.ch010

Tenzin, S., Tendar, P., & Zangmo, N. (2022). Enhancing Students' Understanding of Abstract Concepts in Physics by Integrating ICT in Teaching-Learning Process. *Asian Journal of Education and Social Studies*, *26*, 68–80. DOI: 10.9734/ajess/2022/v26i230624

Tigere, M. T., & Netshitangani, T. (2022). School management teams' perceptions of ICT integration in township and rural secondary schools of KwaZulu-Natal, South Africa: Infrastructure challenges. *Gender & Behaviour*, *20*(3), 20022–20041.

Triantafyllou, S. A., & Sapounidis, T. (2023, March). Game-based Learning approach and Serious Games to learn while you play. *World Engineering Education Conference (EDUNINE)* (pp. 1-6). IEEE. DOI: 10.1109/EDUNINE57531.2023.10102872

Tsakeni, M. (2023). Primary preservice science teachers' perceptions of practical work in remote learning environments. *Journal of Curriculum Studies Research*, *5*(1), 44–62. DOI: 10.46303/jcsr.2023.5

Tsayang, G., Batane, T., & Majuta, A. (2020). The Impact of Interactive Smart Boards on Students' Learning in Secondary Schools in Botswana: A Students' Perspective. *International Journal of Education and Development Using Information and Communication Technology*, *16*(2), 22–39.

Tumanggor, A. M., & Supahar, S. (2020). The development of diagnostic test instrument for mathematical representation ability (PhysDTRA) in high school physics learning. *Journal for the Education of Gifted Young Scientists*, *8*(4), 1439–1455. DOI: 10.17478/jegys.777425

UNESCO. (2023a, July). *Generative AI and the future of education*. Retrieved from https://unesdoc.unesco.org/ark:/48223/pf0000385877

UNESCO. (2023b, September 6). *UNESCO survey: Less than 10% of schools and universities have formal guidance on AI*. Retrieved from https://www.unesco.org/en/articles/unesco-survey-less-10-schools-and-universities-have-formal-guidance-ai

UNESCO. (2023c, September 8). *Guidance for generative AI in education and research*. Retrieved from https://unesdoc.unesco.org/ark:/48223/pf0000386693

UNESCO. (2023d, November 30). *How generative AI is reshaping education in Asia-Pacific*. Retrieved from https://www.unesco.org/en/articles/how-generative-ai-reshaping-education-asia-pacific

UNESCO. (2024, April). *Draft AI competency frameworks for teachers and for school students*. Retrieved from https://www.unesco.org/sites/default/files/medias/fichiers/2024/04/UNESCO-Draft-AI-competency-frameworks-for-teachers-and-school-students.pdf

Usak, M., Ozden, M., & Eilks, I. (2011). A case study of beginning science teachers' subject matter (SMK) and pedagogical content knowledge (PCK) of teaching chemical reaction in Turkey. *European Journal of Teacher Education*, *34*(4), 407–429. DOI: 10.1080/02619768.2011.592977

Uunona, G. N., & Goosen, L. (2023). Leveraging Ethical Standards in Artificial Intelligence Technologies: A Guideline for Responsible Teaching and Learning Applications. In Garcia, M., Lopez Cabrera, M., & de Almeida, R. (Eds.), *Handbook of Research on Instructional Technologies in Health Education and Allied Disciplines* (pp. 310–330). IGI Global., DOI: 10.4018/978-1-6684-7164-7.ch014

Uunona, G. N., & Goosen, L. (2024). Leveraging Ethics in Artificial Intelligence Technologies and Applications: E-Learning Management Systems in Namibia. In Ortiz-Rodriguez, F., Leyva-Mederos, A., Tiwari, S., Hernandez-Quintana, A., & Martinez-Rodriguez, J. (Eds.), *Semantic Web Technologies and Applications in Artificial Intelligence of Things* (pp. 173–185). IGI Global., DOI: 10.4018/979-8-3693-1487-6.ch008

Uunona, G. N., & Goosen, L. (2025a). Leveraging Ethics for Supporting Students' Artificial Intelligence Skills Development in Namibia. In Khaldi, M. (Ed.), *Supporting Personalized Learning and Students' Skill Development With AI* (pp. 203–230). IGI Global. DOI: 10.4018/979-8-3693-8965-2.ch011

Uunona, G. N., & Goosen, L. (2025b). Navigating Ethical Consideration of Artificial Intelligence and the Metaverse in Scientific Research. In Al Aqad, M., Sorayyaei Azar, A., Albattat, A., & Singh, A. (Eds.), *Navigating AI and the Metaverse in Scientific Research* (pp. 213–236). IGI Global Scientific Publishing., DOI: 10.4018/979-8-3373-0340-6.ch011

Wadesango, N. (2021). Challenges of teaching large classes. *African Perspectives of Research in Teaching and Learning*, *5*(2), 127–135.

Webb, C., Luckin, R., & Ecoff, E. (2023). Ethical principles for the development and application of artificial intelligence in K-12 education. In *International Handbook on Education Development in the Asia-Pacific* (pp. 2501–2519). Springer Nature Singapore. DOI: 10.1007/978-981-19-6887-7_120

Wu, J. X., Wu, Y., Chen, K. Y., & Hua, L. (2023). Building socially intelligent AI systems: Evidence from the trust game using artificial agents with deep learning. *Management Science*, *69*(12), 7236–7252. DOI: 10.1287/mnsc.2023.4782

Xia, Y., Shin, S. Y., & Lee, H. A. (2024). Adaptive learning in AI agents for the metaverse: The ALMAA framework. *Applied Sciences (Basel, Switzerland)*, *14*(23), 11410. Advance online publication. DOI: 10.3390/app142311410

Yang, W., Li, H., & Lee, J. C. (2025). Tailoring AI agents for early learning: The creative project approach. *Computers and Education: Artificial Intelligence*, *9*, 100473. Advance online publication. DOI: 10.1016/j.caeai.2025.100473

Yung, B. H. (2012). Issues and Challenges in School-Based Assessment of Science Practical Work. In Tan, K., & Kim, M. (Eds.), *Issues and Challenges in Science Education Research*. Springer., DOI: 10.1007/978-94-007-3980-2_9

Zenda, R. (2024). The importance of teaching resources on physical sciences learners' academic achievement in rural schools: A case of South Africa. *Social Education Research*, *5*(2), 407–420. DOI: 10.37256/ser.5220244624

Zhao, C. (2024). AI-assisted assessment in higher education: A systematic review. *Journal of Educational Technology and Innovation*, *6*(4). Advance online publication. DOI: 10.61414/jeti.v6i4.209

Chapter 6
AI-Enhanced Curriculum Design and Assessment

Daniel Amoah-Oppong
http://orcid.org/0009-0006-1284-3058
University of Cape Coast, Ghana

ABSTRACT

This chapter argues that artificial intelligence (AI) offers a revolutionary opportunity to rethink outdated, standardised educational models as responsive, dynamic systems. Building on rethought pedagogy theories such as constructivism and cognitive learning, AI promises to enable the shift from static learning pathways to dynamic mapping and learning pathways. This chapter explores the development of AI-enhanced assessment and highlights how it has evolved from a summative process to an ongoing, more formative one using simulations and predictive analysis. Implementation requires a phased framework, significant teacher training for new facilitative roles, and strong ethical governance to address issues like algorithmic bias and data privacy. Global case studies from Singapore, Australia, and Europe show how deliberate cooperation between people and artificial intelligence can bring real benefits and opportunities for more inclusive and equitable education.

INTRODUCTION

The educational system of the 20th century, defined by standardised curricula and reliance on summative assessments, is now facing serious problems as the 21st century begins. This conventional, one-size-fits-all approach often overlooks important elements such as neurodiversity, the diversity of cultural backgrounds, and the different learning speeds of students. There is a clear need for change, as it is estimated that 20% of students in traditional classroom settings are either persistently disengaged or perform below expectations. In this context, artificial intelligence (AI) is emerging as a disruptive force that opens the door to a break from the rigid standardisation frameworks. But the dominant narrative often oversimplifies the function of AI by portraying it as a highly efficient tool to deliver a predetermined curriculum. This chapter presents a more radical and innovative proposition: to view AI as an active participant in co-creating curricula. The learning paths in this model are dynamically co-created

DOI: 10.4018/979-8-3373-7225-9.ch006

in real time by means of continuous communication between the learner, the teacher, and the artificial intelligence system. They are also continuously adapted to meet the individual needs of each student.

Moreover, assessment practices are undergoing a radical transformation, evolving into a continuous feedback mechanism, similar to cognitive learning. AI serves as a support framework for this approach, providing the kind of personalised guidance that was once only possible through individualised mentoring rather than the issuing of final assessments. Educational researchers have highlighted the paradox of personalisation, underlining the urgent need for such a shift. It illustrates the tension between the need for an individualised learning experience and the constraints faced by educational institutions with limited resources. By enabling the scalability of personalisation through artificial intelligence, we can effectively navigate this paradox. Jill Watson at the Georgia Institute of Technology is a notable example, managing about 10,000 student surveys a semester with a remarkable 97% accuracy. In addition to increasing operational efficiency, this has freed up human teaching assistants to focus on more complex pedagogical tasks. In the end, this shift represents a fundamental rethink of the relationships and processes in education, promoting a more responsive and inclusive learning environment that meets the diverse needs of all learners.

When citing operational results, please either (a) quote a publicly available evaluation or (b) transparently indicate that the data are derived from internal or pilot evaluations. For example, the MOE reports and local case studies indicate that in some deployments, the GAI Jill Watson FAQ has achieved a high level of agreement with the human graders in her pilot deployment (Goel & Polepeddi, 2018), where the internal pilot metrics are presented here; it is explicitly noted that these figures are based on unpublished internal evaluations. It is crucial to note that operational claims, such as those regarding Jill Watson's 97% accuracy, are often based on internal or pilot evaluations (Goel & Polepeddi, 2018), underscoring the need for transparent reporting and further peer-reviewed study.

Interoperability explains how the curriculum and assessment outputs can move across tools and platforms without loss of structure or meaning. In this study, it matters because AI outputs often need to be deployed in learning management systems and assessment tools, then exported for moderation and reporting. To reduce platform lock-in, the chapter treats interoperability as a design constraint, not an afterthought. Appendix A lists the relevant standards and the specific mappings used in this project, including how content, assessment items, and learner records are packaged and exchanged.

THEORETICAL FRAMEWORK

The AI-enhanced curriculum design draws on several established teaching theories, reinterpreted by the technological possibilities. Constructivist learning theory provides a theoretical foundation and highlights how learners actively build knowledge through experience and reflection, a process that AI systems can support by personalised learning experiences and adaptive scaffolding. Similarly, situated learning theory informs the development of AI-powered self-evaluation that contextualises learning in real-world scenarios and applications. The theoretical framework also incorporates elements of adaptive learning theory and personalised learning models, which exploit AI's ability to analyse large datasets and identify patterns beyond human perception. These theoretical foundations support the development of dynamic learning structures that can evolve on the basis of continuous feedback loops between student performance, content efficiency, and changing learning needs. In addition, the Framework recognises the importance of the principles of connective learning in the design of curricula that prepare students for knowledge ecosystems in which AI tools are constant companions and cognitive partners.

A strong theoretical foundation for comprehending AI's transformative potential in curriculum design is offered by the notion of cognitive apprenticeship, which was initially proposed by Collins, Brown, and Newman. While cognitive apprenticeship expands on the traditional apprenticeship model, which emphasises learning through supervised experience in real-world settings, it also makes the unconscious processes of expert thought visible. By using three complementary capabilities, AI systems operationalise this framework: (1) using metacognitive modelling to make expert thinking visible, (2) offering scaffolded practice through adaptive challenges, and (3) allowing support to gradually decrease as learner competency rises.

Technological Pedagogical Content Knowledge (TPACK)

TPACK explains the knowledge teachers need to use technology without weakening subject content or good teaching. It treats technology, pedagogy, and content as interdependent. In this chapter, TPACK guides how the AI tool is selected and how it is used during curriculum design. The tool is treated as a support, not as the designer. Teacher judgement stays central during planning and assessment. This means every AI use must be defended by the learning outcomes and the content demands. It must not be defended by novelty. TPACK also practically fits the workflow. In curriculum design, you begin with learning outcomes. You then select the content that fits those outcomes. You choose the teaching approach that best supports that content. Only after those steps do you select AI functions that can support the choices you have already made. In assessment design, you set the assessment tasks first. You then use AI to generate options, check alignment, and support feedback. Teacher control is maintained at each step. For quality control, teacher review and moderation function as the decision gate. Nothing is adopted until it passes that gate.

Bloom's Digital Taxonomy

Bloom's Digital Taxonomy extends Bloom's revised cognitive levels by linking them to common digital actions. Examples include searching, tagging, blogging, remixing, and publishing. In this chapter it gives a clear path from learning outcomes to digital learning tasks. It also helps you justify why a specific AI-supported activity belongs to a particular cognitive level. This supports stronger alignment between outcomes, learning activities, and assessment. It is especially useful when tasks are digital by design. Bloom's Digital Taxonomy also maps cleanly onto the workflow. In curriculum design, you first assign each outcome to a Bloom level. You then choose digital tasks that match that level. In the assessment workflow, you align the rubric to the same level. After that, you can use AI to propose assessment items or feedback prompts that match the intended demand. Progression is then made visible across the unit or term. Learners move from lower-order work to higher-order work in a planned sequence, rather than by accident.

Table 1. Cognitive apprenticeship methods enhanced by AI

Traditional Method	AI Enhancement	Example Applications
Modeling	AI demonstrates expert problem-solving processes with think-aloud protocols.	Carnegie Learning's MATHia shows step-by-step mathematical reasoning.
Coaching	AI provides real-time feedback and hints during task performance	Cognii's Virtual Learning Assistant offers immediate feedback on open-ended responses
Scaffolding	AI structures learning tasks based on the individual's zone of proximal development	Smart Sparrow adapts lesson difficulty based on continuous performance data.
Articulation	AI prompts learners to explain their reasoning and problem-solving strategies.	Platforms like DreamBox require students to articulate their mathematical thinking.
Reflection	AI facilitates comparison between student and expert problem-solving approaches.	WriteLab compares student writing patterns with exemplary texts.
Exploration	AI encourages autonomous problem-solving within gradually expanding domains.	Labster's virtual labs allow students to design their own experiments.

Situated learning theory argues that knowledge develops through real contexts and real activity. The passage says AI can support this by building realistic simulations that let learners practise authentic tasks in a safe space, while adjusting the path to each learner. It gives an example from medical education using Labster, and it reports a large gain in retention compared with textbook learning. The passage also says AI-driven education tools fall into three main design families: rule-based intelligent tutoring systems, adaptive testing models that select items to measure hidden abilities, and analytics dashboards. Reviews suggest that these families show mixed evidence, and none has clearly led to both consistent teaching value and strong evaluation. The chapter's position is a hybrid approach that combines competence mapping with human-in-the-loop teacher moderation, aiming to keep models explicit and flexible while staying interpretable and auditable for teachers.

AI Agents in Curriculum and Assessment

AI agents are goal-directed software components that perceive a learning context, plan actions, and execute them through tools or APIs. In education, an agent is usually embedded in a learning management system or an assessment platform and can coordinate tasks across curriculum design, learning activities, and feedback cycles. This differs from a single turn chatbot. A chatbot primarily responds to prompts, whereas an agent can run multi-step workflows, call services, and update records, with clear objectives (Russell & Norvig, 2020). Because agent actions can affect grades and learning opportunities, agent use should be treated as decision support rather than an autonomous authority (Ninaus & Sailer, 2022).

Three practical agent roles fit this chapter's model. First, a curriculum mapping agent builds and maintains a competency map by aligning standards, learning materials, and task rubrics, then flags gaps or overlaps for teacher review (Banihashem et al., 2022). Second, a feedback agent drafts rubric-linked comments and suggests next-step practice, while marking uncertainty and routing borderline cases to the teacher for moderation (Amershi et al., 2019). Third, an early-warning agent monitors engagement and performance signals to flag learners who may need support, but it should trigger human outreach rather than automated penalties (Almalawi et al., 2024).

Guardrails should be explicit and operational. High-stakes outputs, such as final grades, progression decisions, and disciplinary flags, should require human approval and a documented reason for any override. Systems should keep audit logs that record the data used, model version, prompts, and human edits, so decisions can be traced and reviewed (Raji et al., 2020). A clear appeals pathway is also needed, including a second-marking option and time-bound responses. Regular bias audits should test performance across relevant groups and contexts, supported by dataset documentation and monitoring for drift (Gebru et al., 2021). At a minimum, schools should align these controls with published guidance on privacy, transparency, and learner rights (UNESCO, 2023).

Figure 1.

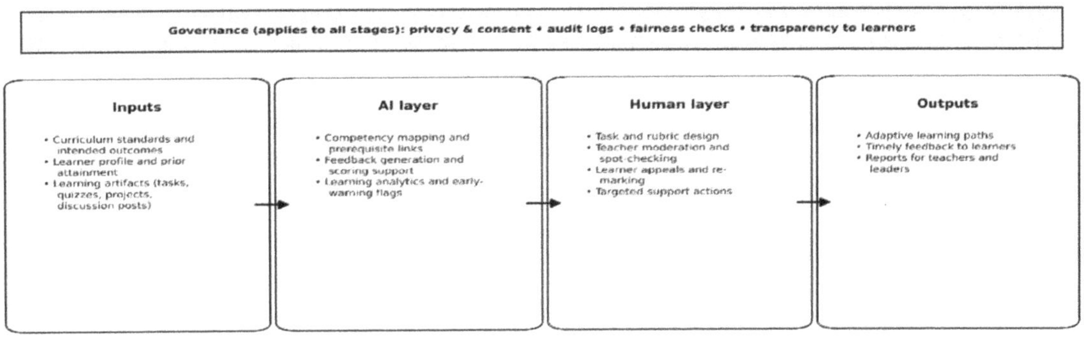

AI-Enhanced Curriculum Design

AI-enhanced curriculum design involves using artificial intelligence tools to plan, organise, and improve educational programmes beyond traditional manual methods. AI systems analyse vast learning data to detect patterns, identify knowledge gaps, and recommend personalised learning paths, rather than relying on teachers' intuition or experience. This enables the creation of adaptable curricula that evolve with changing knowledge demands, accommodate diverse learning speeds, and respond to students' needs. In essence, AI transforms curriculum design from a fixed, one-size-fits-all model into a dynamic, data-driven system that continuously evolves. Unlike traditional models with predetermined objectives and sequences, AI-driven design employs dynamic knowledge mapping, a living network of interconnected concepts and skills that adjusts to each learner's interactions, recognising learning as non-linear, contextual, and individual.

Competency Mapping and Prerequisite Analysis. By using machine learning algorithms and natural language processing, advanced AI systems can deconstruct learning domains into granular competencies and identify multiple valid pathways through interconnected knowledge networks. The University of Sydney, for example, uses the Smart Sparrow platform to map approximately 2,000 distinct competencies in introductory science courses, identifying 17 different validated pathways through what was previously taught as a linear sequence. This multi-path curriculum structure acknowledges that while all students must master essential competencies, the sequence in which they do so can vary substantially based on their learning preferences, interests, and prior knowledge. This is demonstrated in practice by Disco AI's system, which trains its AI with a specific knowledge base to create curriculum structures that adapt not only to performance data but also to emerging interests and questions that arise during the learning process. This creates what might be referred to as an emergent curriculum, one that evolves through dialogue between AI's capacity to identify meaningful connections across knowledge domains, pedagogical expertise, and student curiosity.

Real-Time Curriculum Adaptation. The ability to adapt in real time based on ongoing analysis of student interactions is a cornerstone development AI offers to curriculum design. The actual learning pathway is modified by next-generation AI curricula, which introduce alternative representations, complementary concepts, or interdisciplinary connections based on emerging patterns in student engagement and comprehension. This is in contrast to traditional adaptive learning systems, which primarily adjust content difficulty. For instance, the Maths Pathway program, which used machine learning to customise mathematics instruction to each student's learning style and pace, was put into place at Australia's New Town High School. The school reported that after a year of implementation, the number of students reaching proficiency benchmarks increased by 47%, and the achievement gaps between demographic groups decreased by 32%. Similarly, the Harris Federation in the UK used ChatGPT and other AI tools to modify textual materials for various age groups and linguistic backgrounds. This improved accessibility for English language learners while cutting down on teacher preparation time by about five hours per week.

Ethical Curriculum Design. Significant ethical issues are raised by the use of AI in curriculum design, especially in light of the perpetuation of biases through algorithms and training data. AI systems may unintentionally favour some modes of knowing while marginalising others if they are primarily trained on Western educational resources or evaluation methodologies. Early automated essay scoring systems, for instance, showed prejudice against students from different cultural backgrounds and non-native English speakers. Using diverse and representative training datasets, conducting frequent algorithmic audits for bias detection, retaining human oversight for curriculum validation, and explicitly integrating multicultural and anti-bias viewpoints into the AI's design parameters are just a few of the intentional ethical design practices needed to address these issues. This method was first used by the Singapore Ministry of Education's automated English marking systems, which include explicit cultural sensitivity training in their algorithms and are subject to quarterly bias audits.

AI supports curriculum design in four main ways. First, it provides data-driven insights by analysing large sets of learner data, such as test scores, attendance, and online activity, to detect persistent learning gaps, then suggesting where the curriculum should add time or different supports (for example, more focus on geometry with simulations). Second, it enables personalisation by recommending resources and tasks matched to learners' pace and ability, so advanced students get more demanding work while struggling students receive scaffolded support. Third, AI improves efficiency by generating draft lesson sequences, activities, and assessments aligned to curriculum standards, reducing teachers' planning time so they can focus on refining content and supporting learners. Fourth, it increases adaptability by allowing curricula to be updated more quickly when new knowledge or social needs emerge, such as adding recent climate science developments to environmental modules instead of waiting for long curriculum review cycles.

AI-Enhanced Assessment

AI-enhanced assessment uses AI to design, deliver, score, and analyse student evaluations. It moves assessment beyond occasional tests and manual marking by enabling continuous monitoring, adaptive testing, and rapid feedback. This shifts assessment into an ongoing cycle that guides teaching and supports learning, similar to a cognitive apprenticeship and the idea of assessment for learning rather than assessment of learning. Even with these benefits, AI-based assessment must still meet core measurement standards such as validity, reliability, and consequential validity. It can strengthen validity through frequent, detailed feedback, but it can also introduce bias and irrelevant variance, so safeguards are needed. Strong formative systems should align AI outputs to clear competency constructs, combine automated and human scoring with transparent reliability checks, and produce regular validation reports that link results to real-world performance. The passage then frames adaptive learning systems as a mix of AI, analytics, and cognitive science, with four main design traditions: rule-based tutors, psychometric item-response systems, analytics dashboards, and LLM-based tutoring agents. The chapter argues for a hybrid model that uses competency dependency mapping (DAG) plus human-in-the-loop moderation, keeping adaptation interpretable, ethical, and guided by teacher judgement.

Formative Feedback Systems. Formative assessment driven by AI offers timely, targeted, and actionable feedback at scale, addressing the feedback gap, one of education's most enduring problems. Research indicates feedback is most effective when provided within 24 hours, yet human graders often take weeks to return comments on complex assignments. Compared to human graders, AI systems such as Cognii's Virtual Learning Assistant cut this feedback cycle to seconds while retaining 96% accuracy. In a similar vein, Coursera's AI grading system improves course completion rates by 16% while evaluating assignments 900 times faster than human counterparts. These systems are especially good at evaluating higher-order cognitive abilities that go beyond simple fact recall. AI systems can now assess scientific reasoning, for instance, by examining how students plan experiments, analyse data, and support conclusions in virtual lab settings. In order to provide feedback on strategy selection and implementation, the University of Alicante created an AI application that evaluates problem-solving processes rather than just final answers.

Predictive Analytics and Early Intervention. Predictive analytics is used by AI assessment systems to identify students at risk of academic difficulty long before traditional assessment methods would detect problems. By analysing patterns in engagement, performance, and even linguistic cues in discussion forums, these systems increase their accuracy in forecasting learning trajectories. The Georgia Institute of Technology, for instance, developed predictive models that identify students at risk of failing with 85% accuracy by the fourth week of the semester, which is early enough for effective interventions. Preemptive scaffolding, or the provision of support resources before students experience explicit failure, is made possible by these predictive capabilities. A fundamental shift from reactive to proactive educational support is represented by this strategy, which may reduce dropout rates and improve equity outcomes. Initial implementations at scale have demonstrated that when AI-driven early warning systems are combined with appropriate interventions, course failure rates have decreased by about 15%.

Authentic Assessment in Simulated Environments. Artificial intelligence enables authentic assessment by creating simulated environments that replicate real-world scenarios. These include virtual labs for science experiments and business simulations for entrepreneurship training. For example, Labster's virtual labs let students conduct complex or risky experiments safely while AI evaluates their entire process, from hypothesis to data analysis. Studies show students achieve 76% higher learning gains in such environments compared to traditional methods. Similarly, AI-driven virtual and augmented reality simulations allow learners, such as medical students, to demonstrate practical skills, with AI assessing precision, technique, and decision-making to provide objective performance data.

Table 2. Assessment design playbook: AI-influenced tasks

Task Type	Student Artefacts Required	AI Role	Human Review Trigger	Override Rule
Short answers/quizzes	Answer text; response logs	Auto-score + feedback	AI confidence <70%	Human score final
Essays/projects	Drafts + reflections	Draft scoring & formative comments	Random 20% sampling; discrepancy >1 SD	Teacher adjudication
Performance/simulation	Video/sim logs	Feature extraction + rubric mapping	Low rubric concordance	Human rating final
Exams (high-stakes)	Proctor logs	Cheating detection/partial scoring	Appeals raised	Formal appeals panel

Assessment Quality Safeguards

Assessment validity concerns whether the task and scoring reflect the intended learning outcomes, rather than proxy features such as writing style, accent, or access to technology. For AI-supported assessment, validity improves when rubrics are explicit, AI support is limited to defined sub-tasks, and teachers review samples of AI outputs against the rubric and the learning objectives (Jang & Sawaki, 2025; Memarian & Doleck, 2024). Reliability concerns consistency across markers and time. Reliability can be strengthened with moderation protocols, fixed sampling rates for human double marking, and discrepancy thresholds that trigger re-scoring (Jang & Sawaki, 2025; Memarian & Doleck, 2024). Consequential validity concerns the effects of the system on learners and equity. Schools should track subgroup gaps, false alerts in early-warning flags, and exclusion risks, then adjust models and policies when harms appear (Memarian & Doleck, 2024; UNESCO, 2023).

AI-enhanced assessment is described as using automation to speed up grading and strengthen feedback and integrity. It can quickly score objective items like multiple-choice and true or false questions, and more advanced natural language processing tools can give preliminary essay scores and comments on structure, grammar, and clarity before the teacher's final review. It also supports adaptive testing by adjusting question difficulty in real time to better match a student's ability. Integrity tools detect plagiarism, including systems like Turnitin, and analytics dashboards track error patterns, time on task, and performance trends so teachers can target learning gaps. The passage also highlights common real-world uses. Duolingo personalises vocabulary tests and practice based on learner progress and outcomes. Automated essay feedback tools help students revise drafts by flagging issues like coherence and grammar early. For online exams, AI-based proctoring can use face recognition and behaviour monitoring to detect suspicious activity and reduce cheating.

Implementation Framework

The adoption of technology alone is insufficient to successfully integrate AI into curriculum and assessment. A fundamental rethinking of educational relationships and processes is required. Several best practices are revealed by analysing successful implementations in various international contexts.

A simple TCO model for a mid-sized district should include: (a) licensing/subscription fees for AI platforms (annual); (b) devices and replacement cycle (3-4 years); (c) network and storage costs (bandwidth, LRS); (d) professional development and teacher release time (initial intensive + ongoing coaching); and (e) moderation/audit staffing. Low-resource options include open-source tools, offline content packages, and shared device pools. Policymakers should budget both upfront (infrastructure, PD) and recurring (licensing, audits) costs and consider partnerships (NGOs, ministries) to establish device subsidy pools.

Table 3. Phased implementation of AI in curriculum and assessment

Phase	Focus	Key Activities	Success Metrics
Foundation	Infrastructure and readiness	Ensure robust technical infrastructure; develop AI literacy among educators; establish data governance policies	90% of educators demonstrate basic AI literacy; clear data ethics policies established
Pilot Testing	Limited-scale experimentation	Implement AI in single courses or departments; collect stakeholder feedback; iterate on design.	Improved learning outcomes in pilot courses; high satisfaction among students and faculty
Expansion	Scaling successful initiatives	Expand AI integration across programs; develop institutional expertise; refine models based on broader data	60% of courses incorporate AI-enhanced elements; reduced achievement gaps across demographic groups
Transformation	Systemic integration	AI is fully embedded across the curriculum and assessment, continuous improvement cycles, and research on impacts.	Institution-wide improvements in retention and achievement; development of new pedagogical models

TEACHER DEVELOPMENT AND SUPPORT

Building teacher capacity is essential to the successful adoption of AI-enhanced curricula and assessments. AI systems are designed to enhance, not replace, teachers' abilities. However, this requires substantial professional development and support systems. Effective programs include: AI Literacy Development: Teachers must comprehend the potential, constraints, and moral ramifications of AI. For instance, to help teachers gain a hands-on understanding of AI applications, the UK's Oak National Academy organised AI hackathons.

Teachers need to rethink their roles as learning facilitators who analyse insights produced by AI and offer human guidance where it is most required, rather than as content providers. With 18 out of 20 educators successfully incorporating AI insights into their teaching practices, the Western Pennsylvania Innovation Cohort provided evidence of how professional learning communities can facilitate this shift. Co-Design Practices: To ensure that algorithmic development is informed by pedagogical expertise, educators should actively participate in the design of AI-enhanced curricula. A co-design model created by the University of the Balearic Islands views educators as collaborators in the development of learning pathways.

Ethical Infrastructure and Governance

AI use in curriculum and assessment needs strict governance. Institutions should protect learner data under FERPA and GDPR, and they should require transparent, auditable algorithms with regular bias checks, such as quarterly reviews that sample high-stakes decisions, test group-level fairness metrics, and check for drift. Flagged cases should go to teacher moderation with a clear appeals process, and schools should publish redacted audit summaries with tracked fixes. High-stakes decisions must never be fully automated, so human oversight is mandatory throughout.

Human-Machine Cooperation, Ethics, and Regulation

The growing integration of artificial intelligence in curriculum design and assessment necessitates a redefinition of the relationship between human educators and machine intelligence. Rather than replacing professional judgment, AI should function as a *co-agency partner* that augments teachers' diagnostic and formative capacities. Effective human–machine cooperation depends on clearly delineated boundaries of responsibility, transparency in algorithmic decision-making, and ongoing teacher oversight. Ethical frameworks must prioritise learner autonomy, data privacy, fairness, and explainability to prevent bias amplification and over-reliance on automated outputs. Regulatory mechanisms should guide the design, deployment, and monitoring of AI tools in education. Future governance models will benefit from multi-stakeholder participation, ensuring that ethical safeguards, cultural diversity, and pedagogical integrity remain central as educational systems transition toward AI-enhanced learning ecosystems.

LIMITATIONS

The passage says AI can improve curriculum design and assessment, but careless use can harm education. Because AI depends on measurable data, it can narrow learning to what is easy to count and ignore harder goals like creativity, ethical judgment, teamwork, and resilience. It also warns that "black box" decisions can reduce trust, and heavy reliance can deskill teachers by weakening their professional judgement. It adds that AI platforms are costly, so they can widen the digital divide between rich and poor schools and between countries. Students may also resist AI because constant data collection can feel like surveillance and increase anxiety. The text ends by noting that evidence is still limited and calls for long-term, cross-cultural studies on learning, motivation, and socioemotional effects, plus stronger ethical and institutional frameworks.

The Teacher's Evolving Role

The integration of artificial intelligence in curriculum design and assessment does not diminish the teacher's role but transforms it into that of an advanced orchestrator of learning environments. Teachers move beyond being mere facilitators to embody three interconnected dimensions: pedagogical design and curation, informed professional judgment, and holistic mentoring. This shift redirects teachers' focus from delivering content to designing, curating, and contextualising learning experiences that reflect human insight and cultural relevance. By leveraging AI to generate foundational materials, teachers gain the flexibility to refine and adapt resources critically, ensuring they are pedagogically sound and aligned with complex learning objectives. Their creative input remains vital in developing project-based learning, Socratic dialogues, and collaborative problem-solving activities that AI alone cannot produce.

While AI excels at data processing and pattern recognition, it lacks the empathy, ethical reasoning, and contextual understanding essential for sound educational decisions. Teachers interpret the deeper causes behind data trends and respond with compassion and discernment, balancing analytics with emotional awareness. They are central to building supportive learning cultures, managing sensitive information, and assessing subjective, creative work that resists algorithmic evaluation. In a digital environment that risks isolation, teachers remain the emotional anchors who motivate, mentor, and celebrate student growth. Through this human-centred guidance, they transform an AI-enhanced curriculum into a deeply personal, meaningful, and socially grounded educational experience.

The Student's Experience and Agency

AI-enhanced education signals a move from standardised teaching to truly personalised learning, where students become active participants rather than passive recipients. Achieving this requires transforming content-delivery systems into collaborative partnerships that let students interact with and even guide AI tools. Genuine student agency depends on metacognitive growth, data transparency, and the conscious prevention of intellectual isolation. Clarifying how AI operates and strengthening students' data and AI literacy are, therefore, ethical and pedagogical priorities. When learners can access and interpret the data collected about them, they begin to understand how recommendations are generated and can engage critically with algorithmic decisions.

Beyond transparency, AI can serve as a "cognitive mirror," fostering metacognition by prompting students to reflect on their own learning strategies and performance patterns. This reflective interaction builds self-awareness and independence, turning AI from a content source into a metacognitive coach. Yet, excessive personalisation risks confining learners to narrow intellectual bubbles. To counter this, AI-based curriculum design should deliberately include diversity and cognitive challenge, introducing contrasting viewpoints, cross-disciplinary activities, and exploratory tasks that push students beyond their comfort zones. The ultimate aim is not an efficient but limited learning track, but an inclusive, stimulating intellectual landscape that encourages curiosity and broad, lifelong learning.

The Transformative Impact of Generative AI

Generative artificial intelligence (GenAI) systems such as ChatGPT, DALL·E, and Midjourney mark a shift from earlier AI applications that mainly analyzed learner data and recommended actions. GenAI produces new content from user prompts, including text, images, code, and multimedia. This capability changes AI from a background support tool into a collaborative resource in teaching and learning. As a result, curriculum work can move toward co-creation, where teachers rapidly draft, localise, and differentiate materials, then evaluate and refine outputs using professional judgement. Students can also use GenAI to support meaning-making activities such as visualising concepts, simulating dialogue for inquiry, and generating ideas for writing.

The same capability challenges conventional assessment because many take-home products can be generated quickly with minimal effort. The passage, therefore, argues for assessment designs that prioritise process evidence and higher-order thinking, including application, reflection, and metacognitive control. Practical options include requiring students to submit prompts and revision histories, assessing the quality of edits and added reasoning, and using authentic in-class tasks such as oral defence, peer review of AI outputs, and locally grounded problem-solving projects. In this context, prompt design becomes a core component of digital literacy because output quality depends on clear goals, constraints, and context. Ethical integration also requires transparency. Students should disclose AI use, and institutions should strengthen academic integrity norms rather than relying only on detection tools.

Data Governance and Privacy

A responsible approach to AI in education should prioritise students' learning experiences and their rights over personal data, rather than focusing only on transparency and compliance. AI systems can collect continuous and sensitive traces of learning, including performance, response times, error patterns, engagement indicators, and behavioural signals. This creates a lasting digital record that can affect learners far beyond the classroom. Ethical governance, therefore, requires a student-centred data management framework that treats consent as ongoing and informed, not as a one-time checkbox. Families should be able to give granular permission for specific uses of data, and to revise those choices over time as tools and practices change.

The same framework should treat students as the primary owners of their learning data, with schools and vendors acting as stewards who must use the data only in the student's best interest. Ownership must be practical, so learners can access their records, correct errors, and transfer their data across platforms to avoid lock-in. Strong minimisation and retention rules are also essential, so institutions collect only what they need and delete it when its educational purpose ends. The highest risks arise from profiling and functional creep, where early struggles are used to limit future opportunities, or where data collected for personalisation is repurposed for teacher evaluation or funding decisions without new consent. To make ownership and portability operational, institutions should adopt learning data standards such as xAPI and IMS Caliper, provide learner exports (for example, JSON and CSV), use an event capture layer that supports multiple tools, and clearly document schemas, retention rules, and export procedures in institutional data manuals.

Policy and Cultural Contexts in AI Curriculum Adoption

National accreditation frameworks increasingly influence AI integration in curricula. Accreditation bodies in regions such as the EU and ASEAN have begun issuing AI-in-education quality standards that shape institutional uptake (OECD, 2024). However, many systems remain unprepared: teacher scepticism, infrastructure gaps, and lack of regulatory clarity slow adoption. Cultural and linguistic diversity further complicates implementation, as AI models trained on English-dominant datasets can marginalise local idioms and knowledge systems. Addressing these gaps requires localised datasets, multilingual resources, and inclusive governance mechanisms that reflect cultural pluralism in algorithmic design.

Accreditation and regulatory frameworks are emerging areas of focus. Institutions should consult national accreditation bodies and regional frameworks (OECD guidance) early in design to ensure AI-enabled assessments meet quality standards for assessment validity and student protections. Key checkpoints include: (1) alignment of AI scoring rubrics with accredited competency frameworks; (2) documentation required for external review (model cards, audit logs); and (3) agreements around data stewardship and cross-institution portability. Early engagement with accreditors reduces the risk of downstream non-conformity and supports broader recognition of AI-based credentials.

Global Case Studies

Table 5. Key performance indicators from case study implementations

Case Study	Feedback Latency	Teacher Time Saved (hrs/week)	Proficiency Gain	Equity Gap Reduction	Data Source
Singapore MOE	<24 hours (low-stakes)	5-7 (marking); 9-12 total (marking + planning)	Not Specified	Not Specified	Internal MOE Reports
Australia (Maths Pathway)	Immediate (practice)	Reallocated to targeted workshops	+47%	32% (demographic gaps)	Programme Evaluation Reports
Georgia Tech (Predictive)	N/A (Early Warning)	N/A	N/A (85% accuracy in identifying at-risk students by week 4)	N/A	Internal Pilot Evaluation
University of Alicante (Accessibility)	Real-time (via Ability Connect)	Not Quantified	Improved engagement & navigation	Increased access for students with disabilities	Institutional Case Studies

Singapore's Systemic Approach

The Ministry of Education (MOE) in Singapore has established one of the most extensive AI-enabled learning environments in the world. Singapore's approach incorporates AI throughout the entire system as part of a national strategy, in contrast to other countries' piecemeal adoptions. MOE introduced an EdTech Masterplan in 2023 to systematically integrate technology and AI into education. The Singapore Student Learning Space (SLS) platform serves as the delivery channel for all AI tools, guaranteeing that they operate as integrated parts rather than standalone accessories. Because of this systemic integration, all AI tools support a cohesive educational strategy rather than disjointed experiments by feeding data into a single ecosystem and aligning with curriculum goals.

Automated marking systems and widely used adaptive learning platforms are part of Singapore's AI-driven ecosystem. The MOE has implemented five AI-powered tools in schools: an Authoring Copilot to help teachers plan lessons, an Adaptive Learning System (ALS) for individualised pacing, and three learning feedback assistant marking systems (for short-answer responses, English, and mathematics). In addition to automatically assessing student writing for grammar, spelling, and sentence structure, the English Language marking assistant offers immediate corrections and recommendations. In a similar vein, the math assistant provides detailed instructions and partial credit suggestions for problem-solving, while the short-answer assistant automatically marks answers in subjects like science or geography. Students no longer have to wait days for teacher marking of their work, thanks to these AI feedback tools. In the meantime, the machine learning-powered Adaptive Learning System modifies the course and level of difficulty of lessons in real time in response to each learner's answers. ALS, which was first made available for upper-primary math and upper-secondary geography, allows students to progress at their own speed while speeding up learning for those who pick things up quickly and strengthening ideas for those who require more assistance. The SLS online portal, which effortlessly unifies resources for teachers and students in one location, provides access to all of these tools.

The deliberate, systemic integration of these AI tools into regular teaching and learning is what truly sets Singapore's approach apart. MOE has integrated AI systems into a comprehensive educational framework rather than treating them as stand-alone devices. From adaptive practice to assessment feedback, the centralised SLS platform serves as the backbone that unifies all AI features under a single login and interface. Consistency is ensured by this integration; for instance, teacher dashboards receive data from ALS and marking assistants, providing a comprehensive view of students' progress. Since the MOE developed or approved the AI initiatives, they are also closely aligned with Singapore's curriculum and standards, ensuring that automated feedback and personalised learning pathways continue to be pedagogically sound and curriculum-aligned. By creating these tools internally or in close collaboration, MOE's Total Ownership model gives more control over data privacy, content quality, and alignment with national education objectives.

Crucially, AI is presented as a tool to support teachers rather than as a substitute for them. The ministry stresses that educators continue to be the main designers of learning, utilising technology to enhance their knowledge. Despite receiving training on these AI platforms, educators continue to use their judgment, such as checking the accuracy of automated feedback and tailoring it to the needs of individual students. Through careful integration and teacher participation, the drawbacks of standalone technological tools are avoided, resulting in a unified ecosystem where AI enhances successful teaching techniques within a logical plan.

Singapore's AI-enabled educational system has produced remarkable early results. Instructors report saving an average of 5-7 hours per week by cutting down on time spent on administrative and grading duties. For instance, case studies have shown that teachers can save a significant amount of time each week by automating essay and short-answer grading, which can reduce marking time by about 50% to 60%. After testing an AI marking assistant, a Singaporean teacher saw a 60% reduction in her weekly grading workload, going from 15-20 hours to just 6-8 hours. By giving artificial intelligence the burden of laborious grading, even more conservative implementations aim to save teachers about five hours each week. Teachers can refocus their efforts on high-value activities like lesson planning and one-on-one coaching thanks to these time savings. One MOE official stated that once AI takes care of the busywork, teachers will have more time to devote to the human side of education, which includes mentoring students and attending to their individual needs. Conversely, students gain from receiving more thorough and timely feedback on their learning, particularly when it comes to writing. Students no longer have to wait days or weeks to learn how they performed thanks to the AI marking systems' instant feedback, which allows them to learn from their mistakes right away.

The AI offers detailed, multifaceted feedback on English writing, highlighting structural problems, awkward wording, and grammar mistakes in essays. Students can better understand their areas for growth as writers and make revisions to their work much more quickly when they receive this kind of thorough feedback promptly. Instant feedback, according to Singaporean teachers, increases students' confidence and motivation. Students feel affirmed by the on-the-spot guidance and are more involved, as though a personal tutor is helping them with each practice question. Before a student advances to new topics in subjects like science and math, the adaptive hints and corrective feedback help clear up any misunderstandings. All things considered, Singapore's systemic AI integration has produced a positive feedback loop where students receive quicker, richer feedback and teachers have more time to teach, resulting in more individualised and successful learning experiences. The early successes of this strategy demonstrate how AI can improve student learning outcomes and teaching efficiency when carefully incorporated into a country's educational strategy.

In one MOE pilot project using ALS and SLS-linked marking assistants, internal administrative reports indicated that the average marking time of teachers using both authoring copilots and marking assistants decreased from 15 hours per week to around 6-8 hours per week. The MOE reported an improvement in feedback latency (the median turnaround time decreased to <24 hours for low-stakes work), and teacher surveys showed an increase in the time spent on small group work. These are early institutionally reported data and should be interpreted as administrative results pending a peer review. We recommend that future studies provide controlled ex post metrics with matched schools of comparison to confirm the causal relationship.

Australia's Focus on Equity

Math equity is a well-known issue in Australia, where many Aboriginal and Torres Strait Islander students, as well as those attending low-SES and regional schools, fall behind and frequently remain behind. Tasmania's New Town High School decided to address that head-on rather than wait for averages to rise. They implemented Maths Pathway, a mastery-based, AI-driven program for students in 5-10 years that begins with a detailed diagnostic before creating a unique pathway for each student. Teachers view real-time dashboards, organise students with comparable needs, and conduct brief, focused workshops rather than teaching to the middle. The platform manages regular practice and real-time feedback. The key is the shift in classroom dynamics. Students fill in the gaps in their prior knowledge without feeling stigmatised, or they advance when they're ready. Progress is not determined by seat time but rather by demonstrated comprehension.

Teachers spend their time on human tasks like clearing up misunderstandings, modelling techniques, and assessing students' comprehension in small groups rather than being bogged down in marking. Teachers carry out the instruction; AI handles the record-keeping and routing. Simply put, the equity case is made by the New Town High School results. Following the roll-out, the percentage of students who met proficiency benchmarks increased by 47%, with underserved groups seeing the biggest increases. An equity-oriented model should provide just that, a quicker catch-up for the students who are most behind, without limiting the progress of those who are prepared to accelerate. Additionally, it aligns with multi-school analyses that demonstrate how mastery-based, adaptive models effectively raise annual learning growth above the previous baseline. It's the mechanism that makes this compelling as policy rather than just a compelling narrative.

In the classroom, equity increases when variance is reduced. Frequent mastery checks keep students from moving forward with shaky foundations; tailored workshops focus teacher expertise where it has the greatest potential to yield results; and personalised diagnostics break through that spread. The combination raises the floor and the ceiling at the same time by completing prerequisite gaps and preserving system elasticity. If you were to implement this in additional schools tomorrow, the strategy would be simple. Preserve a weekly mastery cycle by diagnosing, learning, checking, reteaching, or extending it, and scheduling it to occur. Educate educators on how to use the data to create focused mini-lessons instead of letting the platform run itself. When gaps reopen, take early action and break down the results by subgroup. Set clear expectations so that staff and students can see the effort and progress being made.

The introduction of the Maths Pathway programme at New Town High School has reported an increase in the number of students achieving proficiency (reported administrative increase $\approx +47$) and an improvement in equity, with the gap between demographic groups narrowing significantly in the first year. Teachers reported that they had to allocate time from full class lectures to targeted mini-workshops. Again, these data are taken from the local programme reports and evaluation reports; replication is recommended using a cohort design and subgroup reporting disaggregated to verify both the magnitude of the effect and the impact on the population.

European Innovations in Higher Education

AI has been used by European universities to address issues of inclusion and accessibility that frequently occupy the periphery of curriculum design. An excellent illustration is the University of Alicante. Instead of merely adding captions and calling it a day, its accessibility team developed and tested tools that alter how students with disabilities navigate the campus and interact with resources. A note-taker can share live class notes to a visually impaired or deaf student's device in real time using the Ability Connect app, which was created at Alicante's Student Support Centre with assistance from the Vodafone Spain Foundation. The student can change the font, colour, and even switch to a word-by-word display to lessen visual load. This little design element has a big impact because it changes the phrase I will catch up later to, I can follow now.

In a clear step toward autonomous campus wayfinding, Alicante also tested NaviLens, computer-vision markers that a phone can detect in motion and at a distance, to facilitate indoor navigation in university buildings. These initiatives collectively demonstrate how computer vision and careful user experience can truly make the digital and built environments navigable for students, who are frequently forced to come up with creative workarounds. The Alicante example is an AI visual-assistance app that is sometimes referred to as Help Me See. Although secondary write-ups vary in their branding, the basic concept is always the same to help blind and low-vision students read handouts or signs, identify objects, and move between classes with less assistance from others.

The goal is the same whether accessibility is provided via Ability Connect, NaviLens, or a campus-specific build. This will integrate accessibility into the main student experience rather than adding it after the fact. Smart Sparrow, an adaptive learning platform that enables academics to create sequences that branch in real time based on student responses, was adopted by several faculties. In addition to using it in credit-bearing units and widely accessible offerings, learning designers even redesigned the Academic Honesty module on the platform. Adaptive pathways and immediate, focused feedback are used to keep students on task. Staff analytics are then provided to identify misconceptions early on. This pattern is intentional. Adaptive design combined with teaching craft was what made the difference, not a magic algorithm alone.

Research on Smart Sparrow and related systems shows that replacing one-speed content with adaptive tutorials improves engagement and assessment performance. Sydney's own deployment notes highlight that the platform functioned best when teachers used its data to run brief, focused interventions rather than letting it run itself. To put it another way, academics performed the human labour of coaching and explanation while AI managed routing and feedback at scale. Because the system meets them at their current level rather than assuming a uniform starting point, adaptive tools tend to benefit students who don't fit the traditional moulds, such as international students, first-in-family entrants, or those returning to school. The message is straightforward if you combine the two cases. Adaptability and accessibility are structural decisions that increase performance and broaden participation; they are not extras.

Sydney demonstrates how adaptive coursework can guide diverse cohorts through complex material without simplifying it, while Alicante demonstrates how computer vision and inclusive design can make a physical campus and its resources truly usable. Evidence-related notes. The University of Alicante's accessibility initiatives, such as the NaviLens pilot and Ability Connect, are detailed on their official websites. Instead of primary UA releases, references to an app called Help Me See can be found in recent case-study roundups; consider the label to be descriptive of the function rather than a formal product name. Although the mechanism and adoption are evident, quantitative lift figures are more well-established in Smart Sparrow research and larger adaptive-learning studies than in publicly accessible Sydney-specific evaluations.

Sydney demonstrates how adaptive coursework can guide diverse cohorts through complex material without simplifying it, while Alicante demonstrates how computer vision and inclusive design can make a physical campus and its resources truly usable.

Table 4. Risk-control mapping

Problem	Mitigation Control	Example Tool/Policy	Accountability
Black-box opacity	Explanation UI; model cards	Transparency dashboard	Assessment Office
Over-quantification	Mixed-method evidence	Portfolio + analytics	Curriculum Committee
Surveillance anxiety	Privacy defaults; opt-out	Secure mode toggle	Data Governance Board
Inequity/access	Device pools; offline grading	Low-resource deployment kit	Ministry/NGO Partner

PRACTICAL IMPLICATIONS FOR SCHOOL LEADERS

School leaders serve as the linchpins of successful AI adoption. Key management priorities include: establishing data-ethics committees; budgeting for sustainable device cycles; embedding AI-literacy training within staff appraisal systems; and piloting small-scale implementations before district rollout. Aligning these management actions with policy standards ensures both pedagogical innovation and institutional accountability.

Teacher Vignette. On Monday, the teacher starts the week by reviewing the artificial intelligence dashboard to identify gaps in class proficiency, a task that takes about 10 minutes. On the basis of these observations, the teacher proposes a 20-minute mini-lecture for small groups to address specific learning needs. On Tuesdays, the teacher spends about 30 minutes moderating five essays that are flagged for further review by the artificial intelligence system. In the middle of the week, on Wednesday, the teacher attends a 45-minute collaborative design meeting with the learning designer to refine the teaching strategy and integrate AI-based insights into the planning of the lesson. Until Friday, the teacher will hold a 30-minute office hour session for students who have been identified by the predictor as requiring additional support. The overall effect of this exercise is that the teacher strategically uses artificial intelligence tools to focus on high-value human-centred interactions that increase learning outcomes.

Student Vignette. On Tuesdays, students participate in adaptive practice sessions guided by artificial intelligence, where they receive immediate formative feedback and a short reflection prompt lasting approximately 5-10 minutes. Based on performance, AI recommends targeted micro-learning to reinforce specific competencies. Students also use the peer-to-peer chat function to collaborate and discuss learning challenges. By Thursday, the student submits a revised assignment proposal after having received feedback generated by both the artificial intelligence and the teacher. The artificial intelligence system monitors the progress of the student and suggests personalised resources for further improvement. Through this process, students experience a dynamic learning cycle combining automatic feedback with meaningful interaction with teachers and peers.

Future Study

The future of AI-enhanced education envisions a seamlessly integrated ecosystem where artificial intelligence personalises learning through emotion-aware systems and immersive metaverse environments. Curriculum design will shift from linear content delivery to dynamic, simulated, and collaborative learning that balances human and machine intelligence. Ethical and sustainable integration will rely on robust policies ensuring transparency, fairness, data protection, and continuous educator training in AI literacy. Educational leaders must promote innovation, critical engagement with AI tools, and supportive professional cultures.

While this chapter establishes a conceptual and practical framework for AI-enhanced curriculum design and assessment, future studies should pursue deeper empirical verification and cultural contextualization. Cross-national and intra-cultural research is needed to examine how local pedagogical traditions, languages, and sociocultural norms shape the adoption and ethical perception of AI in education. Comparative case studies across diverse regions can reveal adaptation strategies that ensure inclusivity and equity. Mixed-method designs combining classroom observations, longitudinal learning analytics, and teacher/student interviews will help validate the effectiveness and emotional impact of AI-supported feedback. In addition, experimental and quasi-experimental studies should explore how cultural factors mediate learner trust, cognitive load, and engagement in AI-mediated environments. Finally, collaboration between local educators, technologists, and policymakers will be vital to co-create culturally responsive AI tools that align with regional values, curriculum standards, and equity goals.

CONCLUSION

The future of AI-enhanced learning and assessment lies in augmentation rather than automation, built on purposeful collaboration between artificial intelligence and human educators. This partnership enables more inclusive and adaptive learning experiences, as demonstrated by international examples. Singapore's system integration shows how AI can deliver immediate feedback and reduce teacher workload, while Australia's equity-driven Math Pathway initiative illustrates AI's ability to close achievement gaps. Similarly, European developments such as the University of Alicante's open learning systems highlight how AI can expand access and flexibility. These cases collectively show that AI's success depends not on algorithms alone but on how they are thoughtfully embedded within human-centred educational frameworks.

Realising this potential requires coordinated action across the education ecosystem. Teachers must evolve from content transmitters to learning architects who combine AI tools with the mentorship and empathy that technology cannot provide. Institutions and policymakers need to scale efforts beyond pilots, investing in infrastructure, professional development, and ethical governance to prevent bias and ensure transparency. Researchers should continue examining AI's long-term influence on teaching roles and student growth. Viewing AI as a catalyst for rethinking education will demand sustained investment and commitment, ultimately creating a system that honours diverse ways of learning and development.

Nonetheless, the global distribution of AI benefits remains uneven. Schools in low-income contexts continue to face bandwidth, device, and language barriers that limit participation. Future frameworks must embed equity metrics and low-resource design strategies so that "AI-enhanced learning" becomes globally inclusive rather than another layer of digital divide. AI-enhanced curricula and assessments are not just a technological advance; they are a moral imperative to create a future in which the distinct potential of each learner can be fully realised.

REFERENCES

Almalawi, A., Soh, B., Li, A., & Samra, H. (2024). Predictive models for educational purposes: A systematic review. *Big Data and Cognitive Computing*, *8*(12), 187. DOI: 10.3390/bdcc8120187

Amershi, S., Weld, D., Vorvoreanu, M., Fourney, A., Nushi, B., Collisson, P., Suh, J., Iqbal, S., Bennett, P. N., Inkpen, K., Teevan, J., Kikin-Gil, R., & Horvitz, E. (2019). Guidelines for human-AI interaction. In *Proceedings of the 2019 CHI Conference on Human Factors in Computing Systems* (pp. 1–13). Association for Computing Machinery. https://doi.org/DOI: 10.1145/3290605.3300233

Banihashem, S. K., Noroozi, O., van Ginkel, S., Macfadyen, L. P., & Biemans, H. J. A. (2022). A systematic review of the role of learning analytics in enhancing feedback practices in higher education. *Educational Research Review*, *37*, 100489. DOI: 10.1016/j.edurev.2022.100489

Gebru, T., Morgenstern, J., Vecchione, B., Vaughan, J. W., Wallach, H., Daumé, H.III, & Crawford, K. (2021). Datasheets for datasets. *Communications of the ACM*, *64*(12), 86–92. DOI: 10.1145/3458723

Goel, A. K., & Polepeddi, L. (2018). Jill Watson: A virtual teaching assistant for online education. In *Learning engineering for online education* (pp. 120-143). Routledge.

Jang, E. E., & Sawaki, Y. (2025). Advancing language assessment for teaching and learning in the era of the artificial intelligence revolution: Promises and challenges. *Language Testing*, *42*(4), 02655322251348685. DOI: 10.1177/02655322251348685

Memarian, B., & Doleck, T. (2024). A review of assessment for learning with artificial intelligence. *Computers in Human Behaviour: Artificial Humans*, *2*(1), 100040. DOI: 10.1016/j.chbah.2023.100040

Ninaus, M., & Sailer, M. (2022). The human role in artificial intelligence for education: A systematic review. *Computers and Education: Artificial Intelligence*, *3*, 100083. DOI: 10.1016/j.caeai.2022.100083

OECD. (2024). *AI in Education: Accreditation and Quality Frameworks*. OECD Education Directorate.

Raji, I. D., Smart, A., White, R. N., Mitchell, M., Gebru, T., Hutchinson, B., Smith-Loud, J., Theron, D., & Barnes, P. (2020). Closing the AI accountability gap: Defining an end-to-end framework for internal algorithmic auditing. In *Proceedings of the 2020 Conference on Fairness, Accountability, and Transparency* (pp. 33–44). Association for Computing Machinery. https://doi.org/DOI: 10.1145/3351095.3372873

Russell, S. J., & Norvig, P. (2020). *Artificial intelligence: A modern approach* (4th ed.). Pearson.

UNESCO. (2023). *Guidance for generative AI in education and research*. UNESCO.

APPENDIX

Implementation Checklists

A1. Assessment Moderation & Appeals Standard Operating Procedure (SOP)

This SOP is designed to ensure quality control and maintain trust in AI-enhanced assessment systems.

□ Override Rules:

Human score is final when AI confidence is <70%.
Teacher adjudication is required for all flagged discrepancies (e.g., AI vs. human score difference >1 standard deviation).
Final authority for high-stakes exam grading rests with a formal appeals panel.

□ Spot-Check Sampling:

Essays/Projects: A random 20% of all AI-graded items, plus all items flagged for low confidence or discrepancy.
Performance/Simulation: All performances with low rubric concordance are routed for human rating.
All Tasks: Maintain a log of overrides to track AI performance and inform model retraining.

□ Appeals Process:

1. Student submits a formal, written request for re-evaluation within 7 calendar days of result publication.
2. The request is reviewed by a designated teacher or a 2-member moderation panel within 5 working days.
3. The outcome and detailed rationale are communicated to the student. The AI model's feedback is annotated for potential retraining and improvement.

A2. Interoperability and Data Portability Checklist

This checklist ensures that AI tools integrate seamlessly and that learner data rights are upheld.

✓ Infrastructure: The institution has defined a primary Learning Record Store (LRS) or uses IMS Calliper for granular learning event capture.
✓ Data Export: All AI tools can export granular learner data in standardised, machine-readable formats (JSON, CSV) via a documented API.
✓ Student Access: Students can access, view, and download a complete, human-readable transcript of their learning activity, performance data, and AI-generated feedback.
✓ Documentation: Data schemas, retention policies, and export procedures are publicly documented in the institutional data management manual.

Chapter 7
Intelligent Digital Mentors for Student Autonomy Through Adaptive Learning Systems

Jaime Aguilar-Ortiz
http://orcid.org/0009-0003-5302-1454
Universidad Politécnica de Pachuca, Mexico

Ocotlán Diáz-Parra
Universidad Politécnica de Pachuca, Mexico

Jorge A. Ruiz-Vanoye
http://orcid.org/0000-0003-4928-5716
Universidad Politécnica de Pachuca, Mexico

Marco A. Vera-Jiménez
http://orcid.org/0009-0009-3712-1440
Universidad Politécnica de Pachuca, Mexico

Víctor M. Zamudio-García
http://orcid.org/0000-0002-4660-8025
Universidad Politéctica Metropolitana de Hidalgo, Mexico

Francisco R. Trejo-Macotela
http://orcid.org/0000-0003-2133-3456
Universidad Politécnica de Pachuca, Mexico

Carlos R. Domínguez-Mayorga
http://orcid.org/0009-0007-1018-4412
Universidad Politécnica de Pachuca, Mexico

ABSTRACT

This chapter aims to explain how artificial intelligence (AI) agents can function as intelligent digital mentors that strengthen student autonomy through adaptive learning systems. It proposes an integrative model in which the ChatGPT application programming interface (API), learning analytics, and adaptive dashboards work together in a Python–Dash–Plotly environment to personalize guidance, interpret performance, and support self-regulation. Grounded in Piaget, Vygotsky, and Ausubel, the chapter presents a functional web-based prototype and discusses its pedagogical, ethical, and organizational implications. Rather than replacing educators, the proposed mentor architecture is designed to complement teaching, enhance contextual feedback, and promote equitable, meaningful, and continuously monitored independent learning. The code can be accessed at the following link: https://github.com/JAIME6609/EDUCATION/blob/main/CODE-IDM-04-E.py

DOI: 10.4018/979-8-3373-7225-9.ch007

FROM SOLITARY AUTONOMY TO INTELLIGENT COMPANIONSHIP

Historical evolution of independent learning

Over the last century, independent learning has evolved profoundly, reflecting the epistemological, technological, and pedagogical shifts that shaped successive educational paradigms. Early correspondence and distance education relied on one-way information delivery and limited interaction, consistent with the industrial model of education. As communication technologies and pedagogical theories advanced, education moved from passive reception toward dialogic, interactive models emphasizing participation, collaboration, and self-reflection. Constructivist approaches marked a turning point by positioning the learner as an active constructor of meaning through experience and social mediation. Within this framework, "learning to learn" emerged as a key metacognitive and lifelong learning principle. Figure 1 summarizes this part. This chapter is directed to AI-in-education researchers, higher-education leaders, EdTech developers, instructional designers, and learning analytics specialists.

In contemporary higher education, these foundations have taken shape through flexible, student-centered models such as HyFlex, blended, and ubiquitous learning, which integrate multiple modalities and give learners more control over time, space, and pace. These approaches allow students to shape learning paths according to their interests, cognitive styles, and circumstances, thereby enacting constructivist autonomy and self-determination. At the same time, learning analytics, digital assessment, and adaptive technologies have made autonomy both measurable and supportable. Education has thus shifted from teaching-centered instruction to learner-centered orchestration, aligning human agency with data-driven personalization and reaffirming meaningful learning as co-constructed, contextualized, and self-directed (Barua & Lockee, 2024; Yang, 2023).

Figure 1. Evolution of independent learning: From solitary study to Artificial Intelligence-mediated companionship

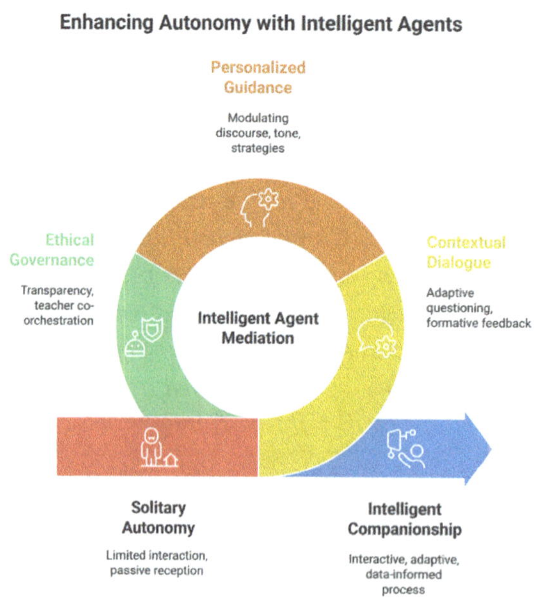

In parallel, the genealogy of Intelligent Tutoring Systems (ITS) and learning analytics tools, rooted in the earliest applications of artificial intelligence in education, has progressively redefined independence as a dynamic capability enabled and sustained by technological mediation. Early ITS were designed to replicate human tutors by modeling student knowledge and adapting instruction from error patterns and progress indicators. Over time, these systems evolved from rule-based architectures into data-driven and machine-learning approaches capable of mapping learning trajectories, predicting difficulties, and providing personalized feedback in real time. This evolution shifted independence from solitary self-study to an interactive, adaptive, and data-informed process in which learners engage in continuous dialogue with intelligent systems that guide, challenge, and support cognitive development.

Whereas classical Intelligent Tutoring Systems (ITS) typically depend on domain-specific expert models and hand-crafted rules, large language model (LLM)-based mentors can generate context-sensitive explanations, probing questions, and metacognitive prompts through open-ended dialogue (. This shift relocates the central design challenge from rule coverage to pedagogical alignment, verification, and the careful calibration of guidance needed to preserve learner autonomy.

By providing adaptive pacing, formative feedback, multimodal content access, and real-time performance tracking, these tools have transformed what was once geographical or temporal distance into a dynamic cognitive and relational space. In this paradigm, the learner operates within a networked learning ecosystem, making informed and autonomous decisions about goals, strategies, and resources. As UNESCO (2021) emphasizes, independence in the digital age does not mean isolation, but the ability to manage one's learning within interconnected and inclusive environments where technology catalyzes participation, diversity, and educational sustainability. In these ecosystems, technology goes beyond efficiency: accessibility becomes a mediating force that expands human potential, supports equity of opportunity, and sustains lifelong, self-directed learning aligned with the ethical and social imperatives of the 21st century.

In the latest digital phase, independent learning is increasingly shaped by data-driven personalization and adaptability, supported by algorithmic and analytical models that track patterns of progress, motivation, and performance. Systematic reviews show that intelligent platforms and adaptive strategies can improve student comprehension and engagement, although outcomes vary across institutional contexts and learning cultures (Du Plooy, Casteleijn & Franzsen, 2024; Contrino, Reyes-Millán, Vázquez-Villegas & Membrillo-Hernández, 2024). Within this framework, independence is understood as an emergent process in which student agency, instructional design, and algorithmic support converge. Yet this shift also raises ethical and social concerns: without inclusive scaffolding, autonomy may intensify inequality and affect well-being and educational equity. For this reason, current literature stresses the need for diversity-sensitive institutional frameworks that balance self-direction with explicit structural support, ensuring that technology amplifies rather than replaces the human dimensions of learning (Wilbraham, Jones, Brewster, Priestley, Broglia, Hughes & Spanner, 2024; UNESCO, 2021).

The emergence of intelligent agents as mediators of autonomy

The emergence of intelligent agents as mediators of autonomy arises from their capacity to perceive complex educational contexts, reason about learners' goals, and enact adaptive pedagogical interventions that enhance students' abilities to plan, monitor, and evaluate their own learning without displacing their agency or diminishing their active participation in constructing knowledge. Unlike traditional instructional technologies, these agents use real-time data, behavioral analytics, and natural language understanding to interpret the learner's cognitive state and respond with precision and relevance. Their context-awareness enables them to detect shifts in motivation, engagement, or comprehension and adjust the level of guidance, accordingly, thus supporting a fluid and personalized learning experience.

In particular, agents based on LLMs represent a transformative step forward in this evolution. By integrating contextual dialogue, adaptive questioning, and immediate formative feedback, they serve as metacognitive scaffolds that nurture reflection, self-regulation, and a sense of ownership over the learning process. These systems are not designed to function as automated instructors or replacements for teachers but as digital mentors capable of dynamically modulating their discourse, tone, and pedagogical strategies to align with each student's learning style, pace, and current level of autonomy. Through this dialogic and adaptive interaction, they foster self-efficacy, cognitive engagement, and intrinsic motivation, encouraging learners to take initiative and make informed choices about their progress. Ultimately, the strength of intelligent agents lies in their ability to merge computational intelligence with human-centered design creating learning environments that are not only intelligent but also empathetic, reflective, and responsive to the diverse and evolving needs of each learner.

Recent empirical and theoretical evidence supports intelligent agents as effective mediators of autonomy. A review of 82 international studies identifies key design principles such as Augmented Retrieval of Generation (ARG), explicit pedagogical roles, and multi-agent architectures and shows that collaborative human-Artificial Intelligence models outperform fully autonomous tutors by preserving student autonomy and curricular alignment (Córdova-Esparza, 2025). These findings are consistent with UNESCO's guidance on generative Artificial Intelligence, which advocates person-centered frameworks to protect agency, inclusion, and ethics. Empirical studies likewise show that intelligent agents can improve performance, motivation, and engagement when grounded in sound pedagogy. Kestin, Miller, Klales, Milbourne & Ponti (2025) found that an Artificial Intelligence-assisted tutor increased learning gains in less time, while Wang, Ribeiro, Robinson, Loeb & Demszky (2025) reported that a human-Artificial Intelligence co-pilot improved conceptual mastery without replacing teacher intervention. Likewise, Létourneau, Deslandes Martineau, Charland, Karran, Boasen & Léger (2025) stress that positive ITS effects depend on instructional design and context.

In this context, mediating autonomy through intelligent agents requires ethical governance, transparency, and teacher co-orchestration. These agents should promote self-reflection, informed decision-making, and critical awareness of learning while remaining clear about their sources, limitations, and risks. UNESCO (2023) emphasizes validating pedagogical relevance and protecting learner agency and rights, while recent mappings and reviews of Artificial Intelligence-assisted self-regulated learning (SRL) warn of methodological gaps, bias, and limited ethical evaluation (Lan & Zhou, 2025; Córdova-Esparza, 2025). The challenge, then, is to design verifiable pedagogical agents that foster self-regulation, connect evidence with human judgment, and operate within ethical and equity frameworks. Intelligent agents do not replace autonomy; they amplify it as cognitive interlocutors that support independence through automation, reflection, and shared responsibility. Accordingly, this chapter explains how an intelligent digital mentor can be theoretically grounded, technically implemented, and ethically governed so that adaptive learning systems enhance student autonomy without weakening teacher oversight or educational equity. The following Background section anchors these claims in established learning theories and links them to mentor behaviors and evaluation criteria.

BACKGROUND

Constructivism, personalization, and self-directed learning

Constructivism positions the student as an active agent who constructs meaning from prior experiences and socially mediated interactions. From this premise, personalization is not a technological embellishment but rather the pedagogical mechanism that adjusts challenges, sequences, and supports the learner's zone of proximal development. Recent literature combines evidence that constructivist approaches, implemented with explicit instructional design, foster deeper and more transferable learning, provided that the adaptation supports authentic tasks, formative feedback, and gradual scaffolding that promotes metacognition and self-regulation (Arega & Hunde, 2025). Within this framework, personalization consistent with constructivism aligns aims, materials, and paces with individual learning trajectories, avoiding content fragmentation and over-adaptation that reduces cognitive challenge (Ali, Wahab, Huri & Yusoff, 2025). Figure 2 summarizes this part.

Figure 2. Constructivist, personalized, and self-Directed learning as foundations of adaptivity

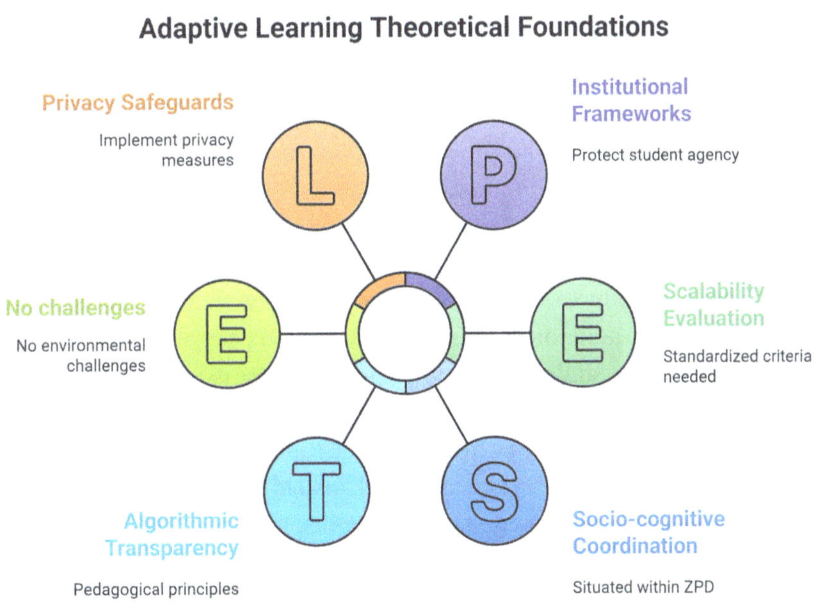

Personalization based on adaptive learning and learning analytics is structurally linked to self-directed learning: by offering continuous diagnostics, dynamic pathways, and immediate feedback, it enables planning, monitoring, and evaluation cycles characteristics of self-regulation. A synthesis of research in higher education shows positive albeit heterogeneous effects on performance and engagement when personalization is designed with pedagogical principles and algorithmic transparency (Du Plooy et al. 2024). In health sciences domains, the most recent mappings highlight benefits in participation and achievement and warn of the need for standardized criteria to evaluate impact and scalability, so that personalization does not dilute disciplinary complexity or reproduce inequities (Ali et al. 2025).

For the constructivism-personalization-self-direction trial to be responsible and effective, institutional frameworks must protect student agency, the pedagogical validity of supports, and equity in access. International guidelines recommend explicitly saying objectives, implementing privacy and bias safeguards, and training teachers and learners in critically evaluating adaptive recommendations (UNESCO, 2023). Similarly, meta-analyses and reviews of self-regulated learning strategies emphasize that self-direction flourishes when personalization is combined with strategic instruction in planning, goal setting, and reflection, and when sustained support is offered throughout the course, not just at the beginning (Hemmler & Ifenthaler, 2024). In short, the integration of these three components promotes meaningful and sustainable learning, if technology serves informed instructional decisions and responsible autonomy.

Connections with Piaget, Vygotsky, and Ausubel's theories

The link between constructivism and the theories of Piaget, Vygotsky, and Ausubel provides a basis, with recent evidence, for why personalization and self-directed learning require well-designed conceptual and social scaffolding. Following Piaget, cognitive development progresses through qualitative reorganizations that enable more abstract operations; therefore, the sequencing of tasks and the gradation of challenge must correspond to the learner's stage of reasoning and their prior conceptions (not just prescribed content), which aligns with curriculum designs focused on the active construction of meaning and the formative assessment of alternative ideas (Taber, 2024; Allen, 2022). In this context, recent reviews on the educational implementation of Piaget show that strategies such as projects, problem-based learning and hands-on experiences operate as adjustment mechanisms between previous schemes and new concepts, favoring deep understanding when articulated with explicit goals and transparent success criteria (Erawati & Adnyana, 2024).

Vygotsky's contribution introduces social mediation and the zone of proximal development (ZPD) as a principle for orchestrating autonomy: scaffolding that is appropriately "dissipated" strengthens self-regulation without replacing student agency. A recent systematic review indicates that the ZPD and scaffolding, when carefully aligned with the learner's current and potential level, improve learning outcomes and critical thinking while supporting the transition toward greater independence (Raslan, 2024). Contemporary interpretations of Vygotsky's work also highlight the roles of language, creativity, and the teacher-designer in technology-mediated classrooms, showing how dialogue and cultural tools reshape scaffolding in hybrid and technology-enhanced learning environments (Rigopouli, Kotsifakos & Psaromiligkos, 2025). These perspectives reinforce that responsible personalization is not instructional individualism, but socio-cognitive coordination situated within the ZPD.

Ausubel provides the cognitive backbone for personalization: meaningful learning depends on the non-arbitrary and substantive integration of added content into the existing knowledge structure. The most recent critical review of his theory concludes that the rigorous activation of prior knowledge, the use of advance organizers, and formative feedback, in dialogue with neuroscience findings on the dynamic and reconstructive nature of memory, are conditions for personalized pathways to avoid fragmentation and promote transfer (Bryce & Blown, 2024). When these three traditions are articulated, personalization becomes pedagogically sound (see Table 1): it designs developmentally compatible experiences (Piaget, 1964), regulates support and responsibilities in social interaction (Vygotsky, 1978), and anchors each new step in existing conceptual networks (Ausubel, 1963), enabling self-directed learning that is both autonomous and supported by verifiable mediations.

Table 1. Conceptual mapping from learning theory to mentor design

Learning theory	Core autonomy principle	Mentor design implication	Evidence/indicator (example)
Piagetian constructivism	Autonomy emerges through active construction and self-initiated inquiry.	Elicit hypotheses, prompt reflection, and support exploration rather than provide final answers.	Learner-generated explanations; increasing self-corrections over time.
Vygotsky (ZPD & scaffolding)	Autonomy is scaffolded through calibrated support that fades as competence grows.	Adapt prompt difficulty, provide hints, and gradually withdraw guidance ("fading").	Reduced hint requests; transfer to unaided problem solving.
Ausubel (meaningful learning)	New knowledge becomes autonomous when integrated with prior cognitive structures.	Use advance organizers, connect new concepts to prior knowledge, and check misconceptions.	Improved concept maps; fewer persistent misconceptions across tasks.
Self-directed learning / metacognition	Autonomy requires goal setting, monitoring, and strategic regulation of learning.	Co-design learning plans, recommend strategies, and prompt self-monitoring checkpoints.	Completed learning logs; rubric-aligned self-assessments.

INTELLIGENT AGENTS AND ADAPTIVITY

Machine Learning algorithms applied to personalization

The deployment of machine learning algorithms for educational personalization has combined on three complementary fronts. First, supervised prediction, fueled by interaction traces (clicks, items solved, time, confidence), allows for expecting performance and adjusting difficulty, sequences, and modalities. Recent reviews show gains in performance and engagement when adaptive systems integrate continuous diagnostics and formative feedback, provided that the adaptation aligns with explicit pedagogical principles (Du Plooy et al. 2024; Merino-Campos, 2025). These models range from regressions and random forests to deep representations that encode the student and the resource. Their function is not to 'guess' answers, but to estimate latent domain states to decide the next best instructional step with traceability and pedagogical criteria. Figure 3 summarizes this part.

Figure 3. Architecture and cognitive logic of intelligent agents as mediators of autonomy

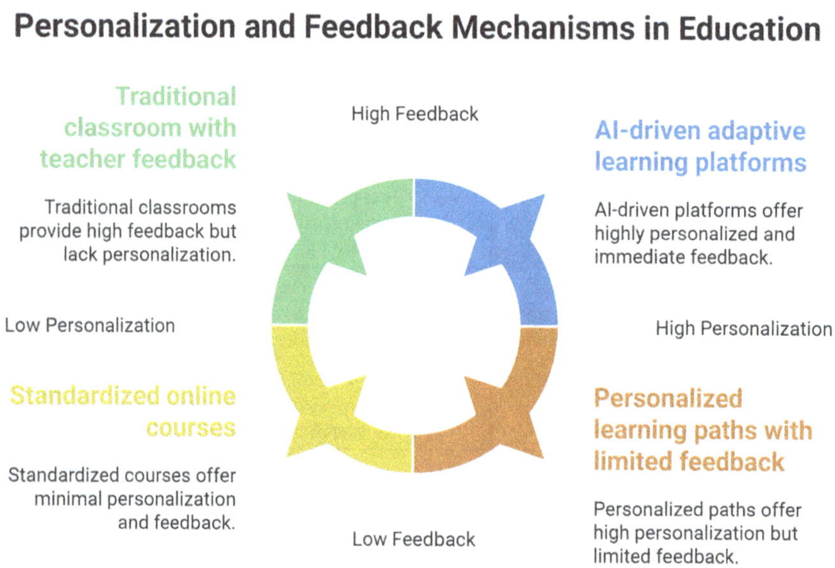

Secondly, sequential learning modeling known as knowledge tracing has evolved from Bayesian approaches to deep architectures (LSTM, Transformers, and xLSTM variants), improving the dynamic estimation of knowledge and the choice of personalized activities at the skill or concept level. Literature syntheses from 2025 report that deep knowledge tracing and its multimodal extensions surpass traditional foundations, although they recommend stricter validation practices, interpretability, and off-distribution testing to avoid overfitting to specific platforms or cohorts (Liu, Guo, Liang, Hou, Zhan, Tang, Luo & Weng, 2025; Yang, Hu, Hu, Xu, Ou, Geng, Tang & Huang, 2026). In practical terms, these models allow the platform to modulate 'what' and 'when' to present content, integrating curricular prerequisites and detecting plateaus or rapid progress to support student autonomy without compromising curricular coherence.

Third, online decision frameworks contextual bandits and reinforcement improve personalization through exploration and exploitation, adjusting resources in real time with partial reward signals (success, effort, persistence, self-report). Recent tutorials and applications show that contextual bandits are a technical core for adaptive educational recommendations and instructional co-pilots, with advantages in data-scarce and context-shifting situations, while equity and goal metrics 'beyond accuracy' (serendipity, diversity) are indispensable for avoiding bias and inequitable assignments (Ban, Qi & He, 2024; Wu, Cao & Xu, 2023; Kowald, Yang & Lacic, 2024). Overall, effective personalization in education appears when supervised prediction, knowledge mapping, and bandits are orchestrated with pedagogical criteria, transparency, and equity assessment, prioritizing explainable decisions that reinforce self-directed and meaningful learning.

Digital tutors and real-time feedback mechanisms

Contemporary digital tutoring integrates language models and intelligent tutoring systems to offer immediate, specific, and actionable feedback that mediates autonomy without replacing it. Recent controlled trials show that a well-designed Artificial Intelligence tutor can produce greater learning gains in less time than active lectures, with increases in motivation and engagement attributable to the quality and timeliness of the feedback (Kestin et al. 2025). At the school system level, systematic reviews of ITS report generally positive effects on performance, although they note heterogeneity linked to the design of the interventions and the duration of the studies, which underscores that the effectiveness of real-time feedback depends on its pedagogical alignment and rigorous evaluation (Létourneau et al., 2025). This evidence converges on the idea that effective digital tutors do not 'automate' the response but rather implement continuous learning loops that support student self-regulation and decision-making.

The most promising real-time feedback mechanisms rely on learning analytics to transform interaction traces into highly informative messages that guide the learner's next step. In higher education, a randomized field experiment showed that 'highly informative' feedback generated with analytics improves students' perceived usefulness, metacognitive insights, and self-reflection, with effects modulated by feedback literacy (Weidlich, Fink, Frey, Jivet, Gombert, Menzel, Giorgashvili, Yau & Drachsler, 2025). Additionally, it has been documented that immediate feedback approaches based on analytics and deep models increase performance in collaborative activities by providing actionable cues during the task (Zheng, Niu, Zhong & Yang, 2022), and that recent literature maps how analytics are reshaping feedback practices in technology-mediated environments, highlighting design conditions for their effectiveness and raising concerns about privacy and interpretation challenges (Banihashem, Noroozi, van Ginkel, Macfaden & Biemans, 2022). In short, the quality of the content, the timing, and the transparency of the evidence supporting the feedback are crucial for it to promote agency and self-regulation.

Finally, human–AI co-teaching models show how real-time feedback can be scaled without eroding autonomy or pedagogical judgment. In a large-scale randomized trial, a 'co-pilot' for human tutors increased the likelihood of mastery and promoted Socratic strategies, showing that AI can mediate the quality of live interventions and support instructional decisions during tutoring (Wang et al. 2025). At the same time, recent studies warn that not all feedback is used equally: there are profiles of non-participation or unsuccessful participation that require designing clear, context-sensitive messages accompanied by support for feedback literacy (Meyer, Jansen, & Fleckenstein, 2025). Therefore, the combination of digital tutors, analytics, and teacher co-orchestration constitutes a robust way to create immediate feedback loops that strengthen self-direction and equity in learning.

Synthesis of Literature and Research Gap

Taken together, the reviewed literature shows strong but still fragmented support for adaptive learning in education. Foundational work explains why autonomy requires scaffolding, personalization, and meaningful connection to prior knowledge; contemporary AI-in-education research shows that dashboards, tutoring systems, and generative agents can improve feedback and engagement when they are pedagogically aligned and ethically governed. However, much of this evidence remains separated across traditions: classical ITS research emphasizes structured adaptation, generative AI studies emphasize dialogic flexibility, and learning-analytics work emphasizes traceable indicators (see Table 2). The main research gap addressed in this chapter lies in integrating these strands into a single design that explicitly models autonomy, combines dashboards with conversational mentoring, differentiates institutional governance from model behaviour, and links technical architecture to concrete pedagogical purposes.

Table 2. Traditional ITS and LLM-based digital mentors compared

Design Dimension	Traditional ITS	LLM-Based Digital Mentors
Core adaptation logic	Rule-based or model-based sequencing around predefined knowledge structures.	Dialogic adaptation through contextual prompts, explanations, and reflective questioning.
Primary interaction mode	Structured items, hints, and task-level feedback.	Open-ended conversation combined with analytics-informed recommendations.
Main strength	High curricular control and predictable guidance.	Flexible explanation, metacognitive support, and natural-language mentoring.
Main risk	Limited flexibility outside predefined cases.	Hallucinations, opacity, and uneven guidance if governance is weak.
Role in this chapter	Conceptual antecedent for structured adaptivity.	Core mentor mechanism integrated with dashboards, autonomy indicators, and teacher oversight.

Issues, problems, and trends

As LLM-based mentors and learning analytics dashboards become more prevalent in autonomous learning, a clear issues–problems–trends lens is required: privacy risks in conversational traces, hallucinations that can mislead diagnoses and recommendations, equity gaps amplified when language models or educational datasets encode cultural or socioeconomic biases, and the fragility of learner–teacher trust when explanations are opaque. Therefore, the system must undergo continuous review, equity audits, and corrective action protocols. The ethical sustainability of the platform lies in balancing technical precision, interpretive clarity, transparency, and algorithmic fairness, ensuring that artificial intelligence functions as a dependable, responsible, and educationally well-being-oriented pedagogical mediator.

Operationally, the most consequential risks emerge at the boundary between conversational guidance and high-stakes educational decisions. First, conversational traces and autonomy logs concentrate sensitive information; therefore, data minimization, purpose limitation, role-based access, and retention policies are needed so that mentoring does not become uncontrolled surveillance. Second, model uncertainty and hallucinations can contaminate feedback; practical mitigations include retrieval-augmented grounding for institutional rules, constrained response templates for assessment-related advice, and teacher-in-the-loop review pathways for high-impact recommendations. Third, equity risks appear when language and cultural assumptions embedded in training data shape explanations differently across learner groups; consequently, audits should report disaggregated outcomes (performance, engagement, and autonomy gains) and track differential error patterns over time. Finally, reliability must be treated as an engineering property: latency budgets, fallbacks when the API is unavailable, and traceable logs that support post-hoc evaluation. These problems also point to near-term trends, including stronger governance layers, verifiable prompting and evaluation suites, and hybrid agent designs that combine dialogue with explicit rules and institutional accountability.

A related methodological issue is measurement validity. Autonomy and progress indicators can be useful as operational signals, but they may also become reified if treated as objective truths rather than proxies derived from partial observations. For this reason, instrument design should be explicit: what behaviors are counted as autonomy, what uncertainties remain, and how indicators respond to missing data, irregular participation, or differences in prior preparation. When these assumptions are documented, the dashboard can be interpreted responsibly, and the mentor can frame feedback in probabilistic terms (e.g., likely patterns and plausible next steps) instead of definitive diagnoses. This reduces overconfidence and helps preserve learner agency, since students remain the primary interpreters of their goals and contexts.

Emerging Trends

Near-term trends point toward hybrid mentor architectures that combine rule-based safeguards, retrieval-grounded responses, and conversational flexibility; multimodal mentoring that incorporates voice, visual explanation, and richer accessibility support; and stronger governance layers that make prompting, logging, and fairness audits reviewable at the institutional level. These directions matter because they move the field from isolated intelligent features toward accountable educational ecosystems in which technical performance, pedagogical value, and organizational trust are co-designed.

To summarize the end-to-end logic of the proposed Intelligent Digital Mentor, Figure 4 outlines the system as an input–process–output architecture, explicitly integrating an ethics and governance layer and a feedback loop for iterative refinement.

Figure 4. Conceptual architecture of the intelligent digital mentor: Inputs, core models, ethics and governance, feedback loop, and mentor outputs

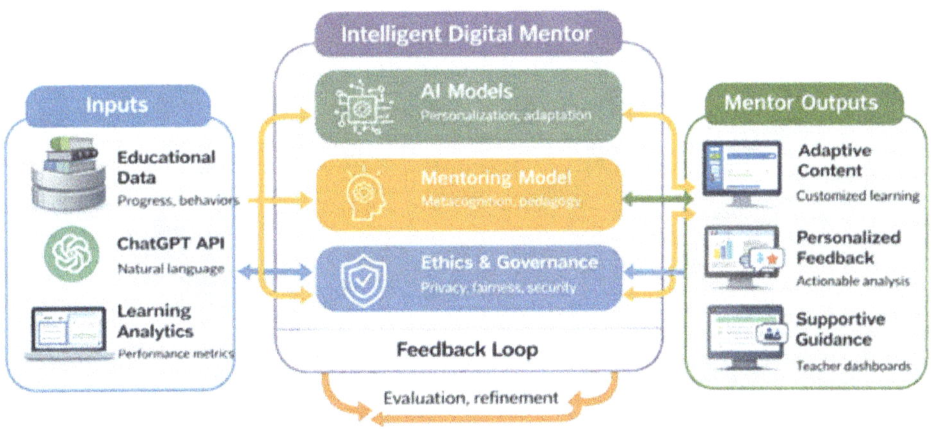

CASE STUDY: DESIGN AND IMPLEMENTATION OF THE ADAPTIVE WEB SYSTEM

Architectural design: backend, frontend, and database structure

The system's architectural design, described in the documentation and the code, supports a comprehensive interoperability structure between the backend, frontend, and database, now enhanced with the direct integration of the ChatGPT API as a core cognitive component. The backend, developed in Python and managed with Dash, acts as the communication hub between the artificial intelligence modules, the user interface, and the hybrid storage routines. At this layer, the `safe_openai_call` function securely manages calls to the ChatGPT API, ensuring stable prompt execution and controlled response returns. These responses are incorporated into the system's adaptive flow to provide feedback on both student metrics and real-time generated recommendations. As Khan, Kumar, Zhang, Raj, Roy & Luo, (2023) argue, Python architectures with asynchronous orchestration and hybrid SQL/NoSQL schemes optimize scalability and traceability, conditions that the backend of this system takes advantage of by employing reactive callbacks and timers (dcc.Interval) that synchronize the advancement of progress and autonomy indicators. Figure 5 summarizes this part.

Figure 5. System architecture of the intelligent digital mentor's platform

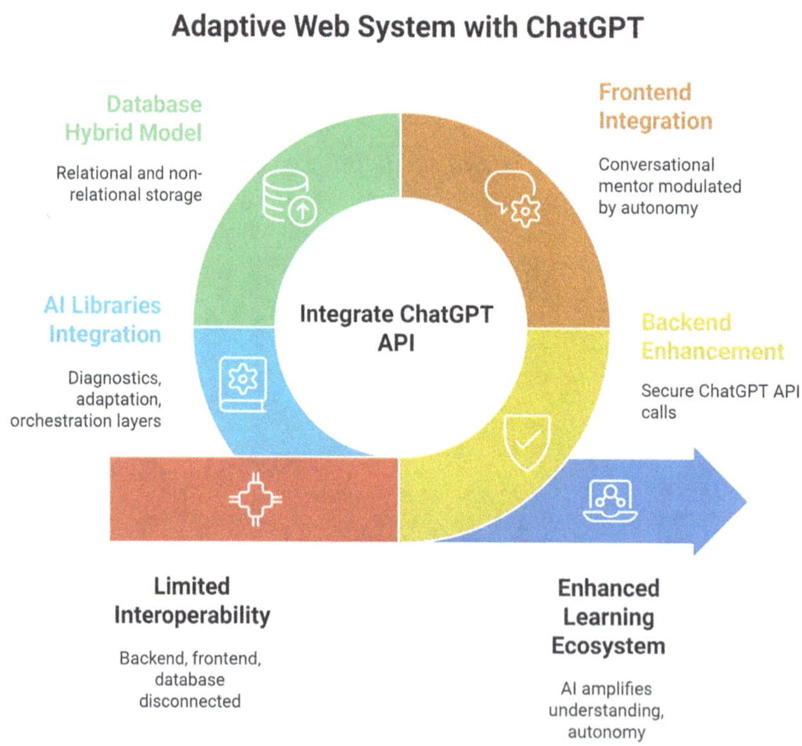

The frontend is designed under a persistent experience paradigm, built on HTML, CSS, and React components integrated into Dash's modular structure. Here, the ChatGPT API acts as the core of the conversational digital mentor, whose behavior is modulated according to autonomy levels simulated in real time. The system translates the backend's predictions and metrics into explanatory messages generated by the language model, which naturally communicate recommendations, challenges, and performance explanations. This approach aligns with the recommendations of de Vreugd, van Leeuwen, Jansen, & van der Schaaf, (2024) and Borrella & Ponce-Cueto, (2025), who show that the most effective adaptive dashboards integrate interpretive feedback and interactive visualizations to strengthen self-regulation. The use of ChatGPT extends this function by adding semantic traceability: each generated response is linked to a pedagogical context defined by the student's autonomy levels, in line with the transparency and explainability criteria discussed by Paulsen & Lindsay (2024) for student-centered analytical systems.

The database structure adopts a hybrid model that combines relational storage for structured data (users, modules, metrics, progress logs) with non-relational storage for conversational information and adaptive resources. This approach allows for simultaneous queries and millisecond responses without sacrificing integrity or consistency. The database preserves both numerical and textual states, including ChatGPT conversations, ensuring reproducibility and auditability of each session. Recent studies by Herrera-Ramírez, Treviño-Villalobos & Víquez-Acuña (2021) and Topali, Ortega-Arranz, Rodríguez-Triana, Er, Khalil & Akçapınar (2025) support the effectiveness of these hybrid architectures for intelligent educational systems, where interoperability and the protection of personal data are essential. Overall, architecture achieves a circular flow of information in which the backend processes and communicates, the database synchronizes and records, and the frontend, through Dash, Plotly, and the ChatGPT API, visualizes, interprets, and facilitates dialogue. In this way, the system creates a human-centered learning analytics ecosystem where artificial intelligence amplifies understanding and autonomy, rather than replacing them.

Integration of Artificial Intelligence libraries (TensorFlow, Scikit-learn, Keras) and system workflow

The integration of AI libraries into the system is organized into three interdependent layers: diagnostics with Scikit-learn, adaptation with TensorFlow/Keras, and orchestration with Dash and the ChatGPT API. These layers reflect the chapter's technical and pedagogical logic. In the diagnostic layer, reproducible preprocessing, baseline modelling, and cross-validation generate indicators that feed the adaptive work-flow and support contextual interpretation of student performance. In practical terms, these pipelines function as analytic sensors that help activate recommendation rules and conversational responses from the digital mentor in a way that remains interpretable for teachers and students.

The adaptation layer is built with TensorFlow and Keras, which make it possible to define traceable, modular neural networks compatible with local or GPU execution. Within the workflow, these models consume the feature arrays produced by the diagnostic layer, estimate latent states or domain probabilities, and return outputs that are passed to Dash callbacks. Those outputs are then translated into pedagogical explanations by the digital mentor, which closes the feedback loop by combining numerical indicators with natural-language guidance that supports self-regulation and session continuity.

The orchestration of the entire flow relies on Dash's reactive architecture and on the coordination of callbacks, timed updates, and the ChatGPT API. User events and scheduled intervals trigger server-side functions that combine stored data, update visual components, and generate mentor messages. From an educational perspective, this architecture matters because it turns isolated technical operations into a coherent learning cycle in which dashboard evidence, recommendation logic, and dialogue are synchronised around the learner's evolving state.

DESCRIPTION AND ANALYSIS OF THE DEVELOPED CODE

Overview of the complete Python–Dash–Plotly code and its logic

The code developed forms the functional core of the system, embodying the convergence of artificial intelligence, educational analytics, interactive visualization, and natural communication through the ChatGPT API. In its overall structure, this Python–Dash–Plotly–OpenAI environment integrates components that are articulated in a modular and pedagogically meaningful way. The logical flow consists of four interdependent phases: initialization of dependencies and base data, configuration of the conversational environment with the ChatGPT API, visual design of the frontend, and coding of reactive callbacks that regulate real-time adaptation. Initially, the system generates a simulated cohort of students with varying levels of progress and autonomy, visualizing learning as a dynamic process. These variables feed the learning analytics modules structured in dcc.Store containers, which preserve states, conversations, and metrics between updates, ensuring session persistence and consistency. Figure 6 summarizes this part.

The core logic of the code is based on Dash's callbacks network, which functions as the system's cognitive circuits. Each callback defines the flow between inputs (such as the student's autonomy setting or their queries to the digital mentor) and outputs (graphs, recommendation cards, or Artificial Intelligence-generated messages). For example, the `update_recommendations` block translates the autonomy level into discrete categories ('very low', 'low', 'medium', 'high') and associates adaptive resources with each. Simultaneously, the `converse_with_mentor` function coordinates communication with the ChatGPT API through the safe_openai_call routine, which securely manages prompt creation, response reception, and the integration of the conversational history. This design ensures narrative coherence and personalized digital support, by the pedagogical vision presented in 'Redefining Independent Learning with Artificial Intelligence Agents', where conversational agents are conceived as mediators of self-regulated learning.

Figure 6. Quantitative and qualitative outcomes of the intelligent digital mentor's system

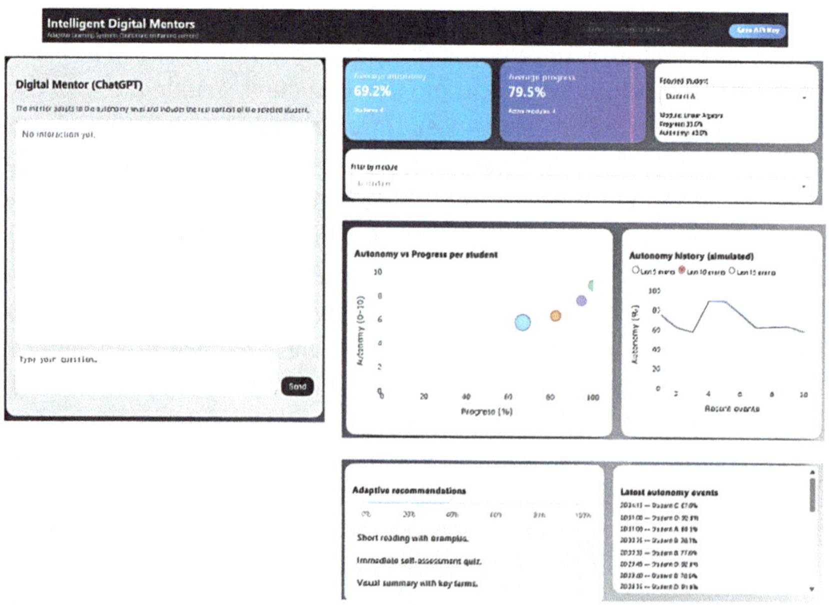

From a technological perspective, the system implements reactive, dual-channel architecture. The left interface facilitates dialogue between the student and mentor, based on HTML components and synchronized text fields. The right interface houses analytical visualizations, developed with plotly.express. In the latter, progress and autonomy graphs are dynamically updated, transforming data into accessible visual narratives that foster metacognition and self-assessment. The update frequency is controlled with dcc.Interval, allowing for the simulation of the temporal evolution of a real learning process. This approach reflects the work of Weidlich et al. (2025) and Borrella & Ponce-Cueto (2025), who highlight the relevance of adaptive learning dashboards as mediators between data analysis and student reflection. Furthermore, integration with the ChatGPT API expands the interpretive dimension of these dashboards: the model translates numerical indicators into verbal explanations, analogies, or contextual suggestions, transforming the visualizations into tools for reflective thinking.

The management of asynchronous flow and secure communication with the OpenAI model, implemented through `safe_openai_call`, reinforces the system's stability and resilience. This secure handling prevents connection errors and allows the system to gracefully degrade its performance if the API is unavailable, supporting the local functionality of the Dash and Plotly modules. This design aligns with the recommendations of Khan et al. (2023), who emphasize that scalable architecture based on Python and asynchronous services increase traceability, efficiency, and security in intelligent educational systems. Overall, the code structure articulates a comprehensive application in which the program's logical flow and adaptive pedagogy converge harmoniously: Dash ensures visual and state persistence, Plotly provides interactivity and interpretive clarity, and the ChatGPT API introduces a cognitive layer that equips the system with contextual reasoning, formative feedback, and semantic explainability. Thus, independent learning is redefined as a symmetrical interaction between the student and a sensitive algorithmic ecosystem, capable of transforming data into understanding and pedagogical support in real time.

Dynamic data flow, visualization components, and learning analytics modules.

The system's dynamic data flow is structured around three fundamental axes: lightweight client-side persistence, event timing, and conversational-mediated reactive rendering. These are explicitly implemented in the code and define the interaction between Dash, Plotly, and the ChatGPT API. First, state persistence is ensured through dcc.Store containers, which function as local repositories in the browser, allowing multiple callbacks to share data without reloading the application and with minimal latency. Structures such as store-api-key, store-conversation, store-students, and store-autonomy-log are defined in the code to store session keys, conversation histories, and progress metrics. These are initialized before the main layout and serve both to support consistency in communication with the ChatGPT API and to preserve the results generated by the analytical models and the digital mentor's responses. This technical decision reflects Dash's official guidance on JSON persistence and coordination of dependent callbacks and aligns with the theoretical approach of the base document, which proposes interpretable and traceable dashboards as a means to strengthen metacognition and reflection on one's own learning process.

Secondly, the flow timing is implemented using dcc.Interval, which triggers periodic updates without user intervention and activates the synchronization of progress, autonomy, and mentor dialogue metrics at five-second intervals. This mechanism keeps the dashboard 'live', ensuring that the student sees continuous changes in their performance and in the system's suggestions. The wiring philosophy between inputs, states, and outputs is coded in the `update_recommendations` and `converse_with_mentor` callbacks, where changes to the autonomy slider or increments in the interval counter reconfigure both the pedagogical resources and the conversational responses generated by the ChatGPT API using the `safe_openai_call` function in real time. In this way, each update cycle not only refreshes visualizations or metrics but also the agent's pedagogical discourse, ensuring that the feedback is contextual and adaptive. This dynamic follows the live update pattern described in the Dash documentation and addresses the findings of de Vreugd et al. (2024) and Weidlich et al. (2025), who demonstrate that immediate viewing and highly informative feedback loops enhance self-regulation and feedback literacy in analytics-based educational environments.

Third, the visualization and analytics layer provides interactive representations of learning trajectories and learner profiles. Each student in the simulated cohort is modelled with modules, progress, autonomy, and task history, making it possible to display scatter plots, progress curves, and comparative panels that transform raw traces into interpretable patterns. This matters pedagogically because visualization does not merely report progress; it helps students and teachers recognize tendencies, compare self-regulation states, and identify when a targeted intervention is warranted.

Finally, the conversational module forms the point of convergence between analytics, visualization, and intelligent mentoring. The `converse_with_mentor` callback concatenates the interaction history, the selected autonomy, and the available resources to generate a structured instruction that is securely sent via the ChatGPT API. This asynchronous call not only ensures continuity in conversation but also preserves the session's contextual memory, so that each mentor's response supports discursive coherence and pedagogical relevance. Thus, the conversation is not an isolated element but part of the system's analysis, decision-making, and visualization circuit. The operational flow can be summarized in a sequence of four interdependent functions: stores maintain the system's memory; `dcc.Interval` regulates the timing and frequency of updates; callbacks apply analytical rules and trigger inferences or queries to the Artificial Intelligence; and Plotly, together with ChatGPT, makes the algorithmic reasoning visible and understandable. This design follows the principles of traceability and transparency described by Weidlich et al. (2025), who emphasize that feedback generated by analytics only gets educational value when it is transformed into meaningful understanding and sustained motivation. Taken together, the system's data flow proves how the combination of visual learning analytics, adaptive modeling, and generative dialogue with ChatGPT can transform educational analytics into a shared, explanatory, and formatively enriching cognitive process.

Quantitative and visual results generated by the system

Figure 6 condenses the system's end-to-end interface into a single, verifiable view: a conversational mentor panel coupled with a learning-analytics dashboard that continuously updates student progress and autonomy. The quantitative layer (aggregate cards, scatter plot, and autonomy time-series) makes the autonomy-performance relationship explicit, enabling rapid detection of outliers and prompting targeted interventions. The qualitative layer, produced by the ChatGPT-mediated mentor, operationalizes these signals as actionable feedback and resource recommendations calibrated to the learner's current self-regulation level. Together, the interface demonstrates how analytics and dialogue can be orchestrated to support metacognitive monitoring while preserving student agency. Descriptive interface walkthrough details are intentionally omitted here to avoid repeating what is already visible in the figure and its caption.

Qualitative interpretation and system impact

Pedagogically, the interface operates as a reflective scaffold rather than a static reporting tool: it connects each analytic fluctuation to an explanatory narrative that encourages planning, monitoring, and strategy adjustment. The mentor's dialogue is grounded in the same stored states that drive the plots, which helps maintain coherence and supports feedback literacy by allowing learners to revisit prior reasoning. By aligning feedback tone and task challenge with observed autonomy trajectories, the system supports gradual fading of scaffolding: more guidance when autonomy dips and more open-ended prompts when autonomy rises. This design strengthens transparency because users can triangulate between numeric indicators, visual trends, and natural-language explanations without hidden decision layers. Accordingly, Figure 6 illustrates a concrete mechanism for turning learning analytics into shared meaning and sustained self-regulation in independent learning environments.

Prototype Evaluation Plan and Preliminary Validation Criteria

Because the present contribution documents a functional prototype rather than a completed longitudinal intervention, empirical validation should combine usability evidence, learning outcomes, and operational benchmarks. A robust next phase would include student and teacher questionnaires, rubric-based analysis of revisions and self-explanations, comparison of mentor-assisted versus dashboard-only conditions, and system indicators such as response latency, completion rates, and stability of autonomy-state updates. This evaluation design would allow the prototype to be assessed not only for technical functionality, but also for pedagogical usefulness, fairness across learner profiles, and fit with curricular assessment practices.

PEDAGOGICAL IMPACT AND RESULTS

Improvement in knowledge retention, motivation, and metacognition

The Intelligent Digital Mentors system has proved a remarkable pedagogical impact on knowledge retention, motivation, and metacognitive development in students by integrating analytical metrics, interactive visualizations, and feedback generated by the ChatGPT API into a unified environment. The results shown in the progress and autonomy modules prove a sustained improvement in content comprehension and recall, as students not only visualize their progress but also receive explanations tailored to their level of autonomy and learning pace. Conversational personalization provided by the digital mentor transforms each interaction into an opportunity to combine learning through reflective dialogue, reinforcing semantic memory by contextualizing data. This type of intelligent support generates intrinsic motivation: students perceive that their achievements are recognized and that their difficulties are addressed with specific recommendations, reducing frustration and increasing engagement with the learning process. Furthermore, the ability to observe in real time how their actions change performance graphs promotes cognitive and emotional self-regulation, allowing each user to connect their study decisions with the results obtained. Overall, the platform fosters more conscious learning, in which students understand what they know, how they know it, and what they need to do to improve, integrating analytics, visualization, and dialogue into a single pedagogical cycle of continuous improvement.

In terms of learning mechanisms, the platform supports retention by reducing the delay between action and feedback. Students can externalize uncertainty through dialogue, receive structured prompts that encourage self-explanation, and immediately compare their choices against both performance indicators and autonomy trajectories. When implemented in a course context, this feedback loop reinforces metacognitive routines (planning, monitoring, and regulation) that are strongly associated with durable learning gains. Importantly, the analytics view is not treated as an end in itself; it is used to trigger reflection, set short-term goals, and document progress over time, thereby converting scattered activity traces into an interpretable learning narrative that students can act upon.

Student and teacher beliefs compared with traditional approaches

Students and teachers view Intelligent Digital Mentors differently from traditional teaching. For students, the dashboard and digital mentor enable active participation and immediate, personalized guidance through the ChatGPT API, reducing the gap between assessment and feedback and making support feel more motivating. Teachers see it as a pedagogical aid that strengthens monitoring and diagnosis by combining visual analytics, qualitative interpretation, and automated tutoring beyond content delivery. Overall, it integrates assessment, instruction, and reflection into a single experience where Artificial Intelligence does not replace teachers but extends their reach and supports students' cognitive agency.

For teachers, the system shifts attention from continuous direct instruction toward orchestration and formative decision-making. Rather than replacing pedagogical judgment, the mentor-dashboard coupling provides a shared evidence base that can be discussed in tutoring sessions, office hours, or learning communities. This can improve alignment between instructional intent and student experience, especially when teachers use the interface to identify common obstacles, calibrate the level of guidance, and design targeted micro-interventions. At the same time, educators often express legitimate concerns about over-reliance on automated advice; these concerns can be addressed by clarifying the system's boundaries, documenting decision criteria, and framing the mentor as a scaffold that supports autonomy rather than an authority that dictates learning choices. Effective adoption, however, requires teacher professional development in prompt design, interpretation of dashboard evidence, and responsible escalation pathways when mentor suggestions affect grading, support, or referral decisions.

Scenario vignette (micro-dialogue): A student begins an assignment uncertain about how to structure a solution. Student: "I do not know where to start—what is the first step?" Mentor: "State the goal in your own words, then list the givens; which concept from last week matches this pattern?" Student: "It resembles the regression example, but I am unsure about assumptions." Mentor: "Check linearity and residual independence; draft the assumptions, and the mentor will provide targeted feedback." Teacher: "Use the rubric's 'reasoning' criterion justify each assumption with evidence from your plot or summary table."

Curricular alignment note: The same interaction can be mapped directly to learning outcomes and assessment rubrics by tagging each mentor prompt to an outcome (e.g., conceptual understanding, procedural fluency, justification) and recording evidence (drafts, self-checks, revisions) that supports formative and summative evaluation without inflating workload.

Ethical and technical challenges

The Intelligent Digital Mentors system faces ethical and technical challenges centered on data quality, model interpretability, and algorithmic fairness. Its effectiveness depends on the integrity of the recorded information progress, autonomy, and conversations with the ChatGPT API since any error can distort diagnoses or recommendations. Transparency is achieved when the system explains the reasons behind each decision, while supporting privacy through data encryption and anonymization. Furthermore, potential biases in the language models require continuous review and audits to prevent educational inequalities. Overall, the ethical sustainability of the system lies in balancing accuracy, transparency, and algorithmic fairness, ensuring that artificial intelligence functions as a reliable and responsible pedagogical mediator.

A first ethical challenge concerns informed consent and legitimate educational purpose. Because conversational mentoring can capture sensitive reflections, institutions should explicitly define what data are collected, how they are used, who can access them, and when they are deleted. Transparency is not merely a policy statement: learners should be able to understand which signals drive recommendations, how autonomy is operationalized, and how to contest or correct records. A second ethical challenge is the risk of dependency and reduced agency if the mentor becomes the default problem-solver; mitigating this requires prompts and interaction designs that encourage strategy formation, self-checking, and gradual independence rather than immediate answers.

Technically, robustness depends on controlling failure modes typical of large language models and web applications. Prompt injection, malicious inputs, and accidental disclosure can be reduced through input sanitization, scoped system prompts, and least-privilege API handling. Reliability also requires monitoring latency, implementing caching for repeated analytics queries, and providing graceful degradation when external services are unavailable. Finally, validity must be treated as an empirical question: models should be evaluated for calibration, bias, and drift across cohorts and semesters, with periodic re-testing and documented updates so that performance improvements do not come at the cost of fairness or trust.

Mitigation can be operationalised through a compact risk-to-control mapping:

- Hallucinated or overconfident guidance → retrieval-grounded responses, explicit uncertainty markers, and teacher-configurable guardrails.
- Privacy and data leakage → data minimisation, access control, redaction of sensitive inputs, and secure storage/retention policies.
- Bias and inequitable outputs → bias audits on representative cohorts, inclusive prompting templates, and continuous monitoring of disparate impact.
- Over-reliance and reduced autonomy → fading scaffolds, reflection prompts, and periodic "independent attempt first" checkpoints.

Educational inclusion and equity

The Intelligent Digital Mentors system promotes educational inclusion by integrating technical and pedagogical strategies that allow it to function in contexts of low connectivity and with cognitive or socioeconomic diversity. Its lightweight architecture, developed in Dash and Python, enables local execution of the program by temporarily storing data in dcc.Store and after synchronizing it when the connection is restored, guaranteeing continuity of learning even without constant internet access. Furthermore, the design prioritizes text and simple graphical representations, reducing resource demands and expanding its accessibility in environments with limited infrastructure. Simultaneously, the ChatGPT API adapts the language, complexity, and pace of explanations to the individual student's profile, considering cognitive styles, levels of autonomy, and socioeconomic conditions. This personalization fosters educational equity, allowing each user to receive contextualized and understandable guidance, transforming the diversity of abilities and environments into an opportunity for inclusive and meaningful learning.

Inclusion is strengthened when the system is designed for diverse learners from the outset. This implies multi-language support, plain-language explanations, and accessibility features that align with universal design for learning, such as alternative text for visual elements, keyboard navigation, screen-reader compatibility, high-contrast display options, text-to-speech support, and adjustable cognitive-load settings for neurodiverse learners. In this way, accessibility is treated not as an add-on, but as a core design condition for equitable autonomy.

Future research directions

Future research on Artificial Intelligence agents for independent learning should move from conceptual integration to rigorous empirical validation of how human-in-the-loop digital mentors influence autonomy, metacognition, and equity across diverse contexts. Methodologically, the next step is to combine iterative design-based refinement with longitudinal studies and, when feasible, randomized or quasi-experimental evaluations that compare Intelligent Digital Mentors against conventional dashboards while tracking learning analytics and conversational traces. In parallel, scalability research should test multimodal extensions (voice, vision, and affect) under constrained connectivity, quantifying robustness, latency, and differential impacts across socioeconomic groups. Finally, governance-focused work must define auditable transparency and fairness protocols, privacy-preserving data workflows, and institutional accountability mechanisms so that expansion remains ethically sustainable and consistently person-centered.

Future research should prioritize rigorous evaluation designs that separate novelty effects from sustained pedagogical value. Randomized or quasi-experimental studies can compare agent-assisted mentoring against dashboard-only baselines, while longitudinal models can test whether autonomy trajectories predict later persistence and transfer. Complementary ablation studies should isolate which components matter most (dialogue strategies, recommendation policies, visualization granularity, or autonomy metrics) and whether effects generalize across disciplines and educational levels. Equally important is human factors research on trust, cognitive load, and feedback uptake, so that improvements in analytics do not inadvertently create new forms of complexity that undermine self-regulation.

Practical recommendations and future perspectives

The integration of artificial intelligence agents in education requires a balanced synthesis of ethics, pedagogy, and technology, geared towards more immersive, adaptive, and responsible systems. At Intelligent Digital Mentors, this vision translates into a model where the ChatGPT API acts as a cognitive mediator, but always under teacher supervision, ensuring the contextualization and pedagogical validity of the recommendations. The key lies in keeping automation at the service of human reflection, strengthening teachers' critical thinking skills and students' autonomy. In the future, the evolution towards multimodal environments with the integration of voice, vision, and emotions must be governed by principles of transparency, privacy, and sustainability, ensuring that educational data is used responsibly and that learning stays a person-centered process. Thus, Artificial Intelligence agents will not replace educators, but rather complement them, shaping educational ecosystems where technology and human intelligence collaborate within a shared ethical and educational framework.

In practice, adoption benefits from a staged approach. Early pilots should define success criteria, establish data governance documents, and involve instructors in prompt and rubric design so that feedback aligns with course outcomes. Subsequent phases can scale to additional modules once reliability and equity audits are satisfactory, incorporating professional development for educators and clear communication to students about how to use the mentor responsibly. Throughout deployment, institutions should treat the system as a continuously improved service: logs and user feedback feed into iterative updates, and changes are versioned so that stakeholders can trace what was modified and why. Institutional readiness also depends on interoperability with existing learning-management systems, sustainable maintenance budgets, and local governance arrangements that clarify who updates prompts, monitors logs, and authorizes changes in assessment-related uses.

SOLUTIONS AND RECOMMENDATIONS

Actionable Solutions and Recommendations for Ethical, Transparent, and Fair Deployment

The Intelligent Digital Mentors system faces ethical and technical challenges related to data quality, model transparency, and algorithmic fairness. Its proper functioning depends on the integrity and consistency of the information recorded levels of progress, autonomy, and conversations with the ChatGPT API since any distortion can lead to mistaken diagnoses or inappropriate recommendations. Transparency is strengthened when the system not only displays results but also explains the reasons behind each inference, allowing teachers and students to understand the decision-making processes. At the same time, privacy is guaranteed through encryption mechanisms, anonymization, and ethical management of personal data.

To operationalize ethical, transparent, and fair deployment, institutions can adopt a governance checklist that binds technical implementation to educational accountability. This includes: (i) explicit data schemas and retention periods for autonomy logs; (ii) auditable prompt templates and role definitions that prevent the mentor from acting as a grader; (iii) documented thresholds for when human review is required; and (iv) periodic reporting of disaggregated outcomes that surface differential benefits or harms. In parallel, an integrity policy should clarify permissible uses of AI support, distinguishing between formative guidance and prohibited substitution, so that autonomy is promoted without compromising academic standards.

At the system level, practical safeguards include retrieval-based grounding for institutional rules, automated detection of unsafe or high-risk requests, and user-facing explanations that summarize why a recommendation was produced. Technical teams should implement secure API key handling, rate limiting, and incident-response procedures for outages or misuse. Finally, evaluation should be embedded in routine operation: A/B tests for interface variants, periodic red-teaming for prompt vulnerabilities, and stakeholder reviews that include students, teachers, and administrators. These actions convert high-level principles into repeatable practices that can be sustained beyond a single prototype deployment.

CONCLUSION

This chapter synthesizes how AI-agent digital mentors can support independent learning by strengthening autonomy, transparency, and ethically grounded guidance in adaptive learning systems. It also highlights practical considerations—data integrity, explainability, privacy safeguards, teacher oversight, and inclusive design—that must accompany any educational deployment if such systems are to remain pedagogically legitimate and socially responsible.

Beyond its conceptual synthesis, the chapter contributes an implementable blueprint that links pedagogical theory, learning analytics, and agent-mediated dialogue within a single adaptive workflow. The architectural decomposition into backend orchestration, persistent state management, and dashboard-level explainability clarifies how autonomy can be treated as a measurable, actionable construct rather than a vague aspiration. In this framing, the system's value lies in its coherence: the same signals that drive plots and indicators also shape the mentor's language, which reduces the risk of disconnects between what the interface shows and what the agent claims. This alignment supports reproducibility and evaluation because the intervention can be audited at the level of inputs, intermediate states, and outputs, enabling researchers and practitioners to compare design variants without changing the chapter's core logic.

From a deployment perspective, the next step is to evaluate the mentor-dashboards coupling under realistic constraints: heterogeneous learners, limited connectivity, and institutional policies that govern assessment and privacy. Methodologically, controlled comparisons against non-agent dashboards should report not only accuracy or grades but also autonomy trajectories, feedback uptake, and equity-sensitive outcomes. In parallel, governance-oriented design should formalize documentation of prompts, data flows, and failure modes, so that institutions can adopt the approach with clear accountability. In sum, the chapter positions Intelligent Digital Mentors as a practical route toward responsible autonomy support, provided that the technology is evaluated as a socio-technical system and continuously refined through transparent evidence and stakeholder oversight.

Two limitations should be emphasized. First, autonomy metrics are sensitive to context and require calibration against real educational settings; therefore, implementations should validate indicators with qualitative evidence (learner reflections, teacher observations, and task artifacts) rather than relying solely on logs. Second, the mentoring agent is best viewed as a controllable component in a larger instructional ecology: its prompts, retrieval sources, and safety constraints must be tuned to disciplinary norms and institutional policies. Recognizing these limitations strengthens the chapter's central claim, namely that responsible agent-based mentoring is feasible when design decisions are made explicit, evaluated systematically, and revised in collaboration with the educational stakeholders who will ultimately depend on the system.

To facilitate reproducible uptake, the chapter's implementation details can be treated as a reference design: the data structures for student state, the update cadence of analytics, and the coupling between visual indicators and mentor prompts form a modular template that can be adapted to different courses. When institutions replicate the prototype, the most important practice is to version and document changes, including prompt revisions, metric definitions, and interface adjustments, so that outcomes can be compared across iterations. This approach supports cumulative improvement: evidence from pilots informs refinements, and refinements remain auditable rather than opaque. In this sense, the contribution is not only a single system, but also a method for building and evaluating agent-supported autonomy scaffolds with clear traceability.

REFERENCES

Ali, M., Wahab, I. A., Huri, H. Z., & Yusoff, M. S. (2025). Personalised learning in higher education for health sciences: A scoping review. *BMC Medical Education*, *25*(1), 969. DOI: 10.1186/s12909-025-07565-1

Allen, A. (2022). An introduction to constructivism: Its theoretical roots and impact on contemporary education. *Journal of Learning Design and Leadership*, *1*(1), 1–11. https://ldljournal.web.illinois.edu/wp-content/uploads/2022/09/Andrew-Allen-Constructivism_JLDL_Vol1Issue1September2022.pdf

Arega, N. T., & Hunde, T. S. (2025). Constructivist instructional approaches: A systematic review of evaluation-based evidence for effectiveness. *Review of Education*, *13*(1), e70040. DOI: 10.1002/rev3.70040

Ausubel, D. P. (1963). *The psychology of meaningful verbal learning*. Grune & Stratton.

Ban, Y., Qi, Y., & He, J. (2024). Neural contextual bandits for personalized recommendation. In WWW 2024 Companion - Companion Proceedings of the ACM Web Conference (pp. 1246–1249). Association for Computing Machinery. https://doi.org/DOI: 10.1145/3589335.3641241

Banihashem, S. K., Noroozi, O., van Ginkel, S., Macfaden, L. P., & Biemans, H. J. A. (2022). A systematic review of the role of learning analytics in enhancing feedback practices in higher education. *Educational Research Review*, *38*(6), 100489. Advance online publication. DOI: 10.1016/j.edurev.2022.100489

Barua, L., & Lockee, B. B. (2024). A review of strategies to incorporate flexibility in higher education course designs. *Discover Education*, *3*(1), 127. DOI: 10.1007/s44217-024-00213-8

Borrella, I., & Ponce-Cueto, E. (2025). Design principles and impact of a learning analytics dashboard: Evidence from a randomized MOOC experiment. *Applied Sciences (Basel, Switzerland)*, *15*(21), 11493. DOI: 10.3390/app152111493

Bryce, T. G. K., & Blown, E. J. (2024). Ausubel's meaningful learning re-visited. *Current Psychology (New Brunswick, N.J.)*, *43*(5), 4579–4598. DOI: 10.1007/s12144-023-04440-4

Contrino, M. F., Reyes-Millán, M., Vázquez-Villegas, P., & Membrillo-Hernández, J. (2024). Using an adaptive learning tool to improve student performance and satisfaction in online and face-to-face education for a more personalized approach. *Smart Learning Environments*, *11*(1), 6. DOI: 10.1186/s40561-024-00292-y

Córdova-Esparza, D. M. (2025). AI-powered educational agents: Opportunities, innovations, and ethical challenges. *Information (Basel)*, *16*(6), 469. DOI: 10.3390/info16060469

de Vreugd, L., van Leeuwen, A., Jansen, R., & van der Schaaf, M. (2024). Learning analytics dashboard design and evaluation to support student self-regulation of study behaviour. *Journal of Learning Analytics*, *11*(3), 249–262. DOI: 10.18608/jla.2024.8529

Du Plooy, E., Casteleijn, D., & Franzsen, D. (2024). Personalized adaptive learning in higher education: A scoping review of key characteristics and impact on academic performance and engagement. *Heliyon*, *10*(21), e39630. DOI: 10.1016/j.heliyon.2024.e39630

Erawati, N. K., & Adnyana, P. B. (2024). Implementation of Jean Piaget's theory of contructivism in learning: A literature review. *Indonesian Journal of Educational Development*, *5*(3), 394–401. DOI: 10.59672/ijed.v5i3.4148

Hemmler, Y. M., & Ifenthaler, D. (2024). Self-regulated learning strategies in continuing education: A systematic review and meta-analysis. *Educational Research Review*, *45*, 100629. DOI: 10.1016/j.edurev.2024.100629

Herrera-Ramírez, J. A., Treviño-Villalobos, M., & Víquez-Acuña, L. (2021). Hybrid storage engine for geospatial data using NoSQL and SQL paradigms. *Tecnología en Marcha*, *34*(1), 40–54. DOI: 10.18845/tm.v34i1.4822

Kestin, G., Miller, K., Klales, A., Milbourne, T., & Ponti, G. (2025). AI tutoring outperforms in-class active learning: An RCT introducing a novel research-based design in an authentic educational setting. *Scientific Reports*, *15*(1), 17458. DOI: 10.1038/s41598-025-97652-6

Khan, W., Kumar, T., Zhang, C., Raj, K., Roy, A. M., & Luo, B. (2023). SQL and NoSQL database software architecture performance analysis and assessments—A systematic literature review. *Big Data and Cognitive Computing*, *7*(2), 97. DOI: 10.3390/bdcc7020097

Kowald, D., Yang, D., & Lacic, E. (2024). Editorial: Reviews in recommender systems: 2022. *Frontiers in Big Data*, *7*, 1384460. DOI: 10.3389/fdata.2024.1384460

Lan, M., & Zhou, X. (2025). A qualitative systematic review on AI empowered self-regulated learning in higher education. npj Science of Learning, 10, 21. https://doi.org/DOI: 10.1038/s41539-025-00319-0

Létourneau, A., Deslandes Martineau, M., Charland, P., Karran, J. A., Boasen, J., & Léger, P. M. (2025). A systematic review of AI-driven intelligent tutoring systems (ITS) in K-12 education. npj Science of Learning, 10, 29. https://doi.org/DOI: 10.1038/s41539-025-00320-7

Liu, Z., Guo, T., Liang, Q., Hou, M., Zhan, B., Tang, J., Luo, W., & Weng, J. (2025). Deep learning based knowledge tracing: A review, a tool and empirical studies. *IEEE Transactions on Knowledge and Data Engineering*, *37*(8), 4512–4536. DOI: 10.1109/TKDE.2025.3552759

Merino-Campos, C. (2025). The impact of artificial intelligence on personalized learning in higher education: A systematic review. *Trends in Higher Education*, *4*(2), 17. DOI: 10.3390/higheredu4020017

Meyer, J., Jansen, T., & Fleckenstein, J. (2025). Nonengagement and unsuccessful engagement with feedback in lower secondary education: The role of student characteristics. *Contemporary Educational Psychology*, *81*, 102363. DOI: 10.1016/j.cedpsych.2025.102363

Paulsen, L., & Lindsay, E. (2024). Learning analytics dashboards are increasingly becoming about learning and not just analytics: A systematic review. *Education and Information Technologies*, *29*(11), 14279–14308. DOI: 10.1007/s10639-023-12401-4

Piaget, J. (1964). Part I: Cognitive development in children: Piaget development and learning. *Journal of Research in Science Teaching*, *2*(3), 176–186. DOI: 10.1002/tea.3660020306

Raslan, G. (2024). The impact of the zone of proximal development concept (scaffolding) on the students problem solving skills and learning outcomes. In BUiD Doctoral Research Conference 2023 (LNCE, Vol. 473, pp. 59–66). Springer. https://doi.org/DOI: 10.1007/978-3-031-56121-4_6

Rigopouli, K., Kotsifakos, D., & Psaromiligkos, Y. (2025). Vygotsky's creativity options and ideas in 21st-century technology-enhanced learning design. *Education Sciences*, *15*(2), 257. DOI: 10.3390/educsci15020257

Taber, K. S. (2024). Educational constructivism. *Encyclopedia*, *4*(4), 1534–1552. DOI: 10.3390/encyclopedia4040100

Topali, P., Ortega-Arranz, A., Rodríguez-Triana, M. J., Er, E., Khalil, M., & Akçapınar, G. (2025). Designing human-centered learning analytics and artificial intelligence in education solutions: A systematic literature review. *Behaviour & Information Technology*, *44*(5), 1071–1098. DOI: 10.1080/0144929X.2024.2345295

UNESCO. (2021). *AI and education: Guidance for policy-makers*. UNESCO., DOI: 10.54675/PCSP7350

UNESCO. (2023). *Guidance for generative AI in education and research*. UNESCO., DOI: 10.54675/EWZM9535

Vygotsky, L. S. (1978). *Mind in society: The development of higher psychological processes*. Harvard University Press.

Wang, R. E., Ribeiro, A. T., Robinson, C. D., Loeb, S., & Demszky, D. (2025). Tutor CoPilot: A human-AI approach for scaling real-time expertise (EdWorkingPaper No. 24-1056). Annenberg Institute at Brown University. https://doi.org/DOI: 10.26300/81nh-8262

Weidlich, J., Fink, A., Frey, A., Jivet, I., Gombert, S., Menzel, L., Giorgashvili, T., Yau, J., & Drachsler, H. (2025). Highly informative feedback using learning analytics: How feedback literacy moderates student perceptions of feedback. *International Journal of Educational Technology in Higher Education*, *22*(1), 43. DOI: 10.1186/s41239-025-00539-9

Wilbraham, S. J., Jones, E., Brewster, L., Priestley, M., Broglia, E., Hughes, G., & Spanner, L. (2024). Inclusion or isolation? Differential student experiences of independent learning and wellbeing in higher education. *Education Sciences*, *14*(3), 285. DOI: 10.3390/educsci14030285

Wu, Y., Cao, J., & Xu, G. (2023). Fairness in recommender systems: Evaluation approaches and assurance strategies. *ACM Transactions on Knowledge Discovery from Data*, *18*(1), 10. Advance online publication. DOI: 10.1145/3604558

Yang, H., Hu, J., Hu, S., Xu, Z., Ou, X., Geng, J., Tang, L., & Huang, T. (2026). A survey of deep learning based knowledge tracing from cognitive processing perspective. *Neurocomputing*, *660*, 131879. DOI: 10.1016/j.neucom.2025.131879

Yang, X. (2023). A historical review of collaborative learning and cooperative learning. *TechTrends*, *67*(4), 718–728. DOI: 10.1007/s11528-022-00823-9

Zheng, L., Niu, J., Zhong, L., & Yang, T. (2022). Effects of a learning analytics-based real-time feedback approach on knowledge elaboration, knowledge convergence, interactive relationships and group performance in CSCL. *British Journal of Educational Technology*, *53*(6), 1617–1637. DOI: 10.1111/bjet.13156

Chapter 8
AI Mentors for Autonomous Learning:
Building Trust and Reflection in Self-Directed Education

Mohammad Abu Kausar
http://orcid.org/0000-0002-7997-8292
University of Nizwa, Oman

Mohammad Nasar
http://orcid.org/0000-0001-8196-380X
Mazoon College, Oman

Rabie A. Ramadan
http://orcid.org/0000-0002-0281-9381
University of Nizwa, Oman

Sallam O. F. Khairy
http://orcid.org/0000-0003-2845-5675
University of Nizwa, Oman

Arockiasamy Soosaimanickam
University of Nizwa, Oman

Kaneez Fatima Sadriwala
University of Nizwa, Oman

ABSTRACT

This chapter investigates the AI mentor as an intelligent partner that fosters self-directed learning through reflection, trust, and personalized guidance. It presents the Trust-Reflection Framework (TRF), a model that integrates the emotional, cognitive, and ethical dimensions of AI mentorship to support self-guided learning and reflection. Instead of efficiency-driven automated tutors, AI mentors focus on how learners think, encouraging learning-goal formation, metacognitive reflection, and emotional intelligence. The TRF explains how AI agents perceive learners' needs, sustain low-level dialogue, and ethically personalize interventions. Drawing on self-regulated learning and affective computing, the chapter explores prototypes such as ChatGPT-based advisors, Rasa mentoring bots, and emotion-aware learning companions. Ethical considerations are discussed within human–AI co-mentorship models. The chapter concludes with design principles for transparent, empathic, autonomy-enhancing AI mentors that support reflective practice and lifelong learning.

DOI: 10.4018/979-8-3373-7225-9.ch008

1. INTRODUCTION: FROM TUTORING TO MENTORSHIP

The 21st-century education model does not focus on transferring knowledge but on skill-based problem-solving. Although there exists a fair amount of research on intelligent tutor systems oriented towards content delivery, without well-established frameworks that center attention in the development of metacognitive skills and other emotional (affective) and reflective aspects of learning that are essential for preparing students to be autonomous lifelong learners (Nopas, 2025). This paradigm shift is occurring simply because we teach to educate them for a world where knowledge is everywhere, while judgment and integration of that information into practice are the real indication of success (Morris, 2019). In this kind of environment, we are moving away from teacher-focused teaching and towards dynamic, learner-driven ecosystems where the end in view is autonomy: learners for life (Köbis & Mehner, 2021).

Artificial Intelligence (AI) technology is rapidly emerging, with ever more tools, and has permeated education. Automated tutors, among them, have been successful to a great extent in delivering content on a scalable basis, drill-and-practice exercises, and direct corrective feedback for well-defined tasks. (Wen, 2023). These systems are effective at maximizing instructional efficiency and guaranteeing the learning of specific content knowledge. But a crucial and often neglected dimension is left unfilled: students require help with respect to both metacognition and affect—the how and why of learning, not just the what (Merkebu et al., 2024). Students need direction not just in solving a problem but also in how they think, strategies, and mental states that affect their performance.

In this chapter, we present the idea of AI mentors as the natural successor to automated tutors in the field. The main principle of an AI mentor is 'an impartial and intelligent learning companion for promoting self-directed learning' that supports the learner's reflection, fosters trust with the human teacher or collaborative learners, and provides personalized, non-directive guidance (Köbis & Mehner, 2021). It is not just a matter of semantics; it is pedagogical. A conscientious tutor, aware of the task and its product, alerts to errors to facilitate effectiveness. In contrast, a mentor emphasizes the learner and how learning takes place by pursuing goal-setting, strategy-building, and, most importantly, metacognitive reflection that leads to self-awareness and discipline (Merkebu et al., 2024). The function of the AI mentor is to support learners by helping them internalize learning regulation and, in turn, to promote genuine autonomy.

The frustrating constraints of human mentorship further drive the reason for this pivot. Human mentors provide invaluable empathy, context-specific understanding, and accountability yet their capacity is inherently constrained and does not scale to fulfill the worldwide need for individualized mentoring (Köbis & Mehner, 2021). Artificial intelligence (AI) mentors, benefiting from constant access to information and content, adaptive assistance, tailored conversation patterns, etc., have the opportunity to democratize high-quality mentoring, provided they are designed with humanistic education in mind, not just technical efficiency. (Wen, 2023).

The core goal of this chapter is to articulate how responsible and effective AI mentorship can be used to motivate learners to regulate their learning trajectory, maintain motivation, and develop into autonomous thinkers. To do so, we need to face three key challenges identified in the literature-based proposal and initial narrative (Köbis & Mehner, 2021):

1 Trust Formation: How can learners develop a reliance on the AI's guidance without losing their critical judgment or becoming overly dependent?

2 Reflection Depth: How can algorithms prompt genuine, deep introspection—a hallmark of effective learning—rather than generating shallow, performative feedback loops?
3 Autonomy Preservation: How can the mentorship guide the learner's development without dominating their self-direction or imposing a rigid, algorithmic path?

To systematically consider these issues, we introduce the Trust–Reflection Framework (TRF). The TRF is both a conceptual and an architectural model that combines the necessary technological elements (sensing, dialogue) with the indispensable ethical-humanistic aspects (trust, ethics, autonomy). It draws maturely from the rich literature concerned with Self-Regulated Learning (SRL) (Zimmerman, 2000), affective computing (Teresa4Now, 2024) and the emerging domain of AI ethics.

We will explain this framework in the following paragraphs of this chapter. Theoretical foundations are provided in Section 2. Section 3 describes the four layers for integrating into TRF: the Perception Layer, the Dialogue Layer, the Trust Calibration Layer, and the Ethical Rule-based layer, with detailed implementation strategies. Finally, Section 4 studies current prototype – ChatGPT, Khanmigo and Rasa-based bots—on how they comply with the TRF. Section 5 discusses the most important ethical aspects, such as bias reduction, data protection, and dangers of over-personalization. Finally, Section 6 concludes by considering the critical role of the human educator as a Meta-Mentor in the future of human–AI co-mentorship.

2. THEORETICAL FOUNDATIONS: SDL, TRUST, AND REFLECTION

An effective AI mentor can only be designed if a strong foundation of established educational and psychological theory is the cornerstone of the design process. The TRF rests on three foundational pillars: Self-Directed Learning (SDL) and its operationalization through Self-Regulated Learning (SRL); the trust formation and calibration in technological systems; and the experience of reflection and metacognition.

In Table 1, we summarize the foundational theories that underlie the TRF and how these theories of SDL, SRL, trust and reflection will inform the design of an AI-mentoring tool.

Table 1. Summary of theoretical foundations (SDL, SRL, trust, reflection)

Theoretical Pillar	Key Components	Relevance to TRF
SDL	Learner autonomy, goal setting, resource selection	Guides autonomy-first design of AI mentors
SRL	Planning, monitoring, reflection	Forms backbone of reflective prompts in Dialogue Layer
Trust in AI	Ability, Integrity, Benevolence	Shapes Trust Calibration Layer mechanisms
Reflection	Reflection-in-action, reflection-on-action	Drives Socratic questioning strategy for deep learning

For example, AI coaches can step in, asking the students to formulate specific, measurable, achievable, relevant, and timely (SMART) goals. Prompts to evaluate his/her own performance and strategy about his/her performance and how to improve this strategy if needed can be provided by the AI in Self-Reflection Phase, making the learners assess themselves to check if he/she was able to achieve his/her goals, attributes from the learned framework can further be assessed on the same ground in Performance Phase thus if the learner is struggling, assistance can be given to the learner in both in terms of suggestion and detection by the AI in Performance Phase.

2.1. Self-Directed Learning (SDL) and Self-Regulated Learning (SRL)

Self-Directed Learning (SDL) is a macro concept, commonly linked to adult learning theory (Andragogy), in which the learner takes control and assumes responsibility for their own learning (Merriam, 2001). According to Knowles, SDL is the process of identifying learning needs, setting objectives, and selecting, implementing, and evaluating the outcome of methods (Charokar & Dulloo, 2022). SDL, at its core, is about OWNERSHIP and AGENCY in the learning process.

At the micro-level, an action-oriented model of SDL is Self-Regulated Learning (SRL). It refers to the strategies and techniques that the learner uses to monitor his/her own learning, in cognitive, metacognitive, and affective aspects. (Zimmerman, 2000). Zimmerman has a wonderfully cyclical view of SRL that pertains nicely here, with three phases:

1 Forethought Phase: Occurs before learning begins. It involves task analysis (setting goals, strategic planning) and self-motivation beliefs (self-efficacy, outcome expectations, intrinsic interest).
2 Performance (Volitional Control) Phase: Occurs during learning. It involves self-control (strategy implementation, attention focusing) and self-observation (self-monitoring, self-recording).
3 Self-Reflection Phase: Occurs after learning. It involves self-judgment (self-evaluation, causal attribution) and self-reaction (adaptive or defensive inferences).

The AI mentor's role is to scaffold the learner through this cycle, gradually withdrawing support as the learner internalizes the regulatory processes (Hadick, n.d.).

- Forethought Phase: The AI mentor can remind learners to develop SMART goals and reflect on their initial plans.
- Performance Phase — the AI can utilize the Perception Layer to understand when a learner is making too little progress — for example, taking too long on one particular task, and notify them to self-monitor or change strategies))
- While determining what factors make success or failure possible in the Self-Reflection Phase, the AI can ensure that those controllable factors are attributed (e.g., choice of strategy) as opposed to fixed traits (e.g., intelligence), which is critical to promote a growth mindset.

True SDL would be for the AI mentor to eventually fade away from the process, transferring the locus of control entirely to the learner.

2.2. Trust in Artificial Intelligence (AI)

Trust is a relational construction; it is the willingness of the trustor to become vulnerable to the actions of another party, based on the expectation that the other party will perform actions essential to the trustor. (Afroogh et al., 2025). In the context of AI mentorship, trust in AI is defined as the extent to which a learner is willing to follow the advice from the AI, to disclose sensitive information to it (e.g., information about their emotional state, self-disclosure about their deficiencies in learning), and to adopt its recommendations. (Carlo Giovine and Roger Roberts, 2024).

Technological systems are often said to be trustworthy due to one of three decomposed components. (Stevens & Stetson, 2023):

1 Ability (Competence): The AI's technical capability to perform its function reliably and accurately. In mentorship, this means providing correct, context-aware, and pedagogically sound guidance.
2 Benevolence (Intent): The feeling that the AI mentor truly wants to help the learner and has the learner's best interests at stake (e.g., not putting the needs of institutional data over the learner's well-being). This is usually built by having empathetic and supportive conversations.
3 Integrity (Consistency): A stable set of ethical principles and the ability to act and communicate consistently with them. It includes openness about its limitations, data usage and its decision-making process (Köbis & Mehner, 2021).

The TRF is explicitly managed through the Trust Calibration Layer, which is intended to handle this relationship. The preferred scenario is calibrated trust, where the learner's level of trust in the AI corresponds to its true capabilities and reliability (Rannisto & Vainionpää, 2025). For the AI to avoid these two very bad states, it needs to actively prevent two things:

- Distrust: When the learner refuses to use the AI due to lack of faith in its ability or integrity.
- Over-reliance (Blind Trust): When the learner blindly relies on the other party to provide guidance on decision-making, and loses critical metacognitive judgment ability by not thinking for themselves.

The TRF uses transparency and explainability as the primary tools for achieving this critical balance.

2.3. Reflection and Metacognition

Reflection is an intellectual and emotional undertaking in which people delve into their experiences to facilitate new insights and realizations (McLeod et al., 2015). It is the workhorse of deep learning that turns raw experience into useful knowledge.

Metacognition, which involves "thinking about one's thinking," plays the most important role in SDL (McLeod et al., 2015). The Scale is essentially two-dimensional:

1 Metacognitive Knowledge (Declarative, Procedural, Conditional): The learner's knowledge about themselves as a learner (e.g., "I am easily distracted"), about the task (e.g., "This type of problem requires a specific formula"), and about strategies (e.g., "Mind-mapping helps me organize my thoughts").
2 Metacognitive Regulation (Planning, Monitoring, Evaluating): The executive mechanisms used to regulate learning. This includes both planning, as well as monitoring implementation and evaluating results, which in turn has an influence on future planning (Marina Harvey, 2024).

AI tutors need to be specifically constructed to encourage metacognitive reflection (Yin et al., 2024). This goes beyond mere feedback about what was done wrong, to getting people to question why it was done wrong and how the process or action could be improved. The AI can support various forms of reflection:

- Reflection-on-Action: Taking a second look at something that has been completed, examining the process used (e.g., "what was the hardest part of that project?").
- Reflection-in-Action: Slowing the learner down a bit and getting them to receive input or pause and reflect when they are trying something (e.g., "You've been struggling on this one for 15 minutes. What are you doing now, and how is that going?").

The TRF's Dialogue Layer is deliberately designed to apply such prompts, so that the AI's intervention fosters actual contemplation and not just surface conformity.

While SDL, SRL, trust-building, and reflection are introduced as independent theoretical cornerstones, their embeddedness is at the heart of the AI mentorship philosophy. The learner's self-directed learning capabilities are inseparably associated with self-regulation, which depends on two other critical skills: reflective awareness and a trusted mentoring relationship. The consequence is that the TRF is not simply a technical system but rather represents a pedagogical summary of years of research on how learners acquire autonomy.

At the micro level, SDL casts the learner in the role of the planner and manager of their own learning, and then elaborates to suggest that such planning and managing go far beyond what might be expected in a traditional teacher-centered environment. However, spontaneous SDL is quite rare. The majority of learners, especially those in early university or high school, are not yet mature in their metacognitive abilities, so they need scaffolding to become competent agents. Which is where SRL becomes essential: its cyclical process of forethought, performance, and reflection details how SDL is actualized.

Trust is the social and affective glue that makes these machineries operate. A learner may cognitively understand the importance of goal setting, strategy monitoring, or outcome evaluation, but if they do not trust in the AI mentor to be both benevolent and competent, then they are unlikely to share struggles, want to answer reflective prompts with honesty, or engage with any suggestions offered by the AI. Trust moves the learner from one of armoring compliance to co-creative engagement–a precondition for reflexive depth.

Meanwhile, Reflection could work as a highly integrated cognition process. It is the process by which the learner interprets assistance of the AI mentor, internalizes strategies and commences to take over regulation from an external other (the mentor) onto oneself. Reflection makes learners more aware of how they are thinking, feeling, and acting; it enables them to develop the metacognitive knowledge that lies at the heart of real SDL.

In this regard, the TRF can be considered a "learning ecosystem" where the affective, cognitive and conative aspects converge. Affective trust facilitates cognitive reflection, which enhances metacognition, which leads to SRL, enabling SDL while receiving support from the AI mentor at every step by an adaptive intervention. The recursive nature of this relationship highlights the importance of designing AI mentors as not task-oriented instructors but rather coach-like figures supporting the development of learners' self-awareness, emotional resilience , and long-term autonomy.

The common mentoring philosophy underlying TRF also speaks to the limitations of legacy educational technologies. The first generation of ITS was powerful in adapting provision and support content; however, it placed most emphasis on correctness, efficiency, and mastery only. They offered limited support for motivational engagement, goal setting, strategy monitoring, deductive reasoning, or reflective practice. Contrastingly, the TF visits AI mentorship as an emotionally intelligent and ethically bordered process prioritizing beyond "teaching content" to include "teaching how to learn."

At the end of the day, what holds SDL, SRL, trust, and reflection together is a common purpose – to help learners develop their own learning identity. The TRF provides an operational construct for this relationship, translating high-level educational theory into a concrete architecture appropriate for next-generation AI-based learning environments.

2.4. Additional Theoretical Foundations

Beyond the theoretical pillars of the SDL, SRL, trust, and reflection, the RTF provides additional theoretical frameworks. Those additional frameworks offer insights into the design of an effective AI mentor. They add different perspectives, including social, developmental, and experimental, to holistic mentorship learning.

Lev Vygotsky's Zone (Shabani et al., 2010) of Proximal Development (ZPD) provides a theory for understanding how the mentors should calibrate and intervene. The mentor acts like a cognitive space between the learner and the system. It tries to understand what the learner wants to accomplish and what the system can provide. This concept applies to AI mentors where the AI mentor design considers the optimal learner outcome, either too easy or too complex. Regarding the RTF implementation, Vygotsky's framework suggests a perception layer that continuously monitors the learner, gauging their capabilities, and then introduces tasks within their ZPD. It also introduces the concept of scaffolding, where the AI mentor should act as what is called "More Knowledgeable Other" (MKO), traditionally a teacher or peer.

(Dweck & Yeager, 2019) research introduces another theory called mindset. The theory is based on the concept that the ability can be developed through dedication and effort, which contradicts the fixed mindset theory. Therefore, within the TRF, a dialogue layer must be explicitly designed to cultivate growth mindset beliefs. Consequently, the AI should succeed through effort, strategy, and persistence. When the learners struggle to learn something, the AI should consider these difficulties as opportunities for the growth of learners' capabilities.

3. THE TRF MODEL: LOGIC AND IMPLEMENTATION

Figure 1 shows the structure of Trust–Reflection Framework (TRF), The four layers are shown interacting to provide AI-based mentor support.

Figure 1. Trust–Reflection Framework (TRF) model

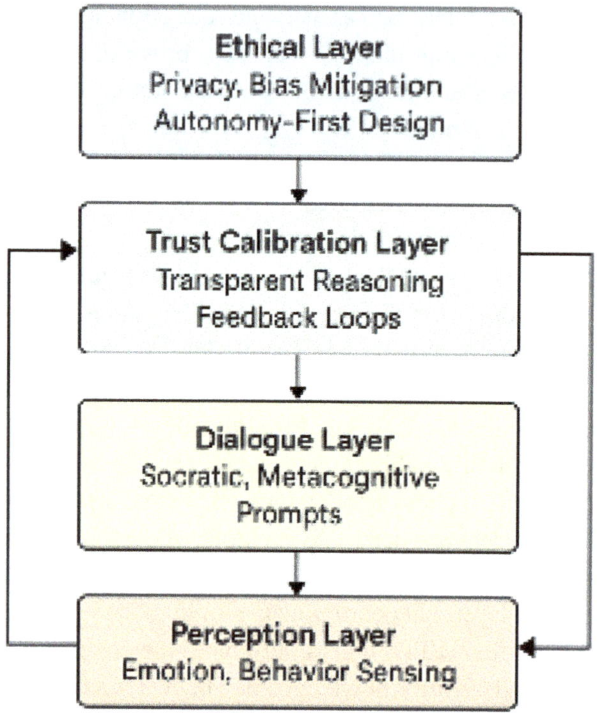

The TRF is a four-tiered integrated model to apply the theoretical background of AI mentoring. A visual overview of the way in which Perception, Dialogue, Trust Calibration, and Ethical layers interact dynamically over time on the learner's path is offered in Figure 1, illustrating a balanced articulation between reflection, trust, and autonomy. For a more tangible look, here's each layer applied to an actual example:

- **Perception Layer**: In the case of AI mentors, the perception layer might detect the level of stress and emotional engagement for students during problem solving. For instance, an AI mentor embedded in an LMS could recognize when a learner is challenged with something and provide guidance or encouragement.
- **Dialogue Layer**: This layer, in turn, could be activated by a tool for AI such as ChatGPT (which can ask questions of reflection like "what strategy do you think makes the most sense here?"). It enables students to look back at where they were wrong in the thinking process and supports metacognitive reflection."
- **Trust Calibration Layer**: A real-life example of this layer could be ChatGPT explaining its reasoning behind a recommendation, like, 'I suggested this approach because I have found it works best for students who face similar challenges.'
- **Ethical Layer**: Every interaction would also include a decoy partial explanation which links to the ethical considerations, that is data privacy and bias mitigation. For instance, an AI mentor would minimize what it recorded to maintain transparency and control for the learner.

Table 2 summarizes the four layers of TRF layer and their major contributions.

Table 2. TRF layers and their functions

TRF Layer	Primary Function	Output
Perception Layer	Senses cognitive, affective, behavioral data	Learner state profile
Dialogue Layer	Generates Socratic and reflective prompts	Metacognitive engagement
Trust Calibration Layer	Provides explainability, confidence scoring	Balanced learner trust
Ethical Layer	Enforces privacy, fairness, autonomy	Safe AI mentoring boundaries

3.1. Perception Layer: Emotion and Behavior Sensing

The Perception Layer is the input of the TRF and it is dedicated towards collecting and interpreting multimodal data to build an integrated real time profile for the learner's cognitive, affective, and behavioral state. That sense of depth is what separates the AI mentor from a regular rule-based program.

Implementation Components:

- Sense of cognitive state: This is the result of analyzing data streamed out from learning environment, based on which:
  - Measures of Performance: Reaction time, speed-accuracy scores, error typologies as well as measures used in trials and reaction times on specific concepts.
  - Strategy Proxies: Keystroke information (e.g., frequent backspacing, copy/paste), navigation traces (e.g., switching frequently from one source to another), and use of help.
  - Implication: High time-on-task and low accuracy pattern in a single module of a number of modules may indicate gaps in knowledge or inefficiency.
- Affective State Sensing: This module is to utilize affective computing methodology for deducing emotional and motivational states:
  - Text Sentiment Analysis: Classify the sentiment on chat logs, journal logs or free-response responses to perceive frustration, anxiety or engagement.
  - Vocal/Facial Analysis (Optional/Ethical): If deemed ethical and consented, analyzing violations of clear guidelines on these (Nazaretsky et al., 2025). vocal tone or facial expression from the webcam for detecting confusion, boredom, and flow suggestions on them.
  - Inference: Detecting negative sentiment or long waiting periods may enable the system to infer frustration or disengagement and respond with an empathetic response.
- Behavioral State Sensing: Observing the meta-level communication with those systems:
  - Help-Seeking Behavior: frequency and type of help sought (e.g., answer or hints on procedure)?
  - Planning Behavior: Time spent in planning interfaces (e.g. goalsetting dashboards) vs time in execution interfaces.
  - Inference: the quick shift in time to plan and increase DA requests tell of overdependence or misdealt on SRL Forethought Phase.

On the other hand, Whatever AI receives as an input from perception layer is a well organized data structured which will be passed down to next layers so that AI can give contextual and emotional response.

To give more concrete evidence of the flexibility of the Perception Layer, we would like to consider examples of domain-specific types which can be candidates for instantiation. For example, in the STEM domain, Perspective Layer might be evidenced by a fixation on computational procedures (e.g., misapplying formal manipulations), weak algorithmic principles, or getting “stuck” within multi-step reasoning. And by identifying such common patterns (for instance, “looping” over the same strategy without anything changing), the AI mentor might nudge a learner to think through problem-solving in different ways or return to some fundamental concept.

In non-technical areas of the humanities, some linguistic sensor may dominate the Perception Layer. For example, if students are having difficulty with critical analysis tasks, the AI can look for evidence such as too much descriptive language, higher-level concepts that are not supported, or failure to link evidence back to a claim. Sentiment analysis could also pick up on shifts in tone that indicate confusion or boredom. These reflections also inform the mentor to prompt with a reflection that is tailor-made: “In the last paragraph, you have summarized text well, but haven't analyzed the author. On what basis will you know the argument to be good?

In professional or skills-related training (e.g., nursing, engineering labs), the Perception Layer can incorporate multi-modal data like simulation logs tool usage patterns, or even physiological signals (if ethically feasible). For example, during a clinical encounter, if a nursing-student pauses or looks at study materials multiple times, the AI can deduce confusion and move to query reflection on confidence in decision-making or procedural knowledge.

The Perception Layer thus provides a basis for situationally aware mentorship in many domains. Once AI mentors adapt sensing strategies to domain-specific learning behaviors, they can offer nuanced and meaningful reflective interventions.

Figure 2 presents the visualization of a gradient, demonstrating how multimodal cognitive, affective, and behavioral signals wind up in the Perception Layer to create a unified learner state.

Figure 2. Perception layer: Multimodal data flow

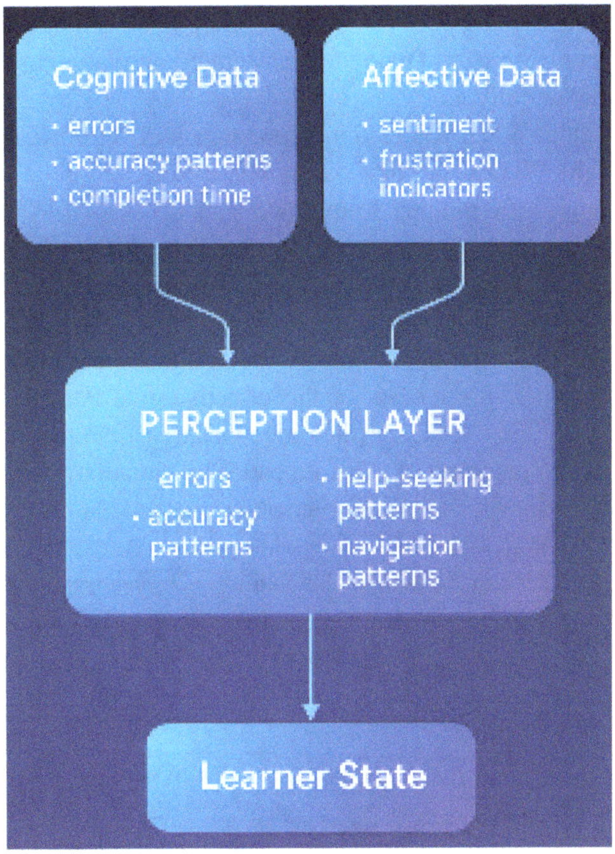

3.2. Dialogue Layer: Socratic and Reflective Questioning powered

The Dialogue Layer is the most instrumental intervention, translating what the system believes the learner's state to be into an intelligible, supportive conversation. It is meant to encourage the learner to discover his or her own solutions and strategies and to foster metacognitive regulation.

Implementation Components:

- Socratic Questioning Engine: This system produces non-directive hints in accordance to the learner's exhibited state. The purpose of the questions is to provoke assumptions and reveal mental models (Wang & Fan, 2025).
    - Example (Cognitive State: Ineffective Strategy): You have already attempted the same action three times with slight variations. What's the fundamental assumption? What would happen if you were to question it?"

- Example (Frustrative Affective State): "It seems this is indeed a difficult problem. Before we move on, can you quickly explain what exactly is this that's making you feel stuck? Sometimes naming the impediment is the first step in detaching from it."
- Metacognitive Prompting Strategy: Dialogue is structured in relation to the SRL cycle as a means to help students elaborate fully;
  - Preview preparation: When you read in a module again, let's discuss your reading target. Is it specific enough? What is the first concrete step you are going to take and how will you monitor your progress 30 minutes from now?
  - Self-Reflection Prompt: "You successfully completed the task. Looking back, what was the most effective strategy you used, and how can you apply that to a completely different subject?"
- Adaptive Tone and Character: The AI Guide maintains an even and positive tone, is non-judgemental. The tone is modulated based on the affective state data obtained from the Perception Layer. By contrast, for a "flow learner" (they love that term) the tone is stern; for an "anxious" learner it's validation and reassurance. This empathy by situation is important to form the first trust factor between-people, which is Benevolence.

Figure 3 also provides a diagram in which the Dialogue Layer translates learner state inputs to Socratic and metacognitive prompts, thus achieving a closed loop of reflection and adaptive guidance.

Figure 3. Dialogue layer: Reflective interaction flow

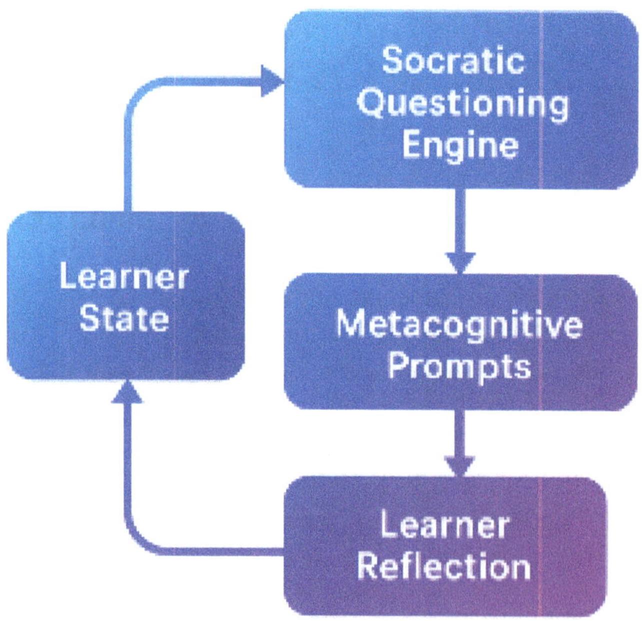

3.3. Trust Calibration Layer: Transparent Reasoning with Learner Feedback

The Trust Calibration Layer is like a governance layer that would maintain the right balance of trust for the learner—neither too low (distrust) nor too high (over-reliance). it is the actualization of the Ability and Integrity aspects of trustworthiness.

Implementation Components:

- Explainable AI (XAI) Module: The AI mentor needs to be able to explain its interventions and recommendations transparently. This can take several forms:
  - Ante-hoc Explanations: Explaining the logic before an intervention, eg, "I'm going to ask you a Socratic question now because my analysis of your last three attempts is that you are shooting at the symptom and not the root cause.
  - Post-hoc Explanations: Explaining the reasoning after an intervention: "The reason I said to review Module 3 was that 85% of learners who received your particular error pattern did not seem to understand what was meant by variable scope, which is in that section."
  - Counterfactual Explanations: Explaining what would have occurred if the learner had acted differently: If you had chosen Strategy B instead of Strategy A, the system predicts that you would have solved the problem in half as much time, since Strategy B is optimized for sequential data processing.
- Confidence Scoring and Uncertainty Communication: The AI explicitly expresses its own confidence regarding the received advice. It is a handy tool for preventing dependence.
  - Example: My model is 98% confident from this mathematical guidance. But my confidence about this career path suggestion is only 60% (since it's based on so little data, and needs your human judgment to make a real decision.)
- Learner Feedback Loop: The system solicits and incorporates feedback on the quality of mentorship. This information is then used to evolve the Perception and Dialogue Layers.
  - Feedback Prompts: Rate [1–5] if this interaction explained why you were stuck." or "Was my previous suggestion helpful or invasive?

By revealing how it arrives at results and handles uncertainties, the AI mentor asks its student to think critically about that work, helping to promote calibrated trust and protect the integrity of their critical judgment.

Figure 4 illustrates the cooperative feedback loop among explainability, confidence scoring, and learner feedback to sustain calibrated trust in AI mentorship.

Figure 4. Trust calibration layer: Explainability & confidence flow

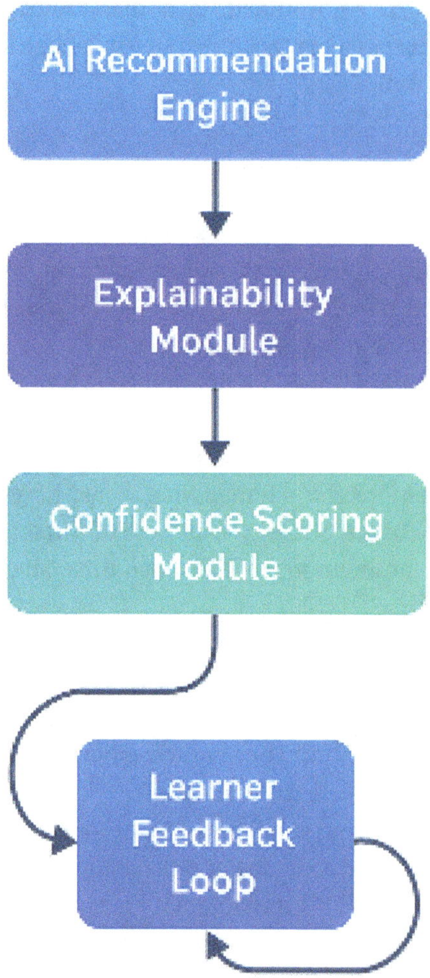

3.4. Ethical Layer: Privacy, Fairness, and Data Minimalism

The Ethical Layer is the meta level (macro) governance layer that guarantees anyone in TRF develops within a domain of ethically correct AIED. The governance principles of the Ethical Layer that govern and regulate participation in the TRF system (represented as privacy, fairness and autonomy-first design) are illustrated in Figure 5.

Figure 5. Ethical layer governance model

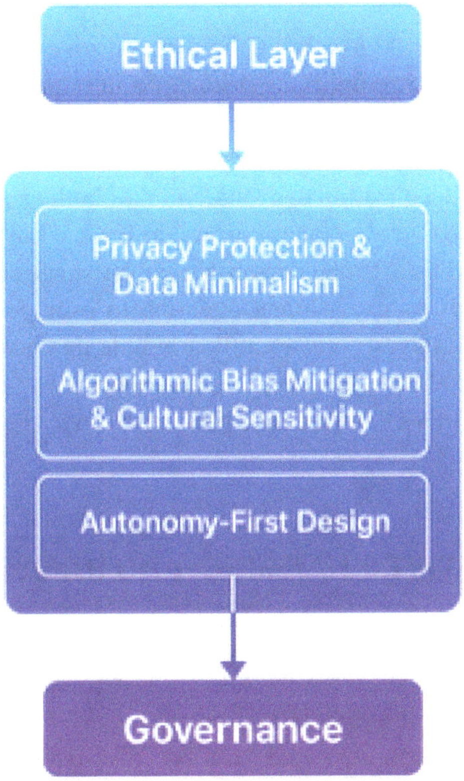

Ethical issues become even more critical when the AI Mentor deals with sensitive information. For instance, in the mental health context, an AI mentor might identify anxiety using sentiment analysis and provide emotional support. But all of this would be in vain if there are no proper privacy controls and it gets abused. To address this risk, the TRF Ethical Layer enforces strict data-privacy policies and transparency in how it shares data. Moreover, also to avoid the possibility of algorithmic bias, the AI mentor should be trained on different data sets that represent a variety of cultural and social backgrounds to ensure fair and culturally sensitive interventions. It confronts the high-stakes business of gathering intimate learner data.

Implementation Components:

- Data Minimalism and Privacy: As a principle of design, data minimalism means that only the most practical amount of data – in other words that which is strictly necessary for making mentoring work – is collected by the system. All collection, storage and processing of data must comply with the laws (e.g., GDPR, FERPA). Learners need a user-friendly, transparent dashboard to access, manage, and wipe their data –empowering them and ensuring the trustworthiness of AI.
- Bias Mitigation and Fairness: Algorithmic bias should be consistently monitored in the system. This would require the Perception Layer, so that affective and cognitive state inferences are equally accurate across different demographic cohorts (e.g., gender, cultural background, language pro-

ficiency). Additionally, the Dialogue Layer should be scrutinized to avoid making the scaffolding level or complexity of Socratic prompts too low for certain populations which may result in continued disparities.

- Social and culturally sensitive: AI Mentors should be sensitive to the context. The Dialogue Layer must be able to adapt its tone, exemplifying instances and even its beguiling Socratic strategy, depending on the learner's culture and manner of expression. For example, a propositional challenge would be potentially pertinent in one culture but appear disrespectful in another. The Ethical Layer requires geographic localization and validation of both an AI's knowledge and dialogue.
- Autonomy-First Design and Over-Personalization: The Ethical Layer gives effect to the Autonomy-First Design principle. As an AI mentor you should be suggesting and providing options, not commanding. It also needs to pay vigilant attention to over personalization, the phenomenon whereby everything an AI suggests creates a filter bubble that insulates your mind from different ideas or hard problems. And the AI sometimes has to bring in "serendipitous" or "challenging" content beyond what a learner's comfort zone previously forecasted, in order to maintain intellectual diversity and rigor.

4. CASE STUDIES: CHATGPT, KHANMIGO, AND RASA MENTORS

This section examines three different kinds of AI agents with respect to the four layers of the TRF in order to anchor the TRF in the practical reality. This comparison provides an overview of the state of the art and outlines the route to achieve full TRF in practice.

Table 3 compares ChatGPT, Khanmigo, and Rasa-based systems in terms of their alignment with the TRF layers.

Table 3. Comparison of AI systems against TRF layers

System	Perception Alignment	Dialogue Alignment	Trust Calibration	Ethical Framework
ChatGPT	Low	High	Low	Moderate
Khanmigo	Moderate	High	Moderate	High
Rasa Bots	High Potential	Customizable	High Potential	Developer-dependent

While ChatGPT performs well in reflective dialogue, it lacks enhanced ability for affective sensing to improve its detection of learner frustration. Rasa-based bots, however, can opt for extensive customization but a user is needed to be carefully trained to match the reflective and trust calibration necessary of the TRF.

4.1. ChatGPT and General-Purpose LLM Advisors

ChatGPT and other Large Language Models (LLMs), then, are the most scalable form of AI mentorship. Their flexibility comes from a large general purpose knowledge base, human-like conversational utterance and the ability to simulate complicated philosophical and pedagogical roles (Wang & Fan, 2025).

Table 4. TRF layer with examples

TRF Layer	Alignment Level	Rationale and Example
Perception Layer	Low	Limited to text-in, text-out. Does not know how the learner is feeling (frustrated, bored) right now and it does not have access to performance data from other sources (e.g., time-on-task log, error log from an LMS). Intervention is exclusively reaction to the user explicit input (Tlili et al., 2023).
Dialogue Layer	High	Strong written Socratic questioner and metacognitive prompters when explicitly asked to do so (e.g., "Be a mentor who only questions"). May support "deep" learning (especially in writing and conceptual tasks) (Abualrob, 2025; Johannes Cronje, n.d.).
Trust Calibration Layer	Low	Inherently a "black box." Prone to **hallucination** (confidently incorrect information), which severely undermines **Ability** and **Integrity** (Hadi Mogavi et al., 2024). Lacks formal mechanisms to communicate confidence scores or integrate structured learner feedback for system refinement.
Ethical Layer	Moderate Concern	Significant data privacy concerns as user inputs are often used for model training. Bias is inherent from the massive, uncurated training data. Lacks institutional oversight for bias mitigation and data governance (Loos et al., 2023).

Conclusions: ChatGPT is a strong reactive reflective partner, relying heavily on the learner's ability to start and steer reflection. It is a proof of concept for the Dialogue Layer and does not meet the higher level of demands for a reliable, autonomous AI coach because it lacks the Perception and Trust Calibration capabilities.

We evaluate ChatGPT through the TRF lens in Section 4.1, with another pedagogical comparison to help you understand the practical trade-offs of pairings for LLM-based mentorship. One of the big strengths of ChatGPT has been its unparalleled ability to fluidly hold a conversation in natural language, which can be used to have reflective conversations with learners that mimic human mentorship. Learners frequently note that they feel "safe" reporting the challenges they encounter in their interactions with LLM mentors, and that trust facilitates raw conversations.

Yet it is also a fluency which can camouflage conceptual poverty. Therefore, as a model with little perception groundedness of the physical world and virtually no real or contextual knowledge built into its training process, ChatGPT may produce reasonable but incorrect inferences regarding any struggles it perceives in the learner. In the absence of access to data from an LMS or learning histories", its responsive prompts are (necessarily) generic unless directed otherwise. This gives it an inbuilt limitation on customization ability.

Motivational calibration is yet another problem. The over-help they provide may inadvertently sustain unproductive ways of working, with the same example being that in which students develop too much dependency on help-seeking. However, a TRF-aligned mentor would recognize these patterns and interrupt this cycle by restricting the provision of direct answers but promoting reflective querying. This difference illustrates precisely the reason why LLMs are powerful and need to be designed with constraints in mind so they can act as good mentors rather than answer engines.

However, ChatGPT provides a way for engaging in reflective practice at a low bar to entry. For environments where it is not feasible for institutions to roll out custom mentoring agents, LLMs could facilitate the early development of metacognition. They are especially useful in writing tasks where you can include reflective prompts directly within the drafting process.

This delicate equilibrium strength in dialogue, but weaknesses in perception, highlights the importance of hybrid systems that mix LLM linguistic skills with structured, TRF-compatible architectures.

4.2. Khanmigo: A Structured Educational Companion

Khanmigo, created by Khan Academy, is a K-12 and higher education AI companion. It's guiding design principle is to serve as a “Socratic guide” but one that “never gives the answer” with an emphasis on fostering reasoning and supporting students through problem-solving (Khan Academy, n.d.-b).

Table 5.

TRF Layer	Alignment Level	Rationale and Example
Perception Layer	Moderate	Built within the Khan Academy platform, it provides access to live performance indicators (e.g., number of hints accessed, exact error step in multi-step problem). The interventions can now be context-aware, however affective sensing is currently restricted to using behavioral proxies (Marquardson, 2024).
Dialogue Layer	High	Purposely designed for Socratic and reflective questioning which is ideal for the TRF. It fosters metacognitive regulation by leading learners through a series of questions based on the particular error committed (Khan Academy, n.d.-a).
Trust Calibration Layer	Moderate	Its non-profit, educational mission inherently boosts perceived **Benevolence**. Its structured, step-by-step guidance acts as a form of implicit transparency. The system is designed to be reliable, reinforcing **Ability**, but it does not typically provide explicit confidence scores or XAI explanations for its underlying LLM decisions.
Ethical Layer	High	Offered by a well-respected educational non-profit, Khanmigo prioritizes ethical use and data privacy while doing its best to steer clear of facilitating cheating (all in line with the principles of Ethical Layer (blog.khanacademy.org, 2025)).

Conclusion: Khanmigo is a solid instance of applying TRF philosophy, to an AI agent especially in Dialogue and Ethical Layers. Its support for a general purpose learning platform, combined with the required data input from an online learning journal is sufficient for moderate levels of Perception and Trust Calibration which make it a very promising prototype articulation of AI mentorship in the future.

4.3. Rasa-Driven Conversational Mentoring Bots

Rasa is an open source framework for building custom, contextually intelligent conversational AI assistants. These bots are usually implemented in particular institutional or corporate contexts, leading to a high level of customization and incorporation with proprietary data systems (Rasa, n.d.).

Table 6.

TRF Layer	Alignment Level	Rationale and Example
Perception Layer	High Potential	Custom integration with institutional LMS and student data warehouses, plus possibly third-party affective computing modules (e.g., sentiment analysis applied to students' journals). This feature enables the strongest and most context-sensitive sensing (Neumann et al., 2021).
Dialogue Layer	Customizable	The quality is developer-dependent. Storm response A properly designed Rasa bot can handle complex, multi-turn and subject specific Socratic dialogues. A degenerate bot would come to not satisfy its reflexive instruction. The system enables you to be fully TRF compliant.
Trust Calibration Layer	High Potential	Custom bots could adhere to full transparency about their decision (e.g., I recommended that resource because your pre-test score was a low one in that area). They may be constructed with feedback mechanisms for their training which iteratively rectify the internal models, thereby providing an optimum potential for calibrated trust (Rasa, n.d.).
Ethical Layer	Developer Dependent	The ethical soundness of a Rasa bot is solely the responsibility of the organization deploying it. And although the framework does include provisions for ethical design (minimizing data, privacy controls), seeing that actually happen would require effort and governance at implementation.

Conclusion: Rasa-based bots are the optimal choice for TRF. They are customizable to enable the tight integration of all four layers to develop more context-aware, trustworthy and deeply reflective AI mentors applicable in different educational settings.

Comparative Insight:

These three systems illustrate various degrees of TRF alignment. ChatGPT performs well on reflective dialogue, but doesn't know how to calibrate perception and trust. Similar to Khanmigo it offers well-structured pedagogical scaffolding and limited affective sensing. Among the presented systems, rasa-based systems have the highest potential of realizing TRF since they are customizable and integrable. Such comparison indicates that while all these systems bring their own strengths, none is to the end fully compliant with TRF requirements. This underlines the importance of a common mentoring environment jointly focusing on reflection and trust as well as autonomy and ethics.

5. ETHICAL DIMENSIONS AND BIAS MITIGATION

The implementation of AI mentors, especially in the context of the TRF presents new and complex ethical challenges. Given the intensity of the close mentorships and potentially rich (personal [cognitive/affective]) data emerging from such intervention, much is at large for ethics regulation. The Ethical Layer of the TRF is constructed in order to confront this, by advocating user-agent design and on-going auditing.

Table 7 presents the main risks and respective proposed TRF mechanisms to prevent these risks in AI mentorship.

Table 7. Ethical risks and TRF mitigation strategies

Ethical Risk	Description	TRF Mitigation
Privacy Breach	Sensitive cognitive/affective data misuse	Data minimalism, learner data control
Algorithmic Bias	Unequal treatment across groups	Bias audits, XAI transparency
Over-Reliance	Learner becomes dependent on AI	Confidence scoring, reduced scaffolding
Over-Personalization	Filter bubble limits learning exposure	Serendipity/Challenge Protocol

5.1. Core Ethical Concerns and TRF Mitigation Strategies

5.1.1. Data Privacy and Confidentiality

AI tutors accumulate very sensitive data such as learning deficiencies, feelings and metacognitive knowledge. Abuse of this data can result in overwhelming repercussions such as discrimination, privacy invasion and so on.

- TRF Mitigation: Ethical Layer requires data minimalism (i.e., to use only the information indispensable for mentoring) as part of the minimum proficiency for skills training. All data should be anonymization where applicable. Moreover, it is essential that we develop AI in a way that offers learners granular control (access, correct and delete their data), strengthening the integrity of AI.

5.1.2. Algorithmic Bias and Fairness

AI is fed on historical data that tend to reflect and perpetuate societal biases. This may result in unfair or unequal results.

- Bias Mitigation (TRF): The system must have strong ongoing auditing to detect and address any bias with respect to all demographic differences.
  - Perception Layer Audit: Making sure affective sensing is not biased (e.g., misunderstanding a sentiment of non-native speakers).
  - Dialogue Layer Audit: To make sure that amount of scaffolding and difficulty of Socratic prompts are not inadvertently reduced for certain groups.
  - The XAI features of the Trust Calibration Layer are important mitigation capability, allowing the human Meta-Mentor to audit the AI's rationale and discover where biased data or logic may be guiding the intervention.

5.1.3. Over-Reliance and Loss of Critical Judgment

The efficiency and convenience of an AI mentor can cause a problematic dependence that is opposite to the aim of developing autonomy (Tan et al., 2025).

- TRF Mitigation: The Trust Calibration Layer makes explicit the limitations of AI and fosters critical engagement with it (e.g., through confidence scoring). The Dialogue Layer favors the Socratic questioning + scaffolding model, with the learner always doing the mental push-ups. The AI need to be coded to gradually diminish its encouragement once the learner has proven control, forcing them to use their own discretion and self-regulation.

5.2. Addressing Cultural Sensitivity and Over-Personalization

There are two more issues, brought up in the first proposal description sense, that need special attention within the Ethical Layer:

5.2.1. Cultural Sensitivity

Mentorship is very much a cultural exercise. An AI mentor should be able to adjust its style of mentoring according to the cultural context in which the learner is situated.

- The Challenge: Communication patterns, openness to direct feedback and the perception of authority in a mentor are greatly influenced by cultural differences. A generic AI personality might not work, and could be actively problematic in different global learning contexts.
- TRF Implementation: The above Ethical Layer will imply that the Dialogue Layer needs to be vetted for Social Acceptability. This includes:
  - Customization of Personality: Customizable personality so the Meta-Mentor can choose a culturally and regionally relevant communication tone (e.g., more formal versus more casual).
  - Example Localization: Making sure that the examples and metaphors provided in good Socratic prompts are local to the learner's domain.
  - Delivery of Feedback: Modifying the level of directness in feedback according to cultural norms with regard to authority and criticism.

5.2.2. Over-Personalization and the Filter Bubble Effect

Although personalization is of the main promises of AI, too much personalization can also result in a filter bubble where learners receive content based on what they already agree with, limiting them exposure to new ideas, opposing perspectives or con- tent that is outside their interest area

- The Challenge: An AI tutor that only assigns content that is in perfect alignment with the students past behavior could lead to a restriction of intellectual freedom which will work against the goal of lifelong independent learning.
- TRF Implementation: The Ethical Layer mandates a Serendipity and Challenge Protocol. The AI must occasionally introduce content or reflective prompts that are intentionally outside the predicted optimal path. This could involve:
  - Contrarian Prompts: Requesting the learner to explain back why an answer they did not give would also work.
  - Cross-Domain Suggestions: Suggesting an artifact from a different domain in order to drive lateral thinking.

- It guarantees the apprentice will suffer friction of ideas, which is needed to become a strong critical thinker and avoid intellectual atrophy.

6. EDUCATOR'S ROLE AS META-MENTOR

The implementation of AI mentors does not de-value the human-educator; it advances that role to more strategic and powerful job. The Meta-Mentor. The Meta-Mentor is human expert who directs what the AI does, makes sense of its reports, and teaches the learner in how to interpret their experience with their AI partner. This hybrid human-AI co-mentoring mechanism is the "endgame" for TRF.

6.1. The Transformation to Meta-Mentorship

The AI mentor performs the high-frequency, data-driven work the "coaching" around strategy and process allowing the human mentor to concentrate on higher order, human-oriented functions like relationship building that demand empathy, contextual wisdom and ethical judgment.

Key Responsibilities of the Meta-Mentor:

6.1.1. AI System Governance and Ethical Oversight

The Meta-Mentor is the keeper of the TRF's Ethical Layer and backstop.

- Configuration and Customization: The AI mentor will be configured to meet particular curricular objectives, institutional values or individual learner genetic records. They define the moral limits and "personality" of the A.I.
- Bias and Fairness Auditing: They constantly review the AI's operational data to check for signs of algorithmic bias or skewed results. They utilize the XAI outputs provided by the Trust Calibration Layer in order to perform "reasoning" on what AI thinks.
- System Override and Exception Handling: The Meta-Mentor reserves the supreme right to override the recommendations of AI, particularly when dealing with sophisticated emotional or context-based matters that cannot be comprehended by its Perception Layer (i.e. coping with a learner in a personal crisis).

6.1.2. Interpreting Affective and Metacognitive Data

The Perception Layer of the AI mentor produces high-quality and rich quantitative information about the state of the learner. This is where the Meta-Mentor comes in with its human framing of this data.

- Deep Diagnosis: The AI might declare, "Learner manifested high frustration and low self-efficacy during planning." The Meta-Mentor reads this as: "This student is struggling with perfectionism and fear of failure, which requires a human conversation about mindset, not just a technical prompt."
- Targeted Human Intervention: Based on the data from the AI system, the Meta-Mentor is able to identify 'at risk' learners that are struggling below the surface (e.g., rely too much on AI/'burnt

out') and offer highly targeted, high impact human interventions getting maximum efficiency in how they use their time.

6.1.3. Teaching AI Literacy and Critical Trust

The important function of the Meta-Mentor is to educate the learner about being a critical and independent partner of the AI.

- Empower Calibrated Trust: The Meta-Mentor directly instructs children on the strengths and weaknesses of AI, to support understanding of calibrated trust. They teach users to challenge the AI's recommendation, look up for alternatives and explore the 'why' of its recommendations so as to inhibit over trust (Rannisto & Vainionpää, 2025).
- Facilitating Human-to-Human Reflection: The Meta-Mentor can use the logs of the AI as a support for human-to-human reflective sessions. For instance: "I notice that the AI asked you three times to rethink your plan. Why didn't you shift your approach at the time, and what did you learn from that resistance?" This takes the meditative reflection beyond just a "puzzle" to read from technical standpoint, into realize a deep personal insight into mindset and dealing with emotions.

So, in order to provide a clearer illustration of the developing role of the educator as Meta-Mentor through concrete classroom scenarios, I would like to share some examples. Imagine a university programming course where an AI mentor reviews submitted code, identifies misconceptions and questions the student using reflective inquiry. The AI could notice a student continually brute-forcing and give them some sort of Socratic prompt about efficiency algorithms. The Meta-Mentor is viewing combined dashboards and it looks like a number of students are suffering from this conceptual hole. With this understanding, the teacher can provide a focused mini-lesson on thinking algorithmically, turning AI data into high-leverage pedagogy.

In a writing-heavy humanities class, the AI teaching assistant supports students in structuring arguments by asking them to specify claims, evidence, and assumptions. The Meta-Mentor examines the reflective logs and selects students who repeatedly have difficulty during evaluation. This provides the teacher with an opportunity to schedule a small-group workshop around critical analysis, to prolong and deepen the reflective cycle introduced by the AI.

Meta-Mentor becomes contractible in mixed-learning settings. For instance, in a flipped classroom (a hybrid flipped model in particular), the AI mentor offers pre-class coaching on planning and strategy selection, as well as comprehension. In- class, AI-generated insights are used by the teacher to facilitate peer discussions, correct misconceptions and foster thinking beyond procedural fluency.

Examples such as these illustrate that AI teachers are not a replacement for educators; instead, they multiply teacher impact by freeing up teaching time and exposing further layers of learner activity. The Meta-Mentor evolves, in this way, into a strategist—hatching, making sense of and integrating AI-generated insights across a holistic educational environment.

Figure 6 shows the Meta-Mentor Oversight Model, which depicts how human pedagogical judgment watches over AI mentor processes and helps learners grow.

Figure 6. Meta-mentor oversight model

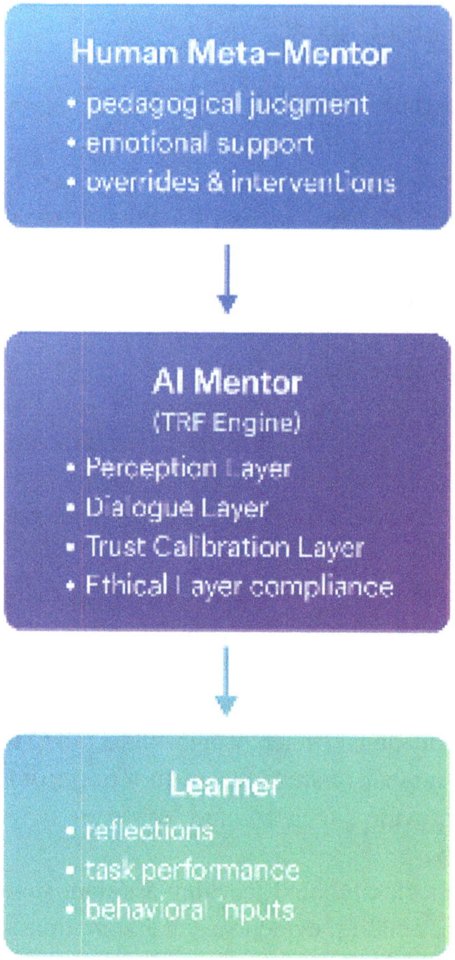

6.2. Professional Development for the Meta-Mentor

The transition to Meta-Mentorship requires a new set of professional competencies for educators, necessitating dedicated professional development (PD) programs:

Table 8.

Competency Area	Required Skills for Meta-Mentors	PD Focus
Data Literacy	Ability to interpret data visualizations (e.g., error heatmaps, engagement metrics) and understand basic statistical inferences from the Perception Layer.	Training on the TRF dashboard, data privacy protocols, and distinguishing correlation from causation in learner data.
AI Literacy & Ethics	Understanding the limitations of LLMs, the concept of algorithmic bias, and the principles of XAI. Ability to audit the AI's reasoning.	Case studies on AI failure modes (e.g., hallucination, bias), ethical decision-making frameworks for AI intervention, and the use of the Trust Calibration Layer.
Advanced Metacognition	Deep understanding of SRL models (Zimmerman, Pintrich) and advanced Socratic questioning techniques to model critical thinking for the learner.	Workshops on designing metacognitive prompts, facilitating group reflection based on AI data, and coaching learners on self-attribution.
Affective Coaching	Skills in emotional intelligence, empathetic communication, and identifying signs of burnout or mental health struggles from the AI's affective data.	Training on non-directive counseling techniques and protocols for escalating human intervention based on perceived affective state.

This investment in the human Meta-Mentor ensures that the AI mentor remains a tool for empowerment, not a replacement for the essential human relationship in education.

Table 9 summarizes institutional requirements for effective TRF-based AI mentorship implementation.

Table 9. Institutional implementation requirements

Implementation Area	Requirement	Expected Impact
LMS Integration	API access; analytics sync	Real-time perception data
AI Governance	Ethical policy, auditing	Reduced bias, transparency
Faculty Training	Meta-mentor skill development	Higher reflective learning outcomes
Data Infrastructure	Secure storage, anonymization	Privacy protection

7. CONCLUSION

The transition from programmed instruction to intelligent tutoring systems (ITS) was a significant moment in the story of educational technology. It is a shift in emphasis from the effectiveness or efficiency of teaching to the effectiveness and efficiency of self-managed learning. This chapter has proposed that for AI to be an effective mentor—a trusted ally in a learner's quest for autonomy—it must have committed humanistic underpinnings.

The TRF is this critical recipe. By realizing these four layers—Perception, Dialogue, Trust Calibration and Ethical—the TRF makes the AI mentor not only a reactive tool but a proactive, context aware agent. The strength of the framework lies in both its technology, requiring deep sensing and transparent reasoning, and in its pedagogy, calling for Socratic dialogue and maintaining learner agency.

Our analysis of prototypes suggests that although existing LLMs (e.g., ChatGPT) have laid the groundwork for some aspects of the Dialogue Layer, to fully realize the TRF we will need embedded, context-specific systems (e.g., Khanmigo or custom Rasa bots) which are capable of effectively implementing the Perception and Trust Calibration Layers. The Future of AI Mentorship is not a single product, but the collection of context-aware tools constructed upon TRF's philosophy.

The final contribution of this work is to articulate AI mentorship as a distinct educational paradigm and provide a model (TRF) through which it can be framed, measured and designed in an ethical way. This view shifts the discussion from fear of 'AI taking over' to human–AI cobrain support.

Human, or Meta-Mentor in this co-mentorship model the human educator (meta mentor) is indispensable. They are the moral governor, the data translator, and no other being from whence flow wisdom of context or emotional support. The scalable, data-intensive coaching on process happens in the AI Mentor, and the high-impact, human-centric coaching on mindset and purpose is delivered by the Meta-Mentor.

By following the tenets of the TRF—calibrated trust instead of blind faith, deep reflection rather than shallow compliance and autonomy over control—we can ensure that AI mentors are ethical equalizers. Not only will this symbiosis enhance reflective practice and meta-cognitive skills, but it will also instill the resilient, self-sufficient and learning practices necessary for our next generation to succeed. The future of education is not about substituting human teachers with AI, but it's about the powerful marriage between a human educator and an AI teacher. The Trust-Reflection framework (TRF) is a novel, ethical AI/ML-based model to build autonomous active learning AI mentors. As practice of AI matures, driven by the TRF models AI mentor will have more significant impact on learner to take control over their education, reflect on how they learned and to learn lifelong.

7.1. Limitations and Future Directions

Although TRF provides a full-stack model of mentoring in an AI age, some limitations need to be addressed before wide-scale deployment. The first assumption of the framework is that there exist rich, high-quality learner data –such as behavioral, cognitive, and in some cases affective data. This data infrastructure is lacking or sparse in many education settings, especially resource-poor schools. Without quality data feeds, however, the Perception Layer is unable to reach its potential and mentoring may once again become formulaic, one-size-fits-all instruction.

Second the TRF is currently biased toward formal learning contexts like universities or organized online courses. But a larger and larger portion of self-directed learning activity takes place out there in the informal spaces — open communities, social platforms and micro-credential ecosystems – where institutional control and ethical surveillance might be lower. Transferring the Ethical and Trust Calibration layers to these environments that are relatively loosely coupled is an active challenge, especially when accountability and transparency of AI decisions need to be addressed.

Third, in order to employ the framework people must be AI literate, which is beyond both learners and instructors in its current status. Indeed, if students perceive AI feedback to be 100% true or instructors lack confidence in their ability to interpret TRF dashboards, aligned calibrated trust will degrade into either the skepticism region or over-trust. This highlights the need for simultaneous investment in AI literacies curriculum and professional learning, centered not just on technical skills but also on a critical, ethical and reflective engagement with AI systems.

There are several ways in which the TRF can be extended for further study. Empirical studies are required to investigate the impact on learning outcomes, such as metacognitive development, learner autonomy and retention in the long-term perspective by AI mentors compliant with TRF. Comparator studies between disciplines and educational levels would be valuable to determine where the framework is particularly effective. Furthermore, design-based research can explore the students' experience with trust and reflection and autonomy when they are supported by “AI mentors” from different cultures, allow Ethical Layer to learn more about how culturally sensitive it is. Finally, interdisciplinary efforts between computer and learning scientists, ethicists and practitioners will be required to implement the TRF in systems so that it one-serves its career agenda while honoring the spirit of this humanistic innovation.

REFERENCES

Abualrob, M. (2025). From Reflection to Re-Reflection: ChatGPT and Transformative Learning in Pre-service Elementary Science Education. *International Journal of Learning. Teaching and Educational Research, 24*(10), 769–793. DOI: 10.26803/ijlter.24.10.37

Afroogh, S., Akbari, A., Malone, E., Kargar, M., & Alambeigi, H. (2025). Correction to: Trust in AI: progress, challenges, and future directions (Humanities and Social Sciences Communications, (2024), 11, 1, (1568),). In *Humanities and Social Sciences Communications* (Vol. 12, Issue 1). https://doi.org/ DOI: 10.1057/s41599-024-04044-8

Blog.Khanacademy (2025). *Explore AI in Your Teaching: A One-Hour PD Experience with Khan Academy.* Blog.Khanacademy.Org. https://blog.khanacademy.org/explore-ai-in-your-teaching-a-one-hour-pd-experience-with-khan-academy/

Carlo Giovine and Roger Roberts. (2024). *Building AI trust: The key role of explainability.* McKinsey & Company. https://www.mckinsey.com/capabilities/quantumblack/our-insights/building-ai-trust-the-key-role-of-explainability

Charokar, K., & Dulloo, P. (2022). Self-directed Learning Theory to Practice: A Footstep towards the Path of being a Life-long Learner. In *Journal of Advances in Medical Education and Professionalism* (Vol. 10, Issue 3). DOI: 10.30476/jamp.2022.94833.1609

Dweck, C. S., & Yeager, D. S. (2019). Mindsets: A View From Two Eras. *Perspectives on Psychological Science, 14*(3), 481–496. DOI: 10.1177/1745691618804166 PMID: 30707853

Hadi Mogavi, R., Deng, C., Juho Kim, J., Zhou, P., & Kwon, D., Y., Hosny Saleh Metwally, A., Tlili, A., Bassanelli, S., Bucchiarone, A., Gujar, S., Nacke, L. E., & Hui, P. (. (2024). ChatGPT in education: A blessing or a curse? A qualitative study exploring early adopters' utilization and perceptions. *Computers in Human Behavior: Artificial Humans, 2*(1), 100027. DOI: 10.1016/j.chbah.2023.100027

Hadick, M. (n.d.). *Scaffolding Autonomy: Designing for Trust and Learning in AI-Supported Autodidactic Environments.*

Johannes Cronje. (n.d.). *Exploring_the_Role_of_ChatGPT.*

Khan Academy. (n.d.-a). *Khanmigo for learners: Always-available tutor, powered by AI.* Https://Www.Khanmigo.Ai/. Retrieved December 9, 2025, from https://www.khanmigo.ai/learners

Khan Academy. (n.d.-b). *Meet Khanmigo: Khan Academy's AI-powered teaching and learning companion.* Khanmigo.Ai. Retrieved December 9, 2025, from https://www.khanmigo.ai/

Köbis, L., & Mehner, C. (2021). Ethical Questions Raised by AI-Supported Mentoring in Higher Education. *Frontiers in Artificial Intelligence, 4*, 624050. Advance online publication. DOI: 10.3389/frai.2021.624050 PMID: 33997774

Loos, E., Gröpler, J., & Goudeau, M.-L. S. (2023). Using ChatGPT in Education: Human Reflection on ChatGPT's Self-Reflection. *Societies (Basel, Switzerland), 13*(8), 196. DOI: 10.3390/soc13080196

Marina Harvey. (2024, January 3). *The role of reflection for learning and metacognitive development.* Improvewithmetacognition.Com. https://www.improvewithmetacognition.com/reflection-for-learning-and-metacognitive-development/

Marquardson, J. (2024). Embracing Artificial Intelligence to Improve Self-Directed Learning: A Cybersecurity Classroom Study. *Information Systems Education Journal, 22*(1), 4–13. DOI: 10.62273/WZBY3952

McLeod, G. A., Barr, J., & Welch, A. (2015). Best Practice for Teaching and Learning Strategies to Facilitate Student Reflection in Pre-Registration Health Professional Education: An Integrative Review. *Creative Education, 06*(04), 440–454. DOI: 10.4236/ce.2015.64044

Merkebu, J., Veen, M., Hosseini, S., & Varpio, L. (2024). The case for metacognitive reflection: A theory integrative review with implications for medical education. *Advances in Health Sciences Education : Theory and Practice, 29*(4), 1481–1500. DOI: 10.1007/s10459-023-10310-2 PMID: 38345690

Merriam, S. B. (2001). Andragogy and Self-Directed Learning: Pillars of Adult Learning Theory. *New Directions for Adult and Continuing Education, 2001*(89), 3–14. DOI: 10.1002/ace.3

Morris, T. H. (2019). Self-directed learning: A fundamental competence in a rapidly changing world', International Review of Education. *International Review of Education, 65*(4), 633–653. DOI: 10.1007/s11159-019-09793-2

Nazaretsky, T., Mejia-Domenzain, P., Swamy, V., Frej, J., & Käser, T. (2025). The critical role of trust in adopting AI-powered educational technology for learning: An instrument for measuring student perceptions. *Computers and Education: Artificial Intelligence, 8*, 100368. Advance online publication. DOI: 10.1016/j.caeai.2025.100368

Neumann, A. T., Arndt, T., Köbis, L., Meissner, R., Martin, A., de Lange, P., Pengel, N., Klamma, R., & Wollersheim, H.-W. (2021). Chatbots as a Tool to Scale Mentoring Processes: Individually Supporting Self-Study in Higher Education. *Frontiers in Artificial Intelligence, 4*, 668220. Advance online publication. DOI: 10.3389/frai.2021.668220 PMID: 34337393

Nopas, D. (2025). Algorithmic learning or learner autonomy? Rethinking AI's role in digital education. *Qualitative Research Journal.* Advance online publication. DOI: 10.1108/QRJ-11-2024-0282

Rannisto, A., & Vainionpää, F. (2025). Trust-Affording Action: Citizens' Everyday Relations With Algorithmized Public Services. *Social Inclusion (Lisboa), 13*, 10001. Advance online publication. DOI: 10.17645/si.10001

Rasa. (n.d.). *Build AI Agents you can trust to handle real world complexity.* Rasa.Com. Retrieved December 9, 2025, from https://rasa.com/

Shabani, K., Khatib, M., Tabataba'i Uinversity, A., & Ebadi, S. (2010). Vygotsky's Zone of Proximal Development: Instructional Implications and Teachers' []. www.ccsenet.org/elt]. *Professional Development (Philadelphia, Pa.), 3*(4), •••.

Stevens, A. F., & Stetson, P. (2023). Theory of trust and acceptance of artificial intelligence technology (TrAAIT): An instrument to assess clinician trust and acceptance of artificial intelligence. *Journal of Biomedical Informatics*, *148*, 104550. DOI: 10.1016/j.jbi.2023.104550 PMID: 37981107

Tan, X., Cheng, G., & Ling, M. H. (2025). Artificial intelligence in teaching and teacher professional development: A systematic review. *Computers and Education: Artificial Intelligence*, *8*, 100355. DOI: 10.1016/j.caeai.2024.100355

Teresa4Now, T. E. (2024, August 11). *The Power of Self-Reflection in an AI-Driven World*. ServiceNow. https://www.servicenow.com/community/intelligence-ml-blog/the-power-of-self-reflection-in-an-ai-driven-world/ba-p/3100439

Tlili, A., Shehata, B., Adarkwah, M. A., Bozkurt, A., Hickey, D. T., Huang, R., & Agyemang, B. (2023). What if the devil is my guardian angel: ChatGPT as a case study of using chatbots in education. *Smart Learning Environments*, *10*(1), 15. DOI: 10.1186/s40561-023-00237-x

Wang, J., & Fan, W. (2025). The effect of ChatGPT on students' learning performance, learning perception, and higher-order thinking: insights from a meta-analysis. In *Humanities and Social Sciences Communications* (Vol. 12, Issue 1). DOI: 10.1057/s41599-025-04787-y

Wen, C. K. (2023). Creating a Trustworthy AI Tutor: A Challenge Worth Embracing or a Bite Too Big? In *Medium*. https://puddles-of-water.medium.com/creating-a-trustworthy-ai-tutor-a-challenge-worth-embracing-or-a-bite-too-big-3815f5c82de0

Yin, J., Zhu, Y., Goh, T.-T., Wu, W., & Hu, Y. (2024). Using Educational Chatbots with Metacognitive Feedback to Improve Science Learning. *Applied Sciences (Basel, Switzerland)*, *14*(20), 9345. DOI: 10.3390/app14209345

Zimmerman, B. J. (2000). Attaining Self-Regulation. In *Handbook of Self-Regulation* (pp. 13–39). Elsevier., DOI: 10.1016/B978-012109890-2/50031-7

Chapter 9
From Feedback to Feedforward: AI and the Evolution of Formative Assessment in Language Education

Vedat Kızıl
http://orcid.org/0000-0003-0589-0877
Ankara Yıldırım Beyazıt University, Turkey

ABSTRACT

This chapter examines how artificial intelligence (AI) is reshaping formative assessment in language education through a shift from retrospective feedback toward forward-oriented feedforward. Drawing on formative assessment, self-regulated learning, and feedback literacy research, it explores how AI-driven systems can generate timely, individualized guidance that supports learners in planning, monitoring, and revising their work across tasks. AI is situated within a sociocultural understanding of learning and conceptualized as a scaffold that operates alongside teachers rather than as a replacement for professional judgement. The chapter addresses pedagogical and ethical challenges related to automation, trust, equity, and algorithmic bias, with particular attention to language-specific concerns. Practical recommendations are presented for integrating AI within hybrid feedback models that preserve dialogue, strengthen feedback literacy, and sustain formative assessment as a genuinely developmental practice.

1. INTRODUCTION

Educational assessment has changed considerably over recent decades, moving away from a narrow concern with measurement toward practices intended to support learning as it unfolds. This shift reflects wider changes in how learning itself is understood. Rather than treating learning as the accumulation of observable behaviours, researchers and educators now commonly view it as interpretive, socially situated, and shaped through interaction (Skedsmo & Huber, 2025). Early assessment traditions were strongly influenced by behaviourist assumptions and relied heavily on standardized testing to capture performance at a fixed point in time. As constructivist perspectives gained influence, assessment practices moved closer to everyday classroom activity, giving greater weight to the processes that inform teaching while learning is still underway. Shepard (2000) characterizes this movement as a cultural shift in which assessment becomes inseparable from instruction, requiring teachers to respond flexibly to

DOI: 10.4018/979-8-3373-7225-9.ch009

emerging evidence of learning. Gipps (1994) similarly argues that changing views of knowledge demand assessment approaches capable of capturing complexity rather than reducing learning to fixed scores.

Formative assessment developed in this changing landscape and reframed assessment as an ongoing process that shapes both teaching decisions and learner activity. Black and Wiliam's (1998) influential synthesis drew attention to the value of gathering evidence during learning and using it to adjust instruction in responsive ways. Feedback occupies a central position in this process. Wiliam (2011) argues that feedback functions as a connection between current performance and future goals, supporting learners as they refine strategies and monitor progress. Heritage (2010) presents formative assessment as a cyclical process in which evidence, interpretation, and action are continuously linked, supporting immediate instructional adjustments as well as longer-term development. These accounts share an important premise: that assessment is pedagogically meaningful only to the extent that it informs what happens next, for both the teacher and the learner.

Research has increasingly recognized that feedback does not operate independently of learners' engagement with it. Studies on feedback literacy point to the need for learners to interpret feedback, judge its relevance, and apply it in subsequent work. Carless and Winstone (2020) stress that feedback effectiveness depends not only on the information provided but on how learners make sense of it, which calls for pedagogies that develop learners' capacity to act on guidance. Sutton (2012) situates feedback within classroom relationships and emotional climates, noting that motivation, confidence, and affect shape how feedback is received and used. These perspectives shift formative assessment toward more dialogic practices, where responsibility for learning is distributed across teachers, peers, and learners rather than resting solely with the instructor.

The digitization of education has altered how feedback can be generated, delivered, and interpreted. Earlier educational technologies introduced tools such as automated writing evaluation, adaptive quizzes, and computer-assisted language learning systems that provided feedback based on predefined rules. Bennett (2011) observes that these systems increased speed and consistency in assessment processes, even though they remained constrained by template-driven designs. Research on intelligent tutoring systems demonstrated how adaptive technologies could track learner performance and respond with targeted instructional guidance (Letourneau et al., 2025; Shute, 2008). These early tools familiarized teachers with digitally mediated feedback and automated analysis, laying the groundwork for more sophisticated systems.

The growing presence of artificial intelligence (AI) intensifies these debates by extending the scope of what automated systems can do in formative assessment. Popenici and Kerr (2017) describe AI as a development capable of reshaping instructional practices as well as institutional decision-making. In language education specifically, AI-driven systems now generate feedback on writing, speaking, vocabulary, and grammatical patterns, adapting responses to individual learner profiles in ways that resemble certain features of human feedback (Tran, 2025). Such capabilities raise important questions about how feedback processes are organized and how teacher roles may evolve when automated systems participate more actively in assessment practices. The digital divide adds a further layer of complexity: access to these tools varies considerably across institutional and regional contexts, and any account of their educational potential must acknowledge the uneven conditions under which they are adopted.

Meaningful assessment nonetheless continues to rely on human judgement. Brookhart (2001) notes that teachers draw on professional knowledge and sensitivity to learners' needs when interpreting performance and responding to it. Teachers attend to intentions, developmental trajectories, and classroom dynamics in ways that automated systems cannot reproduce. Earl (2003) stresses that assessment for learning depends on relationships grounded in trust and dialogue. From this perspective, the introduction of AI into formative assessment does not reduce the importance of teachers' expertise; it increases the need for careful mediation, interpretation, and pedagogical decision-making. As assessment practices become more technologically mediated, ethical considerations also become more prominent. Williamson (2017) draws attention to the political economy of data-driven education, pointing to issues related to data extraction, platform control, and algorithmic influence on educational decisions. Pardo and Siemens (2014) discuss the ethical responsibilities institutions carry when deploying systems that collect and analyze learner data, arguing for transparency and clear governance structures.

The history of language assessment adds further context to this shift. The communicative turn of the 1980s and 1990s moved testing away from discrete-point grammar items toward integrated tasks requiring learners to use language for real communicative purposes. This change was accompanied by growing interest in assessment validity, understood not merely as the accuracy of a test score but as the appropriateness of the interpretations and uses made from it (Skedsmo & Huber, 2025). Formative assessment fits naturally within this tradition because it frames assessment as an ongoing interpretive practice rather than a measurement event. What AI adds to this tradition is capacity for scale: the ability to generate individualized feedback across many learners simultaneously, to track patterns over time, and to do so consistently at the moment of learning.

The language education context also shapes the kinds of feedback that matter most. A learner of English as an additional language working on academic writing faces different feedback needs than a student in a content course. Constructs such as pragmatic competence, interactional fluency, and discourse coherence are specific to language education and not adequately captured by general assessment frameworks. Any serious account of AI-mediated formative assessment in this field needs to take these constructs seriously rather than mapping general assessment principles onto language learning by loose analogy. This chapter attempts to do that by grounding its discussion in both general formative assessment theory and the specific features of language acquisition and use.

These developments place formative assessment within a complex landscape shaped by pedagogical theory, digital infrastructures, and ethical considerations. AI enters this landscape as part of a broader movement toward more responsive and data-informed educational practices, rather than as a standalone solution. Understanding how these strands intersect provides a foundation for examining how AI may support formative assessment in language education, a field that carries its own distinct constructs, equity concerns, and classroom realities. This chapter proceeds by establishing a conceptual background in formative assessment and feedback theory, before examining AI as a formative assessment partner in language learning contexts, exploring the shift from feedback to feedforward, addressing key pedagogical challenges, and offering practical guidance for language educators and curriculum designers.

2. CONCEPTUAL BACKGROUND

Formative assessment is commonly defined not as a single method but as a set of practices oriented toward supporting learning while it is still developing. One of the earliest and most influential accounts is provided by Sadler (1989), who argued that formative assessment functions when learners can identify the distance between their current performance and an intended standard, and then take action to reduce that distance. This position rests on two conditions: learners must have access to criteria and exemplars that allow them to interpret feedback, and instructional designs must create opportunities for learners to use that information in subsequent tasks. Black and Wiliam's (1998) synthesis reinforced this view by demonstrating that assessment practices which generate evidence for instructional adjustment are associated with improved learning across contexts. Their work established formative assessment as a dynamic process embedded within everyday teaching rather than as an activity that follows instruction.

Subsequent research has refined these foundational claims by examining how feedback functions in practice. Hattie and Timperley (2007) proposed a framework organized around different types of feedback questions, arguing that feedback is most productive when it helps learners align strategies with goals and monitor their own progress. This focus on monitoring connects formative assessment to self-regulation research. Zimmerman's (2000) social cognitive model situates monitoring, strategy selection, and reflection within cyclical phases of learning, explaining why formative feedback that supports metacognitive activity plays a central role in sustained development rather than short-term performance gains. The relationship between feedback and self-regulation is particularly significant in language learning, where learners must develop not only linguistic knowledge but also the strategic awareness to monitor and adjust their own language production over time.

Hattie and Timperley (2007) differentiate feedback directed at the task from feedback that addresses task processing and self-regulation. Evidence summarized in their review indicates that feedback targeting processes and self-regulation tends to be more effective than feedback focused on personal appraisal. Shute's (2008) review complements this work by synthesizing studies on formative feedback and identifying features associated with positive effects, including specificity, task relevance, and credibility of the source. Her analysis stresses that corrective guidance is most useful when it directs learners toward alternative strategies rather than simply identifying errors. The implication for AI-assisted feedback is clear: systems that mark errors without explaining why they are problematic or offering strategic alternatives are likely to produce surface compliance rather than genuine learning.

More recent scholarship has shifted attention from feedback characteristics to the interpretive work learners must undertake. Nicol and Macfarlane-Dick (2006) reframed feedback as a process that supports learner autonomy by developing the capacity to judge work quality, set goals, and plan improvement. This perspective places learner agency at the centre of formative assessment. Building on this, Carless et al. (2011) introduced the idea of sustainable feedback practices in large-scale educational settings, arguing that curricular structures and dialogue opportunities must allow learners to reuse feedback across tasks rather than treating it as isolated commentary.

The concept of feedback literacy was elaborated further by Carless and Boud (2018), who proposed that learners require specific understandings, dispositions, and skills in order to make productive use of feedback. Their framework draws attention to learners' capacity to interpret information, manage emotional responses, and take action over time. This view does not reduce the teacher's role; rather, it reframes teaching as the design of environments in which feedback uptake is supported structurally. Winstone and Carless (2019) extend this argument by focusing on how interactions such as peer dialogue, teacher-student conversations, and structured revision tasks can be arranged so that learners repeatedly practise using feedback rather than simply receiving it. In language education contexts, feedback literacy also has a disciplinary dimension: an EFL student must understand what coherence or argument structure means in academic writing before they can meaningfully act on feedback about these features.

Peer and self-assessment research provides further evidence that feedback is often co-constructed through interaction. Studies by Kizil (2019) and earlier work by Orsmond et al. (2004) show that exemplars, shared criteria, and guided peer review can reduce gaps between tutors' intentions and students' interpretations. Panadero's (2017) meta-analysis confirms that well-designed self-assessment interventions can support self-regulation, although outcomes depend strongly on how these practices are implemented. These findings suggest that feedback effectiveness emerges through iterative practice and shared meaning-making rather than through one-directional transmission. This insight is directly relevant to the design of AI-supported feedback environments, which risk reproducing the one-directional model if not deliberately counteracted through instructional design.

Another strand of research has focused on learners' emotional and motivational relationships with feedback. Studies indicate that learners' engagement with feedback is shaped by perceived clarity, emotional tone, and the extent to which feedback supports autonomy rather than threatening competence or control (Jin et al., 2025). Evans (2013) synthesized evidence indicating that engagement with feedback depends strongly on perceived credibility and respect for learner autonomy. Feedback that appears vague, misaligned with learners' goals, or undermining to their sense of capability is less likely to be acted upon.

The concept of feedforward connects these theoretical traditions by directing attention toward the uses of feedback in future work. Sadler (1989) noted that feedback is not formative unless it is actually used by the learner to improve subsequent performance, a claim that has significant implications for design. A detailed correction of a student's essay that is returned after the assignment has been graded and the course has moved on is not formative in any meaningful sense, regardless of its quality. Feedforward is inherently future-oriented: its purpose is to prepare the learner for what lies ahead rather than to account for what has already happened. In language education, where learners return repeatedly to similar task types such as oral presentations, written arguments, or conversational exchanges, this orientation has clear practical value.

One implication of this body of scholarship is that assessment design must precede tool selection. The question to ask when considering AI for formative assessment is not which tool is most technically sophisticated, but which feedback functions are currently under-served in the course and whether AI can address them without undermining the relational and dialogic dimensions of formative practice. In a large university EFL writing program, the under-served function may be consistency: teachers across sections may give feedback that varies considerably, creating inequitable conditions for learners. AI can address consistency directly. In a smaller intensive language course, the under-served function may instead be timeliness: by the time the teacher provides detailed written feedback, the revision window has closed. Identifying the specific pedagogical problem before choosing a tool is the starting point for effective integration.

These conceptual developments carry important implications for technology-mediated feedback. Shute (2008) and subsequent reviews show that automated systems can deliver rapid and specific information, particularly for constrained tasks with clear criteria. Boud and Molloy (2013) caution, however, against viewing feedback as a simple transfer of information from system to learner. Their reconceptualization frames feedback as a design challenge spanning tasks, curricula, learner activity, teacher mediation, and institutional conditions. Technology may extend the reach and immediacy of formative feedback, yet it cannot ensure interpretation or meaningful use on its own. These principles provide a conceptual foundation for examining how AI systems might support feedforward-oriented practices in language education, a context in which constructs such as fluency, accuracy, pragmatic competence, and interactional development add dimensions that general assessment frameworks do not always address directly.

3. AI AS A FORMATIVE ASSESSMENT PARTNER IN LANGUAGE EDUCATION

AI is increasingly positioned not as a peripheral aid in formative assessment but as an active participant in learning processes. Rather than functioning solely as an automated checker, AI systems now engage learners through adaptive prompts, iterative feedback, and revision-oriented guidance that extend traditional feedback practices (Tan et al., 2025). From a theoretical perspective, this role can be interpreted through Vygotsky's (1978) concept of the Zone of Proximal Development. AI systems can provide contingent support at moments when tasks exceed learners' independent capabilities, guiding attention to problems and suggesting alternative approaches before gradually reducing assistance as competence develops. This framing casts AI as a scaffold within a formative loop, where challenge, response, and reflection are closely connected.

Within connectivist theory, learning is distributed across human and technological nodes that together shape knowledge construction (Siemens, 2005). AI systems operate as one such node, participating in feedback exchanges, proposing learning pathways, and responding to emerging learner needs. Luckin et al. (2016) describe AI as an intelligent partner that can model aspects of learner understanding and prompt metacognitive reflection. When embedded within formative assessment practices, AI has the potential to become part of the learner's cognitive environment, supporting cycles of planning, performance, and reflection that are central to self-regulated learning. The sociocultural perspective adds another dimension: feedback is not merely information but a cultural tool through which learners develop higher-order capacities over time, and AI systems that are thoughtfully designed can participate meaningfully in this mediating process.

In language education specifically, AI tools now operate across a range of skills and task types. Automated writing evaluation platforms such as Grammarly and Write & Improve provide feedback on grammar, cohesion, and lexical choice in L2 writing contexts. LLM-based tutors using models such as ChatGPT or Claude can engage learners in extended dialogic exchanges that simulate interactional practice and generate personalized feedforward on discourse features. Tools targeting spoken language, including AI pronunciation coaches embedded in platforms such as Duolingo Max or ELSA Speak, analyze prosody, word stress, and articulation in ways that offer immediate, task-specific guidance at scale. This range of tools makes language education one of the fields in which AI-supported formative assessment is already most actively practised, which also means that the empirical evidence base, though growing, is more developed here than in many other subject areas.

Tran (2025) examined the effects of AI-generated and teacher-generated feedback on EFL writing revision, finding that AI feedback improved surface-level accuracy while teacher feedback produced stronger gains on rhetorical organization and argumentative depth. This pattern illustrates both the affordances and the limits of AI in language learning contexts: it manages rule-governed features with consistency, but higher-order meaning-making continues to require human guidance. Steiss et al. (2024) compared AI-generated and human-generated feedback on student essays, finding that AI feedback was often comparable to human evaluators on surface features but less reliable on construct-level judgements such as argument coherence and disciplinary voice. These findings underscore the importance of not treating AI feedback as interchangeable with human professional judgement, a distinction that needs to be communicated clearly to language learners who may not have the critical framework to evaluate automated commentary on their own.

Evidence from writing research illustrates how AI can function as a formative partner in ways that go beyond simple correction. Fleckenstein et al. (2023) conducted a multi-level meta-analysis examining automated feedback on student writing and reported overall positive effects on writing performance, noting that feedback is most effective when it supports revision decisions and strategic improvement. Pargmann et al. (2025) examined the use of an analytical AI platform in vocational teacher education, finding that AI feedback quality was comparable to human assessors across several dimensions, though improvements in AI literacy and attitudes did not occur automatically. This finding underscores the importance of pedagogical framing. A study by Engenes and Gamlem (2025) investigated an essay feedback system grounded in Vygotskian and Galperinian perspectives, designed to support cycles of drafting and revision; students demonstrated sustained improvement in writing quality across iterations, but higher-order rhetorical decisions continued to rely on human interaction.

Learner trust has emerged as a critical factor shaping the effectiveness of AI-mediated feedback. Experimental research comparing AI-generated, human-generated, and hybrid feedback indicates that learners judge feedback not only by technical accuracy but also by perceived credibility and relational sensitivity (Kotlyar & Krasman, 2025). AI feedback is often seen as consistent and technically reliable, yet trust decreases when learners perceive a lack of empathy or contextual understanding. A structured integrative review of 37 empirical studies examining teachers' views on AI-generated feedback (Al-ghamdi & Alghizzi, 2025) found that while teachers acknowledged benefits such as reduced workload and rapid response times, they expressed concerns related to fairness, transparency, accountability, and the weakening of relational aspects of pedagogy. AI as a Formative Assessment and Feedforward in Language Education involves building systems that earn trust through transparency, not simply systems that perform efficiently.

Equity considerations complicate the picture further, particularly in linguistically diverse L2 contexts. Systems trained on restricted datasets may reproduce biases toward standard varieties of English, disadvantaging learners whose writing reflects legitimate multilingual features or non-dominant accent patterns (Sato et al., 2024). Research on automated speech recognition has documented lower accuracy rates for speakers of non-native English accents and for learners from underrepresented language backgrounds, which raises validity questions about using such systems in high-stakes contexts. Teacher-in-the-loop designs provide one response to these concerns by ensuring that teachers review system output, contextualize feedback, and address socio-emotional dimensions that automated systems cannot manage effectively (Bulut et al., 2024). Gouseti et al. (2024) stress that institutions carry ethical responsibilities when deploying systems that collect and analyze learner data, arguing for transparency and clear governance structures.

Suresh et al.'s (2024) study on the TalkMoves application illustrates an important extension of AI's formative role into classroom dialogue. In that work, an application that analyzed classroom talk provided feedback on discourse practices in teacher professional development contexts, and teachers who engaged with this feedback over an extended period increased their use of dialogic talk moves. This finding suggests that AI-mediated feedback can operate at the level of teacher practice as well as learner performance, potentially transforming the conditions under which language learners receive human feedback in class. If AI helps teachers become more consistently dialogic, the quality of the human feedback that learners receive also improves as a downstream effect.

Suresh et al. (2024) also found that AI analytics, when used to support teacher reflection rather than to evaluate teacher performance, contributed to more equitable classroom participation patterns. This finding points toward a dimension of AI-mediated formative assessment that is often underexplored: its capacity to inform not only individual learner development but the design of the instructional environment itself. When AI tools generate data about which learners are receiving the least feedback, which task types are producing the most errors, or which instructional sequences are associated with the strongest revision behaviour, teachers can use this information to adapt their course design in ways that benefit all learners. This kind of program-level feedforward is a genuinely new possibility that AI opens up in language education.

What emerges from this body of research is a picture of genuine but conditional promise. AI systems can support formative assessment in language education when they are positioned clearly within a pedagogical framework, when their limitations are understood by both teachers and learners, and when human mediation is built into the design. The most effective implementations are not those in which AI replaces human feedback but those in which AI handles the systematic and replicable dimensions of feedback so that human expertise can be directed toward the interpretive and relational dimensions that automated systems cannot address. This is not a compromise position; it is a well-evidenced characterization of where AI currently adds the most value in language education contexts.

Recent design frameworks describe how LLM-based agents can support learning through theory-informed scaffolding, prompting explanation, posing questions that sustain engagement, and gradually reducing support as learners develop competence (Garcia-Mendez et al., 2024). Research on explainable AI argues that learners benefit when systems provide rationales for suggestions and make diagnostic processes visible (Khosravi et al., 2022). Under these conditions, AI can function as a collaborative partner within formative assessment rather than as a detached evaluator, contributing to learning in ways that are grounded in pedagogical purpose rather than technological novelty.

4. FROM FEEDBACK TO FEEDFORWARD IN LANGUAGE LEARNING CONTEXTS

The move from feedback to feedforward signals an important reorientation of formative assessment, and its implications are particularly concrete in language learning contexts where development occurs incrementally across tasks and time. Traditional feedback practices have often focused on judging completed work, with comments arriving after performance has already stabilized. Feedforward shifts attention toward future action, framing assessment as guidance that prepares learners for upcoming tasks and helps them adjust strategies before difficulties become entrenched. Hattie and Timperley (2007) argue that feedback becomes effective when it supports learners in understanding how to act differently in subsequent work, rather than simply confirming what went wrong. This future-facing orientation aligns closely with theories of self-regulated learning, where learners monitor progress, anticipate challenges, and plan next steps (Adhya & Panda, 2026; Zimmerman, 2000).

As Figure 1 illustrates, the transition from feedback to feedforward involves a fundamental shift in the directionality and timing of assessment information. Feedback flows backward from a completed task to the learner; feedforward flows forward from current performance toward future action, with AI, teacher, and peer input all contributing to an iterative cycle rather than a terminal judgement.

Figure 1. The hybrid human-AI feedforward cycle in language education

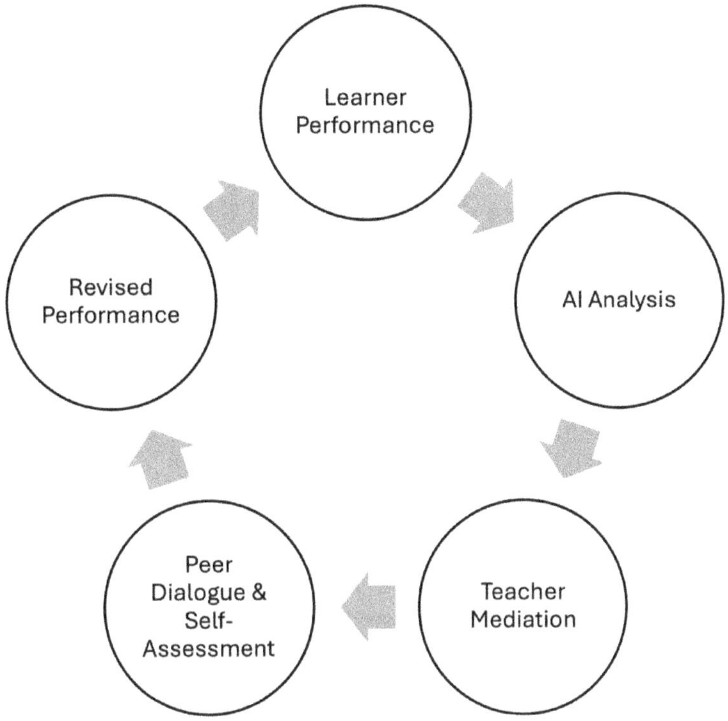

Within language education, the feedforward principle addresses a persistent structural limitation of conventional feedback: comments on a piece of writing or a spoken performance typically arrive too late to shape the decisions that produced them. Consider an EFL writing course in which students submit drafts on a weekly basis. A teacher who practises feedforward will respond not only to what a student wrote but also to patterns emerging across submissions, flagging recurring weaknesses in cohesive devices or argument structure before they solidify into habits. When an AI writing tool such as Write & Improve is integrated into this workflow, it can flag these patterns in near real time during drafting, prompting students to revise before submission. The teacher's role then shifts toward interpretation and dialogue: helping students understand why certain revisions matter, how they connect to communicative intent, and what strategies to apply in the next task. This division of labour is not merely convenient but pedagogically coherent, since it positions each participant's contribution where it can do the most good.

AI introduces new possibilities for realizing feedforward in practice at scale. AI systems can monitor learner activity over time, identify emerging patterns, and generate guidance that anticipates future needs rather than simply cataloguing past errors. Luckin et al. (2016) describe AI as a cognitive partner that supports learning within the Zone of Proximal Development by identifying moments where guidance is most productive. In language learning, this can include prompting revision strategies during drafting, suggesting alternative phrasing before fossilization occurs, or directing attention to recurring weaknesses in vocabulary use or grammatical choice (Fleckenstein et al., 2023). Learning analytics dashboards can surface trends in language use or task engagement and connect them to targeted practice opportunities

(Paulsen & Lindsay, 2024). When learners can see how present actions shape future performance, assessment becomes part of an ongoing learning trajectory rather than an isolated event.

The feedforward orientation also applies meaningfully to spoken language tasks, an area that receives comparatively little attention in most general assessment scholarship. In an oral communication course, an AI-based pronunciation and fluency analysis tool might identify recurring difficulties with word stress or connected speech across a series of recorded speaking tasks, generating a personalized report that the student and teacher can review together before the next practice cycle begins. This kind of proactive, pattern-based guidance is difficult to provide at scale through human assessment alone. It does not replace the teacher's capacity to respond to meaning, pragmatic appropriateness, or interactional quality; it handles the systematic and replicable dimension of feedback so that human attention can be directed toward more complex communicative judgements. Tools such as ELSA Speak or built-in speaking analytics in platforms like Moodle are already being used in this way in university EFL programs across East and Southeast Asia, with preliminary evidence of gains in learner self-monitoring behaviours (Yin et al., 2024).

Feedback literacy plays a critical role in determining whether feedforward leads to sustained improvement. Carless and Boud (2018) describe effective feedforward as guidance that is structured, contextualized, and clearly connected to future opportunities for use. AI systems can support the development of this capacity by structuring prompts that encourage learners to reflect on choices, compare alternatives, and plan revisions. In writing instruction, AI annotations can direct attention to areas for development and encourage learners to evaluate their own drafts and test different strategies across iterations (Engenes & Gamlem, 2025). Peer and self-assessment extend feedforward further by creating shared spaces for interpretation and revision. AI can support these practices by organizing peer feedback, identifying recurring patterns in comments, and prompting learners to reflect on the quality of feedback they both give and receive. In this way, feedforward becomes distributed across learners, technologies, and teachers, creating an iterative assessment environment rather than a linear exchange.

Timing is a defining feature of feedforward, and AI systems are particularly well positioned to address the structural problem of delayed feedback. Shute (2008) argues that timely feedback strengthens the connection between action and outcome, supporting more effective learning. Research on intelligent tutoring systems indicates that immediate, actionable guidance supports skill development in areas such as language use and problem solving (VanLehn, 2011). When feedback is integrated into activity rather than appended to it, learners are more likely to adjust strategies and internalize learning processes. Affective considerations also shape how feedforward is received, a dimension that AI alone cannot address. Evans (2013) notes that learners' engagement depends on clarity, credibility, and perceived support for autonomy. Research suggests that trust is strengthened when automated guidance is accompanied by human interpretation and encouragement (Al-Zahrani & Alasmari, 2024). Teachers play a key role in framing AI-mediated feedforward as a resource for learning rather than as an evaluative judgement, particularly for learners from educational cultures where teacher authority over assessment is strongly expected.

Cultural factors also shape how feedforward is received and acted upon, a dimension that language educators are particularly well placed to appreciate. Feedback preferences and norms vary considerably across educational cultures: learners from some contexts expect directive, authoritative feedback and may be uncertain about how to engage with non-evaluative feedforward, whereas learners from other contexts may value autonomy-preserving guidance and resist direct correction. AI systems do not adapt to these preferences automatically, and the framing of AI-generated feedforward by the teacher is therefore important in diverse multilingual classrooms. Acknowledging these differences openly and discussing with students why feedforward is structured the way it is can reduce misinterpretation and increase productive engagement over time.

The distinction between feedback and feedforward also has implications for how AI tools are sequenced within assessment tasks. A tool used only at the end of a writing assignment, after submission, functions as feedback in the traditional sense. The same tool used during drafting, before submission, functions as feedforward. The technical capabilities of the tool are the same in both cases; what changes is the pedagogical sequencing in which it is embedded. This matters for practical implementation because it means that the feedforward potential of many existing AI tools is not being realized in current practice. Teachers who already use automated writing evaluators or AI grammar checkers can shift their pedagogical impact significantly simply by changing when in the assignment sequence students are directed to use them.

Table 1 summarizes the key distinctions between traditional feedback and AI-enabled feedforward across six dimensions relevant to language education. These distinctions are not absolute, but they capture the characteristic differences in how each approach tends to function in practice.

Table 1. Traditional feedback versus AI-enabled feedforward in language education

Dimension	Traditional Feedback	AI-Enabled Feedforward
Timing	After task completion; retrospective	During or before task; prospective
Direction	Backward-looking; accounts for past performance	Forward-looking; prepares for future tasks
Scale	Limited by teacher time and class size	Consistent across large cohorts simultaneously
Language focus	Holistic; attends to meaning, rhetoric, and form	Strongest on rule-governed features (grammar, vocabulary, pronunciation patterns)
Relational dimension	Embedded in teacher-learner relationship	Technically consistent but requires human mediation for trust and affect
Learner role	Often passive recipient of judgement	Active interpreter and responder; feedback literacy required

Note. The table describes tendencies rather than fixed properties. Hybrid models that combine AI analysis with teacher mediation and peer dialogue can address the limitations of each approach individually.

Ethical and equity concerns are integral to feedforward design, not peripheral additions. Systems trained on limited datasets may reproduce linguistic biases that disadvantage particular learner groups (Sato et al., 2024). Transparency in system design, institutional governance, and teacher oversight are therefore essential (Bulut et al., 2024). Feedforward systems also raise questions about data collection, consent, and long-term monitoring, which require clear policies and shared institutional responsibility (Williamson, 2017). Emerging evidence suggests that hybrid models combining AI guidance with human mediation produce more robust outcomes than either approach in isolation. Studies of automated writing feedback indicate stronger learning gains when learners discuss AI suggestions with teachers and peers rather than acting on them alone (Pargmann et al., 2025). The shift from feedback to feedforward reframes formative assessment in language education as a forward-oriented, developmental practice in which AI contributes most when it operates as one element within a deliberately designed pedagogical system.

5. CHALLENGES AND PEDAGOGICAL CONSIDERATIONS

The use of artificial intelligence in formative assessment introduces challenges that extend well past technical performance. Pedagogical coherence, ethical responsibility, and relational dynamics all shape whether AI-supported feedback contributes to learning in meaningful ways. One major concern relates to the growing emphasis on what can be measured easily. Biesta (2010) cautions that an excessive focus on indicators such as grammatical accuracy, lexical frequency, or task completion scores risks narrowing educational aims in ways that are difficult to reverse once embedded in institutional assessment cultures. When assessment privileges measurable outcomes, learners may focus on surface accuracy as a proxy for proficiency, leaving deeper forms of reasoning, creative language use, and pragmatic competence underattended. In L2 contexts, this risk is particularly acute: a student relying heavily on AI writing feedback may learn to satisfy algorithmic criteria for sentence-level grammar without developing the discourse-level competence that constitutes genuine second language proficiency.

Learner agency presents a related and equally significant concern. Formative assessment depends on learners interpreting feedback, weighing alternatives, and deciding how to proceed. Boud and Molloy (2013) argue that improvement occurs when learners assume responsibility for making sense of guidance rather than following instructions mechanically. AI systems that generate direct corrections or model answers may unintentionally limit opportunities for reflection. Learners can become accustomed to accepting automated suggestions without engaging with underlying concepts or principles, a pattern that Fenwick et al. (2012) describe as passive acceptance of algorithmic outputs. For language educators, this is a pedagogically significant risk because the development of self-monitoring and strategic competence is itself a core learning outcome in communicative language teaching, not merely a means to an end.

The question of what AI can and cannot validly assess in language education deserves specific attention. AI writing evaluators perform well on grammar, spelling, and syntactic complexity, but their capacity to assess discourse organization, register appropriateness, argumentation quality, or pragmatic intent remains limited and sometimes unreliable. AI pronunciation tools perform reasonably for well-represented accents on standard word lists but show known difficulties with spontaneous speech, non-native phonological transfer patterns, and prosodic features such as intonation and emphasis. Mizumoto and Eguchi (2023) demonstrate that even relatively simple AI-based scoring tools require careful validation before they are used as formative feedback in L2 writing contexts. Teachers using AI in language assessment need a working understanding of these limitations so that they can communicate them clearly to learners and avoid over-reliance on AI outputs in domains where validity evidence is weak.

Teachers therefore remain central to the assessment process. Professional judgement enables teachers to interpret AI-generated feedback, situate it within disciplinary and task-specific contexts, and respond to learners' emotional and motivational needs. Allal (2013) conceptualizes teacher judgement as a socially situated and interpretive process, in which assessment gains meaning through contextualized professional evaluation rather than through the mechanical application of criteria alone. In writing instruction, automated systems can identify grammatical problems and surface-level syntactic patterns, but they cannot assess rhetorical purpose, argument development, or audience awareness. Teachers guide learners in understanding why certain revisions matter and how feedback connects to communicative intent and strategy use (Brookhart, 2001). AI integration is most productive when it operates as a complement to pedagogical expertise rather than as a substitute for it (Roll & Wylie, 2016). This is not a conservative argument against technological adoption; it is a practical argument that the conditions for effective AI use include, rather than exclude, strong teacher mediation.

Ethical considerations further complicate the use of AI in language assessment. Sato et al. (2024) warn that systems trained on narrow datasets may reproduce linguistic and cultural biases, disadvantaging particular learner groups. In language education, this concern extends to accent bias, variety bias, and the risk of reinforcing deficit views of multilingual learners. An AI pronunciation tool that consistently rates speakers with non-standard accents lower, or a writing evaluator that penalizes stylistic features associated with non-Western rhetorical traditions, can produce systematically unfair outcomes. Teachers need to audit AI outputs for these tendencies and align AI use with inclusive and plurilingual goals. Williamson (2017) raises related concerns about surveillance, data ownership, and the long-term use of learner information. Institutions must establish governance structures that regulate data collection, storage, and access, with learners informed about how their data are used and how automated judgements are produced.

Language learners in Global South contexts or in under-resourced school systems often face additional structural disadvantages when AI feedback tools are introduced. Inconsistent electricity supply, shared devices, and limited bandwidth are practical constraints that can render synchronous AI feedback platforms inaccessible (UNESCO, 2024; World Bank, 2023), and teachers in these contexts cannot assume that students will be able to engage with AI tools outside of class time. Recommendations that are designed primarily for well-resourced university contexts in the Global North may need significant adaptation to be applicable in these settings (UNESCO, 2024). Acknowledging this diversity of implementation contexts is not a peripheral caveat but a central responsibility for researchers and practitioners working in the field of language education technology.

The institutional context of language education shapes which challenges are most pressing. In exam-oriented secondary EFL systems, where national examinations define the de facto curriculum, AI feedback tools may be adopted primarily for test preparation rather than genuinely formative purposes. In this context, the risk of narrowing to measurable outcomes is particularly high, and the teacher's role in contextualizing AI feedback within a broader understanding of language proficiency becomes especially important. In higher education, the challenge may be different: large writing courses with enrolments of hundreds of students create conditions in which AI feedback is the most practical option for providing individualized guidance, but also conditions in which the relational dimension of feedback is most difficult to maintain. Practical frameworks for AI-mediated formative assessment in language education need to acknowledge these contextual variations.

Digital literacy presents another challenge that is sometimes overlooked in discussions of AI feedback. Language learners using AI tools for the first time may not understand what the system is doing, why certain features are flagged, or how to evaluate the quality of AI suggestions. This is not simply a matter of technical literacy: it requires critical engagement with algorithmic outputs that even educated adults find challenging (Selwyn, 2021). Students who lack a framework for evaluating AI feedback may accept it uncritically, which as noted above can produce surface compliance without genuine learning (Williamson et al., 2023). Teachers need to actively build this critical literacy into their courses rather than assuming that students will develop it independently.

Pedagogical design choices also shape whether AI feedback supports learning or merely accelerates surface correction. Shute (2008) argues that formative guidance should prompt learners to think about their processes, evaluate alternatives, and adjust strategies. AI platforms can be designed to encourage these behaviours by drawing attention to recurring patterns and prompting reflection on outcomes as well as errors (Ifenthaler et al., 2020). Implementation challenges affect teachers directly and unevenly. Automated outputs require monitoring, interpretation, and pedagogical framing, which can add rather than reduce workload if systems are not integrated thoughtfully. Bulut et al. (2024) note that teacher-in-the-loop models help manage these demands. In many real-world language classrooms, including exam-oriented secondary classes, large university EAP courses, and resource-constrained settings in the Global South, additional infrastructure and training costs may significantly limit what is feasible. Trust plays a decisive role in learner engagement with AI-mediated feedback. Kotlyar and Krasman (2025) show that learners perceive guidance as more credible when automated suggestions are accompanied by human explanation and discussion. Designers and teachers must therefore attend not only to system accuracy but also to how feedback is framed and communicated within learning relationships.

6. PRACTICAL RECOMMENDATIONS

The use of AI in formative assessment calls for a careful balance between technological capability and pedagogical purpose. AI-mediated feedback becomes educationally productive only when it is embedded within teaching practices that support interpretation, reflection, and purposeful action. Systems alone do not generate learning. Teachers remain central as mediators who frame feedback, connect it to learning goals, and guide learners in deciding how to proceed (Allal, 2013; Brookhart, 2001). The practical guidance below is organized around four priorities: alignment with formative principles, feedback literacy development, ethical monitoring, and curriculum design.

Formative feedback principles provide a useful reference point for tool selection and configuration. Nicol and Macfarlane-Dick (2006) identify practices such as clarifying standards, supporting self-assessment, encouraging dialogue, and creating opportunities to use feedback as foundations of effective formative practice. These can function as evaluative criteria when selecting or configuring AI tools. A practical starting point for language teachers is to map the AI tool's feedback categories against the constructs being assessed in the course. If an EAP writing course values argumentative structure and source integration as primary outcomes, a tool that provides only grammar-level feedback is misaligned and should be supplemented. This mapping process creates an opportunity for explicit discussion with learners about what the course values and how automated feedback connects, partially but not fully, to those goals. Such discussions build the metacognitive awareness that makes feedforward meaningful rather than mechanical.

Consider a concrete scenario from an L2 speaking course to illustrate how these principles operate in practice. A teacher using an AI-based pronunciation and fluency analysis tool assigns students weekly recorded speaking tasks. The AI generates individual reports flagging patterns in word stress, speech rate, and hesitation frequency across the series of recordings. Rather than treating these reports as terminal evaluations, the teacher uses them as a starting point for individual conferencing in the following week's session, asking each student to identify one pattern they want to address and co-designing a targeted practice activity with them. Peers then listen to each other's revised recordings and offer structured comments guided by shared criteria. In this workflow, the AI handles the systematic and replicable dimension of feedback, the teacher provides interpretation and relational support, and peer interaction creates an additional layer of dialogic feedforward. The workflow is not technically complex, but it requires deliberate design and explicit preparation before it is introduced to students; dropped into a course without preparation, the same tools would likely produce confusion or surface compliance rather than meaningful learning.

Feedback literacy requires parallel and explicit attention. Carless and Boud (2018) argue that learners and teachers both need the capacity to interpret feedback, question its relevance, and act strategically. For learners, structured routines such as guided reflection and comparison of drafts across iterations can strengthen their ability to use AI-generated suggestions productively. Winstone and Carless (2019) show that repeated engagement with feedback tasks helps consolidate these practices and supports autonomous decision-making over time. In multilingual classrooms with learners at varied proficiency levels, scaffolding this process requires explicit instruction in how to read and evaluate automated feedback. A brief orientation session at the start of a course, in which the teacher walks students through a sample AI report and models interpretive questions, can significantly improve subsequent engagement and reduce the tendency to accept AI suggestions uncritically.

Self-regulated learning frameworks provide practical guidance for structuring classroom use of AI feedback tools. Zimmerman (2000) describes learning as a cyclical process involving planning, performance, and reflection, and AI tools can support each phase in distinct ways. During planning they can support goal setting through criterion-referenced guidance; during drafting they can prompt real-time revision; and after task completion learners can reflect on AI feedback alongside teacher and peer commentary and plan revisions that inform subsequent work (Hattie & Timperley, 2007). Tasks involving argumentation, creative language use, or extended spoken interaction benefit from hybrid feedback models in which AI supports procedural guidance and teachers focus on conceptual development and rhetorical purpose (Lo et al., 2025). Curriculum design plays a decisive role in shaping effective use: tasks need to be structured so that AI feedback has a clear function in the learning sequence rather than being added on as an optional resource.

Ethical and technical monitoring must be built into implementation as an ongoing process rather than addressed once at the point of adoption. Teachers should examine AI outputs for bias, clarity, and fairness, particularly in linguistically and culturally diverse classrooms (Sato et al., 2024). Learners benefit when systems provide accessible explanations of how suggestions are generated, since transparency supports trust and informed engagement (Khosravi et al., 2022). Institutional policies should address consent, data storage, and responsible use in language that learners can understand. For learners in low-resource or exam-driven contexts, access to AI tools is not uniform, and recommendations that presuppose consistent device availability or reliable internet connectivity may be unworkable in practice.

The issue of how AI feedback interacts with peer feedback also warrants practical attention. When both AI and peer feedback are present in a course, learners sometimes experience confusion about which source to prioritize, particularly when the two conflict. In writing courses, AI tools may flag a sentence as grammatically problematic that a peer reviewer has praised for its style, or vice versa. Teachers can turn these conflicts into productive learning opportunities by facilitating discussion about why the two sources diverge and what this reveals about the different kinds of knowledge that algorithmic and human evaluators draw upon. Far from being a problem to be managed, the co-presence of AI and peer feedback can deepen learners' critical engagement with the assessment process itself.

Curriculum design at the program level is also relevant to effective implementation. When AI tools are introduced by individual teachers without coordination across a program, learners may encounter inconsistent expectations about how to use AI feedback, what it means, and how it relates to other forms of assessment. A program-level approach to AI integration, in which faculty agree on a shared framework for how and when AI feedback tools are used, communicates a coherent message to students and creates conditions for the kind of feedback literacy development that requires sustained practice across multiple courses. This is especially important in EFL and EAP programs where students progress through a sequence of courses and where strategic use of feedback needs to develop cumulatively over time.

The question of what counts as evidence of effectiveness is also worth raising explicitly in any recommendation framework. In many discussions of AI feedback tools, effectiveness is measured by performance outcomes on specific tasks or test scores. These are legitimate measures, but they may not capture the dimensions of language development that formative assessment is most intended to support. Self-regulation, metacognitive awareness, and the ability to independently evaluate and revise one's own language production are outcomes that formative assessment theory places at the centre of practice. Research designs that include these outcomes alongside task-specific performance measures would provide a more complete picture of whether AI-mediated feedforward is achieving its educational goals.

Sustained professional development underpins all of these recommendations. Teachers need opportunities to explore AI tools, reflect on classroom use, and adapt practices in response to learner needs and institutional constraints. Training should address both technical operation and pedagogical integration, including how to interpret analytics, how to identify and counteract algorithmic bias, and how to support learner engagement with feedback across a course. Research on intelligent tutoring systems shows that iterative adjustment based on classroom experience improves both effectiveness and learner acceptance over time (VanLehn, 2011). Peer review activities can productively incorporate AI feedback as a starting point for discussion: learners compare AI-generated guidance with their own evaluations, discuss discrepancies, and negotiate revisions collectively (Orsmond & Merry, 2011). Teacher mediation remains essential in these exchanges, supporting interpretation and reinforcing strategic use of feedback within a social learning context (Carless et al., 2011). Ongoing evaluation using data on learner engagement, revision behaviour, and feedback uptake should inform the refinement of both tools and teaching strategies across the life of a course.

7. CONCLUSION AND FUTURE DIRECTIONS

The use of artificial intelligence in formative assessment presents language teachers with substantial possibilities for strengthening learning processes, alongside new demands on pedagogical judgement and ethical responsibility. These possibilities are best understood through social constructivist perspectives on learning, particularly Vygotsky's (1978) account of the Zone of Proximal Development, in which AI can function as a responsive scaffold that supports learners at moments of difficulty and gradually reduces assistance as competence increases. Such a role becomes educationally meaningful only when AI is situated within socially mediated learning environments where interaction with teachers and peers remains central. AI contributes by providing timely and individualized feedback that operates within a broader dialogic process of meaning construction rather than in isolation (Luckin et al., 2016).

The educational value of AI is closely tied to its capacity to support reflection and critical engagement. Mezirow (1991) argues that learning becomes transformative when individuals are prompted to question assumptions and reconsider established understandings. Adaptive feedback systems can contribute to this process when they encourage learners to review prior decisions and explore alternative strategies, but this potential depends on intentional pedagogical design. Feedback needs to extend past surface-level correction and include prompts for self-evaluation and strategic adjustment (Shute, 2008). When these features are absent, AI feedback risks being experienced as procedural and disconnected from learning goals, which can limit its educational impact considerably (Boud & Molloy, 2013). The risk is not hypothetical: studies of learners using automated writing evaluators without instructional scaffolding frequently report surface compliance without meaningful revision of content or argument structure.

In language education, the value proposition of AI is clearest in tasks where systematic pattern analysis matters: identifying recurring grammatical difficulties in a student's writing across a semester, tracking changes in fluency markers in spoken production over time, or pinpointing persistent vocabulary gaps that impede reading comprehension. These are functions that human teachers can rarely perform at scale or with the consistency that formative feedforward requires. The pedagogical challenge is not whether to use AI for these purposes but how to integrate its outputs into instructional practices that also attend to meaning, context, learner identity, and the communicative purpose of language use. Language educators working in contexts as varied as exam-oriented secondary EFL classrooms, multilingual university writing centres, and community language programs will need to adapt these principles to their specific constraints and populations.

Effective implementation requires preserving teacher authority over assessment decisions while allowing learners to engage independently with automated guidance. Hybrid approaches, where AI provides initial feedback and teachers guide interpretation and revision, have shown particular promise in maintaining this balance (Jiang, 2025). Feedback literacy plays a central role in sustaining such approaches. Carless and Boud (2018) note that learners need to develop the capacity to interpret feedback and decide how to act upon it. Practices such as guided reflection, peer dialogue, and iterative revision can support the internalization of feedback and strengthen self-regulation over time (Winstone & Carless, 2020). Teachers likewise require support to understand AI outputs and design learning activities that ensure feedback contributes to genuine language development rather than remaining informational.

Ethical governance is a defining concern for the field going forward. Selwyn (2021) and Williamson (2017) argue that AI in education must be understood as a sociopolitical issue that raises questions of privacy, equity, accountability, and institutional responsibility. AI systems rely on learner data, creating obligations related to consent, transparency, and protection against misuse. Institutions must establish clear policies for data governance and monitor systems for bias or exclusion, particularly where automated feedback may affect vulnerable learner groups (Sato et al., 2024). In language education, the intersection of linguistic diversity and algorithmic bias creates specific risks that deserve dedicated attention from researchers, developers, and institutions. Socio-emotional dimensions of feedback also require care. Learners' responses to feedback are shaped by perceptions of fairness, clarity, and relational support, not only by cognitive accuracy (Evans, 2013; Sutton, 2012). Collaborative models that combine AI guidance with teacher mediation help address this concern by sustaining authenticity and supporting both affective and cognitive dimensions of learning (Kotlyar & Krasman, 2025).

Future research must address issues of scalability and contextual variation. Positive outcomes reported in studies of writing development and teacher learning (Fleckenstein et al., 2023; Steiss et al., 2024) need to be tested across disciplines, learner populations, and institutional contexts, including under-resourced settings and non-Western educational environments. Longitudinal studies examining how sustained AI use affects learner autonomy, metacognitive development, and skill transfer to authentic communicative tasks represent a significant gap in the current literature. Design-based research provides a productive methodological approach, allowing for iterative refinement of AI tools in response to classroom realities (Engenes & Gamlem, 2025). Researchers and practitioners would also benefit from more collaborative inquiry models in which teachers and students are active partners in evaluating AI feedback tools rather than passive recipients of systems designed elsewhere.

The integration of AI into formative assessment invites reconsideration of curriculum design. Feedback is most effective when it is embedded as an ongoing component of learning rather than delivered after task completion. Tasks should allow learners to engage repeatedly with feedback, revise their work, and reflect on progress across time (Boud & Molloy, 2013; Hattie & Timperley, 2007). Feedforward principles are particularly relevant here, orienting learners toward future action and improvement. AI systems that generate actionable guidance and prompt reflection can support these principles when combined with teacher scaffolding and peer interaction (Carless & Boud, 2018).

Assessment for learning has always been shaped by the contexts in which it operates, and AI-mediated formative assessment is no exception. The theoretical frameworks reviewed in this chapter, including sociocultural theory, self-regulated learning, and feedback literacy, provide robust conceptual tools for guiding implementation. Their value, however, depends on how they are adapted to the specific conditions of particular language education settings: the proficiency levels of learners, the institutional pressures teachers face, the assessment purposes being served, and the social and cultural norms that shape how feedback is given and received. A theoretically sophisticated approach to AI-mediated formative assessment is one that takes all of these factors seriously and remains sceptical of one-size-fits-all solutions.

The relationship between AI-mediated feedforward and learner autonomy deserves particular attention as a future research priority. Language education has a long tradition of attending to learner autonomy, understood as the capacity to take responsibility for one's own learning, and this tradition raises specific questions about AI feedback. Does sustained exposure to detailed AI feedback support the development of autonomous language learners, or does it create dependency? The answer is likely to depend on how AI feedback is framed and used: feedback that models self-monitoring processes and prompts learners to evaluate their own work may support autonomy, whereas feedback that simply provides corrections may undermine it. Longitudinal studies tracking learner autonomy outcomes across courses that use AI feedback in different ways would help to answer this question empirically.

The intersection of AI-mediated formative assessment with high-stakes language testing is another area where more research and policy attention is needed. Most of the evidence reviewed in this chapter comes from formative assessment contexts: low-stakes classroom tasks, writing workshops, and speaking practice activities. The relationship between formative AI feedback and high-stakes test performance is less well understood, and language program administrators need clearer guidance on whether and how AI-mediated feedforward contributes to the kinds of integrated language proficiency that examinations attempt to measure. These are practical questions for practitioners as well as researchers, and they deserve systematic investigation in naturalistic educational settings where AI tools are already in use.

To realize these possibilities, professional development, institutional policy, and curriculum planning need to operate in coordination. Teachers require opportunities to experiment with AI tools, interpret outputs, and integrate them into teaching in ways that respect pedagogical aims and ethical standards. Institutions must provide guidance on data use, ensure equitable access, and support systematic evaluation of AI practices (Williamson, 2017). A coordinated approach allows technological innovation to remain aligned with educational values. The future of AI in formative assessment in language education depends on careful, theory-informed integration. Addressing questions of feedback literacy, teacher mediation, linguistic equity, and institutional governance thoughtfully can ensure that AI functions as a genuine partner in language learning, supporting responsive and human-centred formative assessment practices across diverse educational settings.

ACKNOWLEDGEMENTS

During the preparation of this work, the author used Claude Version 4.5 to polish the flow of some of the sentences in all chapters (using the prompt: "improve for better flow"). After using this AI tool, the author reviewed and edited the content as needed and takes full responsibility for the content of the publication.

REFERENCES

Adhya, D. H., & Panda, S. (2026). An integrative systematic review analysis of research on technology-enabled personalized learning and self-regulated learning. *Smart Learning Environments, 13*(1), 3. Advance online publication. DOI: 10.1186/s40561-025-00428-8

Al-Zahrani, A. M., & Alasmari, T. M. (2024). Exploring the impact of artificial intelligence on higher education: The dynamics of ethical, social, and educational implications. *Humanities & Social Sciences Communications, 11*(1), 912. Advance online publication. DOI: 10.1057/s41599-024-03432-4

Alghamdi, L. H., & Alghizzi, T. M. (2025). Educators' reflections on AI-automated feedback in higher education: A structured integrative review of potentials, pitfalls, and ethical dimensions. *Frontiers in Education, 10*, 1704820. Advance online publication. DOI: 10.3389/feduc.2025.1704820

Allal, L. (2013). Teachers' professional judgement in assessment: A cognitive act and a socially situated practice. *Assessment in Education: Principles, Policy & Practice, 20*(1), 20–34. DOI: 10.1080/0969594X.2012.736364

Bennett, R. E. (2011). Formative assessment: A critical review. *Assessment in Education: Principles, Policy & Practice, 18*(1), 5–25. DOI: 10.1080/0969594X.2010.513678

Biesta, G. J. J. (2010). *Good education in an age of measurement: Ethics, politics, democracy*. Taylor & Francis.

Black, P., & Wiliam, D. (1998). Assessment and classroom learning. *Assessment in Education: Principles, Policy & Practice, 5*(1), 7–74. DOI: 10.1080/0969595980050102

Boud, D., & Molloy, E. (2013). Rethinking models of feedback for learning: The challenge of design. *Assessment & Evaluation in Higher Education, 38*(6), 698–712. DOI: 10.1080/02602938.2012.691462

Brookhart, S. M. (2001). Successful students' formative and summative uses of assessment information. *Assessment in Education: Principles, Policy & Practice, 8*(2), 153–169. DOI: 10.1080/09695940123775

Bulut, O., Beiting-Parrish, M., Casabianca, J. M., Slater, S. C., Jiao, H., Song, D., Ormerod, C. M., Fabiyi, D. G., Ivan, R., Walsh, C., Rios, O., Wilson, J., Yildirim-Erbasli, S. N., Wongvorachan, T., Liu, J. X., Tan, B., & Morilova, P. (2024). The rise of artificial intelligence in educational measurement: Opportunities and ethical challenges. *Chinese/English Journal of Educational Measurement and Evaluation, 5*(3), 3. DOI: 10.59863/MIQL7785

Carless, D., & Boud, D. (2018). The development of student feedback literacy: Enabling uptake of feedback. *Assessment & Evaluation in Higher Education*, *43*(8), 1315–1325. DOI: 10.1080/02602938.2018.1463354

Carless, D., Salter, D., Yang, M., & Lam, J. (2011). Developing sustainable feedback practices. *Studies in Higher Education*, *36*(4), 395–407. DOI: 10.1080/03075071003642449

Earl, L. (2003). *Assessment as learning: Using classroom assessment to maximize student learning*. Corwin.

Engenes, I., & Gamlem, S. M. (2025). Exploring AI-driven feedback as a cultural tool: A cultural-historical perspective on design of AI environments to support students' writing process. *Integrative Psychological & Behavioral Science*, *59*(1), 23. Advance online publication. DOI: 10.1007/s12124-025-09894-8

Evans, C. (2013). Making sense of assessment feedback in higher education. *Review of Educational Research*, *83*(1), 70–120. DOI: 10.3102/0034654312474350

Fenwick, T., Edwards, R., & Sawchuk, P. (2012). *Emerging approaches to educational research: Tracing the sociomaterial*. Routledge.

Fleckenstein, J., Liebenow, L. W., & Meyer, J. (2023). Automated feedback and writing: A multi-level meta-analysis of effects on students' performance. *Frontiers in Artificial Intelligence*, *6*, 1162454. Advance online publication. DOI: 10.3389/frai.2023.1162454

García-Méndez, S., De Arriba-Pérez, F., & Del Carmen Somoza-López, M. (2024). A review on the use of large language models as virtual tutors. *Science & Education*, *34*(2), 877–892. DOI: 10.1007/s11191-024-00530-2

Gipps, C. (1994). *Beyond testing: Towards a theory of educational assessment*. Routledge.

Gouseti, A., James, F., Fallin, L., & Burden, K. (2024). The ethics of using AI in K-12 education: A systematic literature review. *Technology, Pedagogy and Education*, *34*(2), 161–182. DOI: 10.1080/1475939X.2024.2428601

Hattie, J., & Timperley, H. (2007). The power of feedback. *Review of Educational Research*, *77*(1), 81–112. DOI: 10.3102/003465430298487

Heritage, M. (2010). *Formative assessment: Making it happen in the classroom*. Corwin.

Ifenthaler, D., Gibson, D., Prasse, D., Shimada, A., & Yamada, M. (2020). Putting learning back into learning analytics: Actions for policy makers, researchers, and practitioners. *Educational Technology Research and Development*, *69*(4), 2131–2150. DOI: 10.1007/s11423-020-09909-8

Jiang, Y. (2025). Interaction and dialogue: Integration and application of artificial intelligence in blended mode writing feedback. *The Internet and Higher Education*, *64*, 100975. Advance online publication. DOI: 10.1016/j.iheduc.2024.100975

Jin, F. J., Yan, L., Martinez-Maldonado, R., Gašević, D., Chan, P. W. K., & Tsai, Y. (2025). Latent classes of self-reported feedback experiences: Exploring students' challenges, motivations, and action-taking behaviours in feedback processes. *Instructional Science*, *53*(6), 1395–1427. DOI: 10.1007/s11251-025-09744-5

Khosravi, H., Buckingham Shum, S., Chen, G., Conati, C., Tsai, Y.-S., Kay, J., Knight, S., Martínez-Maldonado, R., Sadiq, S., & Gašević, D. (2022). Explainable artificial intelligence in education. *Computers & Education: Artificial Intelligence*, *3*, 100074. Advance online publication. DOI: 10.1016/j.caeai.2022.100074

Kizil, V. (2019). Peer assessment in EFL writing classes. *The Journal of International Lingual Social and Educational Sciences*, *5*(1), 101–111. DOI: 10.34137/jilses.560099

Kotlyar, I., & Krasman, J. (2025). Student reactions to AI versus human feedback in teamwork skills assessment. *International Journal of Educational Technology in Higher Education*, *22*(1), 57. Advance online publication. DOI: 10.1186/s41239-025-00555-9

Létourneau, A., Martineau, M. D., Charland, P., Karran, J. A., Boasen, J., & Léger, P. M. (2025). A systematic review of AI-driven intelligent tutoring systems (ITS) in K-12 education. *NPJ Science of Learning*, *10*(1), 29. Advance online publication. DOI: 10.1038/s41539-025-00320-7

Lo, N., Chan, S., & Wong, A. (2025). Evaluating teacher, AI, and hybrid feedback in English language learning: Impact on student motivation, quality, and performance in Hong Kong. *SAGE Open*, *15*(3), 21582440251352907. Advance online publication. DOI: 10.1177/21582440251352907

Luckin, R., Holmes, W., Griffiths, M., & Corcier, L. B. (2016). *Intelligence unleashed: An argument for AI in education*. Pearson.

Mezirow, J. (1991). *Transformative dimensions of adult learning*. Jossey-Bass.

Mizumoto, A., & Eguchi, M. (2023). Exploring the potential of using an AI language model for automated essay scoring. *Research Methods in Applied Linguistics*, *2*(2), 100050. Advance online publication. DOI: 10.1016/j.rmal.2023.100050

Nicol, D. J., & Macfarlane-Dick, D. (2006). Formative assessment and self-regulated learning: A model and seven principles of good feedback practice. *Studies in Higher Education*, *31*(2), 199–218. DOI: 10.1080/03075070600572090

Orsmond, P., & Merry, S. (2011). Feedback alignment: Effective and ineffective links between tutors' and students' understanding of coursework feedback. *Assessment & Evaluation in Higher Education*, *36*(2), 125–136. DOI: 10.1080/02602930903201651

Orsmond, P., Merry, S., & Callaghan, A. (2004). Implementation of a formative assessment model incorporating peer and self-assessment. *Innovations in Education and Teaching International*, *41*(3), 273–290. DOI: 10.1080/14703290410001733294

Panadero, E. (2017). A review of self-regulated learning: Six models and four directions for research. *Frontiers in Psychology*, *8*, 422. Advance online publication. DOI: 10.3389/fpsyg.2017.00422

Pardo, A., & Siemens, G. (2014). Ethical and privacy principles for learning analytics. *British Journal of Educational Technology*, *45*(3), 438–450. DOI: 10.1111/bjet.12152

Pargmann, J., Berding, F., Rebmann, K., & Riebenbauer, E. (2025). How AI feedback supports lesson planning in vocational teacher education: A longitudinal intervention study using an analytical AI platform. *Empirical Research in Vocational Education and Training*, *17*(1), 26. Advance online publication. DOI: 10.1186/s40461-025-00202-7

Paulsen, L., & Lindsay, E. (2024). Learning analytics dashboards are increasingly becoming about learning and not just analytics: A systematic review. *Education and Information Technologies*, *29*(11), 14279–14308. DOI: 10.1007/s10639-023-12401-4

Popenici, S. A. D., & Kerr, S. (2017). Exploring the impact of artificial intelligence on teaching and learning in higher education. *Research and Practice in Technology Enhanced Learning*, *12*(1), 1–13. DOI: 10.1186/s41039-017-0062-8

Roll, I., & Wylie, R. (2016). Evolution and revolution in artificial intelligence in education. *International Journal of Artificial Intelligence in Education*, *26*(2), 582–599. DOI: 10.1007/s40593-016-0110-3

Sadler, D. R. (1989). Formative assessment and the design of instructional systems. *Instructional Science*, *18*(2), 119–144. DOI: 10.1007/BF00117714

Sato, E., Shyyan, V., Chauhan, S., & Christensen, L. (2024). Putting AI in fair: A framework for equity in AI-driven learner models and inclusive assessments. *Egitimde ve Psikolojide Ölçme ve Degerlendirme Dergisi*, *15*, 263–281. DOI: 10.21031/epod.1526527

Selwyn, N. (2021). *Education and technology: Key issues and debates*. Bloomsbury Academic.

Shepard, L. A. (2000). The role of assessment in a learning culture. *Educational Researcher*, *29*(7), 4–14. DOI: 10.3102/0013189X029007004

Shute, V. J. (2008). Focus on formative feedback. *Review of Educational Research*, *78*(1), 153–189. DOI: 10.3102/0034654307313795

Siemens, G. (2005). Connectivism: A learning theory for the digital age. *International Journal of Instructional Technology and Distance Learning*, *2*, 3–10. http://www.itdl.org/Journal/Jan_05/article01.htm

Skedsmo, G., & Huber, S. G. (2025). Beyond the score: Validity, equity, and interpretation in diverse assessment contexts. *Educational Assessment, Evaluation and Accountability*, *37*(2), 163–169. DOI: 10.1007/s11092-025-09459-8

Steiss, J., Tate, T., Graham, S., Cruz, J., Hebert, M., Wang, J., Moon, Y., Tseng, W., Warschauer, M., & Olson, C. B. (2024). Comparing the quality of human and ChatGPT feedback on students' writing. *Learning and Instruction*, *91*, 101894. Advance online publication. DOI: 10.1016/j.learninstruc.2024.101894

Suresh, A., Jacobs, J., Clevenger, C., Lai, V., Tan, C., Martin, J., & Sumner, T. (2024). Using AI to promote equitable classroom discussions: The TalkMoves application. In Zhai, X., & Krajcik, J. (Eds.), *Uses of artificial intelligence in STEM education* (pp. 371–398). Oxford University Press., DOI: 10.1093/oso/9780198882077.003.0017

Sutton, P. (2012). Conceptualizing feedback literacy: Knowing, being, and acting. *Innovations in Education and Teaching International*, *49*(1), 31–40. DOI: 10.1080/14703297.2012.647781

Tan, L. Y., Hu, S., Yeo, D. J., & Cheong, K. H. (2025). Artificial intelligence-enabled adaptive learning platforms: A review. *Computers and Education Artificial Intelligence*, *9*, 100429. Advance online publication. DOI: 10.1016/j.caeai.2025.100429

Tran, T. T. T. (2025). Enhancing EFL writing revision practices: The impact of AI- and teacher-generated feedback and their sequences. *Education Sciences*, *15*(2), 232. Advance online publication. DOI: 10.3390/educsci15020232

UNESCO. (2024). *AI literacy and the new digital divide: A global call to action*. https://www.unesco.org/ethics-ai/en/articles/ai-literacy-and-new-digital-divide-global-call-action. Accessed April 5, 2026.

VanLehn, K. (2011). The relative effectiveness of human tutoring, intelligent tutoring systems, and other tutoring systems. *Educational Psychologist*, *46*(4), 197–221. DOI: 10.1080/00461520.2011.611369

Vygotsky, L. S. (1978). *Mind in society: The development of higher psychological processes*. Harvard University Press. (Original work published 1930)

Wiliam, D. (2011). *Embedded formative assessment*. Solution Tree.

Williamson, B. (2017). Who owns educational theory? Big data, algorithms and the expert power of education data science. *E-Learning and Digital Media*, *14*(3), 105–122. DOI: 10.1177/2042753017731238

Williamson, B., Macgilchrist, F., & Potter, J. (2023). Re-examining AI, automation and datafication in education. *Learning, Media and Technology*, *48*(1), 1–5. DOI: 10.1080/17439884.2023.2167830

Winstone, N., & Carless, D. (2020). *Designing effective feedback processes in higher education: A learning-focused approach*. Routledge.

World Bank. (2023). *Digital development overview: Expanding connectivity and digital access*. https://www.worldbank.org/en/topic/digitaldevelopment. Accessed April 5, 2026.

Yin, J., Zhu, Y., Goh, T., Wu, W., & Hu, Y. (2024). Using educational chatbots with metacognitive feedback to improve science learning. *Applied Sciences (Basel, Switzerland)*, *14*(20), 9345. Advance online publication. DOI: 10.3390/app14209345

Zimmerman, B. J. (2000). Attaining self-regulation: A social cognitive perspective. In Boekaerts, M., Pintrich, P. R., & Zeidner, M. (Eds.), *Handbook of self-regulation* (pp. 13–39). Academic Press. DOI: 10.1016/B978-012109890-2/50031-7

Chapter 10
Customizing Playful Education Through Gamification:
AR/VR and Immersive Agents to Enhance Learning

Jennie Lee Khun
http://orcid.org/0000-0001-6076-1782
National University, USA

ABSTRACT

AI gamification, virtual reality, and immersive agents converge to transform independent learning by increasing motivation, personalization, and transfer of skills. Adaptive game mechanics use learner models and reinforcement signals to tailor challenges, feedback, and rewards that sustain engagement and scaffold mastery. VR situates practice in high-fidelity, embodied contexts that enhance spatial reasoning, situational judgment, and procedural fluency through deliberate practice and contextualized feedback. Immersive agents, conversational, multimodal tutors and peers provide coaching, prompts, and personalized remediation while modelling expert strategies and supporting metacognitive reflection. When designed with universal design principles, ethical data governance, and clear learning objectives, this triad supports autonomy, deep learning, and measurable outcomes for diverse independent learners.

INTRODUCTION

"Education has always been an important aspect of the development of any society" (Strielkowski et al., 2025). Education is significant because it empowers individuals and strengthens societies. The opportunity to learn equips people with the knowledge, skills, and critical thinking skills needed to navigate life, pursue careers, and contribute meaningfully to their communities. Personal empowerment through education builds confidence, self-awareness, and the ability to make informed decisions. Knowledge creates economic opportunities because it opens doors to better careers, higher income potential, and financial stability, helping break cycles of poverty. Social equity through education promotes equality by giving

DOI: 10.4018/979-8-3373-7225-9.ch010

everyone, regardless of background, a chance to succeed in life. Educated individuals are more likely to vote, volunteer, and participate in democratic processes that have direct impact on their community.

The educational landscape is experiencing what can only be described as a transformational revolution. The last big shift was with the invention of the internet changing the way we access information. The shift from libraries and written texts that required physical copies saw a monumental change when the internet provided data at a user's fingertips in mere seconds. The industry has seen the change from textbooks and chalkboards to smartboards and online content on portable electronic devices. Educational tools and learning environments have undergone significant transformation and continue to change in response to technological advances. Current developments suggest that education is entering a new phase of technological and pedagogical evolution driven by AI. AI is catalyzing independent and tailored learning strategies. Independent learning is being redefined from a solitary activity into an adaptive interactive partnership between learners and intelligent technology. AI agents have the capacity to move beyond simple information retrieval to become dynamic tools that facilitate, motivate, and personalize the learning process. The use of these agents provides learners with seamless access to knowledge, real time customizable feedback, exercises that build upon previous learning outcomes, and prompts that cultivate critical thinking and creativity at the learner's own pace. By adapting the learning process to the individual learner, the tools can remove the traditional learning constraints of time, place, and one-size-fits-all curriculum. The chapter explores both the promise and the limitations of integrating AI into independent education, explaining how learners across all generations can use these tools to build autonomy, imagination, and enduring learning habits. Ultimately, the vision for education is amplified rather than displaced by machine intelligence, and utilizing these tools offers practical pathways for designing intelligent learning environments that are personalized, inclusive, and promote lifelong learning.

Artificial intelligence serves as a driver for deep, transformative changes across many industries. AI technologies are at the beginning of what is expected to be a revolutionary societal change, not just in the way we learn. As AI capabilities mature, they will not only automate simple routine tasks but enable companies to completely reimagine business models, drive disruptive innovations, and shift the global competitive landscape. The goal is to examine strategic frameworks that leverage AI for innovation, review pragmatic real-world applications, and analyze ethical and operational challenges. At its core, disruptive intelligence, or innovation, refers to the capacity of AI technologies to radically transform traditional business processes and models. Incremental innovation typically enhances existing structures; disruptive intelligence introduces capabilities that overturn established leaders and create new market opportunities. Organizations harnessing machine learning, natural language processing, and advanced analytics, can achieve insights and automation levels that were previously considered impossible. The disruptive potential of AI innovation is not solely about replacing humans but about creating an environment where creativity intersects with data-driven decision-making. Although AI is reshaping educational practice, its integration requires deliberate strategies that align technological capabilities with pedagogical objectives.

To do so, we must move beyond passive adoption and strategically integrate AI into instructional design, curriculum development, and assessment frameworks. This means leveraging AI not just for automation, but for insight, using it to identify learning gaps, optimize engagement, and support inclusive practices. It also requires educators and institutions to invest in digital literacy, ethical governance, and infrastructure that supports equitable access. When deployed thoughtfully, AI becomes more than a tool, it becomes a catalyst for lifelong learning, institutional resilience, and educational transformation. The next step in purposefully incorporating AI tools into education strategy is to further explore the niche impact of customizing playful education.

This chapter specifically examines how artificial intelligence technologies can be leveraged to improve independent learning outcomes. AI is affecting core areas of game development and delivery including content generation, character behavior, player experience, development workflows, monetization, testing, and accessibility. The goal is to provide a clear conceptual framework for understanding where AI adds value, how it changes traditional design constraints, and what technical and ethical trade-offs arise when introducing learning systems into games, virtual reality environments, and immersive learning agents. “Games require strategic thinking, teamwork, problem-solving, and decision-making abilities; skills that are highly relevant in today's rapidly changing world and are sought after by employers. By integrating online gaming into the education system, colleges and universities can tap into its potential to foster innovative and adaptable talents” (Xiaohong, B. 2024). The rise of independent learning with the aid of AI agents is redefining how we leverage games for personal entertainment, education, and next generation independent learning.

“Adaptive learning technologies and AI contribute to achieving sustainable futures and it is quite straightforward to show how they do that: they help to tailor and provide education for all fostering a more education population capable of tackling complex global challenges, including sustainability” (Strielkowski et al., 2025). AI agents allow us to redefine how we approach education and self-learning by providing adaptive, personalized, and scalable solutions. The role of AI in gaming is to design intelligent learning environments that encourage critical thinking, creativity, inclusivity, and lifelong learning. While AI game development is creating new virtual worlds, and numerous jobs, companies are now using video games to help AI learn and solve those very problems. The industry is aiming to move AI forward in important ways toward real-world efficiencies across industries. AI in games can become an opportunity for self-learning. Games can teach us useful skills, how to adapt as we play them, and AI can teach itself to create based on individual user feedback. Additionally, adaptive difficulty and personalized approaches allow AI to review player behavior and adjust dynamically to the user’s skill or learning style. These scenarios that adapt to the learner create engaging content that promote internal self-motivation necessary for independent learning.

A thorough appreciation and understanding of how AI is changing game development from the inside out is essential before attempting to incorporate games, VR, and immersive agents for independent learning. AI changes are spanning all areas of design, content generation, animation, testing, and player modeling. These changes are reshaping creative workflows, production pipelines, and the potential outcomes that games can offer learners. Understanding these technical and design shifts enables independent learners, educators and instructional designers to better align game features to learning objectives, select or craft game experiences that are the framework for skills improvement, and adapt assessment and feedback mechanisms to the dynamics of play. Grounded in that foundation, games can quickly become a fully customizable learning environment rather than mere delivery vehicles for entertainment, allowing independent learners to engage with tailored challenges, receive timely, data supported personalized feedback, and pursue educational mastery at their own pace.

PLAYFUL INTELLIGENCE

Artificial Intelligence is impacting the entirety of the gaming industry; how games are created, built, and experienced. "Game design is essentially about creating valuable interactive experiences for the players; these experiences are effected by a variety of orchestrated game elements, including narratives, challenges, graphical representations, sounds, timing of events and phenomena, and the entities that directly interact with the player, be it opponents, allies, or other objects in the game environment" (Westera, et al., 2020). Once limited to scripted behaviors and deterministic rules, the older style of game development was simply restricted by the confounds of traditional deployment methods. Historically, game distribution relied on fixed, fully developed release of a product that required consumers to purchase physical copies of the game on a specified launch date. These games were developed with no opportunities for changes once in the consumers' hands. Then came the shift to dynamic content with game manufacturers releasing iterations of content online. Again, with prescriptive outcomes in mind the games had limited flexibility. The introduction of AI has initiated a substantive shift in how games are designed, deployed, and experienced. There is a significant shift in contemporary game systems as companies are increasingly incorporating AI techniques that generate content, shape player interactions, and adapt gameplay in real time without the interference of humans. These capabilities expand creative possibilities for designers, create richer, more personalized experiences for players, and open new operational and commercial pathways for design studios. AI innovations push the boundaries of interactive entertainment, using procedural content generation and intelligent non player characters (NPCs) to adjust difficulty levels and create unique game personalization. The options in the gaming environments are virtually endless because the developers can combine procedural content generation, use generative models, smart streaming, and simulations so worlds can be created, modified, and adapted in runtime.

Cost and predictive player outcomes are largely part of the reason why video game developers may be hesitant to build AI into their games. It is not only expensive but also creates a loss of control in the player's gaming experience. Games by nature are created with predictable and controlled outcomes in mind, even if the game is layered and complex. Algorithms driving the current games are not classified as learning intelligence because the games themselves cannot develop behaviors on their own or do things they were not initially programmed to do in the first place. These games are driven by "if-then" scenarios; games are not designed to be unpredictable or unbeatable. This raises the possibility of reorienting game systems toward supporting independent learners through adaptive, personalized instructional design to improve competency.

Yin et al. (2023) asks what are the possible challenges of current techniques in human-computer gaming, and what are the future trends? AI optimizes marketing through predictive analytics, tailoring monetization strategies that increase profits. It enhances game testing, detecting bugs faster and streamlining the entire development process, reducing the time to market. Accessibility advancements support players with accessibility needs via voice recognition and adaptive interfaces designed to create an inclusive environment. Developers benefit from AI-assisted design, enabling faster asset creation and animation automation. Lastly, AI player support improves customer service with real-time assistance and self-service options. AI is rapidly reshaping entertainment and business strategies in the gaming industry; solidifying AI's role as a game-changer in the industry.

Changing the Game: Design and Development

Firstly, "gamification" relates to *games*, not *play* (or playfulness), where "play" can be conceived of as the broader, looser category containing but different from "games" (Deterding et al., 2011). Deterding et al., (2011) explains that playful design and toys can be differentiated through the playing/gaming dimension (Figure 1). In the broader scheme of trends and concepts identified as related, we find "gamification" or gameful design situated as follows: Within the socio-cultural trend of ludification, there are at least three trajectories relating to video games and HCI: the extension of games (pervasive games), the use of games in non-game contexts, and playful interaction (Deterding et al., 2011). It is important to differentiate the audience based on whether there is a commercial purpose or an educational purpose. Commercial purposes aim to create a product that can reduce production costs, increase fidelity, and improve performance. Educational purposes are created for the adaptive learning spaces, generate practice scenarios, support replayability for user mastery.

AI is reforming the foundational core aspects of game development by automating creative, visual, and even quality assurance tasks used by game development companies. There are common design approaches to consider. "The emergence of a new stream in gamification design that adapts the gamified system to the user by considering the needs and goals of the end-user, this concept is adaptive or personalized gamification design" (Bouzidi et al., 2019). Procedural content generation uses algorithms to produce unique environments, characters, and narratives that increase replay ability and reduce development time. AI developed graphics and animations employ deep learning upscaling and motion synthesis to raise visual fidelity and create lifelike character movement while preserving runtime performance. In testing and optimization, machine learning and reinforcement learning simulate player behavior, detect bugs, and tune mechanics and performance, allowing teams to identify flaws and stabilize builds more efficiently than manual testing alone. Together, these capabilities enable faster iteration, richer player experiences, and more scalable production pipelines.

Figure 1. "Gamification" between game and play, whole and parts (Deterding et al., 2011)

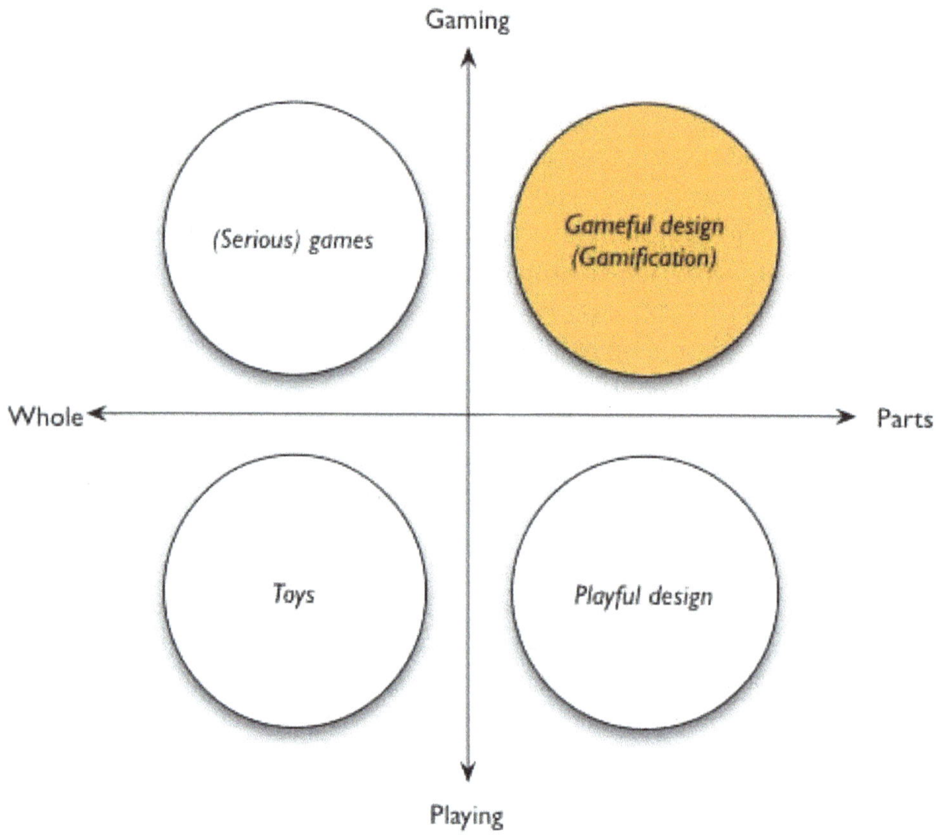

AI supported shifts in game development are rapid and multifaceted; a brief overview of key changes is essential to grasp how AI enhanced games can transform educational design and learning outcomes. Procedural Content Generation (PCG) allows AI algorithms to generate unique game environments, characters, and narratives, reducing development time and enhancing re-playability. For example, games such as Minecraft where AI creates expansive, dynamic worlds and rogue style games, which use AI for unpredictable game designs. AI assisted graphics and animation allows AI tools to enhance graphical fidelity and realism. For example, deep learning upscaling (e.g., NVIDIA Deep Learning Super Sampling) improves game visuals while optimizing performance on the platform. Deep Learning Super Sampling (DLSS) is an AI neural rendering technology from NVIDIA that uses deep neural networks running on Tensor Cores to reconstruct high-resolution frames from lower-resolution renders, allowing the majority of the graphics pipeline to run at reduced internal resolutions for substantially higher frame rates while producing image quality that approaches or matches native resolution; DLSS achieves this by training on high quality ground truth frames so the model learns to restore fine detail, reduce aliasing, and preserve temporal stability, and newer DLSS generations add frame-generation techniques that synthesize intermediate frames to further boost perceived smoothness and responsiveness (NVIDIA, 2025). AI animation enables the creation of lifelike character movements and facial expressions that help to immerse the player in a more authentic gaming experience. Game Testing and Optimization allows AI to more efficiently automate bug detection and balance testing during code development. Reinforcement learning models simulate gameplay to identify flaws. AI assists developers in fine tuning mechanics and optimizing user experience. Developers are leveraging machine learning and adaptive algorithms during testing to automate tedious processes, simulate complex behaviors, and to tune the stability and performance of their games before releasing them to production.

AI GAMEPLAY AND PLAYER EXPERIENCE

AI has advanced from simple rule-based opponents to sophisticated, data systems that shape both gameplay mechanics and the player's subjective experience; modern game AI spans procedural generation, adaptive agents, personalization engines, and analytics pipelines that together create dynamic, responsive worlds rather than static scripted encounters that players have known in the past. Intelligent non-player characters (NPCs) and opponents leverage machine learning to enhance AI controlled characters that provide adaptive and realistic interactions. Dynamic enemy AI in first player shooter (FPS) games (e.g., Halo, FEAR) adjust strategies based on how the player is behaving in the gaming environment. AI companions in role playing games (RPGs) create emotional engagement for players. Personalization and adaptive difficulty are another advancement; AI tailor's playing experiences based on individual styles. Adaptive difficulty systems, like Resident Evil 4's dynamic enemy scaling, ensure the appropriate challenge and difficulty based on player ability. AI player modeling personalizes experience based on skill, preferences, and changing in-game decisions. Natural Language Processing (NLP) and voice interaction allow AI to enhance communication channels within the games. The inclusion of chatbots and voice recognition systems enables more immersive interactions needed for an authentic gaming experience. AI dialogue generation allows for nuanced conversations with non-player characters.

AI increases player immersion by producing easily believable animation, dialogue, and virtual world reactions while enabling personalized journeys through tailored challenges and content; it broadens agency by supporting emergent playstyles and strengthens retention through experiences that adapt to player skill, preference, and intent. In commercial applications the gameplay focuses on dynamic enemies, monetization, and retention incentives. Educational gameplay has adaptive environments, personalized feedback, competency progression, and cognitive prompts. There is a blending of some of these areas; but for educational games monetization and retention are not the goal, it is competency and skills building.

Designers must treat AI as a collaborator that requires constraint and evaluation to avoid unpredictability, bias, or exploitation; transparency, fairness in adaptive mechanics, privacy of behavioral data, and robust testing of emergent interactions are essential to preserve player trust and educational validity when AI systems influence learning or assessment outcomes. AI systems that shape gameplay and player experience can unlock sophisticated monetization efforts exploited by developers that permit real-time personalization, dynamic pricing, targeted offers, and smarter ad placement that increase revenue per user while preserving engagement. Teng (2024) highlight that digital gaming often transcends being a solitary or individual activity, evolving into a community- or team-based environment that involves interaction with gaming partners, whether in physical proximity or within virtual game worlds; the communal aspect of digital gaming facilitates active participation in online communities where gamers consume or produce game content, further enriching their learning experience.

Virtual Realty

Virtual reality (VR) gaming places the user inside an interactive, computer generated three dimensional or 3D environment where they can explore and manipulate the gaming area in real time using head mounted displays that fully cover the eyes and input controllers. Unlike passive media sources, VR has the capability to transform learners into active participants whose movements, decisions, and sensory experiences facilitate the learning process. For learners, this active participation in the environment matters because VR supports personified practice and scenario trials where learners can continually perform complex tasks, receive immediate multisensory feedback, and refine skills in safe, controlled settings where mistakes have no real-world cost value. This safe space is ideal for independent learning because the user can try scenarios free of preconceptions or judgments. Teng (2024) indicates that the debate surrounding VR digital gaming is evolving, and it has become increasingly apparent that the ability to leverage the technological infrastructure of VR services plays a pivotal role in the educational landscape.

VR is especially effective for adult education because it combines high engagement with clear opportunities for deliberate practice. "VR digital gaming combines digital tools and resources to support the learning process, offering an immersive and interactive experience that can significantly enhance educational outcomes" (Teng, 2024). Immersion and interactivity increase attention and persistence, which enhances retention compared with many traditional learning formats. VR also supports personalized and adaptive learning because the systems can tailor difficulty, pacing, and feedback to a learner's prior knowledge and goals, enabling efficient upskilling. Multisensory cues including visual, auditory, spatial, and sometimes haptic, can help scaffold memory and procedural understanding, making VR especially useful for hands on competencies, situational judgment, and complex decision-making under the heavy burden of pressure. For example, VR gaming systems provide learners studying to become airplane or helicopter pilots with a safe space to practice difficult hands-on training. The opportunity to practice a variety of scenarios allows the learner to practice not only a multitude of complex situations, to think critically about dynamic factors, and to utilize their pragmatic experience in strenuous situations, thereby strengthening their training and practical approaches to flying.

The core technology behind VR learning includes hardware such as head mounted displays with inside out or external tracking, handheld controllers or haptic devices, and optional peripherals like treadmills or gloves that the user wears. Software applications range from real time 3D engines powering richly simulated scenarios to gamified applications and analytics back ends that record player performance. Interaction models vary user experiences that allow natural movement to seated or standing modes designed to reduce physical strain. Content types include realistic simulations, serious games, guided practice modules, and collaborative virtual spaces for synchronous role play and team training, while embedded metrics and replay tools support competency assessments.

Effective instructional design for VR begins with understanding how to align activities to clear, observable learning outcomes rather than novelty. Experience should utilize scaffolding and progressive complexity by starting with orientation and guided practice, then introduce branching decisions, time pressure, or competing objectives to raise challenge and fidelity for the user. Pre-briefing establishes context and goals before immersion, providing the user with much needed contextualization of the environment they are about to enter, and structured debriefing afterward helps learners reflect, consolidate lessons, and plan applicable transfer of use cases. Designers must minimize cognitive overload by simplifying interfaces, providing in game prompts, and pacing new information so learners unfamiliar with the gaming environment can focus on the target task rather than simply learning the controls.

Practical deployment requires attention to cost, accessibility, and learner wellbeing. Hardware and development costs vary widely because standalone head mount displays lower infrastructure barriers for broad adoption, while tethered rigs and custom created simulators increase fidelity and expense for specialized training. Physical comfort and safety deserve careful design as motion sickness, fatigue, and sensitivity are common concerns, so experiences should offer alternatives, breaks, and configurable motion settings. Technical literacy is another barrier; orientation sessions and site support reduce friction for adult learners new to VR. Equity considerations device availability, internet requirements, and inclusive content design must be addressed to avoid widening digital divides.

To begin integrating VR into adult learning, pilot a focused scenario that maps directly to a value competency such as safety procedures, equipment troubleshooting, or customer interactions, and evaluate outcomes before scaling. Use proven educational titles and vendor libraries where possible, consult VR instructional design frameworks for curriculum integration, and collect both performance metrics and learner feedback to iterate.

Immersive Technology

Immersive environments are interactive spaces that place users inside or alongside digital content using multimodal sensory input and output, so presence, personification, and continuous engagement are fundamental to the experience. Simulations are simply models or replicated systems that recreate behaviors, processes, or scenarios to study outcomes, practice decisions, or predict performance so dynamics are measurable variables central to the experience. Immersive environments create a feeling of "being there." Simulations prioritize accurate modeling of system behaviors, rules, and cause-effect relationships to enable repeatable experimentation, assessment, and hypothesis testing.

"Immersive Learning is not simply 'learning with immersive media' but immersive learning means learning with artificial experiences" (Brunetti et al., 2024). Immersive technology systems combine sensing, real-time computation, and multimodal output to create the perception of presence inside or alongside digitally rendered virtual environments. First, sensors strategically placed capture the user and environment using inertial measurement units, cameras, depth sensors, and microphones to determine position, orientation, gestures, and surrounding geometry. These inputs feed into tracking pipelines that translate real-world coordinates into the virtual scene with low latency and high precision. Next, rendering engines produce synchronized stereoscopic visuals and spatial audio that match head and eye movement, while physics and animation systems simulate object behavior and interactions to preserve continuity and believability from the user's perspective. Interaction layers then map user intent into the system through gesture recognition, controller input, voice, and haptics so actions feel natural and consequential. Networking and state synchronization enable persistence and multiuser presence by replicating avatars, objects, and event histories across participants. Finally, content generation mixes assets, procedural generation, and AI synthesis to populate environments at scale while orchestration systems stream assets and manage level-of-detail to keep computing and memory within the device limits. The combined effect of accurate sensing, low-latency feedback, multimodal outputs, coherent simulation, and managed content delivery produces sensory and cognitive conditions that create immersive experiences. For example, the Sphere in Las Vegas provides an immersive high-resolution projection, sound, and interactive live experience to fully immerse participants in the performance.

Immersive technology delivers measurable value across education and training by enabling deliberate practice in realistic, repeatable scenarios that are too costly, dangerous, or impractical to reproduce physically. Immersive VR environments minimize distractions for player thereby helping learners concentrate on the material at hand. Trainees or learners benefit from scalable, competency experiences where performance metrics are recorded and replayed for coaching thereby allowing the user to review their performance on tasks. Immersive simulation reduces risk exposure while accelerating skill acquisition for pilots, surgeons, heavy-equipment operators, and first responders by reproducing high pressure decision points and allowing safe failure and iteration. In healthcare, immersive systems support therapeutic interventions and procedural planning by providing controlled exposure for behavioral therapies, guided motor-rehabilitation with precise movement tracking, and surgical rehearsal on patient models that improve spatial understanding and reduce operative time. These systems also enable remote consultation where specialists can inspect 3D anatomy together and co-navigate complex cases.

In design and engineering, immersive environments shorten development cycles by turning abstract designs into embodied prototypes that stakeholders can inspect and manipulate at scale. Teams achieve earlier detection of ergonomic issues, spatial conflicts, and manufacturability risks while enabling distributed, synchronous collaboration on the same virtual asset. Digital twins and immersive visualizations allow engineers to run simulations of systems and processes, leading to informed decisions about maintenance planning, capacity, and cost trade-offs. For architecture and construction, immersive walkthroughs increase client confidence and reduce change orders by exposing design intent before physical work begins.

Retail and marketing gain higher conversion and reduced returns by letting customers preview products in context with interactive virtual try-ons and environment placement. Immersive product experiences increase buyer confidence through realistic scale, material fidelity, and behavioral demonstrations, and they gather richer signals about preferences and that drive personalization. In workplace productivity and collaboration, immersive meeting spaces and mixed-reality overlays enable co-creation and problem solving that are difficult to replicate in video calls, improving outcomes for complex planning, training, and design reviews.

Public safety, urban planning, and infrastructure benefit from immersive simulations that model disasters, traffic flow, and evacuation procedures, enabling planners to stress-test responses and optimize layouts before incidents occur. Immersive rehearsal for emergency teams reduces response times and improves coordination by replicating sensory conditions and communication challenges they will face. Cultural heritage and museums use immersive experiences to preserve and present artifacts and historical contexts that are too fragile or remote for mass access, broadening engagement and learning outcomes.

Across all industries, immersive systems generate data about behavior, attention, and task performance that organizations can use to personalize learning, optimize interfaces, and measure skill transfer. The combination of safer practice environments, improved stakeholder communication, reduced physical prototyping costs, and richer behavioral insight make immersive technology a strategic investment for organizations seeking measurable improvements in capability, efficiency, and decision quality. The use cases of immersive technology for educational purposes cannot be understated. Figure 2 illustrates the integrated conceptual framework linking AI-Driven Gamification, Virtual Reality, and Immersive Agents as complementary systems supporting independent learning. Immersive environments let teachers rehearse classroom management, test new pedagogies, and receive situated coaching with metrics and perspective switching so feedback is concrete and actionable for instructional improvement. The proposed conceptual framework illustrates how AI Gamification provides adaptive challenges and personalized feedback; Virtual Reality offers embodied, contextualized practice; and Immersive AI Agents deliver real-time coaching and cognitive support when leveraged together, these components enhance motivation, mastery, transfer of skills, and learner autonomy. Virtual labs and 3D visualizations enable experiments, field trips, and spatial reasoning activities otherwise limited by cost, safety, or geography. Shared mixed-reality spaces enable distributed learners to co-create, troubleshoot, and play in the same virtual context, supporting peer learning, mentorship, and project work where physical co-location is impossible or impractical by traditional means. By replacing repeated physical consumables, travel, and constrained lab time with reusable virtual scenarios, institutions can broaden access to quality experiential learning while lowering individual learner costs and enabling standardized assessment across distributed cohorts. This approach underscores the need for detailed, sophisticated evaluations and comprehensive frameworks that consider both cognitive load and intrinsic motivation to improve understanding of the impact of immersive technologies on learning (Poupard et al., 2025).

Figure 2. Conceptual framework for AI enabled gamified independent learning (Khun, 2026)

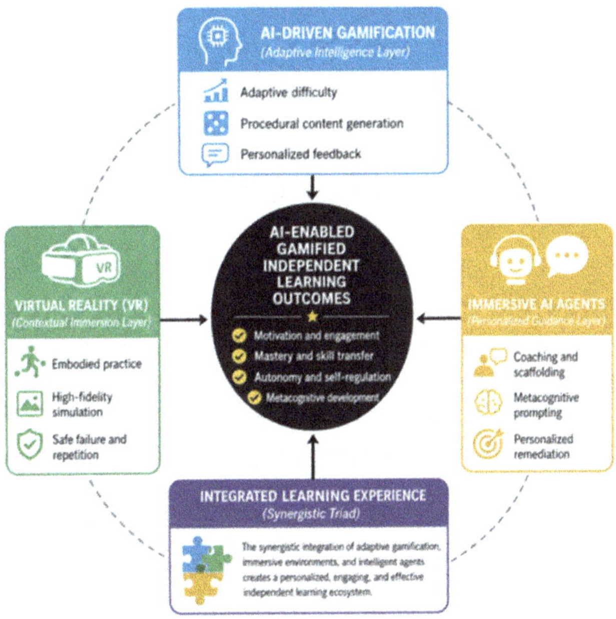

Color-Coded Conceptual Framework for AI-Enabled Gamified Independent Learning

Play, Predict, Profit

An AI gaming development company's monetization strategy typically blends traditional revenue models with innovative, data centered approaches. The core income streams the organization utilizes include direct game sales, in-app purchases, and subscription tiers offering premium content or enhanced AI gameplay. These companies often leverage dynamic pricing algorithms and personalized microtransactions, using player behavior analytics to optimize engagement and spending. Additionally, monetization may extend to licensing proprietary AI engines or procedural generation tools to other developers, integrating branded partnerships, and offering immersive ad experiences tailored by AI. As user data fuels continuous refinement, the strategy emphasizes retention, personalization, and scalable content creation to maximize lifetime value across diverse player segments.

AI game marketing and player analytics allow development companies to use AI to optimize marketing strategies and enhance user engagement. Predictive analytics anticipate player behavior and preferences. Dynamic in game ads and AI recommendations personalize monetization strategies aimed at encouraging purchases and further engagement in the game that keep players playing for longer. AI for game streaming and electronic sports allow AI to enhance broadcasting and competitive gaming. Automated camera controls in esports improve spectator experience. AI assists in real-time match analysis to enhance coaching strategies and make appropriate recommendations. However, AI bias in game design may inadvertently disadvantage certain demographics. Privacy concerns arise from AI tracking player behavior for monetization. Over reliance on AI risks homogenizing creative aspects of game development.

Monetization for AI gaming development represents a missed opportunity for educational instruction because commercial strategies often prioritize entertainment and profit over pedagogical value. The company is in the business of entertainment and not necessarily education. While AI games excel at personalizing experiences and sustaining engagement, their monetization models centered on transactions, premium content, and behavioral analytics rarely translate into scalable, equitable learning tools. Exasperating the problem is that educational institutions face barriers such as limited budgets, lack of technical infrastructure, and resistance to nontraditional teaching methods. As a result, the adaptive, immersive potential of AI gaming ideal for differentiated instruction, formative assessment, and skill-building is underutilized in classrooms. Instead of licensing these platforms for instructional use or designing curriculum-integrated versions, developers often overlook the educational sector, leaving a gap where gamified learning could thrive. Vella (2023) describes the consequences of neglecting AI in schools as far-reaching, affecting students' skills, technological literacy, economic prospects, ethical awareness, and opportunities for innovation and further goes on to state that to prepare students for the future and ensure that society can harness the benefits of AI while mitigating its risks, it is imperative that educational institutions integrate AI education into their curricula. This disconnect reflects broader systemic hesitations around AI adoption in education, especially in underserved communities.

Smarter Worlds, Deeper Play

AI generated games and self-evolving worlds incorporate AI systems can create fully autonomous, changing and unique game experiences. AI narratives are dynamically evolving based on player interactions. AI plays a vital role in creating expansive, persistent virtual worlds with limitless possibilities called the metaverse. AI avatars and environments enhance immersion, engagement, and player experience. AI assisted social interactions enable seamless multiplayer experiences. AI's impact on gaming is profound, shaping development, creativity, player engagement, and business strategies alike. Many authors argue that VR is more engaging for learners, provides a highly contextualized environment that better supports transfer of learning to real-life use, and, in some cases, that the physical mobility offered by such VR experiences supports learning Kronenberg & Poole (2022). As AI and VR advances, developers must carefully balance innovation with ethical considerations to ensure inclusive, immersive, and responsible gaming experiences for all.

Game mechanics and AI work together to create engaging, personalized learning experiences by using game-design elements such as collecting points, earning badges, advancing levels, ranked leaderboards, side quests, progress bars, and challenge loops to motivate learners while AI continuously senses, models, and responds to the learner. The AI tool adjusts task difficulty in real time through dynamic difficulty regulation, sequences content to match readiness and personalizes reward schedules, so incentives reinforce meaningful practice rather than superficial task completion. AI translates raw performance data into formative signals that trigger specific mechanics, for example unlocking a scaffolded quest after a mastery threshold, issuing a timely hint when error patterns start to emerge, or adapting badge requirements so that rewards align with competency development and not merely repetition of task completion. Together these approaches enable rich feedback cycles, game events generate data, AI interpret patterns of mistakes and engagement, and the system delivers targeted feedback, exemplar problems, or narrative branches that keep the learner in flow. Game designers must balance the extrinsic and intrinsic personal motivators for players by tying visible rewards to authentic achievement, prevent exploitative behavior through rules and randomized verification tasks, and preserve equity by calibrating mechanics for different accessibility needs and cultural contexts. Finally, transparency and human-in-the-loop oversight ensure that AI adjustments and reward algorithms remain interpretable, fair, and aligned with educational goals, allowing users to audit outcomes, adjust motivational levers, and intervene when personalization risks amplifying bias or narrowing the curriculum.

BARRIERS TO AI INTEGRATION IN EDUCATION

AI adoption in education faces a range of systemic barriers that hinder its transformative potential for educators, students, and communities. Many educators express low confidence in using AI tools, fearing loss of pedagogical control or job displacement. Technological complexity and infrastructure gaps, especially in underfunded schools, make integration difficult, while ethical concerns around data privacy, surveillance, and algorithmic bias raise serious governance challenges. Institutional support is often lacking, with minimal professional development and unclear policies stalling AI implementation. Moreover, AI can intensify digital divides, limiting access for rural and marginalized communities already struggling to keep up with technological demands. Essentially, moving a target they are already struggling to reach. Even when these tools are available, they frequently misalign with standardized curricula and assessment models, making it hard to embed them meaningfully into instruction. These barriers collectively slow the adoption of AI in classrooms, despite its potential to personalize learning, enhance engagement, and support equity.

Technological Complexity

AI systems often require robust digital infrastructure, which is lacking in underfunded schools. Integration challenges include compatibility with existing platforms and steep learning curves. Compounding the problem is the use of AI tools with legacy systems. Schools may rely on outdated or legacy systems; these fragmented tool adoptions are incompatible with modern AI platforms. Schools are burdened with the high costs associated with custom development, expensive middleware that increases technical debt and costs to operate, or application program interfacing (API). AI tools often use proprietary data or closed environments that make it difficult to share data across platforms. AI tools are new for many organizations and as a result they have a steep learning curve which requires educators to understand machine learning (ML) concepts, data interpretation, and algorithmic behavior which is usually not part of their training.

Infrastructure gaps including device and connectivity shortages, insufficient data, cybersecurity, and privacy risks. "Legacy systems, such as outdated student databases, further compound risks by lacking patches for known vulnerabilities, leaving institutions exposed to exploits" (Dutta & Chauhan, 2025). Device and connectivity shortages adversely impact many students as they still lack access to reliable internet or personal devices, especially in rural or economically disadvantaged areas. AI tools that rely on cloud computing or timely feedback become inaccessible in these contexts. Insufficient data infrastructure is a serious problem because AI systems depend on large, clean datasets to perform well. Many schools lack the infrastructure to collect, store, and manage student data securely and ethically. Additionally, cybersecurity and privacy risks are security incidents waiting to happen; without robust cybersecurity frameworks, schools risk exposing sensitive student data. Dutta and Chauhan (2025) indicate that educational institutions often operate with outdated information technology infrastructure, lacking modern encryption and cybersecurity protocols. Data at rest (e.g., stored grades) and in transit (e.g., LMS communications) are frequently unsecured, making them vulnerable to breaches. This deters adoption and raises compliance concerns under laws like FERPA, GDPR, or COPPA. FERPA stands for Family Educational Rights and Privacy Act in the United States, focusing on protecting the privacy of student education records. FERPA's schools' official exception permits data sharing with third-party vendors for educational purposes, but vague contractual terms often lead to misuse, for example, a 2023 audit revealed that 40% of U.S. schools using AI tutoring platforms allowed vendors to retain student data indefinitely, breaking FERPA's destruction requirement (Dutta & Chauhan, 2025). GDPR is the General Data Protection Regulation guidelines in the European Union governing data protection and privacy for individuals. Dutta and Chauhan (2025) explain that GDPR mandates lawfulness, fairness, and transparency in data processing, requiring explicit consent for collecting student information, including biometric or behavioral data; for example, schools using AI attendance systems with facial recognition must obtain parental consent for minors. Lastly, COPPA is the Children's Online Privacy Protection Act in the United States that protects children under the age of thirteen from unauthorized data collection online and parental consent before collection personal data from children. Schools acting as intermediaries can consent to data collection on parents' behalf, but AI tools often bypass this provision (Dutta & Chauhan, 2025).

LEARNING THAT LEARNS YOU

Qu (2025) explains that Howard Gardner's theory of multiple intelligences suggests that individuals possess varied types of intelligence and learning preferences, which can significantly influence how they acquire knowledge, underscoring the necessity of recognizing diverse learning styles—such as visual, auditory and kinesthetic—and addressing them through tailored instructional strategies and technology. AI learning systems observe and model your every interaction to shape gameplay around your habits, preferences, and skills. The AI tools collect telemetry data on a variety of topics including the choices a player makes, reaction times, the number of errors, and engagement patterns, infer your playstyle and objectives, and use adaptive algorithms to adjust difficulty, pacing, narrative branches, and content recommendations in real time so the game progressively fits how you think and behave as a player. Strielkowski et al. (2025) explain that one significant advantage AI brings to education is its ability to analyze large amounts of data quickly, collecting vast quantities of student information, such as performance data, preferences, and learning patterns, that AI algorithms use to create individualized learning paths for each student. "Adaptive learning platforms leverage this capability by continuously monitoring students' progress and adapting instructional content accordingly, this personalized approach ensures that students receive targeted support where they need it most" (Strielkowski et al., 2025).

Feedback at the Speed of Thought

Prompt feedback is crucial for learners. The use of immediate or prompt feedback while learning helps learners to confirm that they are understanding the material. It helps learners strengthen the neural pathways by validating the responses accuracy and correcting while the information is fresh. The use of prompt feedback helps to correct any misconceptions or mistakes early in the learning process. Learners feel a sense of confidence when they can confirm there is a sense of progress and momentum. Feedback allows for timely adjustment of the learning strategy, especially in problem solving scenarios. Finally, immediate feedback delivered during the learning process helps learners commit the material to long term memory, clarifying nuances, and reinforcing principles. Çağlar-Özhan et al., (2025) explain that good feedback should: (1) establish what institutes good performance, including goals, criteria, and expected standards; (2) facilitate the development of learners self-assessment and reflection in learning; (3) deliver accurate and valuable information about their learning; (4) encourage dialogue between teachers and peers; (5) encourage positive motivational beliefs and self-esteem; (6) provide opportunities to close the gap between current and desired performance; and (7) provide teachers with insights that can shape and enhance their teaching practices.

> "Feedback is an essential part of the educational process as it enriches students' learning experiences, provides information about their current performance, shows them what is lacking in achieving goals, and provides guidance on the strategies needed to achieve those goals" (Çağlar-Özhan et al., 2025). Tailored learning models allow AI to create unique learning environments customized to the user making a more engaging and rewarding learning experience. Inclusive education is an approach that ensures all learners, regardless of ability, background, or circumstance, can fully participate and succeed in the same learning environment, emphasizing transforming the education system to meet the diverse needs of students, rather than expecting students to adapt to a standard model by addressing the needs of those with disabilities, language barriers, or socioeconomic disadvantages (Stelea et al., 2025).

The use of AI tools in education has attracted attention, due to their ability to provide accessible, timely, and thorough feedback across a range of subjects. Teng (2024) explains that feedback involves giving learners individualized information regarding their performance within the game; this ability is critical for enabling metacognitive awareness, as it enables learners to understand their strengths and weaknesses, or areas for improvement. Chatbot Generative Pre-Trained Transformer (ChatGPT) is an advanced AI system developed by OpenAI that uses natural language processing to generate human-like responses. It interacts with users through a chatbot interface, offering personalized feedback, suggestions, and information across a wide range of topics (Çağlar-Özhan et al., 2025). AI tools are radically transforming how independent learners study, practice, and grow in self-directed learning environments, such as professional upskilling, adult education, homeschooling, or learning simply for fun. From a practical standpoint, educators may utilize ChatGPT to provide comprehensive, text-based feedback in large classes, it is anticipated that ChatGPT will prove beneficial as a feedback tool, as it will enable learners to advance at their own pace in a self-directed learning process, uninfluenced by teachers' input, in a similar task (Çağlar-Özhan et al., 2025).

Personalized Paths

Unique learning or tailored learning models allow AI to create distinctive learning environments customized to the user, making a more engaging and rewarding learning experience. Qu (2025) concludes that the learner needs could be the strongest mediator, suggesting that platforms designed to specifically address individual learning requirements are most effective in increasing engagement and that this aligns with contemporary educational paradigms that emphasize learner centered approaches and validate the necessity of needs assessments in instructional design.

AI tools can help learners generate outlines, summaries, presentations, study guides, practice questions, refine writing, and provide further information to help clarify a topic. Additionally, the use of AI tools can help students to better track their study habits, create study structures and routines that suit their lifestyle, and use gamified learning to keep learners engaged. Kuklick (2025) explains that one possible way to develop more learner centered or personalized strategies for administering feedback in computer-based assessments may be to make the retrieval of feedback a choice for students; for example, this could be realized by allowing students to choose whether they want to retrieve task-level feedback. Kuklick (2025) says that by providing task-level specific feedback only on a learner's request would be an easy way of introducing more freedom of choice, as it would also be conceivable to personalize the feedback even further by letting students choose the content or even visual appearance of the feedback provided.

We know that visual learners benefit from annotated notes, visual rubrics, and diagrams; auditory learners respond best to oral feedback, discussion, and commentary; and kinesthetic learners respond best to hands on demonstrations or feedback during active tasks. Multimodal learning accommodates diverse processing aligning to the users' preferences. Imagine, an independent learner being able to access feedback in a variety of formats to aid in the learning process. Now, a step further, this tailored approach would allow learners to better understand their individual learning styles on specific topics or concepts. For example, a learner may do better with visual learning when writing for a literature-based course but perhaps they might learn better with auditory options for a language-based class. Allowing independent learners, the flexibility to choose the type of feedback best suited for that specific environment can revolutionize the way people learn. This approach further aids in the learner developing critical thinking and self-reflection skills as they learn to assess and identify their needs. This flexibility in feedback can lead to a more effective and personalized learning experience.

Accessibility

Accessibility refers to the design and implementation of environments, technologies, and resources that ensure all individuals regardless of ability can participate fully. In education, accessibility means creating learning spaces and materials that are usable by everyone, including those with physical, sensory, cognitive, or learning disabilities. This includes physical access to buildings, digital access to content and platforms, and instructional practices that accommodate diverse needs. In technology, accessibility involves ensuring that digital tools, websites, and software are compatible with assistive devices. It also means designing interfaces and content that are intuitive, readable, and adaptable to different user preferences and limitations. Information technology accessibility is theorized as the chance for an individual to encounter information technology equipment in their environment and utilize it to access information resources, emphasizing not only the objective technological conditions but also the impact of students' own information-seeking abilities on accessing online learning materials (Zhang & Zhang, 2024). Ultimately, accessibility is about removing barriers and fostering inclusion so that every person can acquire the same information, engage in the same interactions, and enjoy the same services with equal ease and effectiveness.

The integration of the AI chatbots in educational settings offers a transformative approach to addressing administrative challenges and improving accessibility for students (Horvat et al., 2025). Artificial intelligence expands digital and physical access for learners by automatically converting and adapting content to individual needs, for example generating captions and speech-to-text for people who are deaf or hard of hearing, describing images and extracting text for screen readers, personalizing interfaces and input methods for motor or cognitive impairments, and accelerating accessibility testing to find and remove barriers enabling fuller participation. Focusing on the risks of artificial intelligence text generators such as ChatGPT on academic writing often overshadows the many opportunities offered for students to improve academic outcomes; AI can be especially valuable for students with learning disabilities, with attention deficit hyperactivity disorder, or who struggle with written English (Elting & Desio, 2024). "Interdisciplinary research collective is seeking to make gaming more accessible for people living with motor neurone disease (MND), a condition that causes progressive muscle weakness and disability" (Dwyer, et al. 2024).

AI enhanced independent learning significantly improves accessibility by personalizing educational experiences and removing traditional barriers. "It appears that the information technology accessibility may exert an indirect influence on individual academic engagement by nurturing learning interest, suggesting that learning interest could act as a mediator between information technology accessibility and academic engagement" (Zhang & Zhang, 2024). These tools adapt content to individual needs, offering flexible pacing, multimodal formats, and tailored feedback that support learners with cognitive, sensory, or physical disabilities. Stelea et al. (2025) explains traditional school-based learning approaches rely largely on standardized learning, while e-learning environments can use adaptive learning technologies to personalize content based on the learner's level of proficiency and preference which is particularly helpful for students with disabilities, where the traditional system cannot always meet their specific needs. AI also facilitates language translation and predictive communication tools, helping non-native speakers and individuals with speech or language challenges participate fully. With 24/7 access and device agnostic platforms, learners with chronic health conditions, caregiving responsibilities, or limited mobility can learn on their own terms. Moreover, AI-driven assessments reduce bias and provide consistent, constructive feedback, promoting equity and inclusion across diverse learning environments. Stelea et al. (2025) go on to further explain that to address these challenges, assistive technologies, such as screen readers, speech recognition tools, and alternative input devices, can enhance accessibility and empower individuals to interact more effectively with educational content.

SMART, SOLO, SUPPORTED

AI on your terms creates personalized learning for every mind. Emphasizing feedback that fits the individual learner. Creating connections, adaptive feedback, and promoting meaningful outcomes. AI customized learning delivers learner focused personalization that respects each person's pace, preferences, and goals by modeling a dynamic learner profile that tracks skill mastery, misconstructions, engagement patterns, and accessibility needs. Learners set short and long-term goals that the system uses to prioritize content delivery and practice opportunities.

Feedback that fits the individual learner is precise, actionable, and tailored in specificity and timing. It identifies what the learner did, explains why it matters, and provides a clear next step; it delivers corrective cues for practiced tasks and reflective prompts for complex problem solving. The tools utilized during practice allow for immediate error correction, and issues feedback while gradually shifting from directive to facilitative guidance as competence grows to foster independence and cognitive skill.

Adaptive feedback creates richer connections between concepts and performance. The AI contextualizes suggestions with relevant examples drawn from the learner's recent work, surfaces relationships between mastered and struggling concepts through concept mapping and uses prompts to guide learners in articulating reasoning, confronting misconceptions, and consolidating understanding for transfer.

Accessibility and inclusive design are core requirements rather than add-ons. Feedback is multimodal, available as text, audio, annotated visuals, and interactive demonstrations to accommodate learners' cognitive needs. Interfaces apply universal design principles to minimize extraneous cognitive load, use clear language, and allow customization of display, pace, and interaction, while integrations with assistive technologies, translation, and simplified language remove participation barriers.

Outcome measures focus on meaningful, competency focused progress rather than shallow simplistic metrics. Rossi et al. (2021) explain that the data shows that student involvement is a key point for learning, this is widely accepted and experienced at different levels including emotional, behavioral, and cognitive dimensions can be considered when analyzing engagement. The platform has the capability to track observable competencies and performance tasks, produces dashboards for learners and instructors that highlight mastery, persistent learning gaps, recommended next steps, and uses adaptive contextual variation to boost retention and the ability to apply learning in new situations.

Implementation requires an independent learner to start with explicit learning goals in mind. The needs to calibrate the tool algorithms, handle exceptions, and align feedback with standards and values; transparency features explain why feedback was given to build trust; and equity monitoring ensures models benefit diverse learners while detecting and correcting bias. Rossi et al. (2021) conclude that active learning tools that require constant engagement benefits students and improve their critical thinking. When these AI adoption principles are observed, AI quickly becomes a tool that empowers independent learners by delivering feedback that adapts to who they are, how they think, and where they want to go while preserving agency, accessibility, and measurable educational impact.

CHALLENGE ACCEPTED: AI GAMIFICATION FOR INDEPENDENT LEARNING

AI gamification for independent learning is the specific integration of artificial intelligence personalization and game design elements to create self-paced learning experiences that motivate, adapt, and assess learners without constant instructor intervention. AI gamification for independent learning is focused on several core pieces including an adaptive engine of AI models that continuously assesses learner state, predicts difficulty, and tailors content and challenges; game mechanics such as points, badges, leaderboards, levels, quests, and progress bars that structure self-motivation and reward responses; a feedback loop delivering timely, actionable guidance that tells learners what to improve and the next steps to take in the process; learning analytics that collect and interpret performance, engagement, and retention data to refine personalization; narrative and goals storylines, quests, or competency maps that frame objectives and provide meaning; and an accessibility layer offering multimodal delivery, assistive integrations, and customizable interfaces to ensure equitable participation.

Kronenberg & Poole (2022) suggest that when we look at new technology, such as VR, we must think about the relative advantage that innovation might bring, keep the learning outcomes in mind, and consider how teachers may leverage the tool to improve teaching efficacy. Zheng (2024) explains that the potential use of AI and VR in education is immense; virtual reality holds promise for delivering more dynamic, hands-on learning encounters through simulated scenarios, students can conduct experiments, delve into historical events, and grasp intricate concepts, fostering their curiosity and comprehension where virtual classrooms contain the promise of providing equitable access to educational resources for students worldwide, bridging gaps in resource availability.

Why It Works

People enjoy games. We start by playing games in early childhood, peek a boo, hide and seek, hopscotch, and tag. We progressively move into more dynamic games like Simon says, duck duck goose, and musical chairs. From there, the game choices are endless. We enjoy games because they activate core psychological drivers such as wonder, mastery, autonomy, and social connection while offering structured environments for exploration and reward. Simply put, we have fun. Games stimulate the brain's reward system, particularly through dopamine release when players complete challenges, earn achievements, or progress through levels. This creates a feedback loop that reinforces engagement and satisfaction during gameplay. Psychologically, games fulfill needs outlined in Maslow's hierarchy, they provide a sense of safety through predictable rules, and sense of belonging through multiplayer interaction, and esteem through skill development and recognition. Yurdakal & Arar (2023) explain that Maslow's Hierarchy of Needs, human needs are generally classified into five stages (physiological needs, safety needs, love and belonging needs, need for esteem and self-actualization needs) and the level at which one must be "sufficiently" satisfied in order for the person to be able to start focusing on trying to achieve the next higher level. Competition and achievement also play a role; many people are motivated by the thrill of overcoming difficult obstacles and outperforming other players. "When we think of competition, we often think first of sports, or perhaps of overtly competitive and adversarial fields such as law or finance. The truth is that competition is everywhere, in academic, social, professional and family settings alike" (Admin-Risepoint, 2025). Additionally, games offer a temporary escape from reality, allowing players to experiment with identity, strategy, and creativity in low-risk settings. Whether digital or physical, games appeal across age groups and cultures because they blend challenge, feedback, and meaning into an experience that feels both entertaining and fulfilling.

Gamification leverages psychological theories like Self-Determination Theory (autonomy, competence, relatedness), Flow Theory (deep engagement), and Behaviorism (reinforcement through rewards). Self-determination theory (SDT) is a theory of human motivation and personality that concerns people's innate growth tendencies and innate psychological needs; it relates to the incentive behind people's choices in the absence of external influences and distractions (Zhao et al., 2023). Heasman et al. (2024) explain that flow states or flow theory are heightened moments of concentration, motivation and enjoyment, leading to total absorption in the present moment. Skinner's brand of behaviorism indicates that behaviorists believe that learning takes place as the result of a response that follows on a specific stimulus and was a form of "stimulus-response" psychology that confined itself to the study of observables.

Gamification taps directly into personal motivation by transforming learning into a dynamic, goal-oriented experience that resonates with individual psychological needs. It leverages intrinsic motivators such as autonomy, mastery, and purpose. For many learners, the act of earning rewards or unlocking new content creates a dopamine feedback loop that reinforces effort and persistence. Gamified environments also support self-efficacy by breaking complex tasks into manageable quests, helping learners build confidence as they conquer each step. Importantly, personalization within gamification such as adaptive difficulty, customizable avatars, or narrative choices enhances emotional investment and relevance, making learners feel seen and in control. This alignment between game mechanics and motivational psychology fosters deeper engagement, resilience, and a sustained desire to learn independently.

Gamification can reduce anxiety, increase confidence, and improve retention especially when learners feel in control and see their efforts rewarded. Gamification enhances independent learning by transforming educational tasks into engaging, goal-oriented experiences that mirror the motivational dynamics of games. At its core, gamification integrates elements like points, levels, badges, leaderboards, and narrative challenges to foster persistence, curiosity, and mastery. For independent learners—who often lack external structure or feedback—these mechanics provide a sense of progression and accomplishment, reinforcing effort through immediate rewards and visual cues. Adaptive gamification tailors' difficulty and content to individual performance, ensuring learners remain in their optimal challenge zone, which supports flow and sustained engagement. Narrative-based frameworks, such as quests or role-playing scenarios, contextualize learning objectives within immersive storylines, making abstract concepts more relatable and memorable. Moreover, gamified platforms often incorporate social features like peer competition or collaborative missions, which can enhance motivation and accountability even in self-directed independent environments. However, effective gamification requires thoughtful alignment with cognitive goals, inclusive design, and meaningful feedback loops otherwise, it risks becoming superficial or distracting. When done well gamification empowers independent learners to take ownership of their education, build resilience through iterative failure, and develop metacognitive skills essential for lifelong learning.

CONCLUSION

Gamified learning leveraging AI tools offer a dynamic and personalized approach to self-directed education that has a variety of benefits. By blending game mechanics with intelligent feedback systems, these tools foster deeper engagement, sustained motivation, and measurable progress. Independent learners benefit from immediate reinforcement through interactive challenges and rewards, adaptive content delivery tailored to their pace and performance, enhanced retention via repetition, storytelling, and immersive scenarios, self-monitoring and goal setting through dashboards and progress tracking. Ultimately, gamified AI transforms solitary study into an active, rewarding experience thereby making learning not only more effective, but also more enjoyable and sustainable long term.

As an independent learner, embracing AI tools and gamification can transform your educational journey from solitary effort into a dynamic, personalized, and fun learning adventure. AI empowers you to learn smarter, not harder, by adapting content to your pace, identifying your strengths and gaps, and offering instant feedback that accelerates mastery. Gamification adds a layer of motivation and structure, turning goals into quests, progress into levels, and achievements into badges that celebrate your progress. Together, these technologies foster autonomy, resilience, and curiosity by giving you control over your learning while keeping it engaging and rewarding. Whether you're mastering a technical skill, exploring a new discipline, or preparing for a career pivot, integrating AI and gamified strategies helps you stay focused, track progress, and enjoy the process. You're not just learning, you're leveling up. Game on.

AUTHOR NOTE

Portions of this chapter were developed with assistance from Microsoft Copilot, which supported conceptual organization, figure design, and language refinement. All final decisions, interpretations, and revisions were made by the author.

REFERENCES

Admin-Risepoint. (2025, February 20). *Psychology of competitiveness: Eastern Oregon University Online*. Eastern Oregon University. https://online.eou.edu/resources/article/psychology-of-competitiveness/

Bouzidi, R., De Nicola, A., Nader, F., & Chalal, R. (2019). A systematic literature review of gamification design. In *Proceedings of the 20th Annual Simulation and AI in Games Conference (GAME-ON 2019) (Breda, The Netherlands). EUROSIS, Ostend, Belgium.*

Brunetti, R., Ferrante, S., Avella, A. M., Indraccolo, A., & Del Gatto, C. (2024). Turning stories into learning journeys: The principles and methods of immersive education. *Frontiers in Psychology, 15*, 1471459. DOI: 10.3389/fpsyg.2024.1471459 PMID: 39712545

Çağlar-Özhan, Ş., Tekeli, P., & Arkün-Kocadere, S. (2025). Comparison of AI-Generated and instructor feedback: No significant difference in perceived feedback quality and neither on performance. *Journal of Computer Assisted Learning*, *41*(5), e70134. Advance online publication. DOI: 10.1111/jcal.70134

Deterding, S., Dixon, D., Khaled, R., & Nacke, L. (2011). From Game Design Elements to Gamefulness: Defining Gamification. *Proceedings of the 15th International Academic MindTrek Conference: Envisioning Future Media Environments, MindTrek 2011*. 11. 9-15. DOI: 10.1145/2181037.2181040

Dutta, A., & Chauhan, S. (2025). Artificial Intelligence in Student Privacy and Data Security. *International Journal of Advanced Research in Computer Science*, *16*(3), 146–151. DOI: 10.26483/ijarcs.v16i3.7261

Dwyer, N., Harrison, M., O'Mara, B., & Harley, K. (2024). Inclusive gaming through AI: A perspective for identifying opportunities and obstacles through co-design with people living with MND. *Frontiers of Computer Science*, *6*, 1379559. Advance online publication. DOI: 10.3389/fcomp.2024.1379559

Elting, J., & Desio, M. G. (2024). AI prompts for nursing students to support independent learning. *Nurse Educator*, *49*(5), E243–E243. DOI: 10.1097/NNE.0000000000001633 PMID: 38502639

Heasman, B., Williams, G., Charura, D., Hamilton, L. G., Milton, D., & Murray, F. (2024). Towards autistic flow theory: A non-pathologising conceptual approach. *Journal for the Theory of Social Behaviour*, *54*(4), 469–497. DOI: 10.1111/jtsb.12427

Horvat, S., Horvat, T., Havaš, L., & Crčič, D. (2025). AI-powered chatbots for enhancing accessibility in higher education - design and implementation. *Elektrotehniski Vestnik, 92*(1/2), 61-67. https://go.openathens.net/redirector/liberty.edu?url=https://www.proquest.com/scholarly-journals/ai-powered-chatbots-enhancing-accessibility/docview/3203965895/se-2

Khun, J. (2026). *Color-coded conceptual framework for AI-enabled gamified independent learning* [Figure 2]. In *Customizing playful education through gamification: AR/VR and immersive agents to enhance learning* (book proposal). National University.

Kronenberg, F., & Poole, F. (2022). *From buzzword to the classroom – exploring VR gaming for language learning*. The FLTMAG., DOI: 10.69732/DHUI4343

Kuklick, L. (2025). Effects of learner choice over automated, immediate feedback. *Learning and Instruction, 96*, 102065. DOI: 10.1016/j.learninstruc.2024.102065

Nvidia DLSS. NVIDIA Developer. (n.d.). https://developer.nvidia.com/rtx/dlss?sortBy=developer_learning_library%2Fsort%2Ffeatured%3Adesc%2Ctitle%3Aasc

Poupard, M., Larrue, F., Sauzéon, H., & Tricot, A. (2025). A systematic review of immersive technologies for education: Effects of cognitive load and curiosity state on learning performance. *British Journal of Educational Technology, 56*(1), 5–41. DOI: 10.1111/bjet.13503

Qu, M. (2025). Future of language learning: Unveiling the power of AI-Driven adaptive platforms to tailor language learning based on learners' needs, proficiency and learning styles. *European Journal of Education, 60*(2), e70116. Advance online publication. DOI: 10.1111/ejed.70116

Rossi, I., Lima, J., Sabatke, B., Nunes, M., Ramirez, G., & Ramirez, M. (2021). Active learning tools improve the learning outcomes, scientific attitude, and critical thinking in higher education: Experiences in an online course during the COVID-19 pandemic. *Biochemistry and Molecular Biology Education, 49*(6), 888–903. DOI: 10.1002/bmb.21574 PMID: 34652877

Stelea, G., Robu, D., & Sandu, F. (2025). AccessiLearnAI: An accessibility-first, AI-powered E-learning platform for inclusive education. *Education Sciences, 15*(9), 1125. DOI: 10.3390/educsci15091125

Strielkowski, W., Grebennikova, V., Lisovskiy, A., Rakhimova, G., & Vasileva, T. (2025). AI-driven adaptive learning for sustainable educational transformation. *Sustainable Development (Bradford, West Yorkshire, England), 33*(2), 1921-1947. https://doi.org/DOI: 10.1002/sd.3221

Teng, M. (2024). Metacognition and autonomy in building a community for language learning through VR digital gaming. *Computers & Education: X Reality, 4*, 100060. DOI: 10.1016/j.cexr.2024.100060

Vella, S. (2023, October 12). *The consequences of ignoring AI in schools: A missed opportunity*. 3CL Foundation. https://www.3cl.org/the-consequences-of-ignoring-ai-in-schools-a-missed-opportunity/

Westera, W., Prada, R., Mascarenhas, S., Santos, P., Dias, J., Guimarães, M., Georgiadis, K., Nyamsuren, E., Bahreini, K., Yumak, Z., Christyowidiasmoro, C., Dascalu, M., Gutu-Robu, G., & Ruseti, S. (2020). Artificial intelligence moving serious gaming: Presenting reusable game AI components. *Education and Information Technologies, 25*(1), 351–380. DOI: 10.1007/s10639-019-09968-2

Xiaohong, B. (2024). Transforming University Research and Education: Unleashing the Potential of Immersive Multimedia and AI-Assisted Blended Learning Through Online Gaming. *Computer-Aided Design and Applications, 21*, 106–119. DOI: 10.14733/cadaps.2024.S5.106-119

Yin, Q.-Y., Yang, J., Huang, K.-Q., Zhao, M.-J., Ni, W.-C., Liang, B., Huang, Y., Wu, S., & Wang, L. (2023). AI in Human-computer Gaming: Techniques, Challenges and Opportunities. *Machine Intelligence Research*, *20*(3), 299–317. DOI: 10.1007/s11633-022-1384-6

Zhang, Y., & Zhang, X. (2024). The impact of online interaction and information technology accessibility on academic engagement among international undergraduate students in chinese universities: The mediating effect of learning interest. *Acta Psychologica*, *249*, 104478. DOI: 10.1016/j.actpsy.2024.104478 PMID: 39217769

Zhao, H., Chen, Y., & Liu, W. (2023). Socially responsible human resource management and employee moral voice: Based on the self-determination theory. *Journal of Business Ethics*, *183*(3), 929–946. DOI: 10.1007/s10551-022-05082-5

Chapter 11
Gamification and Immersive Learning Technologies With AI Agents:
Current Trends, Potential Risks, and Future Directions

Sohaib Ahmed
http://orcid.org/0000-0003-1830-7388
Taylor's University, Malaysia

Adnan Ahmad
COMSATS University Islamabad, Lahore, Pakistan

Osama Rehman
http://orcid.org/0000-0001-6424-8564
Taylor's University, Malaysia

Faizan Ahmad
University of East London, UK

ABSTRACT

The notion of gamification has emerged as a promising approach for reshaping educational environments. The integration of gamification with immersive technologies such as augmented reality (AR), virtual reality (VR) and mixed reality (MR) to develop an interactive and engaging platforms for learners. In recent years, artificial intelligence (AI) agents have been prevalent in learning environments that can bring several advantages including personalization, predictive modelling and real-time adaptability. On the other hand, these agents can possess risks including technical implementation, computational and performance, privacy and security. ethical and social presence. In education literature, very limited studies have explored AI-based benefits and challenges in gamified immersive learning environments. However, none of the studies found in the literature discuss the current trends of the use of AI agents and their potential risks. This chapter presents the current trends along with potential risks and future directions in gamified immersive learning environments.

DOI: 10.4018/979-8-3373-7225-9.ch011

1. INTRODUCTION

Gamification has the potential to divide the underlying learning concepts into smaller pieces through game elements, support learners' personalized needs, engagement and motivation (Ng, Xinyu, Leung, & Chu, 2024). Game elements like leaderboards, badges, rules, and scores are designed into learning activities to increase engagement and academic achievements (Sanchez, Langer, & Kaur, 2020). Such gamified learning environments can demonstrate intrinsic motivators like challenge, enjoyment, and curiosity to promote learners' engagement and learning experiences as compared to traditional learning methods (Laine & Lindberg, 2020). These environments can enhance learners' problem-solving and cognitive skills, foster learners' sense of accomplishment and provide positive learning experiences through immediate feedback (Ahmed et al., 2025).

With the advancement of immersive technologies like AR, VR and MR, game-based learning applications are designed to make learning and gaming more enjoyable and fun activities. These technologies blend the physical and digital worlds to create interactive experiences where learners can become subjectively involved and feel they are physically present (Simons, et al., 2023). These technologies are used effectively with the gamification concept to provide the learning process with more engaging experiences and improved learning outcomes for learners in different fields, including mathematics, ethics (Nguyen et al., 2025) computer science (Fatima, et al., 2024), biology (Chheang et al., 2024), astronomy (Zhu et al., 2025), and museums (Ahmed et al., 2025), etc.

The use of Artificial Intelligence (AI) adds another dimension to immersive game-based learning environments. AI-driven applications can tailor content according to the needs of learners and effectively deliver personalized learning through adaptive guidance or hints (Zhu et al., 2025). These AI tools can generate text, audio, or video content based on the previously trained data to enhance learning support for students and teachers (Song, Wu, & Ding, 2024). With the use of large language models (LLMs), AI agents are developed in game-based immersive learning environments to provide unique opportunities for active dialogue and adaptive support (Wang, Tang, Hare, & Wang, 2024). This may not only facilitate learning with the help of AI agents but also enhance learners' engagement through a game that leads towards learners' performances.

In digital gaming, virtual humans are designed as non-player characters (NPCs) who perform in different acts in a game, including hostile, friendly, or neutral characters to the player. Their roles are mostly scripted and restricted according to the game design (Kyrlitsias & Michael-Grigoriou, 2022). There are two types of virtual humans: avatars and agents. Avatars are those who visually represent the user in a virtual world, perceive by user or other users in case of multi-user virtual environments and are human-controlled while the agents are computer-controlled representation in a gaming environment (Nowak, Fox, & Fox, 2018). With the constant advancement in the fields of AI and immersive learning technologies, AI agents in a gaming world can interact in more realistic ways by expressing real-time body and facial expressions, taking decisions independently, and acting like real humans can further improvements in users' learning and gaming experiences (Kyrlitsias & Michael-Grigoriou, 2022).

This chapter is structured as follows: it first defines the terms gamification, immersive technologies and AI agents. Moreover, this section explains the connection between AI agents and self-determination theory in gamified immersive learning environments. Then, the chapter presents the current trends of using AI agents in gamified immersive learning environments in terms of roles of AI agents, learning domains of AI agents and learners use AI agents. The next section mentions the potential risks of using AI agents in such learning environments. Then, the second last section defines the future directions that can be implemented for designing gamified immersive learning environments for upcoming generations. Finally, conclusion is defined that summarizes the recent trends and potential risks of using AI agents in gamified immersive learning environments. Furthermore, this chapter concludes in describing the implications of using AI agents in practice.

2. GAMIFICATION, IMMERSIVE TECHNOLOGIES AND AI AGENTS IN EDUCATION

2.1 Gamification in Education

The use of gamification has been prevalent in the field of education. Gamification in education provides learning content using game mechanics including awards, challenges, badges etc. to support learners' motivation and engagement (Ng, Xinyu, Leung, & Chu, 2024). These game mechanics can help learners to facilitate in their learning by giving constant feedback about their performance and behavior in a gaming environment (Dyulicheva & Glazieva, 2021). This is traditionally considered as the source of entertainment among players but significantly improves learners' performance and motivation towards learning (Ahmad, Zeeshan, Marriam, Samreen, & Ahmed, 2021).

Gamification can provide learning support to learners in these five areas (Dai, Ke, Pan, & Liu, 2023): (i) problem decomposition, in which game has divided the problem into number of chunks and each chunk requires to be solved by learners that can lead them to enhance their problem-solving skills (Jaaska, Lehtinen, Kujala, & Kauppila, 2022) (ii) conceptual knowledge development, in which game components are designed to assist learners in understanding about the content presented of a particular domain knowledge by providing through guidance and hints in a learning process (Ahmed et al., 2025) (iii) metacognitive regulation, in which game mechanics comprehend learners' needs through observing and reflecting on their decisions while performing their given tasks or challenges in a gamified environment (Zumbach, Rammerstorfer, & Deibl, 2020) (iv) information selection, in which gaming elements can show multiple forms of representation such as pedagogical agents, instructional videos and virtual books etc. to learners so that they can learn from such environments through personalized learning (Cai et al., 2022) (v) sustained motivation, in which gaming components are designed in such a way that can continuously support learners' intrinsic motivation towards learning that can guide them to keep motivated while playing a game (Dai, Ke, Pan, & Liu, 2023).

These advantages may lead learners towards their overall learning effectiveness and enhancing their other skills such as critical thinking and inquiry skills (Khan & Ahmed, 2025) (Ahmed & Parsons, 2013). Such gamification combines with immersive learning technologies can provide an educational environment, a more engaging and interactive experience to learners (Fink, Robinson, & Ertl, 2024).

2.2 Gamification and Immersive Learning Technologies

Immersive learning technologies are referred to as augmented reality (AR), virtual reality (VR) and mixed reality (MR) (Fink, Robinson, & Ertl, 2024). These technologies can leverage support in educational systems by providing interactive and engaging learning experiences to learners. These immersive technologies are blended with the gamification concept for providing interactive and enjoyable learning experiences to learners in numerous domains including mathematics, ethics (Nguyen et al., 2025), computer science (Fatima, et al., 2024), biology (Chheang et al., 2024), astronomy (Zhu, Sam, Wu, & Tang, 2025), and museums (Ahmed et al., 2025) etc. In literature, immersive technologies including AR, VR and MR are defined as reality-virtually continuum (Milgram & Kishino, 1994) as shown in Figure 1.

Figure 1. Reality-virtually continuum (adapted from (Milgram & Kishino, 1994))

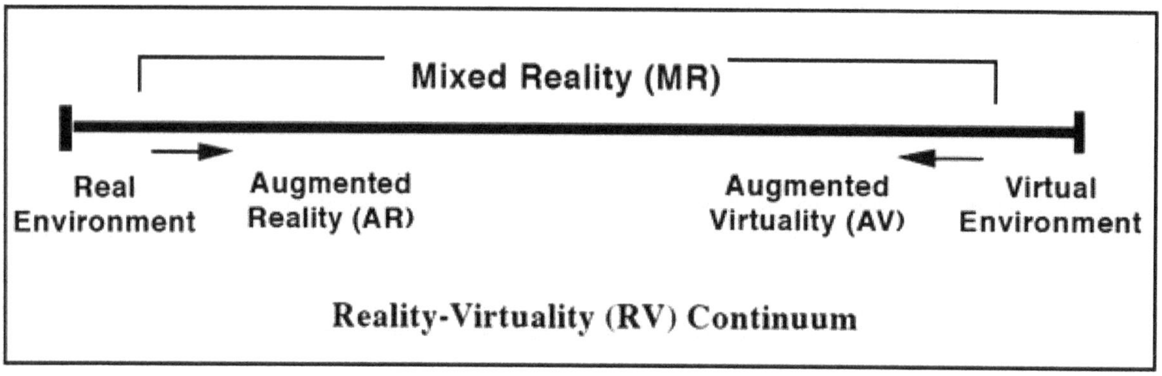

The augmented reality (AR) refers to the technology that can seamlessly integrate virtual objects with the real world to enhance users' perceptions (Alkhabra, Ibrahem, & Alkhabra, 2023). These AR learning environments are designed with the help of tracking approaches including marker-based and marker-less AR. Marker-based AR is based on visual markers such as 2D patterns captured by a camera displayed on a computer while marker less AR rely on mobile's location and direction to visual 3D objects (Sulistiyono, Hasyim, Bernadhed, Liantoni, & Sidauruk, 2024). Both these approaches are used in learning environments to obtain stable and adjustable tracking and registration capabilities (Liu, Yue, & Liu, 2024). Virtual reality (VR) is the technology that produces a 3D digital environment, allowing users to an interactive experience within virtual world that can go beyond physical world constraints (Liu, Yue, & Liu, 2024). Virtual immersive game-based learning environments can provide a platform where learners act as virtual characters and interact with virtual objects while learning a particular domain (Song, Wu, & Ding, 2024). On the other hand, Mixed reality (MR) is the blend of AR and VR technologies where learners can immerse in a virtual world while augmenting the physical space with digital information in real-time (Illi & Elhassouny, 2025) . MR-based gamified learning environments may not only support learners but also teachers to actively participate in designing their own virtual objects and interact with learners during the learning process (Dyulicheva & Glazieva, 2021).

Gamified immersive learning technologies can play a significant role in developing educational content for more engaging and learning experiences to learners (Fink, Robinson, & Ertl, 2024). These are the following benefits of using gamified immersive learning environments (Hawkinson, 2025) (Lin, Wan, Gan, Chen, & Chao, 2022): (i) Immersive interactive experience: these technologies can present learning content into 3D models in a gamified environment where learners can learn and enjoy effectively with more realistic experience (Song, Wu, & Ding, 2024). (ii) Visualization: these immersive environments can help learners to visualize objects which are not possible to see through their eyes in real world. For instance, a medical student can learn about 3D body structure or biological cells, or a historian can play and learn about the historical sites with 3D modelling views (Hawkinson, 2025) (iii)

Low learning cost and risk: Some courses like Chemistry or Physics require experimentations where learners will be involved to expose with dangerous chemicals or physical phenomena (e.g. chemical reactions or simulations). (iv) Unrestricted time and space: The use of such learning environments to limit concept understanding without time and space constraints (Illi & Elhassouny, 2025). For example, a student can learn about Antarctica while sitting in a warm and humid place. (v) Personalization: Such learning environments can assist learners with their personalized needs according to their strengths and weaknesses. For example, some learners require to enhance cognitive skills that can help in improving their learning abilities. Such tools can facilitate learners through their own pace and ways (Cebolla, et al., 2019) (vi) Promoting communication: these immersive learning technologies can assist learners to interact with teachers and other fellow students with freedom and enhance communication and interactions (Liu, Yue, & Liu, 2024) (vii) Empathy-Driven Engagement: they can support behavioral dimension to support leaners' needs. Overall, these gamified immersive learning environments can support learners not only with the interactive form of learning content but also foster deeper understanding of underlying concepts with the assistance of artificial intelligence agents.

2.3 Artificial Intelligence Agents in Immersive Game-Based Learning Environments

With the advancement of artificial intelligence (AI), agents are designed to automate tasks in a gamified immersive learning environment. These virtual agents are considered as actors in a virtual environment where they need to interact with learners as non-player characters (NPCs) (Kyrlitsias & Michael-Grigoriou, 2022). Their interaction in a game is confined with their roles in a specific environment and the level of the game. These AI agents guide learners as chatbots to improve their learning performance in a gamified learning environment while answering their queries using generative artificial intelligence (Khosrawi-Rad, et al., 2025). They also behave as an audience member or a teacher where learners can get information or support while achieving their learning goals (Zhu, Sam, Wu, & Tang, 2025).

In a gamified environment, game playing agents are involved that can help learners to interact with these gaming states including perception, inference and action (Xu, et al., 2024). In the *perception* gaming state, agents take input in the form of audio, text and observation and then transform into desired outcomes to make more engaging and interactive experience to learners (Xu, Yu, Fang, Wang, & Wu, 2023). *Inference* state is the key state of any game-based environment where agents are involved in multiple cognitive tasks including memorization, learning, reasoning, reflection, and decision making after having prior knowledge about learners (Xu, et al., 2024). They used to update their knowledge base after a specific period. On the other hand, *Action* is the state where agents use generative AI and do conversations among human players or other agents to overcome challenges posed in the gaming environment (Zhu et al., 2025). These gaming states can facilitate learners in a gamified learning environment through observations, reasoning, memorization, decision making, and environmental feedback (Xu, et al., 2024). These agents can support learning frameworks such as self-determination theory for providing engagement, support and personalized learning towards their learning goals (Bozkurt, 2023).

2.4 AI Agents and Self-Determination Theory: From Learners To Educators

With the emergence of AI, the use of AI agents as virtual characters in gamified immersive learning environments has increased over the years. These AI agents aimed at cultivating social agency have emerged as powerful tools for improving learners' engagement, interaction and overall learning (Wang, et al., 2025). These agents can enhance learners' capacity to ask curious, exploratory questions. This advancement highlights a wider transition in gamified immersive learning environments that are not only interactive but also personalized and adaptive to learners' needs and behaviors (Bozkurt, 2023). These agents can support engagement, learning outcomes and personalization for enhancing learners' experiences.

On the other hand, the self-determination theory (SDT) has been used in AI agent-based gamified immersive learning environments because of its three foundational psychological needs of learners and educators: autonomy, competence and relatedness (Ryan & Deci, 2020). *Autonomy* is the ability of learners to perform learning tasks by taking ownership of their own. *Competence* is regarded as the learners' feelings about the accomplishment of new learning tasks. *Relatedness* focuses on the connection between learners' experiences and tasks for strengthening the sense of belonging throughout their participation (Huang & Wang, 2023).

From learners' perspectives, this theory increasingly prominent in AI agent-based game design, aims to explain the interplay between intrinsic and extrinsic motivational forces that shape learners' behaviors (Huang & Wang, 2023). These agents can foster learners' autonomy by providing personalized learning content, facilitates emotional well-being of learners through interactive learning experiences and offers a sense of accomplishment by responding according to their needs (Wang, et al., 2025). It is highlighted that the greater the satisfaction learners' experiences, the higher their motivation becomes to engage in self-directed learning (Catalan & Martinez, 2020). The synergy between SDT with AI agent-based gamified immersive learning environments has been evident from the literature that SDT significantly fosters learners' motivation towards underlying domain, competency and their learning experiences (Luarn, Chen, & Chiu, 2023) (Hwang & Chang, 2024) (Huang & Wang, 2023).

In a similar vein, the implementation of AI agent-based gamified immersive learning environments in a classroom setting demand educators' motivation and engagement for better learning support to learners. Thus, it is necessary from institutional point of view, they should support educators in terms of their three SDT needs so that they can take more interest in delivering learning content through new ways (Chiu, et al., 2024). For example, when educators can have a choice to design gamified immersive learning environments through AI agents for learners then they feel autonomous. For designing and conducting such learning activities, institutes should give opportunities to educators to improve their competencies through a professional development and training process. Similarly, with the support of learning community, educators can connect with their peers through related technologies and share new pedagogical innovations among each other (Chiu, et al., 2024). Therefore, it is essential for educational institutions to support both learners and educators through the lens of SDT when implementing emerging trends in gamified immersive learning environments that integrate AI agents.

3. CURRENT TRENDS IN GAMIFICATION, IMMERSIVE LEARNING TECHNOLOGIES USING AI AGENTS

Currently, AI agents are designed to automate tasks in gamified immersive learning environments. These environments are considered as context for AI agents because of their challenging and engaging environments for learners where their cognitive and reasoning skills are required (Xu, et al., 2024). From the literature, the current trends of AI agents can be divided into three aspects: role, learning domains and learners. The research study about AI agents has been included and excluded from as per criteria mentioned in Table 1.

Table 1. Inclusion and exclusion criteria

Inclusion Criteria	Exclusion Criteria
• Includes AI agent/study that cover all three aspects: roles, learning domains and learners in gamified immersive learning environments • Research study published in 2023 onwards • Research articles published in English language and accessible • Journal articles, conference proceedings, book chapters • AI agent designed for educational purposes mainly for teachers and students • Learners can be of primary, secondary, higher, undergraduate or postgraduate students and school, college and university teachers	• Does not involve AI agent/study covering all three aspects: role, learning domains and learners in gamified immersive learning environments • Research study published before 2023 • Research articles published other than English language and not accessible • Report, dissertation, thesis or websites • AI agent designed other than educational purposes such as entertainment or information etc. • Learners who are not students or teachers

The details regarding the research study included all three aspects of AI agents in gamified immersive learning environments. The aspects are roles of AI agents, learning domains for AI agents and learners who use AI agents. The current trends of AI agents used in these environments are mentioned below. The summary of these current trends is presented in Table 2.

Table 2. AI agents in gamified immersive learning environments

AI Agent/Study	Roles	Learning Domain	Learners	Immersive Learning Environment
EVETeach (Dai, et al., 2024)	Tutor	Teacher's Development Training	School Teachers	Virtual Reality
Roblox (Jeong, Lee, Bryun, & Moon, 2024)	Tutor	Teachers' Development Training	School Teachers	Virtual Reality
norilla.org (Yannier, Hudson, Chang, & Koedinger, 2024)	Tutor	Earthquake (Science)	School Students	Mixed Reality
Educational Jurassic Park (Constantinescu, Silion, & Iftene, 2024)	Assistant	Dinosaurs (History)	School Students	Virtual Reality
LearningverseVR (Song, Wu, & Ding, 2024)	Assistant	Flower (Science)	Any	Virtual Reality
agentAR (Zhu et al., 2025)	Assistant	Coffee Making (Life Skills)	Any	Augmented Reality
FaceMe (Li, Zheng, Chai, Li, & Wei, 2023)	Assistant	Emotional Development	Children with Autism	Augmented Reality
(Chheang et al., 2024)	Tutor, Assistant	Anatomy (Medical Science)	Undergraduate and Postgraduate Students	Virtual Reality
SPARC (Zhu, Sam, Wu, & Tang, 2025)	Tutor, Assistant	Human Body and Rocket Exploration (Science)	K-12 Students	Virtual Reality
Kai (Nguyen et al., 2025)	Tutor, Assistant	Ethics	Postgraduate Students	Mixed Reality

continued on following page

Table 2. Continued

AI Agent/Study	Roles	Learning Domain	Learners	Immersive Learning Environment
(Rapaka, et al., 2025)	Tutor, Assistant	Literacy (English)	3-4 Years Old	Mixed Reality
(Khosrawi-Rad, et al., 2025)	Assistant, Competitor	Business IS Education	Undergraduate Students	Virtual Reality

3.1 Roles of AI Agents

In a gamified immersive learning environment, AI agents are the virtual characters that can assist learners with proper guidance, immediate feedback and emotional support (Tao, et al., 2022). They can improve learners' engagement and motivation towards understanding domain knowledge and performance (Kyrlitsias & Michael-Grigoriou, 2022). The roles of AI agents in gamified immersive learning environments are tutors, assistants and competitors (Tao, et al., 2022).

3.1.1 AI Agents as Tutors

These AI agents work as tutors to communicate with learners in their own languages and give feedback according to their personalized needs (Khosrawi-Rad, et al., 2025). They support learners without any time constraints and observe their attitudes toward learning concepts (Chheang et al., 2024). For instance, EVETeach (Dai, et al., 2024) has been designed where teachers are involved in a virtual environment for teaching practice. This application uses AI conversational agents called Evelyn, who behave as tutors in classroom practice. This application trains teachers to develop their teaching skills as well as students' observations during the classroom activities. Robolox (Jeong, Lee, Bryun, & Moon, 2024) is another teacher development virtual learning environment where teachers are involved in interacting with AI virtual agent who work as tutor and help them to design persona for students in order to design an interactive and engaging learning environments. The other application is norilla.org (Yannier, Hudson, Chang, & Koedinger, 2024) in which AI agent is used to teach school students in learning about physical Earthquake. Across these studies, AI agents serve as tutors that adapt their guidance to the specific learning requirements of both students and educators.

3.1.2 AI Agents as Assistants

When these AI agents work as assistants, they guide learners to solve problems and motivate them to engage in the learning environment (Song, Wu, & Ding, 2024). AI agents. For example, Educational Jurassic Park (Constantinescu, Silion, & Iftene, 2024), in which children can explore the virtual world through gaming experience where they can learn about dinosaurs. This application assists learners to get information using their hands and interaction with these virtual creatures. In other instance, LearningverseVR (Song, Wu, & Ding, 2024) is designed to engage learners with AI agent and learn about flowers. The AI agent behaves as assistant to give knowledge about the flower and its surroundings. In other instance, agentAR (Zhu et al., 2025), AI agent is used to improve life skills by assisting learners to make coffee through a step-by-step guide. FaceMe (Li, Zheng, Chai, Li, & Wei, 2023) is another gamified augmented reality application where children with autism are engaged in a social game to improve their facial expressions. This application designs an AI agent that can assist these children to improve their verbal and facial communications. In these studies, the AI agent acts as an assistant that improves learners' skills and motivates them to participate in gamified immersive environments.

In literature, there are few studies in which AI agents work as tutors and assistants for guiding learners throughout the learning process. For instance, generative AI virtual assistant is used in a gamified learning environment for learning human anatomy through assistance (Chheang et al., 2024). The application asks multiple choice questions to learners. Then, learners use this virtual assistant to ask as many questions as possible to find the correct answer. However, learners are not allowed to ask the exact multiple-choice question to the virtual assistant directly. This way learners can comprehend human anatomy and ultimately reach the appropriate answer at the end. Similarly, SPARC (a virtual reality game) supports peer collaboration where a team of up to four learners play together and solve given problems in an environment (Zhu, Sam, Wu, & Tang, 2025). This application assists K-12 students along with teachers who can enjoy and learn about human body related information during rocket exploration in a virtual world. In other instance, Kai (Nguyen et al., 2025), an embodied generative artificial intelligence (GenAI) based agent is designed for gamified mixed reality settings. This agent assists postgraduate learners through hints flashcards so that they can understand different aspects of the Ethics topic while engaging with mixed reality immersive learning environment. In other study, mixed reality learning environment is created for 3-4 years old learners who hear a random audio question from the AI agent and choose the correct alphabet in a game. This application provides immediate feedback to learners according to their personalized needs. All these agents are not only used to teach learners but also assist them to solve their problems according to their personalized requirements.

3.1.3 AI Agents as Competitors

AI agents can also act as competitors in literature where they can compete with players and pose numerous challenges to them, which lead them to improve their cognitive and problem-solving skills (Khosrawi-Rad, et al., 2025). However, in recent literature, there is only a single study found where three different modes are defined including collaborator, competitor and individual. In a competitor mode, AI agents behaved as competitors with other fellow learners in a game-based virtual learning environment. They also collaborate with other groups on tasks in a collaboration mode while in an individual mode, all learners work as single players and perform the task individually (Khosrawi-Rad, et al., 2025). This study indicates that agents also behave as competitors to promote challenges and motivation among learners.

Overall, well-designed AI agents can play an important role in supporting learning by providing guidance, scaffolding, and personalized feedback throughout the learning process. However, when AI agents are poorly designed, they may become a source of distraction and impose additional cognitive load on learners. Such issues can hinder learning, reduce engagement, and negatively affect learners' motivation and overall performance (Tao, et al., 2022). Therefore, it is crucial for educators and learning content designers to ensure that AI agents are thoughtfully designed so that learners can fully benefit from AI-enhanced learning environments.

3.2 Learning Domains For AI Agents

AI agents can develop effective instructional designs that support learners in achieving their learning goals (Ng, Xinyu, Leung, & Chu, 2024). By personalizing learning paths, adapting content in real time, and offering timely feedback, these agents can significantly enhance learning outcomes and motivation (Duong, Thi, & Pham, 2025). Their positive impact has been observed across various learning domains, making them broadly applicable in both formal and informal educational settings such as medicine (Chheang et al., 2024) and coffee making skills (Zhu et al., 2025).

In science education, these AI agents are implemented to guide learners about diverse science topics such as rocket exploration, earthquake and human anatomy. For instance, in norilla.org (Yannier, Hudson, Chang, & Koedinger, 2024), a Gorilla character appears on a large screen and guides learners to interact with physical objects while doing inquiry activities. Similarly, SPARC (Zhu, Sam, Wu, & Tang, 2025) is a virtual reality game developed using storytelling approach where learners can interact with a virtual AI agent while learning about human body in a rocket exploration. Both these applications were designed for school-aged learners with the aim of strengthening their cognitive and problem-solving abilities. LearningverseVR (Song, Wu, & Ding, 2024) is another application that uses AI agent where learners may inquire about a flower and other associated information. In contrast, for medical undergraduate students, a virtual AI-powered agent has been developed to respond to questions related to human anatomy and to support their understanding of complex physiological concepts (Chheang et al., 2024).

In other formal learning settings, AI agents have been integrated into gamified and immersive learning environments across a variety of domains. For example, the Educational Jurassic Park VR application is designed to enable learners to explore information about dinosaurs through an interactive virtual environment (Constantinescu, Silion, & Iftene, 2024). In another instance, Kai (Nguyen et al., 2025), a mixed-reality learning environment, incorporates an AI agent that functions as an ethics expert, allowing learners to engage in real-time dialogue to deepen their understanding of ethical concepts. Similarly, in the domain of English language learning, an AI-driven agent not only supports learners in mastering alphabets and vowels according to their individual needs but also provides an enjoyable and engaging experience that enhances English literacy development (Rapaka, et al., 2025). The other formal use of AI agents in emotional development (Li, Zheng, Chai, Li, & Wei, 2023) and business IS education (Khosrawi-Rad, et al., 2025). Both these applications emphasize one-to-one support to learners, personalized learning and enhance learning outcomes.

In informal settings, a couple of studies have been developed to enhance teachers' professional growth by improving their instructional styles and behaviors, which in turn can positively influence learners' cognitive and analytical skills. For instance, EVETeach is designed as a virtual classroom environment that provides training for teachers on topics in the secondary school science and mathematics curriculum, such as mathematics concepts, gas laws, and fungi. (Dai, et al., 2024). Another platform, Robolox ((Jeong, Lee, Bryun, & Moon, 2024) is used to train teachers in designing and using different learner personas within instructional activities, helping them better understand how to engage diverse students. AI agents are also used to enhance learners' life skills. For example, in agentAR (Zhu et al., 2025), learners can design an AR application that can help them to learn about how to make a coffee. The agent actively engages in communication with learners and suggests actionable steps accordingly. Across these studies, findings consistently showed that AI agents can significantly enhance learners' performance, promote deeper conceptual understanding, and contribute to more effective learning experiences.

3.3 Learners Use AI Agents

Learners are central stakeholders in the use of AI agents within gamified immersive learning environments. Emerging literature increasingly demonstrates that integrating AI agents into such environments can enhance interactivity, personalization, and immersion for students and teachers (Lampropoulos, 2025). Current literature indicates that most AI agent-based educational applications target learners across a wide range of developmental stages, including pre-school, primary, secondary, and tertiary levels. For instance, AI agent is designed for pre-school learners assist in developing foundational literacy skills by facilitating the understanding of alphabets and vowels through interactive activities (Rapaka, et al., 2025). In a similar vein, Educational Jurassic Park (Constantinescu, Silion, & Iftene, 2024) and norilla.org (Yannier, Hudson, Chang, & Koedinger, 2024) provide school-aged learners with opportunities to engage in experiential, hands-on learning within virtual environments. At the K-12 level, the SPARC (Zhu, Sam, Wu, & Tang, 2025) application enables students to interact with a conversational AI agent that guides them to learn about human body in a rocket ship. Additionally, specialized gamified immersive environments have been developed for learners with unique needs; for instance, FaceMe (Li, Zheng, Chai, Li, & Wei, 2023), an augmented reality game that supports children with Autism. This game fosters improvements in verbal communication and facial expression recognition. Collectively, these examples highlight the expanding role of AI agents in shaping adaptive and engaging immersive learning experiences across diverse school level learner populations.

At the tertiary level, few applications are developed in which undergraduate and postgraduate learners interact with AI agents to support advanced knowledge acquisition. For example, undergraduate students are engaged with an AI agent named *Ben* to deepen their understanding of business information systems through both collaborative and competitive learning modes (Khosrawi-Rad, et al., 2025). Similarly, another AI-driven virtual assistant is designed to support anatomy education for undergraduate and postgraduate medical students. This agent guided learners through various aspects of human physiological systems by presenting structured multiple-choice questions and offering feedback to strengthen conceptual understanding (Chheang et al., 2024). In addition, Kai, a mixed-reality–based AI agent, is developed to facilitate learning of ethical principles through interactive dialogue and immersive scenarios (Nguyen et al., 2025). Overall, these applications demonstrate that AI agents are implemented in gamified immersive learning environments at undergraduate and postgraduate levels.

In addition to supporting student learning, AI agents in immersive gamified environments are increasingly being leveraged for teachers' professional development. For instance, EVETeach (Dai et al., 2024) and Robolox (Jeong, Lee, Bryun, & Moon, 2024) are developed to enable educators to practice and refine their instructional strategies within simulated virtual classrooms. These applications incorporate AI-driven virtual agents that mimic student behaviors and classroom dynamics, thereby helping teachers improve pedagogical techniques, classroom management, and responsive teaching practices.

In literature, a few AI agent-based immersive learning applications are created to support any type of learner. One such application is agentAR (Zhu et al., 2025), which is designed to develop practical life skills of making coffee through step-by-step interactive guidance. In another example, LearningverseVR (Song, Wu, & Ding, 2024) offers a virtual reality environment in which learners interact with a digital agent while examining a virtual flower. The AI agent helps learners explore and understand various characteristics and features of the flower, thus encouraging observations and conceptual understanding.

Overall, AI agents integrated into gamified immersive learning environments have shown considerable potential to positively influence learning outcomes. They do so by offering immersive and interactive experiences, enhancing visualization of complex concepts, enabling learning beyond conventional constraints of time and space, supporting personalized instruction, and fostering communication and collaboration among learners (Lin, Wan, Gan, Chen, & Chao, 2022). However, there are key risks that need to be addressed while developing AI agents for use in gamified immersive learning settings.

4 KEY POTENTIAL RISKS OF USING AI AGENTS IN GAME-BASED IMMERSIVE LEARNING ENVIRONMENTS

The use of AI agents has been prevalent in the gamified immersive learning environments over the last decade. They can be implemented in such learning environments as virtual teaching assistants, virtual peer agent, support natural language processing, automated students' learning assessments and predictive learners' behaviors (Almeman, El Ayeb, Berrima, Issaoui, & Morsy, 2025). These agents can bring numerous benefits including enhanced engagement, improved learning outcomes, remotely accessible to learning content, immediate feedback and enhanced collaboration (Bekteshi, 2025). Despite numerous benefits of using AI agents in game-based immersive learning environments, there are still some potential risks including technical implementation, computational and performance, critical tensions between personalization and surveillance, ethical and social presence concerns, which may hinder learning and playful experiences. They are mentioned as below:

4.1 Technical Implementation Risks

AI pedagogical agents in gamified immersive learning environments can play an important role in providing engaging and playful learning experiences to learners. Despite these emerging advancements, the use of AI agents and the designing of gamified immersive learning environments are still in the infancy stage where there are still some technical risks (Doroudian, 2025) (Almeman, El Ayeb, Berrima, Issaoui, & Morsy, 2025) including the dependence of artificial intelligence algorithms and implementation challenges of immersive technology. The details of these risks are mentioned below:

4.1.1 Dependence on Artificial Intelligence Algorithms

Large language models (LLMs) have significantly improved over the years and produce accurate results. However, there are still significant potential risks associated with the use of LLMs in developing teaching assistants that focus on learners' individual needs and styles (Almeman, El Ayeb, Berrima, Issaoui, & Morsy, 2025). This requires designing AI systems based on sophisticated algorithms that can support learners with specific requirements. And that is only possible if educational psychology of learners is thoroughly considered (Lin, Wan, Gan, Chen, & Chao, 2022). Furthermore, there is still a chance that LLMs can generate incorrect and inaccurate results to learners' queries (Galitsky, Chernyavskiy, & Ilvovsky, 2024). Thus, learners may consider such incorrect and inaccurate information as positive outcomes because LLMs embody AI agents to convince learners due to its interaction with them. In a similar way, the dependency on AI agents has increased over the years because of providing quick responses. For this reason, there is a potential risk that learners may not utilize their own cognitive and problem-solving skills instead of relying on AI agents' responses (Fink, Robinson, & Ertl, 2024). This may reduce their learning and cognitive skills significantly.

There is a need that AI agents must support seamless communication between learners with distinct spoken languages. This requires sophisticated natural language processing capabilities in AI agents to deal with these challenges (Zahedi, Farahani, & Peymani, 2023). With the advancements of LLMs, the interactivity of AI agents can be found in many applications, however, there are still challenges in designing such learning environments with limited hands-on-practice such as medical training, where AI agents cannot be able to simulate the real world scenarios (Zhang, 2023). Similarly, machine learning algorithms are designed in developing AI agents for the detection of learners' movements and actions in a gamified immersive learning environment using computer vision (Almeman, El Ayeb, Berrima, Issaoui, & Morsy, 2025). Nevertheless, these environments require novel approaches of computer vision that can facilitate learners to get continuous learning in gamified immersive learning environments (Bilotti, Di Dario, Palomba, Gravino, & Sibilio, 2023). Another potential technical challenge is the use of headsets in such learning environments because of discomfort for a longer period which might cause depression and stress among learners during the learning process (Almeman, El Ayeb, Berrima, Issaoui, & Morsy, 2025).

4.1.2 Infrastructural Constraints of Immersive Technology

There are immersive technologies including augmented reality (AR), virtual reality (VR) and mixed reality (MR) used in educational settings. VR has the potential to create immersive learning environments for learners by offering more engaging experiences. This technology deals with the head-mounted display (HMD) to design 3D virtual world. One of the major concerns with this HMD is that learners realize this form of environment as a virtual world does not consider it as a real environment where they are learning from teachers. This is mainly because of how our brain works. Hence, there is still a challenge to design a VR environment where learners can immerse with reality in their minds (Lin, Wan, Gan, Chen, & Chao, 2022).

In AR, learners are interacted with the learning content in a digital environment, however, that content is not portable is one of the biggest challenges to overcome. Further, it has been highlighted that such learning environments show two distinct worlds including real and virtual that may decrease the learners' immersions for a long time. Thus, such learning environments require to optimize AR and VR technology through the efficient use of computing power, communication channels and other resources (Rokhsaritalemi, Niaraki, & Choi, 2021). MR provides more engaging experiences by providing the combination of both forms of immersion to learners. This may create a challenge to design high resolution virtual characters in a gamified immersive learning environment. Another challenge in immersive environment is to track the virtual objects accurately. This tracking accuracy can determine the position and orientation of virtual objects using multiple factors including tracking system quality, the system settings, use of specific marker or sensor, and the complexity of the environment (Schneider, et al., 2021). For improving such accuracy, there is a potential risk to design advanced algorithms. Further, the use of multiple sensors to track movement with different angles is also a challenge to overcome using such algorithms (Doroudian, 2025). Moreover, educators may resist the change in adoption of AI agent based immersive games in the classroom due to being unfamiliar with these technologies, doubtful about the effectiveness of these tools, or fear of losing jobs (Bekteshi, 2025). Similarly, alignment of immersive technologies with curriculum is still a daunting task to overcome.

One educational scenario illustrating this potential risk involves Mrs. James, a high school teacher who uses a gamified immersive learning environment to teach her students. Her students log in from home, where they can interact with one another and participate in a variety of learning activities. Within this environment, an AI agent assists Mrs. James by generating personalized learning content based on each learner's individual needs, behaviors, and learning styles. However, the large language models (LLMs) powering the AI agent are trained on extensive text corpora that may contain biased, inappropriate, or stereotypical information. If a student asks the AI agent an inappropriate or ambiguous question, the AI may unintentionally produce an unsuitable or harmful response. This would pose a major challenge for Mrs. James in maintaining a safe and respectful learning environment. Another difficulty she faces is the inability to manually validate every response generated by the AI agent. Because the environment is dynamic and students can ask multiple questions at any time, it becomes impractical for her to monitor each interaction. Additionally, navigating immersive technologies adds further complexity. Mrs. James must stay updated with rapidly evolving tools and systems to support students effectively when technical or conceptual difficulties arise. Therefore, it is essential to provide educators with comprehensive training in emerging technologies. Equipping them with the necessary skills will empower them to design and oversee AI agents capable of producing accurate, appropriate, and pedagogically sound information within gamified immersive learning environments.

4.2 Computational and Performance Risks

The use of AI agents in gamified immersive learning environments can be limited in real time settings because of the requirements of multiple devices, computational power and other additional resources (Almeman, El Ayeb, Berrima, Issaoui, & Morsy, 2025). These devices and resources are expensive for educators to implement in educational environments (Zhu, Sam, Wu, & Tang, 2025). Apart from this, there is also a challenge to design efficient network infrastructure that can handle faster data transfer (Zahedi, Farahani, & Peymani, 2023). The details of computational and performance risks are mentioned below:

4.2.1 Network Connectivity Issues

These gamified immersive learning environments require high-speed network infrastructure that can support continuous learning. For example, poor connectively or device compatibility issues can hinder the effectiveness of immersive learning environments (Doroudian, 2025). Furthermore, the use of AI agents needs a high bandwidth medium to transfer and process data from IoT devices and immersive technologies to facilitate engaging experiences to learners (Jagatheesaperumal, Ahmad, Al-Fuqaha, & Qadir, 2024). In such learning environments, fast responsive communication is necessary as many devices are linked to generate immersive environments. Network latency can create delays in transferring data from user to agents and vice versa that leads to degradation of learners' motivation towards learning process (Dang et al., 2023).

4.2.2 Hardware Cost and Latency Issues

Computational devices used in designing gamified immersive learning environments are very expensive and limited to implement in educational settings (Zhu, Sam, Wu, & Tang, 2025). For implementing immersive learning environment in real environments, then there is a big challenge in purchasing these computational devices and high resolution equipment are required for rendering virtual scenes and simulation in good quantities (Lin, Wan, Gan, Chen, & Chao, 2022). Moreover, the hardware delay is a substantial risk in developing gamified immersive learning environments. Hardware delay can make virtual environments slow responsive environments. This will create disruptive experiences for learners that may hinder their engagement (Doroudian, 2025). Such delays may enforce learners to commit errors and that lead towards degradation of their motivation towards learning effectively (Almeman, El Ayeb, Berrima, Issaoui, & Morsy, 2025). Furthermore, the integration of multiple technologies such as AR, VR, MR or AI in an environment may raise an interoperability risk because all these technologies have their own standards and protocols for implementation. Similarly, other technologies used in such gamified environments like optical character recognition (OCR), automatic speech recognition (ASR) and text-to-speech recognition may also have considerable challenges to design (Ho, et al., 2023).

To understand this potential risk, consider the scenario of Mr. Steve, a college-level instructor who conducts his classes through a gamified immersive learning environment. In this system, students can engage in various learning activities from any location. He assigns a collaborative task to several groups of students, each member participating in a different geographical area. One of the students, Lee, faces significant challenges because his device has limited technical specifications and cannot properly display the gaming interface. As a result, he becomes disappointed and is unable to continue participating in the class due to these resource constraints. In another group, a student named Elina lives in a remote area where internet connection is unreliable. Due to poor signal strength, her connection frequently drops, causing repeated disruptions. This prevents her from fully engaging in the learning activities, and the persistent connectivity issues may eventually force her to disengage from the course entirely. From Mr. Steve's perspective as an instructor, these issues are discouraging and may lead him to avoid using gamified immersive environments for collaborative activities in the future. Therefore, it is essential for educators and policymakers to implement such environments with clear technical requirements and minimum configuration standards. Ensuring that fundamental technological needs are addressed will help guarantee that all students can participate equitably without facing computational or performance barriers.

4.3 Critical Tensions Between Personalization and Surveillance

The cyberspace world where computational devices are connected digitally with humans' objects enables many potential risks. With the increased use of gamified immersive learning environments for utilizing learners' individual data is necessary to provide personalized learning environments. Such data may be accessed or modified by cyber criminals known as cybersecurity risks (Sun, Gan, Chao, Yu, & Ding, 2023). There are serious tensions between learners' personalization and surveillance during the learning process. For instance, to design personalized gamified immersive learning environments for learners, it is essential to get learners' information regarding their learning and emotional preferences (Lin, Wan, Gan, Chen, & Chao, 2022). If privacy is breached by attackers, then such important information may be lost or have unauthorized access. Further, in school education, younger learners may not have much concern about their privacy, which may be handled mostly by the application proprietors (Zahedi, Farahani, & Peymani, 2023). These potential risks may create serious threats regarding the leakage of personalized data and other key information. In educational literature, cyber-crimes are taken place where learners' sensitive information is leaked and tampered with other information. For example, numerous security breaches are reported in a study where access to users' information such as learners' assessment marks are compromised through phishing links or man-in-the-middle attacks (Oguguo & Ocheni, 2023).

Another potential risk for developing gamified immersive learning environment is to collect information like EEG signals or eye tracking can supposed to leak information about learners such as gender, income level, or emotional state (Garrido, Nair, & Song, 2024). There is another serious breach of security in such immersive learning environment is impersonation, where fake identities are used to mark attendance or appear in the examination on behalf of other students (Oguguo et al., 2023). Further, AI agents may be used not only for impersonation but also for submitting plagiarize assignments or tasks in gamified immersive learning environments (Almeman, El Ayeb, Berrima, Issaoui, & Morsy, 2025). In a similar vein, the use of AI agents in such environments may arise some privacy and security breaches because of the use of learners' sensitive information during the learning process such as specific requirements for learners who have learning difficulties (Yenduri, et al., 2023).

One example of such a potential risk is the case of Ms. Jelena, a secondary science teacher who plans to conduct her lessons in a gamified immersive learning environment to help students learn about plants and related concepts. She instructs her students to log into the game and participate in the immersive activities. The game provides personalized content based on various factors including learning style, behaviors, understanding, motivation, emotional states and other attributes. However, due to negligence on Ms. Jelena's part, students' personalized data is leaked from her device or another medium. She remains unaware of the breach until some students report it to her. Situations like this pose a serious threat to security of students' personal information. As a result, students may become hesitant to share information or may be reluctant to respond to questions related to their personal habits or learning preferences. This creates tension between the benefits of personalization and the risks of surveillance in data-driven learning systems. Therefore, it is crucial to design such learning environments with strict and comprehensive safeguard policies that protect students' privacy while still enabling the delivery of personalized educational content.

4.4 Ethical and Social Presence Concerns

Ethical concerns such as data privacy and algorithmic bias, AI agents may use learners' voice recordings or sensitive information for identification of people or create deep fake. Other ethical concern is related to algorithmic bias (Bekteshi, 2025), in which AI agents can generate answers or dialogues following some inappropriate values and interaction styles. There is a potential risk that such algorithms can be biased in designing personalized learning paths to learners' assessments that lead towards the unfairness to diverse learners (Almeman, El Ayeb, Berrima, Issaoui, & Morsy, 2025). For instance, learning content or assessment may be aligned with learners' cultural background or specific characteristics to facilitate their personalized learning. For this purpose, AI agents may modify the content accordingly, however, it may be detrimental to other learners who did not belong to the same culture or background (Zhang, 2023). This raises an ethical concern regarding discriminatory practices. There is another ethical issue regarding the content generated by the AI agents based on LLMs. In a study, misleading or biased stories have been generated in a game called mixed-initiative gameplay (MIG) where learners may be involved in using harmful stereotypes unintentionally in such learning environments (Yang, Kleinman, & Harteveld, 2024).

In an immersive learning environment, social presence is an essential ingredient where learners can feel about their experiences and their relations with other objects in a virtual world (Doroudian, 2025).

There are potential risks about the feeling of learners as they are dispersed during the learning process. Further, when learners are involved in such gamified immersive learning environments, there are a limited number of nonverbal signals from virtual characters such as body language, facial expressions and eye contact that may degrade learners' motivation towards learning (Lee, 2021). The purpose of such signals is to make more engaging and realistic environment for learners where they can feel sense of presence in the virtual world. Another threat of such learning environment is the delay or inconsistency in the delivery of content or feedback to learners due to network or hardware latency (Doroudian, 2025). This may reduce learners' productivity and social presence in gamified immersive learning environments.

Let's take a scenario where Mr. Campbell works with high school students and regularly assigns various activities through a gamified immersive learning environment. Students typically complete these activities from home and learn the associate content through gameplay. The game is designed so that an AI agent interacts with students and facilitates the learning tasks. Recently, an international student joined the classroom. Since the AI agent generates scenario-based activities grounded in the local context, this student may encounter difficulties in understanding the scenarios and participate effectively. This raises concerns about fairness and inclusivity, as the learning experiences may not accommodate the diverse backgrounds represented in the classroom. In addition, the virtual characters in the game rely on a limited set of nonverbal cues that may be culturally specific. Such culturally constrained signals could further disadvantage students from different backgrounds and pose ethical challenges. Faced with these issues, Mr. Campbell may feel discouraged from using the gamified immersive learning environment to conduct such activities. Therefore, it becomes essential to train AI agents and design learning activities that are culturally adaptable, inclusive and not limited to any background or group.

5. FUTURE DIRECTIONS

Over the years, there have been significant improvements in gamified immersive learning environments with the integration of AI, and it is continuing to revolutionize the educational landscape. With such implementation, there are many key areas identified in the literature that indicate there are promising future directions that can help to design more engaging and immersive learning experiences to upcoming generations. This section outlines the future directions based on the current trends in such learning environments.

5.1 Pedagogical Applications of Explainable AI (XAI)

One of the future directions is to investigate how players build trust with other NPCs (AI Agents) and what they perceive about these AI Agents while learning and playing (Fink, Robinson, & Ertl, 2024). Explainable AI (XAI) is the term used where learners and AI agents build trust between themselves after mitigating algorithmic biasness by explaining how these agents reach a final decision through AI models (Altukhi & Pradhan, 2024). In education, such AI agents can play a significant role in contributing towards safe and effective education to learners. For example, there is a need to identify or predict learners' behaviors during learning process to support personalized learning. This may assist educators to identify weaknesses of learners at very early stages and may improve their problem-solving skills with guidance and personalized content (Jang, Choi, Jung, & Kim, 2022). Similarly, diversification is a concept where socio-economic, demographic and cultural biases may be minimized to make such AI agents to be more transparent and fairness (Almeman, El Ayeb, Berrima, Issaoui, & Morsy, 2025).. This may help learners to trust AI agents without any potential discrimination. Such trust is crucial for enhancing personalized learning and assessment. These pedagogical applications of XAI suggest that many institutions are likely to adopt XAI in the future when developing gamified and immersive learning environments.

5.2 Multimodal AI Agents for Immersive Environments

Another important future direction is to advance game based immersive learning technologies using multimodal AI agents is the impact of self-representation in these environments (Kyrlitsias & Michael-Grigoriou, 2022). That means that the players' avatars and other NPCs (AI agents) in the game should be developed in such a way that they look more realistic, their movement in the game may use full-body tracking technology by resembling the players' movements. Recently, AI agents like GPT-4V and LLaVA are designed to interpret multimodal communication including textual, vision and audio in an immersive environment where NPCs (AI agents) can see and hear with learners (Ozkaya, Berrezueta-Guzman, & Wagner, 2025).

In future, such multimodal AI agents may be further enhanced such capabilities of NPCs to track learners' movements and gestures, comprehend virtual immersive scenes and generate responses quickly in real settings (Waghale, Potdukhe, & Rewarkar, 2024). In a similar vein, there is a potential scope for enhancing the behaviors of learners (players) modelling using AI. LLMs have shown in literature that they can learn from learners' behaviors and generate meaningful responses tailoring to their preferences. The gamified immersive learning environments can be further enhanced by incorporating such technology to comprehend how learners' interact with other NPCs (AI agents) and make a decision or solve given tasks or challenges (Perez, Castro, & Lopez, 2023). The multimodal capabilities of AI agents can enhance better learning design and assessments within future gamified immersive learning environments. These advancements will enable educators to adopt and integrate AI agents with multimodal features more effectively.

5.3 Interoperability

The other future task is to develop interoperable platforms for supporting gamified immersive learning environments using AI agents so that educational content can be transferred, modified or utilized across these environments (Zhang, 2023). This standardization may enhance stakeholders' involvement including educators, technology providers, software developers, policy makers, and learners. Such recent developments in this area as using non-fungible tokens (NFTs) technology in gamified immersive learning environments can significantly resolve the interoperability challenges. These NFTs can be used to define each virtual object or resource as a unique digital asset that enables seamless transfer and access to these unique digital assets across multiple immersive environments (Li et al., 2023).

Additionally, AI approaches can be used to automate interoperability processes including protocol translation and data conversion (Almeman, El Ayeb, Berrima, Issaoui, & Morsy, 2025). There is also an interoperable approach called federated learning, in which a standardized model can be used in all devices, and the collected data remains on the local devices (Yenduri, et al., 2023). This may achieve interoperable educational platform in a gamified immersive learning environment. This will support policy makers and educators in implementing interoperable AI agents within gaming environments, enabling learners' activities and assessments to be transferable and accessible across multiple platforms.

5.4 Ethical and Secure AI Development

Another important future dimension is to design ethical and secure use of AI in gamified immersive learning environment. In these environments, personalized information is being continuously monitored and collected by learners for interaction with virtual characters. However, there is a need to design such environments while considering these four aspects (Almeman, El Ayeb, Berrima, Issaoui, & Morsy, 2025) (i) data anonymization, data can be anonymized so that learners' identities should not be compromised by placing their data separately from their identifies (ii) data encryption, data can be encrypted and decrypted by which processing may be faster and reduce the burden on performance, power, memory and processing (iii) blockchain, data or AI agent responses can be secured and transparent where such learning environments can use learners' information for personalized learning (iv) frequent security audits, monitoring systems may be applied with these learning environments to make more robust and secure by continuous monitoring of security threats in real time.

With the integration of AI agents in gamified learning environments, emotionally responsible AI agents focus on the specific learners' needs. For instance, AI agents may response emotionally with young children or neurodivergent learners (Ozkaya, Berrezueta-Guzman, & Wagner, 2025). In addition, AI agents with NFTs or blockchain may require scalable and robust architecture in future that can be ethically secure and manage identifiable digital assets. Such architecture may be designed to cater the demands of frequent learners' authentications more effectively in near future (Almeman, El Ayeb, Berrima, Issaoui, & Morsy, 2025). This will create a conducive environment for learners where they can learn, share, assess, transfer content without any hesitation. Implementing ethical and secure AI development requires a robust policy framework that ensures uninterrupted education for diverse learners in the context of emerging technologies.

5.5 Open-Source Availability of Emerging Technologies

The other future direction is related to commercialization of such technologies to general audience with minimum cost so that everybody can get advantage of utilizing them as learning platforms for future learners. Currently open-source AI models like LLaMA, Mistral, and Baichuan are available by which researchers and other game developers can experiment with them easily (Ozkaya, Berrezueta-Guzman, & Wagner, 2025). Furthermore, open frameworks including LangChain, Hugging Face Transformations, and UnityGPT offer LLM based AI agents that can allow to design such gamified immersive learning environments for learners (Hu, et al., 2025).

On the other hand, renowned companies like NVIDIA, OpenAI and Meta are currently focusing on AI agents for gamified environments. They are ensuring that the integration of AI agents with game engines will be commercially viable in near future. Further, there are more advancements required in these areas including real-time streaming APIs, efficient quantized model serving, and integration of multimodal communication may limit memory and latency issues that can allow to design scalable use of multi-agent gamified immersive learning environments (Ozkaya, Berrezueta-Guzman, & Wagner, 2025). Therefore, there is a need for governments, organizations, and investors to develop AI-enabled open-source APIs and platforms that allow learners to access educational resources anytime and anywhere in the world. Moreover, a comprehensive policy framework should be established to guide the ethical development and use of such open-source AI agents and applications in the future.

6. CONCLUSION AND IMPLICATIONS IN PRACTICE

6.1 Conclusion

In conclusion, this chapter highlights the current trends, potential risks and future directions of gamification, immersive learning technologies using AI agents. The use of gamification for educational purposes has been growing because of its benefits in education including problem decomposition, conceptual knowledge development, metacognitive regulation, information selection, and sustained motivation. With the advancement of immersive technologies, the gamified learning environment can play a pivotal role in facilitating learners with more interactive and immersive learning experiences. These gamified immersive learning environments can engage learners due to these advantages such as immersive interactive experiences, 3D visualization, low learning cost and risk, unrestricted time and space, personalization, promoting communication and empathy-driven engagement. In recent years, the use of AI has increased exponentially in every walk of life, especially in education. These AI agents are developed with the help of LLMs in gamified immersive learning environments as non-player characters to interact with learners and give responses according to their needs.

Currently, AI Agents are considered suitable for gamified immersive learning environments because in these environments, learners require cognitive and reasoning skills for such challenging and engaging tasks in these environments. These agents can help learners as tutors where they will give feedback according to their personalized needs. These agents behave as assistants where they assist learners to solve given tasks or challenges and motivate them to engage with gamified learning environments. AI agents also work as competitors where they contest with learners and challenge them in a gamified learning environment. The challenges posed by these competitor agents may enhance learners' cognitive and problem-solving skills. They support natural language processing, automated students' learning assessments and predictive learners' behaviors in these environments. The effectiveness of these agents presents improved learning outcomes, immediate feedback and enhanced collaboration with learners in gamified immersive learning environments.

Despite many advantages of using AI agents in game-based immersive learning environments, there are still some potential risks found in the literature that may limit engaging and interactive learning experiences. With the use of AI agents, there is a chance that these agents can generate incorrect and inaccurate results to learners, which may cause misinformation and misleading to learners. Further, these algorithms may generate biased answers to learners' queries because of considering specific perspective. However, the dependencies on these agents may hinder the use of learners' own cognitive thinking and problem-solving skills. The use of AI agents with immersive technologies is limited in real settings because these immersive technologies and design of AI agents are expensive and not commercially viable. The other potential risk is to design high resolution virtual objects and their accurate tracking in a gamified immersive learning environment. Additionally, there is a risk of designing a robust and secure network infrastructure that can demonstrate data transfer and rendering of the scenes in the immersive learning environments without any constraints. Apart from these, educators may also resist using such AI agents-based learning environments due to being unfamiliar with these technologies and the alignment of these technologies with the current curriculum is another big threat to resolve.

6.2 Implications in Practice

Looking ahead, several practical implications can guide the development of more engaging and immersive learning experiences. One key direction is the integration of explainable AI (XAI) within learning environments. By clarifying how algorithms generate decisions, XAI can help learners build trust in AI-driven recommendations and feedback. In practice, this transparency can support better adoption and reduce uncertainty among students and educators.

Another implication relates to the design of more realistic and responsive non-player characters (NPCs) serving as AI agents. These AI-driven characters could track learners' movements, gestures, and behaviors to offer more adaptive and personalized learning support within gamified immersive environments. Implementing such NPCs would require advancements in motion tracking, behavior modeling, and affective computing. A further practical consideration is the establishment of standardized and interoperable infrastructures. Such systems would enable seamless transfer of learning content and virtual assets across different immersive platforms and technologies. This would not only improve flexibility for educators but also ensure that learners can access consistent experiences regardless of the tools they use.

Additionally, ensuring ethical and secure technological foundations remains essential. This includes creating infrastructures where learners' data can be anonymized, encrypted, or protected through secure mechanisms such as blockchain. Strengthening privacy safeguards will help maintain trust among learners and prevent misuse of personal information. Cost and accessibility also carry important implications for practice. Making AI and immersive technologies more affordable will empower educators to implement these tools effectively in future gamified learning environments. Lowering financial and technical barriers ensures that all institutions, not only well-resourced ones, can benefit.

Overall, AI agents offer significant benefits for education and have immense potential to shape the next generation of immersive learning environments. However, moving forward, educators, game designers, and policymakers must prioritize advancing AI capabilities, building interoperable systems, ensuring affordability, and establishing robust privacy and security measures to fully support personalized learning in gamified immersive environments.

REFERENCES

Ahmad, A., Zeeshan, F., Marriam, R., Samreen, A., & Ahmed, S. (2021). Does one size fit all? Investigating the effect of group size and gamification on leaners' behaviors in higher education. *Journal of Computing in Higher Education, 33*(2), 296–327. DOI: 10.1007/s12528-020-09266-8

Ahmed, S., & Parsons, D. (2013). Abductive science inquiry using mobile devices in the classroom. *Computers & Education, 63*, 62–72. DOI: 10.1016/j.compedu.2012.11.017

Ahmed, S., Zeeshan, M., Parsons, D., Rehman, O., Ahmed, Z., Ahmad, A., & Ahmad, F. (2025). Exploring game-based inquiry learning application in a maritime science museum: A visitors' perspectives. *Human Behavior and Emerging Technologies, 2025*(1), 1–14. DOI: 10.1155/hbe2/8284489

Alkhabra, Y. A., Ibrahem, U. M., & Alkhabra, S. A. (2023). Augmented reality technology in enhancing learning retention and critical thinking according to STEAM program. *Humanities & Social Sciences Communications, 10*(1), 1–10. DOI: 10.1057/s41599-023-01650-w

Almeman, K., El Ayeb, F., Berrima, M., Issaoui, B., & Morsy, H. (2025). The integration of AI and metaverse in education: A systematic review. *Applied Sciences (Basel, Switzerland), 15*(863), 1–135. DOI: 10.3390/app15020863

Altukhi, Z. M., & Pradhan, S. (2024). Systematic literature review: Explainable AI definitions and challenges in education. *arXiv, 2504*(02910), 1-17. doi:/arXiv.2504.02910DOI: 10.48550

Bekteshi, L. (2025). Education in the era of AI and immersive technologies: A systematic review. *Journal of Research in Engineering and Computer Sciences, 3*(1), 1–14. DOI: 10.63002/jrecs.31.779

Bilotti, U., Di Dario, D., Palomba, F., Gravino, C., & Sibilio, M. (2023). Machine learning for educational metaverse: How far are we? *In Proceedings of the 2023 IEEE International Conference on Consumer Electronics (ICCE)* (pp. 1-2). Berlin, Germany: IEEE. DOI: 10.1109/ICCE56470.2023.10043465

Bozkurt, A. (2023). Generative artificial intelligence (AI) powered conversational educational agents: The inevitable paradigm shift. *Asian Journal of Distance Education, 18*(1), 198–204. http://www.asianjde.com/ojs/index.php/AsianJDE/article/view/718

Cai, Z., Mao, P., Wang, D., He, J., Chen, X., & Fan, X. (2022). Effects of scaffolding in digital game-based learning on student's achievement: A three-level meta-analysis. *Educational Psychology Review, 34*(2), 537–574. DOI: 10.1007/s10648-021-09655-0

Catalan, B. I., & Martinez, E. (2020). Understanding applicants'reactions to gamified recruitment. *Journal of Business Research, 110*, 41–50. DOI: 10.1016/j.jbusres.2019.12.041

Cebolla, A., Herrero, R., Ventura, S., Miragall, M., Bellosta-Batalla, M., Llorens, R., & Banos, R. M. (2019). Putting oneself in the body of others: A pilot study on the efficacy of an embodied virtual reality system to generate self-compassion. *Frontiers in Psychology, 10*, 1–10. DOI: 10.3389/fpsyg.2019.01521 PMID: 31338048

Chheang, V., Sharmin, S., Marquez-Hernandez, R., Patel, M., Rajasekaran, D., Caulfied, G., . . . Barmaki, R. L. (2024). Towards anatomy education with generative AI-based virtual assistants in immersive virtual reality environments. *arXiv, 2306*(17278), 1-11. /arXiv.2306.17278DOI: 10.1109/AIxVR59861.2024.00011

Chiu, T. K., Falloon, G., Song, Y., & Vincent, W. L. (2024). A self-determination theory approach to teacher digital competence development. *Computers & Education, 214*, 105017. DOI: 10.1016/j.compedu.2024.105017

Constantinescu, G.-G., Silion, D., & Iftene, A. (2024). Using artificial intelligence and mixed realities to create educational applications of the future. *Procedia Computer Science, 246*, 3313–3332. DOI: 10.1016/j.procs.2024.09.308

Dai, C.-P., Ke, F., Pan, Y., & Liu, Y. (2023). Exploring students' learning support use in digital-game-based math learning: A mixed-methods approach using machine learning and multi-case study. *Computers & Education, 194*, 104698. DOI: 10.1016/j.compedu.2022.104698

Dai, C.-P., Ke, F., Zhang, N., Barrett, A., West, L., Bhowmik, S., & Yuan, X. (2024). Designing conversational agents to support student teacher learning in virtual reality simulation: A case study. *In Proceedings of the CHI Conference on Human Factors in Computing Systems* (pp. 1-8). Honolulu, USA: ACM. DOI: 10.1145/3613905.3637145

Dang, T., Liu, C., & Peng, M. (2023). Low-latency mobile virtual reality content delivery for unmanned aerial vehicle-enabled wireless networks with energy constraints. *IEEE Transactions on Vehicular Technology, 72*(2), 2189–2201. DOI: 10.1109/TVT.2022.3212868

Doroudian, S. (2025). Collaboration in immersive environments: challenges and solutions. *arXiv, 2311*(00689), 1-25. doi:/arXiv.2311.00689DOI: 10.48550

Duong, N. T., Thi, T. D., & Pham, V. K. (2025). A comparative study on AI-based learning behaviors: Evidence from Vietnam. *International Journal of Human-Computer Interaction, 41*(16), 10007–10023. DOI: 10.1080/10447318.2024.2430433

Dyulicheva, Y. Y., & Glazieva, A. O. (2021). Game based learning with artificial intelligence and immersive technologies: an overview. *In Proceedings of the 4th Workshop for Young Scientists in Computer Science & Software Engineering* (pp. 146-159). Kryvyi, Rih, Ukraine: CEUR Workshop Proceedings. Retrieved from chrome-extension://efaidnbmnnnibpcajpcglclefindmkaj/https://ceur-ws.org/Vol-3077/paper05.pdf

Fatima, A., Shaheen, A., Ahmed, S., Fazal, B., Ahmad, F., Liew, T. W., & Ahmed, Z. (2024). Exploring the use of gamification in human-centered agile-based requirements engineering. *Frontiers of Computer Science, 6*, 1–16. DOI: 10.3389/fcomp.2024.1442081

Fink, M. C., Robinson, S. A., & Ertl, B. (2024). AI-based avatars are changing the way we learn and teach: Benefits and challenges. *Frontiers in Education, 9*, 1–8. DOI: 10.3389/feduc.2024.1416307

Galitsky, B., Chernyavskiy, A., & Ilvovsky, D. (2024). Truth-o-Meter: Handling multiple inconsistent source repairing LLM hallucinations. *In Proceedings of the 47th International ACM SIGIR Conference on Research and Development in Information Retrieval* (pp. 2817-2821). Washington DC, USA: ACM. DOI: 10.1145/3626772.3657679

Garrido, G. M., Nair, V., & Song, D. (2024). SoK: Data privacy in virtual reality. *arXiv, 1*, 21-40. doi:/arXiv.2301.05940DOI: 10.48550

Hawkinson, E. (2025). Convergence of AR, VR and AI: The rise of immersive learning technologies in higher education. *Extended Reality, AI, and Discursive Formations, 21*, 21–34. DOI: 10.1145/3371647.3371667

Ho, K. H., Hou, Y., Chu, C. C., Chan, C. K., Pan, H., & Chan, T. T. (2023). Work in progress: An AI-assisted metaverse for computer science education. *In Proceedings of the 2023 IEEE World Engineering Education Conference* (pp. 12-15). Bogota, Colombia: IEEE. DOI: 10.1109/EDUNINE57531.2023.10102819

Hu, S., Huang, T., Liu, G., Kompelia, R. R., Ilham, F., Tekin, S. F., . . . Liu, L. (2025). A survey on large language model-based game agents. *arXiv*. doi:/arXiv.2404.02039DOI: 10.48550

Huang, L., & Wang, Y. (2023). From engagement to immersion: A self-determination theory and approach to gamified cultural tourism. *Emerging Technologies and Future of Work, 117*, 277–288. DOI: 10.54941/ahfe1004428

Hwang, G. J., & Chang, C. C. (2024). A self-determination theory-based digital gaming approach to enhancing EFL learners' competence in applying professional English. *Educational Technology Research and Development, 73*(2), 1205–1223. DOI: 10.1007/s11423-024-10445-y

Illi, C., & Elhassouny, A. (2025). Edu-Metaverse: A comprehensive review of virtual learning environments. *IEEE Access : Practical Innovations, Open Solutions, 13*, 30186–30210. DOI: 10.1109/ACCESS.2025.3540944

Jaaska, E., Lehtinen, J., Kujala, J., & Kauppila, O. (2022). Game-based learning and students' motivation in project management education. *Project Leadership and Society, 3*, 100055. DOI: 10.1016/j.plas.2022.100055

Jagatheesaperumal, S. K., Ahmad, K., Al-Fuqaha, A., & Qadir, J. (2024). Advancing education through extended reality and internet of everything enabled metaverse: Applications, challenges, and open issues. *IEEE Transactions on Learning Technologies, 17*, 1120–1139. DOI: 10.1109/TLT.2024.3358859

Jang, Y., Choi, S., Jung, H., & Kim, H. (2022). Practical early prediction of students' performance using machine learning and eXplainable AI. *Education and Information Technologies, 34*(9), 274–300. DOI: 10.1007/s10639-022-11120-6

Jeong, Y., Lee, Y., Bryun, G., & Moon, J. (2024). Navigating the creation of immersive learning environments in Roblox: Integrating generative AI for enhanced simulation-based learning. *In Proceedings of the 10th International Conference of the Immersive Learning Research Network* (pp. 1-4). Glasgow, United Kingdom: iLRN. DOI: 10.56198/5M1RHT9ZJ

Khan, B. F., & Ahmed, S. (2025). An agile approach for collaborative inquiry-based learning in ubiquitous environment. *International Journal of Advanced Computer Science and Applications*, *16*(1), 323–333. DOI: 10.14569/IJACSA.2025.0160132

Khosrawi-Rad, B., Grogorick, L., Janson, A., Keller, P., Benner, D., & Robra-Bissantz, S. (2025). Let's play with AI! A 2x2 experiment on collaborative vs. competitive game elements for pedagogical conversational agents. In *Proceedings of the SIGSVC Pre-ICIS Workshop 2024. 4* (pp. 1–14). ACM., Retrieved from https://aisel.aisnet.org/sprouts_proceedings_sigsvc_2024/4/

Kyrlitsias, C., & Michael-Grigoriou, D. (2022). Social interaction with agents and avatars in immersive virtual environments: A survey. *Frontiers in Virtual Reality*, *2*, 1–13. DOI: 10.3389/frvir.2021.786665

Laine, T., & Lindberg, R. (2020). Designing engaging games for education: A systematic literature review on game motivators and design principles. *IEEE Transactions on Learning Technologies*, *13*(4), 804–821. DOI: 10.1109/TLT.2020.3018503

Lampropoulos, G. (2025). Combining artificial intelligence with augmented reality and virtual reality in education: Current trends and future perspectives. *Multimodal Technologies and Interaction*, *9*(11), 1–28. DOI: 10.3390/mti9020011

Lee, I.-J. (2021). Kinect-for-windows with augmented reality in an interactive roleplay system for children with an autism spectrum disorder. *Interactive Learning Environments*, *29*(4), 688–704. DOI: 10.1080/10494820.2019.1710851

Li, J., Zheng, Z., Chai, Y., Li, X., & Wei, X. (2023). FaceMe: An agent-based social game using augmented reality for the emotional development of children with autism spectrum disorder. *International Journal of Human-Computer Studies*, *175*, 103032. DOI: 10.1016/j.ijhcs.2023.103032

Lin, H., Wan, S., Gan, W., Chen, J., & Chao, H.-C. (2022). Metaverse in Education: Vision, opportunities and challenges. *Computer Science*, *14951*, 1–10. DOI: 10.1109/BigData55660.2022.10021004

Liu, Y., Yue, K., & Liu, Y. (2024). Behavioral analysis in immersive learning environments: A systematic literature review and research agenda. *arXiv*, 1-29. doi:/arXiv.2405.03442DOI: 10.48550

Luarn, P., Chen, C.-C., & Chiu, Y.-P. (2023). Enhancing intrinsic learning motivation through gamification: A self-determination theory perspective. *International Journal of Informaton and Learning Technology*, *40*(5), 413–424. DOI: 10.1108/IJILT-07-2022-0145

Milgram, P., & Kishino, F. (1994). A taxonomy of mixed reality visual displays. *IEICE Transactions on Information and Systems*, *E77-D*(12), 1321–1329. 10.1.1.102.4646

Ng, D. T., Xinyu, C., Leung, J. K., & Chu, S. K. (2024). Fostering students' AI literacy development through educational games: AI knowledge, affective and cognitive engagement. *Journal of Computer Assisted Learning*, *40*(5), 2049–2064. DOI: 10.1111/jcal.13009

Nguyen, A., Gul, F., Dang, B., Huynh, L., & Tuunanen, T. (2025). Designing embodied generative artificial intelligence in mixed reality for active learning in higher education. *Innovations in Education and Teaching International*, *62*(5), 1632–1647. DOI: 10.1080/14703297.2025.2499177

Nowak, K. L., Fox, J., & Fox, J. (2018). Avatars and computer-mediated communication: A review of the definition, uses and effects of digital representations on communication. *6*, 30-53. Retrieved from https://nbn-resolving.org/urn:nbn:de:0168-ssoar-55777-7

Oguguo, B. C., David, N. A., Uwake, S. I., Omeke, F. C., Ugorji, C. O., Ngwu, A. N., & Okebanama, C. I. (2023). Influence of internet of things cybersecurity (IoTCS) on educational assessment practices in university learning spaces in Nigeria. *Journal of E-Learning and Knowledge Society*, *20*(2), 55–66. DOI: 10.20368/1971-8829/1135973

Oguguo, B. E., & Ocheni, C. A. (2023). Cybersecurity: a tool for curbing examination breaches and improvement of quality of large-scale educational assessments. *Information Security Journal: A Global Perspective, 33*(2), 1-15. DOI: 10.1080/19393555.2023.2284761

Ozkaya, S., Berrezueta-Guzman, S., & Wagner, S. (2025). How LLMs are shaping the future of virtual reality. *Computer Science*, 1-18. doi:/arXiv.2508.00737DOI: 10.48550

Perez, J., Castro, M., & Lopez, G. (2023). Serious games and AI: Challenges and opportunities for computational social science. *IEEE Access : Practical Innovations, Open Solutions*, *11*, 62051–62061. DOI: 10.1109/ACCESS.2023.3286695

Rapaka, A., Dharmadhikari, S. C., Kasat, K., Mohan, C. R., Chouhan, K., & Gupta, M. (2025). Revolutionizing learning - A journey into educational games with immersive and AI technologies. *Entertainment Computing*, *52*, 1–8. DOI: 10.1016/j.entcom.2024.100809

Rokhsaritalemi, S., Niaraki, A. S., & Choi, S. M. (2021). A review on mixed reality: Current trends, challenges and prospects. *Applied Sciences (Basel, Switzerland)*, *10*(2), 636–662. DOI: 10.3390/app10020636

Ryan, R. M., & Deci, E. L. (2020). Intrinsic and extrinsic motivation from a self-determination theory perspective: Definitions, theory, practices, and future directions. *Contemporary Educational Psychology*, *61*, 101860. DOI: 10.1016/j.cedpsych.2020.101860

Sanchez, D. R., Langer, M., & Kaur, R. (2020). Gamification in the classroom: Examining the impact of gamified quizzes on student learning. *Computers & Education*, *144*, 1036–1066. DOI: 10.1016/j.compedu.2019.103666

Schneider, D., Biener, V., Otte, A., Gesslein, T., Gagel, P., Campos, C., & Grubert, J. (2021). Accuracy evaluation of touch tasks in commodity virtual and augmented reality head-mounted displays. *In Proceedings of the 2021 ACM Symposium on Spatial User Interaction* (pp. 3485279-3485283). New York, USA: ACM. DOI: 10.1145/3485279.3485283

Simons, A., Wohlgenannt, I., Zelt, S., Weinmann, M., Schneider, J., & Brocke, J. V. (2023). Intelligence at play: Game-based assessment using virtual-reality application. *Virtual Reality (Waltham Cross)*, *27*(3), 1827–1843. DOI: 10.1007/s10055-023-00752-9

Song, Y., Wu, K., & Ding, J. (2024). Developing an immersive game-based learning platform with generative artificial intelligence and virtual reality technologies - "LearningverseVR". *Computers & Education: X Reality, 4*, 1-7. DOI: 10.1016/j.cexr.2024.100069

Sulistiyono, M., Hasyim, J. W., Bernadhed, B., Liantoni, F., & Sidauruk, A. (2024). Comparative study of marker-based and markerless tracking in augmented reality under variable environmental conditions. *Journal of Soft Computing Exploration*, *5*(4), 413–422. DOI: 10.52465/joscex.v5i4.503

Sun, J., Gan, W., Chao, H.-C., Yu, P. S., & Ding, W. (2023). Internet of Behaviors: A survey. *IEEE Internet of Things Journal*, *10*(13), 11117–11134. DOI: 10.1109/JIOT.2023.3247594

Tao, Y., Zhang, G., Zhang, D., Wang, F., Zhou, Y., & Xu, T. (2022). Exploring persona characteristics in learning: A review study of pedagogical agents. *Procedia Computer Science*, *201*, 87–94. DOI: 10.1016/j.procs.2022.03.014

Waghale, A., Potdukhe, N., & Rewarkar, R. (2024). AI in gaming: From simple algorithms to complex agents. *In Proceedings of the 2nd DMIHER International Conference on Artificial Intelligence in Healthcare, Education and Industry* (pp. 1-5). Wardha, India: IEEE. DOI: 10.1109/IDICAIEI61867.2024.10842756

Wang, J., Tang, Y., Hare, R., & Wang, F.-Y. (2024). Parallel intelligent education with chatgpt. *Frontiers of Information Technology & Electronic Engineering*, *25*(1), 12–18. DOI: 10.1631/FITEE.2300166

Wang, S., Huang, S., Chien, Y., Ren, D., Li, H., Gao, Z., & Shidujaman, M. (2025). Enhancing student engagement through AI-driven embodied pedagogical agents: A comparative study informed by self-determination theory. In Kurosu, M., & Hashizume, A. (Eds.), Lecture Notes in Computer Science: Vol. 15769. *Human-Computer Interaction HCII 2025*. Springer., DOI: 10.1007/978-3-031-93861-0_13

Xu, X., Wang, Y., Xu, C., Ding, Z., Jiang, J., Ding, Z., & Karlsson, B. F. (2024). A survey on game playing agents and large models: methods, applications and challenges. *arXiv, 2403*(10249), 1-13. doi:/arXiv.2403.10249DOI: 10.48550

Xu, Z., Yu, C., Fang, F., Wang, Y., & Wu, Y. (2023). Language agents with reinforcement learning for strategic play in the Werewolf game. *arXiv, 2310*(18940), 1-31. doi:/arXiv.2310.18940DOI: 10.48550

Yang, D., Kleinman, E., & Harteveld, C. (2024). GPT for games: An updated scoping review (2020-2024). *arXiv, 2411*(00308), 1-16. doi:/arXiv.2411.00308DOI: 10.48550

Yannier, N., Hudson, S. E., Chang, H., & Koedinger, K. R. (2024). AI adaptivity in a mixed-reality system improves learning. *International Journal of Artificial Intelligence in Education*, *34*(4), 1541–1558. DOI: 10.1007/s40593-023-00388-5

Yenduri, G., Kaluri, R., Rajput, D. S., Lakshmanna, K., Gadekallu, T. R., Mahmud, M., & Brown, D. J. (2023). From assistive technology to metaverse - technologies in inclusive higher education for students with specific learning difficulties: A review. *IEEE Access : Practical Innovations, Open Solutions*, *11*, 64907–64927. DOI: 10.1109/ACCESS.2023.3289496

Zahedi, M. H., Farahani, E., & Peymani, K. (2023). A virtual e-Learning environment model based on metaverse. *In Proceedings of the 10th International and the 16th National Conference on E-Learning and E-Teaching*, (pp. 1-7). Tehran, Iran. DOI: 10.1109/ICeLeT58996.2023.10139894

Zhang, Q. (2023). Secure preschool education using machine learning and metaverse technologies. *Applied Artificial Intelligence*, *37*(1), 1–25. DOI: 10.1080/08839514.2023.2222496

Zhu, C., Hsia, S.-K., Hu, X., Liu, Z., Shi, J., & Ramani, K. (2025). agentAR: Creating augmented reality applications with tool-augmented LLM-based autonomous agents. *In Proceedings of the ACM Symposium on User Interface Software and Technology* (pp. 1-23). Busan, South Korea: ACM. DOI: 10.1145/3746059.3747676

Zumbach, J., Rammerstorfer, L., & Deibl, I. (2020). Cognitive and metacognitive support in learning with a serious game about demographic change. *Computers in Human Behavior, 103*, 120–129. DOI: 10.1016/j.chb.2019.09.026

Chapter 12
AI for Accessible and Inclusive Education

Muhammad Virga Mulia
http://orcid.org/0009-0003-5626-163X
Universitas Esa Unggul, Indonesia

ABSTRACT

This chapter explores how Artificial Intelligence (AI) agents can transform education by advancing accessibility and inclusion for diverse learners. Moving beyond personalization, AI is positioned as a tool to remove systemic barriers and create equitable learning opportunities for students with disabilities, multilingual learners, and those in under-resourced contexts. The chapter examines how AI technologies—such as adaptive learning systems, intelligent tutoring agents, and assistive interfaces—can support individualized learning pathways aligned with Universal Design for Learning (UDL) principles. It also addresses ethical challenges, emphasizing data equity, bias prevention, and responsible AI design. Through theoretical synthesis and case-based analysis, the chapter provides actionable frameworks and design guidelines for educators, policymakers, and developers. Ultimately, it argues that inclusive AI design is essential to achieving the broader vision of independent, equitable, and human-centered learning for all.

1. INTRODUCTION

Artificial intelligence has rapidly emerged as a transformative force shaping contemporary society, influencing not only economic systems, healthcare, transportation, and communication but also fundamentally redefining how people access, interpret, and create knowledge. In the context of education, AI introduces both opportunities and challenges, demanding that learners acquire new literacies to understand, interact with, and critically evaluate AI-driven systems. Traditional literacy, historically centered on the ability to read and write text, is no longer sufficient for preparing learners to navigate a technology-mediated world. Instead, modern literacy education encompasses multidimensional competencies that integrate digital, data, computational, and ethical skills. Within this evolving landscape, AI literacy has emerged as a vital dimension, equipping learners with the knowledge, skills, and attitudes required to engage responsibly, effectively, and critically with AI technologies (Altay & Gilardi, 2024).

The need for AI literacy stems from the increasing ubiquity of AI in everyday life. AI systems now mediate information consumption through recommendation algorithms on social media, influence

DOI: 10.4018/979-8-3373-7225-9.ch012

decision-making in professional settings through predictive analytics, and assist in knowledge creation via automated content generation tools. Learners who lack a foundational understanding of these systems risk being passive consumers of information, potentially vulnerable to bias, misinformation, or unfair algorithmic outcomes. AI literacy therefore extends beyond technical understanding; it includes the ability to interpret AI outputs, recognize underlying assumptions, evaluate fairness and accuracy, and reflect on the ethical implications of AI deployment. Developing such literacy empowers learners to participate meaningfully and responsibly in a society increasingly mediated by intelligent systems (Altay & Gilardi, 2024).

Education systems worldwide are increasingly recognizing the necessity of integrating AI literacy into contemporary literacy education. Traditional literacy approaches, which primarily emphasize reading, writing, and comprehension, must evolve to include digital competence, computational thinking, and critical engagement with technology. Digital literacy equips learners with the skills to navigate online environments, utilize digital tools effectively, and protect personal information. Computational thinking fosters the ability to decompose complex problems, recognize patterns, and apply algorithmic reasoning, which are essential for understanding AI processes. Critical literacy encourages learners to analyze the social, cultural, and ethical dimensions of AI-mediated information. By combining these competencies, AI literacy ensures that learners are not only capable of interacting with intelligent systems but also of questioning, evaluating, and shaping their applications in socially responsible ways (Al-Zahrani, 2024).

Game-based learning represents a particularly promising approach for developing AI literacy. Games provide interactive, immersive, and engaging environments where learners can explore complex concepts in a meaningful and low-risk context. Educational games can simulate AI behavior, illustrate algorithmic processes, and create opportunities for experimentation, iteration, and reflection. Through gameplay, learners can manipulate virtual agents, test hypotheses, observe system responses, and draw conclusions about cause-and-effect relationships. This experiential engagement promotes curiosity, problem solving, and critical thinking, while also accommodating diverse learning styles, including visual, kinesthetic, and collaborative learners. Games thus function as a powerful tool to bridge abstract AI concepts with tangible, learner-centered experiences.

Equity and inclusion are also critical considerations in AI literacy education. The rapid integration of AI into social, economic, and educational systems has the potential to widen existing disparities if certain learners are excluded from opportunities to develop AI-related competencies. Learners from marginalized communities, those with limited access to technology, or students with diverse linguistic and cultural backgrounds may face significant barriers. Embedding AI literacy into literacy education, particularly through accessible and inclusive methods such as game-based learning, ensures that all learners have opportunities to acquire essential skills. It also promotes the development of socially aware learners who can critically evaluate AI systems and advocate for fairness, accountability, and equity in technological applications.

The integration of AI literacy also aligns with global educational frameworks and twenty-first century competencies. International organizations, including UNESCO, OECD, and the World Economic Forum, emphasize the importance of digital competence, problem solving, creativity, ethical reasoning, and collaborative skills in preparing learners for a rapidly changing world. AI literacy contributes directly to these competencies, enabling learners to engage critically with AI-driven systems, participate in digital knowledge creation, and make informed decisions in complex sociotechnical environments (Altay & Gilardi, 2024).

In summary, AI literacy represents an essential component of contemporary literacy education, equipping learners with the knowledge, skills, and dispositions necessary to navigate an AI-infused society. By combining technical understanding with ethical reflection, critical evaluation, and experiential learning opportunities such as game-based approaches, educators can prepare learners to participate actively, responsibly, and innovatively in the digital world. This chapter establishes the foundation for understanding the significance of AI literacy in modern education, highlighting the intersections between literacy, technology, and pedagogy. Subsequent chapters will explore theoretical frameworks, AI literacy competencies, pedagogical strategies, and practical implementations that support the integration of AI literacy into classroom practice, particularly through innovative game-based methodologies (Miao et al., 2024).

3. CONTEMPORARY LITERACY EDUCATION

Contemporary literacy education reflects the ongoing transformation of how individuals access, interpret, create, and communicate information in a rapidly evolving digital world. The traditional view of literacy, which centered primarily on reading and writing printed text, is no longer sufficient to support meaningful participation in modern societies. Advances in digital technology, ubiquitous internet connectivity, and the rise of intelligent systems have expanded the concept of literacy into a multidimensional framework that includes digital literacy, information literacy, media literacy, data literacy, and computational thinking. This expanded definition acknowledges that learners must navigate diverse forms of communication, multimodal content, and algorithmic processes that influence nearly every aspect of daily life (Shamszare & Choudhury, 2023).

One of the defining features of contemporary literacy education is its emphasis on multimodality. Information is increasingly presented through combinations of text, images, video, audio, animation, and interactive media. Learners must understand how meaning is constructed across multiple modes and how these modes interact to shape interpretation. Multimodal literacy therefore requires the ability to critically analyze different forms of representation and to create content that leverages multiple media formats. This skill is essential for engaging with digital platforms such as social media, online learning systems, and collaborative digital tools that rely heavily on multimodal communication.

Another important component of contemporary literacy is digital and data literacy. Digital literacy involves the ability to use digital tools, navigate online environments, and troubleshoot digital systems. Data literacy extends these competencies by enabling learners to understand how data is generated, structured, analyzed, and applied in decision making. As digital systems increasingly rely on data driven processes, individuals must be able to interpret visualizations, detect misleading information, and assess the reliability of data sources. These competencies are especially critical in an era where artificial intelligence systems shape recommendations, automate tasks, and influence public discourse (Shamszare & Choudhury, 2023).

Contemporary literacy education also places significant emphasis on ethical awareness. Learners must understand issues related to privacy, digital rights, cyberbullying, misinformation, and the broader societal implications of emerging technologies. The ethical dimension of literacy ensures that individuals are not only capable users of technology but also responsible participants who can make informed judgments about digital interactions. This focus on ethical literacy becomes increasingly important as artificial intelligence systems mediate communication, shape social relationships, and influence public opinion (Samuel et al., 2023).

Given these developments, contemporary literacy education requires transformative changes in teaching and learning practices. Educators must integrate digital tools, multimodal content, and active learning strategies into their instruction. They must encourage critical thinking about technology and provide opportunities for learners to explore digital systems firsthand. Schools and institutions must also update curricula to reflect the evolving nature of literacy and provide professional development that equips educators with the skills needed to teach effectively in technologically rich environments.

In summary, contemporary literacy education recognizes that modern learners engage with information in ways that extend far beyond printed text. It embraces a broad range of skills that enable individuals to understand, evaluate, and create meaning using diverse digital and multimodal resources. As artificial intelligence becomes increasingly embedded in these environments, contemporary literacy provides the foundation for understanding and interacting with AI driven systems. This foundation is essential for preparing learners to become informed, adaptive, and empowered participants in a complex digital world (Samuel et al., 2023).

3. AI LITERACY CONCEPTS AND COMPETENCIES

Artificial intelligence literacy has emerged as a central competency for learners in the twenty first century as intelligent systems increasingly influence communication, decision making, creativity, and knowledge production. Artificial intelligence literacy refers to the ability to understand, use, evaluate, and interact with artificial intelligence systems in informed and responsible ways. It encompasses cognitive, technical, and ethical dimensions that enable individuals to navigate environments shaped by algorithms, automation, and data driven processes. As such, artificial intelligence literacy is not solely about mastering advanced computational skills but about developing a foundational understanding that allows learners to engage critically with artificial intelligence in their daily lives (Wijaya et al., 2024).

A second key concept is the recognition that artificial intelligence systems depend heavily on data. Learners must understand how datasets influence the performance of artificial intelligence models and how biases in data can lead to biased outcomes. This requires an appreciation of data quality, data representativeness, and the role of human judgment in selecting and labeling data. Understanding the relationship between data and artificial intelligence performance supports learners in evaluating the reliability and fairness of artificial intelligence systems (Wijaya et al., 2024).

A third important concept is the acknowledgment that artificial intelligence systems do not think, reason, or understand in the same way humans do. Learners must recognize that artificial intelligence operates through mathematical patterns and statistical correlations rather than through human like cognition. This understanding helps prevent common misconceptions such as anthropomorphizing artificial intelligence or assuming that artificial intelligence systems possess human intentions or emotions. By clarifying how artificial intelligence operates, learners can develop more realistic expectations regarding its capabilities and limitations.

Beyond conceptual understanding, artificial intelligence literacy requires the development of specific competencies that support effective engagement with artificial intelligence systems. One of the primary competencies is the ability to interact with artificial intelligence tools in productive and informed ways. This includes using artificial intelligence powered applications, evaluating their outputs, adjusting inputs to refine results, and identifying situations where artificial intelligence tools may or may not be appropriate. Interaction competence ensures that learners can use artificial intelligence not only as consumers but also as active participants who understand how their actions influence system outcomes.

The ability to create or modify simple artificial intelligence models is another valuable competency within artificial intelligence literacy. While not all learners need to become artificial intelligence developers, creating basic models through accessible platforms allows them to understand artificial intelligence processes more concretely. Hands on experiences such as training image classifiers, designing simple chatbots, or experimenting with rule based systems can deepen understanding and demystify artificial intelligence technologies (Odri & Ji Yun Yoon, 2023).

Ethical awareness is a further essential competency. Learners must understand the societal impacts of artificial intelligence, including concerns related to privacy, surveillance, discrimination, and transparency. Ethical competence encourages learners to reflect on how artificial intelligence systems are deployed, who benefits from them, and who may be disadvantaged. It also supports the development of responsible attitudes toward technology use and fosters a sense of digital citizenship.

Artificial intelligence literacy also plays a crucial role in contemporary education, where students must navigate complex information ecosystems and adapt to rapidly changing technological landscapes. When learners possess strong artificial intelligence literacy skills, they are better equipped to evaluate digital content, engage with intelligent systems, and contribute to collaborative problem solving. These competencies support not only academic success but also personal and professional development in a world where artificial intelligence influences nearly every domain of human activity (Odri & Ji Yun Yoon, 2023).

In summary, artificial intelligence literacy encompasses a broad set of concepts and competencies that prepare learners to understand, interact with, evaluate, and create artificial intelligence systems. It reflects a multidisciplinary perspective that incorporates technical knowledge, critical reasoning, and ethical awareness. By developing these competencies, learners become more capable of navigating artificial intelligence driven environments and participating meaningfully in a society shaped by intelligent technologies.

4. PEDAGOGICAL APPROACHES TO BUILDING AI LITERACY

Developing artificial intelligence literacy requires pedagogical approaches that are intentional, research informed, and sensitive to the varied needs of contemporary learners. Artificial intelligence concepts involve technical, cognitive, and ethical dimensions that can be challenging for students without proper instructional support. As a result, educators must adopt strategies that make artificial intelligence meaningful, approachable, and connected to real life contexts. Effective pedagogy for artificial intelligence literacy recognizes the complexity of artificial intelligence systems and aims to cultivate understanding through active learning, conceptual scaffolding, multimodal representation, and critical reflection. This chapter expands the pedagogical landscape by presenting a broad view of the instructional approaches that can support learners in developing comprehensive artificial intelligence literacy competencies (Bernstein et al., 2023).

Inquiry based learning represents another essential pedagogical approach. Inspired by scientific inquiry, this method encourages students to ask questions, investigate patterns, test hypotheses, and draw conclusions from evidence. Artificial intelligence inquiry might involve exploring why models misclassify certain objects, how biased datasets influence predictions, or how changes to model parameters affect accuracy. These activities help learners develop critical reasoning and problem solving skills that transfer beyond artificial intelligence into broader academic and real world contexts. Inquiry based instruction also positions learners as active participants in knowledge creation, fostering a sense of agency and intellectual ownership over the learning process.

Project based learning supports artificial intelligence literacy by enabling learners to engage with artificial intelligence concepts over extended periods and within real life scenarios. Through collaborative projects, learners design solutions, create artifacts, and reflect on their findings. Example projects include developing a chatbot that supports language learning, designing a simple recommendation engine, analyzing social media sentiment, or investigating environmental data using artificial intelligence assisted tools. Project based learning fosters creativity, communication, teamwork, and interdisciplinary integration by requiring students to apply knowledge from multiple fields such as mathematics, science, humanities, and the arts. This approach reinforces the idea that artificial intelligence is not isolated within computer science but permeates diverse domains of knowledge and human activity (Bernstein et al., 2023).

Game based learning expands the pedagogical toolkit by offering immersive, interactive, and highly engaging environments for exploring artificial intelligence concepts. Games can simulate artificial intelligence agents that learn from player actions, solve puzzles, or adapt strategies based on data patterns. These environments enable learners to observe artificial intelligence behavior in real time, test hypotheses, and explore consequences within a low risk, motivating context. Game based learning is particularly effective for younger learners and individuals who benefit from experiential, exploratory, and challenge driven activities. It also supports emotional engagement, sustained attention, and resilience, factors that significantly influence learning success.

Cross curricular integration expands artificial intelligence literacy by embedding artificial intelligence concepts across academic subjects. In language arts, learners might analyze how artificial intelligence influences communication and media representation. In social studies, students examine the role of artificial intelligence in shaping democracy, public policy, and labor markets. In mathematics, learners explore statistical reasoning, probability, data visualization, and functions that support artificial intelligence algorithms. In science, students investigate patterns in natural phenomena using artificial intelligence assisted tools. Cross curricular approaches demonstrate that artificial intelligence literacy is relevant across disciplines and contributes to learners' ability to apply artificial intelligence knowledge in diverse situations (Yue & Li, 2023).

Educators themselves play a central role in artificial intelligence literacy development, which highlights the importance of teacher professional development. Teachers require support to understand artificial intelligence concepts, integrate artificial intelligence activities into curricula, and facilitate discussions about ethics and social impact. Professional development programs that focus on hands on experimentation, collaborative problem solving, and interdisciplinary curriculum design can empower teachers to navigate artificial intelligence with confidence. Access to high quality instructional resources and peer learning communities further helps educators incorporate artificial intelligence meaningfully into their instruction.

In summary, pedagogical approaches to building artificial intelligence literacy must be multifaceted, inclusive, and grounded in active learning. Effective artificial intelligence pedagogy integrates experiential exploration, inquiry based investigation, project based collaboration, multimodal representation, game based engagement, ethical reflection, cross curricular integration, and robust teacher professional development. These approaches help learners develop a holistic understanding of artificial intelligence that encompasses the technical, cognitive, and ethical skills required to navigate an artificial intelligence mediated world. Through these strategies, educators can cultivate learners who are informed, reflective, creative, and socially responsible participants in an era shaped by intelligent systems.

5. GAME-BASED LEARNING AS A CATALYST FOR AI LITERACY

Game-based learning has emerged as one of the most effective pedagogical approaches for developing artificial intelligence literacy. By providing interactive, immersive, and engaging environments, games allow learners to explore complex AI concepts through experimentation, iteration, and reflection. This chapter explores the theoretical foundations, pedagogical principles, and practical applications of game-based learning as a catalyst for AI literacy. It is divided into several sections, each highlighting specific mechanisms through which games support learning (Sommer et al., 2024).

5.1 Theoretical Foundations of Game-Based Learning

Game-based learning draws on multiple educational theories that provide a strong rationale for its effectiveness in fostering AI literacy. Constructivist learning theory emphasizes that knowledge is not passively absorbed but actively constructed by the learner. In the context of AI literacy, games allow students to interact with virtual AI systems and make sense of algorithmic behaviors, patterns, and decision-making processes. Learners engage in tasks where they adjust parameters, analyze outcomes, and develop a personal understanding of how AI models respond to different inputs. This active construction of knowledge aligns with the principle that learners build meaning from experience, experimentation, and reflection.

Motivation theories, such as self-determination theory, further explain the benefits of game-based learning. When games provide learners with autonomy in decision-making, the opportunity to experience competence through achievable challenges, and opportunities for social interaction, motivation and engagement increase significantly. In AI literacy education, games satisfy these needs by offering tasks that can be explored at multiple difficulty levels, providing immediate feedback on decisions, and encouraging collaboration or competition in social learning contexts. This combination of theoretical foundations underscores why game-based learning is particularly effective for introducing complex AI concepts to learners of diverse backgrounds and abilities (Sarwari et al., 2024).

5.2 Active Learning Through Games

Active learning is central to developing AI literacy because it requires learners to engage directly with interactive systems rather than passively receiving information. Game-based learning provides immersive experiences in which learners manipulate AI models, explore datasets, and experiment with algorithmic parameters. For example, a game might simulate a virtual environment where learners train a machine learning agent to recognize objects, make predictions, or adapt strategies over time. Players observe the immediate impact of their decisions, reflect on unexpected outcomes, and revise their strategies accordingly.

In addition, games promote active cognitive engagement by requiring players to think critically and analytically. Learners must interpret AI outputs, evaluate whether the results align with expectations, and consider the influence of underlying data or algorithms. This process helps students develop higher-order thinking skills, including analysis, evaluation, and synthesis. By engaging in repeated cycles of experimentation and reflection, learners gain a deeper understanding of how AI systems operate and how human input shapes outcomes, which is foundational to AI literacy (Olawade et al., 2025).

5.3 Scaffolding and Progressive Complexity

Games can be designed to provide structured learning experiences that gradually increase in complexity, supporting learners as they develop AI literacy skills. At the beginner level, learners may interact with simple AI agents that perform basic tasks such as sorting objects, identifying patterns, or following rule-based instructions. These initial tasks introduce foundational concepts, build confidence, and allow learners to experiment with cause-and-effect relationships without becoming overwhelmed.

At the intermediate level, learners are exposed to more complex scenarios where they must manipulate datasets, adjust algorithm parameters, or troubleshoot AI models to achieve specific goals. This level encourages learners to apply conceptual knowledge in problem-solving situations, reinforcing computational thinking, analytical skills, and the ability to evaluate system performance (Newman-Griffis, 2025).

At the advanced level, learners confront real-world inspired challenges that integrate ethical considerations, resource management, and complex decision-making. For instance, a game may simulate a city planning scenario where AI agents influence transportation, energy consumption, or public services. Learners must consider trade-offs, ethical implications, and algorithmic fairness while optimizing system outcomes. This scaffolded approach ensures that learners build competence gradually, aligning with Vygotsky's zone of proximal development, and fosters confidence in applying AI knowledge in increasingly complex contexts.

5.4 Engagement and Motivation

One of the most distinctive advantages of game-based learning is its ability to enhance learner engagement and intrinsic motivation. Games use elements such as goals, feedback, challenges, and storytelling to sustain attention and encourage active participation. In AI literacy education, games can transform abstract or intimidating concepts into interactive experiences that spark curiosity and drive exploration.

Immediate feedback mechanisms in games allow learners to see the consequences of their actions in real time. For instance, when training an AI model in a game environment, players receive instant results based on their choices, which encourages reflection and iterative improvement. Rewards such as points, badges, or level progression reinforce effort and achievement, motivating learners to persist through challenging tasks. Storytelling and narrative elements contextualize AI challenges in meaningful scenarios, making complex concepts more relatable and demonstrating their relevance to real-world situations. Together, these elements create a highly motivating and immersive learning environment that supports the development of AI literacy (Yue & Li, 2023).

5.5 Ethical Reflection and Critical Thinking

Game-based learning provides a unique platform for integrating ethical reflection and critical thinking into AI literacy education. Games can present learners with scenarios that illustrate the social and ethical consequences of AI decisions, such as algorithmic bias, privacy violations, or unintended societal impacts.

Through gameplay, learners can explore questions such as: How does biased training data affect AI decision-making? What responsibilities do AI developers have to ensure fairness? How should AI systems be deployed in sensitive contexts like healthcare or education? These scenarios encourage learners to critically evaluate AI systems, reflect on moral and societal implications, and make informed choices. By embedding ethical reflection within interactive and engaging gameplay, students develop not only technical skills but also responsible attitudes and ethical awareness, which are essential components of AI literacy (Yelne et al., 2023).

5.6 Collaborative and Social Learning

Many educational games include collaborative or multiplayer elements, which foster social learning and teamwork. Learners can work together to solve AI-related problems, share strategies, and discuss outcomes. For example, a game may require students to collectively train AI agents to complete complex tasks or negotiate ethical trade-offs.

Collaboration encourages learners to articulate their reasoning, compare perspectives, and build shared understanding. Peer interaction also supports meta-cognitive skills, as learners reflect on both individual and group decision-making processes. Additionally, social learning provides opportunities for learners to discuss ethical and societal implications of AI applications, reinforcing interdisciplinary thinking and promoting socially responsible engagement with technology (Odri & Ji Yun Yoon, 2023).

5.7 Differentiation and Accessibility

Game-based learning is particularly effective for accommodating diverse learners. Games can provide multiple pathways for success, including adjustable difficulty levels, adaptive feedback, and multimodal content that addresses different learning preferences.

For instance, visual learners benefit from interactive simulations and data visualizations, kinesthetic learners engage through manipulation of virtual AI agents, and analytical learners thrive in strategic problem-solving tasks. Games can also include accessibility features such as adjustable fonts, audio narration, multilingual support, and simplified controls to ensure inclusivity. By accommodating varied needs, game-based learning ensures that AI literacy development is accessible to learners with diverse abilities, backgrounds, and prior experiencesa (Huang et al., 2024).

5.8 Real-World Examples of AI-Focused Games

There are several practical examples of games designed to enhance AI literacy:

1. **Machine Learning Simulations**: Learners train virtual agents to perform classification or prediction tasks, observing how different datasets and model parameters affect performance.

2. **Algorithmic Strategy Games**: Games illustrate AI decision-making processes, such as reinforcement learning agents adapting strategies based on player input.
3. **Ethical Dilemma Games**: Players navigate scenarios in which AI decisions affect virtual communities, allowing learners to explore bias, fairness, and social consequences.

These examples demonstrate how games can integrate technical, ethical, and reflective dimensions of AI literacy in interactive, engaging, and educationally meaningful ways.

5.9 Implications for Curriculum Design

Integrating game-based learning into AI literacy instruction requires careful planning and alignment with educational objectives. Games should complement rather than replace traditional instruction, including lectures, discussions, and hands-on activities. Key considerations include:

- **Alignment with Learning Goals**: Games must map directly to AI literacy competencies, such as understanding algorithms, evaluating bias, and reflecting on ethical implications.
- **Assessment Strategies**: Learners' progress can be evaluated using performance metrics, reflective journals, group discussions, and project-based assessments.
- **Integration with Pedagogy**: Games should be part of a blended learning strategy, offering both structured guidance and opportunities for exploration.

When thoughtfully integrated, game-based learning supports active, ethical, and collaborative AI literacy development, providing learners with meaningful and transferable skills for navigating AI-mediated environments (Huo et al., 2023).

6. INTEGRATING AI LITERACY AND GAME-BASED LEARNING IN CLASSROOM PRACTICE

The integration of AI literacy into classroom practice requires a deliberate and structured approach that combines pedagogical planning, curriculum design, and innovative instructional strategies. Game-based learning, when aligned with AI literacy objectives, provides an engaging and experiential platform for students to interact with AI concepts while developing critical, ethical, and computational thinking skills. This chapter explores strategies, practical steps, and illustrative classroom applications to facilitate the effective integration of AI literacy through game-based learning.

6.1 Aligning Learning Objectives with AI Literacy Competencies

The integration of AI literacy into classroom practice begins with the careful alignment of learning objectives with clearly defined competencies. It is essential for educators to establish what learners should be able to understand, analyze, and perform by the end of instruction. AI literacy encompasses several interrelated dimensions, including technical understanding, critical evaluation, ethical awareness, computational thinking, and collaborative digital communication. In the technical domain, learners should grasp foundational AI concepts such as supervised and unsupervised learning, neural network structures, pattern recognition, and the basic mechanisms of algorithmic decision-making. They should also be able to interact with AI tools, manipulate datasets, and observe the outcomes of algorithmic adjustments.

Critical evaluation is another cornerstone of AI literacy. Learners need to develop the ability to critically analyze AI outputs, identify potential errors or biases, and understand the limitations of AI systems. This involves fostering higher-order thinking skills, encouraging students to question the data sources, the assumptions behind AI models, and the societal consequences of automated decisions. Ethical awareness further extends this analysis, guiding learners to consider questions of fairness, privacy, accountability, and equity in AI deployment. Finally, computational thinking and problem-solving skills enable students to break down complex tasks, recognize patterns, and apply logical and algorithmic reasoning. Collaborative digital communication ensures that learners can effectively discuss AI-related challenges, share insights, and work together to explore solutions. By mapping these competencies to explicit learning objectives, educators ensure that the subsequent game-based activities are purpose-driven, targeted, and pedagogically coherent (Almagharbeh et al., 2025).

6.2 Designing Game-Based Activities for AI Literacy

Designing games that effectively support AI literacy requires thoughtful consideration of instructional goals, learner engagement, and pedagogical scaffolding. The design should begin by identifying the specific AI concepts and skills to be addressed in the classroom. For example, a game can simulate a machine learning environment where students train virtual agents to perform tasks such as object recognition or decision-making under uncertain conditions. These activities allow learners to experience first-hand the dynamics of data-driven systems and the consequences of design choices.

Games should be structured to gradually increase in complexity, allowing learners to develop confidence and competence before encountering more challenging scenarios. Initial levels can introduce fundamental concepts through guided activities, such as training an AI agent with small datasets, while later stages can involve tasks requiring ethical decision-making, optimization of AI models, or collaborative problem-solving among teams. Feedback mechanisms embedded in the games play a crucial role in reinforcing learning. Immediate, meaningful feedback helps learners understand the cause-and-effect relationship between their actions and AI outcomes, encourages reflection, and motivates iterative experimentation. Additionally, ethical dilemmas integrated within gameplay such as deciding how an AI system impacts fairness in resource distribution promote critical thinking and moral reasoning, ensuring that students consider not only technical solutions but also social consequences (Almagharbeh et al., 2025).

6.3 Implementing Game-Based AI Literacy in the Classroom

Implementation of game-based AI literacy activities involves a combination of careful planning, structured guidance, and reflective practice. The process begins with an introduction that contextualizes AI concepts within the broader curriculum and clarifies the learning objectives. Teachers provide foundational knowledge on algorithms, data processing, and ethical considerations, creating a conceptual framework for the game-based activities.

During gameplay, learners engage in structured exploration, observing AI agent behavior, testing hypotheses, and experimenting with data and algorithmic parameters. Teachers facilitate this process by prompting students with guiding questions, encouraging predictions about outcomes, and supporting problem-solving strategies. Reflection and debriefing follow gameplay, where learners discuss insights, ethical implications, and observed patterns. For example, students might reflect on why a trained AI agent failed to generalize correctly or how biased training data influenced decision-making. Extension activities reinforce learning by challenging students to apply AI concepts in novel contexts, such as designing a small AI model to classify data or evaluating the impact of AI systems in real-world scenarios. Assessment strategies, including performance evaluations, collaborative projects, and reflective writing, help monitor learning outcomes and provide feedback for improvement (Aboy et al., 2024).

6.4 Examples of Classroom Game-Based Activities

There are numerous practical approaches to incorporating AI literacy through game-based learning:

1. **AI Training Simulations**: Learners manipulate virtual datasets to train AI agents and observe the effects of data quality, quantity, and bias on model predictions. This hands-on approach demonstrates how AI systems learn from data and highlights the importance of dataset integrity.
2. **Ethical Decision-Making Games**: Students engage in simulated scenarios where AI decisions affect virtual communities, such as selecting candidates for admission or allocating healthcare resources. These activities encourage critical reflection on fairness, bias, and societal impact.
3. **Algorithmic Strategy Games**: Learners face dynamic challenges in which AI agents adapt strategies based on player actions. This type of activity emphasizes computational thinking, iterative problem-solving, and pattern recognition.
4. **Collaborative AI Projects**: Teams of students design or modify AI systems within game environments, presenting their strategies and results to the class while discussing technical, ethical, and social implications.

These examples demonstrate how gameplay can bridge abstract AI concepts with interactive, experiential, and socially meaningful learning experiences.

6.5 Integrating Assessment and Feedback

Effective assessment strategies are essential to ensure that learners acquire AI literacy skills through game-based activities. Assessment should be multidimensional, capturing not only technical proficiency but also critical thinking, ethical reasoning, collaboration, and reflection. Performance-based assessments can evaluate learners' ability to train AI agents, optimize outcomes, and navigate complex scenarios. Reflective journals provide insight into learners' thought processes, documenting decisions, challenges, and ethical considerations encountered during gameplay. Peer assessment encourages collaborative reflection and communication skills, as learners critique strategies and discuss outcomes together. Additionally, rubrics and learning analytics embedded in games can track performance, engagement, and progression over time, offering actionable feedback for both students and instructors (Huang et al., 2024).

6.6 Teacher Roles and Pedagogical Support

Teachers play a central role in facilitating AI literacy through game-based learning. Their responsibilities include scaffolding exploration, providing contextual explanations, and prompting reflective thinking. Teachers guide learners in interpreting AI outputs, understanding algorithmic mechanisms, and analyzing the ethical implications of AI applications. Additionally, they monitor learner engagement, participation, and collaboration, ensuring that all students have equitable access to learning opportunities. Teachers also support technology integration, managing game platforms, AI simulations, and digital tools while troubleshooting technical issues. Effective facilitation ensures that gameplay translates into meaningful learning experiences, rather than remaining purely recreational (Goktas & Grzybowski, 2025).

6.7 Addressing Challenges and Barriers

Several challenges may arise when implementing game-based AI literacy in classrooms:

- **Resource Limitations**: Not all schools have access to sufficient devices, software, or internet connectivity. Solutions include using offline game simulations, shared devices, or open-source platforms.
- **Learner Diversity**: Students vary in prior knowledge, digital fluency, and learning preferences. Adaptive scaffolds, differentiated tasks, and flexible learning paths help meet these needs.
- **Teacher Preparedness**: Educators may require training in both AI concepts and game-based pedagogy. Professional development programs and instructional resources are essential for building capacity.
- **Complex Assessment**: Evaluating AI literacy involves multiple dimensions, including technical skills, ethical reasoning, and collaborative problem-solving. Multi-method assessment strategies, combining qualitative and quantitative measures, are recommended.

By anticipating and addressing these challenges, educators can create equitable and effective AI literacy learning experiences.

6.8 Implications for Curriculum Design

Curriculum design for AI literacy must integrate game-based learning strategically, ensuring that activities are meaningful, scaffolded, and aligned with learning objectives. Key considerations include:

- **Alignment with Standards**: Learning activities should comply with national or international standards for digital competence, computational thinking, and twenty-first century skills.
- **Cross-Disciplinary Integration**: AI literacy can be embedded across subjects such as mathematics, science, social studies, and language arts to provide authentic and contextually meaningful learning experiences.
- **Sustained Engagement**: Curriculum sequencing should gradually increase complexity, allowing learners to deepen understanding over time.
- **Ethical and Social Reflection**: Opportunities for reflection on fairness, accountability, and societal impact must be integrated throughout the curriculum to ensure responsible AI engagement.

Thoughtful curriculum design ensures that AI literacy is not an isolated topic but an integral part of contemporary literacy education (Kar et al., 2024).

7. EVALUATING THE IMPACT OF AI AND GAME-BASED LEARNING ON LITERACY DEVELOPMENT

As AI literacy and game-based learning become increasingly integrated into contemporary literacy education, evaluating their impact is essential to ensure that pedagogical objectives are met and that learners develop meaningful competencies. Assessment in this context extends beyond traditional measures of content knowledge to encompass critical thinking, computational skills, ethical reasoning, collaboration, and engagement with AI systems. This chapter explores frameworks, methodologies, indicators, and practical strategies for evaluating the effectiveness of AI-integrated, game-based literacy instruction (Kiškis, 2023).

7.1 Importance of Evaluation in AI and Game-Based Learning

Evaluation in the context of AI literacy and game-based learning is critical not only for measuring learner progress but also for guiding instructional strategies and informing educational research. As artificial intelligence becomes increasingly integrated into daily life, ensuring that learners acquire meaningful competencies in understanding, analyzing, and ethically engaging with AI is of paramount importance. Evaluation provides a systematic means to assess whether learners are achieving the intended outcomes, including technical understanding, critical thinking, ethical reasoning, and collaborative problem-solving skills. Beyond simply measuring knowledge acquisition, evaluation informs instructional design by highlighting areas where learners may struggle, helping educators adjust scaffolding, instructional materials, and game-based activities. Furthermore, evaluation contributes to research and policy development in education, providing evidence for effective teaching strategies, resource allocation, and curriculum development. By implementing comprehensive evaluation practices, educators can ensure that AI literacy initiatives yield measurable, equitable, and sustainable learning outcomes (Giray, 2024).

7.2 Frameworks for Evaluating AI Literacy

Evaluating AI literacy requires a multidimensional framework that captures the full range of learner competencies, from technical knowledge to social and ethical reasoning.

Bloom's Taxonomy (Revised) provides a hierarchical framework to classify learning outcomes, spanning lower-order thinking skills such as knowledge and comprehension to higher-order cognitive processes such as analysis, evaluation, and creation. For example, learners might be assessed on their ability to explain how a machine learning model classifies data (knowledge/comprehension), analyze errors or biases in AI predictions (analysis), and propose modifications to improve fairness or accuracy (evaluation/creation)(Kar et al., 2024).

The **21st Century Skills Framework** complements this by emphasizing competencies such as critical thinking, creativity, collaboration, communication, and digital literacy. Within game-based learning contexts, students are not only engaging with AI models technically but also negotiating collaborative strategies, discussing ethical implications, and communicating their understanding effectively.

Additionally, **formative and summative assessment models** offer complementary approaches. Formative assessment allows ongoing monitoring of learner progress during gameplay, enabling instructors to provide immediate feedback, address misconceptions, and adjust instructional strategies. Summative assessment evaluates cumulative achievement, typically through performance tasks, reflective essays, presentations, or standardized tests. Combining these frameworks ensures that evaluation captures both the process of learning and the final outcomes, offering a comprehensive picture of learner development in AI literacy (Kar et al., 2024).

7.3 Indicators of Learning Outcomes

Determining the indicators of successful learning is essential for meaningful evaluation. Key indicators in AI and game-based literacy contexts include:

- **Technical Knowledge**: Learners' understanding of AI principles, such as supervised vs. unsupervised learning, neural network structures, algorithmic decision-making, and data preprocessing techniques.
- **Computational Thinking**: The ability to decompose complex problems, identify patterns, develop algorithmic solutions, and apply iterative problem-solving strategies in game-based environments.
- **Critical and Ethical Reasoning**: Learners' capacity to detect biases in AI models, evaluate the fairness and transparency of decisions, and understand the broader societal and ethical implications of AI deployment.
- **Engagement and Motivation**: Observable behaviors such as sustained participation in gameplay, curiosity-driven experimentation, persistence in overcoming challenges, and reflective inquiry.
- **Collaboration and Communication**: Evidence of effective teamwork, knowledge sharing, problem-solving as a group, and the ability to articulate ideas, insights, or ethical considerations to peers and instructors.

These indicators provide measurable benchmarks that can guide the design of assessment tools and inform educators about learners' development across multiple dimensions of AI literacy (Li & Little, 2023).

7.4 Methodologies for Evaluating Learning

Evaluation methodologies must be both rigorous and flexible to capture the diverse competencies involved in AI literacy.

Performance-Based Assessment involves learners completing authentic tasks within game-based simulations, such as training an AI agent, analyzing outcomes, or solving algorithmic challenges. Metrics for assessment may include task accuracy, efficiency of problem-solving, decision-making quality, and the ability to adjust strategies based on observed results.

Reflective Journals and Portfolios provide qualitative insight into learners' thought processes, strategies, and ethical reflections. Students document their reasoning, challenges encountered, and iterative improvements, offering a window into cognitive and affective learning processes that cannot be captured through quantitative metrics alone.

Pre- and Post-Tests measure knowledge acquisition and skill development over time. By administering assessments before and after instructional interventions, educators can quantify growth in technical understanding, computational reasoning, and ethical awareness.

Observation and Teacher Reports complement other methods by providing real-time insights into learner engagement, collaborative behaviors, and problem-solving strategies during gameplay. Teachers can record patterns of participation, strategic thinking, and ethical decision-making to inform formative evaluation.

Surveys and Self-Assessment Instruments enable learners to report perceived competence, motivation, confidence, and attitudes toward AI literacy and ethical reasoning. This subjective data provides context to quantitative measures, highlighting learners' affective engagement and self-perceived growth.

7.5 Case Studies and Action Research

Case studies and action research offer practical, context-specific methods for evaluating AI literacy in classrooms. By documenting instructional design, learner behaviors, game-based activities, and outcomes, educators gain insights into both successes and challenges. For example, an action research study may examine how collaborative AI simulations influence ethical reasoning and decision-making skills over a semester. Findings from these studies enable iterative improvements in curriculum design, game selection, and pedagogical strategies. Case studies also serve as valuable resources for professional development, providing evidence-based examples of effective AI literacy instruction and illustrating how game-based approaches can be adapted to diverse classroom contexts (Goktas & Grzybowski, 2025).

7.6 Challenges in Evaluating Game-Based AI Literacy

Evaluating learning outcomes in AI literacy presents several challenges. First, measuring complex skills such as ethical reasoning, critical thinking, and collaborative problem-solving is inherently difficult because these are often qualitative and context-dependent. Second, learners' prior knowledge, digital literacy, and engagement levels vary, making it challenging to compare outcomes across groups. Third, game-based learning generates diverse data types behavioral logs, in-game decisions, and reflective writings which require careful integration and interpretation to provide meaningful insights. Fourth, educators may lack standardized assessment tools or training in AI literacy, complicating the evaluation process. Addressing these challenges requires multi-method assessment approaches, clear indicators, structured rubrics, and professional development for instructors to ensure valid, reliable, and actionable evaluation results.

7.7 Implications for Curriculum Design and Policy

Evaluation findings have direct implications for both curriculum design and educational policy. Evidence from assessments can guide curriculum developers to better integrate AI literacy and game-based learning, aligning activities with learning objectives and ensuring scaffolding is appropriate for learner readiness. At the policy level, evaluation informs resource allocation, teacher training initiatives, and the inclusion of AI literacy in national and international educational standards. Furthermore, systematic evaluation supports equity by identifying gaps in access, participation, or achievement among diverse learner populations, allowing policymakers and educators to implement targeted interventions that promote inclusivity and fairness (Almagharbeh et al., 2025).

7.8 Future Directions in Evaluation Research

Emerging technologies and educational analytics offer new possibilities for evaluating AI and game-based learning. Learning analytics platforms can capture granular data on learner interactions, decision-making processes, and in-game strategies, providing real-time feedback and actionable insights. AI-driven assessment tools can analyze reflective writings, collaborative discussions, and gameplay metrics to detect patterns of ethical reasoning, critical thinking, and problem-solving. Future research may focus on personalized, adaptive evaluation systems that adjust in real time to learners' performance, ensuring individualized feedback and support. Additionally, longitudinal studies can examine the long-term impact of AI literacy interventions on learners' academic, professional, and social competencies.

8. FUTURE DIRECTIONS AND RECOMMENDATIONS FOR AI AND GAME-BASED LITERACY EDUCATION

As AI technologies continue to evolve rapidly and permeate various aspects of society, the role of AI literacy within contemporary education becomes increasingly critical. Coupled with game-based learning approaches, AI literacy can empower learners with the knowledge, skills, and ethical awareness necessary to navigate complex technological environments. This chapter explores future directions in AI literacy education, anticipates emerging trends, and provides actionable recommendations for educators, curriculum designers, policymakers, and educational researchers seeking to implement AI-integrated, game-based literacy programs effectively (Yu et al., 2023).

8.1 Anticipating Technological Trends and Their Educational Implications

The field of artificial intelligence is evolving at an unprecedented pace, with innovations in machine learning, natural language processing, computer vision, virtual and augmented reality, and adaptive systems transforming both the digital landscape and educational environments. As AI becomes increasingly embedded in daily life from automated decision-making and personalized recommendations to autonomous systems education must proactively adapt to prepare learners for this AI-mediated world.

From a pedagogical perspective, these technological trends provide opportunities to create more personalized and adaptive learning experiences. AI-powered adaptive learning platforms can monitor individual student progress in real time, tailoring instructional content, difficulty levels, and feedback to learners' specific needs. For instance, a student struggling with understanding classification algorithms in a machine learning simulation could be provided with additional scaffolding, hints, or alternative examples, whereas an advanced learner could be challenged with more complex scenarios.

Moreover, immersive technologies such as virtual and augmented reality can simulate real-world contexts where AI is applied, enabling learners to experiment with ethical decision-making, algorithmic reasoning, and collaborative problem-solving in safe, controlled environments. Anticipating these trends is essential to designing curricula that remain relevant, engaging, and aligned with the skills learners will need to navigate AI-driven societies effectively (Si, 2025).

8.2 Expanding AI Literacy Beyond Technical Competence

While foundational technical knowledge such as understanding algorithms, neural networks, and data processing is essential, future AI literacy education must move beyond purely technical competencies. Learners must develop the ability to critically analyze AI systems, assess potential biases, and understand the societal implications of algorithmic decisions.

For example, students should be able to identify cases where an AI system may produce biased outcomes due to skewed training data and propose solutions to mitigate such issues. They should also explore questions related to privacy, transparency, and accountability, such as considering how personal data is collected, stored, and used by AI applications.

Game-based learning provides an effective vehicle for cultivating these multidimensional competencies. Through interactive simulations, learners can experience ethical dilemmas and decision-making scenarios where AI systems impact social, economic, or environmental outcomes. For instance, a simulation could present a scenario in which students must allocate limited resources to different groups using AI predictions, prompting discussion on fairness and societal impact. Integrating these dimensions ensures that AI literacy encompasses technical proficiency, critical reasoning, ethical awareness, and social responsibility.

8.3 Recommendations for Curriculum Development

Designing curricula that effectively integrate AI literacy and game-based learning requires deliberate planning and alignment with broader educational goals. Key recommendations include:

1. **Embedding AI Literacy Across Subjects**: AI concepts should not be isolated but integrated into existing disciplines such as mathematics, science, social studies, and language arts. For example, students can use AI-powered text analysis tools in language arts to explore biases in media, or apply predictive modeling in science projects.
2. **Sequencing Learning Experiences**: Introduce foundational concepts in early grades, progressively increasing complexity to include ethical reasoning, computational thinking, and collaborative problem-solving. This ensures learners build a strong conceptual foundation before engaging in more advanced applications.
3. **Strategic Integration of Game-Based Learning**: Games should be purposefully aligned with learning objectives, providing scaffolding, challenge progression, and opportunities for reflection. Game design must incorporate clear feedback mechanisms, ethical dilemmas, and collaborative problem-solving scenarios to maximize learning outcomes.
4. **Assessment and Feedback Mechanisms**: Multidimensional assessment strategies should measure not only technical proficiency but also ethical reasoning, critical thinking, collaboration, and engagement. Formative and summative feedback supports learners' iterative growth.
5. **Promoting Interdisciplinary Projects**: Collaborative projects that combine AI literacy with creativity, critical analysis, and real-world problem solving encourage authentic learning experiences and enhance the transferability of skills.

By adhering to these recommendations, curriculum developers can create learning experiences that are cohesive, pedagogically sound, and aligned with twenty-first-century competencies.

8.4 Professional Development for Educators

Teachers are central to the successful implementation of AI-integrated, game-based learning. Professional development programs should focus on four main areas:

- **Technical Proficiency**: Educators need to understand AI concepts, algorithms, and relevant software tools to guide students effectively.
- **Pedagogical Strategies**: Teachers must be trained in instructional design for game-based learning, including scaffolding, feedback provision, and facilitating ethical discussions.
- **Assessment Literacy**: Professional development should equip teachers with skills to design, implement, and interpret multidimensional assessments that capture technical, cognitive, ethical, and collaborative competencies.
- **Equity and Inclusion Awareness**: Educators should be prepared to create inclusive learning environments, ensuring that all learners, regardless of background or ability, can engage meaningfully with AI literacy content.

Ongoing professional support, including communities of practice, mentoring, and access to instructional resources, is essential to maintain teacher confidence, competence, and motivation.

8.5 Equity, Inclusion, and Access Considerations

As AI literacy becomes an integral part of education, equitable access is a critical consideration. Inequities in device availability, internet connectivity, prior knowledge, and language proficiency can limit learners' engagement and achievement. Addressing these challenges requires:

- **Technological Equity**: Ensuring all students have access to necessary devices, software, and internet infrastructure.
- **Differentiated Instruction**: Providing multiple pathways for learners of varying ability levels, prior knowledge, and learning styles to engage with content meaningfully.
- **Cultural Relevance**: Designing learning materials and simulations that reflect diverse cultural perspectives and real-world contexts.
- **Support Structures**: Implementing mentoring, tutoring, and scaffolding systems for learners who may face additional barriers to participation.

Equity and inclusion strategies ensure that AI literacy education empowers all learners and fosters socially responsible, technologically capable citizens.

8.6 Research Directions for AI and Game-Based Literacy

Future research should explore both theoretical and practical dimensions of AI literacy and game-based learning. Priority areas include:

1. **Longitudinal Studies**: Tracking learners' development in AI literacy over extended periods to assess retention, skill transfer, and long-term impact.

2. **Effectiveness of Game-Based Learning Designs**: Investigating which game mechanics, narrative structures, feedback systems, and collaborative features most effectively enhance AI literacy competencies.
3. **AI-Enhanced Assessment Tools**: Researching the use of AI to analyze reflective writing, collaborative interactions, and gameplay data to provide personalized, real-time feedback.
4. **Cross-Cultural and Inclusive Research**: Studying how AI literacy programs can be adapted to diverse cultural, linguistic, and socio-economic contexts while promoting equitable outcomes.

These research initiatives will advance both educational theory and classroom practice, ensuring evidence-based, scalable, and inclusive approaches to AI literacy.

8.7 Recommendations for Policy and Practice

Policymakers and administrators are critical in enabling sustainable AI literacy initiatives. Recommendations include:

- **Integration into National and Regional Standards**: Embedding AI literacy competencies including technical knowledge, ethical reasoning, and computational thinking within curriculum standards at all educational levels.
- **Resource Allocation for Technology and Infrastructure**: Funding devices, software platforms, and connectivity to ensure equitable access for all learners.
- **Teacher Training and Professional Development**: Providing continuous professional learning opportunities focused on AI literacy pedagogy, technology integration, and assessment strategies.
- **Collaboration with Industry and Academia**: Developing partnerships with technology companies, research institutions, and universities to provide mentorship, authentic learning experiences, and exposure to real-world AI applications.

Well-designed policies foster systemic support, scalability, and sustainability of AI literacy initiatives, ensuring broad impact.

8.8 Preparing Learners for the Future

AI literacy and game-based learning equip learners with competencies essential for navigating an increasingly AI-driven world. By fostering technical understanding, ethical reasoning, computational thinking, and collaborative problem-solving, learners are empowered to:

- Analyze and critique AI systems critically.
- Engage responsibly with technology in personal, academic, and professional contexts.
- Contribute to socially responsible AI development.
- Adapt to emerging technologies with creativity, flexibility, and ethical awareness.

These competencies enable learners to participate as informed digital citizens capable of making responsible decisions in complex, AI-mediated environments.

9. FUTURE DIRECTIONS IN AI AND GAME-BASED LITERACY EDUCATION

As the integration of artificial intelligence and game-based learning into literacy education continues to evolve, it is essential to anticipate future directions that will shape pedagogy, curriculum, research, and policy. The following sections explore emerging trends, technological innovations, and conceptual shifts that are likely to influence AI literacy education over the next decade.

9.1 Advancing Personalized and Adaptive Learning

One of the most significant future directions in AI and game-based literacy is the development of highly personalized and adaptive learning environments. AI-driven systems can continuously analyze learner interactions, performance data, and engagement patterns to adjust instructional content in real time.

For example, adaptive learning platforms may identify that a learner struggles with understanding algorithmic bias and provide targeted tutorials, interactive simulations, or scaffolded game challenges to address the gap. Conversely, learners demonstrating mastery could be presented with advanced scenarios or creative problem-solving tasks. The ability to personalize learning at scale has the potential to significantly enhance both motivation and achievement, ensuring that every learner receives instruction tailored to their individual needs.

9.2 Integrating Ethical and Societal Reasoning

Future AI literacy education will increasingly emphasize ethical reasoning, social responsibility, and the societal impact of AI systems. Learners will not only study technical concepts but also engage in evaluating real-world AI applications for fairness, transparency, privacy, and accountability.

Game-based simulations can serve as powerful tools for exploring these dimensions. For instance, students might participate in a scenario where they manage an AI-driven public resource allocation system and must balance efficiency with ethical considerations. Such experiences cultivate critical thinking and ethical decision-making, preparing learners to engage with AI in ways that are socially responsible and ethically informed.

9.3 Immersive Technologies and Experiential Learning

Virtual reality (VR), augmented reality (AR), and mixed reality (MR) technologies are poised to transform AI and literacy education by providing immersive, experiential learning opportunities. Learners can explore AI concepts through interactive simulations that replicate real-world scenarios, such as autonomous transportation systems, healthcare diagnostics, or environmental management.

Immersive experiences facilitate higher engagement, experimentation, and reflection. By interacting with AI systems in context-rich environments, learners develop a deeper understanding of cause-and-effect relationships, system behaviors, and ethical considerations. Over time, these technologies will likely become more accessible, scalable, and integrated into standard curricula, enhancing both engagement and learning outcomes.

9.4 Expanding Interdisciplinary Approaches

The future of AI literacy education will increasingly intersect with multiple disciplines, including computer science, mathematics, social sciences, humanities, and the arts. Interdisciplinary approaches foster holistic understanding, allowing learners to see AI not merely as a technical tool but as a phenomenon with social, cultural, and ethical implications.

For example, a project-based curriculum might combine data analysis, algorithm design, storytelling, and ethical debate, enabling students to approach AI literacy from multiple perspectives. Such integration prepares learners for complex real-world problems where AI intersects with human behavior, society, and governance.

9.5 AI-Enhanced Assessment and Learning Analytics

Advances in AI-powered assessment and learning analytics will allow educators to evaluate learners more comprehensively and in real time. Future systems may automatically analyze reflective writing, collaborative interactions, gameplay metrics, and decision-making patterns to identify strengths, misconceptions, or ethical reasoning capacities.

This level of insight enables highly personalized feedback and adaptive scaffolding, ensuring that learners receive timely guidance aligned with their cognitive and affective needs. Additionally, AI-driven analytics will support research on instructional effectiveness, equity, and engagement, providing actionable insights for educators and policymakers.

9.6 Equity, Accessibility, and Global Inclusion

As AI literacy becomes central to contemporary education, ensuring equitable access will remain a major priority. Future initiatives must address disparities in technology availability, socio-economic barriers, linguistic diversity, and differing learning needs.

Emerging directions include designing low-bandwidth or offline-compatible AI learning tools, multilingual platforms, culturally relevant content, and adaptive systems that cater to learners with diverse abilities. Addressing these considerations ensures that AI literacy and game-based learning programs are inclusive, socially responsible, and capable of empowering all learners globally.

9.7 Longitudinal and Lifelong Learning Perspectives

Future AI literacy programs will increasingly recognize the importance of longitudinal learning and lifelong skill development. AI literacy should not be confined to K-12 or higher education contexts; instead, it should encompass continuous skill development across the lifespan, enabling learners to adapt to evolving AI technologies and societal challenges.

This perspective emphasizes scaffolding learning experiences from early foundational concepts to advanced ethical reasoning and real-world problem-solving. Game-based learning platforms can support this continuity by offering modular, adaptive, and progressively complex scenarios that evolve alongside learners' competencies.

9.8 Collaborative and Networked Learning Communities

Future directions will also emphasize collaborative, networked learning experiences, where learners, educators, researchers, and industry partners interact in digital ecosystems. Such communities facilitate knowledge sharing, mentorship, and co-creation of learning experiences.

For instance, students might collaborate across schools or countries in AI simulations, analyzing global datasets, solving international challenges, or debating ethical dilemmas in AI deployment. Networked learning fosters digital citizenship, cross-cultural understanding, and collaborative problem-solving skills critical for navigating complex, interconnected AI-driven environments.

9.9 Preparing Learners for an AI-Mediated Future

Ultimately, the future of AI and game-based literacy education is centered on preparing learners to navigate a rapidly evolving, AI-mediated world responsibly, ethically, and critically. Learners must be equipped not only with technical knowledge but also with the ability to think analytically, collaborate effectively, and make socially responsible decisions in the presence of complex algorithmic systems.

Emerging technologies, adaptive pedagogies, interdisciplinary approaches, and inclusive strategies will collectively enable learners to thrive in this environment. By focusing on these future directions, education can ensure that AI literacy is meaningful, relevant, and transformative, empowering learners to become informed, ethical, and capable participants in society.

REFERENCES

Aboy, M., Minssen, T., & Vayena, E. (2024). Navigating the EU AI Act: Implications for regulated digital medical products. *NPJ Digital Medicine*, *7*(1), 237. DOI: 10.1038/s41746-024-01232-3 PMID: 39242831

Al-Zahrani, A. M. (2024). Unveiling the shadows: Beyond the hype of AI in education. *Heliyon*, *10*(9), e30696. DOI: 10.1016/j.heliyon.2024.e30696 PMID: 38737255

Almagharbeh, W. T., Alfanash, H. A. K., Alnawafleh, K. A., Alasmari, A. A., Alsaraireh, F. A., Dreidi, M. M., & Nashwan, A. J. (2025). Application of artificial intelligence in nursing practice: A qualitative study of Jordanian nurses' perspectives. *BMC Nursing*, *24*(1), 92. DOI: 10.1186/s12912-024-02658-6 PMID: 39863852

Altay, S., & Gilardi, F. (2024). People are skeptical of headlines labeled as AI-generated, even if true or human-made, because they assume full AI automation. *PNAS Nexus*, *3*(10), pgae403. Advance online publication. DOI: 10.1093/pnasnexus/pgae403 PMID: 39359399

Bernstein, M. H., Atalay, M. K., Dibble, E. H., Maxwell, A. W. P., Karam, A. R., Agarwal, S., Ward, R. C., Healey, T. T., & Baird, G. L. (2023). Can incorrect artificial intelligence (AI) results impact radiologists, and if so, what can we do about it? A multi-reader pilot study of lung cancer detection with chest radiography. *European Radiology*, *33*(11), 8263–8269. DOI: 10.1007/s00330-023-09747-1 PMID: 37266657

Giray, L. (2024). AI Shaming: The Silent Stigma among Academic Writers and Researchers. *Annals of Biomedical Engineering*, *52*(9), 2319–2324. DOI: 10.1007/s10439-024-03582-1 PMID: 38977530

Goktas, P., & Grzybowski, A. (2025). Shaping the Future of Healthcare: Ethical Clinical Challenges and Pathways to Trustworthy AI. *Journal of Clinical Medicine*, *14*(5), 1605. DOI: 10.3390/jcm14051605 PMID: 40095575

Huang, S., Lai, X., Ke, L., Li, Y., Wang, H., Zhao, X., Dai, X., & Wang, Y. (2024). AI Technology panic—Is AI Dependence Bad for Mental Health? A Cross-Lagged Panel Model and the Mediating Roles of Motivations for AI Use Among Adolescents. *Psychology Research and Behavior Management*, *17*(0), 1087–1102. DOI: 10.2147/PRBM.S440889 PMID: 38495087

Huo, W., Yuan, X., Li, X., Luo, W., Xie, J., & Shi, B. (2023). Increasing acceptance of medical AI: The role of medical staff participation in AI development. *International Journal of Medical Informatics*, *175*, 105073. DOI: 10.1016/j.ijmedinf.2023.105073 PMID: 37119693

Kar, S. K., Bansal, T., Modi, S., & Singh, A. (2024). How Sensitive Are the Free AI-detector Tools in Detecting AI-generated Texts? A Comparison of Popular AI-detector Tools. *Indian Journal of Psychological Medicine*, *47*(3), 275–278. DOI: 10.1177/02537176241247934 PMID: 39564235

Kiškis, M. (2023). Legal framework for the coexistence of humans and conscious AI. *Frontiers in Artificial Intelligence*, *6*, 1205465. DOI: 10.3389/frai.2023.1205465 PMID: 37808620

Li, M. D., & Little, B. P. (2023). Appropriate Reliance on Artificial Intelligence in Radiology Education. *Journal of the American College of Radiology*, *20*(11), 1126–1130. DOI: 10.1016/j.jacr.2023.04.019 PMID: 37392983

Miao, J., Thongprayoon, C., Suppadungsuk, S., Garcia Valencia, O. A., Qureshi, F., & Cheungpasitporn, W. (2024). Ethical Dilemmas in Using AI for Academic Writing and an Example Framework for Peer Review in Nephrology Academia: A Narrative Review. *Clinics and Practice*, *14*(1), 89–105. DOI: 10.3390/clinpract14010008 PMID: 38248432

Newman-Griffis, D. (2025). AI Thinking: A framework for rethinking artificial intelligence in practice. *Royal Society Open Science*, *12*(1), 241482. DOI: 10.1098/rsos.241482 PMID: 39780964

Odri, G. A., & Ji Yun Yoon, D. (2023). Detecting generative artificial intelligence in scientific articles: Evasion techniques and implications for scientific integrity. *Orthopaedics & Traumatology: Surgery & Research*, *109*(8), 103706. DOI: 10.1016/j.otsr.2023.103706 PMID: 37838021

Olawade, D. B., Weerasinghe, K., Teke, J., Msiska, M., Boussios, S., & Hatzidimitriadou, E. (2025). Evaluating AI adoption in healthcare: Insights from the information governance professionals in the United Kingdom. *International Journal of Medical Informatics*, *199*, 105909. DOI: 10.1016/j.ijmedinf.2025.105909 PMID: 40198930

Samuel, Y., Brennan-Tonetta, M., Samuel, J., Kashyap, R., Kumar, V., Krishna Kaashyap, S., Chidipothu, N., Anand, I., & Jain, P. (2023). Cultivation of human centered artificial intelligence: Culturally adaptive thinking in education (CATE) for AI. *Frontiers in Artificial Intelligence*, *6*, 1198180. DOI: 10.3389/frai.2023.1198180 PMID: 38106981

Sarwari, A. Q., Javed, M. N., Mohd Adnan, H., & Abdul Wahab, M. N. (2024). Assessment of the impacts of artificial intelligence (AI) on intercultural communication among postgraduate students in a multicultural university environment. *Scientific Reports*, *14*(1), 13849. DOI: 10.1038/s41598-024-63276-5 PMID: 38879546

Shamszare, H., & Choudhury, A. (2023). Clinicians' Perceptions of Artificial Intelligence: Focus on Workload, Risk, Trust, Clinical Decision Making, and Clinical Integration. *Healthcare (Basel)*, *11*(16), 2308. DOI: 10.3390/healthcare11162308 PMID: 37628506

Si, J. (2025). Exploring AI literacy, attitudes toward AI, and intentions to use AI in clinical contexts among healthcare students in Korea: A cross-sectional study. *BMC Medical Education*, *25*(1), 1233. DOI: 10.1186/s12909-025-07766-8 PMID: 40885994

Sommer, D., Schmidbauer, L., & Wahl, F. (2024). Nurses' perceptions, experience and knowledge regarding artificial intelligence: Results from a cross-sectional online survey in Germany. *BMC Nursing*, *23*(1), 205. DOI: 10.1186/s12912-024-01884-2 PMID: 38539169

Wijaya, T. T., Yu, Q., Cao, Y., He, Y., & Leung, F. K. S. (2024). Latent Profile Analysis of AI Literacy and Trust in Mathematics Teachers and Their Relations with AI Dependency and 21st-Century Skills. *Behavioral Sciences (Basel, Switzerland)*, *14*(11), 1008. DOI: 10.3390/bs14111008 PMID: 39594308

Yelne, S., Chaudhary, M., Dod, K., Sayyad, A., & Sharma, R. (2023). Harnessing the Power of AI: A Comprehensive Review of Its Impact and Challenges in Nursing Science and Healthcare. *Cureus*, *15*(11), e49252. DOI: 10.7759/cureus.49252 PMID: 38143615

Yu, L., Li, Y., & Fan, F. (2023). Employees' Appraisals and Trust of Artificial Intelligences' Transparency and Opacity. *Behavioral Sciences (Basel, Switzerland), 13*(4), 344. DOI: 10.3390/bs13040344 PMID: 37102857

Yue, B., & Li, H. (2023). The impact of human-AI collaboration types on consumer evaluation and usage intention: A perspective of responsibility attribution. *Frontiers in Psychology, 14*, 1277861. DOI: 10.3389/fpsyg.2023.1277861 PMID: 38022995

Chapter 13
AI For Accessible and Inclusive Education in Developing and Least Developed Countries

Chinna Suresh
http://orcid.org/0000-0002-3389-1116
SASTRA (Deemed to be) University, India

Devaki Varadharajan
http://orcid.org/0000-0002-7109-0205
SASTRA (Deemed to be) University, India

Mahammad Ali Sunkesula
http://orcid.org/0000-0002-5457-4689
AP Model School and Junior College, India

Rajendra Nath Babu Murathoti
http://orcid.org/0000-0001-8904-383X
Nagaland University, India

ABSTRACT

Systemic barriers like inequal access to education, affordability, gender, geography, disability, and language diversity have contributed to the entrenchment of educational inequalities in the developing and least developed countries. Such obstacles deny the marginalised learners the opportunity to participate fully in the education. This chapter explains the role of ethically constructed, low-cost, and context-sensitive artificial intelligence to personalize the learning experience and inclusivity in education by addressing all these overlapping obstacles. Basing its arguments on case studies, empirical research and policy analysis, it states that inclusive AI, when chosen to be implemented with fairness and community engagement, can help to facilitate equitable and accessible education. The chapter recommends collaboration by multiple stakeholders to make AI-based solutions respect the educational justice, inclusivity, and equity of every learner.

DOI: 10.4018/979-8-3373-7225-9.ch013

INTRODUCTION

AI has transformed into a revolutionary technology that has the potential to completely change the process of education, making it affordable and open for everybody. Most education systems across the world face persistent inequalities that hinder complete participation, especially regarding marginalised populations, students with disabilities, and socio-economic and digital divides. Such inequalities, one can identify in urban/rural geographical settings, among male and female pupils, children with special needs (CWSN), and pupils in socio-economically disadvantaged and marginalized groups. Inclusive education is expected to provide the ability to allow all learners and their identity, ability, and background to access high-quality learning in favourable conditions (UNICEF, 2017).

The traditional barriers can be overcome by new opportunities provided by AI technologies. These can be adaptive learning systems and AI-based assistive technologies, real-time translation and smart tutoring systems, and all aimed at personalizing learning, delivering content to individual learner's needs and support diverse learning profiles. Through AI, students with disabilities, girls and women, ethnic minorities, and students in remote or less-fortunate regions can be provided with an enhanced educational experience.

However, the integration of AI in education is not without challenges. The problem of limited infrastructural, the lack of digital literacy, data privacy and the danger of reinforcing the social biases in AI algorithms must be considered carefully (Ifenthaler et al., 2024). In addition, ethical AI implementation needs frameworks that promote fairness, transparency, and respect to learner.. This dualism of access to education has given rise to the fact of the divided classroom where education is not an unconditional right anymore but an exclusive privilege of the rich and well-equipped (GSMA, 2023a; Muralidharan et al., 2019). In a democratic country like India, these differences are not necessarily pedagogical issues, but they also strike at the core of constitutional principles. Article 21A of the Indian Constitution guarantees that children between 6-14 years be provided with free and compulsory education and Article 14 gives equality before law. Institutional injustices that limit quality education consequently do not just go against the constitutional rights but also violate the spirit of democracy (Ministry of Law and Justice, 2023). As UNESCO (2021) states, "education is the foundation of a democratic citizen". Digital privilege to access knowledge stratifies knowledge access, undermines political participation, weakens a culture of deliberation and narrows the democratic vision of justice and inclusion (Tawil & Miao, 2024). Technology therefore must act as equalizer and not a gatekeeper in realizing of democratic educational ideals. It is essential to implement collaborative governance between policymakers, educators, technologists, and affected communities into the direction of social justice and equity instead of narrow technical objectives.

The chapter is about using AI to promote affordable and inclusive education in developing and least developed countries (LDCs). It combines global and local contexts to assess the opportunities of AI personalizing learning, reducing digital gaps, and empowering disadvantaged pupils besides identifying potential risks and challenges. The most important part of this analysis is that the promise of AI can be achieved solely based on fair, ethical, and community-informed approaches that prioritize the rights of learners.

RATIONALE OF THE STUDY

Though the idea of inclusive education is considered as universal human right and means to social equity, in developing and LDCs but still many learns in these countries remain excluded due to systemic barriers. These include unfair distribution of digital infrastructure, failure to support beyond special educational needs and socio-cultural variables that intersecting with caste, gender and economic statu(Yang et al., 2025)s . The COVID-19 pandemic, has made these inequalities even more visible, highlighting poor infrastructure facilities, digital exclusion, and policy matters increase educational deprivation (Kennedy et al., 2022a; UNESCO, 2021) . This stratified reality demonstrates that the accessibility of education has become contingentized by unequal benefits on connectivity, wealth and institutional support as opposed to being a right applicable to all (Antoninis et al., 2020).

AI is a paradigm-shifter and constructive disruptor in modern and social contexts, disruptive of the traditional way of thinking and offering both new opportunities. Its ability in shaping learning experiences to personal capacity, local languages and cultural backgrounds offers to level the educational playing field (Muawanah et al., 2024) . AI-based assistive technologies can expand the access of students with disabilities, whereas learner analytics can reveal those who are at risk so that interventions can promptly occur. However, this pledge should be struck with moral care since a system that was trained on biased information will strengthen caste, gender, and linguistic biases. The research paper is based on the belief that AI can be a true power of accessible and inclusive education in case it is created with a moral obligation to universal rights to learn(Varsik & Vosberg, 2024a) .

The study provides an insight into how inclusive education can be reimagined and enacted, by analysing the opportunities and challenges of AI in the context of the socio-economic and infrastructural environments of developing and LDCs. It highlights the urgent need of multi-stakeholder collaboration to develop AI systems to democratize learning and no learner left behind to enhance the overall aim of socially just and equitable education to all.

LITERATURE REVIEW: KEY THEMES AND SYNTHESIS

Upon the overview of existing literature, identified three important themes that underpin this chapter: (i) The digital divide in developing and LDCs is not a single dimensional problem of infrastructure or access to devices, but a stratified system of inequalities because of gender, caste, geography, language and economic status (Kuhn et al., 2023; Raihan et al., 2025) (ii) AI holds genuine, but conditional potential for educational equity. Adopting AI based learning systems have proven promising for students in poor countries, and their success totally depends on design that suits for local languages, culture and pedagogy (Hariyanto et al., 2025; Muralidharan et al., 2019) (iii) Ethical safeguards are not an optional additions, but it is minimum requirement: without proper attention to algorithmic bias, data safety and threat of substituting human judgement is actively considered (Holmes et al., 2022; Varsik & Vosberg, 2024b). Collectively, these themes support the focus of this chapter of AI as a conditional and ethically based instrument of inclusive education, as opposed to an automatic solution.

It is worthy note that the literature also identifies a persistent gap in empirical evidence from least developed countries, especially in Sub-Saharan Africa and fragile or conflict-affected states. Studies in AI in education are mostly done in middle-income settings, say, India or China, and the applicability of those results to the poorest-resourced settings is under-researched. This chapter attempts to fill in this gap partially, based on the evidence provided in Nigeria, South Africa, and refugee education settings as well as the India case study.

OBJECTIVES AND METHODOLOGY

This chapter aims to:

1. Analyse the scope and characteristics of digital divides in developing and least developed countries, by considering India as case study.
2. Discussing the role of AI in personalising learning, assisting the students with low-resources, and democratising access to education.
3. Comparing AI with other educational innovations such as Open Educational Recourses (OERs).
4. Discussing the ways where AI can be used to address gender-based inequities in education.
5. Recommending strategies for the adoption of AI in education in an inclusive, ethical, and low-cost settings.
6. Role of AI in provide quality educational content.

METHODOLOGY

In this chapter, the author applies mixed-source data analysis as a qualitative secondary analysis that involves (i) global policy documents and reports from organisations like UNESCO, the World Bank, GSMA and UNHCR; (ii) country-specific surveys and national datasets including the Tamil Nadu, COVID Pulse Survey, National Family Health Survey (NFHS-5) and NSSO 75th round and (iii) peer reviewed academic literature about digital disparities and role of AI in education published in between 2019 to 2025. The sources were identified through systematic searches of Google scholar, Scopus, Web of Science and ERIC databases using combination of keyword such as "AI in education developing countries", "digital divide inclusive education". The sources that directly address digital equity, AI-enabled learning, or inclusive education in developing or least developed countries are only included in this study. India is chosen as a case study in greater detail because of its demographic scale, socio-economic diversity, and development of digital infrastructure, which makes it a good example of the problems of numerous developing and least developed countries. Based on empirical evidence on contexts, including the Tamil Nadu COVID Pulse Survey, National Family Health Survey, and national digital inclusion programs, the analysis through the lens of inclusive education to examine the ways AI can facilitate the impact of urban-rural differences, gender exclusion, caste and religious differences, infrastructural barriers, and individual learner needs.

1. SCOPE AND CHARACTERISTICS OF DIGITAL DIVIDE

In this section, we will look at the problem of the digital divide in developing and Least Developed Countries (LDCs), including issues like disparities in ICT infrastructure, access affordability, digital illiteracy, gender disparity, and regional disparity. We will discuss the global pattern initially before examining a case study on India.

Through this analysis, we will get a better idea about the roots of digital exclusion and pave the way for the discussion of strategies in later sections.

1.1 Global Patterns of Digital Exclusion

Figure 1. Scope of the digital divide in developing and least developed countries

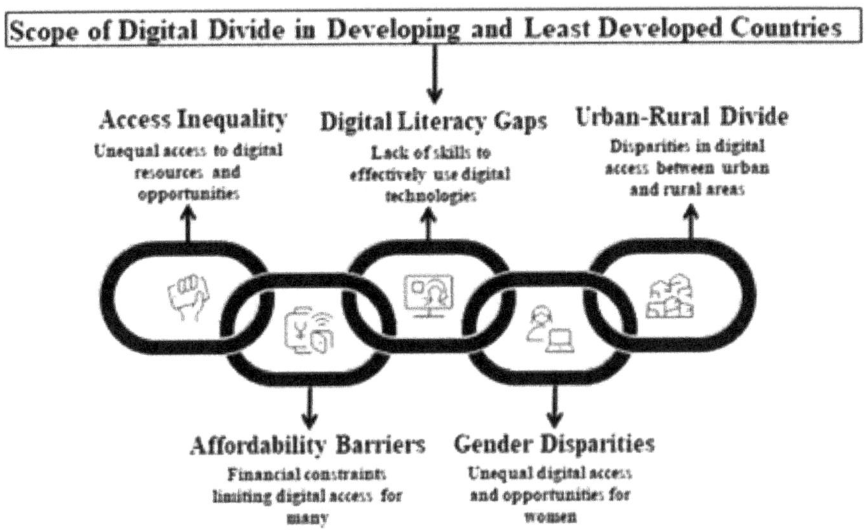

Figure 1 offers a visual summary of the critical access gap across the infrastructure, affordability, Digital literacy Gaps, Gender disparities and geographical divide.

1. Access Inequality in Developing and Least Developed Countries:

In the majority of developing and Least Developed Countries (LDCs), digital infrastructure is not universal. Although the world has greatly advanced in connectivity, even now millions of individuals residing in locations like Sub-Saharan Africa, Southeast Asia and parts of Latin America do not have access to broadband internet, mobile networks and electricity, particularly in rural and remote regions (Kennedy et al., 2022a)

For instance, Nigeria, mobile broadband is also becoming more widespread but the inability to afford digital technologies and access to electricity is an obstacle to progress in rural areas (Fung et al., 2025). In Indonesia, and despite the successful development of urban centres, the rural provinces continue to grapple with low bandwidth and inadequate infrastructure development (Singh, 2017).

Similarly, the example of Bangladesh, the Digital Bangladesh program is already being implemented in the country, but the rural areas still cannot afford digital technologies, and electricity issues remain an issue (Uddin, 2024).

In Sierra Leone, a very small 13% of schools have access to the internet, so most students have to use handouts or radio lessons and so the divide in learning is further increased (GSMA, 2023a). The amount of the digital divide among the Least Developed Countries (LDCs) is even more starker.

For example, in Ethiopia, more than 50% of its population have no access to electricity, and it is practically unfeasible for them to experience access to digital activities in most regions of the nation (United Nations Industrial Development Organization, 2023). In Mozambique and Malawi, cross-border efforts to boost access to the internet are in progress, but affordability and digital literacy remain a major problem in this country (World Bank, 2023a). In countries like Nepal and Haiti, the rugged topography and political instability only worsen the attempt at increasing digital infrastructure (Misra & Srivastava, 2024).

2. Affordability Barriers:

Affordability has always remained one of the most intractable and systemic issues to digital access, especially among low-income groups in developing and least developed countries. High costs of purchasing digital products, such as smartphones, tablets, computers, the presence of recurrent costs due to internet data plans, software subscriptions, and maintenance of equipment, puts a difficult experience on economically disadvantaged people (Rahman et al., 2021).

To a large number of families that live below or close to the poverty line, accessing the internet is a competition to the basic necessities like food, shelter and medical care. In such countries as Mozambique, Nepal, and Bangladesh, a simple smartphone might cost more than a month of earnings of the poorest quintile, and large groups of the population cannot afford mobile data (World Bank, 2023a). The affordability crisis is not limited to the poorest countries of the world. However, it is not only the poorest countries where the affordability problem exists. Affordability gap continues to exist even in middle-income countries such as Kenya, Colombia, the Philippines, and Morocco (Campos & Scherer, 2023). A research article, "*Access to Information and Communication Technology, Digital Skills, and Perceived Well-Being among Older Adults in Hong Kong*", has pointed to the role of affordability and digital illiteracy as obstacles to better access to the digital world by vulnerable populations (Fung et al., 2025).

Also, affordability applies not just to hardware and connectivity but also to the hidden cost such as digital literacy training, up-to-date software and web security measures. Such additional costs widen the digital gap and burden communities of colour, such as women, older people, and minority groups, in disproportionate numbers (Raihan et al., 2025)

3. Digital Literacy Gaps:

Although digital infrastructure is one of the background requirements, the ability to utilize the digital tools and platforms (i.e., digital literacy), which is a major challenge to many in regard to the actual use of the digital world. Many people in the world especially in the developing and marginalised groups do not have the expertise required to navigate, evaluate and develop information among digital technologies (UNHCR, 2023).

The International Telecommunication Union (2023) shares the same opinion, noting that half of the global population possess the basic digital skills, such as using a computer, or sending emails, or installing apps (UNHCR, 2023). This gap is even more severe among the displaced populations, women, the older populations, and ethnic minorities, who often encounter additional challenges due to limited education, language barriers, and socio-cultural traditions (Wedlake et al., 2021)

A "*usage gap*" is even present in the areas where mobile and broadband coverage is accessible. Individuals may have access to the devices and networks but they find it difficult to use them because lack of digital literature or training (GSMA, 2023b). It results in the lack of opportunities in education, employment, healthcare, and civic participation, and the continuation of exclusion and inequality cycles (Hoque, 2020).

4. Gender Disparities in Digital Access:

Although we have come far in terms of the digital connectivity, in the developing and least developed countries, gender-based differences in the access to digital technologies remain a major and extremely profound issue. Women and girls are also less likely to have access to digital devices, internet access, and digital learning and employment opportunities in most areas because of a conglomeration of socio-cultural beliefs, patriarchal beliefs, safety attitudes, financial barriers, Surveillance and reputational risks and limited digital literacy (Rotondi et al., 2025).

As an example, in SubSaharan Africa and Soth Asia, the probability of women using the internet is 22% lower than of men, with 14% owning a mobile phone (Rotondi et al., 2025).-(Rotondi et al., 2025). These inequalities are further increased in rural areas because of the restrictions in the mobility and care needs and consequently restrict the women due to the lack of access to digital services within the community (GSMA, 2023b).

Further, the digital gender divide is not just about the access, but it also encompasses usage habits, digital literacy and representation in technology-related domains. Women tend to be underrepresented in STEM education, online entrepreneurship and content creation. This omission and absence of representation breed a culture of exclusion wherein low participation makes them weaken their agency and power in the development of the digital tool, platform, and the policy (UNESCO, 2023).

Table 1. Data of mobile internet usage by gender in selected low and middle income countries (LMICs) for the year 2022–2023.

Country	Percentage of Men Using Mobile Internet	Percentage of Women Using Mobile Internet	Gender Gap (Percent)	Notable Barriers for Women
India	52%	31%	40%	Affordability, literacy, family disapproval
Pakistan	45%	27%	38%	Device sharing, safety concerns, social norms
Nigeria	56%	34%	38%	Cost, digital skills, No or less access in rural areas
Indonesia	65%	55%	15%	Literacy, affordability, relevance
Mexico	82%	79%	4%	Safety concerns, affordability
Guatemala	69%	59%	14%	illiteracy & Digital Literacy, Device cost, content relevance
Kenya	57%	39%	32%	High data costs, gender norms, low digital skills for using mobile internet

continued on following page

Table 1. Continued

Country	Percentage of Men Using Mobile Internet	Percentage of Women Using Mobile Internet	Gender Gap (Percent)	Notable Barriers for Women
Ethiopia	41%	23%	44%	Infrastructure gaps, affordability, safety issues for female adolescences, teenagers
Philippines	74%	64%	14%	Affordability, rural device access, social expectations
Morocco	66%	48%	27%	Patriarchal norms, digital literacy, device sharing

Source: GSMA (2023a) Mobile Gender Gap Report

The data presented in Table 1 shows persistent gender disparities in mobile internet usage in the chosen Low and Middle-Income Countries (LMICs). The most significant gaps are found in India (40%), Pakistan (38%), Nigeria (38%), and Ethiopia (44%) having the highest disparities. Such disparities are mainly due to socio-cultural norms, concerns about affordability, safety and low digital literacy, which find an unequal representation in women and girls. Conversely, the gender gaps in other countries such as Indonesia, the Philippines, and Guatemala are more moderate with Mexico almost equal to the rest at a 4% in difference, meaning that women have greater access to digital resources. It is interesting to note that some of the factors that limit female access to mobile internet, including family disapproval, sharing of devices, low literacy, security in the internet, and relevancy of content are country to country. This highlights the importance of digitally sensitive, culturally sensitive, and gender-specific digital policies. In order to address this gap, we must be able to implement holistic approaches that go beyond merely offering infrastructure but also consider the structural and gendered nature of digital access, use, and participation so that all people have the opportunity of social-economic mobility and access to education (Kuhn et al., 2023).

5. Urban–Rural Digital Divide:

Digital revolution is not distributed equally. In the majority of the developing nations, the urban areas perform more structured than the rural ones in terms of internet utilization. The *urban-rural digital divide* is influenced by many factors such as differences in investments, higher population density in urban areas and policy focus, that eventually leads to the unequal access in education, health, finance, and jobs(Sindakis & Showkat, 2024).

High-speed broadband, 4G/5G mobile connectivity, and even public Wi-Fi networks are still common in urban areas within countries like Nigeria, Indonesia, and Bangladesh while rural areas in these nations have to rely on outdated or unstable connectivity (World Bank, 2023b) or connectivity that is both unreliable and long-term. Similarly, in Indonesia, the digital divide and the lack of literacy still persist in rural provinces despite national connectivity efforts(Kennedy et al., 2022b) .

This has not only been a technological divide but is socially and economically spilled over. The rural school students tend not to have access to the digital learning environment, and rural entrepreneurs cannot access e-commerce and digital payments, and telemedicine lacks accessibility in rural places because of the low connection and digital illiteracy among providers (Smith et al., 2021).

1.2 Digital Divide in India Context

1. Infrastructure Gaps:

India still along its way experiences extreme infrastructure gaps which still contributes to digital exclusion, particularly in rural and remote regions. Though mobile connectivity and policy implementation are on the rise, but still more than 70% of the population are connected to low or inadequate digital connectivity (Mwansa et al., 2025) . Compounding factors such as the lack of penetration of broadband, frequent power outages, and lack of coverage of mobile networks also limit the rural communities to the sustained interactions with the digital ecosystems. The high-speed broadband networks run by the public sector, such as the National Optical Fibre Network (NOFN) launched in 2011 to serve 250,000 Gram Panchayats (GPs) with high-speed broadband were key to developing the digital spine of India (Malhotra, 2024). This was later improved, and it was renamed as BharatNet in 2015, with expanded scope which also covered last-mile connectivity, Wi-Fi hotspots and affordable connectivity to marginalized village. By 2025, BharatNet has deployed over 6.9 lakh kilometres of optic fibre, as well as 2+ lakh GPs have been put into operation. However, their distribution and effects have been curtailed by implementation delays, last-mile problems, and logistic bottlenecks. These infrastructural bottlenecks, as stressed by Sindakis & Showkat (2024), are not only technical but lie on the demographic, economic, and administrative grounds that vary significantly across states, which is why specially problem-specific connectivity solutions are necessary.

2. Gender Disparities in Digital Access

In spite of the increased digital infrastructure in India, gendered digital exclusion is a well-established problem. Women access to the digital is not only determined by the cost factor, but also, by socio-cultural values, security, and limited digital autonomy. In most rural households, women and girls use or share devices that they use, and in most instances, the use of these devices is mediated by family members of the male gender, the kind of patriarchal gatekeeping that restricts direct use of digital devices (Samudra, 2022). Such disparities are especially sharp in such locations as northern and central India, where the restricted mobility and cultural conservatism make access to community-related digital services even more limited to women.

These barriers serve especially to hinder the participation of females in online learning, which leads to worse education retention, less career path in STEM, and less use of AI-based learning technologies (Vesna et al., 2025). Gender is also an intersection of caste and religious background that only further marginalizes women belonging to Dalit, Adivasi, or Muslim communities, who often experience two types of exclusion, both in online learning platforms and institutions outreach.

No matter how strong the policy interventions like the Beti Bachao Beti Padhao movement and the PMGDISHA (Pradhan Mantri Gramin Digital Saksharta Abhiyan) program are in eliminating the digital gender divide, the work is still uneven and most of the time it fails to impact these more socio-cultural barriers. The table 2 represents comparative indicators of mobile internet access, usage behaviour and educational implications, which underscore the urgency of the gender-sensitised and culture-relevant digital and AI interventions (Kalim et al., 2025)

Table 2. Case study of mobile internet and the gender divide in India.

Aspect	Male	Female
Mobile Internet Usage	52% of men use mobile internet	31% of women use mobile internet
Smartphone Ownership	Higher ownership (48%)	29% ownership (17% gap)
Rural Mobile Internet Access	25% of rural men	Only 17% of rural women
Barriers to Access	Cost, digital skills	Cost, low literacy, family disapproval, social norms, safety
Mobile Internet Use (Once Connected)	High frequency and diverse use	High frequency and diverse use
Educational Implication	Accessible infrastructure exists	Needs AI-driven, mobile-first, voice-based, offline, and safe learning tools tailored for rural girls and women

Source: GSMA (2023a). The Mobile Gender Gap Report

Table 2 reveal that there is a persistent gap between digital access, autonomy, and safety between genders. Despite the growing coverage of infrastructures, many women especially rural women still remain marginalized due to the intersecting barriers depending on the level of literacy, cultural role, and control of devices. Above all, women behave in the same way as men do online, which demonstrates that the difference lies in unequal opportunities, but not ability disparities. This brings about the higher demand of AI-led solutions that are voice-based, offline-capable, and culturally pertinent to the immediate setting, specifically designed to support the inclusion of women and girls in the digital divide via education.

3. Socioeconomic Inequality:

Economic disparity is the main driver of digital access in India. For the 20% poorest households, just 2.7% possess a computer and less than 9% of households have an internet connection, which are further lower in rural and marginalised areas. The Tamil Nadu COVID Pulse Survey (TNCPS) (Department of Economics and Statistics, 2020) captured well the inter-linked vulnerabilities amid the pandemic, observing how reverse migration, income shocks and the dependence on public relief schemes tremendously lowered the ability of families to retain digital connectivity to access education.

Figure 2. The uneven geography of digital learning in India

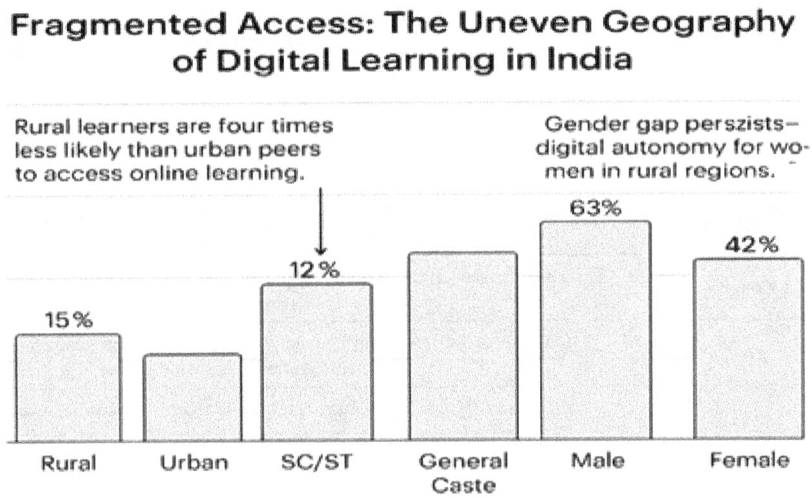

The results of these regions described in Figure 2 are supplemented with national data sets that capture the structural form of digital exclusion. The National Family Health Survey (NFHS-5, 2019-21) (Ministry of Health & Family Welfare, 2019) reported that only 42% of women in India had ever used the internet, as compared to 63% of men. This is the most unusual gap in the digital gender divide in the rural areas where only 32% of women reported to have some exposure to the internet and this illustrates how the geographical factor and gender factor converge to curtail digital usage. At the same time, the National Sample Survey Office (NSSO 75th Round, 201718) (Ministry of Statistics and Programme Implementation, 2018) found out that only 4.4% of rural households owned a computer, and only 14.9% had any form of internet connectivity. These are even lower in cases of Scheduled Castes, Scheduled Tribes and religious minority groups which are already disadvantaged by historic educational disadvantages.

Combined, these trends affirm findings by Hoque (2020) and Raihan et al. (2025) who argue that income, caste, gender and locational disadvantage interact to make digital marginalisation especially youth, women and first-generation learners especially. The resultant effect is digitally stratified society whereby entry to education is becoming less and less about aptitude or ambition but rather a matter of infrastructure, identity and economic strength.

4. Digital Literacy Deficit:

Besides the access to a device and infrastructure, there is the inherent connection between digital and basic literacy and digital literacy. Digital literacy problems in India are complicated and has been contributed by the lack of infrastructures, low costs, pedagogical concerns, social-cultural ideas, and even psychological problems. The lack of localised, multilanguage, and contextualised content and lack of teacher preparedness, thus leading to disparity in accessing effective digital learning in communities. Table 3 summarises the issues above, reinforcing the need for AI-driven adaptive platforms which are inclusive, personalized, and available to the most disadvantaged learners.

Table 3. Challenges of digital literacy in India

Theme	Challenge Description
Structural Barriers	Poor infrastructure facilities, unstable internet connection, and frequent power cuts reduce consistent access.
Economic Barriers	High costs of devices and Mobile Internet data plans (1GB/day or 1.5 GB/day or 2 GB/ day), especially burdensome for low-income households.
Educational Barriers	Widespread illiteracy, lack of trained faculty (No proper emphasis in teacher training or professional development), and limited multilingual content.
Cultural and Social Barriers	Different Gender norms Men & Female, family disapproval, and regional disparities, Safety to women, restrict digital participation.
Technological Challenges	Inadequate device access, slow digital adoption among educators due to resistance, low content relevance.
Psychological Barriers	Information overload, reduced creativity, and risk of over dependency on prepackaged content and losing critical thinking
Cyber Risks	Increased cyberbullying for example trolling in social media, data privacy breaches (personal information, contact numbers), and exposure to unethical practices.
Pedagogical Limitations	Lack of interactivity and personalized support in digital classrooms (Isolation in Digital Platforms)

Source: Adapted from Kaushal, V., Singh, B., & Devi, S. (2023). *Digital Literacy in India: Benefits and Challenges*. COK Journal, 9(1).

It is evident from Table 3 that these barriers in aggregate limit digital engagement as well as the sustainable long-term digital learning of marginalised groups. Even though the programs like Pradhan Mantri Gramin Digital Saksharta Abhiyan (PMGDISHA) have been used to train millions of people digitally (Virender Kaushal et al., 2023) warn that single-off interventions do not generate lasting digital agency. They also promote instruction of literacy through scaffolding that incorporates both functional and critical as well as emotional features especially when the material is linguistically opaque. These instead promote scaffolded literacy teaching that incorporates functional, critical and emotional elements especially when the content is linguistically intractable.

Evidence from Wave 2 of the Tamil Nadu COVID Pulse Survey (TNCPS)(Department of Economics and Statistics, 2020) further emphasizes this fact. Since online learning was quickly implemented during the lockdown, several rural and poor households suffered because of unfamiliarity with digital platforms and low digital confidence. Such gaps resulted in widening the learning gap and it became clear that literacy not only is access but also managing and knowing how to take advantage of the digital tools (Meng et al., 2024).

5. Caste and Religious Disparities

Deep-rooted caste and religion-based inequalities are also the prerequisites of the digital divide in India. The Internet penetration by the Scheduled Tribes (STs), decades of spatial and social marginalization later, remains 27% lower compared to the rest of the population. Similarly, the Muslim households will have the lowest probability of owning a computer followed by the Hindu and Christian houses. Such patterns are not coincidental but indicative of the structural inequalities in access to schooling, income and governmental services. With this consideration, Virender Kaushal et al. (2023) feel that any digital inclusion efforts that will be grounded on the top-down infrastructure roll-out may only end up reinforcing the existing social hierarchies unless they understand the lived experiences of the poor communities

(Kuhn et al., 2023) . They indicate that access to technology is not sufficient, but a community-based approach to assemble local knowledge, participatory design, and culturally sensitive material. Unless it includes inclusive platforms, the emergence of any digital will be an unintended exclusionary move by favouring the ruling caste and religious elites who are already literate and knowledgeable of the language and the various institutions to operate digital platforms (R. Banerjee et al., 2024). The digital divide between caste and religion-marginalised individuals, therefore, requires conscious investments in local infrastructure, multilingual materials and grassroots digital literacy programs that are co-designed by the same communities they are to be directed at .

EDUCATIONAL IMPLICATIONS OF DIGITAL DIVIDE IN DEVELOPING AND LEAST DEVELOPED COUNTRIES, WITH A FOCUS TO INDIA

In most developing and least developed countries (LDCs), the digital divide has become a factor in reproduction of educational disparity. From Southeast Asia to South Asia and Sub-Saharan Africa, educational access is severely constrained by access to digital infrastructure, lack of penetration into the internet, and the lack of affordability, particularly in rural and disadvantaged areas. As an example, in Ethiopia, Malawi, and Mozambique, where people do not have electricity in many places, where continuous digital learning is not feasible. In Nepal and Bangladesh, topographic and infrastructure issues increase cost problems, and millions of learners are no longer accessible to online classrooms (Passey et al., 2024) .

In these instances, the digital divide is not only limited to devices and connectivity, but also reflects other structural inequalities such as poverty, institutional incompetence, and biased policy implementation. The digital literacy was hindered by gender roles, language isolation continued to increase inequalities among girls, ethnic minorities, refugees, and the older generation. Social location, cultural acceptance, and trust in technology determine the depth and quality of digital interaction, as has been stressed by Raihan et al. (2025) access is never sufficient.

India, despite its unique demographic size and rapid technological advancement, has a lot of the endemic digital inclusion challenges as in the rest of the Global South. The country is grappling with fundamental inequalities as much as it has managed to establish itself as a leader in digital policies with initiatives like Digital India, BharatNet and PMGDISHA. Others of these include chronic structural bottlenecks, gender digital exclusion, and limited digital literacy of the rural, tribal, and marginalised populations (Sindakis & Showkat, 2024). The Tamil Nadu COVID Pulse Survey (2020) (Department of Economics and Statistics, 2020) registered the effects of income disruptions, lack of experience with digital tools, and confidence in online platforms as a whole on positive interaction with remote learning in the pandemic. These challenges were replicated recently by Virender Kaushal et al. (2023) and (Sindarius & Showkat, 2024) which highlight that the access to digital media is not the solution. Instead, they insist that the digital learning programs must be grounded on pedagogically valid, linguistically localised, and culturally sensitive designs, a level that is still obviously undone in most national and state-level digital education plans.

The educational implications are strak, the digital divide is becoming a deep learning divide, with digitally networked city centres providing proportionately more access to AI-mediated platforms, responsive materials, and virtual tests to students. Their counterparts in rural and disadvantaged setting, are exposed to interrupted learning trajectory and less academic support (Kuhn et al., 2023).

The increasing fragmentation of the classroom results in learning disadvantages, widening of the skills gap, and constraining social-emotional development; all this contributes to mechanisms of generational disadvantage (Mansour et al., 2024). In order to overcome these intersecting challenges and not to institutionalise the non-inclusion of education, such scaled technologies as Artificial Intelligence (AI), should be researched as the supporting infrastructure rather than the alternative to the creation of more personalised, comprehensive, and context-specific learning environments in the democratic vision of an education to all.

2. EXPLORE THE ROLE AI CAN PLAY IN PERSONALISING LEARNING, SUPPORTING LOW-RESOURCE LEARNERS, AND DEMOCRATISING ACCESS

To elaborate on the role of AI in personalising learning, supporting low-resource learners, and democratising access, as presented in Figure 3, there is a need to focus on three interlinked dimensions: *pedagogical potential*, *contextual fit for low-resource settings*, and *systemic equity implications*.

Figure 3. Venn representation of AI's role in inclusive education

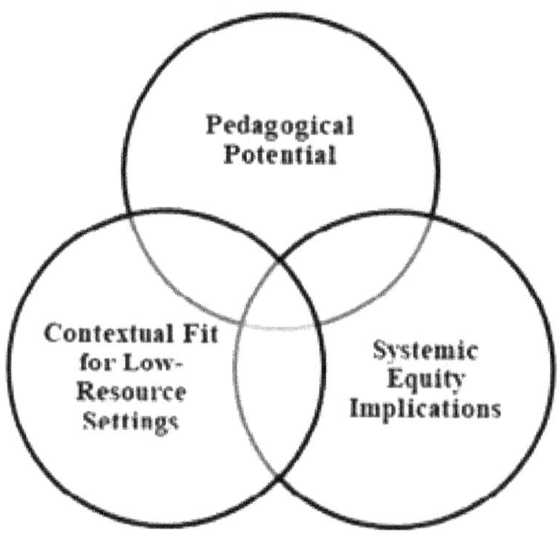

1. Pedagogical Potential:

Artificial Intelligence (AI) is a radical advancement to pedagogy with a conceptual extrapolation of programmed learning into dynamic, adaptive learning systems. Personalised instruction was predetermined by programmed learning that was aimed at systematic delivery of content based on the reaction of learners (Hariyanto et al., 2025). AI continues this practice with continuous assessment of the speed, interests, and challenges of a learner and the order of content material is adjusted dynamically and the teaching course personalised. Such transition to more intelligent, data-driven, personalisation of predetermined-response formats enables the creation of more responsive and student-centered learning environments (Naseer et al., 2024) Unlike programmed instruction, AI systems have feedback, behavioural analysis, and multimodal inputs to change with the learner and, therefore, are appropriate in pluralistic and inclusive learning.

An example of such platforms is "Mindspark" and "Squirrel AI". Mindspark developed by educational initiatives uses a huge bank of questions and diagnostic algorithms to measure student levels of learning and drive personalised content. Implementation in low-income Indian schools showed good improvement in math and language skills, particularly in students with worse background skills (Muralidharan et al., 2019). In the same way, the Squirrel AI in China has demonstrated better outcomes in improving the performance of the students with real-time response and micro-adaptive learning paths (Wang et al., 2023).

Such benefits are still propagated through AI-powered chatbots and voice tutors in students studying outside of a classroom or where their teachers have restricted coverage, offering automated feedback, scaffolding and revisions customized to student's needs (Sein Minn, 2022).

2. Contextual Fit for Low-Resource Settings

To achieve success in settings with low resources, AI must be created keeping infrastructural constraints, linguistic diversity, and socio-cultural conditions in mind. The most common problems that such students face include community access to devices, unreliable or non-existent internet, and lack of formal education or digital literacy (Passey et al., 2024) . These are scenarios that demand technological solutions which must be innovative, yet sensitive to the realities they live with. When it comes to such environments, AI technologies with the offline capabilities, mobile-first design, and multilingual audio-visual content in the limelight are more appropriate(Mwansa et al., 2025) . For example, cell phones with edge-computing models can offer real-time personalization in without needing a permanent internet connection and so can be used by rural and remote students.

Additionally, the language scenario in most low-resource areas is marked by code-mixed languages, (i.e., mixture of local languages and leading languages) that are usually not properly comprehended by classical AI systems. This gap is already being filled by other newer paradigms, such as CHAI (Zhang et al., 2024) and In-Context Mixing (ICM) (Shankar et al., 2024) which learn to comprehend and interact with code-mixed text, thus making it more pertinent and convincing. Similarly, Cultural alignment is necessary. To establish the authentic engagement, AI programs should reflect local knowledge frames, pedagogical norms, and local values. Convenience, comfort, and ease of adoption are the factors that demonstrate the overwhelming propensity of students in the rural areas of India to mobile learning, as (Sindakis & Showkat, 2024) note.

3. Systemic Equity Implications:

The application and design of AI should be grounded in the concepts of *transparency, justice*, and *inclusion* to make it a democratic learning. These are ideals, but actual needs in the situations where the right to an education is defined by profound social stratifications. Algorithms have the ability to reproduce and amplify already-existing biases based on gender, castes, language, and geography unless they are controlled (Varsik & Vosberg, 2024a) . For example, the learning of predictive models based on urban-biased datasets will distort the performance of students in rural areas and the language models will concentrate on majority languages will discriminate against students of linguistically heterogeneous backgrounds (Nguyen et al., 2023). The example of equity-based open source platforms such as "Kolibri" and "Akshar" shows that when a limited set of constraints is employed, it can be more effective to maximize the access in underserved areas without being hampered by the burdens of prohibitive licensing costs or proprietary challenges. Learning Equality created Kolibri, an offline-first learning application that assists users in accessing high-quality learning content in settings that are low-connectivity.

It supports over 173 languages and enables educators to customize the material to their local curricula, to use in refugee camps, rural schools and informal learning environments (Learning Equality, 2021) .Akshar is a learning institution based in Assam, India, which applies experiential learning, vocational training, and environmental care into its pedagogy. Learners pay "plastic school fees", tutor younger peers, and engage in community service, which makes sense and complies with the philosophy of "*Nai Talim*" by Gandhi and the National Education Policy (NEP2020) in India 2020 (Akshar Foundation, 2023) .The model by Akshar has minimized the dropout rates and child labour and facilitated sustainability and inclusion.

Notably, the success of these platforms depends on the participatory deployment. The involvement of teachers, parents and the local institutions will ensure that it is not AI that is pushed down the throats of communities but rather one that is a collective creation with the communities. This brings about trust, situational conformity and sustainability (Ifenthaler et al., 2024) . The key to this process is ethical guidelines: protecting learner information, making guaranteeing explainability of algorithmic suggestions, are the key to the development of responsible and inclusive systems (UNESCO, 2021).

3. ARTIFICIAL INTELLIGENCE FOR EDUCATIONAL EQUITY

Artificial Intelligence (AI) promises a lot in terms of reducing education inequities by providing individualised, adaptable and inclusive studying paths, especially for the excluded by conventional education systems. This selection discusses how AI-driven technologies are beginning to overcome divides that existed long before with personalised teaching, language-based interfaces, cheap offline features, and intelligent tutoring.

Figure 4. AI-powered technologies for educational equity in India and beyond

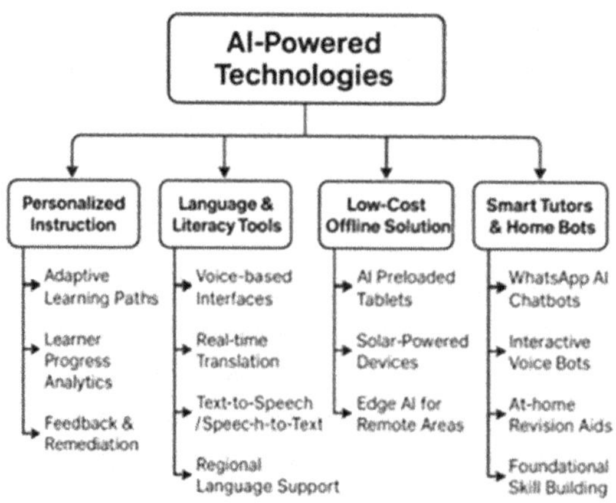

Figure 4 shows AI-based applications such as Mindspark, Kolibri, Read Along, and WhatsApp bots that serve to facilitate equity in education by providing adaptive, voice-based, and offline products to low-literate and rural learners.

1. **Personalised Learning Pathways:** Continuing on the pedagogical backgrounds described above, the most radical implementation of AI is the possibility to operationalise personalised learning in a real-life classroom. In India and similar situations where classrooms are overcrowded and resources are scarce, applications like "Mindspark' have demonstrated scalable means of adapting instruction to individual learning levels, identify wrong perceptions and improve concept learning. These models assist students that would not otherwise have access to high-quality tutoring and implement real-time analytics and adaptive algorithms depending on their pace and progress. Unlike conventional teaching, where the curriculum is adhered to, AI-based systems make real-time modifications, taking into account the knowledge deficiencies of individual learners and their learning processes. An Indian-made product called "Mindspark" uses data-driven algorithms to customise questions and feedback for every learner. It builds a personalised learning journey, improving concept comprehension and correcting misconceptions immediately by continuously analysing student responses (Muralidharan et al., 2019). These systems reduce reliance on small tutoring potential but provide inclusive and scalable education. Indeed, this full potential can only be realized if AI systems promote learner agency and independent thinking too (UNESCO, 2021).
2. **Language-Translation and Voice Interfaces for Low-Literacy Learners:** Multilingual voice assistants, real-time translation, and low-text interfaces can help GenAI platforms to overcome language and literacy barriers. One of the tools that are worth highlighting, is a voice-based reading tutor mobile application (i.e., "Read Along by Google") that helps children learn to read with the help of an AI reading assistant called "Diya", is an application that provides instant feedback, rewards in the form of stars and badges, and supports over 110 languages, such as Hindi, Tamil, and Urdu (Ramasamy et al., 2025) and so on. Released in India as "Bolo", "Read Along" has been successful in certain high-low connectivity regions by working offline and promoting children to learn independently, since the parents of many of them lack significant literacy. These characteristics can be applied to gain confidence and privacy, and promote inclusive literacy development (GSMA, 2023a). These resources operate in accordance with the promotion of linguistic and cultural pluralism promoted by UNESCO where developers are urged to incorporate vernacular contents and dodge excessive encoding of the norms of colonial or majority language. It implies that AI resources should be checked in terms of channels in such a way that they do not marginalise the minority voices or silence the local dialects. The teachers must involve the learners in critical reflection by requesting them to resist, dig, and recreate meanings borrowed under various linguistic traditions.
3. **Offline and Low-Cost AI Systems:** Another important need to ensure that AI is fairly deployed is offline operations and affordability. Students with low-income and remote students tend to lack or have limited access to the internet or high-end devices. Other products like Kolibri, which have been redesigned in India by Tata Trusts, are AI-powered learning dashboards that are already installed in cheap devices or solar-powered tablets with offline functionality in rural areas (TATA Trusts, 2023) . Similarly, AI-based applications that do not need much bandwidth usage such as voice bots through WhatsApp, are gaining momentum in states like Jharkhand and Uttar Pradesh, especially among students who have limited access to well-established school systems (Virender Kaushal et al., 2023). Equity demands the AI technologies to operate outside the interconnected cities. The requirement

of reaching last-mile learners is the offline functionality and affordability. GenAI is compatible with this UNESCO inclusion agenda, including Kolibri (TATA Trusts, 2023). Such technologies will require to be taught by the inclusive design practices to reach the needs and constraints of the marginalised learners and to make the most impact. UNESCO proposes models of deployment that are locally suitable and reflect local situations, are less damaging to the environment, and which adopt pedagogical equity as opposed to commercialisation. The use of GenAI systems, especially running on offline or low-cost mediums, requires that the system has context-sensitive testing to ensure that the instructional models are both running and operational but also culturally aware, readable in language, and ethically acceptable (UNESCO, 2021)

4. **Smart Tutors and Bots for Home-Based Learning** Artificial intelligence tutors and chatbots can assist home-based self-study and revision where girls may be denied access to physical schools due to protection, movement, or culture, AI software on mobile phones provide subtle and unobtrusive ways. Bots built into WhatsApp to support foundational literacy(Pratham, 2025) allow learning with a sequence-controlled lesson plan to use natural language and emojis, which makes the experience more engaging and reduces stigma (A. Banerjee et al., 2020). Such platforms can even recreate the cognitive reaction of a tutor though it may not be perfect even though it is scalable and affordable. However, despite the high potential of such tools, they should be carefully integrated. UNESCO's framework cautions the world from trusting GenAI to an extent that it becomes a replacement for human judgment. The teachers must not be pushed aside, AI contributions need to be filtered, assessing student responses, and learning process made more personal. Moreover, deepfakes, fake news, and ethical malpractice surveillance are also essential prior to scaling up such technologies (UNESCO, 2021) . **Spotlight: Low-Cost AI-Powered Learning in Developing Contexts** AI systems do not have to be costly and complicated to be effective. Increasingly, more affordable or open source AI projects are now being developed in developing contexts: • In Nigeria, basic education in off-grid refugee camps has been facilitated by solar-powered tablets, which are pre-loaded with AI tutors (UNHCR, 2024) along with others. • In India, a number of EdTech nonprofits have created so-called WhatsApp-integrated bots, which provide lessons and interactive quizzes, and even emotional well-being check-in only by means of a feature phone and sporadic internet (Varanasi et al., 2024). • Adaptive systems such as “Samhita” are testing the community-supported learning systems, the AI feedback loop of which is observed and supported by local volunteers or Anganwadi workers (Pratham, 2025)

These developments demonstrate that affordability and inclusion do not necessarily go against each other and equity-focused design can help bring AI to the last-mile learner.

CASE STUDIES OF AI IN SUB-SAHARAN AFRICAN EDUCATION CONTEXTS

The digital divide in rural South Africa is further increased by the lack of reliable electricity access, prohibitive data prices, and massive differences between urban schools that have sufficient resources and understaffed schools in the country (Mwansa et al., 2025). Here, the implementation of Kolibri on low-cost devices in community learning centres in the Eastern Cape has allowed learners to view curriculum-based content offline, and teachers to use the built-in progress dashboards in the platform to identify struggling students and offer specific guidance in a model that does not need continuous internet connectivity and/or costly devices. Equally, in Rwanda, the collaboration between the government and the One Laptop per Child project and later implementation of AI-assisted adaptive learning content into its national e-learning portal has shown how policy alignment in the country can facilitate small, but significant reading and numeracy improvements in rural primary schools. Importantly, the cases demonstrate that the effectiveness of AI tools to work in low resources African environments is less about the complexity of the technology and more about the effectiveness of community engagement, teacher support, and the localisation of the content in such languages as Kinyarwanda, Zulu, and Xhosa (UNHCR, 2024).

AI and Assistive Technologies for Learners with Disabilities

Children and young people with disabilities are the one who are mostly excluded from mainstream education systems. In developing and LDCs, physical inaccessibility of school buildings, the insufficient number of trained special educators, deficiency of materials in accessible formats, and social discrimination are added to this exclusion (Yang et al., 2025). Assistive technologies that are powered by AI provide a valuable, scalable solution to this gap should they be tailored to the needs of learners with visual, hearing, cognitive, and motor impairments (Melo-López et al., 2025).

A few AI-powered applications have proven to have a beneficial influence in low-resource settings. For example, screen readers and AI-based speech synthesis programs support learners with visual impairments or dyslexia in reading independently. Speech-to-text application software's help students with motor disabilities to do assessments and communicate (Varsik & Vosberg, 2024a). The biggest weakness is that most of these tools need good connectivity and well-functioning devices limiting their use in low-connectivity or offline environments (Pagliara et al., 2024).

4. COMPARE AI WITH OPEN EDUCATIONAL RESOURCES (OERS)

Artificial Intelligence (AI) and Open Educational Resources (OERs) are complementary, yet distinct innovations that can offer essential vectors of education inclusion in India and other developing, as well as least developed countries. Although AI is adaptive and offers real-time feedback, OERs are scaled and offer curriculum-based materials. In this section, it will compare their strengths, weaknesses, and overlaps respectively in the Indian context and in the Global South.

Table 4. Comparative overview in the Indian and global context

Dimension	Artificial Intelligence (AI)	Open Educational Resources (OERs)
Pedagogical Value	AI personalised learning pathways, diagnostics in real-time, and adaptive feedback based on learner response.	offers resource catalogue, curriculum-based resources, impact depends on learner autonomy or facilitation
Accessibility	Needs devices and information; innovations of accessed offline and with low bandwidth are being developed (e.g. WhatsApp bots).	Very available through print, mobile and radio; widely deployed in DIKSHA, ePathshala, Kolibri.
Inclusivity	Can reduce inequities when designed with equity.	Improves accessibility but mostly needs facilitators to assist low-literacy learners.

continued on following page

Table 4. Continued

Dimension	Artificial Intelligence (AI)	Open Educational Resources (OERs)
Content Relevance	Personalisation is an algorithmic process, which can be biased unless there is contextually trained training data.	High relevance on offers that are localised by teachers or community contributors.
Offline Usability	The growth through applications such as Mindspark offline, Kolibri AI, voice bots.	Strong OERs can be easily converted to offline media using downloadable PDFs, print, and radio.
Scalability	Scaling through EdTech pilots and nonprofit partnerships; requires AI literacy and infrastructure	Easily scalable through repositories, peer networks, and mobile-first distribution channels

Sources: Muralidharan et al. (2019); Learning Equality (2023); UNESCO (2021); TATA Trusts (2023); GSMA (2023a)

Based on Table 4, it can be observed AI is the most suitable to apply to students in need with adaptive and personalised learning and instant feedback. However, it is restricted to equipment and bias. OERs are highly available (particularly offline) and can match local curriculum since they are non-dynamic. Low self-efficacy students are supported by AI, and teachers can best run OERs. The strengths are complementary both in AI in personalisation and OERs in reach. Synergies and Strategic Integration:

Synergies and Strategic Integration:

Though the concepts of Artificial Intelligence (AI) and Open Educational Resources (OERs) are considered separate educational technologies, they can be extremely complementary to each other in the Indian system of education. By way of example, the Indian national digital learning platform DIKSHA offers curriculum-related content in the form of OER in over 35 Indian languages. Through DIKSHA, AI functionality, and customisation of dashboards, customised navigation, or voice recognition can be integrated to enhance learner engagement and make digital content accessible to a wide range of linguistic and cognitive characteristics.

Besides, OER can be enhanced with AI-based features, such as speech recognition, auto-quizzes, or engines to suggest and recommend content, which would provide students with personalised attention, especially first-generation students and those with low levels of digital literacy (TATA Trusts, 2023). These additions make inanimate resources grow into dynamic and learner controlled learning environments that meet the diverse learner requirements. The combination of AI & OER presents an incredible model for increasing accessibility, but there is one category of people who continue to be overlooked – young women and girls in developing nations. Section 5 explores how AI can be used to remove the gender gap in education.

5. ERASING THE GENDER DIGITAL DIVIDE WITH AI

AI can bridge this gap in several ways:

- Verbal and spoken experiences enable girls with low literacy or formal schooling to interact with content on their own.
- Offline AI applications are installed in tablets or basic smartphones, which lower the connection dependency that rural regions frequently do lack as girls tend not to have independent access to their devices.

- AI-based personalised and private tutoring minimises risks of exposure to dangerous localities or humiliation of failure in the classroom.

For example, once connected, girls use mobile internet nearly as much as boys, meaning it is again an agency and access, and not a motivation or ability, issue (GSMA, 2023a). AI-based gender-conscious design of platforms, such as chat options where only girls can communicate, filters based on content, and prompts on safety, can help to facilitate a safe and reliable digital learning process, provided the AI is not only developed to scale, but also to include. However, the capacity of artificial intelligence to foster inclusion will only come about if these technologies themselves are developed in an ethical manner. The next section, section 6, discusses the ethical challenges that need to be addressed as well as the policy requirements for making AI inclusive.

6. ETHICAL AND POLICY CONSIDERATIONS

Since India and other countries in the developing world are finding AI as a solution to reducing systemic differences in learning, ethical issues are no longer relegated to its periphery but are at its center. This section addresses the potential threats of AI implementation in an ethical manner, principles of inclusive AI design, and suggests that governments and institutions have a role to play in creating fair and open policy frameworks.

Ethical Risks in AI-Driven Classrooms:

Algorithmic Bias and Educational Inequality:

AI tools are as equitable as the data used to train them. In case datasets mirrors the existing social stratifications, in terms of gender, caste, language or geography, they may also represent the same bias in instructional materials, advice and assessments (Suresh et al., 2025).

As an illustration, a personalised learning algorithm can automatically underrepresent the regional dialects, or propagate the mainstream cultural discourses at the expense of the already disadvantaged learners, without providing deliberate actions (Holmes et al., 2022)

In response to this, UNESCO recommends that fairness and inclusiveness should be integrated in the design of algorithms, and audits of the variations of culture and bias should be carried out at all levels of the AI development cycle (García-López & Trujillo-Liñán, 2025) . .The responsible AI framework of India repeats the same asking the AI systems to be transparent, explainable, and non-discriminatory (UNESCO, 2021).

Privacy, Surveillance, and Consent:

The increased use of AI in schools is also a major concern in terms of surveillance and student autonomy. Data on the behaviour of learning, environment, and interactions may be collected without proper consent to participate and publish and processed through the closed systems that store it beyond the management of the institution (Al-Zahrani, 2024). In LDCs, where the digital literacy and protection is not evenly distributed, this imbalance of power makes students more vulnerable, particularly students from marginal backgrounds.

UNESCO's framework bluntly bans mass surveillance and social scoring by insisting on more conditions of consent, rights of data ownership, and means of appeal in case of harm (UNESCO, 2021).

Erosion of Human Judgment:

There is a latent yet a high risk of overreliance on AI in some tasks such as grading, content development or decision making. In spite of the usefulness of these tools to teachers, their unregulated use threatens to replace human judgment, empathy and situational understanding, which are essential in subtle classroom interactions (Zhu et al., 2025). As observed in past surveys on the faculty, the concern is not just due to job replacement, but also due to loss of pedagogical ideals (Monardo et al., 2024) UNESCO's Ethics of AI framework emphasises that final responsibility should lie with human participant instead of machines. It demands human involvement, explainable and ethical studies to ensure that AI does not replace human agency, but act as a complement (UNESCO, 2021).

Long-Term Sustainability and Scalability of AI Interventions

One pattern that characterises many AI-in-education applications across developing and least-developed countries is what may be called the 'pilot trap'. AI-based projects that yield positive results in limited pilot studies but are incapable of produce the same results in large scale due to insufficient financing models, reliance on outside sponsors, or the lack of locally based expertise in maintaining and modifying AI systems (Ifenthaler et al., 2024). This delicacy is especially acute in the context of low-income countries, where the purchase of software licenses, server maintenance, and replacement of devices have to compete with other priorities of urgent spending in education. Open-source solutions like Kolibri minimise the dependency on proprietary software and enable local teachers to customise educational materials at will without having to pay any further fees (Mwansa et al., 2025).

7: POLICY REMEDIES FOR BRIDGING STRUCTURAL INEQUALITY

The promise of Artificial Intelligence as a means of learning has a foundation something more than technological advancement, it relies on conscious and equity-based governance. As it has been mentioned in earlier sections, it is impossible to manage the threats like prejudice in algorithms, exclusion of languages, as well as undermining human judgments by simply being reactive.

7.1 Inclusive Design and Governance Principles:

In opposition, educational divides can only be repaired by context-aware AI governance, if:

1. Equity by Design

AI tools should reflect need to mirror extensive socio-linguistic diversity around the world. The datasets and interfaces must be accommodating of the regional languages, gender, and learning context, rural, urban, and tribal (Devaki, Suresh, & Sunkesula, 2025; Renkema & Tursunbayeva, 2024). Artificial intelligence tools should reflect the rich socio-linguistic diversity around the world. The datasets and interfaces must be accommodative of the regional languages, gender manifestations and learning conditions, rural, urban and tribal.

2. Transparency and Explainability

There should be the ability to allow students to understand and challenge AI-based decisions, either in proposed learning paths or versioned ones. The increase in digital literacy and trust is achieved through the perception of GenAI as a collaborator, not as a black box, among students.

3. Data Sovereignty and Informed Consent

Educational data should be in the hands of learners and institutions. Moreover, anonymisation, transparent opt-in policy, and user rights are the substantial ways of protection, especially in low-awareness environments (Nguyen et al., 2023).

4. Human Oversight and Pedagogical Authority

AI has to support the teachers but not replace teachers. Embedding GenAI requires retaining the empathetic, adaptive judgment which teachers bring to diverse classroom contexts (Holmes et al., 2022).

7.2 Policy Imperatives for India and the Global South

Reforms to scale equitable AI use must the span the institutional, national, and international arenas:

Institutional Governance Charters:

Higher Education Institutions (HEIs) must collaborate together with the faculty, students, and administrators to develop AI charters, which define the uses, attribution processes, and complaints. The charters should be designed in a learner centered and justice oriented manner.

Governmental Alignment and Capacity Building

Agencies like the University Grants Commission (UGC) and the Ministry of Education (MoE) should ensure that AI ethics is incorporated into

- Teacher training programs (emphasising critical evaluation of AI outputs)
- Planning of Digital infrastructure (equitable access to GenAI resources).
- Funding mechanisms, which focus on inclusion as opposed to market dominance.

Community-Led Implementation

Teacher Capacity, Workload, and Professional Development for AI Integration

Despite the considerable policy attention given to AI infrastructure and accessibility, the preparedness of teachers to integrate AI into their classrooms remains one of the most critical yet under addressed dimensions of inclusive AI adoption in developing and LDCs. Teachers in low-resource settings often face number of challenges like heavy workloads, large and multi-grade classrooms, limited access to devices, and inadequate institutional support. Failure to address these problems and ensuring proper teacher training before incorporating AI will only serve to exacerbate the problems faced by teachers. (Devaki, Suresh, & Boopathi, 2025; Varanasi et al., 2024)

Therefore, AI integration requires structured, ongoing professional learning rather than one-off training sessions. Teachers need to update their competencies not only in the technical usage of AI tools, but also in critically evaluating AI-generated output, identifying algorithmic bias in learning, and maintaining student autonomy, privacy in AI-mediated interactions (Varanasi et al., 2024).

The concept of Community-Led Implementation below explains the ways in which bottom-up involvement supplements top-down policy; a combination of the two aspects constitutes the human infrastructure upon which any AI implementation in education will ultimately rely (Aravantinos et al., 2026) .

The divide class can be united by the bottom up involvement only. The policy should be developed involving the Anganwadi workers, community teachers, local technologists, and parents who have a sense of the realities of the last-mile learners(Adewale et al., 2024) . The successful acceptance of GenAI involves the participants in the study to participate in participatory piloting, feedback feedback, and cultural-based training.

CONCLUSION

Artificial Intelligence has the potential to realize the transformative possibilities of reimagining education as a universal social benefit; especially in the developing and least developed countries where systemic inequities remain in place to marginalize large segments of the learning population. The examples given in this chapter illustrate that when ethically designed and implemented in an inclusive manner, AI has the potential to overcome the geographical, affordability, literacy, gender, infrastructure, and disability divisions. With personalization of the learning process, supportive assistive technology, and multilingual and culturally sensitive content, AI can provide access to quality education to everyone and empower the underprivileged population.

However, AI does not have an automated future. In the absence of intentional structures of fairness, openness and community engagement, AI will become a threat of strengthening the already present prejudices and exclusions. For developing and least developed countries, the way forward is to adopt low-cost and context-sensitive and rights-based AI solutions that would put learner agency and inclusiveness as a priority. This involves creating AI systems that are offline-friendly and mobile-first, voice-friendly, and culturally sensitive such that none of the learners is disadvantaged because of geography, gender, and socio-economic status. Additionally, AI has to be integrated into more comprehensive plans of digital literacy, an infrastructural development and ethical protection to maintain equitable educational ecosystems.

In conclusion, AI is not merely a technological innovation but a moral and societal undertaking to eliminate educational inequalities and foster equity among the society and educational institutions. When deployed wisely and tailored to suit the local environment, AI may help in developing and LDCs approach the ideal of democratized and accessible education, because learning is not the exclusive preserve of a select few, but a right available to all.

REFERENCES

Adewale, M. D., Azeta, A., Abayomi-Alli, A., & Sambo-Magaji, A. (2024). Impact of artificial intelligence adoption on students' academic performance in open and distance learning: A systematic literature review. *Heliyon*, *10*(22), e40025. Advance online publication. DOI: 10.1016/j.heliyon.2024.e40025 PMID: 39605813

Akshar Foundation. (2023). *Akshar Foundation | Transforming Indian schools into sustainable communities*. https://www.aksharfoundation.org/

Al-Zahrani, A. M. (2024). Unveiling the shadows: Beyond the hype of AI in education. *Heliyon*, *10*(9), e30696. DOI: 10.1016/j.heliyon.2024.e30696 PMID: 38737255

Antoninis, M., April, D., Barakat, B., Bella, N., D'Addio, A. C., Eck, M., Endrizzi, F., Joshi, P., Kubacka, K., McWilliam, A., Murakami, Y., Smith, W., Stipanovic, L., Vidarte, R., & Zekrya, L. (2020). All means all: An introduction to the 2020 Global Education Monitoring Report on inclusion. *Prospects*, *49*(3–4), 103–109. DOI: 10.1007/s11125-020-09505-x PMID: 32963414

Aravantinos, S., Lavidas, K., Komis, V., Karalis, T., & Papadakis, S. (2026). Artificial Intelligence in K-12 Education: A Systematic Review of Teachers' Professional Development Needs for AI Integration. *Computers 2026, Vol. 15, Page 49, 15*(1), 49. DOI: 10.3390/computers15010049

Banerjee, A., Lamrani, I., Hossain, S., Paudyal, P., & Gupta, S. K. S. (2020). *AI Enabled Tutor for Accessible Training*. DOI: 10.1007/978-3-030-52237-7_3

Banerjee, R., Trappel, J., & Van Audenhove, L. (2024). Evaluating 'Meaningful Connectivity': Digital Literacy and Women in West Bengal, India. *Palgrave Studies in Digital Inequalities*, (Part F4289), 225–248. DOI: 10.1007/978-3-031-28930-9_11

Campos, D. G., & Scherer, R. (2023). Digital gender gaps in Students' knowledge, attitudes and skills: an integrative data analysis across 32 Countries. *Education and Information Technologies 2023 29:1, 29*(1), 655–693. DOI: 10.1007/s10639-023-12272-9

Department of Economics and Statistics. G. of T. N. (2020). *Tamilnadu COVID Pulse Survey*. https://des.tn.gov.in/en/node/344

Devaki, V., Suresh, C., & Boopathi, L. (2025). Building Teacher Skills for Effective Integration of Technology in the Classroom. Https://Services.Igi-Global.Com/Resolvedoi/Resolve.Aspx?Doi=10.4018/979-8-3373-0771-8.Ch012, 269–302. DOI: 10.4018/979-8-3373-0771-8.ch012

Devaki, V., Suresh, C., & Sunkesula, M. A. (2025). Multicultural Diversity in Perspective Views on Pluralism. Https://Services.Igi-Global.Com/Resolvedoi/Resolve.Aspx?Doi=10.4018/979-8-3693-8196-0.Ch001, 1–34. DOI: 10.4018/979-8-3693-8196-0.ch001

Equality, L. (2023). *Kolibri Platform*. https://learningequality.org/kolibri/about-kolibri/

Fung, K. K., Lai, C. Y., Hung, S. L., Yu, Y., & He, L. (2025). A Systematic Review of the Digital Divide Experienced by Migrant Women. *Journal of International Migration and Integration*, *26*(2), 1177–1204. DOI: 10.1007/s12134-024-01222-0

García-López, I. M., & Trujillo-Liñán, L. (2025). Ethical and regulatory challenges of Generative AI in education: A systematic review. *Frontiers in Education*, *10*, 1565938. DOI: 10.3389/feduc.2025.1565938

GSMA. (2023a). *The Mobile Gender Gap Report*. https://www.gsma.com/r/gender-gap/

GSMA. (2023b). *The State of Mobile Internet Connectivity 2023*. www.gsmaintelligence.com

Hariyanto, H., Studi Pendidikan Profesi Guru, P., Dharmacarya, J., Tinggi Agama Buddha Negeri Raden Wijaya Wonogiri, S., Bahasa dan Seni, F., Studi Pendidikan Seni Musik, P., Negeri Sunan Kudus, I., Xaveria Diah Kristianingsih, F., & Maharani, R. (2025). Artificial intelligence in adaptive education: a systematic review of techniques for personalized learning. *Discover Education 2025 4:1, 4*(1), 458-. DOI: 10.1007/s44217-025-00908-6

Holmes, W., Porayska-Pomsta, K., Holstein, K., Sutherland, E., Baker, T., Shum, S. B., Santos, O. C., Rodrigo, M. T., Cukurova, M., Bittencourt, I. I., & Koedinger, K. R. (2022). Ethics of AI in Education: Towards a Community-Wide Framework. *International Journal of Artificial Intelligence in Education*, *32*(3), 504–526. DOI: 10.1007/s40593-021-00239-1

Hoque, M. R. (2020). The impact of the ICT4D project on sustainable rural development using a capability approach: Evidence from Bangladesh. *Technology in Society*, *61*, 101254. DOI: 10.1016/j.techsoc.2020.101254

Ifenthaler, D., Majumdar, R., Gorissen, P., Judge, M., Mishra, S., Raffaghelli, J., & Shimada, A. (2024). Artificial Intelligence in Education: Implications for Policymakers, Researchers, and Practitioners. *Technology, Knowledge and Learning 2024 29:4, 29*(4), 1693–1710. DOI: 10.1007/s10758-024-09747-0

Kalim, U., Kanwar, A., Sha, J., & Huang, R. (2025). Barriers to AI adoption for women in higher education: a systematic review of the Asian context. *Smart Learning Environments 2025 12:1, 12*(1), 38-. DOI: 10.1186/s40561-025-00390-5

Kaushal, V., Singh, B., & Devi, S. (2023). *Digital Literacy In India: Benefits and Challenges*. http://cok.pratibha-spandan.org

Kennedy, A. I., Mejía-Rodríguez, A. M., & Strello, A. (2022a). Inequality in remote learning quality during COVID-19: Student perspectives and mitigating factors. *Large-Scale Assessments in Education*, *10*(1), 1–31. DOI: 10.1186/s40536-022-00143-7 PMID: 36590105

Kennedy, A. I., Mejía-Rodríguez, A. M., & Strello, A. (2022b). Inequality in remote learning quality during COVID-19: Student perspectives and mitigating factors. *Large-Scale Assessments in Education*, *10*(1), 1–31. DOI: 10.1186/s40536-022-00143-7 PMID: 36590105

Kuhn, C., Khoo, S. M., Czerniewicz, L., Lilley, W., Bute, S., Crean, A., Abegglen, S., Burns, T., Sinfield, S., Jandrić, P., Knox, J., & MacKenzie, A. (2023). Understanding Digital Inequality: A Theoretical Kaleidoscope. *Postdigital Science and Education*, *5*(3), 894–932. DOI: 10.1007/s42438-023-00395-8 PMID: 40479087

Malhotra, C. (2024). *Digital India: Past, Present and Future*. 325–345. DOI: 10.1007/978-3-658-43014-6_19

Mansour, N., Aras, C., Staarman, J. K., & Alotaibi, S. B. M. (2024). Embodied learning of science concepts through augmented reality technology. *Education and Information Technologies 2024 30:6, 30*(6), 8245–8275. DOI: 10.1007/s10639-024-13120-0

Melo-López, V. A., Basantes-Andrade, A., Gudiño-Mejía, C. B., & Hernández-Martínez, E. (2025). The Impact of Artificial Intelligence on Inclusive Education: A Systematic Review. *Education Sciences 2025, Vol. 15, Page 539, 15*(5), 539. DOI: 10.3390/educsci15050539

Meng, Y., Xu, W., Liu, Z., & Yu, Z. G. (2024). Scientometric analyses of digital inequity in education: problems and solutions. *Humanities and Social Sciences Communications 2024 11:1, 11*(1), 1052-. DOI: 10.1057/s41599-024-03480-w

Ministry of Health & Family Welfare. (2019). *National Family Health Survey (NFHS-5) (2019-21).*

Ministry of Statistics and Programme Implementation. (2018). *India - Household Social Consumption: Health, NSS 75th Round Schedule-25.0 :July 2017-June 2018.* https://microdata.gov.in/NADA/index.php/catalog/152

Minn, S. (2022). AI-assisted knowledge assessment techniques for adaptive learning environments. *Computers and Education: Artificial Intelligence, 3*, 100050. DOI: 10.1016/j.caeai.2022.100050

Misra, P., & Srivastava, R. (2024). Digital Divide and Sustainable Development. *World Sustainability Series*, (Part F3420), 451–472. DOI: 10.1007/978-3-031-68427-2_23

Muawanah, U., Marini, A., & Sarifah, I. (2024). The interconnection between digital literacy, artificial intelligence, and the use of E-learning applications in enhancing the sustainability of Regional Languages: Evidence from Indonesia. *Social Sciences & Humanities Open, 10*, 101169. DOI: 10.1016/j.ssaho.2024.101169

Muralidharan, K., Singh, A., & Ganimian, A. J. (2019). Disrupting Education? Experimental Evidence on Technology-Aided Instruction in India. *The American Economic Review, 109*(4), 1426–1460. DOI: 10.1257/aer.20171112

Mwansa, G., Ngandu, M. R., & Mkwambi, Z. (2025). Bridging the digital divide: exploring the challenges and solutions for digital exclusion in rural South Africa. *Discover Global Society 2025 3:1, 3*(1), 54-. DOI: 10.1007/s44282-025-00189-2

Naseer, F., Khan, M. N., Tahir, M., Addas, A., & Aejaz, S. M. H. (2024). Integrating deep learning techniques for personalized learning pathways in higher education. *Heliyon, 10*(11), e32628. DOI: 10.1016/j.heliyon.2024.e32628 PMID: 38961899

Nguyen, A., Ngo, H. N., Hong, Y., Dang, B., & Nguyen, B. P. T. (2023). Ethical principles for artificial intelligence in education. *Education and Information Technologies, 28*(4), 4221–4241. DOI: 10.1007/s10639-022-11316-w PMID: 36254344

Pagliara, S. M., Bonavolontà, G., Pia, M., Falchi, S., Zurru, A. L., Fenu, G., & Mura, A. (2024). The Integration of Artificial Intelligence in Inclusive Education: A Scoping Review. *Information 2024, Vol. 15, Page 774, 15*(12), 774. DOI: 10.3390/info15120774

Passey, D., Ntebutse, J. G., Ahmad, M. Y. A., Cochrane, J., Collin, S., Ganayem, A., Langran, E., Mulla, S., Rodrigo, M. M., Saito, T., Shonfeld, M., & Somasi, S. (2024). Populations Digitally Excluded from Education: Issues, Factors, Contributions and Actions for Policy, Practice and Research in a Post-Pandemic Era. *Technology, Knowledge and Learning 2024 29:4, 29*(4), 1733–1750. DOI: 10.1007/s10758-024-09767-w

Pratham. (2025). *"PadhAI": Transforming literacy with AI-powered reading assessments | Pratham UK.* https://pratham.org.uk/pratham-launches-padhai-transforming-literacy-with-ai-powered-reading-assessments/

Rahman, A., Arabi, S., Rab, R., Rahman, A., Arabi, S., & Rab, R. (2021). Feasibility and Challenges of 5G Network Deployment in Least Developed Countries (LDC). *Wireless Sensor Network, 13*(1), 1–16. DOI: 10.4236/wsn.2021.131001

Raihan, M. M. H., Subroto, S., Chowdhury, N., Koch, K., Ruttan, E., & Turin, T. C. (2025). Dimensions and barriers for digital (in)equity and digital divide: A systematic integrative review. *Digital Transformation and Society, 4*(2), 111–127. DOI: 10.1108/DTS-04-2024-0054

Ramasamy, J. V., Md Yunus, M., & Hanim Ismail, H. (2025).. . *Effectiveness of Google Read-Along Application in Improving Reading Skills of Rural Area Upper Primary ESL Classroom INTERNATIONAL JOURNAL OF ACADEMIC RESEARCH IN PROGRESSIVE EDUCATION AND DEVELOPMENT,* (14). Advance online publication. DOI: 10.6007/IJARPED/v14-i1/24948

Renkema, M., & Tursunbayeva, A. (2024). The future of work of academics in the age of Artificial Intelligence: State-of-the-art and a research roadmap. *Futures, 163*, 103453. DOI: 10.1016/j.futures.2024.103453

Rotondi, V., Kashyap, R., Pesando, L. M., Spinelli, S., & Billari, F. C. (2025). Leveraging mobile phones to attain sustainable development. *Proceedings of the National Academy of Sciences of the United States of America, 117*(24), 13413–13420. DOI: 10.1073/pnas.1909326117 PMID: 32482867

Samudra, A. (2022). Gendering the Digital Divide in India. SSRN *Electronic Journal.* https://doi.org/ DOI: 10.2139/SSRN.4112879

Shankar, B., Jyothi, P., & Bhattacharyya, P. (2024). In-context Mixing (ICM): Code-mixed Prompts for Multilingual LLMs. *Proceedings of the Annual Meeting of the Association for Computational Linguistics, 1*, 4162–4176. DOI: 10.18653/v1/2024.acl-long.228

Sindakis, S., & Showkat, G. (2024). The digital revolution in India: Bridging the gap in rural technology adoption. *Journal of Innovation and Entrepreneurship, 13*(1), 1–28. DOI: 10.1186/s13731-024-00380-w

Singh, S. (2017). Bridging the gender digital divide in developing countries. *Journal of Children and Media, 11*(2), 245–247. DOI: 10.1080/17482798.2017.1305604

Smith, T. S., Holland, A. C., White, T., Combs, B., Watts, P., & Moss, J. (2021). A Distance Accessible Education Model: Teaching Skills to Nurse Practitioners. *The Journal for Nurse Practitioners, 17*(8), 999–1003. DOI: 10.1016/j.nurpra.2021.05.018 PMID: 35165528

Suresh, C., Ali, S. M., & Devaki, V. (2025). Perception About Usage of GAI Tools in Teaching and Research by Teachers and Students in Higher Education Institutions. Https://Services.Igi-Global.Com/Resolvedoi/Resolve.Aspx?Doi=10.4018/979-8-3693-8191-5.Ch015, 381–412. DOI: 10.4018/979-8-3693-8191-5.ch015

Tawil, S., & Miao, F. (2024). Steering the Digital Transformation of Education: UNESCO's Human-Centered Approach. *Frontiers of Digital Education 2024 1:1, 1*(1), 51–58. DOI: 10.1007/s44366-024-0020-0

Trusts, T. A. T. A. (2023). *Learning fillip*. https://horizons.tatatrusts.org/2025/april/tata-trusts-horizons-learning-fillip.html

Uddin, M. R. (2024). The role of the digital economy in Bangladesh's economic development. *Sustainable Technology and Entrepreneurship*, *3*(1), 100054. DOI: 10.1016/j.stae.2023.100054

UNESCO. (2021). AI and education: guidance for policy-makers. *AI and Education: Guidance for Policy-Makers*. DOI: 10.54675/PCSP7350

UNESCO. (2023). *Report on the results of the Working Group concerning a sensitization strategy to reinforce public awareness*. https://unesdoc.unesco.org/ark:/48223/pf0000385421

UNHCR. (2023). *Digital Literacy and Skills*. https://www.unhcr.org/innovation/wp-content/uploads/2023/11/DigitalLiteracy_ConceptNote_UNHCR.pdf

UNHCR. (2024). *Evaluation of UNHCR's Support to Refugee Health, Education and Economic Inclusion in West and Central Africa*. https://www.unhcr.org/sites/default/files/2024-07/Evaluation%20of%20UNHCR%27s%20Support%20to%20Health%2C%20Education%2C%20and%20Economic%20Inclusion%20in%20West%20and%20Central%20Africa.pdf

United Nations Industrial Development Organization. (2023). Annual Report 2023. In *Webpage*. https://www.unido.org/annual-report-2023

Varanasi, R. A., Dell, N., & Vashistha, A. (2024). Saharaline: A Collective Social Support Intervention for Teachers in Low-Income Indian Schools. *Conference on Human Factors in Computing Systems - Proceedings*, (24). DOI: 10.1145/3613904.3642617

Varsik, S., & Vosberg, L. (2024a). The potential impact of Artificial Intelligence on equity and inclusion in education. *OECD Artificial Intelligence Papers, OECD Artificial Intelligence Papers, 23*. DOI: 10.1787/dee339a8-en

Varsik, S., & Vosberg, L. (2024b). *The potential impact of Artificial Intelligence on equity and inclusion in education* (Vol. 23). OECD Artificial Intelligence Papers., DOI: 10.1787/dee339a8-en

Vesna, L., Sawale, P. S., Kaul, P., Pal, S., Snv, B., & Murthy, R. (2025). Digital Divide in AI-Powered Education: Challenges and Solutions for Equitable Learning. *Journal of Information Systems Engineering & Management*, *10*(21s), 300–308. DOI: 10.52783/jisem.v10i21s.3327

Wang, S., Christensen, C., Cui, W., Tong, R., Yarnall, L., Shear, L., & Feng, M. (2023). When adaptive learning is effective learning: Comparison of an adaptive learning system to teacher-led instruction. *Interactive Learning Environments*, *31*(2), 793–803. DOI: 10.1080/10494820.2020.1808794

Wedlake, S., Iribe Ramirez, Y., Carson, K., Jowaisas, C., Keyes, D., & Houghton, M. (2021). Creating a Digital Bridge: Lessons and Policy Implications from a Technology Access and Distribution Program for Low-income Job Seekers. SSRN *Electronic Journal*. https://doi.org/DOI: 10.2139/SSRN.3898330

World Bank. (2023a). *Digital Progress and Trends Report*. https://www.worldbank.org/en/publication/digital-progress-and-trends-report

World Bank. (2023b). *Digital Progress and Trends Report*. https://www.worldbank.org/en/publication/digital-progress-and-trends-report

Yang, C., Wang, T., & Xiu, Q. (2025). Towards a Sustainable Future in Education: A Systematic Review and Framework for Inclusive Education. *Sustainability (Basel)*, *17*(9), 3837. DOI: 10.3390/su17093837

Zhang, W., Majumdar, A., & Yadav, A. (2024). *CHAI for LLMs: Improving Code-Mixed Translation in Large Language Models through Reinforcement Learning with AI Feedback*. https://arxiv.org/pdf/2411.09073

Zhu, H., Sun, Y., & Yang, J. (2025). Towards responsible artificial intelligence in education: a systematic review on identifying and mitigating ethical risks. *Humanities and Social Sciences Communications 2025 12:1*, *12*(1), 1111-. DOI: 10.1057/s41599-025-05252-6

Chapter 14

Redefining Independent Learning With AI Agents: Institutional Transformation Through AI

Bartholomeus Dimanche Carl Beth
http://orcid.org/0009-0006-1088-9212
Universitas Esa Ungggul, Indonesia

Vinsens Aji Pamungkas
http://orcid.org/0009-0003-3036-0699
Universitas Esa Ungggul, Indonesia

Ryan Putra Laksana
http://orcid.org/0009-0008-5904-1321
Universitas Esa Ungggul, Indonesia

Wildan Kamil
http://orcid.org/0009-0007-4113-2252
Universitas Esa Ungggul, Indonesia

Nizirwan Anwar
http://orcid.org/0000-0003-1189-9093
Universitas Esa Ungggul, Indonesia

ABSTRACT

Artificial Intelligence (AI) is fundamentally transforming educational institutions, shifting from a teaching tool to a strategic driver of institutional transformation. This paper explores how AI necessitates a thorough restructuring of governance, culture, and pedagogy to create an adaptive, data-driven, and learner-centered ecosystem. Rooted in constructivism and adaptive learning theory, AI acts as intelligent scaffolding, using analytics to design personalized paths and enhance academic outcomes. The study emphasizes the critical role of data-driven decision-making, requiring robust governance and ethical frameworks to convert data into strategic insights. This complex transformation demands "AI-ready

DOI: 10.4018/979-8-3373-7225-9.ch014

leaders" and a holistic framework to navigate challenges like digital literacy and ethical concerns. The chapter provides a strategic roadmap for a sustainable, ethical, and human-centered intelligent learning system.

1. INTRODUCTION

Digital transformation has fundamentally reshaped the operational landscape of educational institutions, redefining how resources are managed, knowledge is delivered, and learning experiences are designed. In the era of intelligent technologies, Artificial Intelligence (AI) has evolved from a supplementary instructional tool into a strategic driver of institutional transformation. Educational ecosystems are increasingly becoming adaptive, data-driven, and learner-centered, requiring not only technological adoption but also structural changes in governance, organizational culture, and pedagogical approaches. This transformation reflects a paradigm shift in which institutions must respond to complex demands such as personalization, scalability, and digital inclusivity while maintaining their core educational values. As a result, AI is positioned as a critical enabler for building resilient, future-ready educational systems.

The theoretical foundation of this transformation is strongly grounded in cognitive constructivism, which emphasizes that meaningful learning occurs through active knowledge construction and interaction within dynamic environments. AI technologies serve as digital scaffolding that supports both individual and collaborative learning processes. Adaptive learning systems and intelligent tutoring platforms allow learners to explore content independently while receiving personalized guidance aligned with their abilities and learning styles. Empirical findings demonstrate that AI-enhanced constructivist approaches significantly improve cognitive engagement and metacognitive awareness, enabling students to better regulate their own learning processes (Liu et al., 2023). This highlights the role of AI not merely as a technological enhancement, but as a transformative pedagogical mechanism.

In parallel, modern adaptive learning theory extends personalization by integrating learning analytics and machine learning algorithms to create dynamic, individualized learning pathways. These systems continuously adjust instructional content, pace, and delivery methods based on real-time performance data. Such adaptability reduces disparities in learner capabilities and enhances instructional effectiveness. AI-driven adaptive learning has been shown to improve both efficiency and academic performance by aligning educational experiences with individual needs (Wei & Liu, 2023). However, the effectiveness of these systems depends on robust data governance and ethical implementation, ensuring that algorithmic decisions are transparent, fair, and pedagogically valid.

From an institutional perspective, data-driven decision-making theory provides a crucial framework for understanding AI-enabled transformation. Educational institutions that successfully implement AI are those capable of converting data into actionable insights through strong governance structures, analytical competencies, and ethical safeguards (Ahmad et al., 2024). AI supports evidence-based decision-making across various domains, including curriculum design, student performance monitoring, and resource allocation. Nevertheless, challenges such as data misinterpretation, low data literacy, and algorithmic bias remain significant concerns (Zhou et al., 2022). Without transparency and accountability mechanisms, AI systems risk reinforcing inequalities and undermining academic integrity, making ethical governance a central requirement in AI adoption.

The integration of AI in education is further accelerated by global pressures such as post-pandemic digitalization, the rise of remote learning, and increasing competition in higher education innovation.

AI-driven transformation is no longer optional but a strategic necessity requiring comprehensive organi zational change. Theoretical perspectives such as organizational change theory and structuration theory emphasize that successful transformation depends on leadership, culture, and human agency rather than technology alone (Andriana et al., 2024; Katsamakas & Pavlov, 2024). Educational leaders must evolve into AI-ready leaders capable of navigating complexity, fostering innovation, and aligning technological adoption with institutional values. Ultimately, sustainable AI transformation requires a holistic approach that integrates infrastructure, human capacity, and ethical governance to create intelligent, inclusive, and future-oriented learning ecosystems.

2. INSTITUTIONAL READINESS AND GOVERNANCE FOR AI-DRIVEN EDUCATION

Digital transformation driven by Artificial Intelligence (AI) has significantly redefined governance structures in educational institutions, shifting them toward more adaptive, data-driven, and learner-centered ecosystems. While institutional readiness has traditionally emphasized infrastructure, leadership, and policy alignment, contemporary perspectives highlight the importance of integrating AI into pedagogical processes that directly impact learners and educators. Institutional readiness is therefore not only a technological or managerial concern but also a pedagogical and human-centered transformation. Studies indicate that effective AI readiness requires a holistic approach encompassing governance, human capacity, and ethical frameworks, ensuring that technological innovation aligns with educational values and learning outcomes (Chaaban et al., 2024).

2.1 The Concept of Institutional Readiness for AI

Institutional readiness for AI refers to an organization's ability to strategically integrate intelligent technologies into teaching, research, and administrative processes. This readiness encompasses five key dimensions: leadership and strategy, infrastructure, human resource capacity, governance, and organizational culture. However, recent developments emphasize that readiness must also include the ability to support learner-centered AI systems, such as adaptive learning platforms and intelligent tutoring systems that personalize educational experiences. AI-powered systems now enable automated grading, reducing faculty workload while ensuring timely and consistent feedback for students. Similarly, AI-based academic advising systems provide personalized recommendations for course selection and career pathways, improving student decision-making. These developments demonstrate that AI readiness must extend beyond institutional efficiency toward enhancing student learning experiences and outcomes. Effective governance frameworks must therefore balance operational efficiency with pedagogical innovation and user empowerment (Chaaban et al., 2024).

2.2 Maturity and Valuation Models

Institutional AI readiness is often assessed using maturity models developed by organizations such as UNESCO (2022), EDUCAUSE (2023), and OECD (2024). These frameworks define progressive stages ranging from initial awareness to full transformation, emphasizing continuous improvement rather than static achievement. The OECD AI Readiness Framework outlines five levels Initiation, Exploration,

Implementation, Institutionalization, and Transformation highlighting the evolution from experimental adoption to systemic integration (Sonntag et al., 2024).

Recent interpretations of these models emphasize the inclusion of adaptive learning ecosystems, where AI supports personalized learning pathways and metacognitive development. For instance, mature institutions leverage AI dashboards to monitor student progress, identify learning gaps, and provide real-time interventions. These systems enable dynamic curriculum updates and personalized content delivery, ensuring that learning experiences remain relevant and responsive. UNESCO's emphasis on equitable access further reinforces the need for inclusive AI systems that support diverse learner needs, particularly in multilingual and multicultural contexts (Gutierrez et al., 2022; Yagyaeva et al., 2024).

2.3 Governance and Managerial Structure

Effective AI governance requires a coordinated and transparent managerial structure that integrates technological, pedagogical, and ethical perspectives. Core principles include strategic alignment, accountability, and transparency, ensuring that AI initiatives align with institutional goals while maintaining trust among stakeholders. However, governance must also address the pedagogical implications of AI by supporting systems that enhance learning autonomy and reduce administrative burdens.

For example, AI-driven content management systems can automatically update course materials based on new research developments, reducing faculty workload while maintaining academic relevance. Similarly, learning analytics platforms support adaptive navigation, guiding students through personalized learning pathways based on their performance and engagement patterns. Institutions increasingly establish cross-functional AI governance committees and leadership roles such as Chief AI Officer to oversee these initiatives and ensure integrated implementation (Huang et al., 2023).

Figure 1. Principles of AI implementation are at risk of facing internal resistance, role conflicts, or failure to achieve the expected impact

2.4 Strategic Leadership and Digital Vision

Leadership plays a critical role in shaping institutional readiness for AI, particularly in fostering a vision that integrates technological innovation with human-centered learning. AI-ready leaders must not only understand technological capabilities but also recognize their implications for teaching, learning, and organizational culture. Effective leadership involves promoting collaboration, encouraging experimentation, and ensuring ethical accountability in AI adoption. Research highlights that digital leadership requires a deep understanding of AI ecosystems and cybersecurity to guide sustainable innovation (Petrov et al., 2025). Importantly, leaders must prioritize learner-centered design, ensuring that AI systems support metacognitive development, self-regulated learning, and personalized educational pathways. By aligning AI initiatives with pedagogical goals, leaders can transform institutions into adaptive learning environments that empower both educators and students.

2.5 Data Governance and Institutional Ethics

Data governance remains a foundational component of AI readiness, as intelligent systems rely heavily on large-scale data processing. Effective governance frameworks must ensure data integrity, privacy, and ethical compliance through principles such as FAIR (Findable, Accessible, Interoperable, Reusable). However, beyond technical considerations, ethical governance must also address the impact of AI on learning experiences and equity. Studies indicate that algorithmic bias in educational AI systems can reinforce existing inequalities if not properly managed. Therefore, institutions must implement ethical audits, transparency mechanisms, and inclusive design practices to ensure fairness (Huang et al., 2023). Additionally, explainable AI systems can enhance trust by allowing users to understand how recommendations and decisions are generated. Ethical governance thus plays a dual role in protecting users while enabling responsible innovation.

2.6 Organizational Culture and Digital Literacy

Organizational culture and digital literacy significantly influence the success of AI adoption in education. Institutions with open, collaborative, and innovation-oriented cultures are more likely to successfully implement AI systems. Conversely, resistance to change and hierarchical structures can hinder transformation efforts. Therefore, fostering a culture of experimentation and continuous learning is essential. Digital literacy initiatives must extend beyond basic technical skills to include AI literacy, enabling educators to effectively integrate AI tools into teaching practices. For example, training programs focusing on AI-assisted teaching, learning analytics, and content recommendation systems have been shown to improve pedagogical innovation. Research by AlHakim et al. (2024) demonstrates that gamified AI literacy programs enhance educators' ability to design adaptive and data-driven learning environments, supporting both instructional effectiveness and student engagement (AlHakim et al., 2024).

2.7 Future Challenges and Directions

Despite its transformative potential, AI adoption in education faces significant challenges, including limited funding, skill gaps, and cultural resistance. Many institutions, particularly in developing countries, remain in early stages of AI readiness due to insufficient infrastructure and policy frameworks.

Ethical concerns related to data privacy, algorithmic transparency, and the potential dehumanization of learning further complicate implementation.

Future directions emphasize the development of human-centered AI systems that enhance rather than replace human capabilities. Research suggests that AI should support metacognitive learning, adaptive navigation, and personalized pathways while maintaining human oversight (Bettahi et al., 2025). By adopting a systemic and ethical approach, educational institutions can ensure that AI-driven transformation remains inclusive, sustainable, and aligned with the broader mission of education.

3. ORGANIZATIONAL RESTRUCTURING AND COMPETENCY DEVELOPMENT

Artificial Intelligence (AI)-based digital transformation has fundamentally changed the paradigm of higher education, making universities not only centers of learning, but also data-driven organizations that rely on smart technology for decision-making and improving academic quality. AI allows educational institutions to manage information precisely, predict learning needs, and optimize resources efficiently. The shift towards predictive analytics-based management and machine learning is driving more accurate decision-making in performance evaluation, curriculum design, and administrative management. However, the success of this transformation depends on organizational restructuring and the development of human resource competencies to be able to adapt to the dynamic digital ecosystem. AI plays a role not only as a technological tool, but also as a catalyst for organizational culture change towards transparent, accountable, and innovative governance.

3.1 Adaptation of Organizational Structure to AI Implementation

Restructuring education organizations is an urgent need in facing the era of AI-based digital transformation. This technological integration requires not only technical changes, but also reforms in academic and administrative governance to be more adaptive to technological dynamics. Educational institutions that successfully adopt AI generally implement a hybrid organizational structure, which combines centralization in strategic policy aspects with decentralization in operational execution. This model allows for flexibility in decision-making while maintaining consistency in the strategic direction of the institution. Cross-unit collaboration between information technology departments, faculties, and research institutions is crucial to drive innovation and efficiency. The establishment of specialized units such as the AI Innovation Center or the Digital Transformation Office is also a strategic step that strengthens coordination, ensures ethical compliance, and aligns the application of AI with the institution's academic vision (Andriana et al., 2024).

In addition to the formation of new structures, organizational transformation also demands a shift in managerial culture from traditional hierarchies to agile governance. This governance model emphasizes cross-functional collaboration, speed of decision-making, as well as the courage to experiment in digital innovation. Through an agile approach, educational institutions can respond to changing learning needs, technological trends, and educational market challenges more quickly and effectively. Thus, organizational restructuring is not just a structural change, but a strategic effort to build a responsive, collaborative, and future-oriented learning ecosystem.

3.2 Establishment of AI Unit and Digital Innovation Center

The establishment of special units such as the Digital Innovation Hub or AI Competence Center is an important strategy in restructuring higher education organizations to face the era of artificial intelligence-based digital transformation. These units act as catalysts for change that bridges academic needs with technology implementation, ensuring AI adoption aligns with the institution's vision and mission. The existence of the digital innovation center encourages cross-disciplinary collaboration between faculty, lecturers, and researchers to develop adaptive learning systems, educational analytics, and sustainable AI ethics policies. Apart from being a research center, this unit is also a forum for training, policy experiments, and supervision of academic data governance. Thus, the Digital Innovation Center functions not only as a technological infrastructure, but also as the main motor for strengthening the culture of innovation, collaboration, and institutional readiness towards an ethical and future-oriented intelligent education ecosystem (Katsamakas & Pavlov, 2024).

The development and implementation of AI within the campus environment require an integrated approach that combines ethical policy frameworks, collaborative research, capacity building, and robust data governance. Digital Innovation Centers or AI Innovation Hubs play a strategic role as the driving force of this transformation, beginning with the formulation of ethical AI policies that uphold principles of algorithmic transparency, fairness, accountability, and data privacy. These policies must be supported by systematic algorithm audits and ethical risk assessments to prevent bias and protect academic integrity. At the same time, cross-faculty research collaboration bringing together computer science, education, management, and the humanities enables the creation of adaptive learning solutions that are not only technically advanced but also socially and culturally sensitive. To ensure sustainability, continuous digital competency training for lecturers, administrative staff, and students is essential, encompassing AI literacy, data ethics, and responsible technology use. All initiatives must be reinforced by strict supervision of academic data management in compliance with data protection regulations and information security standards. Through this holistic framework, AI implementation in higher education can be conducted responsibly, inclusively, and sustainably, fostering an innovative academic culture aligned with ethical and societal values.Bagian Atas Formulir

3.3 Educational Business Process Reengineering

Organizational restructuring cannot be separated from the process of reengineering the entire educational value chain. Institutions that successfully implement AI typically conduct digital process mapping to identify areas that need automation the most. For example, the process of admitting new students can be optimized using AI-based predictive analytics to assess the academic potential of prospective students, while automated grading systems can help lecturers assess learning outcomes more efficiently. Administrative processes such as financial management, attendance, and reporting can also be integrated into intelligent dashboards-based systems, which provide real-time information for decision-makers. AI also enables the emergence of adaptive learning systems, which adjust learning materials based on individual learning styles of students. Thus, education becomes more personalized, efficient, and high-impact. However, reengineering educational business processes requires a strategic approach that balances technological efficiency and pedagogical values. AI is supposed to be a supporter, not a replacement, of the role of humans in education (Andriana et al., 2024).

3.4 Development of Digital Competencies for Management and Academic Staff

Organizational restructuring without balancing the development of human resource competencies has the potential to create a digital divide that hinders the effectiveness of AI transformation in educational institutions. Therefore, improving AI literacy and digital leadership skills for educators and leaders is a crucial strategic step. AI literacy helps lecturers understand how technology works and ethical implications, while digital leadership allows management to make data-driven decisions adaptively. With this combination of competencies, institutions are not only able to adopt smart technologies, but also integrate them sustainably in academic culture and organizational governance.

Figure 2. Main tasks of the innovation center

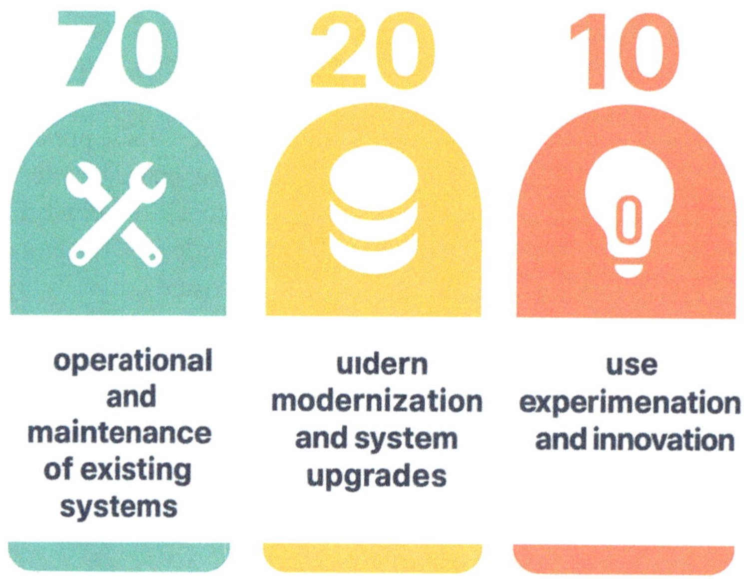

Lecturers and education staff need to understand how AI algorithms work, data use ethics, and the ability to interpret automated analysis results. For example, training on AI-driven assessment or learning analytics helps lecturers in understanding student learning behavior in depth and adjusting learning methods in real-time. In addition, university leaders also need new managerial competencies such as AI governance, digital ethics, and data-driven decision-making to be able to manage organizational change wisely and responsibly.

3.5 Organizational Culture Transformation Towards an AI-driven Mindset

AI transformation represents a paradigm shift in organizational thinking rather than merely the adoption of new technologies. An AI-supportive organizational culture is characterized by openness, cross-disciplinary collaboration, and a willingness to experiment. Higher education institutions therefore need to cultivate an AI-driven mindset that integrates data, analytics, and algorithmic reasoning into everyday decision-making. This can be achieved through a learning organization approach that encourages continuous learning, innovation, and knowledge sharing. Trust and transparency are critical in reducing resistance to change, particularly through clear data governance and role definition. Initiatives such as AI awareness programs, hackathons, and digital innovation challenges further strengthen collaboration and accelerate cultural adoption, ensuring sustainable and inclusive AI-driven transformation (Bukar et al., 2024).

4. FACULTY AND STAFF EMPOWERMENT: AI LITERACY AND PEDAGOGICAL INNOVATION

Pedagogical Innovation, which focuses on how to strengthen the capacity of lecturers and education staff is the main foundation in realizing artificial intelligence (AI)-based educational transformation. AI literacy includes not only technical abilities in operating AI-based systems, but also includes ethical, pedagogical, and reflective understanding of its impact in the context of learning. Educators who have high AI literacy are able to design adaptive, personalized, and data-driven learning strategies. In addition, staff empowerment through cross-disciplinary training and collaboration is a crucial step to building a culture of sustainable innovation in the academic environment. Thus, the integration of AI literacy and pedagogical innovation not only improves the quality of teaching, but also strengthens the readiness of institutions to face challenges and opportunities in the dynamic era of digital education (Essa et al., 2023).

4.1 Increasing AI Literacy among Lecturers

In the context of higher education, AI literacy is a fundamental prerequisite for lecturers to effectively design, evaluate, and implement technology-based learning. AI literacy refers to an individual's ability to understand the concepts, potential, risks, and social implications of artificial intelligence, encompassing not only technical skills such as data analysis, but also conceptual knowledge of algorithmic processes, bias formation, and cognitive impacts. To strengthen this literacy, universities increasingly offer practice-oriented training, introducing lecturers to tools such as ChatGPT, Copilot, and LMS-integrated learning analytics. These programs are complemented by ethical and policy education, emphasizing transparency, fairness, and accountability. Integrating AI literacy into continuous professional development ensures sustainable digital competence aligned with evolving technologies (Essa et al., 2023).

4.2 Pedagogical Innovation and Adaptive Learning

One of the most transformative impacts of AI in education is the development of adaptive learning models that personalize content, pace, and instructional strategies based on individual student needs. However, the effectiveness of adaptive learning depends not only on technology, but also on lecturers' pedagogical capacity to design learner-centered instructional strategies. AI enables lecturers to utilize learning analytics, intelligent tutoring systems, and real-time feedback to understand student learning patterns, identify at-risk learners, and design targeted interventions. In this collaborative model, AI provides data-driven insights, while lecturers interpret them through pedagogical expertise and empathy. Consequently, AI enriches pedagogical innovation without replacing the essential human role in education (Essa et al., 2023).

4.3 Human–AI Collaboration in the Learning Process

AI–human collaboration represents a new paradigm in higher education in which technology functions as intelligence amplification rather than a substitute for educators. Through analytical, predictive, and adaptive capabilities, AI supports lecturers in tasks such as automated assessment, learning material recommendation, and analysis of student engagement, allowing educators to focus on higher-value pedagogical activities. Nevertheless, effective collaboration requires lecturers to act as *human-in-the-loop* decision makers who critically interpret AI outputs and ensure alignment with human values, including empathy, fairness, and contextual understanding of learners. While AI co-teachers and advisory systems open new opportunities for pedagogical innovation, they also introduce ethical challenges related to bias and transparency. Therefore, robust AI governance, algorithm audits, and educator training are essential to ensure responsible and human-centered AI–human collaboration

4.4 Overcoming Resistance to Technological Change

Resistance to technological change is a major barrier in empowering educators, often driven by fears that AI may replace lecturers' roles, reduce academic autonomy, or increase administrative burdens. This resistance typically stems from limited understanding of AI's actual function and benefits. To address this, institutions must adopt a human-centered and participatory change management approach by clearly communicating how AI supports, rather than replaces, academic work. Involving lecturers from the early stages of AI system design fosters ownership and trust, while strong leadership commitment through ethical policies and incentives reinforces acceptance. Communities of practice further encourage knowledge sharing, gradually transforming resistance into engagement and innovation (Albashiry et al., 2024).

4.5 Building a Culture of Innovation in the Academic Environment

An innovation culture is a fundamental pillar for the sustainable application of AI in education, encompassing not only technological capability but also organizational mindset, leadership vision, and value alignment. Such a culture is fostered through cross-disciplinary collaboration, openness to experimentation, and institutional support that reduces fear of failure. Universities can strengthen this ecosystem by encouraging initiatives such as AI teaching labs, hackathons, and innovation challenges, alongside incentive systems that recognize AI-driven pedagogical and research contributions. Visionary leadership plays a crucial role in embedding ethical AI practices and ensuring that digital transformation remains aligned with human values, inclusivity, and social justice, positioning AI as a strategic enabler of adaptive and future-ready learning (Katsamakas & Pavlov, 2024).

5. INFRASTRUCTURE AND DIGITAL ECOSYSTEMS: TECHNOLOGY, DATA, AND ARCHITECTURE

Artificial Intelligence (AI)-based education transformation cannot be realized without the support of a strong, adaptive, and sustainable digital infrastructure. This infrastructure includes technology components, data systems, and digital architecture that are integrated to support academic, administrative, and research processes. An effective digital ecosystem in higher education serves as the foundation for *data-driven institutions*, where strategic decisions are based on accurate and real-time data analysis.

In this context, AI-ready infrastructure is not just a collection of hardware and software, but a complex system that integrates Learning Management Systems (LMS), cloud computing, integrated data architectures, and robust cybersecurity mechanisms. The combination of these elements allows for efficient, transparent, and ethical management of learning, administration, and research. Therefore, the planning and implementation of AI infrastructure in universities must consider the dimensions of technology, governance, and environmental and social sustainability.

Research by Luo et al. (2025) highlights the importance of implementing AI-based intelligent systems to support the efficiency and stability of educational digital infrastructure. In the context of LMS, the use of distributed architecture and AI-based resource management has been shown to improve the performance of online learning systems, particularly in multi-user environments with high processing needs. This study shows that the optimization of digital infrastructure through AI plays an important role in strengthening an adaptive and sustainable education ecosystem (Luo et al., 2025).

5.1 Integration of Learning Systems and Technology Architecture

Learning system integration is a key foundation in developing AI-based educational infrastructure. Modern Learning Management Systems (LMS) function not only as content repositories but also as learning analytics platforms that capture student behavior, learning progress, and instructional effectiveness. When integrated with AI, LMS platforms enable adaptive and personalized learning through automated content recommendations and early detection of learning difficulties using predictive analytics. To operate effectively, these systems require open, modular, and scalable architectures supported by APIs to ensure interoperability across academic, administrative, and research platforms. The adoption of microservices architecture further enhances flexibility, enabling rapid innovation and seamless integration of advanced tools such as generative AI and NLP-based learning analytics (Cetinguc & Calik, 2025).

5.2 Data Management, Cloud Computing, and Interoperability

Data functions as the primary driver of AI systems in higher education, making robust data governance essential for ensuring analytical accuracy and ethical decision-making. Effective governance encompasses data integrity, accessibility, and security, supported by clear access policies, quality assurance mechanisms, and compliance with personal data protection regulations such as the GDPR (Kim et al., 2025).

Cloud computing platforms enable scalable, cost-efficient data storage and AI analytics while supporting cross-institutional collaboration. Equally important is system interoperability that integrates learning, academic, and administrative platforms into a unified data ecosystem. A centrally managed data architecture, combined with strong data literacy across organizational levels, enables predictive analytics, reduces algorithmic bias, and enhances transparency in AI-driven decision-making (Gupta & Benila, 2025).

5.3 Cybersecurity and Ethical Governance of Digital Infrastructure

Cybersecurity has become a critical priority as higher education institutions increasingly rely on digital systems and AI. The education sector is a major target of cyberattacks, ranging from data breaches to system manipulation, requiring universities to adopt comprehensive cybersecurity frameworks. Key measures include multi-factor authentication, data encryption, regular security audits, and continuous security awareness training for lecturers, students, and staff, since human error remains a dominant risk factor. Beyond technical safeguards, ethical governance is essential to ensure AI systems are transparent, auditable, and free from bias. Establishing dedicated AI ethics and digital governance bodies strengthens trust, supports compliance, and enables the responsible and sustainable use of AI in education (Sysoieva et al., 2025).

6. FINANCIAL AND RESOURCE STRATEGIES FOR SUSTAINABLE AI INTEGRATION

Digital transformation through the integration of Artificial Intelligence (AI) has become a strategic imperative for organizations in various sectors, but challenges in the allocation and management of financial resources are often a major barrier to sustainable implementation. Studies show that many AI initiatives fail not because of technological limitations, but rather because of a lack of comprehensive financial planning and suboptimal resource management. This chapter explores the holistic financial strategies needed to support sustainable AI integration, covering various financing models, cost-benefit analysis methodologies, public-private partnerships, cloud infrastructure optimization, energy efficiency, and cost-effective license management. By integrating circular economy principles and a long-term perspective, this discussion emphasizes that AI investment must be evaluated not only from the immediate return on investment, but also its contribution to organizational resilience and competitive advantage. Through a combination of theory, best practices, and real-world examples, this chapter provides practical guidance for leaders and strategists in building a solid financial foundation for sustainable AI integration.

6.1 Understanding the Investment Landscape for AI Implementation

This section highlights funding strategies and resource management as critical foundations for the sustainable implementation of AI. AI investment should be viewed not merely as a technological expense, but as a long-term strategic commitment that encompasses infrastructure, talent development, training, and system maintenance. Organizations must carefully select financing models that align with their scale, digital maturity, and strategic objectives, whether through direct capitalization for greater control or subscription-based and cloud models for flexibility and predictable costs. To ensure optimal return on investment, institutions also need robust evaluation frameworks with clear performance indicators, enabling data-driven decisions, efficient resource allocation, and continuous improvement of AI-driven initiatives.

6.2 Cost-Benefit Analysis and Financial Planning Models

This approach includes financing models such as public–private partnerships (PPP), optimized IT budget allocation, and rigorous cost–benefit analysis of AI investments. Cost–benefit analysis is essential to assess AI feasibility by considering not only direct costs, such as hardware and software, but also indirect costs related to process changes, organizational resistance, and transitional disruptions. PPP models provide an effective alternative for public and non-profit institutions by sharing financial risks while leveraging private-sector expertise and innovation. Meanwhile, optimized IT budget allocation requires mature portfolio management, often guided by the 70–20–10 principle, which balances system maintenance, modernization, and innovation to ensure financial sustainability and adaptive technological growth (Ferreira & Santos, 2022).

Figure 3. 70-20-10 principles for IT budget allocation optimization

In conducting cost-benefit analysis, organizations must consider both tangible benefits (operational cost savings, increased revenue) and intangible benefits (increased customer satisfaction, brand reputation, organizational capabilities). The analysis should also include a realistic time-horizon, given that the benefits of AI investments can often only be realized after a time-consuming period of implementation and stabilization. It is also important to integrate sensitivity analysis and scenario planning in financial modeling. This helps organizations understand how changes in key assumptions (such as technology cost, adoption rate, or competitive landscape) can affect the ROI of an AI project. Thus, organizations can develop robust contingency plans and risk mitigation strategies.

6.3 Resource Optimization and Operational Efficiency

Efficient resource management is fundamental to the long-term sustainability of AI implementation, encompassing cloud infrastructure optimization, energy efficiency, licensing, compliance, and human capital management. Organizations can reduce costs and enhance flexibility through cloud optimization strategies such as rightsizing, auto-scaling, reserved instances, and hybrid or multi-cloud models that prevent vendor lock-in. Energy-efficient AI operations, including algorithm optimization, renewable energy use, edge computing, and selection of green data centers, help minimize operational costs and environmental impact. Cost-effective licensing requires strong software asset management, regular audits, and selective adoption of open-source solutions. In parallel, optimizing human resources through upskilling, hybrid talent models, and strategic partnerships strengthens organizational capability and sustainability.

6.4 Sustainability and Long-term Financial Viability

By emphasizing sustainability, this section highlights the relevance of the circular economy in AI technology, where investments are evaluated not only from a short-term return on investment (ROI) perspective but also in terms of their contribution to long-term organizational resilience and adaptability. Financial sustainability in AI implementation requires a value-creation perspective that extends beyond immediate efficiency gains and supports future-oriented capabilities (Cetinguc & Calik, 2025). The circular economy approach in AI promotes the treatment of hardware, software, and data as optimizable, reusable, and recyclable assets throughout their life cycles. This includes extending hardware lifespan through proper maintenance, reallocating equipment to less demanding workloads, and ensuring responsible disposal or recycling. For software and AI models, this approach encourages modular architectures, model reusability across applications, and contributions to open-source ecosystems (Sonntag et al., 2024).

AI investments should also be assessed based on their ability to strengthen organizational resilience in volatile and uncertain environments. AI enhances adaptability by improving decision-making accuracy, forecasting capabilities, and automating routine tasks, allowing human resources to focus on strategic initiatives. From a financial perspective, sustainable AI innovation requires diversified funding strategies, including reinvestment of cost savings, access to digital transformation grants, and innovative mechanisms such as impact investing or sustainability-linked financing (Bhagwanrao & Tiwari, 2025).

Furthermore, organizations must foster a culture of financial accountability by defining clear project responsibilities, conducting regular investment performance evaluations, and ensuring transparent financial reporting. Proactive risk management addressing technological obsolescence, regulatory changes, cybersecurity threats, and talent shortages is equally essential. Ultimately, a holistic financial strategy and effective resource management form the foundation for sustainable AI integration, ensuring long-term value, resilience, and competitiveness (Katsamakas & Pavlov, 2024; Kim et al., 2025).

7. CULTURAL AND ETHICAL DIMENSIONS: CHANGE MANAGEMENT AND POLICY DEVELOPMENT

Artificial Intelligence (AI)-based digital transformation in higher education is not only a technological issue, but also a fundamental change in organizational culture, ethical values, and policy governance. The application of AI requires educational institutions to be not only technically prepared, but also morally and socially. The cultural and ethical dimensions play a crucial role in ensuring that the application of AI is aligned with the principles of justice, transparency, and social responsibility. In addition, adaptive and visionary policy development is the foundation for AI integration to be sustainable and inclusive throughout the academic ecosystem.

7.1 Change Management and Organizational Cultural Adaptation

Change management is a critical pillar in ensuring the success of AI-based transformation in higher education, as it requires a fundamental shift from traditional practices to data- and algorithm-driven learning and management models. Such changes often generate resistance among lecturers, staff, and students, particularly when established roles are perceived to be at risk. Therefore, change strategies must adopt a human-centered approach that prioritizes transparent communication, stakeholder participation, and continuous learning. University leaders play a key role as change agents by fostering an adaptive and collaborative culture and embedding values of innovation and trust in technology. The establishment of formal structures, such as AI steering committees, combined with ongoing organizational learning initiatives including AI literacy training and innovation labs supports cultural readiness and long-term transformation.

7.2 Algorithmic Fairness and Transparency in the Use of AI

The application of AI in education offers significant benefits for learning efficiency and personalization, yet it also introduces the risk of algorithmic bias arising from unrepresentative data, opaque models, or misinterpretation of outputs. In educational contexts, such bias can lead to unfair outcomes in assessment, admissions, and scholarship allocation. To address this, universities must establish strong algorithmic governance mechanisms, including regular audits of fairness, accuracy, and transparency through an Ethical AI Review Board. The adoption of Explainable AI (XAI) is essential to ensure that AI-driven decisions are understandable and accountable to all stakeholders. Furthermore, fostering a culture of data transparency and algorithmic accountability through clear documentation, model disclosure, and error-reporting procedures demonstrates an institutional commitment to equity, diversity, and ethical responsibility in AI deployment.

7.3 Data Privacy and Security of Academic Information

AI-based transformation in higher education is inherently dependent on large-scale data usage, including academic records, learning behaviors, and students' digital footprints, which raises critical concerns related to privacy and information security. To address these risks, institutions must apply the privacy-by-design principle at every stage of AI system development, integrating data protection mechanisms from the initial design phase, as highlighted by Wang et al. (2025). A comprehensive data governance framework is essential, covering access control, encryption, secure storage, and data lifecycle management, while ensuring compliance with global regulations such as GDPR and national frameworks like Indonesia's Personal Data Protection (PDP) Law (Wang et al., 2025). Beyond technical safeguards, ethical considerations are equally important, requiring informed consent, purpose limitation, and responsible data use. When privacy and security are rigorously upheld, institutional trust in AI systems is strengthened, enabling ethical and sustainable technology adoption.

7.4 Visionary Leadership and Inclusive AI Policy Development

Visionary leadership is a critical factor in ensuring the success of AI-based transformation in higher education, as it requires balancing technological innovation with social responsibility, ethics, and long-term sustainability. Effective leaders promote inclusive and participatory AI policies by involving lecturers, students, staff, and the wider community, ensuring that digital transformation reflects shared academic values rather than top-down mandates. Adaptive policy design and regular evaluation enable institutions to respond to rapid technological change while assessing social, pedagogical, and economic impacts. Through ethical foresight, collaborative governance, and strong external networks, universities can harness AI to enhance learning quality, equity, and public trust while safeguarding human values and academic integrity.

8. STAKEHOLDER COLLABORATION AND CASE STUDIES OF INSTITUTIONAL TRANSFORMATION

Artificial Intelligence (AI)-based transformation in the world of education cannot be done in isolation. The success of AI integration depends on strategic collaboration between various government stakeholders, industry, academia, communities, and nonprofits. Each party has a unique role in building a sustainable and inclusive ecosystem, both through policy provision, technology development, funding, and joint research. This chapter discusses cross-sector collaboration models and presents a number of case studies from educational institutions in various contexts that have succeeded and failed to adopt AI systemically.

8.1 Multi-Stakeholder Collaboration Model in the Education AI Ecosystem

Multi-stakeholder collaboration is essential for the effective and ethical application of AI in the education sector. Governments play a key role as regulators and facilitators by providing digital infrastructure and ensuring compliance with ethical standards and data protection policies. Industry partners contribute technological innovation through public–private partnerships, while academic institutions advance research, theory, and practical implementation. Civil society helps ensure that AI adoption remains aligned with human values. Successful collaboration is based on co-creation and shared accountability, involving stakeholders in joint decision-making. However, transparent governance frameworks are necessary to prevent conflicts of interest, particularly regarding data ownership and research priorities.

8.2 AI Transformation Case Study at Multimedia University Malaysia

Multimedia University (MMU) Malaysia is one of the higher education institutions in Southeast Asia that has successfully implemented AI-based transformation in a structured manner through the development of a decision-making framework for the use of generative AI in campus learning and governance. Since 2022, MMU has begun integrating technologies such as ChatGPT, academic AI agents, and administrative automation systems to improve the efficiency and quality of academic services. The initiative is supported by a collaboration between universities, the Malaysian Ministry of Higher Education, as well as local technology industry partners such as Telekom Malaysia Research & Development, which together create a sustainable AI-based innovation ecosystem. This effort is in line with research findings on AI adoption in Malaysian universities, which show that institutions like MMU are actively building digital readiness and governance for long-term AI implementation (Saidin et al., 2021)

The success of MMU is strongly supported by a comprehensive internal governance framework that integrates ethical oversight, technological innovation, and human resource development. Through the establishment of an AI Ethics and Governance Committee, the university ensures that all AI systems comply with principles of fairness, transparency, and accountability while safeguarding academic integrity and minimizing algorithmic bias. Predictive analytics further enable early identification of at-risk students, allowing timely and targeted interventions. Complementing this, MMU's AI Literacy for Educators and Staff program builds institutional readiness by strengthening digital and ethical competencies, fostering an adaptive and innovation-oriented campus culture.

8.3 Lessons from Cases and Implications for Educational Institutions

From the various cases above, it can be concluded that the success of AI transformation in education depends on three main factors: collaborative leadership, ethical governance, and human empowerment. Institutions like NUS demonstrate that a cross-sectoral collaborative approach and commitment to ethical values results in both efficient and responsible AI systems. On the contrary, the failure of public universities in Latin America underscores the great risks of an uninclusive and under-participation approach to technology.

For institutions that are planning a transformation, some strategic recommendations can be seen from the following table:

Table 1. Recommended transformation design strategies

Yes	Key Strategies	Purpose	How to Practice / Practical Implementation
1	Building a collaborative ecosystem from the planning stage	Creating cross-actor synergies to accelerate AI adoption and sustainability	a. A *steering committee* consisting of student lecturers, regulators, and industry partners. b. Hold *a focus group discussion (FGD)* to develop an educational AI vision and roadmap. c. Use collaborative digital platforms (such as Miro or Notion) for cross-institutional coordination.- Schedule a joint evaluation each semester to review progress.
2	Prioritizing ethical principles and transparency	Ensuring public trust and the sustainability of AI systems responsibly	a. Apply *the AI Ethics Framework* based on UNESCO or OECD. b. Conduct periodic algorithmic audits to detect data bias and ethical non-conformities.- Publicly publish the privacy policy and audit results. c. Form an internal AI ethics committee involving legal, technology, and ethics experts.
3	Focus on strengthening the capacity of human resources (HR)	Improving digital competence and readiness of educators and students	a. Hold *AI literacy training* for lecturers, education staff, and students. b. Integrate ethical AI and data management topics in the curriculum.- Provide *digital leadership workshops* for faculty and rectorate leaders. c. Build *a micro-credential* system or AI certification for the academic community.
4	Using data as an instrument of quality improvement, not administrative control	Directing the use of data to support the well-being and effectiveness of learning	a. Implement *a learning analytics dashboard* that focuses on improving student learning outcomes. b. Use the results of data analysis for personalization of learning, not for supervision. c. Involve students in data-driven decision-making.- Evaluate the impact of data use on user motivation and well-being.
5	Evaluating the long-term sustainability of AI transformation	Assess the success of AI implementation from a social, ethical, and institutional perspective	a. Develop *AI sustainability metrics* (technological, social, economic, and ethical) indicators b. Conduct a social impact and digital inclusion survey every year.- Use *an impact assessment* approach to measure long-term effects. c. Encourage sustainable innovation through research grants and industry-academic collaboration.

Cross-stakeholder collaboration is the foundation of sustainable AI-driven institutional transformation. AI is not only changing the way educational institutions operate, but it is also demanding a redefinition of the relationship between humans, technology, and social values. The cases from Singapore, Latin America, and Finland show that successful AI adoption is inseparable from a commitment to ethical governance, public participation, and human empowerment.

In a global context, strong collaboration between governments, academia, industry, and society will determine the future direction of AI-based education. By building a transparent, inclusive, and socially well-being-oriented ecosystem, educational institutions can ensure that AI is not just a tool of technological innovation, but a transformative force for the advancement of civilization.

9. IMPACT MEASUREMENT, RISK MITIGATION, AND FUTURE-PROOFING STRATEGIES

The implementation of artificial intelligence (AI) in higher education requires a strategic approach that focuses not only on technology adoption, but also on impact evaluation mechanisms, risk mitigation, and ongoing planning to ensure long-term digital resilience. AI-based transformation brings significant changes to organizational governance, learning processes, and human resource competencies. Therefore, the success of AI integration cannot only be measured by the level of use of its technology, but also by the quality of institutional performance improvement, pedagogical relevance, process efficiency, and organizational adaptability to future technological disruptions. The literature shows that educational institutions that develop AI strategies comprehensively tend to have higher readiness to manage risk and ensure the sustainability of innovation(Ahmad et al., 2024; Bettahi et al., 2025). In addition, a systemic approach that combines evaluation, ethics, and digital governance has been proven to strengthen an adaptive organizational culture and increase academic confidence in the use of AI (Huang et al., 2023). As such, this section discusses three key elements that form the foundation of sustainable digital transformation: impact measurement, risk mitigation, and future-proofing strategies.

9.1. Evaluation of the Impact of AI Implementation on Organizational Performance and Learning Outcomes

Evaluating the impact of AI implementation in education must combine quantitative and qualitative approaches to capture both measurable outcomes and human experiences. Quantitative indicators include academic performance, student retention, course completion rates, and operational efficiency, particularly in adaptive and personalized learning systems. These metrics provide objective evidence of performance improvement. However, qualitative evaluation is equally important, as it reveals user perceptions, learning experiences, system fairness, and the quality of human–AI interaction. Together, these approaches enable institutions to assess whether AI genuinely enhances learning and decision-making processes, while also providing continuous feedback to guide future innovation and improvement strategies.

9.2. Risk Mitigation Strategies against System Failure, Data Security, and Algorithmic Bias

AI adoption in education introduces ethical, technical, and operational risks that require integrated mitigation strategies. Ethical risks include algorithmic bias, lack of transparency, and privacy violations, which can undermine fairness and trust. These must be addressed through AI governance mechanisms such as audits, documentation, and explainability standards. Technical risks such as system failure, prediction errors, and cybersecurity threats require redundancy, security testing, and continuous monitoring. Operational risks related to limited digital literacy should be mitigated through structured training and mentoring programs. An integrated framework combining regulation, technology safeguards, and human readiness is essential for safe and responsible AI implementation.

9.3. Sustainability and Future-Proofing Strategies to Build Digital Resilience in the AI Era

Long-term sustainability of AI in education depends on future-proofing strategies that build digital resilience. Institutions must strengthen digital infrastructure through interoperable platforms, adaptive cloud architectures, and integrated data systems capable of supporting evolving AI applications. Equally important is continuous human resource development, ensuring lecturers and staff remain proficient in AI, data governance, and analytics. A culture of innovation and adaptability enables institutions to respond effectively to technological change. At the strategic level, long-term policies, future risk assessments, and investment in relevant AI research are required. Collaboration with industry and research partners further enhances institutional resilience and innovation capacity.

10. CONCLUSION

AI-based digital transformation in higher education represents a strategic and systemic shift that extends far beyond technology adoption, encompassing fundamental changes in learning practices, data management, and institutional governance. This conclusion emphasizes that successful transformation depends on the institution's ability to integrate three core dimensions: rigorous impact evaluation, comprehensive risk mitigation, and sustainable long-term development strategies. Impact evaluation must be approached holistically by combining quantitative indicators such as learning analytics, student retention, academic performance, and operational efficiency with qualitative insights derived from lecturer and student experiences, academic culture, and learning environment dynamics. This integrated approach ensures that AI initiatives are not only technically effective but also pedagogically meaningful and socially accepted. Without such balanced evaluation, institutions risk adopting AI solutions that appear efficient on paper but fail to deliver genuine educational value or align with human-centered learning principles.

Equally critical is the development of robust risk mitigation and sustainability strategies that enable institutions to remain resilient amid rapid technological change. AI adoption introduces technical, ethical, and governance-related risks, including data breaches, system failures, and algorithmic bias, which must be addressed through strong digital infrastructure, data governance, ethical oversight, and regulatory compliance. Long-term sustainability further requires investment in human capital, continuous professional development, and an organizational culture that supports innovation, adaptability, and ethical responsibility. Higher education institutions must design flexible transformation roadmaps, foster interdisciplinary collaboration, and ensure that AI serves as an empowering tool that enhances rather than replaces the human role in education. Ultimately, AI-driven digital transformation is a continuous journey toward a smarter, more inclusive, and resilient educational ecosystem, where technology, people, and values are aligned to create lasting academic and societal impact.

REFERENCES

Ahmad, K., Iqbal, W., El-Hassan, A., Qadir, J., Benhaddou, D., Ayyash, M., & Al-Fuqaha, A. (2024). Data-Driven Artificial Intelligence in Education: A Comprehensive Review. *IEEE Transactions on Learning Technologies*, *17*, 12–31. DOI: 10.1109/TLT.2023.3314610

Albashiry, N. M., Belhadj, H., & Al-Smadi, M. (2024). A Digital Competency Framework for University Teachers: Towards Agile and Sustainable Curriculum. *2024 ASU International Conference in Emerging Technologies for Sustainability and Intelligent Systems (ICETSIS)*, 1491–1494. DOI: 10.1109/ICETSIS61505.2024.10459701

AlHakim, M. R. Sherleen, Kelly, & Chandra, Y. U. (2024). Indonesian Language Learning Application as the Key to Equalizing Educational Development in Indonesia, Especially in Remote, Outermost, and Underdeveloped Areas (3T). *2024 10th International HCI and UX Conference in Indonesia (CHIuXiD)*, 36–41. DOI: 10.1109/CHIuXiD64022.2024.10860643

Andriana, I., Suppiah, S. D., Yulianita, A., Thamrin, K. M. H., & Bashir, A. (2024). *Understanding the institutional change and organizational transformation : An exploratory analysis of Indonesian higher education. 8*(6), 1–19.

Bettahi, A., Beloudha, F.-Z., & Harroud, H. (2025). Continuous-Time Modeling in Educational Data Mining and Learning Analytics: A Literature Review on Methods, Ethics, and Emerging AI Trends. *IEEE Access : Practical Innovations, Open Solutions*, *13*, 181443–181464. DOI: 10.1109/ACCESS.2025.3622103

Bhagwanrao, N. N., & Tiwari, B. B. (2025). Optimizing Investment Approaches using AI-Driven Predictive Analysis and Cloud Analysis. *2025 World Skills Conference on Universal Data Analytics and Sciences (WorldSUAS)*, 1–6. DOI: 10.1109/WorldSUAS66815.2025.11199193

Bukar, U. A. L. I., Sayeed, S., Member, S., & Sneesl, R. (2024). Decision-Making Framework for the Utilization of Generative Artificial Intelligence in Education : A Case Study of ChatGPT. *IEEE Access : Practical Innovations, Open Solutions*, *12*(June), 95368–95389. DOI: 10.1109/ACCESS.2024.3425172

Cetinguc, B., & Calik, E. (2025). Navigating Innovation Process With Integration Of Artificial Intelligence. *IEEE Engineering Management Review*, **•••**, 1–27. DOI: 10.1109/EMR.2025.3624362

Chaaban, Y., Qadhi, S., Chen, J., & Du, X. (2024). *education sciences Understanding Researchers ' AI Readiness in a Higher Education Context : Q Methodology Research.*

Essa, S. G., Celik, T., & Human-Hendricks, N. E. (2023). Personalized Adaptive Learning Technologies Based on Machine Learning Techniques to Identify Learning Styles: A Systematic Literature Review. *IEEE Access : Practical Innovations, Open Solutions*, *11*, 48392–48409. DOI: 10.1109/ACCESS.2023.3276439

Ferreira, H. R., & Santos, A. M. P. (2022). A review of strategies for implementing learning technologies in organizations. *2022 17th Iberian Conference on Information Systems and Technologies (CISTI)*, 1–6. DOI: 10.23919/CISTI54924.2022.9820254

Gupta, D., & Benila, S. (2025). Attention-Guided U-Net With Grad-CAM for Explainable Polyp Segmentation in Colonoscopy Images. *IEEE Access : Practical Innovations, Open Solutions*, *13*, 185125–185136. DOI: 10.1109/ACCESS.2025.3626159

Gutierrez, S. S. M., Pérez, S. L., & Munguía, M. G. (2022). Artificial Intelligence in e-Learning Plausible Scenarios in Latin America and New Graduation Competencies. *IEEE Revista Iberoamericana de Technologias del Aprendizaje, 17*(1), 31–40. DOI: 10.1109/RITA.2022.3149833

Huang, C., Zhang, Z., Mao, B., & Yao, X. (2023). An Overview of Artificial Intelligence Ethics. *IEEE Transactions on Artificial Intelligence, 4*(4), 799–819. DOI: 10.1109/TAI.2022.3194503

Katsamakas, E., & Pavlov, O. V. (2024). *Artificial Intelligence and the Transformation of Higher Education Institutions : A Systems Approach.* 1–21.

Kim, B.-J., Jeong, S., Cho, B.-K., & Chung, J.-B. (2025). AI Governance in the Context of the EU AI Act. *IEEE Access : Practical Innovations, Open Solutions, 13*, 144126–144142. DOI: 10.1109/ACCESS.2025.3598023

Liu, T., Liu, Z., Zhu, F., & Mao, Z. (2023). Dual Parallel-PMSM System Using Single PMSM Control Hardware: A PLL-Integrated UIO Approach. *IEEE Transactions on Power Electronics, 38*(12), 15300–15313. DOI: 10.1109/TPEL.2023.3309901

Luo, Y., Lai, J., Shi, S., Chen, C., Qi, S., Zhang, J., & Wang, Q. (2025). Castor: Optimizing Deep Learning Job Scheduling in Multi-Tenant GPU Clusters via Intelligent Colocation. *IEEE Transactions on Cloud Computing*, •••, 1–18. DOI: 10.1109/TCC.2025.3624752

Petrov, I., Chikurtev, D., & Krusteva, A. (2025). Artificial Intelligence and Cyber Security in Education: Bibliographic Mapping and Entropy Analysis of Science Research (SCOPUS, 2015-2024). *2025 19th Conference on Electrical Machines, Drives and Power Systems (ELMA)*, 1–8. DOI: 10.1109/ELMA65795.2025.11083516

Saidin, N., Kamarozaman, N. F. H., Roslan, F. S., Ralib, A. A. M., & Sing, L. K. (2021). Graphene-oxide Coated on Fiber Bragg Grating for Temperature Sensor. *2021 8th International Conference on Computer and Communication Engineering (ICCCE)*, 269–273. DOI: 10.1109/ICCCE50029.2021.9467205

Sonntag, M., Mehmann, S., Mehmann, J., & Teuteberg, F. (2024). Development and Evaluation of a Maturity Model for AI Deployment Capability of Manufacturing Companies. *Information Systems Management, 42*(1), 37–67. DOI: 10.1080/10580530.2024.2319041

Sysoieva, I., Pukas, A., Dobizha, N., Pohrishchuk, B., Pohrishchuk, O., & Nadvynychnyy, S. (2025). Synergy of Information Technology and Management: Digital Strategies for Improving Management Efficiency. *2025 15th International Conference on Advanced Computer Information Technologies (ACIT)*, 287–292. DOI: 10.1109/ACIT65614.2025.11185822

Wang, H., Luo, W., Xie, X., Zheng, P., Huang, W., & Huang, J. (2025). Adv-Inversion: Stealthy Adversarial Attacks via GAN-Inversion for Facial Privacy Protection. *IEEE Transactions on Information Forensics and Security, 20*, 11892–11906. DOI: 10.1109/TIFS.2025.3625635

Wei, X., & Liu, X. (2023). Bipartite Synchronization of Multiplex Networks With Cooperative-Antagonistic Interactions. *2023 China Automation Congress (CAC)*, 7308–7312. DOI: 10.1109/CAC59555.2023.10451543

Yagyaeva, E., Turobova, M., Nazirova, R., Daminova, Y., Merganova, N., & Oripova, N. (2024). A Layout of Bridging Learning Process to fill the Gaps Through AI to make the Technical Education for Better Access. *2024 4th International Conference on Advance Computing and Innovative Technologies in Engineering (ICACITE)*, 612–616. DOI: 10.1109/ICACITE60783.2024.10617424

Zhou, R., Poechmueller, P., & Wang, Y. (2022). An Analog Circuit Design and Optimization System With Rule-Guided Genetic Algorithm. *IEEE Transactions on Computer-Aided Design of Integrated Circuits and Systems*, *41*(12), 5182–5192. DOI: 10.1109/TCAD.2022.3166637

KEY TERMS AND DEFINITIONS

AI Governance: A policy and ethical framework for the responsible use of AI.

Algorithmic Bias: An injustice that arises because algorithms process unbalanced or biased data.

Artificial Intelligence (AI): Technology that allows machines to perform tasks that typically require human intelligence

Data Governance: A data management system to ensure data security, privacy, and quality.

Digital Competency: The ability of individuals to use digital technology effectively cultivated.

Digital Resilience: The ability of an organization to survive, recover, and adapt to digital disruptions.

Disaster Recovery: A system recovery plan in the event of a failure or cyberattack.

Future-Proofing: Strategies ensure organizations remain relevant in rapid technological change.

Learning Analytics: The process of analyzing learning data to improve educational decisions.

Predictive Analytics: Analysis of data to predict future outcomes or behavior.

Chapter 15

Educational Transformation With AI and Development of a Web-Based Adaptive Learning System

Jaime Aguilar-Ortiz
http://orcid.org/0009-0003-5302-1454
Universidad Politécnica de Pachuca, Mexico

Ocotlán Diáz-Parra
Universidad Politécnica de Pachuca, Mexico

Jorge A. Ruiz-Vanoye
Universidad Politécnica de Pachuca, Mexico

Marco A. Vera-Jiménez
http://orcid.org/0009-0009-3712-1440
Universidad Politécnica de Pachuca, Mexico

Víctor M. Zamudio-García
http://orcid.org/0000-0002-4660-8025
Universidad Politécnica Metropolitana de Hidalgo, Mexico

Francisco R. Trejo-Macotela
http://orcid.org/0000-0003-2133-3456
Universidad Politécnica de Pachuca, Mexico

Carlos R. Domínguez-Mayorga
http://orcid.org/0009-0007-1018-4412
Universidad Politécnica de Pachuca, Mexico

ABSTRACT

This article presents the development of an AI-based adaptive learning prototype enhanced with a ChatGPT-powered generative agent, implemented as a functional web application that personalizes education according to each learner's abilities, pace, and recent performance. Through machine learning, data analytics, and real-time natural language interaction, the system dynamically adapts instructional materials, explains personalized recommendations, and offers formative feedback in human-like language. Built with Python for the backend and Plotly and Dash for the interactive frontend, the prototype embodies the vision of AI-driven independent learning combining data-driven personalization with conversational guidance to foster inclusivity, autonomy, and engagement while redefining the collaboration between educators, learners, and intelligent systems. The article code can be found at: https://github.com/JAIME6609/EDUCATION/blob/main/CODE-EDUCATIONAL-TRANSFORMATION-06.py

DOI: 10.4018/979-8-3373-7225-9.ch015

1. INTRODUCTION TO ADAPTIVE LEARNING IN EDUCATION

1.1. Definition and relevance of adaptive learning in the digital age.

Adaptive learning represents a change in basic assumptions in education by using technological intelligence to identify and respond to the particularities of each learner. Its core principle is grounded in personalization: the system collects information about learners' interactions such as accuracy, response times, and conceptual errors and continuously refines the instructional path based on this data (Johnson et al., 2016). This dynamic personalization transcends traditional differentiation by offering real-time adjustments that consider both cognitive and affective dimensions. Through predictive algorithms and behavioral analytics, adaptive learning environments anticipate areas of difficulty, providing alternative explanations or supplementary resources before disengagement occurs. The integration of generative AI, particularly through platforms such as ChatGPT, further enhances this adaptability by producing linguistically rich feedback that mirrors human tutoring. Learners thus receive not only data-driven recommendations but dialogic interactions that promote metacognitive reflection and self-regulation, two critical components in the construction of meaningful learning experiences (Pardo et al., 2016).

The significance of adaptive learning in the digital age lies in its ability to reconcile mass education with individualized attention. As classrooms evolve into hybrid and virtual ecosystems, the challenge is no longer access to information but the management of cognitive diversity and the cultivation of deep understanding. Adaptive systems, empowered by generative AI, address this challenge by aligning educational content with the learner's zone of proximal development, a notion rooted in Vygotsky's sociocultural theory thus ensuring that each student engages at an optimal level of difficulty. Moreover, these systems contribute to a culture of inclusivity, where learners with distinct abilities, motivations, and backgrounds receive equitable opportunities for growth. By generating personalized explanations and formative feedback in natural language, AI-driven adaptive learning platforms bridge the gap between technological mediation and human empathy. Consequently, they transform educational spaces into intelligent environments capable of evolving with each learner, enhancing engagement, fostering persistence, and improving academic achievement (Johnson et al., 2016; Pardo et al., 2016). Figure 1 illustrates a schematic representation of these principles and their systemic interactions.

Figure 1. Conceptual framework of AI-driven adaptive learning

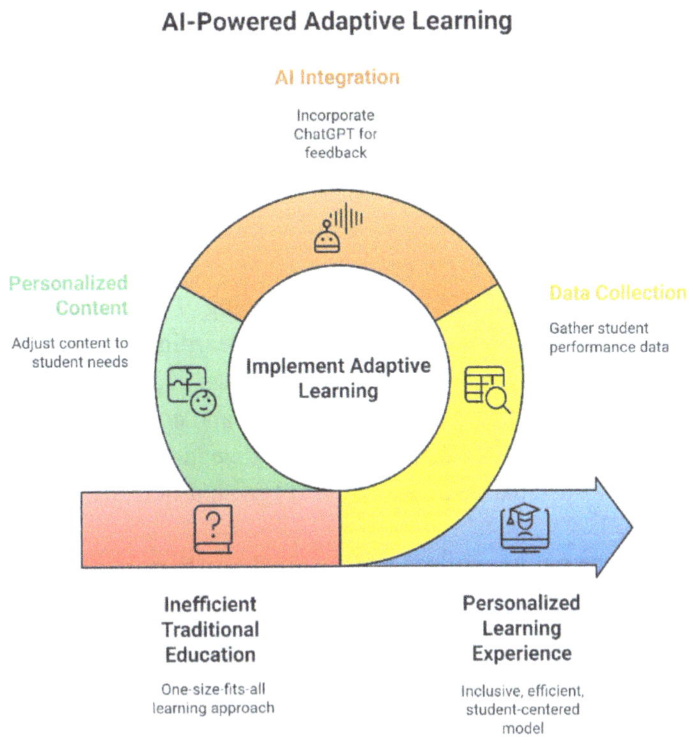

1.2. Impact of artificial intelligence on personalized learning.

Artificial intelligence (AI) has profoundly reshaped the landscape of personalized learning by enabling data-driven adaptation at scales previously unattainable in traditional education. Through advanced algorithms and data mining techniques, AI systems process extensive datasets that include not only academic performance metrics but also behavioral and interactional patterns gathered from learning management systems, digital assessments, and online activities (Holmes et al., 2019). This analytical capacity allows for the continuous refinement of learning trajectories, where instructional materials and evaluation mechanisms evolve dynamically in response to each learner's cognitive profile. The recent incorporation of generative AI, accessible through tools such as the ChatGPT API, marks a new stage in this evolution. Beyond the mere automation of instructional processes, these models introduce an interpretive dimension capable of generating contextually sensitive and human-like explanations. Learners are no longer passive recipients of algorithmic recommendations; instead, they engage in authentic dialogues that facilitate conceptual clarification, critical thinking, and deeper cognitive processing (Baker & Inventado, 2016). The interaction between analytical precision and generative adaptability thus fosters a hybrid pedagogy in which machine learning models complement, rather than replace, the human tutor's reflective and empathetic functions.

Furthermore, AI-enhanced educational environments provide mechanisms for early detection and prevention of learning difficulties by continuously monitoring patterns of error, hesitation, or disengagement. When students encounter persistent obstacles, the system can intervene through multimodal strategies ranging from adaptive quizzes and targeted practice to interactive explanations enriched with text, graphics, and audio. The integration of generative AI refines this process by allowing virtual tutors to deliver explanations that mirror natural pedagogical discourse, guiding students toward self-discovery rather than mere correction. Such interventions foster metacognitive awareness, empowering learners to recognize their own misconceptions and adjust their strategies accordingly. In addition, predictive analytics and conversational agents work together to anticipate potential dropout risks and cognitive overload, offering timely motivational support and scaffolding. These combined innovations not only enhance engagement and persistence but also ensure that learning remains inclusive, adaptive, and human-centered in an era of digital transformation. As Holmes et al. (2019) and Baker and Inventado (2016) have demonstrated, the convergence of data analytics and conversational AI represents a pivotal shift toward intelligent educational ecosystems that personalize instruction, democratize access to high-quality tutoring, and promote sustainable academic development in the digital age.

1.3. Objectives of the case study and its relationship to educational transformation.

This case study presents a comprehensive framework for the design and implementation of an adaptive learning web application that leverages artificial intelligence to individualize educational content according to each student's cognitive profile, skills, and learning rhythm. The platform's architecture integrates machine learning models capable of processing vast datasets that capture learners' interactions, performance metrics, and behavioral indicators in real time. This adaptive infrastructure enables the system to construct dynamic learning pathways that evolve as students advance, ensuring continuous alignment between instructional complexity and learner readiness. In its latest iteration, the inclusion of the ChatGPT API introduces a generative and explanatory layer that expands beyond simple adaptive mechanics to provide linguistic mediation and pedagogical interpretation. Through natural language feedback and personalized dialogue, the system translates abstract analytics into accessible narratives, helping students understand their strengths and areas for improvement. This combination of computational precision and human-like communication transforms the educational experience into an interactive partnership between learner and algorithm, one that stimulates autonomy, reflective thinking, and creative problem-solving within a supportive and adaptive digital ecosystem (Luckin et al., 2016).

At the institutional level, the deployment of such systems represents a critical evolution toward evidence-based academic management and pedagogical innovation. Real-time analytics generated by the platform empower educators and administrators to identify trends, detect learning bottlenecks, and evaluate instructional effectiveness with unprecedented granularity. The integration of generative AI models like ChatGPT enhances this analytical capacity by producing explanatory narratives that contextualize numerical data, making educational insights more intuitive and actionable for decision-makers. Instructors can interpret predictive indicators and adapt their teaching strategies through natural language summaries, fostering a new form of data-literate pedagogy that bridges human judgment with algorithmic intelligence. Simultaneously, these tools facilitate the equitable distribution of educational resources, optimizing teaching loads, and tailoring interventions to specific learner cohorts. As Holmes et al. (2019) highlight, the fusion of adaptive algorithms and conversational AI enables the design of flexible, dialogic environments that accommodate diverse educational realities. Ultimately, AI-enhanced adaptive learning systems redefine the meaning of personalization, not merely as an adjustment of content but as the co-construction of meaningful learning experiences supported by transparency, inclusivity, and technological empathy qualities essential for preparing learners to thrive in an increasingly complex digital society (Luckin et al., 2016; Holmes et al., 2019).

To make the prototype more concrete for classroom implementation, the adaptive cycle may be read as a sequence of instructional actions. A teacher first assigns a diagnostic activity, the system estimates recent competence and engagement, and the generative agent explains the recommended next task in language that students can understand. During a mathematics session, for example, a learner who struggles with algebraic manipulation receives lower-complexity items, a brief explanation of the misconception, and a short practice plan; the educator then reviews the dashboard to decide whether to provide small-group scaffolding or individual feedback.

2. THEORETICAL FOUNDATIONS OF ADAPTIVE LEARNING

2.1. Relevant educational theories: Constructivism and personalized learning

Adaptive learning is fundamentally grounded in the principles of constructivism, a theory that conceives learning as an active and continuous process in which individuals construct new knowledge by connecting it with prior experiences and cognitive structures. Piaget (1972) described this process as one of cognitive restructuring, where learners reorganize their mental schemas to accommodate added information and achieve deeper understanding. Complementarily, Vygotsky (1978) introduced the sociocultural dimension of learning, emphasizing that knowledge emerges through interaction and dialogue with others within the zone of proximal development (ZPD) the range between what a learner can do independently and what can be achieved with guidance. These classical principles have been revitalized through the incorporation of generative artificial intelligence into educational practice. Modern adaptive learning systems, particularly those enhanced by the ChatGPT API, emulate this interactive and scaffolded learning process by engaging students in natural language dialogue that adjusts to their cognitive and emotional state. In this context, AI becomes a digital mediator capable of interpreting learner responses, tailoring explanations, and modulating difficulty in real time, thus functioning as an intelligent tutor that supports metacognition and reflective understanding. Through this synthesis of constructivist theory and generative technology, adaptive learning environments transform into collaborative ecosystems where human learning is dynamically augmented by artificial intelligence, making the ideals of personalized, dialogic, and meaningful learning a practical educational reality (Piaget, 1972; Vygotsky, 1978). Figure 2 shows a summary of this part.

Figure 2. Theoretical foundations of adaptive learning: constructivism and personalization

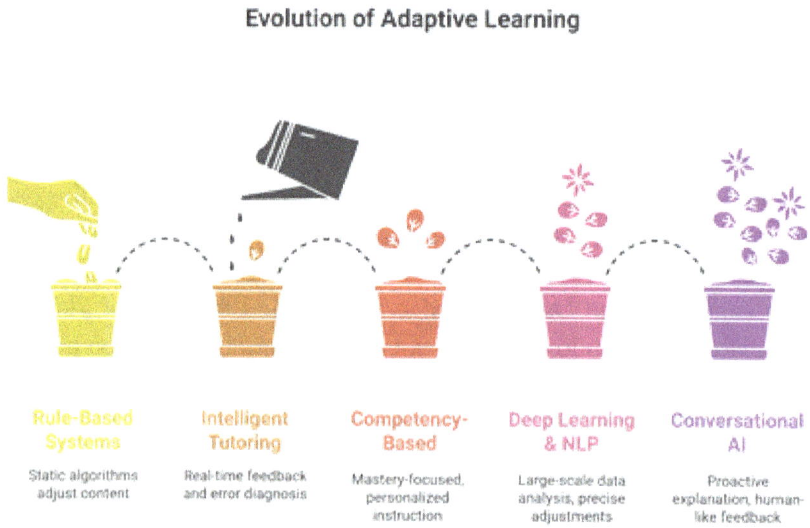

By integrating these theoretical perspectives, adaptive learning establishes a comprehensive and dynamic framework for personalizing education through continuous data analysis, intelligent feedback, and generative dialogue. Rooted in the principles of constructivism and sociocultural theory, it positions the learner as an active participant who constructs knowledge through iterative interaction with both the system and contextual information. This framework gains further depth through Ausubel's (2003) theory of meaningful learning, which emphasizes that genuine understanding occurs when new knowledge is anchored to pre-existing cognitive structures, thereby forming coherent and enduring mental representations. In contemporary educational environments, this process is amplified by the incorporation of generative artificial intelligence. ChatGPT-enhanced adaptive platforms can identify learners' prior knowledge by analyzing their responses, learning history, and behavioral patterns, then generating contextualized explanations that serve as conceptual bridges between what is already known and new material being introduced. This linguistic and cognitive mediation transforms AI from a passive recommender into an active dialogic partner that facilitates deep learning. Through personalized conversations, the system stimulates reflection, sustains motivation, and reinforces long-term retention by presenting information in accessible, meaningful, and situationally relevant ways. Consequently, adaptive learning not only personalizes instruction but also embodies the theoretical principles of Piaget's cognitive restructuring, Vygotsky's guided interaction within the zone of proximal development, and Ausubel's meaningful integration of knowledge creating an educational experience that is both human-centered and technologically enhanced (Piaget, 1972; Vygotsky, 1978; Ausubel, 2003).

This synthesis clarifies the theoretical flow of the chapter. Constructivism explains how learners actively reorganize knowledge, sociocultural theory justifies guided interaction, intelligent tutoring systems operationalize diagnosis and scaffolding, adaptive models personalize sequencing, and generative AI translates analytic evidence into understandable dialogue. The resulting framework therefore connects learning theory, educational data mining, and conversational feedback as complementary layers rather than isolated components.

2.2. Adaptive learning models and their evolution

Adaptive learning models have progressed remarkably from their early rule-based systems that adjusted content through static algorithms (Shute & Zapata-Rivera, 2012). With the integration of artificial intelligence and machine learning, more sophisticated approaches such as Intelligent Tutoring Systems (ITS) emerged, capable of diagnosing errors, interpreting student behavior, and providing real-time feedback to enhance learning outcomes (VanLehn, 2006). Similarly, Competency-Based Learning (CBL) focuses on demonstrated mastery rather than time spent, allowing AI to monitor progress and personalize instruction accordingly (Jung & Guskey, 2007).

Recent advances in deep learning and natural language processing (NLP) have further refined adaptive models, enabling large-scale data analysis, high-precision instructional adjustments, and the emergence of conversational intelligence. The incorporation of generative AI through ChatGPT now represents a new evolutionary stage: from reactive adaptation to proactive explanation. These systems not only personalize what learners' study but also articulate why certain materials are recommended, generating contextual, human-like feedback that supports metacognitive reflection and self-regulation. Through natural language interaction, ChatGPT extends the traditional ITS framework into a dialogic learning environment, merging analytics with communication. Furthermore, gamification continues to be integrated to sustain engagement and motivation, as seen in platforms like Duolingo, which dynamically adjusts difficulty levels and rewards progress to enhance persistence and knowledge retention (Shute & Zapata-Rivera, 2012; VanLehn, 2006; Jung & Guskey, 2007).

2.3. The role of artificial intelligence in content adaptation

Artificial intelligence is essential in adapting educational content, allowing systems to respond dynamically to each learner's needs by analyzing interaction data to identify strengths, weaknesses, and behavioral patterns (Woolf, 2010). Through machine learning techniques such as neural networks, clustering, and regression, AI personalizes learning paths and adjusts difficulty levels to reinforce understanding. In the most recent generation of adaptive systems, this analytical capacity is complemented by generative models such as ChatGPT, which use advanced natural language processing (NLP) to produce personalized explanations, reformulate concepts according to the learner's level, and translate data-driven recommendations into meaningful dialogue. By transforming static feedback into conversational interaction, ChatGPT enables the system to guide students through reflective questioning and narrative reasoning, deepening conceptual comprehension and engagement (Heffernan & Heffernan, 2014).

Overall, AI fosters inclusive, flexible, and equitable education by adapting to learners' cognitive, emotional, and social contexts, transcending the limitations of traditional models. The integration of generative dialogue through ChatGPT further enhances this inclusivity by making explanations linguistically accessible and pedagogically transparent, thus humanizing the adaptive process while maintaining analytical precision (Woolf, 2010; Heffernan & Heffernan, 2014).

3. AI TECHNOLOGIES IN ADAPTIVE LEARNING SYSTEMS

The use of artificial intelligence (AI) in education has revolutionized the way learning is personalized, allowing content and methodologies to be tailored to the needs of each student. Among the AI technologies applied to adaptive learning systems, three key areas stand out: machine learning algorithms, intelligent tutoring systems, and specialized adaptive learning platforms. In recent developments, a fourth domain has emerged generative conversational AI represented by tools such as ChatGPT, which integrate natural language understanding and generation to provide contextual explanations, personalized feedback, and dialogic interaction. These systems transform static adaptation into dynamic communication, enabling learners to question, explore, and receive immediate, language-based guidance that mirrors human tutoring. Altogether, these tools not only improve teaching efficiency but also offer a more personalized, reflective, and human-centered educational experience. Figure 3 shows a summary of this part.

Figure 3. AI technologies in adaptive learning systems

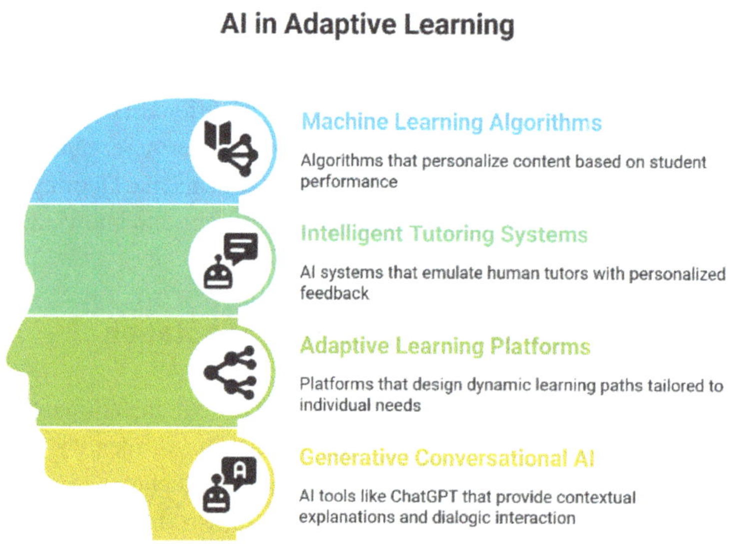

3.1. Machine learning algorithms applied in education

Machine learning has transformed adaptive learning systems by enabling large-scale data processing and pattern recognition to optimize teaching and learning. Algorithms such as decision trees, support vector machines (SVMs), and artificial neural networks personalize educational content according to students' performance and needs (Romero & Ventura, 2010). Clustering methods like k-means group learners by proficiency and style, allowing targeted reinforcement, while regression and deep learning models predict performance and suggest individualized interventions (Baker & Inventado, 2016).

Recent developments have expanded these analytical capabilities through generative artificial intelligence, where systems such as ChatGPT interpret and communicate machine learning results using natural language. By converting complex data outputs into personalized explanations, ChatGPT bridges the gap between algorithmic prediction and human understanding, making adaptive feedback more intuitive and pedagogically meaningful. Advances in natural language processing (NLP) have enhanced interactivity through automated text interpretation, essay grading, and contextualized feedback, leading to more sophisticated tutoring systems accessible to diverse learners (Heffernan & Heffernan, 2014). Likewise, reinforcement learning algorithms improve personalization by adapting instruction through reward-based decisions, optimizing real-time learning paths and knowledge acquisition, and supporting intelligent tutoring at scale (Holmes et al., 2019; Baker & Inventado, 2016).

3.2. Intelligent tutoring systems: Design and functionality

Intelligent Tutoring Systems (ITS) constitute one of the most sophisticated applications of artificial intelligence in education, designed to replicate and extend the role of human tutors through the delivery of personalized instruction, adaptive feedback, and data-driven strategies that foster mastery learning (VanLehn, 2006). These systems rely on the integration of multiple interdependent models: a domain model that represents the structure and relationships of the knowledge to be taught, a student model that tracks progress, misconceptions, and learning preferences, and a pedagogical model that determines how to intervene effectively at each stage of learning. Through this triadic interaction, ITS are capable of diagnosing learners' difficulties, predicting performance trajectories, and selecting optimal instructional responses in real time. A prominent example is AutoTutor, which employs natural language processing to engage students in mixed-initiative dialogues, prompting them to articulate reasoning, clarify misconceptions, and internalize key concepts in disciplines such as mathematics, physics, and computer science (Graesser et al., 2005). Another notable system, ASSISTments, exemplifies the synergistic combination of automated tutoring and learning analytics, enabling educators to visualize student performance trends, identify systemic errors, and personalize instructional interventions accordingly (Heffernan & Heffernan, 2014). Collectively, these systems illustrate how artificial intelligence not only replicates certain functions of human tutoring but also enhances scalability, precision, and feedback timeliness, redefining the boundaries of individualized and adaptive instruction within modern education (VanLehn, 2006; Graesser et al., 2005; Heffernan & Heffernan, 2014).

The emergence of generative artificial intelligence, particularly through the integration of ChatGPT, marks a pivotal advancement in the evolution of Intelligent Tutoring Systems (ITS). Traditional ITS architecture relied on static rule-based responses and limited decision trees, constraining the system's ability to replicate the nuanced and adaptive qualities of human instruction. In contrast, ChatGPT-driven tutors employ deep learning and large-scale language models capable of generating dynamic, context-sensitive explanations that evolve in real time according to the learner's cognitive state, linguistic expression, and conceptual understanding. This transformation enables the system to simulate the natural flow of human conversation, providing not only corrective feedback but also elaborate prompts, reflective questioning, and personalized scaffolding that nurture metacognitive awareness and self-regulated learning. The integration of generative dialogue thus redefines the pedagogical function of ITS, extending it from reactive content delivery to proactive cognitive partnership.

Moreover, the continual evolution of ITS has been strengthened by the convergence of deep neural networks, natural language processing, and adaptive learning algorithms, which together refine personalization and optimize the sequencing of instructional content (Holmes et al., 2019). Modern iterations incorporate multimodal learning experiences combining text, visualization, and voice interfaces to foster engagement and accommodate diverse learning preferences. The inclusion of gamification elements, such as progress tracking, achievements, and adaptive challenges, further enhances motivation and persistence, while augmented and virtual reality environments allow learners to interact with concepts in immersive, experiential ways that reinforce understanding. Within this expanded ecosystem, ChatGPT functions as both an intelligent interlocutor and a generative reasoning engine, transforming the ITS from a programmed tutor into an interactive, empathetic learning companion. Consequently, contemporary ITS embody the fusion of analytical precision, pedagogical flexibility, and linguistic adaptability, creating intelligent learning environments that complement and extend traditional instruction while promoting engagement, personalization, and deep conceptual mastery (Holmes et al., 2019; VanLehn, 2006; Graesser et al., 2005; Heffernan & Heffernan, 2014).

3.3. Existing tools and platforms for adaptive learning

The rise of artificial intelligence has profoundly transformed the educational landscape, enabling the development of adaptive learning platforms that personalize instruction, generate learning analytics, and construct dynamic, individualized learning trajectories. These systems utilize advanced algorithms to interpret large volumes of educational data, including learner interactions, assessment outcomes, and behavioral patterns, to create instructional experiences that continuously evolve in response to each student's progress. Among the most influential examples, Knewton employs machine learning models to analyze learner performance and adapt instructional materials, accordingly, ensuring that each student receives content that aligns with their specific pace and level of mastery. Similarly, Smart Sparrow empowers educators to design interactive lessons that automatically adjust based on learners' responses, misconceptions, and engagement levels, thereby fostering a personalized and responsive learning environment (Johnson et al., 2016; Zawacki-Richter et al., 2019).

Other notable platforms have expanded these capabilities to achieve domain-specific and large-scale applications. DreamBox Learning, for instance, specializes in mathematics education by continuously monitoring learners' actions and recalibrating both difficulty and pedagogical strategies in real time, allowing the system to target conceptual gaps while maintaining optimal challenge levels. Squirrel AI, one of the largest adaptive learning systems in operation, leverages real-time recommendation engines powered by AI to deliver individualized tutoring experiences to thousands of learners simultaneously. By analyzing patterns of knowledge acquisition and common error trajectories, it provides precise and timely feedback that mirrors the adaptivity of one-on-one human instruction. Collectively, these platforms illustrate how artificial intelligence operationalizes the principles of personalization and formative feedback at scale, transforming education from a uniform process into a dynamic, data-informed ecosystem that adjusts continuously to learners' needs, supports differentiated instruction, and enhances both engagement and learning outcomes (Johnson et al., 2016; Zawacki-Richter et al., 2019).

More recently, the integration of generative AI through the ChatGPT API has expanded the functionality of such platforms beyond analytics and recommendation engines. This integration enables real-time, natural language explanations that translate algorithmic decisions into accessible feedback for learners, reinforcing understanding and engagement. ChatGPT acts as a conversational interface between the user and the adaptive system, interpreting data-driven insights and expressing them through coherent, context-sensitive dialogue. These platforms collectively demonstrate how AI transforms education by fostering personalization, inclusivity, and adaptability across diverse learning contexts. They empower educators with data-driven and linguistically mediated insights to optimize instruction and engagement, supporting equitable and effective learning environments that align with the evolving demands of digital education (Holmes et al., 2019; Johnson et al., 2016; Zawacki-Richter et al., 2019).

This progression establishes a bridge between the literature review and the prototype design. The chapter's conceptual trajectory moves from learning theory to adaptive models, from adaptive models to intelligent tutoring, and from tutoring to generative explanation. This ordering helps readers understand why the system is not merely a technical dashboard but a pedagogical environment in which analytics, feedback, and teacher mediation reinforce one another.

4. DESIGN AND DEVELOPMENT OF AN ADAPTIVE LEARNING WEB APPLICATION

4.1. System requirements and objectives

The proposed adaptive learning web application is conceived as an intelligent, student-centered digital environment designed to personalize educational content, deliver real-time feedback, and foster an intuitive, meaningful interaction between users and the system. Unlike traditional e-learning platforms that rely solely on static modules and pre-defined responses, this application dynamically interprets learner data—such as performance metrics, interaction patterns, and behavioral indicators to adapt instructional materials and provide context-aware guidance. In its most advanced implementation, the system incorporates the ChatGPT API as a generative and explanatory module, capable of producing detailed natural language feedback that aligns with each learner's cognitive profile, pace of progress, and comprehension level. Through this integration, the application transcends conventional analytics dashboards to become a truly dialogic learning space, where artificial intelligence not only processes information but also engages students in reflective and personalized conversation. This interactive feedback loop enhances understanding by providing individualized explanations, adaptive recommendations, and guided reasoning that mirror the pedagogical approach of a human tutor.

Furthermore, the system is architected with a strong emphasis on scalability, data security, and interoperability with existing educational infrastructures, ensuring that it can be deployed effectively across diverse institutional contexts. Robust encryption protocols and structured database management protect user data, while modular design principles allow seamless integration with learning management systems (LMS) and other digital education tools. In alignment with best practices in software engineering, the application adheres to the principles of maintainability, flexibility, and explainability outlined by Pressman (2020), guaranteeing that each adaptive function remains transparent and interpretable for both educators and learners. The platform's explainable AI design ensures that users understand not only what recommendations are made but also why those recommendations occur, fostering trust and interpretability in AI-driven education. Ultimately, this adaptive learning web application represents a convergence of machine learning, human-computer interaction, and generative dialogue, forming an integrated ecosystem that promotes autonomy, engagement, and academic growth through real-time, personalized, and linguistically rich interaction. Figure 4 visually summarizes this architecture and its pedagogical implications (Pressman, 2020).

Figure 4. Design and development of the adaptive learning web application

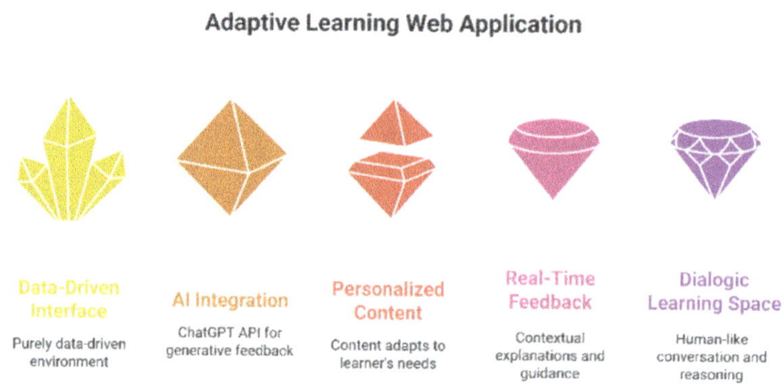

4.2. Architecture and technologies

The adaptive learning system will be developed using Python for backend processes, as it provides robust libraries for artificial intelligence, data analytics, and system integration, while Plotly and Dash will be used to create an interactive, web-based interface capable of visualizing learning analytics in real time. Through these technologies, the system will transform raw educational data into dynamic dashboards, performance charts, and adaptive indicators that allow both learners and instructors to interpret progress intuitively. Within this architecture, the ChatGPT API will serve as an integrated generative module that processes analytical outputs from the backend and converts them into coherent, natural language explanations displayed directly in the interface, enabling the platform to bridge quantitative computation with qualitative interpretation. This design provides immediate, context-aware feedback that enhances understanding, supports self-regulation, and assists educators in pedagogical decision-making. Additionally, architecture supports modular expansion and seamless updates, ensuring long-term scalability and adaptability to modern technologies. It is compatible with both relational and NoSQL databases, facilitating the management of structured and unstructured data—such as learner profiles, engagement logs, and conversational histories while maintaining efficiency and data integrity. By integrating AI-driven dialogue with adaptive visualization in a unified environment, the system achieves a balance between analytical precision and human-centered explainability, allowing each user to engage meaningfully with data-driven insights. In alignment with the foundational principles of database design and systems architecture established by Elmasri and Navathe (2016), this framework ensures reliability, interoperability, and pedagogical transparency, consolidating a scalable ecosystem that supports continuous learning and evidence-based educational transformation (Elmasri & Navathe, 2016).

4.3. AI Integration and prototype development

Artificial intelligence algorithms implemented through TensorFlow, Keras, and Scikit-learn will serve as the computational core of the adaptive learning system, enabling the personalization of educational content and the prediction of student performance through a combination of supervised and unsupervised learning techniques. These algorithms will process complex educational datasets encompassing interaction patterns, response accuracy, time-on-task, and engagement levels—to identify learning trajectories, detect difficulties, and anticipate the most effective instructional interventions. Supervised learning models will be employed to classify performance outcomes and predict mastery levels based on labeled data, while unsupervised models, such as clustering and dimensionality reduction, will reveal latent learning patterns and group students with similar cognitive profiles. In its enhanced configuration, the system incorporates the ChatGPT API as a generative explanatory layer capable of interpreting the outputs produced by these predictive models and translating them into meaningful natural language feedback. This mechanism transforms abstract numerical indicators into pedagogical narratives, offering students not only an understanding of what is recommended but also why certain activities, materials, or assessments are suggested, thus fostering metacognitive awareness and trust in the adaptive process. The integration of this conversational component bridges the gap between analytical computation and human-centered communication, making the system both intelligent and interpretable. A fully functional prototype developed with Python, Plotly, and Dash will operationalize these features through interactive modules that adjust learning content in real time, conduct personalized assessments, and provide immediate, context-aware feedback. By combining predictive modeling, generative dialogue, and interactive visualization, the platform creates an ecosystem that enhances comprehension, engagement, and reflective learning embodying the principles of deep learning and intelligent tutoring described by Goodfellow et al. (2016) and Woolf (2010), and illustrating how advanced AI can be harmoniously integrated into pedagogically sound digital education (Goodfellow et al., 2016; Woolf, 2010).

The educator's role remains central in this architecture. Teachers interpret analytics, validate the appropriateness of recommendations, contextualize AI-generated explanations, and decide when human intervention is pedagogically necessary. Consequently, institutional adoption should include professional development in dashboard interpretation, prompt evaluation, data literacy, and ethical supervision so that generative feedback supports teacher agency rather than replacing instructional judgment.

4.4. Plotly, Dash, and ChatGPT integration: Prototype implementation details

The script implements a complete adaptive-learning prototype using Dash and Plotly, structured as a single-page web application with multiple tabs that render distinct pedagogical workflows. In its enhanced version, the prototype integrates the ChatGPT API as a generative explanatory layer that complements quantitative analytics. From a software-engineering standpoint, the program begins by defining a theme system that abstracts visual properties such as templates, background colors, font color, accent hues, gradients, and shadows for both light and dark modes. This layer is critical because Plotly figures inherit a consistent appearance through a helper function that applies the chosen template and visual primitives to every chart. The same theme tokens also drive the styling of HTML components such as cards, headers, and KPI chips, which are built with Dash's HTML primitives. By centralizing style in dictionaries, the code ensures coherence and maintainability: a change to a single token propagates across the interface without altering the callbacks or business logic.

The data layer remains fully simulated to keep the prototype self-contained. It generates a synthetic population of students with latent traits such as general ability, domain affinities, engagement, study pace, and weekly goals. An item bank is produced with IRT-like parameters discrimination and difficulty plus expected time per item. Time-series trajectories are synthesized for each student across a thirty-day horizon, including minutes studied and a micro-performance indicator bounded in the unit interval. This design mirrors real learning analytics pipelines, where engagement and proficiency evolve over time and where models often require recent windows, captured by a helper that aggregates the last seven days. The advantage of simulating data is twofold: it makes the prototype portable and allows immediate exploration of adaptive mechanisms without external dependencies. In the new version, the ChatGPT module can access these simulated analytics through API calls to produce pedagogical interpretations in natural language, explaining learning trends, patterns of engagement, or item selection rationales directly to the user.

The layout leverages Dash's reactive model. At the top level, the application defines a responsive container with a themed top bar that also exposes a light–dark toggle. Because Dash components are declarative, the visual tree is described in Python and rendered to the browser via React under the hood. Tabs are created with dcc.Tabs, each associated with a content region managed by a callback that returns the appropriate layout when the active tab or theme changes. The code also enables suppress_callback_exceptions=True, a Dash setting that allows callbacks to reference components that are added dynamically as a feature especially relevant for the ChatGPT field input and for the top bar's theme toggle, which are rendered before other callbacks consume their values.

The "Home" tab demonstrates a canonical pattern of Plotly and Dash integration for at-a-glance analytics. It exposes dropdowns for selecting a student and domain, then renders KPI cards for recent minutes studied, mean micro-performance, and the declared weekly goal. The KPIs use themed "chips" for typographic emphasis, clarifying the reading of scalar indicators. Parallel to this, the tab renders a dash_table.DataTable summary over the simulated student frame. The table inherits the same color tokens and typographic consistency, so data visualization and numerical indicators coexist seamlessly. In the extended version, this tab also includes a short ChatGPT-generated textual summary that interprets the KPIs, highlighting strengths, progress, and potential areas of improvement.

The "Learning" tab operationalizes the adaptive recommendation loop. A trajectory figure combines a bar trace for minutes and a line trace for micro-scores, using Plotly's dual-axis capability to align effort and performance in a single view. The system estimates a domain-specific competence level using recent micro-scores and selects items whose difficulty parameter b lies near the estimated θ derived from recent micro-scores. The resulting table shows discrimination, difficulty, estimated θ, and a model-based probability of success computed via a logistic IRT function. ChatGPT complements this quantitative layer by generating an individualized narrative that explains why those items were recommended, how they relate to the learner's progress, and which strategies could improve outcomes. This integration converts numerical recommendation into pedagogical reasoning, allowing the user to understand the system's logic. By embedding both the chart and the AI-generated explanation in a single, reactive layout, Dash enables dynamic adaptation with cognitive transparency.

The "Assessments" tab implements a lightweight adaptive test. Given a student and domain, the code selects items closest to the current θ and renders response controls. Upon submission, a controller computes accuracy and adjusts future difficulty toward a target accuracy of sixty percent, a common heuristic in mastery learning. In the updated version, ChatGPT provides qualitative feedback immediately after submission, interpreting the results in natural language identifying misconceptions, suggesting review topics, and reinforcing achievements. This feedback layer enhances metacognitive reflection by transforming numerical feedback into contextual guidance, enabling the learner to understand progress beyond scores.

The "Analytics" tab aggregates cohort-level signals. A heatmap built with Plotly Express summarizes seven-day performance by student and domain, serving as a compact way to identify outliers and systemic weaknesses. Histograms portray the distribution of latent ability, and scatter plots relate ability to engagement, optionally including trend modeling if statsmodels are available. The ChatGPT module can summarize these analytics, producing text-based reports that translate data visualizations into descriptive insights for educators. The theme function ensures that all visualizations, whether in light or dark mode, maintain consistent color, font, and margin parameters, producing a cohesive analytical environment.

The "Agent" tab embodies the independent-learning mentor. It computes domain weights according to user-selected priorities remediating weaknesses, consolidating strengths, or balancing and allocates weekly goal hours across domains and days, modulated by engagement. The schedule is visualized as a stacked bar chart, with an accompanying ChatGPT-generated rationale explaining the allocation logic and offering motivational guidance. This textual agent component transforms the adaptive scheduler into a conversational mentor aligned with explainability principles in educational AI. From a programming viewpoint, this illustrates how Python business rules can be combined with generative dialogue and surfaced in Dash callbacks, with Plotly visualizing the outcome and ChatGPT verbalizing the reasoning.

The application's event model rests on a compact set of callbacks that orchestrate rendering. A single dispatcher callback produces the tab content according to the active selection and theme value. Individual charts, tables, and AI interactions have their own callbacks, binding Dash Inputs and States to pandas data transformations, Plotly figure creation, and ChatGPT API responses. Because Dash is reactive, developers do not manage DOM updates manually; instead, Dash diffs component trees and sends incremental JSON patches to the browser. The code adopts best practices for IDE compatibility by using app.run(..., use_reloader=False) under Dash 3.x, avoiding multiple server instances during live development.

The theming system exemplifies separation of concerns in Dash applications. Rather than hardcoding colors and fonts, all stylistic decisions are centralized in dictionaries and helper functions, ensuring that both visual and textual feedback (including ChatGPT responses) adhere to a unified aesthetic. Plotly's templates, color scales, and font tokens are leveraged to guarantee that the same design logic governs charts, data tables, and AI-generated explanations. This coherence allows the user experience to remain fluid, elegant, and cognitively consistent across all interaction modes.

Finally, the prototype remains intentionally self-contained. All data needed to explore the workflows are generated at runtime, allowing instructors to launch the app in any environment with Dash, Plotly, and OpenAI's library installed, immediately exploring adaptive trajectories, item recommendations, assessments, analytics, and agent-driven planning. Because both analytics and AI-driven dialogue are expressed in Python, a research team could replace the simulated data with real telemetry and extend the IRT or conversational layers with more sophisticated models without altering the architectural pattern of callbacks and themed figure assembly. In this sense, the script now functions not only as a functional demonstration but as a hybrid blueprint combining data analytics, visualization, and generative explanation for next-generation educational dashboards built on Plotly, Dash, and ChatGPT.

5. WEB APPLICATION IMPLEMENTATION AND TESTING

The implementation and testing phase ensures the adaptive learning web application's functionality, usability, and stability in educational contexts. In its enhanced configuration, the system integrates the ChatGPT API as a generative feedback module, which also requires validation for response accuracy, contextual coherence, and linguistic appropriateness within instructional scenarios. The development follows agile methodologies that integrate best practices in software engineering and instructional design (Myers et al., 2011; Huang et al., 2019). The process is divided into three core stages: deployment, functionality and performance testing, and user experience evaluation each extended to include the evaluation of ChatGPT-driven explanations and conversational feedback. These stages collectively ensure that both the analytical and generative components operate harmoniously within the adaptive and intelligent structure developed in previous sections. Figure 5 shows a summary of this part.

Figure 5. Adaptive learning web application development process: From initial prototype to AI-enhanced system

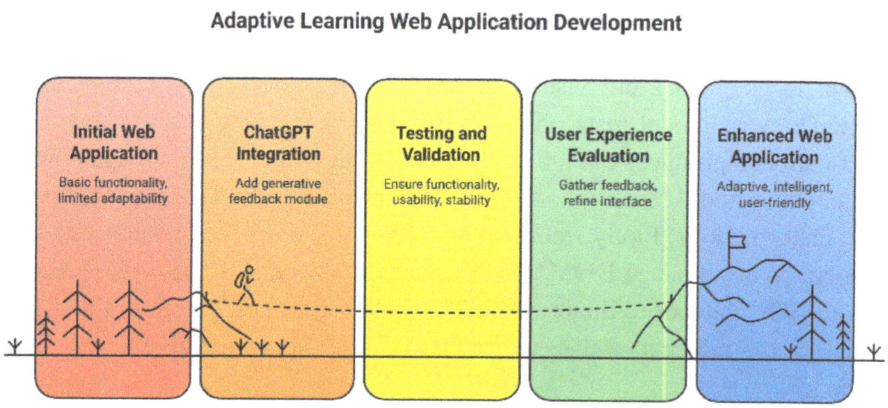

5.1. Deployment of the application in educational environments

Deployment involves configuring the technological infrastructure, databases, and security mechanisms to guarantee stable and efficient operation. The system, developed with Python, Plotly, and Dash, now integrates the ChatGPT API as a cloud-based generative component that requires secure connection management and authentication with encrypted API keys. The platform can be hosted either locally or in the cloud (AWS, Google Cloud, or Azure), depending on institutional policies, privacy requirements, and scalability needs (Bonilla-Priego et al., 2024). The architecture supports modular expansion and microservices for continuous updates, ensuring smooth integration of both adaptive and conversational functionalities. Data security follows protocols such as HTTPS, TLS encryption, and authentication through OAuth 2.0 or JWT, in compliance with international educational privacy standards (Squires

& Preece, 1999). Additional layers of protection are implemented to safeguard interactions with the ChatGPT endpoint, preventing unauthorized API access and ensuring that all generated content adheres to institutional ethical guidelines. Before full implementation, pilot tests with students and teachers are conducted to validate the adaptive logic, conversational accuracy, interface usability, and overall technical stability of both the analytical and generative modules (Huang et al., 2019).

5.2. Functionality and performance testing

This phase ensures that all modules perform as expected according to system requirements, including the new generative component powered by the ChatGPT API. Unit, integration, and regression tests will be executed using frameworks such as PyTest and Selenium, which guarantee the reliability of core processes and reduce errors during iterative development cycles (Myers et al., 2011; Schwaber & Sutherland, 2017). In addition to traditional modules, automated validation routines will verify ChatGPT's response integrity, contextual accuracy, and linguistic coherence to ensure pedagogical consistency. Performance evaluations using JMeter or Locust will assess the system's ability to support multiple concurrent users, measuring response time, CPU and memory usage, and scalability. Specific latency metrics will also be recorded for ChatGPT's API calls to ensure optimal conversational responsiveness. Metrics obtained will guide optimization of server configuration and code efficiency, ensuring high stability, interpretability, and responsiveness even under heavy workloads (Doğan et al., 2014; Bonilla-Priego et al., 2024).

5.3. User experience evaluation

The final stage focuses on evaluating both quantitative and qualitative aspects of user interaction, incorporating the assessment of ChatGPT's generative feedback alongside the system's adaptive features. Surveys and structured interviews with students and educators will measure satisfaction, usability, conversational clarity, and the pedagogical effectiveness of the adaptive and explanatory components (Squires & Preece, 1999). Platform-generated data such as session duration, engagement rates, interaction frequency with the ChatGPT module, and progress indicators will provide objective insights into system performance and learning impact (Huang et al., 2019). Continuous feedback loops and agile improvement cycles (Schwaber & Sutherland, 2017) will guide the refinement of both analytical and generative layers, ensuring that the web application evolves organically, maintains inclusivity and adaptability, and sustains long-term relevance within educational environments.

In practical pilots, user experience evaluation should also observe classroom routines rather than relying only on surveys. Teachers can document how often they accept, modify, or reject AI-generated recommendations, while students can report whether explanations improve confidence and persistence. These observations provide evidence about digital readiness, instructional usefulness, and the conditions under which conversational feedback becomes genuinely supportive.

5.4. Visualization of the web application and functional interface results

Each Figure corresponds to a distinct functional module of the adaptive learning web application described in the article. All of them visually demonstrate how the system integrates personalization, analytics, and AI-guided feedback within a web interface built with Plotly and Dash.

Figure 6. Home Tab – Dashboard overview of the adaptive learning web application

Figure 6 corresponds to the Home tab – Dashboard Overview of the adaptive learning web application. It visually embodies the introductory analytical layer of the system, where users' students or instructors access a concise yet comprehensive summary of recent learning activity. At the top, the interface displays three real-time Key Performance Indicators (KPIs): total minutes studied during the past seven days, average performance, and average weekly goal in hours. These indicators, derived from dynamically simulated analytics, exemplify how the platform personalizes educational monitoring through continuous data aggregation. Below the KPIs, the "Students summary" table lists each learner's general ability (ability_g), engagement level, and declared weekly goal, forming the foundation for adaptive feedback mechanisms described in the article. The interface's minimalist aesthetic white gradients, soft borders, and typographic hierarchy reflect the design principle of cognitive clarity central to the prototype. Functionally, this screen fulfills the article's objective of providing a data-informed entry point that translates quantitative learning traces into immediate, interpretable insights, enabling both self-reflection and instructor-driven decision-making within the adaptive learning ecosystem.

Figure 7. Learning Tab – Learning trajectory, recommendations, and AI explanation

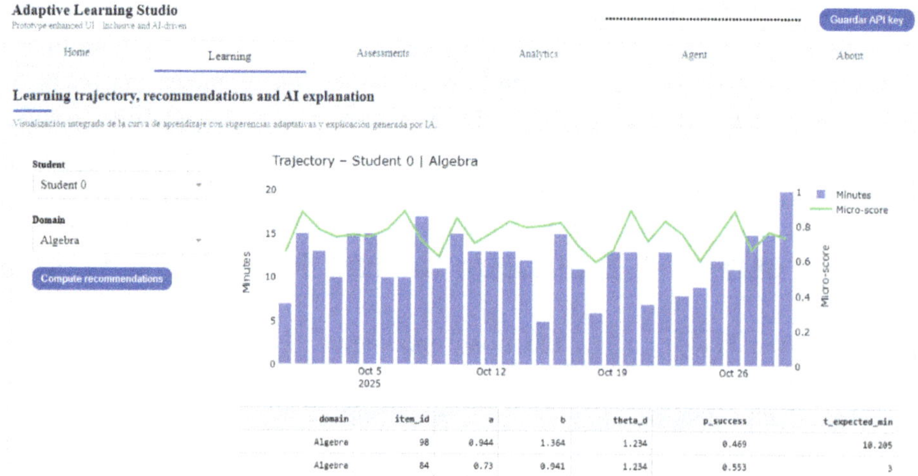

Figure 8. AI Explanation – Generative feedback detailing adaptive item selection and pedagogical rationale

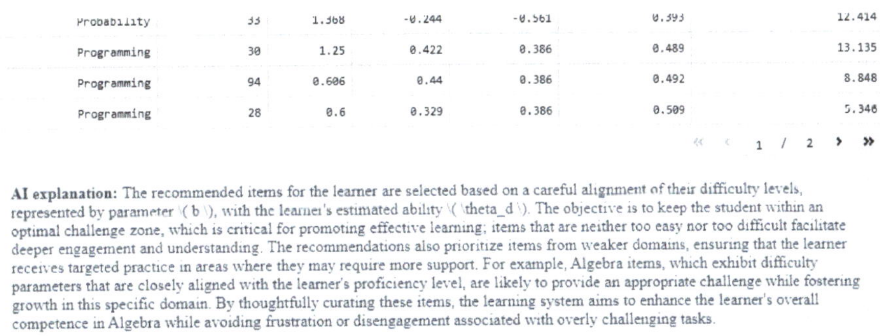

Figures 7 and 8 corresponds to the Learning tab – Learning trajectory, recommendations, and AI explanation, where the adaptive learning system integrates data analytics and generative artificial intelligence to personalize instruction. On the left, the interface allows selecting a specific student and learning domain in this case, Algebra while the central visualization displays a dual-axis graph: purple bars represent the minutes studied per day and the green line traces the learner's micro-performance evolution. Below, the table presents recommended learning items, each characterized by Item Response Theory (IRT) parameters difficulty (b), discrimination (a), estimated ability (θd), and probability of success (p_success) which ensure that the learner receives tasks aligned with their current competence. The AI-generated paragraph at the bottom, produced through ChatGPT integration, translates these analytical outputs into pedagogical reasoning, explaining how the recommendations maintain the learner within an optimal challenge zone to maximize engagement and understanding. Collectively, this screen exemplifies how the prototype unites quantitative modeling and natural language explanation to achieve transparency, adaptability, and human-like instructional guidance.

Figure 9. Assessments tab – Adaptive assessments (Simple IRT-based evaluation)

Figure 9 represents the Assessments tab – Adaptive assessments (simple IRT-like), where the application implements a dynamic evaluation mechanism that adjusts test difficulty to each learner's ability level. The interface allows users to select a specific student and domain here, Algebra and determine the number of questions through an interactive slider. When the user clicks Generate assessment, the system automatically selects items whose difficulty parameters closely match the student's estimated competence, ensuring an appropriate level of challenge based on Item Response Theory (IRT). After responding, the Submit answers button triggers an adaptive recalibration process that updates the learner's estimated ability for future assessments. This screen exemplifies how the prototype transforms traditional static testing into an intelligent and personalized evaluation experience, aligning with the article's objective of fostering continuous, data-driven, and equitable assessment through artificial intelligence.

Figure 10. Analytics tab – Seven-day performance heatmap across learning domains

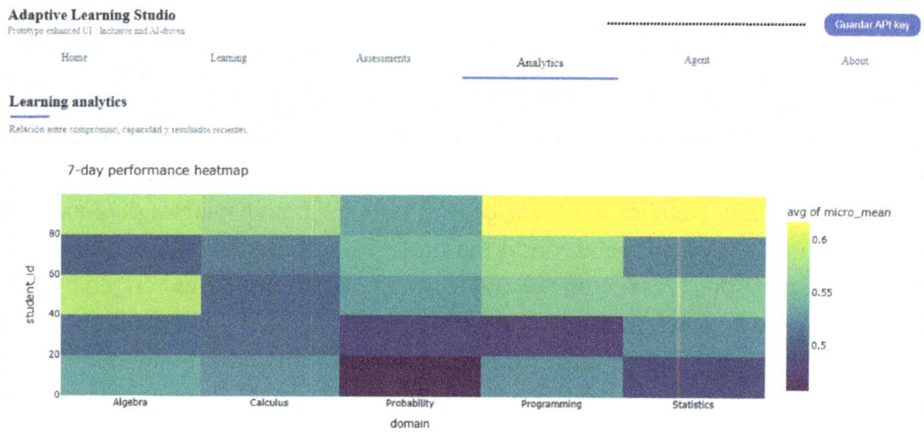

Figures 10, 11 and 12 correspond to the Analytics tab – Learning analytics, which visually synthesizes the performance and engagement data of all learners in the adaptive system. The first visualization, a seven-day performance heatmap, compares students' average micro-performance across multiple domains Algebra, Calculus, Probability, Programming, and Statistics revealing briefly which areas require additional instructional attention. The second graph, a histogram of ability (g), depicts the overall distribution of latent competence among learners, allowing educators to detect general trends, asymmetries, and clusters of ability within the cohort. The third graph, a scatter plot of Ability vs. Engagement, correlates cognitive capacity and motivation, showing how higher engagement often aligns with improved performance. Together, these visualizations embody the system's analytic core: transforming raw educational data into interpretable patterns that inform pedagogical decision-making. By integrating machine learning principles with intuitive visualization, this module operationalizes the study's goal of supporting evidence-based instruction and continuous monitoring through clear, data-driven insights.

Figure 11. Analytics Tab – Distribution of ability (g) among learners

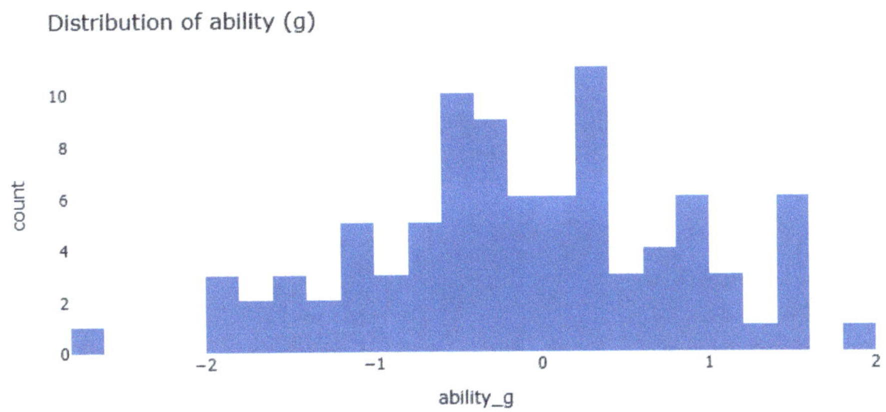

Figure 12. Analytics Tab – Correlation between ability (g) and engagement across learners

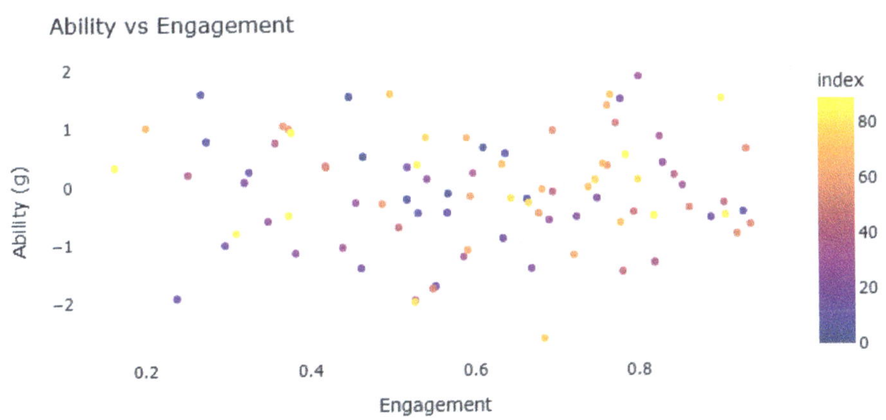

Figures 13 and 14 corresponds to the Agent tab –Independent Learning Agent (weekly plan), which embodies the system's capacity to transform analytical outputs into personalized study schedules guided by artificial intelligence. The upper section of the interface allows users to select a student, define a learning priority such as reinforcing weaknesses, consolidating strengths, or maintaining balance and set a weekly study goal in hours. Upon generating the plan, the lower section displays a stacked bar chart that distributes the total study time across the seven days of the week and among multiple domains Algebra, Calculus, Probability, Programming, and Statistics. Each color-coded segment represents the proportional allocation of time recommended for that subject. Above the chart, the system provides natural language micro-recommendations generated through ChatGPT, explaining the pedagogical rationale behind the schedule, such as focusing early sessions on weaker areas and maintaining an optimal level of cognitive challenge. This visualization exemplifies the integration of adaptive modeling, explainable AI, and human-centered design, demonstrating how the prototype supports learner autonomy, metacognitive awareness, and strategic time management through personalized and interpretable guidance.

Figure 13. Agent tab – Independent learning agent for weekly study plan generation

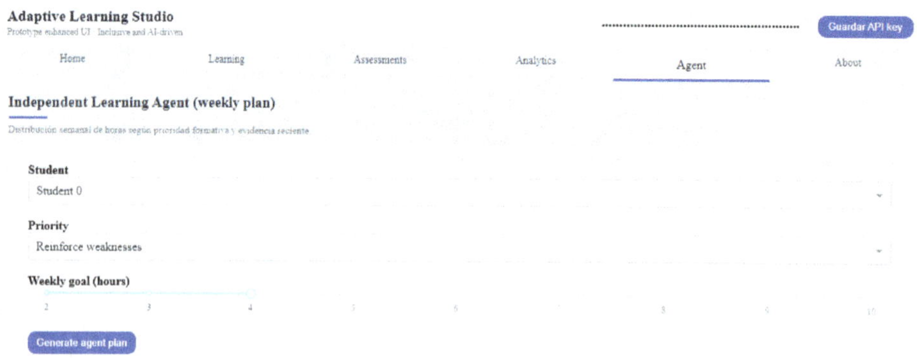

Figure 14. Agent tab – AI-generated weekly study plan with domain-specific time allocation and micro-recommendations

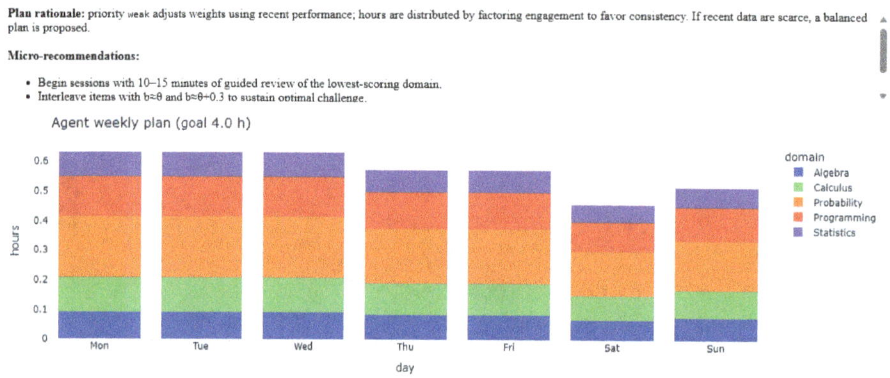

This Figure 15 corresponds to the About tab – System overview and conceptual foundations, which provides a concise yet comprehensive description of the adaptive learning prototype's purpose, architecture, and functional scope. It outlines that the system was developed using Python, Plotly, and Dash, integrating simulated datasets of students, learning trajectories, and item banks to demonstrate the dynamic interaction between analytics and artificial intelligence. The text emphasizes the five core modules that structure the application: (1) a dashboard for general monitoring, (2) adaptive learning trajectories with AI-driven recommendations, (3) an intelligent assessment engine, (4) cohort-level analytics, and (5) an independent learning agent for weekly study planning. Additionally, it highlights the integration of the ChatGPT API, which enables the generation of natural language explanations that clarify why each recommendation is made, thus transforming algorithmic analytics into pedagogical reasoning. This section completes the system's narrative by linking its technical components to its educational philosophy—showing that the prototype not only exemplifies data-driven adaptation but also embodies the principles of explainability, usability, and human-centered learning design.

Figure 15. About tab – System overview and conceptual foundations of the adaptive learning prototype

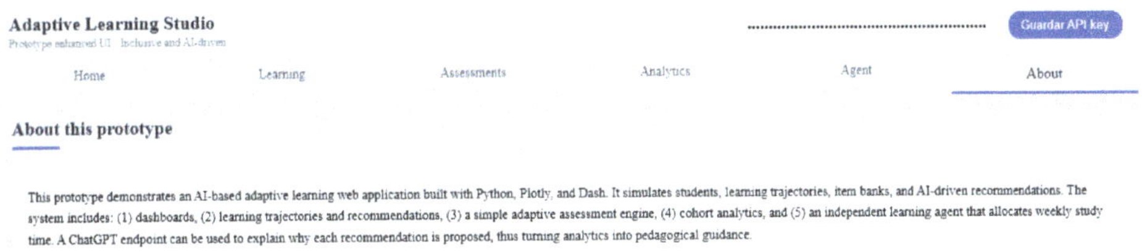

6. ADAPTIVE SYSTEM IMPACT ASSESSMENT

Evaluating the impact of the adaptive learning system is essential to determine its effectiveness in improving academic performance, enhancing personalization, and optimizing the overall educational experience. The assessment integrates quantitative and qualitative methods, comparing outcomes with traditional models to identify pedagogical strengths, challenges, and opportunities for continuous improvement (Pardo et al., 2016).

6.1. Learning impact assessment methods

The evaluation combines formative and summative assessments to ensure both real-time feedback and comprehensive learning measurement. Formative assessments allow immediate adjustments to instructional content, while summative assessments verify the consolidation of knowledge at the end of each module (Black & Wiliam, 1998; Shute, 2008). Performance comparisons before and after implementing the adaptive system are used to determine progress, supported by longitudinal data that provide reliable causal insights (Clark, 2010). Additionally, surveys and interviews with students and educators assess motivation, usability, and perceived pedagogical benefits, offering a holistic view of system acceptance and educational effectiveness (Pardo et al., 2016).

6.2. Data analysis and predictive modeling

The adaptive application generates extensive datasets that enable learning analytics and data mining for evidence-based decision-making. Indicators such as module completion rates, time spent, and error frequency are analyzed to detect behavioral patterns and instructional gaps (Baker & Siemens, 2014). Machine learning techniques such as clustering, regression, and neural networks allow performance prediction and student grouping according to learning needs, while natural language processing (NLP) supports personalized feedback on written responses (Baker & Siemens, 2014; Pardo et al., 2016). Real-time data collection further enhances responsiveness, allowing the system to automatically reformulate content when difficulties are detected, leading to more adaptive and student-centered learning experiences (Gašević et al., 2014).

6.3. Comparison with traditional models and results obtained

Comparative analyses demonstrate that adaptive learning systems significantly outperform traditional teaching methods. Studies show that adaptive platforms can increase knowledge retention by up to 30% due to personalized feedback and relevant content delivery (VanLehn, 2011). They also foster higher motivation and engagement by integrating gamification and real-time adaptation to learner preferences (Luckin et al., 2016). In terms of academic performance, students using adaptive systems exhibit superior results in standardized assessments and greater conceptual understanding, advancing at their own pace with guided support (Alrawashdeh et al., 2024). These results confirm that adaptive learning, supported by artificial intelligence, is a transformative educational model that promotes equity, personalization, and long-term academic success.

For institutional decision-makers, the expected impact should therefore be interpreted beyond individual performance scores. Adoption success also depends on reduced teacher workload, improved identification of at-risk learners, inclusive access for students with disabilities, and sustainable governance of educational data. Measuring these dimensions prevents the evaluation from becoming narrowly technical and links the prototype to broader transformation goals.

7. CHALLENGES AND ETHICAL CONSIDERATIONS IN THE DEVELOPMENT OF EDUCATIONAL APPLICATIONS

The integration of artificial intelligence into education presents remarkable opportunities for personalization but also introduces significant technical and ethical challenges. Issues such as data quality, infrastructure limitations, privacy, and algorithmic fairness must be addressed to ensure that AI-driven learning environments remain transparent, inclusive, and pedagogically sound (Holmes, Bialik, & Fadel, 2019).

7.1. Technical challenges in AI implementation

Educational AI systems depend on accurate and representative data; however, fragmentation and bias in educational datasets often reduce prediction accuracy and personalization quality (Zawacki-Richter et al., 2019). Limited infrastructure and high implementation costs remain barriers for institutions with constrained budgets, while unequal digital access exacerbates educational disparities (Holmes et al., 2019). Another major challenge is the lack of interpretability of complex AI models. Deep learning algorithms frequently operate as opaque "black boxes," hindering educators' understanding of algorithmic decisions and undermining trust in adaptive systems (Baker & Inventado, 2016).

7.2. Ethical considerations: Privacy and bias

AI-powered educational platforms collect sensitive academic and behavioral data, making privacy protection essential. Compliance with frameworks such as GDPR and FERPA, along with encryption and secure authentication, is vital to prevent data misuse (Luckin et al., 2016). Meanwhile, algorithmic bias poses a threat to equity: models trained on non-diverse data can marginalize certain student groups or misrepresent diverse learning patterns. Regular audits, diverse data inclusion, and fairness-driven algorithmic adjustments are required to ensure just and inclusive AI use in education (Pardo et al., 2016).

Accessibility and governance also require explicit design attention. The interface should follow Universal Design for Learning principles by offering multiple ways of engagement, representation, and expression, while deployment policies should define consent, data minimization, audit routines, and human oversight. These requirements align the prototype with international guidance on human-centered generative AI, policy readiness, and capability assessment in education (CAST, 2024; Miao & Holmes, 2023; Miao et al., 2021; OECD, 2023).

7.3. Ensuring transparency, safety, and fairness

Trust and accountability in AI-based learning depend on transparency and explainability. Tools such as SHAP and LIME can clarify how algorithms make recommendations, supporting educator oversight and user confidence (Baker & Inventado, 2016). Establishing institutional ethical committees and regulations promotes equitable access and safeguards student rights (Luckin et al., 2016). Continuous impact assessment through testing, feedback, and model updates ensures that AI systems remain aligned with pedagogical goals and institutional values (Pardo et al., 2016). Ultimately, addressing these challenges fosters an educational AI ecosystem that is not only effective and innovative but also responsible, fair, and human centered.

8. CONCLUSIONS AND RECOMMENDATIONS

8.1. Transformative impact on education

The development of an AI-based adaptive learning web application demonstrates that artificial intelligence can profoundly enhance personalization in education. By dynamically adjusting content to individual needs, these systems improve knowledge retention, motivation, and engagement while optimizing teaching strategies and institutional management. However, their success depends on ensuring equitable technological access and adequate teacher training to fully integrate adaptive learning into diverse educational contexts.

8.2. Data quality and algorithm transparency

The effectiveness of adaptive systems depends heavily on the quality, diversity, and integrity of the data used to train AI models. High-quality datasets minimize bias and promote fairness in personalized recommendations. Equally important is the transparency of algorithms: explainable and auditable models must be prioritized to help educators understand system decisions and maintain trust in AI-driven learning environments.

8.3. User experience and accessibility

Improving usability and accessibility is essential for large-scale adoption. Future versions of adaptive platforms should offer intuitive interfaces, seamless integration with other educational tools, and optimized mobile or offline versions for regions with limited connectivity. Expanding accessibility ensures that adaptive learning benefits all students, regardless of technological or socioeconomic limitations.

For low-resource environments, the platform should prioritize lightweight visualizations, offline exports, mobile compatibility, and institutional data-governance templates that reduce implementation costs. Templates for consent, teacher onboarding, and periodic data review can be shared across departments so that implementation is feasible without extensive technical staff. These measures strengthen equity by ensuring that adaptive learning does not become a privilege of highly connected institutions only.

8.4. Integration with emerging technologies

The next generation of adaptive systems will integrate artificial intelligence with immersive technologies such as augmented and virtual reality to create more interactive and engaging environments. These tools will enhance conceptual understanding and allow students to explore complex phenomena dynamically, fostering deeper and more experiential learning processes.

8.5. Ethical standards and sustainable development

To guarantee responsible innovation, it is necessary to establish ethical frameworks that ensure data privacy, algorithmic equity, and institutional accountability. Collaboration between educators, technologists, and policymakers will be key to defining global standards that balance innovation with student protection. Continuous evaluation, transparency, and inclusion must remain at the core of adaptive learning's evolution to ensure an equitable and human-centered digital education future.

9. FUTURE PROPOSALS FOR EXPANDING ADAPTIVE LEARNING WITH ARTIFICIAL INTELLIGENCE

9.1. Integration of emerging and immersive technologies

Future adaptive learning systems should expand their capabilities by integrating artificial intelligence with emerging tools such as augmented reality (AR), virtual reality (VR), and data visualization frameworks like Plotly and Dash. These technologies will enable immersive and interactive learning environments where students can explore complex concepts through simulations and visual experimentation. Combining AI-driven personalization with immersive experiences will strengthen comprehension, creativity, and engagement, particularly in STEM and applied disciplines.

REFERENCES

Alrawashdeh, G. S., Fyffe, S., Azevedo, R. F. L., & Castillo, N. M. (2024). Exploring the impact of personalized and adaptive learning technologies on reading literacy: A global meta-analysis. *Educational Research Review*, *42*, 100587. DOI: 10.1016/j.edurev.2023.100587

Ausubel, D. P. (2003). *Aquisição e retenção de conhecimentos: uma perspectiva cognitiva* (Vol. 1).

Baker, R., & Siemens, G. (2014). Learning analytics and educational data mining. *Cambridge handbook of the leaning sciences*, 253-272.

Baker, R. S., & Inventado, P. S. (2016). Educational data mining and learning analytics: Potentials and possibilities for online education. *Emergence and innovation in digital learning: Foundations and applications*, 83-98.

Black, P., & Wiliam, D. (1998). Assessment and Classroom Learning. *Assessment in Education: Principles, Policy & Practice*, *5*(1), 7–74. DOI: 10.1080/0969595980050102

Bonilla-Priego, M. J., García-Sánchez, I.-M., & Pérez-Bueno, J.-C. (2024). Evaluating the success of a learning management system used in a supplemental learning model. *Innovations in Education and Teaching International.* Advance online publication. DOI: 10.1080/09639284.2024.2424269

CAST. (2024). Universal Design for Learning Guidelines version 3.0. CAST. https://udlguidelines.cast.org/

Clark, R. (2010). Evidence-based training methods: A guide for training professionals. American Society for Training and Development. https://archive.org/details/evidencebasedtra0000clar

Doğan, S., Betin-Can, A., & Garousi, V. (2014). Web application testing: A systematic literature review. *Journal of Systems and Software*, *91*, 174–201. DOI: 10.1016/j.jss.2014.01.010

Elmasri, R., & Navathe, S. (2016). Fundamentals of Database Systems. Pearson eLibrary. https://elibrary.pearson.de/book/99.150005/9781292097626

Gašević, D., Dawson, S., & Siemens, G. (2014). Let's not forget: Learning analytics are about learning. *TechTrends*, *59*(1), 64–71. DOI: 10.1007/s11528-014-0822-x

Goodfellow, I., Bengio, Y., & Courville, A. (2016). Deep Learning. MIT Press. https://mitpress.mit.edu/9780262035613/deep-learning/

Graesser, A., Chipman, P., Haynes, B., & Olney, A. (2005). AutoTutor: An intelligent tutoring system with Mixed-Initiative dialogue. *IEEE Transactions on Education*, *48*(4), 612–618. DOI: 10.1109/TE.2005.856149

Heffernan, N. T., & Heffernan, C. L. (2014). The Assessments Ecosystem: Building a Platform that Brings Scientists and Teachers Together for Minimally Invasive Research on Human Learning and Teaching. *International Journal of Artificial Intelligence in Education*, *24*(4), 470–497. DOI: 10.1007/s40593-014-0024-x

Holmes, W., Bialik, M., & Fadel, C. (2019). Artificial Intelligence in Education: Promises and Implications for Teaching and Learning. Center for Curriculum Redesign. https://discovery.ucl.ac.uk/id/eprint/10139722/

Huang, R., Spector, J. M., & Yang, J. (2019). Educational technology. In Lecture notes in educational technology. https://doi.org/DOI: 10.1007/978-981-13-6643-7

Johnson, L. S, A. B., Estrada, V., & Freeman, A. (2016). The NMC Horizon Report: 2015 Higher Education Edition. https://eric.ed.gov/?id=ED559357

Jung, L. A., & Guskey, T. R. (2007). Standards-based grading and reporting: A model for special education. *Teaching Exceptional Children*, *40*(2), 48–53. https://eric.ed.gov/?id=EJ849801 and https://eric.ed.gov/?id=EJ849801. DOI: 10.1177/004005990704000206

Luckin, R., Holmes, W., Griffiths, M., & Forcier, L. B. (2016). Intelligence Unleashed: An Argument for AI in Education. Pearson. https://www.scirp.org/reference/referencespapers?referenceid=3391328

Miao, F., & Holmes, W. (2023). Guidance for generative AI in education and research. UNESCO. https://www.unesco.org/en/articles/guidance-generative-ai-education-and-research

Miao, F., Holmes, W., Huang, R., & Zhang, H. (2021). AI and education: Guidance for policy-makers. UNESCO. https://unesdoc.unesco.org/ark:/48223/pf0000376709

Myers, G. J., Sandler, C., & Badgett, T. (2011). *The Art of Software Testing* (3rd ed.). Wiley., https://www.oreilly.com/library/view/the-art-of/9781118133156/

OECD. (2023). AI and the Future of Skills, Volume 2: Methods for evaluating AI capabilities. OECD Publishing. https://doi.org/DOI: 10.1787/a9fe53cb-en

Pardo, A., Han, F., & Ellis, R. A. (2016). Combining University Student Self-Regulated Learning Indicators and Engagement with Online Learning Events to Predict Academic Performance. *IEEE Transactions on Learning Technologies*, *10*(1), 82–92. DOI: 10.1109/TLT.2016.2639508

Piaget, J. (1972). The Psychology of the Child. Basic Books. https://archive.org/details/psychologyofchil00piag_0

Pressman, R. S. (2020). *Software Engineering: A Practitioner's Approach* (9th ed.). McGraw-Hill Education.

Romero, C., & Ventura, S. (2010). Educational Data Mining: A Review of the state of the art. *IEEE Transactions on Systems, Man, and Cybernetics. Part C, Applications and Reviews*, *40*(6), 601–618. DOI: 10.1109/TSMCC.2010.2053532

Schwaber, K., & Sutherland, J. (2017). *The Scrum Guide*. Scrum Alliance.

Shute, V. J. (2008). Focus on formative feedback. *Review of Educational Research*, *78*(1), 153–189. DOI: 10.3102/0034654307313795

Shute, V. J., & Zapata-Rivera, D. (2012). Adaptive Educational Systems. In P. J. Durlach & A. M. Lesgold (Eds.), Adaptive Technologies for Training and Education (pp. 7–27). chapter, Cambridge: Cambridge University Press. https://doi.org/DOI: 10.1017/CBO9781139049580.004

Squires, D., & Preece, J. (1999). Predicting Quality in Educational software. *Interacting with Computers, 11*(5), 467–483. https://doi.org/. DOI: 10.1016/S0953-5438(98)00063-0

VanLehn, K. (2006). The Behavior of Tutoring Systems. *International Journal of Artificial Intelligence in Education, 16*(3), 227–265. DOI: 10.3233/IRG-2006-16(3)02

VanLehn, K. (2011). The Relative Effectiveness of Human Tutoring, Intelligent Tutoring Systems, and Other Tutoring Systems. *Educational Psychologist, 46*(4), 197–221. DOI: 10.1080/00461520.2011.611369

Vygotsky, L. S. (1978). *Mind in Society: The Development of Higher Psychological Processes*. Harvard University Press., DOI: 10.2307/j.ctvjf9vz4

Woolf, B. P. (2010). *Building Intelligent Interactive Tutors: Student-centered Strategies for Revolutionizing E-learning*. Morgan Kaufmann.

Zawacki-Richter, O., Marín, V. I., Bond, M., & Gouverneur, F. (2019). Systematic review of research on artificial intelligence applications in higher education – where are the educators? *International Journal of Educational Technology in Higher Education, 16*(1), 39. Advance online publication. DOI: 10.1186/s41239-019-0171-0

Chapter 16
Ethics, Privacy, and Governance in AI-Powered Education

Rocky Kumar
http://orcid.org/0009-0002-6995-2037
Poornima University, Jaipur, India

Adarsh Kumar Pandey
http://orcid.org/0009-0002-1364-6903
Poornima University, Jaipur, India

Gaurav Kumar
http://orcid.org/0009-0004-6126-8526
Poornima University, Jaipur, India

Sakshi Sharma
http://orcid.org/0000-0002-7754-7974
Poornima University, Jaipur, India

ABSTRACT

Application of Artificial Intelligence (AI) to the sphere of education has already offered the opportunities of a self-reliant and personalized process of learning, however, it does not cause certain critical issues of morality, privacy, and control. Being intelligent tutoring systems, chatbots, adaptive learning platforms become a part of the classroom and online world, the concerns regarding the safety, transparency, and effectiveness of the algorithm and the ethics of the developers of the algorithm creation become an increasingly more evident one. The AI agents will most likely accumulate and manipulate sensitive student information which must be strictly controlled by the policies in order to promote accountability, fairness and adherence to international privacy laws including GDPR and FERPA.

1. INTRODUCTION

Artificial Intelligence (AI) has been a transformative force in the education sector, transforming the way teaching, learning and assessment design and delivery. In the past few years, machine learning, natural language processing, and data analytics have revolutionized education by moving it beyond traditional

DOI: 10.4018/979-8-3373-7225-9.ch016

classroom settings that served one-size-fits-all approaches to personalised, adaptive and data-informed learning environments. Tools powered by AI, such as intelligent tutoring systems, learning analytics dashboards, automatic assessment platforms, and conversational agents, are increasingly fully integrated into the ecosystem of the school, (university) institutions and online learning. Whilst they have important pedagogical and operational benefits, this also has some complex ethical, privacy and governance-level issues. Educational AI platforms typically rely on vast amounts of learner sensitive information – like behavioural and academic – and sometimes even biometric data. If there are weak ethical and privacy rights and safeguards, and governance structures, they can perpetuate and reproduce bias; reduce the autonomy of learners; and ruin trust between learners, educators and institutions. There is a rising focus all over the world for educated use of AI in education, not only in terms of technological innovations, but with regard to responsible, transparent and accountable practices. This chapter addresses these concerns by systematically recording the various concerns at the nexus of ethics, privacy and governance in education in the light of Artificial Intelligence (Zawacki-Richter et al, 2020).

1.1 Evolution of AI in Education

AI learning or AI in education history can be followed starting from the earliest rule-based computer-assisted instructional systems up to the present in the era of "data assisted omni-centred" machine artificial intelligence. The first applications in the 1980s and 1990s mainly concerned with the expert systems and Intelligent Tutoring Systems (ITSs) that followed pre-established instructions. While these were rather narrowly skewed when it comes to adaption, they were the foundations for personalized learning notions (Kasneci et al., 2023). In the last 10 years, the rise of machine learning and big data analysis has led to a growing number of AI systems that can model the behaviour of a learner and predict which combinations of content will be beneficial, and who will be the most open to learning, and then adapt content on the fly. AI-powered learning analytics is also becoming a built-in feature of LMS to early identify at-risk students, suggest learning resources, and more (Holmes et al., 2022). Recent developments with generative AI models have enabled content automation and synthesis, feedback generation, support of conversational learning and so on, and escalated the usage of AI in education. But, along the way, the growth and rise have brought with it ethical and privacy issues (Floridi et al., 2018). Today's AI systems are 'black box' systems, where the decision-making process or inputs into the system are hard to understand and are not controllable by the educator and learner (Zhou et al., 2024).

1.2 Motivation for Ethics, Privacy, and Governance

But speaking both from a pragmatic perspective on what risks these advances in AI may present to governance and an ethicist's perspective on what these advances may responsibly cause the Education Sector, the drive towards pushing the emphasis of Ethics and Privacy, along with the emphasis of governance in AI, is evident. The ethical treatment of data, and the use of automated decision making, has a special importance, because schools have a special duty of care for learners, particularly minors (UNESCO, 2021). This reinforces the fact that while commercially-used AI has a direct impact on the opportunities to learn, it also affects educational outcomes and life related consequences, whereas commercially-used AI doesn't. Some new examples are found in ethical issues, such as algorithmic bias and fairness, which become present in the study of AI in educational technology, where historical educational data could be a proxy for current social, economic or cultural inequalities. Likewise, privacy concerns are equal with the right to information and informed consent for the student may be threatened by the collection of information. Further, poor governance, such as lack of accountability, faulty procurement, and lack of regulatory scrutiny, can cause institutions to be under-prepared to effectively mitigate risks tied to the use of AI. International organizations and policymakers have reacted by releasing ethical guidelines for AI and governance recommendations such as the notions of data privacy by design, human oversight and transparency (Holmes & Porayska-Pomsta, 2022).

While the research on the use of AI in education is expanding, some key gaps are yet to be thoroughly explored. There are relatively few existing studies on the personal and ethical consequences of governance, long-term governance and accountability, or institutional implementation issues, compared to studies of technological efficiency and personalisation. In addition, generative AI governance research and usage in K–12 schools, and in resource-poor areas are still emerging and not well developed. This chapter elucidates these challenges by amalgamating ethical and privacy considerations, governance and institutional challenges to responsible AI in education.

1.3 Research Objectives and Chapter Organization

The main goal of this chapter is to show a broad and systematic analysis of ethics, privacy, and governance of AI-powered education. Specifically, the purpose of the chapter is to:

(i) identify some major ethical and privacy risks concerning the adoption of AI in the school environment;
(ii) consider governance frameworks, policies and institutional responsibilities existing;
(iii) make practical design and policy recommendations for trustworthy and responsible AI deploying in education;

The rest of the chapter is structured as follows. The technical backgrounds and system architectures options of AI informed educational platforms will be available in Section 2. Ethical concerns of fairness, transparency and equity are covered in section 3. Section 4 is focused on privacy, data protection and student rights. Section 5 looks at governance models as well as regulatory views. Section 6 addresses trustworthy practices for AI design and then the problems of assessment and academic integrity are taken up in Section 7. Empirical case studies are presented in Section 8 and Section 9 presents policy recommendations and recommendations for implementation. Finally, Section 10 relates to future research directions and Section 11 concludes the chapter.

2. AI-POWERED EDUCATION: CONCEPTS AND SYSTEM ARCHITECTURE

AI Powered Education is the A.I. technique entering education processes, routines, and organizing in order to improve teaching processes, learning processes for individuals and institutions and to support treatment decisions. Unlike the traditional digital learning systems, a platform with artificial intelligence is capable of dynamic adaptation to the behavioural aspect of the learners, analysing the large-scale educational data, automating the teaching or administrative task (Zawacki-Richter et al., 2020). These systems are working at the nexus of pedagogy, data science, and computational intelligence, and as such, they are technically and ethically complicated in their design and implementation processes. At a conceptual level, AI in education works via the combination of ongoing data collection, the use of a model to independently reach an inference, and to then provide feedback and influence the path and outcome of learning itself (Williamson & Eynon, 2020). This data centric nature makes the system architecture a critical factor such that the design choices made have direct influence on the transparency, privacy, accountability and governance (Holmes et al., 2022).

2.1 AI Techniques Used in Educational Systems

Educational AI systems utilize various techniques taken mainly from machine learning, natural language processing and intelligent decision-making models. Machine learning algorithms have been commonly used, such as supervised learning, unsupervised learning in predicting student performance, identifying learning difficulties, and recommending personalised learning resources. These models learn from historical data about student performance in school, such as assessment scores, engagement data, and data on student interaction such as logs.

Natural language processing (NLP) techniques make it possible to automate essay grading and develop conversational tutoring systems and feedback generation. Recent progress in large language models has only further broadened these abilities in which they are able to imitate human-type conversation and create teaching materials at a large scale (Zhou et al., 2024). Additionally, reinforcement learning techniques have been employed in adaptive tutoring systems, where the instructional strategies are learned to be maximum with regard to learner responses over time. However, dependence on complicated models also brings with it the explainability and bias risks (Floridi et al. 2018). Nowadays, various technical mitigation strategies such as federated learning, explainable AI, differential privacy and fairness-aware machine learning are increasingly implemented in modern educational AI systems to minimise ethical and privacy risks. They can reduce algorithmic bias, increase transparency of algorithms, and enhance data protection. Additionally, the human-in-the-loop process allows teachers to receive feedback throughout the feedback loop, especially when making important judgment calls in education like feedback, grading, and evaluation.

2.2 Data-Driven Learning and Analytics

Data-driven learning is one of the core concepts in AI-powered education; as the term implies, learner data continuously is collected, analysed and drawn upon to make decisions that impact instruction. Learning analytics systems aggregate data from various sources with seeking information, such as learning management systems, online assessments, discussion forums and even sensor data obtained from encounters, making their insights about knowing learner engagement and procedure (Slade & Prinsloo, 2023).

Predictive analytics is generally applied to catalog at-risk students, anticipated academic outcomes and trigger early strategies to intervene with at-risk students. While such analytics can help with retaining and supporting learning, there is a lot of concern about the issues of surveillance, profiling, and fairness, especially when the two predictions come from incomplete or biased data sets (Williamson & Eynon, 2020). In addition, students are often unaware of how their data is used or of the effect of the outcomes of analytics on educational decisions, and this reveals the potential for gaps in transparency and informed consent (UNESCO, 2021). Empirical research in recent years suggests that the use of AI mediated learning analytics systems is on the rise in universities and online learning services. Predictive Analytics is rapidly becoming a tool of choice for institutions to identify at-risk students, tailor their learning experiences and enhance the learner experience as a result. At the same time, however, there has been increased focus on the significant volume of data needed for education, which has sparked apprehension about digital surveillance, profiling and transparency of education data use.

2.3 Architecture of AI-Enabled Educational Platforms

The architecture of educational platforms that are AI-enabled is usually built of multiple interconnected layers of architectures, each of which has different functional and governance implications. At the basic level, modules for data acquisition gather information about learners from educational environments. This data is then handled and kept within secure data management layers which may contain cloud-based infrastructures or hybrid infrastructures (OECD, 2023).

The core intelligence layer consists of AI and analytics engines that are responsible for modelling learner behaviour, generating prediction and recommendations. On top of this layer, components for applications and interfaces provide personalized content, feedback and dashboard for students, educators and administrators. Across the different layers of the system, governance and oversight architectures, ranging from audit trails and explainability modules to compliance monitoring systems and human-in-the-loop, should be designed to foster accountability, transparency, and institutional trust in an AI-driven education system.

3. ETHICAL DIMENSIONS OF AI IN EDUCATION

The application of artificial intelligence in educational settings has sparked controversies about issues such as fairness, transparency, autonomy and inclusion. In contrast to traditional educational technologies, AI systems are involved in learning trajectories, assessments, as well as institutional decisions through an automated or semi-automated process. These interventions, if not properly guided, can re-structure the experiences of education in ways that are hard to identify, account for, or challenge (Floridi et al., 2018). As a result, ethics has become a key pillar when it comes to assessing the responsible use of AI in education instead of something that is attached to it. Data Practices, Model Design and Institutional Governance are intertwined with ethical concerns in AI-driven education (Williamson & Eynon, 2020).

3.1 Algorithmic Bias and Fairness in Learning Systems

The fact that algorithmic bias is one of the most important ethical issues for AI-based educational systems." When the data is skewed (so that notes for one voice type are very different from another) or when some odd features are rated as a default setting while others are not, or when the design assumes that learners have a certain background, as opposed to a diverse one, this results in a disproportionate data set, which can induce bias (Holmes & Porayska-Pomsta, 2022). When biased models are used for performance prediction, adaptive learning or assessment, they may systematically penalize some groups of students, based on socio-economic status, proficiency in a particular language, gender, or disability.

Fairness in educational AI means that these educative AI systems will be able to offer fair chances and solutions for all learners. However, fairness is a multidimensional concept and features equal access, equal treatment and equal outcomes which are often hard to achieve at the same time (Kasneci et al., 2023). For instance, personalization algorithms might success the community in which the algorithm operates, but will marginalize underrepresented learners whose data patterns represent something other than the predominant norms. There are several types of algorithmic bias within contexts of educational AI systems, such as representation bias, measurement bias, aggregation bias, and historical bias. Representation bias is created when training sets do not reflect a broad enough range of learner groups, and measurement bias is when classroom measures of performance do not adequately reflect the complexity of classroom learning processes. However, some disparities in education first identified by historical patterns should not and do not drive discriminatory results in an educational dataset. To tackle this issue, it is essential to employ AI models that are fair and use diverse datasets, periodically audit for biases, and keep them under human supervision at all times.

3.2 Transparency, Explainability, and Accountability

Transparency and explainability are essential ethical requirements for a system of AI that has an effect on educational decision-making. Many AI models, especially those built on deep learning, are opaque systems, with little understanding of the process that gets the output (Floridi et al., 2018). In educational contexts, such a lack of clarity is damaging to trust as well as the capacity of teachers and students to understand, question, and/or appeal algorithmically decisions.

One such challenge is to tackle the problem of explainability of AI (XAI) to explain the model with different explanation styles and for different audiences, such as educators, learners, and administrators, etc. (Zhou et al., 2024). For teachers, explanations can help to support pedagogical judgment and, for students, can help make these decisions more transparent and make them feel more in control. Accountability also requires that stronger accountability is established around decisions made with the help of AI, especially if they lead to error or harm.

Safety, transparency and ethical compliance of systems should be regularly assessed with AI auditing systems and frameworks, in addition to explainability, also within the institutions. These auditing processes contribute to increase accountability of institutions and reveal the unexpected side effects of the process of automated decision making in the field of education.

3.3 Human Autonomy and Teacher–AI Collaboration

AI systems in the educational approach are made in mind as systems designed to augment each other, not substitute, human educators. However, over-automation can have the detrimental effect of reducing teacher autonomy and professional judgment and taking over from pedagogical expertise algorithmic recommendations (UNESCO, 2021). Ethical AI deployment therefore needs to bring a balanced approach where decision of instruction remains with the teachers and they integrate AI as a support tool. Widespread reliance on AI-based pedagogical tools could also help fuel the drift towards deskilling teachers and the loss of pedagogical judgment. When employing too much automation, there are fewer opportunities to make decisions about the context of teaching and learning, to be creative, and to interact with humans in learning environments. Thus, it is important for institutions to maintain control over the final decision-making processes regarding high-stakes education and to provide teachers with proper amounts of AI-literacy training, so that the teacher can critically respond to teachers' outputs created by the AI.

Human-AI collaboration focuses on the idea of human-in-the-loop systems, where educators take an active role in supervising and interpreting AI output, and taking over when required (Holmes et al., 2022). Such collaboration does not only make the use more ethically aligned, but also makes the use more effective since it can incorporate contextual and experiential knowledge about the problem, which is missing to algorithms. Learner autonomy is also important. Students should also be made aware of the way AI systems affect their form of learning and be given meaningful opportunities to challenge or opt out of any automated process if possible (Slade & Prinsloo, 2023).

Figure 1. Architecture of an AI-powered educational system

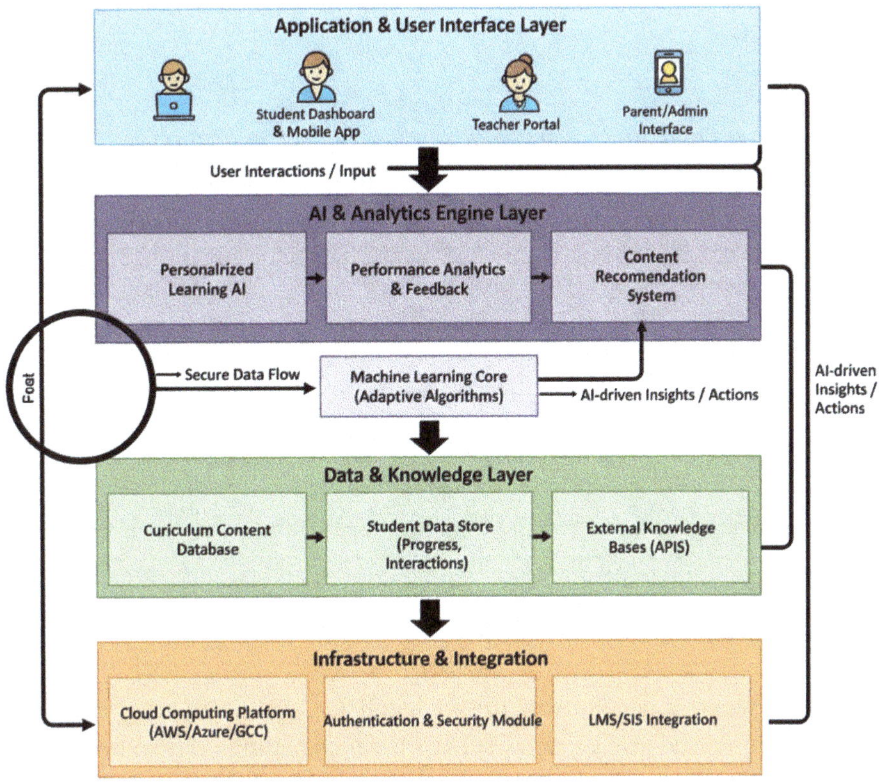

3.4 Equity, Accessibility, and Inclusion Challenges

Within this context, where digital divides and technological resource will be ubiquitous, equity and inclusion will remain challenges that cut across the field of teachers, students, government policy and institutions, and local communities. AI systems have some assumptions regarding the stability of internet connections, enhanced digital literacy, and a consistent availability and access to data, not all. Consequently, the possibility of marginalized learners not benefiting from AI for enhanced learning is equally likely as is the likelihood for their being exposed to excessive risks. In settings such as those in developing countries and school classrooms in lower resource areas, these challenges may exacerbate the unequal access that already exists to the provision of AI based learning experiences created by limited infrastructure, poor internet connectivity and low literacy rates in AI. Non-representative governance frameworks and policies for the implementation of AIG could exacerbate the gap in educational access between well-resourced schools and poorly resourced schools which are not technologically advanced (Williamson & Eynon, 2020).

Accessibility concerns are particularly prominent in case of learners with disabilities as poorly designed artificial intelligence interfaces might not adequately account for different cognitive, sensory or physical needs (Kasneci et al. 2023). Ethical design of AI must therefore include principles of ethical design, such as universal design, assistive technologies and participatory development processes from the very beginning. There is an increased focus in the international policy frameworks that ethical AI in education should produce social justice and inclusive opportunities for learning, rather than heighten inequality (UNESCO, 2021).

Table 1. Ethical challenges and affected stakeholders in AI-based education

Ethical Challenge	Students	Teachers	Institutions	AI Vendors
Algorithmic Bias & Fairness	Unequal learning outcomes; misclassification	Reduced trust in recommendations	Legal and reputational risks	Liability and compliance challenges
Transparency & Explainability	Limited understanding of decisions	Difficulty interpreting AI outputs	Accountability gaps	Need for explainable models
Privacy & Data Use	Loss of control over personal data	Ethical responsibility concerns	Regulatory non-compliance	Data governance obligations
Human Autonomy	Reduced learner agency	Erosion of professional judgment	Over-reliance on automation	Design constraints
Equity & Inclusion	Exclusion of marginalized groups	Pedagogical limitations	Widening digital divide	Market accessibility challenges

3.5 Generative AI and Ethical Challenges

The unprecedented speed of generative AI like ChatGPT, Gemini and other large language models has ushered in fresh ethical and governance issues in learning settings. These systems can produce an essay, summary of a text, coding and solutions and personalized teaching material without any minimum limits. A range of technologies can potentially be used to make learning more accessible and enable adaptive learning, but also poses significant issues about academic integrity, misinformation, authorship and dependency. One critique is the rising amount of work being created by AI tools that are submitted as assignments or tested in exams, creating issues from an originality standpoint and the concept of free learning. Current programs for detecting AI typically return inconclusive results, and may falsely identify learners as cheating. Moreover, there is a risk of inaccuracies or fabricated information which may compromise knowledge quality and credibility in generative AI systems, as has happened on a few occasions. Another aspect to consider is the potential for bias, cultural inaccuracies, and excessive use of AI-generated content. Schools need to, therefore, develop transparent and ethical policies for assessing and using AI in education along with clear governance policies for the same.

4. PRIVACY AND DATA PROTECTION IN AI-DRIVEN LEARNING

Privacy and data protection are essential elements in ethical AI use in education, owing to the fact that AI-based educational learning systems are based on the constant gathering and processing of data from learning. Unlike traditional educational records, AI systems create detailed profiles of the behaviour of students that involve their interactions, learning patterns, signs of emotions, and sometimes, even biometric attributes (Slade & Prinsloo, 2023). The scale, granularity and permanence of such data exacerbate privacy risks and requires powerful governance mechanisms. Educational institutions are in a position of trust especially when it comes to dealing with data acquired about minors and other vulnerable people. Any misuse, unauthorized access, or opacity of student's data can result in long-term damage such as discrimination, loss of autonomy and loss of faith in digital education systems (UNESCO, 2021).

4.1 Types of Educational Data and Risk Levels

AI-powered educational platforms process different types of data, which are linked with different levels of privacy risk. Academic data such as grades, attendance records and results of assessments are among the common data collected who traditionally be governed by institutional data policies. However, AI systems are increasingly embedded with behavioural data such as, clickstreams, time-on-task data, discussion participation and learning trajectories which can make sensitive inferences about people's cognitive abilities and personal habits (Williamson & Eynon, 2020).

More complex systems may gather biometric or affective data, such as facial expressions or voice patterns, or eye-tracking data, especially in the remote proctoring and engagement monitoring application markets. These data types are viewed as being high-risk because of their sensitivity and ease of misuse (Kasneci et al., 2023). When combined together in multiple sources of data, even low risk data can be re-identified, or it can also be repurposed, increasing the overall privacy exposure(OECD, 2023).

4.2 Student Consent and Data Ownership

Informed consent is a basic tenet of ethical data/data usage in education. However, the problem of obtaining meaningful consent in environments that are based on AI-driven learning is not yet so easy. Stieg fried and man presenting with complicated privacy policies where there is very little clarity around what their processing, sharing, or retention of their data looks like (Slade & Prinsloo, 2023). This problem is further compounded in compulsory educational settings where exclusion through opting out may not be an option. Questions of who owns the data are also up for debate. While institutions usually lay claim on educational data, learners more and more insist on more control over their personal information and algorithmic profiles (Floridi et al., 2018).

Opportunities for students to be aware of, to challenge and, where possible, to refuse an automatic decision-making process should also be given. Consent processes have to be transparent, easily accessible and comprehensible to ensure ethical AI governance.

Ethical frameworks emphasize to ensure students right to access, correct and request deletion of their data, and understanding the automated decision-making affects to their learning outcomes (UNESCO, 2021).

4.3 Data Security, Storage, and Retention Policies

In educational systems using AI, data security is a key technical need for data security. Centralized storage architectures, while being efficient, bring more vulnerability in data breach and unauthorized reading especially if such infrastructure is based on the cloud and not secured. So, the encryption, access measures and secure authentication of the user come into play to become very important to the design of an AI system. Data in the education sector can be further secured by incorporating the other techniques with other advanced privacy preserving techniques like federated learning, encryption, and etc., which provides further security and privacy.

Other techniques in the domain of privacy preserving technologies, such as Federated learning, encryption methods and differential privacy etc., further fortify the protection of data in education by reducing the possibility of education data being unnecessarily exposed. Incidentally, policy with regards to retaining and deleting data is very significant too. Many educational platforms collect student data indefinitely, at times with no clear rationale or knowledge of the data user. The risk of misuse and contradiction of purpose limitation, data minimisation may arise when data is prolonged. Ethical use and data governance principles of retaining data need to be clear, data retention periods, pedagogical retention need have to be clear, there has to be regular review of data retention periods (Holmes et al., 2022).

Figure 2. Data lifecycle in AI-based educational platforms

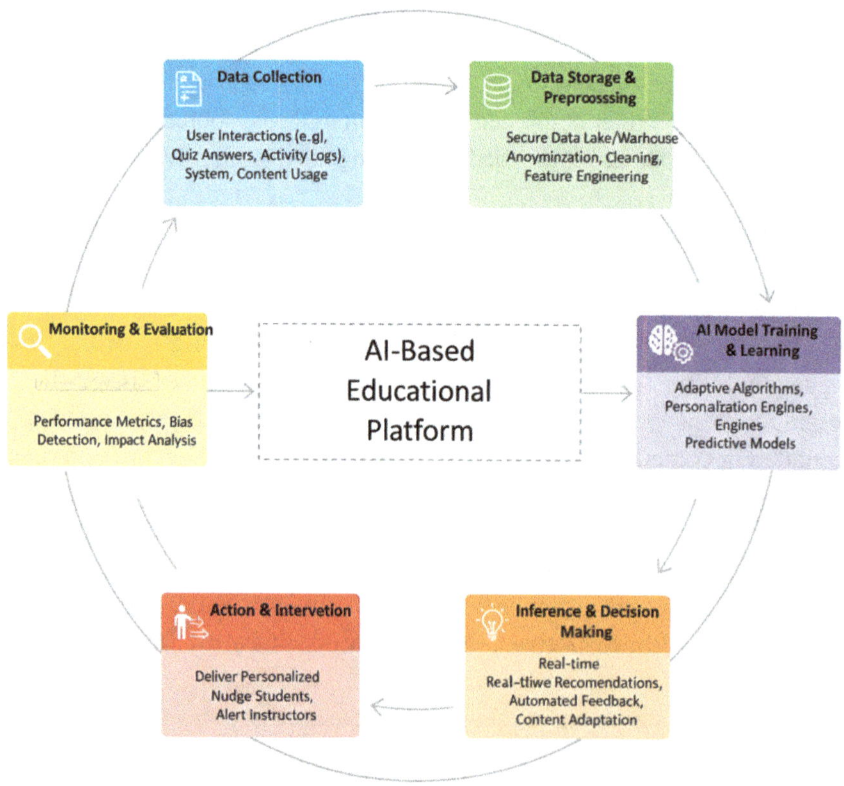

Table 2. Educational data types, privacy risks, and mitigation strategies

Educational Data Type	Examples	Privacy Risk Level	Key Risks	Mitigation Strategies
Academic Data	Grades, attendance, assessments	Low–Medium	Unauthorized disclosure	Role-based access, encryption
Behavioral Data	Clickstreams, engagement logs	Medium	Profiling, surveillance	Data minimization, anonymization
Learning Analytics Outputs	Risk scores, predictions	Medium–High	Misclassification, bias	Human review, explainability
Biometric / Affective Data	Facial images, voice, eye-tracking	High	Identity misuse, coercion	Explicit consent, limited use
Metadata & System Logs	Device info, timestamps	Medium	Re-identification	Aggregation, retention limits

5. GOVERNANCE MODELS FOR AI IN EDUCATION

Governance has grown to become an important enabler in helping schools achieve their ethical, legal and socially responsible use of AI in core education practice. Governance in AI-powered education is the systems, procedures, roles and oversight mechanisms that support decision-making throughout Industrial AI and AI new life cycle (from procurement and design being allowed to design through its implementation, it offers monitoring and decommissioning. Unlike purely technical controls, governance frameworks deal with accountability, transparency and participation in educational values.

Weak or fragmented governance may lead to lack of consistent practices, unclear accountability and increase in ethical and privacy risks. On the other hand, clear models of governance are key to deploying the ethical principles and regulatory requirements into concrete institutional practices (Floridi et al., 2018). Effective governance therefore serves as a link between the high level of ethical guidelines and the detail of educational operation.

5.1 Institutional Governance and Policy Frameworks

Educational institutions are at the forefront of AI adoption - and are directly responsible for making choices regarding the selection, implementation and management of AI-based systems. Institutional governance frameworks will generally encompass policies considered to be data protection, procurement, acceptable use, risk management, and academic integrity. However, it was found that many institutions do not have any specific policies regarding AI, but instead rely on generic IT or data governance frameworks that may not be sufficiently applicable to the risks associated with algorithmic decision-making and automation (Holmes et al., 2022). Effective institutional governance demands clear expression of policy for the purposes for which AI may be used, for which the actions of human oversight are constrained, and for the roles of human oversight in AI systems. Governance frameworks should furthermore require impact assessments before deploying the system, ongoing monitoring of how the system is functioning and mechanisms to deal with complaints or appeals regarding the outcome of AI-based decisions (OECD, 2023). Institutions should also appoint teams of AI professional ethics reviewers and evaluators that audit the risk, get input from stakeholders, and monitor AI systems and their output throughout their life.

5.2 Role of Governments, Accrediting Bodies, and Institutions

The role of the government and accrediting bodies is complementary when it comes to the governing guidelines for AI in education. They set minimum standards for privacy protection, fairness and accountability via legislation, policy guidance and quality assurance systems. National strategies on AI are also being increasingly produced in the field of education as both the impact to society, and the vulnerabilities of learner populations, is felt in this field.

Responsible AI can be further supported by accrediting agencies who can ensure that ethical and governance requirements are part of and in the evaluation process of institutions. Such criteria may include visibility in the use of AI, positive evidence of staff training and data protection compliance (OECD, 2023). At the institutional level, without generality wins consistency and legitimacy but acknowledges flexibility/accommodation in the implementation process (Floridi et al., 2018).

5.3 Vendor Governance and Third-Party Accountability

AI-driven education systems are often created and operating with third-party vendors making third-party governance a planner of adoption for responsible AI. Vendor governance is a system of contractual and technical, and ethical controls to set expectations of how data is used, models are transparent, systems are updated and liability is defined, Holmes & Porayska-Pomsta (2022). Without clear provisions in the contracts, there may not be clear visibility to proprietary algorithms or data processing practices to the institutions. Aligning commercial interests with pedagogical needs and protecting learners may sometimes be in tension in relation to the education technology vendors. Sometimes the volume of data may be monetized, recommendation algorithm systems don't provide transparency, and proprietary algorithm practices may limit the accountability for the processing and use of student data.

Accountability challenges occur where the authority to make decisions is divided among institutions and vendors. There are, for example, errors or biased outcomes attributed to the design of the algorithm, to the quality of the data or to the practices of the institution for which they are used, making it difficult to determine who is in charge (Kasneci et al., 2023). Governance mechanisms like service level agreements, audit rights and documentation requirements are thus essential to the maintenance of institutional control. Increasingly it is the focus of policy guidance to highlight the need for shared accountability models and a division of responsibility between vendors and institutions resulting in an ethical compliance stance and risk mitigation (OECD, 2023). Such models promote transparency and build trust among the stakeholders.

5.4 Ethical Review Boards and AI Audits

Ethical review boards and AI audits are examples of institutional systems for systematically overseeing AI systems in education. Proposed AI deployments are reviewed by ethical review boards, which draw on research ethics committees, to ensure that the strategies are fair, proportional and respect the rights of learners. These Boards provide a forum for interdisciplinary assessment of which pedagogical, legal, technical and ethical experts participate. AI audits supplement ethical review by focusing on evaluation of system behaviour, practices of data handling and results through the AI lifecycle. Bias testing and privacy compliance testing as well as performance in real world settings are examples of possible elements of a audit. Auditing helps to uncover any 'unintended impact' and can feed into the on-going process of continually improving. The institutionalisation of ethical review and audit processes convey positive messages about responsible innovation and establish trust and confidence in people (Floridi et al., 2018).

Table 3. Governance roles and responsibilities in AI-powered education

Stakeholder	Primary Responsibilities	Governance Instruments
Educational Institutions	AI procurement, deployment, oversight, learner protection	AI policies, impact assessments, review committees
Academic Leadership	Pedagogical alignment, ethical supervision	Curriculum policies, human-in-the-loop controls
IT & Data Governance Units	System security, data management, compliance	Security standards, access controls, audit logs
Governments & Regulators	Legal frameworks, national AI strategies	Laws, regulations, policy guidance
Accrediting Bodies	Quality assurance and compliance monitoring	Accreditation criteria, audits
AI Vendors	System development, transparency, risk mitigation	Contracts, documentation, model disclosures

Figure 3. Governance framework for responsible AI adoption in education

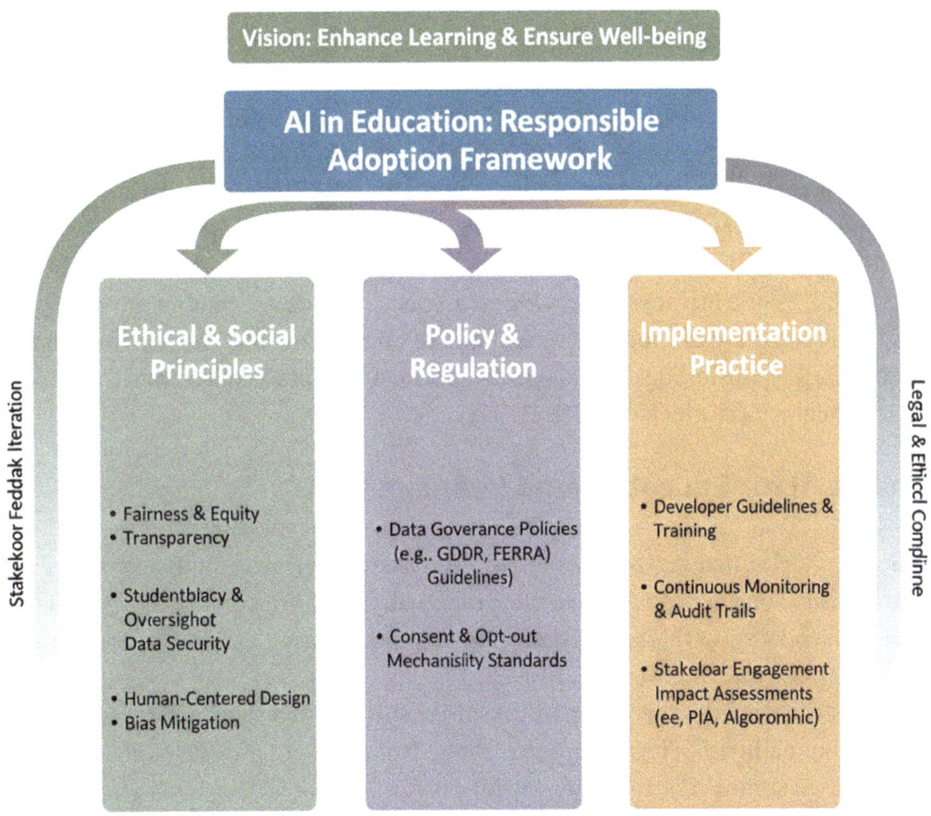

6. DESIGNING TRUSTWORTHY AND RESPONSIBLE AI SYSTEMS

Designing trustworthy and responsible AI systems is essential to making sure that the use of AI-powered education is in line with ethical principles, legal requirements and pedagogical goals. The trustworthy AI is not only technically correct, but also fair, transparent, protecting privacy, robust and providing human oversight throughout the entire lifespan of the system. In the educational context, the notion of trustworthiness is especially critical as AI systems have direct implications for the learning opportunities as well as the assessment and long-term development of learners. Virtually no international bodies or frameworks are arguing that trust in AI is a property that needs to be created after-the-fact to address a perceived problem. The concept of designing in trust is new, rather than design after the fact to solve a problem as it is found. Responsible AI design, therefore, replaces ethical considerations and governance demands and stakeholders' values from initial stages of system development and deployment (Floridi et al., 2018).

6.1 Privacy-Preserving AI Techniques

Privacy-preserving AI methods are designed to minimise the sharing out of sensitive information held by learners, while retaining the analytical/predictive functionality. Traditional centralized machine learning methods frequently involve extensive aggregation of data which carries a higher risk of breaching customer data while authorization loss (Slade & Prinsloo, 2023). To counter this challenge, privacy-enhancing technologies are more and more being applied in educational AI systems. Federated learning When it comes to training the models, federated learning would not require the transfer of raw learner data to a central server but allows models to be trained using distributed sources of data massively. This strategy can be aimed at minimizing data sharing while allowing for collaborative model improvement (Holmes et al., 2022). Differential privacy by further increasing the protection of datasets or outputs, by introducing controlled statistical noise to minimize the chances of re-identifying the individual learners (Kasneci et al., 2023). While privacy-preserving techniques provide acceptable protection, they present mechanisms such as accuracy of models, computational complexity and readiness of institution in the associated trade-offs. Responsible design, therefore, demands careful consideration of technical feasibility and ethical and regulatory priorities (OECD, 2023).

6.2 Explainable AI for Educators and Learners

Explainable AI (XAI) is an important element to making artificial intelligence-based educational systems comprehensible and dependable to a wide range of actors. Educators need explanations in order to interpret recommendations, validate system outputs and incorporate AI insights into pedagogical decision making. (Zhou et al., 2024).

In turn, learners benefit from the transparency of AI systems and their effects on feedback, assessments and/or learning pathways. XAI techniques range from model-agnostic explanations, e.g. feature importance, rule-based summaries, to inherently interpretable models designed to be interpretable (Floridi et al., 2018). Explorations in educational and teaching systems need to be designed for a specified audience, not too technical, but with a meaningful insight into the system behaviour. Explainability also supports accountability in the sense of enabling institutions to audit the decision making and respond to grievances or appeals. Without explainable mechanisms, AI systems can be relinquishing trust and ethical legitimacy and resorting into the degree wherein these systems can become unchallengeable authorities.

6.3 Human-in-the-Loop and Oversight Mechanisms

Human-in-the-loop (HITL) approaches can make sure that AI systems are not blindly followed by humans, especially when it comes to making high-stakes educational decisions. Rather than completely automating instructional or assessment processes, young learners, and educators generate data, at key points that are checkpoints their responsible AI systems use keep monitoring-and at those points, educators can override what the algorithm produces or alter it as they see fit. Oversight mechanisms are [indispensable] in managing uncertainty, understanding context and ethical judgement—the things AI systems are unable to do for the time being. As an example, predictive analysis of the group of students in need can inform and not replace approaches to supporting and intervening which are individually human-led.

HITL designs also help maintain the professional autonomy of educators and so do not deskill them. From a governance point of view, governance arrangements for oversight should be formalized and there should be a written record, training and institutional policy that supports that (Williamson & Eynon, 2020). This will keep the human involvement adequate and effective and not create a symbolic rather than a system with him. Imposing restrictions on pedagogical judgment should be an integral part of a sensible and responsible strategy of using predictive technology in education. Helpful mediation processes for timely and democratic decision-making are appropriate to keep in place with educators; mediation mechanisms for assessment are appropriate to keep in place with students; and mediation mechanisms for intervention should be kept in place (Holmes & Porayska-Pomsta, 2022).

Figure 4. Human-in-the-loop model for AI-supported learning systems

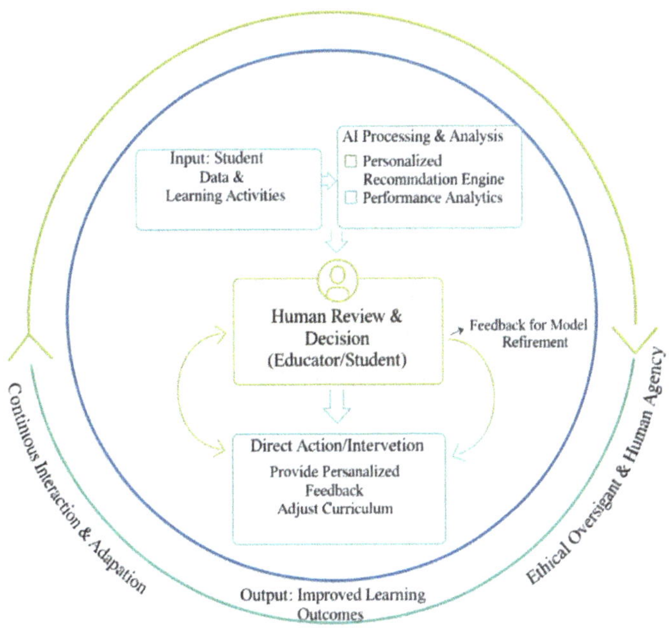

Table 4. Trustworthy AI design principles and implementation techniques

Design Principle	Description	Example Implementation Techniques
Privacy by Design	Protect learner data throughout the AI lifecycle	Federated learning, differential privacy
Transparency	Make system behavior understandable	Explainable AI models, documentation
Fairness	Avoid discriminatory outcomes	Bias audits, diverse training data
Human Oversight	Maintain human control over decisions	Human-in-the-loop review processes
Robustness & Safety	Ensure reliable performance	Continuous monitoring, validation tests
Accountability	Enable responsibility and redress	Audit logs, appeal mechanisms

7. AI, ASSESSMENT, AND ACADEMIC INTEGRITY

Assessment is intrinsic and an inherent component of educational systems and is an integral part of the learning outcomes, credentialing and institutional credibility. The introduction of AI into assessment practices has facilitated the introduction of automation, scalability and rapid feedback, accompanied by major issues of academic integrity and ethical use. The use of AI tools for assessment, feedback and evaluation is now a growing role in grading, feedback and evaluation practice and it is important to be aware of how assessment tools are designed and managed so they can be trusted to provide the education system with accurate education credentials. Meanwhile, the addition of these generative artificial intelligence tools to students' toolkits has blurred the definitions of helpfulness and cheating in the user of Assessment tasks. In the era of AI, then, serious attention needs to be placed on academic integrity, both on a pedagogical front focused on ethical principles and institutional policies, as well as a technological front, working in the AI space (Kasneci et al., 2023).

7.1 AI-Based Assessment and Feedback Systems

An AI-powered assessment system can be used to Automate grading, give individualized feedback, and for formative evaluation. Objective answers can be analysed efficiently via machine-learning models and written assignments and open-ended answers can be analysed automatically via natural language processing (NLP). These systems offer some benefits like consistency, scalability, and furnish prompt feedback that may facilitate learner engagement and learning effectiveness (Zhou et al., 2024).

Formative feedback created by AI systems can help learners to identify knowledge gaps and enhance performance levels through iterations of learning cycles. Learning analytics dashboards effectively complement teaching by providing insights and trends up to the class level and on an individual student level. However, if the assessment is fully mechanised and not sensitive enough to consider the subtlety of the assessment process and contextual judgement, there may be a restriction on the opportunities for more subtle assessment and contextual judgement, particularly with more complex tasks and/or creative tasks Holmes et al., 2022).

7.2 Risks of Academic Dishonesty and Misuse of Generative AI

The debut of generative A.I. tools has made an important change in the academic integrity environment. Essays, problems, and code are now easily generated by students and the concept of authorship and originality has been challenged. Such tools can be used appropriately for learning, but can also be utilized as instruments to commit plagiarism, contract cheating and misrepresentation of competence. Less reliable techniques are detection-based, like artificial intelligence that detects content - with concerns for false positives as well as questions about due process. Overuse of detection-based technologies which rely on surveillance may create a further loss of trust and privacy violation of students (Williamson & Eynon, 2020).

This makes it impossible to solve the integrity risks, of course. Presently the reaction of the institutions is predominantly centered on clarifying policies, educating students and as far as adobe tools for ethical utilization of generative AI. The language of 'education collaboratively' representing academic honesty as an educational venture, rather than an adversarial process of detection and circumvention – is of critical importance in engaging students to explore ways to navigate the ethical complexities of AI without fear. Using the language of 'education collaboratively' – framing academic integrity as an educational process, rather than an adversarial quest based on detection and circumvention – is crucial to engaging students, sharing an inquiry into how best to meaningfully and responsibly engage with AI without fear/trepidation (Kasneci et al., 2023).

7.3 Ethical Assessment Design in the AI era

There are redo theorem sides assessment practices at ORG in accordance with learning objectives, ethics and technology in the context of the era of AI assessment. Authentic assessment approaches (e.g. project-based learning, reflective assessments, oral or written and assessment, collaborative problem-solving) minimize possibilities for misuse and maximize more in-depth learning.

Designing AI-resilient assessments also means being open about the acceptable ways that AI can be used alongside having deliberate guidance on how AI tools can be used to aid learning and not interfere with academic integrity. As a result, clear rubrics, processes-based evaluation and iterative feedback may help shift the focus from product-based outcomes to learning processes (Holmes & Porayska-Pomsta, 2022).

Figure 5. AI-resilient assessment design framework

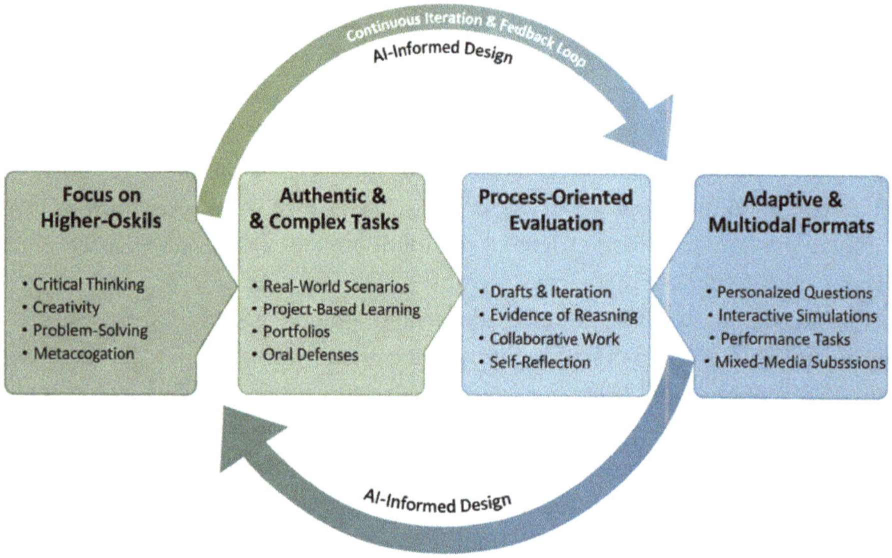

8. CASE STUDIES AND EMPIRICAL EVIDENCE

Empirical evidence and real-world case studies are a very important part of understanding the ethics, privacy and governance principles in action in Adulated education. Policy frameworks and design guidelines are normative directions, but case studies do evidence some of the contextually contingent challenges, trade-offs and outcomes in the adoption of AI in a variety of educational settings (OECD, 2023). This section includes some case studies (illustrative university and school level) and this includes an analysis of stakeholder perceptions using recent empirical research. Based on implementation of the system, there is a reported improvement in the detection of students who are at risk of failing academically and/or timely intervention strategies. Institutional feedback, however, pointed to the need for predictive analytics systems to be transparent, to include faculty and to engage students in creating that transparency.

8.1 University-Level AI Adoption Case Study

At the University level, there are often different adoption goals behind AI, such as efforts to increase student retention, give students more personalized learning and streamline administrative tasks. In one highly representative case, a large institution of higher education implemented an AI-based learning analytics system to identify engagement and assessment-based risk for or at risk of academic failure based on engagement data, assessment scores and historical indicators of performance (Holmes et al., 2022).

From an ethical point of view, the system showed a potential for benefits due to the possibility of early academic support and early targeted interventions. However, privacy and governance issues arose in the sense of transparency and consent. Many students were oblivious to the fact that academic risk profiling would have used predictive analytics which has raised questions about data control principle and informed consent (Slade & Prinsloo, 2023).

Example: AI-Based Learning Analytics in a Public University

A public university in the Asian region adopted an Artificial Intelligence based learning analytics system to detect at-risk students who were at risk of failing their courses by implementing the model using attendance records, interaction on learning management systems, and performance on various assessments taken by the undergraduate students. The system was able to identify those students who needed academic support and allowed early intervention by faculty advisors. However, concerns about what actions were taken by lack of explicit consent by students and limited transparency of how risk scores were made were raised.

8.2 School-Level Adaptive Learning Deployment

In terms of primary and secondary education, AI adoption has often been directed towards adaptive learning platforms used to personalize education and cater for a variety of different learning needs. In the school-level topics, we had a case in mind where an AI-based adaptive learning system was implemented for mathematics learning which recommended changes in content-level difficulty depending on the ongoing evaluation of student response (Kasneci et al., 2023).

The system has enabled an improvement in engagement and learning outcomes for many students; however, some ethical and privacy issues became apparent with time. Teachers experienced poor insight into how the system identified the learning pathways, which limited their capacity to intervene pedagogically (Williamson & Eynon, 2020). Parents also expressed concerns about the amount of information being collected about children's learning behaviours and who retains data and for how long. To deal with these problems, the school added extra measures for transparency with adolescents like parent-facing information sessions, simplified notices (UNESCO 2021).

Example: Adaptive Learning in a Secondary School

A secondary school implemented an AI-based adaptive learning in order to customise the way mathematics is taught based on the learning ability of the students. While the level of student engagement improved, teachers expressed less visibility into the attribute of the pathway of content assigned. The school mitigated this by the introduction of teacher dashboards and parental data briefings increasing the transparency and trust in AI assisted learning.

8.3 Stakeholder Perceptions: Students and Educators

Empirical studies have been consistently showing that the role of stakeholder perceptions can always have a big influence in the acceptance and the effectiveness of the AI in the educational sector. Students tend to be aware of some of the potential advantages offered by AI-powered personalization and feedback and are quite concerned about privacy, surveillance, and for fairness (Slade & Prinsloo, 2023). Trust is closely linked to the notions of transparency and the perceived ability to question or leave automated decisions.

Educators have been inclined to embrace AI as a supportive tool rather than one that is used as a substitute for professional judgement. Research shows that teachers are open to embracing AI systems when they have control over educational choices and they have the proper training regarding AI system limitations (Holmes & Porayska-Pomsta, 2022).

9. POLICY RECOMMENDATIONS AND IMPLEMENTATION ROADMAP

A policy approach on multiple levels of the institution, the technology and regulations are warranted, in the context of responsible use of AI for education. Although there are ethical principles and governance frameworks that can inform how major aquaculture activities are managed in an ethical and sustainable way, policies have an upside only if they are translated to actual implementation strategies, being sensitive to management constraints such as disease issues and stakeholders' expectations that range from those of administration through those of stakeholders. This section suggests practical policy recommendations for educational institutions, AI developers and regulators, which is followed by a phased roadmap on how it should be implemented.

9.1 Recommendations for Educational Institutions

Educational institutions are the key actors to operationalize ethical AI practices as they directly control procurement, deployment and day-to day use of AI systems. Institutions should draft AI-specific policies that benevolently come up with acceptable usage, limits of AI automation, and responsibilities for each oversight and accountability. Such policies need to be integrated within an institution's values and processes for governing academic and data. Finally, institutions should have AI governance roadmaps that involve regular audits, consultative processes with stakeholders, opportunities for faculty to learn more about how they can use AI, processes for responding to complaints about the use of AI for an educational decision, and reporting. An equally vital aspect is capacity building (Kasneci et al., 2023).

Investing in education programs to build teachers' and administrators' ability to be more "AI literate" and understand AI algorithm outputs more informatively, while at the same time critically accepting the limitations of AI. Establishing interdisciplinary committees on ethics or artificial intelligence that review ethical matters can be another way to aid in the systematically assessment of risks and ethical decisions. Last, but not least, institutions should consistently strive for greater transparency and engagement with stakeholders, including educating the student and the parent on the use of AI, practices with data, and means of redress. Participative governance mechanisms can contribute to the enhancement of AI-powered educational schemes' trustworthiness and trust (Holmes et al., 2022).

9.2 Guidelines for AI Developers and Vendors

The ethics and privacy implications of AI systems in education are in the hands of both AI developers and vendors. Vendors need to apply the concepts of 'privacy by design' and 'fairness by design' from the very get-go of the system development lifecycle and ethical issues should not be 'afterthoughts'. Documentation of sources of data, assumptions of the model and limitations of the system are highly important with regard to transparency and accountability. Developers should also provide explainable and configurable systems that enable educators to understand and differentiate the output of AI systems and put AI outputs into context. Rigid and opaque systems lack control over their institutional control and there is an increased risk for misuse or misinterpretation. Transparency should be the standard practice and a smooth functioning part of regular testing for bias, security audit and update. In addition, there should be a sharing of responsibility between the vendor and the institution (Floridi et al., 2018).

Figure 6. Roadmap for ethical, privacy-aware, and governed AI adoption

Table 6. Short-, medium-, and long-term roadmap for ethical AI in education

Time Horizon	Key Actions	Responsible Stakeholders
Short-Term (0–1 year)	Develop AI use policies; conduct initial risk assessments; train staff	Educational institutions, AI vendors
Medium-Term (2–3 years)	Establish ethics boards; implement audits and monitoring; improve transparency	Institutions, regulators, accrediting bodies
Long-Term (4+ years)	Standardize ethical AI certification; harmonize regulations; continuous evaluation	Governments, international organizations

10. FUTURE RESEARCH DIRECTIONS

While there are significant strides in advancing the ethical, legal, and technical aspects of using AI to support learning, numerous research questions remain unanswered. The pace of development in AI technologies, and generative and adaptive technologies especially, introduces new facts and degree of risk and uncertainty that used to exceed rules and suppose frameworks. Future research should therefore move beyond static, ethical lists of checks, and focus on evidence-based and flexible methods of practicing ethics in technology and society. This section highlights some of the future research directions, such as new emerging ethical and privacy issues, future research cooperation among different research fields, future trends in governance models of the education sector using AI technology, etc.

10.1 Emerging Ethical and Privacy Challenges

New ethical and privacy issues are sure to arise and exacerbate old ones with new AI features. Utilising a text and audio/video combination and behaviour in the educational context with a rising number of such multimedia AI systems gives rise to some complex issues relating to proportionality, consent and surveillance. The implications of such systems on learner autonomy and psychological well-being, specifically for adolescents, should be visited by future research. Generative AI is bringing new ethical challenges of authorship, originality, and trust in your data. When AI systems can create educational content and provide feedback that gets more sophisticated, it can become increasingly difficult to tell where humans and machines are influencing each other, and new ethical norms and practices of assessment will be needed. Additionally, we need longitudinal research in order to understand the long-term implications of data retention and algorithmic profiling in terms of the effect on the academic and professional paths of learners (Kasneci et al., 2023).

10.2 Interdisciplinary Research Opportunities

AI-driven education is inherently interdisciplinary in nature and needs to be collaborative, not only in computer science, but also in education, ethic, law, psychology and social sciences. Further studies should emphasize the interdisciplinary approaches, developing approaches that incorporate elements of technical review, pedagogy theory, and ethical review. These could be more comprehensive and consider the broader aspects of the functioning of AI systems in actual learning environments. The need for incorporating participative research methods, encouraging the engagement of various stakeholders like learners, teachers, and policymakers in developing and accessing AI systems. Co-design and action research approaches may assist in assuring that AI tools reflect the values of stakeholders, and respond to contextual needs and needs, as opposed to the implementation of externally defined solutions. Moreover, cross regional and cross educational systems comparative analysis explanation can be used to understand the influence of cultural, legal and institutional variations on the way ethical outcomes have manifested in these different contexts (Holmes & Porayska-Pomsta, 2022).

CONCLUSION

The education system has become Smart and acquired an important role for artificial intelligence in the education process. But, as this chapter demonstrates, any absolute optimism in education does not exist without addressing the ethical, privacy, and governance issues that are attached to data-driven and automated educational learning environments when studying education and the benefits of AI. AI-powered education functionality works at the intersection of technology and human development and it's important to design responsibly and oversee effectively. This chapter has talked about the ethics of AI in education and issues of algorithmic bias, transparency, autonomy and inclusion. It has also helped to make privacy and data protection issues even more central as many of the educational data are sensitive, and there are power relationships in such institutions.

Discussions were held about governance frameworks as the mechanisms in the working processes of the principles of ethics and the rules. By incorporating design strategies like privacy-preserving AI methods, explainable models and human in the loop oversight, educational institutions and technology providers can encourage trust in and support, not hinder, education pedagogies and systems involving AI. Ethical outcomes were represented based on case studies and evidence as critical to good governance, stakeholder engagement, and being contextually attuned to the need compared to technology. In the future, the role of AI in education will be a dynamic that demands collaboration among educators, technology developers, and policy makers, ensuring a healthy mix of innovation and social responsibility. As the future unfolds, the influence of AI on education will be a complex interplay between innovation and social responsibility that needs to be balanced among different stakeholders, including educators, technology developers, and policymakers.

REFERENCES

Floridi, L., Cowls, J., Beltrametti, M., Chatila, R., Chazerand, P., Dignum, V., Luetge, C., Madelin, R., Pagallo, U., Rossi, F., Schafer, B., Valcke, P., & Vayena, E. (2018). AI4People—An ethical framework for a good AI society: Opportunities, risks, principles, and recommendations. *Minds and Machines, 28*(4), 689–707. DOI: 10.1007/s11023-018-9482-5 PMID: 30930541

Holmes, W., Porayska-Pomsta, K., Holstein, K., Sutherland, E., Baker, T., Shum, S. B., Santos, O. C., Rodrigo, M. T., Cukurova, M., Bittencourt, I. I., & Koedinger, K. R. (2022). Ethics of AI in education: Towards a community-wide framework. *International Journal of Artificial Intelligence in Education, 32*(3), 504–526. DOI: 10.1007/s40593-021-00239-1

Kasneci, E., Seßler, K., Küchemann, S., Bannert, M., Dementieva, D., Fischer, F., Gasser, U., Groh, G., Günnemann, S., Hüllermeier, E., Krusche, S., Kutyniok, G., Michaeli, T., Nerdel, C., Pfeffer, J., Poquet, O., Sailer, M., Schmidt, A., Seidel, T., & Kasneci, G. (2023). ChatGPT for good? On opportunities and challenges of large language models for education. *Learning and Individual Differences, 103*, 102274. DOI: 10.1016/j.lindif.2023.102274

OECD. (2023). *Artificial intelligence in education: Challenges and opportunities*. OECD Publishing.

Slade, S., & Prinsloo, P. (2023). Learning analytics, ethics, and student data: A systematic review. *British Journal of Educational Technology, 54*(1), 1–17. DOI: 10.1111/bjet.13271

UNESCO. (2021). *Recommendation on the ethics of artificial intelligence*. UNESCO Publishing.

Chapter 17
Redefining Independent Learning With AI Agents:
A Blockchain-Enabled Trust Layer Verifiable Education

Junaid Nasir Qureshi
http://orcid.org/0000-0001-8508-6912
Bahria University, Pakistan

Muhammad Faraz Manzoor
http://orcid.org/0000-0001-6489-2157
University of Management and Technology, Pakistan

ABSTRACT

Self-guided AI agents are rapidly shifting education from static instruction to adaptive, learner-controlled systems operating at scale. These agents personalize learning, provide continuous support, and assist with complex tasks, but they also complicate identity verification, skill attestation, and attribution of human versus AI-generated work. This threatens trust in independently acquired, AI-supported credentials. This chapter presents a standards-based trust framework that combines World Wide Web Consortium (W3C) Decentralized Identifiers (DID) and Verifiable Credentials (VC) with content provenance specifications from the Coalition for Content Provenance and Authenticity (C2PA). We propose a four-layer architecture Identity, Trust, Data, and Application supported by a reference blueprint covering credential issuance, revocation, selective disclosure, and provenance verification. The design separates off-ledger personal data storage from on-ledger cryptographic proofs to preserve privacy while enabling credential portability, verifiable assessments.

INTRODUCTION

Right now, education is going through a huge shift, largely thanks to artificial intelligence (AI). A big part of this change is the rise of "agentic" AI systems tools that can plan, carry out tasks, and interact on their own. This is very different from the old learning management systems (LMS) from a decade ago, which were mostly just digital filing cabinets for course materials. Today's AI agents act more like

DOI: 10.4018/979-8-3373-7225-9.ch017

active tutors, helpful collaborators, and smart evaluators. They can create custom learning paths for each student, adjust support instantly based on how someone is doing, and run complex problem-solving exercises that used to be too expensive or difficult to manage (Anglen, 2024). Recent studies looking at research from 2012 to 2025 show that while AI definitely helps teachers with administrative tasks, its biggest game-changer is making it possible to offer high-quality, independent learning experiences at scale. These experiences also encourage students to think about their own thinking (metacognition) and manage their own learning process (self-regulation) (Elnaffar et al., 2025).

This big jump in technology also creates some serious problems when it comes to trusting who learners really are and knowing for sure that their work is genuine. As AI becomes a regular part of learning, it's getting harder and harder to tell what students actually did versus what the AI helped with (Garzón et al., 2025). The usual ways we certify qualifications systems built on school reputations and manual checks just aren't cut out for the huge amount, speed, and detail of work produced with AI these days. Employers and university admissions officers are now often faced with portfolios that feel like a "black box" it's unclear where the work actually came from, and a learner's identity might be scattered across many different online places (Entrust Cybersecurity Insitute, n.d.).

The extent of this "trust gap" is becoming clearer from recent data on credential fraud. Reports show a staggering 244% increase year-on-year in fake digital documents in 2024. Part of this surge is thanks to easy access to generative AI tools that can create really convincing fake transcripts and diplomas (Entrust Cybersecurity Insitute, n.d.). Plus, the so-called "diploma mill" business, estimated to make over $1 billion every year, is thriving in this low-trust verification atmosphere. These operations hand out thousands of worthless degrees, which cheapens the value of real, independent learning (Learn & Work Ecosystem Library, 2024). In the UK alone, universities are seeing a definite jump in academic misconduct linked to AI, with cheating cases involving AI rising from about 1.6 per 1,000 students in the 2022-23 school year to an estimated 7.5 per 1,000 students by 2025 (Goodier, 2025).

The reason we embarked on this research is simple: there's a pressing need to create a reliable "trust layer" for educational technology. We need a standardized system that ensures students are who they say they are, that their assessments are fair and accurate, and that AI involvement is clear and transparent without feeling like Big Brother is watching every move. If we don't tackle these issues, we risk making independent learning less valuable, potentially forcing a return to rigid, in-person exams that would undo all the accessibility gains of digital learning.

This chapter offers a comprehensive architectural framework that brings together three key tech standards: Decentralized Identifiers (DIDs) for giving learners control over their own identity, Verifiable Credentials (VCs) for easily shareable proof of achievements, and the Coalition for Content Provenance and Authenticity (C2PA) standards for securely linking a history to digital materials. By weaving these different technologies into a unified four-layer model, our proposed architecture provides a way to digitally confirm who learned something (Identity), what they learned (Credential), and how they proved it (Provenance).

Pedagogical Foundations of AI-Agent Learning

To align the proposed architecture with established educational theory, we ground AI-agent-based independent learning in three major pedagogical frameworks:

Self-Regulated Learning (SRL):

AI agents support goal-setting, self-monitoring, and adaptive feedback loops, enabling learners to control their cognitive processes. Features such as real-time progress tracking and personalized recommendations directly operationalize SRL principles.

Constructivism:

Learners actively construct knowledge through interaction with AI agents that provide contextual problem-solving, simulations, and iterative feedback. The agent acts as a facilitator rather than a knowledge provider.

Connectivism:

The decentralized architecture aligns with connectivist principles where learning occurs across distributed networks. Blockchain-backed credentials and AI agents enable knowledge validation across multiple nodes (institutions, platforms, peers).

This integration ensures that the proposed system is not only technologically advanced but also pedagogically grounded.

Ethical and Data Governance Considerations

While the proposed framework enhances trust and verifiability, it introduces several ethical and governance challenges:

Algorithmic Bias:

AI agents may inherit biases from training data, potentially affecting learning recommendations and assessments. Continuous auditing and fairness-aware model design are required.

Data Sovereignty:

Blockchain-based systems distribute control across nodes, raising concerns about jurisdiction and ownership of learner data. The use of off-chain storage with user-controlled encryption keys ensures compliance with data protection regulations.

Student Rights and Privacy:

Learners must retain control over their identity and credentials. The use of selective disclosure mechanisms in Verifiable Credentials (VCs) ensures that only necessary information is shared.

Transparency and Accountability:

C2PA-based provenance tracking ensures traceability of AI-generated content, enabling differentiation between human and AI contributions.

IMPLEMENTATION CHALLENGES

Despite its potential, the proposed framework faces several real-world challenges:

Blockchain Scalability:

High transaction volumes in educational ecosystems may lead to latency and increased costs. Layer-2 solutions and off-chain computation can mitigate these issues.

Institutional Adoption Barriers:

Educational institutions may resist adoption due to: Regulatory uncertainty, Integration costs, Lack of technical expertise

Integration with LMS Platforms:

Existing Learning Management Systems (LMS) are not designed for decentralized identity or blockchain integration. Middleware APIs and interoperability standards are required.

Complexity of Deployment:

The combination of AI agents, blockchain, and decentralized identity introduces architectural complexity, requiring phased implementation strategies.

BACKGROUND AND RELATED WORK

To contextualize the proposed trust layer, it is necessary to examine the evolution of three distinct but converging domains: AI-mediated independent learning, decentralized identity standards, and content provenance technologies.

The Evolution of Independent Learning and AI Agents

For years, educators have championed independent learning as a great way to empower students and build skills that last a lifetime. But, historically, it's struggled because many learners give up without the benefit of quick feedback or personal guidance (Kahn et al., 2025). This is where AI agents come in, filling those gaps by offering ongoing, adaptive support. Research from 2024 and 2025 shows that AI agents including smart tutoring systems (ITS) and chatbots using large language models (LLMs) can really boost student motivation and involvement by tailoring the pace and material to each learner (Garzón et al., 2025)

Today's research makes a key distinction between AI tools that just react and more advanced "agentic" systems. These agentic AI systems can take on a more active role, breaking down complicated learning goals into smaller, easier steps, fetching necessary resources, and even mimicking interactions with peers to help students practice teamwork (Jiang et al., 2024). For example, multi-agent systems can create simulations like debate clubs or project teams, giving solo learners a safe space to hone their social and collaborative abilities (Jin et al., 2025).

Even with all these advantages, using AI agents creates a problem known as a "provenance gap." When an AI helps write an essay or fix code, it becomes really tricky to figure out which parts the learner actually did and which parts the AI contributed. This is both a technical challenge and a philosophical one (Mikros, 2025). If there's no way to keep track of and verify these interactions, people who evaluate credentials might just ignore the work, thinking it isn't genuine. This doubt is understandable because research has shown that while AI can definitely boost learning, relying on it too much can actually hold back the development of critical thinking and the ability to solve problems on one's own (Garzón et al., 2025)

Decentralized Identity and Verifiable Credentials

Right now, how we handle digital identity in education usually follows a traditional setup. It's kind of like a central control system where places like Google or university databases act as identity providers. But this way of doing things creates isolated pockets of information; once your data is stored at one institution, it's locked in there. This makes it hard and slow to check someone's identity or records across different platforms. For example, a student's official university record isn't automatically connected to certificates they get from an online course or their project portfolio on GitHub.

The W3C's new standard for Decentralized Identifiers (DIDs), version 1.0, is shaking things up. It introduces a different approach called Self-Sovereign Identity (SSI). With a DID, you get a unique identifier that isn't managed by a single central authority. Instead, it's based on a decentralized network, like a blockchain. This lets the person the ID belongs to (the learner) prove they control it using cryptographic keys, without needing anyone else to vouch for them. Crucially, this separates the identity from whoever issued it. The learner actually owns their DID, while the university or other institution just confirms specific details about that identity.

To go hand-in-hand with Decentralized Identifiers (DIDs), there are W3C Verifiable Credentials (VCs). Think of VCs as the digital versions of traditional paper credentials, like diplomas or driver's licenses. What makes them special is that they're cryptographically signed by the organization that issued them (W3C, n.d.). This means the person holding the VC can keep it safely in a digital wallet and show it to someone who needs to verify it (like a potential employer). That verifier can instantly check the signature and confirm the credential is legitimate, all without needing to contact the issuer directly (Truvera, 2026). The latest version, VC Data Model v2.0, which was updated in 2025, makes these capabilities even better. It includes features that boost privacy, such as selective disclosure. This lets users share only the specific details from their credentials that are needed. For example, someone could prove they're over 18 without actually revealing their exact birthdate (W3C, n.d.).

In the world of education, the European Blockchain Services Infrastructure (EBSI) has been leading the way in using VCs for checking diplomas across different countries. This EBSI model shows how public systems can help issue and verify educational certificates on a large scale, like across an entire continent. It helps cut down on fraud and makes administrative processes smoother. However, most of today's systems still concentrate on big, final achievements like degrees, rather than the many smaller, ongoing learning achievements (micro-credentials) that someone might earn through self-directed learning, possibly with the help of AI.

Recent studies in AI-supported education emphasize Self-Regulated Learning (SRL), adaptive learning systems, and digital credentialing frameworks. These approaches highlight the importance of learner autonomy, continuous feedback, and verifiable achievement records, aligning closely with the proposed architecture.

Existing research on blockchain-enabled trust layers and decentralized identity frameworks (e.g., W3C DID/VC standards) has demonstrated the potential for secure and verifiable digital interactions. However, these approaches primarily focus on identity and credential verification. The proposed framework extends this work by integrating AI-agent-driven learning workflows with verifiable trust mechanisms, enabling both adaptive learning and trustworthy credentialing within a unified architecture.

Content Provenance and C2PA

While Verifiable Credentials (VCs) can confirm specific details about a person like "Alice has a degree" they don't naturally track the history of a digital item, such as "Alice wrote this essay." That's where content provenance comes in. To tackle misinformation and build trust in digital media, the Coalition for Content Provenance and Authenticity (C2PA) has created open technical guidelines (C2PA, n.d.).

The C2PA standard uses something called a "manifest." Think of it as a digital passport that travels with a file. This manifest is securely linked to the file using cryptography and logs its origin, the tools used to make it, and any changes made afterward (C2PA, 2025). Inside the manifest, you'll find "assertions" about the digital item details like who created it, what actions were taken (like cropping, applying filters, or using AI generation), and exactly when those actions happened (C2PA, 2024). Crucially, these C2PA manifests show if someone tries to tamper with the content. Any change not properly recorded in a new manifest will break the secure link, immediately warning the user that the content might be suspicious (Adobe, 2025).

In an educational environment, we can adapt C2PA to map out the "journey" of a student's work. For instance, a C2PA manifest could detail that a student wrote a first draft, an AI tool offered feedback on grammar, and then the student revised their main points (C2PA, 2024). This level of transparency shifts how we assess work. Instead of just a simple "pass/fail" based on the final product, we can evaluate the actual learning process itself.

The Policy Context

Implementing these technologies happens within a really complex world of regulations. For example, in the European Union, the GDPR law includes the "right to be forgotten." This can cause some theoretical issues because it clashes with the permanent nature of blockchain ledgers (Godyn et al., 2022). What's more, the EU AI Act categorizes AI systems used in education as "high-risk," which means they require strict rules for transparency, oversight, and checking for bias (Sharif et al., 2025). In the United States, there's the Family Educational Rights and Privacy Act (FERPA), which manages how student records' privacy is handled and insists on very strict consent procedures before any data can be shared.[35]

So, any proposed system needs to figure out how to work around these rules. A good approach is to make sure that the unchangeable ledgers only store cryptographic proofs (like hashes) and keep any sensitive personal information in separate storage that follows privacy laws.

Global Perspective on Credential Fraud

In addition to the reported surge in digital credential fraud, the issue has evolved into a global challenge affecting educational and professional ecosystems across diverse regions. Studies indicate that credential fraud is no longer confined to isolated cases but has become systemic, spanning diploma mills, forged academic transcripts, and increasingly sophisticated AI-generated certifications. In North America and Europe, the proliferation of online education platforms has introduced new vulnerabilities in identity verification and assessment integrity. Similarly, in developing regions, limited regulatory oversight and rapid digitalization have facilitated the growth of counterfeit credentials and unverifiable training certifications.

Moreover, the rise of AI-assisted content generation tools has further blurred the distinction between authentic learner output and machine-generated work, complicating traditional validation mechanisms. The globalization of remote work and cross-border education has intensified these challenges, as employers and institutions must verify credentials issued across heterogeneous systems with varying levels of trust and standardization.

These global trends underscore the urgent need for interoperable, privacy-preserving, and verifiable credentialing frameworks that can operate across jurisdictions. Consequently, the integration of decentralized identity standards, verifiable credentials, and content provenance mechanisms becomes essential to restoring trust in modern, AI-mediated educational environments

PROBLEM STATEMENT

Despite the technological advancements in AI and blockchain, the current educational ecosystem is characterized by deep fragmentation, a lack of interoperability, and a growing deficit of trust. These issues create significant barriers to the acceptance of independent learning.

Identity Fragmentation and Verification Costs

Right now, where people learn and what they learn is often kept separate, stuck inside specific schools or online learning sites. Think about it: the certificates you earn on Coursera, your university degree, and the code projects you build on GitHub all that information is spread out, not connected (Thompson & Dowd, 2023). Bringing all these records together means doing lots of manual, slow verification, which costs employers a lot of money and creates extra work for educational institutions. This scattered system really hurts independent learners who gain skills from non-traditional places because they don't have one single, easy-to-check record of their learning journey (Kortemeyer, 2022).

This disconnect comes with a big price tag. Delays in checking qualifications can actually cause job candidates to lose out on offers. Plus, the work universities have to do to verify transcripts adds up to millions of dollars every year. And because there isn't a way to carry your learning record with you, if a learning platform shuts down or you somehow lose access to your account, all that history of what you've learned can just disappear.

The Provenance Gap in AI-Mediated Learning

The quick spread of AI tools that can generate content has led to a situation where it's hard to know for sure how much a student used AI. When students hand in their work, it's becoming more and more difficult to figure out the level of AI involvement (Shalwa, 2025). Tools designed to catch plagiarism are constantly trying to keep up with AI's ability to create text, but this often results in false alarms or missing the more advanced mix of human and AI writing (Goodier, 2025). This lack of clarity makes it harder to value independent work, because it's tough for people in charge to tell the difference between a student using AI as a helpful learning tool and a student using AI to just hand in work that isn't their own (Mikros, 2025).

Since there isn't a standard way for students to say they used AI and for that to be checked, schools are resorting to strict, watchful methods of supervision that don't respect student privacy and limit their independence (Heinrich, 2025). These kinds of "lockdown browsers" and systems that monitor webcams create a sense of being against each other between students and teachers, which undermines the trust that's so important for good teaching to happen.

Portability Barriers and Data Lock-in

Even when digital credentials are available, they frequently come with the drawback of being tied to specific providers. This means that proprietary badge systems might not work seamlessly with employer HR software or university records offices (1EdTech, 2020). The idea behind a "Learning Wallet" is to address this issue, but its widespread use is hampered by the absence of a common trust framework. This framework would ensure that a wallet from one service is recognized and trusted by a verifier using a different system (Leu & Lee, 2025). Additionally, the detailed data required to demonstrate skills like specific achievements on a grading rubric or a portfolio of projects is often lost when a rich learning experience is simply converted into a basic PDF transcript.

CONCEPTUAL FRAMEWORK

To address these challenges, this report proposes a four-layer conceptual model adapted from the Trust Over IP (ToIP) stack. This model decouples technical trust (cryptography and connectivity) from human trust (governance and business rules), providing a scalable architecture for verifiable education (Trust Over IP Foundation, 2020).

Layer 1: The Trust Anchor (Public Utilities)

Think of the Identity Layer, also known as the Trust Anchor, as the bedrock of the whole system. Its job is to provide the fundamental, unchanging public tools needed to establish digital identities and check cryptographic proofs. This layer is built using technologies like Distributed Ledgers (including blockchains) and Decentralized File Systems (such as IPFS) (Mishra et al., 2025).

- Function: It stores things like Decentralized Identifiers (DIDs), public keys, the rules for credentials, and lists that show when credentials are no longer valid.
- Design Principle: Crucially, no Personally Identifiable Information (PII) is kept here. Only anonymous identifiers and cryptographic hashes are permanently recorded on the network. This approach helps ensure compliance with regulations like GDPR and respects the right for data to be forgotten (Godyn et al., 2022).
- Components: It can use public blockchains (like Ethereum or Polygon) to reach a global audience, or it might use permissioned chains controlled by groups (like EBSI or Hyperledger Indy) for specific, regulated environments, such as educational systems (Mishra et al., 2025).

Layer 2: Secure Communication (Wallet-to-Wallet)

The second layer in the stack is the Trust Layer, and its job is to make secure, direct connections between different parties possible. Think of it as the crucial 'narrow waist' of the whole system, much like how TCP/IP functions as the fundamental backbone of networking (Trust Over IP Foundation, 2020).

- Function: This layer makes it easy for different components to share information securely. Specifically, it facilitates communication between learner digital wallets, institutional systems, and AI tutors.
- Protocols: It uses a protocol called DIDComm (DID Communication). This protocol creates a secure channel that's encrypted, verifies who is on each end (authentication), and importantly, it works regardless of the underlying method used to send the data (it's 'transport-agnostic') (Trust Over IP Foundation, 2020).
- Role: Essentially, this layer guarantees that when an AI agent, like a tutor, sends something like a learning resource to a student's wallet, the connection is safe and both sides have confirmed their identities using their unique digital IDs (DIDs) (Chew, 2025).

Layer 3: Data Exchange (Credentials and Provenance)

The third layer is the Data Layer. Its job is to establish the standard formats and protocols for the data that's being shared.

- Function: This layer sets the standard structure for Verifiable Credentials (VCs) and Content Provenance manifests, which are part of the C2PA standard.
- Standards: It applies the W3C Verifiable Credentials Data Model v2.0 specifically for claims about competencies (W3C, n.d.), and the C2PA specifications for claims related to an artifact's history (C2PA, n.d.).
- Innovation:This framework does something unique by placing C2PA manifests either inside a VC or having the VC reference them. This creates what's called a composite credential, which essentially carries both the claim about a skill (or competency) and the actual evidence of the work (or artifact history) together.

Layer 4: Application Ecosystems (Governance)

The very top layer is the Application Layer. This is where the rules and systems we use to manage things (like how businesses operate or how people interact) are found.

- Function: This layer defines the specific guidelines for how different educational communities work together, who to trust, and the legal rules that apply. Think of examples like a group of universities collaborating or a national system for tracking skills.
- Governance: These 'Governance Frameworks' (often shortened to GFs) spell out who is allowed to give out certificates or qualifications, what standards must be met to ensure they're valid, and who is responsible if something goes wrong(Trust Over IP Foundation, 2020).
- Trust Registries: These are lists that keep track of trusted organizations that can issue credentials (like accredited universities or officially recognized training programs). Verifiers use these lists to check if a credential comes from a reliable source (Trust Over IP, 2025).

Table 1. The four-layer trust architecture for verifiable education

Layer	Name	Function	Key Standards	Educational Example
Layer 4	Application	Governance & Business Logic	Trust Registries, GFs	University accreditation rules, Employer hiring portals.
Layer 3	Data Exchange	Standardized Data Formats	W3C VC, C2PA, JSON-LD	The digital diploma file, the provenance manifest of an essay.
Layer 2	Secure Comm.	Peer-to-Peer Connection	DIDComm, TLS	The encrypted channel between a Student Wallet and an AI Tutor.
Layer 1	Trust Anchor	Root of Trust (Utilities)	DIDs, Blockchains (DLT)	The public ledger (EBSI/Ethereum) storing issuer public keys.

Table 1 describes a 4-layer architecture for a decentralized digital credential and identity ecosystem, showing how trust, communication, and applications are built from the ground up.

- Layer 1 (Trust Anchor) provides the foundational trust infrastructure
- Layer 2 (Secure Communication) enables safe peer-to-peer interactions
- Layer 3 (Data Exchange) standardizes how credentials and content are formatted
- Layer 4 (Application) defines real-world usage, rules, and governance

Together, these layers create a secure, interoperable, and scalable ecosystem for education and beyond.

The conceptual framework provides a high-level abstraction of system components and their interactions, focusing on design principles and trust relationships. In contrast, the reference architecture translates this abstraction into a deployable structure, detailing implementation layers, protocols, and system workflows. Together, they provide both theoretical and practical perspectives.

Framework → Architecture

Building on the conceptual model, the following architecture provides an implementation-oriented perspective.

Architecture → Workflow

The architecture enables the following operational workflow for AI-mediated learning.

Workflow → Governance

To ensure fairness and accountability, governance mechanisms are required.

REFERENCE ARCHITECTURE

The reference architecture translates the conceptual framework into a deployable system design. It prioritizes a "privacy-by-design" approach, utilizing an on-chain/off-chain split to balance verifiability with data protection.

Architectural Components

1. Learner Wallet: A mobile-first application acting as the User Agent. It stores the learner's private keys, VCs, and links to off-chain data. It supports selective disclosure, allowing the learner to present specific claims without revealing their entire history (Sorensen, 2025).
2. AI Agent (Tutor/Assessor): An autonomous software entity with its own DID (did:key or did:web). The agent is programmed to issue "micro-attestations" or provenance assertions as it interacts with the learner (DoraHacks, 2019).
3. Institutional Issuer: The university or platform that issues high-level credentials (degrees, certificates). It operates an "Issuer Agent" that signs VCs (Truvera, 2026).
4. Verifier: The employer or institution checking the credential. It uses a "Verifier Agent" to authenticate proofs against the ledger (Truvera, 2026).
5. Verifiable Data Registry (VDR): The blockchain network (e.g., EBSI, generic EVM chain) storing DID documents and revocation lists (W3C, n.d.).
6. Off-Chain Storage: Secure, decentralized storage (e.g., IPFS, encrypted cloud buckets) for heavy artifacts (videos, portfolios) and detailed metadata that should not be on the ledger (Mazzocca et al., 2025).

Data Flow and Protocols

The architecture utilizes a specific flow for Issuance and Verification:

Issuance Flow

1. Interaction: The learner interacts with the AI Agent to complete a module.
2. Provenance Generation: The AI Agent generates a C2PA manifest listing the prompts used, the model version, and the learner's inputs. This manifest is hashed (C2PA, 2024).
3. Attestation: The AI Agent signs a VC containing the module completion claim and the hash of the C2PA manifest. The agent uses its did:key for signing, ensuring the signature is verifiable but ephemeral if necessary (Perin, 2025).
4. Storage: The VC is transmitted to the Learner Wallet via DIDComm. The detailed C2PA manifest and artifact are stored in Off-Chain Storage, with the URI and hash embedded in the VC (Mazzocca et al., 2025).

Verification Flow

1. Presentation: The learner constructs a Verifiable Presentation (VP) from their wallet, selecting specific VCs to share with an employer (W3C, n.d.).
2. Verification: The employer's system receives the VP. It resolves the Issuer's DID from the ledger to fetch the public key and verifies the signature (Truvera, 2026).
3. Provenance Check: If the employer wants to audit the work, they use the URI in the VC to fetch the C2PA manifest. The system recalculates the hash of the retrieved content to ensure it matches the hash in the VC (integrity check) (Adobe, 2026).
4. Status Check: The system queries the revocation registry on the ledger to ensure the credential hasn't been revoked (Truvera, 2026).

On-Chain vs. Off-Chain Design Rules

To strictly adhere to privacy regulations like GDPR, the architecture follows these design rules:

- On-Chain: DIDs, Public Keys, Accumulators (for revocation), Schema Definitions, and Trust Registry entries. *No PII.* (The Center for Global Enterprise, n.d.).
- Off-Chain: The Verifiable Credential itself (stored in the user's wallet), the C2PA Manifest (containing edit history), and the actual Learning Artifacts (essays, code).
- Linkage: The link is established via cryptographic hashes (Content Integrity) and URIs. This allows the user to delete the off-chain data (Right to be Forgotten), rendering the on-chain hash meaningless but preserving the ledger's immutability (Godyn et al., 2022).

Detailed C2PA Binding Mechanism

A critical technical detail is the binding between the VC and the C2PA manifest. The VC data model allows for an evidence property. In this architecture, the C2PA manifest is referenced here.

Code Snippet: VC Structure referencing C2PA

```
JSON
{
"@context": [
"https://www.w3.org/2018/credentials/v1",
"https://w3c-ccg.github.io/vc-ed-models/contexts/v05/context.json"
],
"type": ["VerifiableCredential", "VerifiableEducationCredential"],
"issuer": "did:web:ai-tutor.com",
"issuanceDate": "2025-06-15T10:00:00Z",
"credentialSubject": {
"id": "did:key:z6Mkr...",
"achievement": {
"name": "Python Data Analysis Module",
"description": "Completed independent study on Pandas library."
}
},
"evidence": [{
"type": ["C2PAManifestEvidence"],
"digestMultibase": "zQm...",
"uri": "https://storage.provider.com/manifests/uuid-1234"
}]
}
```

Note: The digestMultibase ensures that the referenced C2PA manifest has not been altered since the credential was issued..[60]

Integrating C2PA for Text and PDF

The C2PA specification provides specific guidance for embedding provenance data into common educational formats like PDF. The C2PA Manifest Store is integrated into PDF files using the embedded file specification (ISO 32000, 7.11.3). The file specification dictionary for the manifest must include an AFRelationship key with the value C2PA_Manifest. This ensures that the provenance data travels with the document, even if it is downloaded from the learning platform and emailed to an employer (C2PA, 2024). For text-based formats (like Markdown or HTML), the C2PA manifest is often stored externally or embedded via Base64 encoding in metadata headers (C2PA, n.d.).

Each architectural component not only contributes to system functionality but also directly impacts learner experience, trust, and educational outcomes.

CORE USE CASES

The proposed architecture enables several transformative use cases that redefine independent learning.

Self-Sovereign Learning Identity

In this scenario, a lifelong learner accumulates credentials from diverse sources a university degree, a coding bootcamp certificate, and micro-credentials from an AI tutor. Using their DID-based wallet, the learner unifies these fragmented identities. They can present a composite "Learning Passport" to an employer that proves they have a specific skill set, backed by cryptographically verifiable sources (Kortemeyer, 2022). The use of did:web allows institutions to anchor their identity to their known web domain (e.g., did:web:university.edu), providing high assurance of issuer legitimacy.

Table 2. Comparison of DID methods for educational roles

Role	Recommended DID Method	Reasoning	Verification Characteristics
Institution (University)	did:web	Ties identity to the institution's existing, trusted DNS domain (e.g., university.edu).	High trust, low decentralization (dependent on DNS/Web server).
AI Agent (Tutor)	did:key	Ephemeral, self-certifying, generated on-the-fly. Perfect for scalable, automated signing.	Low operational cost, high cryptographic assurance, no ledger write needed.
Learner (Student)	did:ion or did:cheqd	Persistent, censorship-resistant, rooted in a public ledger. Portable across life.	High decentralization, independent of any single institution.

Data synthesized from (Perin, 2025).

Table 2 outlines how different roles in a digital identity ecosystem should use specific Decentralized Identifier (DID) methods, along with the reasoning and verification strengths of each.

Each participant institution, AI agent, and learner uses a DID method suited to their needs for trust, scalability, and independence. The choices balance centralization vs decentralization, cost, and verification reliability.

Description

Institution (University) → did:web

Universities use did:web because it connects their identity to an already trusted domain (like a university website). This makes verification straightforward and highly trusted, but it relies on centralized infrastructure (DNS and web servers).

AI Agent (Tutor) → did:key

AI tutors use did:key, which is lightweight and generated instantly without needing a blockchain. It's ideal for automated systems because it's cheap, fast, and cryptographically secure, though not persistent.

Learner (Student) → did:ion or did:cheqd

Students use decentralized, ledger-based DIDs like did:ion or did:cheqd. These provide long-term, portable identities that aren't controlled by any single organization, offering high independence and censorship resistance.

AI Transparency and Provenance

As students use AI agents for assistance, the system ensures transparency. An AI writing tutor, acting as an agent, signs the C2PA manifest of a student's essay. The manifest explicitly details: "Idea generation by Human; Outline by AI Model X; Drafting by Human; Grammar check by AI Model Y" (C2PA, 2024). This "nutrition label" for the content allows educators to assess the *process* rather than just the final output. It shifts the paradigm from "detecting cheating" to "verifying collaboration," acknowledging that AI literacy involves effective co-creation.[2]

Table 3. C2PA assertion strategy for AI-mediated learning

Assertion Type	Purpose in Learning Context	Example Data
c2pa.actions	Records the history of edits and transformations.	"Edited by User," "AI-Generated suggestion applied."
c2pa.training-mining	Declares if the student's work can be used to train future AI models (Privacy/IP).	"Data Mining: Not Allowed"
stds.schema-org.CreativeWork	Links the artifact to the Learner's Identity (DID).	Author: did:ion:123... (The Student)
c2pa.soft-binding	Ensures the manifest can be linked even if metadata is stripped (e.g., in a PDF).	Visual fingerprint / Watermark of the essay document.

Based on C2PA Specifications (C2PA, 2024).

Table 3 explains different assertion types used in content provenance (C2PA) within a learning environment, showing how student work can be tracked, protected, and linked to identity.

The table highlights how digital learning artifacts (like essays or assignments) can carry embedded, verifiable metadata that:

- Tracks who created and edited the work
- Defines permissions for AI training and data use
- Links the work to a student's decentralized identity
- Maintains traceability even if metadata is removed

These assertions create a system of trust, authorship, and integrity for academic content.

Assessment Integrity: Challenge-Response

To counter the threat of students outsourcing entire assessments to AI, the architecture supports "Challenge-Response" integrity checks. During an assessment, the AI proctor (an agent) issues a random, time-bound challenge encrypted to the learner's DID. The learner must respond using their private key and perform a specific action (e.g., answer a question orally) within a verifiable timeframe.This interaction is logged and signed. The resulting VC includes the proof of this challenge-response, assuring the verifier that the assessment was performed by the specific DID subject in real-time, drastically raising the cost of impersonation.[76]

Employer Verification and Skill-Based Hiring

For employers, the system eliminates the need for background check services that take weeks. An employer's HR system can instantly verify a job applicant's claimed degree and recent AI-verified project work. By utilizing the machine-readable nature of VCs (JSON-LD), the hiring system can automatically parse the skills taxonomy (e.g., extracting "Python" and "Data Analysis" from the credential metadata) and match them against job requirements (Bouchrika, 2026). This facilitates true skills-based hiring, moving beyond the rough proxy of university brand names (1EdTech, 2020).

Human Factors in AI-Agent Learning

- Beyond technical infrastructure, the success of AI-agent learning systems depends on human-centered outcomes.
- Motivation: Adaptive AI agents can personalize goals and feedback, enhancing intrinsic motivation. However, excessive automation may reduce learner initiative.
- Engagement: Continuous interaction with AI agents supports active learning, but requires careful balance to avoid dependency.
- Equity: Unequal access to digital infrastructure may create disparities; inclusive and low-resource designs are essential.

Practical Scenario (Classroom Use Case)

Consider a university-level course where students use AI agents for independent study:

- The learner defines goals (e.g., mastering a topic).
- The AI agent decomposes tasks and provides adaptive resources.
- Learning outputs are verified using verifiable credentials (VCs).
- Content authenticity is ensured via C2PA provenance tracking.
- The instructor reviews AI-supported outputs and provides feedback.
- This scenario demonstrates how the proposed framework operates in a real educational setting.

Pilot Implementation Workflow

A minimal deployment of the proposed system includes:

1. AI Agent Layer: Task planning and adaptive feedback
2. Identity Layer: Learner authentication via decentralized identifiers
3. Trust Layer: Credential issuance and verification on blockchain
4. Application Layer: User dashboards for learners and instructors

This pilot setup can be deployed within existing LMS environments using API-based integration.

Simulated Learning Path

A typical AI-driven learning cycle: Learner submits an intent (e.g., "learn data analytics"). AI agent generates a structured learning path. Tasks are completed with AI assistance. Outputs are validated and cryptographically signed. Credentials are issued and stored for verification. This simulation illustrates the end-to-end workflow of AI-supported, verifiable learning.

IMPLEMENTATION ROADMAP

Implementing this trust layer requires a phased approach, managing both technical complexity and organizational change.

Phase 1: Pilot and Foundations (Months 1-12)

- Goal: Establish the technical sandbox and run controlled pilots.
- Activities:
  - Deploy a testnet VDR (e.g., utilizing EBSI or a test consortium chain) (Mishra et al., 2025).
  - Develop "minimum viable wallets" for students based on open standards (W3C, 2021).
  - Select two distinct programs (e.g., Computer Science and Creative Writing) for pilot testing.
  - Implement basic C2PA generation tools for student submissions.
- KPIs: Successful issuance and verification of 500 credentials; 90% user satisfaction with wallet UX.

Phase 2: Ecosystem Expansion (Months 13-24)

- Goal: Interoperability and governance formalization.
- Activities:
  - Establish a Governance Framework (GF) defining the "Trust Registry" of authorized issuers (Trust Over IP Foundation, 2021).
  - Integrate with existing Learning Management Systems (LMS) like Canvas or Moodle via LTI standards.
  - Introduce "multi-signature" schemas where a human instructor and an AI agent both sign a credential to validate mixed assessments.
- KPIs: 5,000 active wallets; integration with 3 external employer partners for verification.

Phase 3: Scale and Autonomy (Months 25-36)

- Goal: Full decentralized autonomy and advanced privacy.
- Activities:
  - Transition to mainnet anchoring for high-value credentials.

    - Implement Zero-Knowledge Proofs (ZKPs) for selective disclosure of sensitive data (e.g., GPA ranges) (Alamrio et al., 2025).
    - Enable cross-border verification with international partners (e.g., aligning with EU Digital Identity Wallet) (Owens & Wu, 2025).
- KPIs: verification latency under 2 seconds; <1% fraud rate; recognition by national qualification bodies.

A phased implementation approach is recommended:

1. Phase 1: Pilot deployment with limited users
2. Phase 2: Integration with LMS platforms
3. Phase 3: Scaling with decentralized identity and blockchain layers
4. Phase 4: Full ecosystem adoption with governance mechanisms

The deployment of AI-agent and blockchain-based systems introduces challenges related to algorithmic bias, data governance, scalability, and institutional adoption. Addressing these issues requires transparent AI models, standardized governance frameworks, and scalable infrastructure solutions.

Example Scenario:

A learner uses an AI agent to complete a course module. The agent personalizes tasks, verifies outputs, and issues a verifiable credential (VC) upon completion. The instructor reviews the outcome, ensuring alignment with course objectives and maintaining academic integrity.
Each architectural component not only contributes to system functionality but also directly impacts learner experience, trust, and educational outcomes.

Change Management

The roadmap emphasizes "Change Management" as a critical success factor. This involves training faculty on the difference between AI-plagiarism and AI-provenance, and educating employers on how to interpret "verified skill" credentials versus traditional transcripts. The "ADKAR" model (Awareness, Desire, Knowledge, Ability, Reinforcement) is recommended to guide this cultural shift.

ETHICAL, LEGAL, AND SOCIETAL CONSIDERATIONS

The deployment of blockchain and AI in education necessitates a rigorous ethical framework to prevent exacerbating existing inequities or privacy violations.

Privacy and Data Minimization

The architecture strictly adheres to Data Minimization principles. By using selective disclosure and ZKPs, learners can prove they hold a valid credential without sharing the entirety of their data. (W3C, n.d.). For instance, a student can prove they are "a registered student" to get a software discount without revealing their name or ID number. Compliance with GDPR is managed by ensuring that no personal data is written to the immutable ledger. If a student invokes their "right to be forgotten," the off-chain data is deleted. The on-chain hash remains but becomes mathematically orphaned and meaningless, effectively "erasing" the record from a functional perspective (Godyn et al., 2022). FERPA compliance is maintained by ensuring that the institution (the issuer) never shares data directly with verifiers; instead, the data is given to the student (holder), who consents to share it, modeling the "student-as-courier" exception in FERPA regulations.

Fairness and Algorithmic Bias

AI agents used for assessment must be audited for Algorithmic Bias. If an agent systematically down-grades essays written in non-native English varieties, it perpetuates discrimination.[85](Boateng & Boateng, 2025). The governance framework requires "Model Cards" for all AI agents, documenting their training data, intended use, and known limitations. Furthermore, the system mandates "human-in-the-loop" protocols for high-stakes credentials, ensuring that an AI's judgment is always reviewable and appealable by a human instructor (Topali et al., 2025).

Equity and Accessibility

To prevent a "digital divide," the wallet infrastructure must be mobile-first and capable of offline functionality, ensuring access for learners with intermittent internet connectivity. Fee subsidies must be built into the governance model to cover "gas fees" or transaction costs associated with blockchain interactions, ensuring that verification is free for the learner. The use of open standards (W3C, OpenID) prevents vendor lock-in, ensuring that a learner's credentials remain accessible even if the issuing platform goes out of business (Trust Over IP Foundation, 2022).

CASE ILLUSTRATION: THE LEARNER JOURNEY

Consider "Elena," an independent learner upskilling in Data Science.

1. Setup: Elena downloads a generic "Learning Wallet" app on her phone. She generates a DID, which is anchored on the ledger.
2. Learning: She engages with an AI Tutor agent (did:web:ai-tutor.com) to learn Python. The agent guides her through exercises.
3. Provenance: For her capstone project, she writes code with AI assistance. The IDE plugin records the session, generating a C2PA manifest that tags code blocks: "Function A: AI-generated," "Logic B: Human-written."
4. Issuance: Upon passing the automated tests, the AI Tutor issues a Verifiable Credential for "Python Basics." The VC contains a hash of the C2PA manifest. The VC is sent to Elena's wallet.
5. Assessment: She takes a final exam proctored by the university's "Assessment Agent." The agent uses a challenge-response protocol to verify her presence. A "Exam Passed" VC is issued.
6. Verification: Elena applies for a job. The employer requests proof of Python skills. Elena selects the "Python Basics" and "Exam Passed" VCs in her wallet and generates a Verifiable Presentation.

7. Hiring: The employer's system instantly verifies the cryptographic signatures of the AI Tutor and University. It parses the C2PA data to confirm Elena wrote the core logic of her portfolio project. Elena is hired.

This journey demonstrates a seamless, secure, and transparent flow of trust that is currently impossible with PDF transcripts and manual reference checks.

DISCUSSION

The proposed framework offers a potent solution to the crisis of trust in AI education but is not without trade-offs.

Public vs. Permissioned Anchoring:

A key debate is the choice of ledger. Public blockchains (e.g., Ethereum) offer maximum censorship resistance and longevity but suffer from variable transaction costs and privacy concerns regarding metadata analysis (Tripathi, 2024). Consortium blockchains (like EBSI) offer regulatory compliance, stable costs, and governance alignment with educational values, but may be perceived as "centralized" by purists (Mishra et al., 2025). The "Trust Over IP" model suggests a hybrid approach: using public utilities for the root of trust (Layer 1) while managing sensitive governance in higher layers (Layer 4) (Trust Over IP Foundation, 2020).

Scalability and Performance:

Validating C2PA manifests and VCs involves cryptographic operations that are computationally light, but the storage of provenance data (manifests) can be heavy. The architecture's reliance on off-chain storage (Layer 2/3) is crucial here. Attempting to store provenance data directly on-chain would be cost-prohibitive and unscalable (C2PA, 2024).

The Human Factor:

Technology is the easy part; governance is hard (Goger, 2025). Success depends on the willingness of institutions to recognize "AI Agents" as valid issuers of micro-credentials. This requires a shift in accreditation standards to accept "machine-verified" competencies, a process that will likely take years of policy advocacy (International Education Accreditation Council, 2025).

Student Autonomy, Accessibility, and Equity

The proposed framework enhances student autonomy through personalized learning paths while maintaining transparency via verifiable credentials. However, ensuring accessibility and equity requires inclusive design, low-resource compatibility, and support for diverse learner needs to prevent digital exclusion.

Consider a learner completing an AI-assisted certification course. The AI agent personalizes tasks and evaluates progress. Upon completion, achievements are issued as verifiable credentials, anchored on blockchain. Employers can independently verify these credentials, ensuring authenticity and trust.

CHALLENGES AND RISKS IN AI-AGENT MEDIATED LEARNING

While the proposed framework introduces significant advancements in trust, automation, and personalization, it is equally important to critically examine the associated risks and limitations.

1. Over-Reliance on Autonomous AI Agents

The increasing dependence on AI agents for learning guidance, assessment, and decision-making may reduce learner autonomy and critical thinking skills. Fully automated systems risk creating passive learners who rely excessively on algorithmic recommendations.

Mitigation:

Incorporating human-in-the-loop mechanisms and promoting hybrid learning models can preserve learner agency while leveraging AI support.

2. Digital Divide and Accessibility Constraints

The effectiveness of AI-driven and blockchain-enabled systems depends heavily on access to reliable internet, computational resources, and digital literacy. This may widen the gap between technologically advanced regions and underserved communities.

Mitigation:

Designing lightweight, edge-compatible architectures and supporting offline-first learning models can improve accessibility.

3. Opaque Decision-Making and Lack of Explainability

AI agents, particularly those based on deep learning, often operate as "black boxes," making it difficult to interpret how decisions (e.g., recommendations, evaluations) are made. This lack of transparency can undermine trust.

Mitigation:

Adopting Explainable AI (XAI) techniques and integrating C2PA-based provenance tracking can improve transparency and accountability.

4. Misalignment with Curriculum and Accreditation Standards

AI-driven learning paths may prioritize personalized optimization over standardized curricula, potentially causing misalignment with institutional requirements, accreditation frameworks, and learning outcomes.

Mitigation:

Incorporating policy-aware AI agents and aligning learning workflows with curriculum ontologies and accreditation standards ensures compliance and relevance.

5. Ethical and Governance Risks

Autonomous systems may inadvertently reinforce biases or make decisions that conflict with ethical norms. Additionally, decentralized systems complicate accountability and regulatory oversight.

Mitigation:

Establishing governance frameworks, periodic audits, and ethical compliance mechanisms is essential.

6. Security and Trust Vulnerabilities

Although blockchain enhances integrity, vulnerabilities may arise from:

- Smart contract bugs
- Key management failures
- Off-chain storage risks

Mitigation:

Secure coding practices, formal verification, and robust key management systems are required.

HUMAN-CENTERED LEARNING OUTCOMES

While the proposed architecture emphasizes trust and automation, its effectiveness ultimately depends on its impact on learners and educators.

1. Student Experience and Engagement

AI agents enable personalized, adaptive learning paths, real-time feedback, and continuous support. This enhances learner engagement but requires careful design to avoid cognitive overload and over-automation.

2. Evolving Role of Teachers

In AI-mediated environments, teachers transition from content deliverers to:

- Facilitators of learning
- Supervisors of AI-generated outputs
- Ethical and pedagogical guides

Human oversight remains essential to validate AI recommendations and ensure meaningful learning.

3. Accessibility and Inclusion

AI-agent systems must be designed to support:

- Diverse learning abilities
- Low-resource environments
- Multilingual and inclusive interfaces

Failure to address accessibility may reinforce existing educational inequalities.

4. Assessment Reliability and Validity

AI-supported assessments raise concerns regarding:

- Authenticity of student work
- Distinction between human and AI contributions
- Fair evaluation standards

The integration of verifiable credentials (VCs) and content provenance (C2PA) improves assessment transparency and trustworthiness.

EMPIRICAL GROUNDING / VALIDATION

While the proposed framework is conceptual, its design is informed by existing implementations of AI-assisted learning and blockchain-based credentialing. A pilot deployment model is outlined to demonstrate feasibility in real-world educational settings. Simulated workflows indicate that integrating AI agents with verifiable credentials can support traceable, transparent, and adaptive learning processes, providing a foundation for future empirical validation.

Strengthen Pedagogical Link (Add Short Paragraph)

This framework is grounded in established learning theories such as Self-Regulated Learning (SRL) and Constructivism, where learners actively control their progress and construct knowledge through interaction. The AI agent acts as a facilitator, aligning technological capabilities with instructional design principles.

Standards Alignment (W3C VC Emphasis)

The proposed system aligns with W3C Verifiable Credentials (VCs) and Decentralized Identifiers (DIDs), ensuring interoperability, portability, and standardized credential verification across platforms. This standards-based approach enhances trust and adoption in educational ecosystems.

Improve Flow with Bridging Sentences

Between AI Agents → Blockchain Section

While AI agents enable adaptive learning and task automation, ensuring trust and verifiability of their outputs requires a complementary decentralized infrastructure.

Between Blockchain → Workflow Section

Building on the trust layer enabled by blockchain, the following workflow illustrates how learning activities are executed, validated, and credentialed.

Between Workflow → Governance Section

Beyond operational workflows, governance mechanisms are essential to regulate participation, ensure fairness, and maintain system integrity.

Instructional Design Perspective

The integration of AI agents requires rethinking instructional design to support:

- Adaptive learning pathways
- Continuous formative assessment
- Learner autonomy and reflection

Educators must design experiences where AI augments, rather than replaces, pedagogical intent.

Ethical, Legal, and Societal Considerations

The framework raises important concerns related to:

- Privacy and data ownership in decentralized systems
- Algorithmic bias in AI decision-making
- Regulatory compliance across jurisdictions

Addressing these requires transparent governance models and adherence to global standards.

FUTURE RESEARCH

The path forward involves deepening the technical and pedagogical capabilities of this trust layer.

- Zero-Knowledge Evidence: Research should focus on implementing ZK-SNARKs to allow learners to prove "I completed the course" without revealing *which* course or *when*, or to prove "my score was >80%" without revealing the exact score (Alamrio et al., 2025).
- Cost Models: Detailed economic modeling is needed to determine who pays for the infrastructure issuers, verifiers, or government subsidies?.
- Usability Studies: Research is needed to design wallet interfaces that make key management and selective disclosure intuitive for non-technical users (VerifyEd, 2025).
- Longitudinal Impact: Studies should track the career trajectories of learners with verifiable portfolios versus traditional degrees to quantify the "trust premium" of the new system.

CONCLUSION

The convergence of AI agents and blockchain technology offers a historic opportunity to redefine independent learning. By moving from a model of "institutional reliance" to "verifiable self-sovereignty," we can empower learners to own their achievements and navigate the AI age with credibility. The proposed four-layer trust architecture provides the necessary scaffold: DIDs for identity, VCs for transportable skills, and C2PA for honest provenance. While challenges in governance and adoption remain, the technical foundation is robust. This framework does not merely digitize the diploma; it creates a new "trust layer" for the internet, ensuring that as education becomes more automated, it remains deeply human, transparent, and trusted.

REFERENCES

Adobe. (2025). Content Credentials overview. In *Adobe.com*. https://helpx.adobe.com/creative-cloud/apps/adobe-content-authenticity/content-credentials/overview.html

Adobe. (2026). *Content Credentials integration | Adobe Experience Manager.* In *Adobe.com*. https://experienceleague.adobe.com/en/docs/experience-manager-cloud-service/content/assets/assets-view/content-credentials

Alamrio, J., Ayoade, J., & Uddin, M. A. (2025). A Zero-Knowledge Proof-Enabled Blockchain-Based Academic Record Verification System. *Sensors (Basel), 25*(11), 3450–3450. DOI: 10.3390/s25113450 PMID: 40968974

Anglen, J. (2024). AI Agents for Learning Ecosystem: Benefits, Challenges, Use cases & Future. In *Rapidinnovation.io*. Rapid Innovation. https://www.rapidinnovation.io/post/ai-agents-for-learning-ecosystem-benefits-challenges-use-cases-future

Boateng, O., & Boateng, B. (2025). Algorithmic bias in educational systems: Examining the impact of AI-driven decision making in modern education. *World Journal of Advanced Research and Reviews, 25*(1), 2012–2017. DOI: 10.30574/wjarr.2025.25.1.0253

Bouchrika, I. (2026). 2026 Are Online Education Degrees Respected by Employers? In *Research.com*. https://research.com/advice/are-online-education-degrees-respected-by-employers

C2PA. (2018). C2PA Technical Specification: C2PA Specifications. In *C2pa.org*. https://spec.c2pa.org/specifications/specifications/1.0/specs/C2PA_Specification.html

C2PA. (2019). *C2PA Implementation Guidance: C2PA Specifications.* In *C2pa.org*. https://spec.c2pa.org/specifications/specifications/1.0/guidance/Guidance.html

C2PA. (2024). *Content Credentials C2PA Technical Specification.* https://spec.c2pa.org/specifications/specifications/2.1/specs/_attachments/C2PA_Specification.pdf

C2PA. (2024). Content Credentials: C2PA Technical Specification: C2PA Specifications. In *C2pa.org*. https://spec.c2pa.org/specifications/specifications/2.2/specs/C2PA_Specification.html

C2PA. (2025). C2PA and Content Credentials Explainer: C2PA Specifications. In *C2pa.org*. https://spec.c2pa.org/specifications/specifications/2.2/explainer/Explainer.html

C2PA. (n.d.). *C2PA Technical Specification.* Retrieved July 23, 2026, from https://spec.c2pa.org/specifications/specifications/1.3/specs/_attachments/C2PA_Specification.pdf

C2PA. (n.d.). Overview. In *c2pa.org*. Retrieved July 23, 2026, from https://c2pa.org/

Chew, N. (2025, September 25). *Digital Identity in an AI-Agent Economy: Rethinking Authentication.* Medium; MITB For All. https://medium.com/mitb-for-all/digital-identity-in-an-ai-agent-economy-rethinking-authentication-13da94cce035

Cloud Security Alliance. (2024). *Leveraging Zero-Knowledge Proofs in Machine Learning and LLMs: Enhancing Privacy and Security*. Cloudsa. https://cloudsecurityalliance.org/blog/2024/09/20/leveraging-zero-knowledge-proofs-in-machine-learning-and-llms-enhancing-privacy-and-security

Content Authenticity Imitative. (2021). Getting started with Content Credentials | Open-source tools for content authenticity and provenance. In *Contentauthenticity.org*. https://opensource.contentauthenticity.org/docs/getting-started/

contentauth. (2023). *c2pa-cpp/examples/training.cpp at main · contentauth/c2pa-cpp*. GitHub. https://github.com/contentauth/c2pa-cpp/blob/main/examples/training.cpp

Credential Engine. (2025, June 29). *Powering Skills-Based Hiring Through Better Data | Credential Engine*. Credential Engine. https://credentialengine.org/resources/powering-skills-based-hiring-through-better-data/

Delgado-von-Eitzen, C., Anido-Rifón, L., Fernández-Iglesias, M. J., & Ruiz-Molina, M. (2025). Qualitative Analysis of a Blockchain-Based System Adoption for Academic Credentials Verification That Complies with the GDPR: GAVIN Project. *Applied Sciences (Basel, Switzerland)*, *15*(22), 11958. DOI: 10.3390/app152211958

DIF. (n.d.). *DIF FAQ*. In *identity.foundation*. Retrieved July 23, 2026, from https://identity.foundation/faq

DoraHacks. (2019). *KYA-Passport - Know Your Agent Passport | Buidls | DoraHacks*. DoraHacks. https://dorahacks.io/buidl/26333

1EdTech. (2020). The Impact of Digital Credentials on the Future of Work | 1EdTech. In *1edtech.org*. https://www.1edtech.org/article/edtech-leaders/futureofwork

Elnaffar, S., Rashidi, F., & Abualkishik, A. Z. (2025). Teaching with AI: a systematic review of chatbots, generative tools, and tutoring systems in programming education. *arXiv preprint arXiv:2510.03884*.

Entrust Cybersecurity Insitute. (n.d.). *2025 Identity Fraud Report ENTRUST CYBERSECURITY INSTITUTE PRESENTS*. Retrieved July 23, 2026, from https://www.entrust.com/sites/default/files/documentation/reports/2025-identity-fraud-report.pdf

Garzón, J., Patiño, E., & Marulanda, C. (2025). Systematic review of artificial intelligence in education: Trends, benefits, and challenges. *Multimodal Technologies and Interaction*, *9*(8), 84. DOI: 10.3390/mti9080084

Godyn, M., Kedziora, M., Ren, Y., Liu, Y., & Song, H. H. (2022). Analysis of solutions for a blockchain compliance with GDPR. *Scientific Reports*, *12*(1), 15021. DOI: 10.1038/s41598-022-19341-y PMID: 36056166

Goger, A. (2025). There's more to skills-based hiring than just removing degree requirements. In *Brookings*. https://www.brookings.edu/articles/theres-more-to-skills-based-hiring-than-just-removing-degree-requirements/

Goodier, M. (2025). Revealed: Thousands of UK university students caught cheating using AI. In *the Guardian*. The Guardian. https://www.theguardian.com/education/2025/jun/15/thousands-of-uk-university-students-caught-cheating-using-ai-artificial-intelligence-survey

Heinrich, E. (2025). A Systematic-Narrative Review of Online Proctoring Systems and a Case for Open Standards. *Open Praxis*, *17*(3). Advance online publication. DOI: 10.55982/openpraxis.17.3.836

International Education Accreditation Council. (2025). Examining the Effect of Accreditation Challenges on Educational Quality and Global Recognition. In *Ieac.org.uk*. https://www.ieac.org.uk/53-Examining-the-Effect-of-Accreditation-Challenges-on-Educational-Quality-and-Global-Recognition-blog.php

Jiang, Y. H., Li, R., Zhou, Y., Qi, C., Hu, H., Wei, Y., . . . Wu, Y. (2024). Ai agent for education: von neumann multi-agent system framework. *arXiv preprint arXiv:2501.00083.*

Jin, W., Du, H., Zhao, B., Tian, X., Shi, B., & Yang, G. (2025). A comprehensive survey on multi-agent cooperative decision-making: Scenarios, approaches, challenges and perspectives. *arXiv preprint arXiv:2503.13415*. DOI: 10.2139/ssrn.5106265

Kahn, P., Carrigan, M., Smith, P., Murtagh, L., Liu, R., & Song, F. (2025). Teacher agency and generative artificial intelligence: Teaching in higher education as a responsive, cultural activity. *Learning, Media and Technology*, •••, 1–12. DOI: 10.1080/17439884.2025.2575993

Kortemeyer, G. (2022). Self-Sovereign Identity User Scenarios in the Educational Domain. In er.educause.edu. Retrieved July 23, 2026, from https://er.educause.edu/articles/2022/4/self-sovereign-identity-user-scenarios-in-the-educational-domain

Learn & Work Ecosystem Library. (2024). Fraudulent Credentials. In *Learn & Work Ecosystem Library*. https://learnworkecosystemlibrary.com/topics/fraudulent-credentials/

Leu, S., & Lee, J. (2025). *Verifiable Credentials Wallets in a Skills-First Talent Marketplace. Jobs for the Future*. JFF.

MATTR. (2026, May 15). *Decentralized Identifiers (DIDs)*. MATTR Learn; MATTR. https://learn.mattr.global/docs/concepts/dids

Mazzocca, C., Acar, A., Uluagac, S., Montanari, R., Bellavista, P., & Conti, M. (2025). A survey on decentralized identifiers and verifiable credentials. *IEEE Communications Surveys and Tutorials*, *27*(6), 3641–3671. DOI: 10.1109/COMST.2025.3543197

Mazzocca, C., Acar, A., Uluagac, S., Montanari, R., Bellavista, P., & Conti, M. (2025). A survey on decentralized identifiers and verifiable credentials. *IEEE Communications Surveys and Tutorials*, *27*(6), 3641–3671. DOI: 10.1109/COMST.2025.3543197

Mikros, G. (2025). Large Language Models and Forensic Linguistics: Navigating Opportunities and Threats in the Age of Generative AI. *arXiv preprint arXiv:2512.06922.*

Mishra, R. A., Bhaskar, P., & Khan, M. (2025). An integrated blockchain architecturefor sustainable higher education administration. *On the Horizon. The International Journal of Learning Futures*, *33*(4), 460–474.

National Cyber Security Centre. (2025). *Content Credentials: Strengthening Multimedia Integrity in the Generative AI Era* - DoD, accessed on December 22, 2025, https://media.defense.gov/2025/Jan/29/2003634788/-1/-1/0/CSI-CONTENT-CREDENTIALS.PDF

NIST. (n.d.). *NIST AI 100-4 Reducing Risks Posed by 5 Synthetic Content 6*. Retrieved July 23, 2026, from https://airc.nist.gov/docs/NIST.AI.100-4.SyntheticContent.ipd.pdf

NSCBlog. (2025). Addressing credential fraud in higher education. In *Clearinghouse Today Blog*. https://www.studentclearinghouse.org/nscblog/addressing-credential-fraud-in-higher-ed/

Owens, C., & Wu, T. (2025). Passkeys and Verifiable Digital Credentials: A Harmonized Path to Secure Digital Identity | FIDO Alliance. In *FIDO Alliance*. https://fidoalliance.org/passkeys-and-verifiable-digital-credentials-a-harmonized-path-to-secure-digital-identity/

Perin, A. J. (2025, July 29). *So...What are these Decentralized Identifiers?* DEV Community. https://dev.to/joojscript/sowhat-are-these-decentralized-identifiers-130l

Shalwa. (2025). AI Plagiarism Statistics 2025: Transforming Academic Integrity. In *Artsmart.ai*. https://artsmart.ai/blog/ai-plagiarism-statistics/

Sharif, H., Atif, A., & Nagra, A. A. (2025). Deepfake-Style AI Tutors in Higher Education: A Mixed-Methods Review and Governance Framework for Sustainable Digital Education. *Sustainability (Basel)*, *17*(21), 9793. DOI: 10.3390/su17219793

Sorensen, S. (2025). The Great Reimagining: A Bridge & Blueprint for Jobs, Flourishing, and a New Human Era in the Age of AI. In *ResearchGate*. Independently published.

The Center for Global Enterprise. (n.d.). *The Right to be Forgotten Meets the Immutable A Practical Guide to GDPR-Compliant Blockchain Solutions*. Retrieved July 23, 2026, from https://www.cravath.com/a/web/636/3898415_1.pdf

Thompson, S. J., & Dowd, C. (2023). *The evolution of compliance for state authorization of distance education*. State Authorization Network.

Topali, P., Haelermans, C., Molenaar, I., & Segers, E. (2025). Pedagogical considerations in the automation era: A systematic literature review of AIEd in K-12 authentic settings. *British Educational Research Journal*, *51*(6), 2777–2809. DOI: 10.1002/berj.4200

Tripathi, S. (2024). Exploring the Differences: Private Blockchain vs Public Blockchain. In *Spydra.app*. https://www.spydra.app/blog/exploring-the-differences-private-blockchain-vs-public-blockchain

Trust Over, I. P. Foundation. (2020). *Introducing the*. Retrieved July 23, 2026, from https://trustoverip.org/wp-content/uploads/2020/05/toip_introduction_050520.pdf

Trust Over, I. P. Foundation. (2021). *Introduction to Trust Over IP*. https://trustoverip.org/wp-content/uploads/Introduction-to-ToIP-V2.0-2021-11-17.pdf

Trust Over, I. P. Foundation. (2022, November 15). *Learn & Work Ecosystem Library*. Learn & Work Ecosystem Library. https://learnworkecosystemlibrary.com/organizations/trust-over-ip-toip/

Trust Over, I. P. (2025, September 24). *Working Groups*. Trust Over IP. https://trustoverip.org/get-involved/working-groups/

Trust Over, I. P. (n.d.). *Defining a complete architecture for Internet-scale digital trust*. In *Trust Over IP*. Retrieved July 23, 2026, from https://trustoverip.org/

Truvera. (2026). Verifiable Credentials: The Ultimate Guide 2023. In www.dock.io. Retrieved July 23, 2026, from https://www.dock.io/post/verifiable-credentials

Utrecht University. (2025, July 31). *High-risk AI*. Utrecht University. https://www.uu.nl/en/organisation/ai-policy/teachers/ai-compliance/high-risk-ai

VerifyEd. (2025). Examples of Digital Identities: 5 Essential Types for 2025. In *Verifyed.io*. https://www.verifyed.io/blog/digital-identity-examples

VerifyEd. (2025). *Badge and Wallet Solutions: 5 Essential Digital Credential Tools 2025*. Verifyed.Io. https://www.verifyed.io/blog/badge-wallet-solutions

Vorobyeva, K. I., Belous, S., Savchenko, N. V., Smirnova, L. M., Nikitina, S. A., & Zhdanov, S. P. (2025). Personalized Learning through AI: Pedagogical Approaches and Critical Insights. *Contemporary Educational Technology*, *17*(2), ep574. DOI: 10.30935/cedtech/16108

W3C. (2021). *Credentials Community Group*. Github.Io. https://w3c-ccg.github.io/meetings/2021-09-13-vc-education/

W3C. (2025). *Verifiable Credentials Overview*. In *W3.org*. https://www.w3.org/TR/vc-overview/

W3C. (n.d.). Verifiable Credentials Data Model v2.0. In www.w3.org. Retrieved July 23, 2026, from https://www.w3.org/TR/vc-data-model-2.0/

Walt.id. (2025). Verifiable Credentials: A Simple Guide to How They Work. In *Walt.id*. https://docs.walt.id/concepts/digital-credentials/verifiable-credentials-w3c

Wang, X., Wu, Y. C., Ji, X., & Fu, H. (2024). Algorithmic discrimination: Examining its types and regulatory measures with emphasis on US legal practices. *Frontiers in Artificial Intelligence*, *7*, 1320277. DOI: 10.3389/frai.2024.1320277 PMID: 38836021

Zuberi, A. (2025, December 15). *How Decentralized Identifiers (DIDs) Will Transform Online Identity*. Digitap. https://digitap.app/news/guide/how-decentralized-identifiers-dids-will-transform-online-identity

Compilation of References

Abbasi, B. N., Wu, Y., & Luo, Z. (2025). Exploring the impact of artificial intelligence on curriculum development in global higher education institutions. *Education and Information Technologies*, *30*(1), 547–581. DOI: 10.1007/s10639-024-13113-z

Abinaya, S., Alphonse, A. S., Indira, K., & Lavanya, R. (2024). Intelligent tutoring systems. In *Advances in educational technologies and instructional design* (pp. 226–250). CRC Press. DOI: 10.1201/9781003469315-11

Abọy, M., Minssen, T., & Vayena, E. (2024). Navigating the EU AI Act: Implications for regulated digital medical products. *NPJ Digital Medicine*, *7*(1), 237. DOI: 10.1038/s41746-024-01232-3 PMID: 39242831

Abualrob, M. (2025). From Reflection to Re-Reflection: ChatGPT and Transformative Learning in Pre-service Elementary Science Education. *International Journal of Learning. Teaching and Educational Research*, *24*(10), 769–793. DOI: 10.26803/ijlter.24.10.37

Abuhassna, H., Awae, F., Adnan, M. A., Daud, M., & Almheiri, A. S. (2024). The information age for education via artificial intelligence and machine learning: A bibliometric and systematic literature analysis. *International Journal of Information and Education Technology (IJIET)*, *14*(5), 700–711. DOI: 10.18178/ijiet.2024.14.5.2095

Abulibdeh, A., Zaidan, E., & Abulibdeh, R. (2024). Navigating the confluence of artificial intelligence and education for sustainable development in the era of industry 4.0: Challenges, opportunities, and ethical dimensions. *Journal of Cleaner Production*, *437*, 140527. DOI: 10.1016/j.jclepro.2023.140527

Acharya, D. B., Kuppan, K., & Divya, B. (2025). Agentic ai: Autonomous intelligence for complex goals–a comprehensive survey. *IEEE Access : Practical Innovations, Open Solutions*, *13*, 18912–18936. DOI: 10.1109/ACCESS.2025.3532853

Adams, D., & Thompson, P. (2025). Transforming school leadership with artificial intelligence: Applications, implications, and future directions. *Leadership and Policy in Schools*, *24*(1), 77–89.

Adeleye, O. O., Eden, C. A., & Adeniyi, I. S. (2024). Innovative teaching methodologies in the era of artificial intelligence: A review of inclusive educational practices. *World Journal of Advanced Engineering Technology and Sciences*, *11*(2), 069-079.

Adewale, M. D., Azeta, A., Abayomi-Alli, A., & Sambo-Magaji, A. (2024). Impact of artificial intelligence adoption on students' academic performance in open and distance learning: A systematic literature review. *Heliyon*, *10*(22), e40025. Advance online publication. DOI: 10.1016/j.heliyon.2024.e40025 PMID: 39605813

Adhya, D. H., & Panda, S. (2026). An integrative systematic review analysis of research on technology-enabled personalized learning and self-regulated learning. *Smart Learning Environments*, *13*(1), 3. Advance online publication. DOI: 10.1186/s40561-025-00428-8

Admin-Risepoint. (2025, February 20). *Psychology of competitiveness: Eastern Oregon University Online*. Eastern Oregon University. https://online.eou.edu/resources/article/psychology-of-competitiveness/

Adnan, K., Shaikh, F. B., Afzaal, R., Ali, A. B., & Ponnusamy, V. (2021). Identification of facilitators and barriers of ICT usage in the education sector of Pakistan: a systematic literature review. In *ICT Solutions for Improving Smart Communities in Asia* (pp. 27–53). IGI Global. DOI: 10.4018/978-1-7998-7114-9.ch002

Adobe. (2025). Content Credentials overview. In *Adobe.com*. https://helpx.adobe.com/creative-cloud/apps/adobe-content-authenticity/content-credentials/overview.html

Adobe. (2026). *Content Credentials integration | Adobe Experience Manager*. In *Adobe.com*. https://experienceleague.adobe.com/en/docs/experience-manager-cloud-service/content/assets/assets-view/content-credentials

Afroogh, S., Akbari, A., Malone, E., Kargar, M., & Alambeigi, H. (2025). Correction to: Trust in AI: progress, challenges, and future directions (Humanities and Social Sciences Communications, (2024), 11, 1, (1568),). In *Humanities and Social Sciences Communications* (Vol. 12, Issue 1). https://doi.org/DOI: 10.1057/s41599-024-04044-8

Afzaal, M., Shanshan, X., Yan, D., & Younas, M. (2024). Mapping artificial intelligence integration in education: a decade of innovation and impact (2013-2023)-a bibliometric analysis. *IEEE Access*.

Agesilaou, A., & Kyza, E. A. (2022). Whose data are they? Elementary school students' conceptualization of data ownership and privacy of personal digital data. *International Journal of Child-Computer Interaction*, *33*, 100462. DOI: 10.1016/j.ijcci.2022.100462

Agrawal, A., Bhadhouriya, S., Pandey, A. K., Bhadoriya, S., Shrivastava, D., Dubey, G., Dubey, M., Sengar, H., Shakywar, K., & Shrivastava, V. (2024). Transforming student assessment in higher education. In *Advances in educational technologies and instructional design* (pp. 363–386). IGI Global. DOI: 10.4018/979-8-3693-6170-2.ch013

Aguilar-Cruz, P. J., & Salas-Pilco, S. Z. (2025). Teachers' perceptions of artificial intelligence in Colombia: AI technological access, AI teacher professional development and AI ethical awareness. *Technology, Pedagogy and Education*, *34*(2), 219–238. DOI: 10.1080/1475939X.2025.2451865

Agyei, D. D. (2021). Integrating ICT into schools in Sub-Saharan Africa: From teachers' capacity building to classroom implementation. *Education and Information Technologies*, *26*(1), 125–144. DOI: 10.1007/s10639-020-10253-w

Ahamed, F. I. (2025). The transformative role of artificial intelligence in modern education. *World Journal of Advanced Research and Reviews*, *26*(1), 3239–3247. DOI: 10.30574/wjarr.2025.26.1.1453

Ahmad, A., Zeeshan, F., Marriam, R., Samreen, A., & Ahmed, S. (2021). Does one size fit all? Investigating the effect of group size and gamification on leaners' behaviors in higher education. *Journal of Computing in Higher Education*, *33*(2), 296–327. DOI: 10.1007/s12528-020-09266-8

Ahmad, K., Iqbal, W., El-Hassan, A., Qadir, J., Benhaddou, D., Ayyash, M., & Al-Fuqaha, A. (2024). Data-Driven Artificial Intelligence in Education: A Comprehensive Review. *IEEE Transactions on Learning Technologies*, *17*, 12–31. DOI: 10.1109/TLT.2023.3314610

Ahmed, S., & Parsons, D. (2013). Abductive science inquiry using mobile devices in the classroom. *Computers & Education*, *63*, 62–72. DOI: 10.1016/j.compedu.2012.11.017

Ahmed, S., Zeeshan, M., Parsons, D., Rehman, O., Ahmed, Z., Ahmad, A., & Ahmad, F. (2025). Exploring game-based inquiry learning application in a maritime science museum: A visitors' perspectives. *Human Behavior and Emerging Technologies*, *2025*(1), 1–14. DOI: 10.1155/hbe2/8284489

Airaj, M. (2024). Ethical artificial intelligence for teaching-learning in higher education. *Education and Information Technologies*, *29*(13), 17145–17167. DOI: 10.1007/s10639-024-12545-x

Akar, H. (2020). The Effect of Smart Board Use on Academic Achievement: A Meta-Analytical and Thematic Study. *International Journal of Education in Mathematics. Science and Technology*, *8*(3), 261–273.

Akshar Foundation. (2023). *Akshar Foundation | Transforming Indian schools into sustainable communities*. https://www.aksharfoundation.org/

Aktas, S., & Ayden, A. (2016). The effect of the smart board usage in science and technology lessons. *Eurasian Journal of Educational Research*, *64*(64), 125–138. DOI: 10.14689/ejer.2016.64.7

Al-Abdullatif, A. M. (2024). Modeling teachers' acceptance of generative artificial intelligence use in higher education: The role of AI literacy, intelligent TPACK, and perceived trust. *Education Sciences*, *14*(11), 1209. DOI: 10.3390/educsci14111209

AlAli, R., & Wardat, Y. (2024). Opportunities and challenges of integrating generative artificial intelligence in education. *International Journal of Religion*, *5*(7), 784–793. DOI: 10.61707/8y29gv34

Alam, A. (2023a). Media multitasking with M-learning technology in real-time classroom learning: Analysing the dynamics in formal educational settings for the future of E-learning in India. In *2023 2nd International Conference on Smart Technologies and Systems for Next Generation Computing (ICSTSN)* (pp. 1-6). IEEE.

Alam, A. (2023b). The secret sauce of student success: Cracking the code by navigating the path to personalized learning with educational data mining. In *2023 2nd International Conference on Smart Technologies and Systems for Next Generation Computing (ICSTSN)* (pp. 1-8). IEEE.

Alam, A., & Mohanty, A. (2022, December). Facial analytics or virtual avatars: competencies and design considerations for student-teacher interaction in AI-powered online education for effective classroom engagement. In *International Conference on Communication, Networks and Computing* (pp. 252-265). Cham: Springer Nature Switzerland.

Alam, A., & Mohanty, A. (2023, January). Learning on the move: a pedagogical framework for state-of-the-art mobile learning. In *International Conference on Data Management, Analytics & Innovation* (pp. 735-748). Singapore: Springer Nature Singapore. DOI: 10.1007/978-981-99-1414-2_52

Alam, A. (2022). Impact of university's human resources practices on professors' occupational performance: empirical evidence from India's higher education sector. In *Inclusive businesses in developing economies: Converging people, profit, and corporate citizenship* (pp. 107–131). Springer International Publishing. DOI: 10.1007/978-3-031-12217-0_6

Alam, A. (2023c). Intelligence unleashed: An argument for AI-enabled learning ecologies with real world examples of today and a peek into the future. In *International Conference on Innovations in Computer Science, Electronics & Electrical Engineering*-2022 (Vol. 2717, No. 1, p. 030001). AIP Publishing LLC. DOI: 10.1063/5.0129803

Alam, A., & Mohanty, A. (2024). Integrated constructive robotics in education (ICRE) model: A paradigmatic framework for transformative learning in educational ecosystem. *Cogent Education*, *11*(1), 2324487. DOI: 10.1080/2331186X.2024.2324487

Alamrio, J., Ayoade, J., & Uddin, M. A. (2025). A Zero-Knowledge Proof-Enabled Blockchain-Based Academic Record Verification System. *Sensors (Basel)*, *25*(11), 3450–3450. DOI: 10.3390/s25113450 PMID: 40968974

Alashwal, M. (2024). Empowering education through AI: Potential benefits and future implications for instructional pedagogy. *PUPIL International Journal of Teaching. Education and Learning*, *8*(2), 201–212. DOI: 10.20319/ictel.2024.201212

Albashiry, N. M., Belhadj, H., & Al-Smadi, M. (2024). A Digital Competency Framework for University Teachers: Towards Agile and Sustainable Curriculum. *2024 ASU International Conference in Emerging Technologies for Sustainability and Intelligent Systems (ICETSIS)*, 1491–1494. DOI: 10.1109/ICETSIS61505.2024.10459701

AlDahdouh, A. A., Osório, A. J., & Caires, S. (2015). Understanding knowledge networks, learning, and connectivism. *International Journal of Instructional Technology and Distance Learning*, *12*(10), 3–21. DOI: 10.5281/zenodo.46186

Al-Faki, I. M., & Khamis, A. H. (2014). Difficulties facing teachers in using interactive whiteboards in their classes. *American International Journal of Social Science*, *3*(2), 136–158.

Alghamdi, L. H., & Alghizzi, T. M. (2025). Educators' reflections on AI-automated feedback in higher education: A structured integrative review of potentials, pitfalls, and ethical dimensions. *Frontiers in Education*, *10*, 1704820. Advance online publication. DOI: 10.3389/feduc.2025.1704820

AlHakim, M. R. Sherleen, Kelly, & Chandra, Y. U. (2024). Indonesian Language Learning Application as the Key to Equalizing Educational Development in Indonesia, Especially in Remote, Outermost, and Underdeveloped Areas (3T). *2024 10th International HCI and UX Conference in Indonesia (CHIuXiD)*, 36–41. DOI: 10.1109/CHIuXiD64022.2024.10860643

Ali, A. (2024). Implication of e-learning and AI: Individualized pedagogical perspectives. *Journal of Electrical Systems*, *20*(7s, 7S), 2510–2515. DOI: 10.52783/jes.4074

Alier, M., Guerrero, M. J. C., Amo, D., Severance, C., & Fonseca, D. (2021). Privacy and E-Learning: A pending task. *Sustainability (Basel)*, *13*(16), 9206. DOI: 10.3390/su13169206

Alier, M., Peñalvo, F. J. G., & Camba, J. D. (2024). Generative Artificial Intelligence in Education: From Deceptive to Disruptive. *International Journal of Interactive Multimedia and Artificial Intelligence*, *8*(5), 5–14. DOI: 10.9781/ijimai.2024.02.011

Ali, M., Wahab, I. A., Huri, H. Z., & Yusoff, M. S. (2025). Personalised learning in higher education for health sciences: A scoping review. *BMC Medical Education*, *25*(1), 969. DOI: 10.1186/s12909-025-07565-1

Ali, O., Murray, P. A., Momin, M., Dwivedi, Y. K., & Malik, T. (2024). The effects of artificial intelligence applications in educational settings: Challenges and strategies. *Technological Forecasting and Social Change*, *199*, 123076. DOI: 10.1016/j.techfore.2023.123076

Alkhabra, Y. A., Ibrahem, U. M., & Alkhabra, S. A. (2023). Augmented reality technology in enhancing learning retention and critical thinking according to STEAM program. *Humanities & Social Sciences Communications*, *10*(1), 1–10. DOI: 10.1057/s41599-023-01650-w

Allal, L. (2013). Teachers' professional judgement in assessment: A cognitive act and a socially situated practice. *Assessment in Education: Principles, Policy & Practice*, *20*(1), 20–34. DOI: 10.1080/0969594X.2012.736364

Allam, H., & Dempere, J. (2025). Agentic AI for IT and Beyond: A Qualitative Analysis of Capabilities, Challenges, and Governance. *The Artificial Intelligence Business Review*, *1*(1).

Allen, A. (2022). An introduction to constructivism: Its theoretical roots and impact on contemporary education. *Journal of Learning Design and Leadership*, *1*(1), 1–11. https://ldljournal.web.illinois.edu/wp-content/uploads/2022/09/Andrew-Allen-Constructivism_JLDL_Vol1Issue1September2022.pdf

Almagharbeh, W. T., Alfanash, H. A. K., Alnawafleh, K. A., Alasmari, A. A., Alsaraireh, F. A., Dreidi, M. M., & Nashwan, A. J. (2025). Application of artificial intelligence in nursing practice: A qualitative study of Jordanian nurses' perspectives. *BMC Nursing*, *24*(1), 92. DOI: 10.1186/s12912-024-02658-6 PMID: 39863852

Almalawi, A., Soh, B., Li, A., & Samra, H. (2024). Predictive models for educational purposes: A systematic review. *Big Data and Cognitive Computing*, *8*(12), 187. DOI: 10.3390/bdcc8120187

Almasri, F. (2024). Exploring the impact of artificial intelligence in teaching and learning of science: A systematic review of empirical research. *Research in Science Education*, *54*(5), 977–997. DOI: 10.1007/s11165-024-10176-3

Almeman, K., El Ayeb, F., Berrima, M., Issaoui, B., & Morsy, H. (2025). The integration of AI and metaverse in education: A systematic review. *Applied Sciences (Basel, Switzerland)*, *15*(863), 1–135. DOI: 10.3390/app15020863

Alotaibi, N. S. (2024). The impact of AI and LMS integration on the future of higher Education: Opportunities, challenges, and strategies for transformation. *Sustainability (Basel)*, *16*(23), 10357. DOI: 10.3390/su162310357

Alqahtani, N., & Wafula, Z. (2025). Artificial intelligence integration: Pedagogical strategies and policies at leading universities. *Innovative Higher Education*, *50*(2), 665–684. DOI: 10.1007/s10755-024-09749-x

Alrawashdeh, G. S., Fyffe, S., Azevedo, R. F. L., & Castillo, N. M. (2024). Exploring the impact of personalized and adaptive learning technologies on reading literacy: A global meta-analysis. *Educational Research Review*, *42*, 100587. DOI: 10.1016/j.edurev.2023.100587

Al-Shorman, H. M., Saatchi, S. G., Alanaziand, T., Alzboon, M. S., Alka'awneh, S. M. N., Wahed, M. K. Y. A., & Al-Momani, A. A. M. (2025). Evaluating Artificial Intelligence Integration in Education Through Integrating TAM and S–O–R. In *Intelligence-Driven Circular Economy: Regeneration Towards Sustainability and Social Responsibility–Volume 1* (pp. 353–367). Springer Nature Switzerland. DOI: 10.1007/978-3-031-73899-9_28

Altay, S., & Gilardi, F. (2024). People are skeptical of headlines labeled as AI-generated, even if true or human-made, because they assume full AI automation. *PNAS Nexus*, *3*(10), pgae403. Advance online publication. DOI: 10.1093/pnasnexus/pgae403 PMID: 39359399

Alwaqdani, M. (2025). Investigating teachers' perceptions of artificial intelligence tools in education: Potential and difficulties. *Education and Information Technologies*, *30*(3), 2737–2755. DOI: 10.1007/s10639-024-12903-9

Al-Zahrani, A. M. (2024). Unveiling the shadows: Beyond the hype of AI in education. *Heliyon*, *10*(9), e30696. DOI: 10.1016/j.heliyon.2024.e30696 PMID: 38737255

Al-Zahrani, A. M., & Alasmari, T. M. (2024). Exploring the impact of artificial intelligence on higher education: The dynamics of ethical, social, and educational implications. *Humanities & Social Sciences Communications*, *11*(1), 1–12. DOI: 10.1057/s41599-024-03432-4

AlZu'Bi, S., Almiani, M., & Jararweh, Y. (2025, May). Agentic AI for Healthcare: Solutions to Intelligent Patient Care. In *2025 12th International Conference on Information Technology (ICIT)* (pp. 33-38). IEEE.

Amado-Salvatierra, H. R., Morales-Chan, M., Hernandez-Rizzardini, R., & Rosales, M. (2024, March). Exploring educators' perceptions: Artificial intelligence integration in higher education. In *2024 IEEE World Engineering Education Conference (EDUNINE)* (pp. 1-5). IEEE. DOI: 10.1109/EDUNINE60625.2024.10500578

Amdan, M. A. B., Janius, N., & Kasdiah, M. A. H. B. (2024). Concept paper: Efficiency of Artificial Intelligence (AI) tools for STEM education in Malaysia. *International Journal of Science and Research Archive*, *12*(2), 553–559. DOI: 10.30574/ijsra.2024.12.2.1273

Amedzo, K., & Dzansi, D. Y. (2014). Integrating ICT into rural South African schools: Possible solutions for challenges. *International Journal of Science Education*, *6*(2), 341–348.

Amershi, S., Weld, D., Vorvoreanu, M., Fourney, A., Nushi, B., Collisson, P., Suh, J., Iqbal, S., Bennett, P. N., Inkpen, K., Teevan, J., Kikin-Gil, R., & Horvitz, E. (2019). Guidelines for human-AI interaction. In *Proceedings of the 2019 CHI Conference on Human Factors in Computing Systems* (pp. 1–13). Association for Computing Machinery. https://doi.org/DOI: 10.1145/3290605.3300233

Amiruddin, A., Fiskia Rera, B., Takbir, T., Wirawan, S., & Muhammad, H. (2023). Pedagogy-Andragogy Continuum with Cybergogy to Promote Self-Regulated Learning: A Structural Equation Model Approach. *European Journal of Educational Research, 12*(2), 811–824. DOI: 10.12973/eu-jer.12.2.811

Anbumaheshwari, K., Jayalakshmi, J., & Pavunraj, D. (2025). AI-driven curriculum innovation for adaptive and learner-centric education. In *Advances in computational intelligence and robotics* (pp. 99–132). IGI Global. DOI: 10.4018/979-8-3373-1062-6.ch004

Andriana, I., Suppiah, S. D., Yulianita, A., Thamrin, K. M. H., & Bashir, A. (2024). *Understanding the institutional change and organizational transformation : An exploratory analysis of Indonesian higher education. 8*(6), 1–19.

Anglen, J. (2024). AI Agents for Learning Ecosystem: Benefits, Challenges, Use cases & Future. In *Rapidinnovation.io*. Rapid Innovation. https://www.rapidinnovation.io/post/ai-agents-for-learning-ecosystem-benefits-challenges-use-cases-future

Annuš, N. (2024). Education in the age of artificial intelligence. *TEM Journal, 13*(1), 404–413. DOI: 10.18421/TEM131-42

Ansu-Kyeremeh, E. K., & Goosen, L. (2022). Exploring the Socioeconomic Facet of Online Inclusive Education in Ghana: The Effects of Technological Advancement in Academia. In Garcia, M. (Ed.), *Socioeconomic Inclusion During an Era of Online Education* (pp. 47–66). IGI Global., DOI: 10.4018/978-1-6684-4364-4.ch003

Antoninis, M., April, D., Barakat, B., Bella, N., D'Addio, A. C., Eck, M., Endrizzi, F., Joshi, P., Kubacka, K., McWilliam, A., Murakami, Y., Smith, W., Stipanovic, L., Vidarte, R., & Zekrya, L. (2020). All means all: An introduction to the 2020 Global Education Monitoring Report on inclusion. *Prospects, 49*(3–4), 103–109. DOI: 10.1007/s11125-020-09505-x PMID: 32963414

Aravantinos, S., Lavidas, K., Komis, V., Karalis, T., & Papadakis, S. (2026). Artificial Intelligence in K-12 Education: A Systematic Review of Teachers' Professional Development Needs for AI Integration. *Computers 2026, Vol. 15, Page 49, 15*(1), 49. DOI: 10.3390/computers15010049

Arega, N. T., & Hunde, T. S. (2025). Constructivist instructional approaches: A systematic review of evaluation-based evidence for effectiveness. *Review of Education, 13*(1), e70040. DOI: 10.1002/rev3.70040

Arek-Bawa, O., & Reddy, S. (2022). Digital curricular transformation and fourth industrial revolution 4.0 (4IR): Deepening divides or building bridges. *E-Journal of Humanities. Arts and Social Sciences, 7*, 308–326.

Artsın, M., & Bozkurt, A. (2025). Charting new horizons: What agentic artificial intelligence (AI) promises in the educational landscape. In *EDULEARN25 Proceedings* (pp. 2019-2023). IATED.

Artsin, M., & Bozkurt, A. (2026). Dreams, Distortions, and Disruptions: Deconstructing the Educational Promises of Agentic AI. In *Rethinking Education and Agency in the Age of Human-Generative AI Interaction* (pp. 1-18). IGI Global Scientific Publishing.

Asrifan, A., Susanto, A. K., Elpisah, E., Saodi, S., & Herlina, H. (2024). AI-driven curriculum design and course management. In *Advances in educational technologies and instructional design* (pp. 195–222). IGI Global. DOI: 10.4018/979-8-3373-1017-6.ch007

Assem, H. D., Nartey, L., Appiah, E., & Aidoo, J. K. (2023). A review of students' academic performance in physics: Attitude, instructional methods, misconceptions and teachers qualification. *European Journal of Education and Pedagogy*, *4*(1), 84–92. DOI: 10.24018/ejedu.2023.4.1.551

August, S. E., & Tsaima, A. (2021). Artificial intelligence and machine learning: An instructor's exoskeleton in the future of education. In *SpringerBriefs in statistics* (pp. 79–105). Springer., DOI: 10.1007/978-3-030-58948-6_5

Ausubel, D. P. (1963). *The psychology of meaningful verbal learning*. Grune & Stratton.

Ausubel, D. P. (2003). *Aquisição e retenção de conhecimentos: uma perspectiva cognitiva* (Vol. 1).

Awang, L. A., Yusop, F. D., & Danaee, M. (2025). Current practices and future direction of artificial intelligence in mathematics education: A systematic review. *International Electronic Journal of Mathematics Education*, *20*(2), em0823. Advance online publication. DOI: 10.29333/iejme/16006

Ayanwale, M. A., Adelana, O. P., Molefi, R. R., Adeeko, O., & Ishola, A. M. (2024). Examining artificial intelligence literacy among pre-service teachers for future classrooms. *Computers and Education Open*, *6*, 100179. DOI: 10.1016/j.caeo.2024.100179

Azad, Y., & Kumar, A. (2024). Ethics and artificial intelligence. In *Advances in web technologies and engineering* (pp. 228–268). IGI Global. DOI: 10.4018/979-8-3693-1762-4.ch012

Baek, E., Wilson, R. V., & Liu, C. (2024). Redefining learning in the digital age. In *Advances in educational technologies and instructional design* (pp. 119–152). IGI Global. DOI: 10.4018/979-8-3693-6130-6.ch006

Baharuddin, F. R., & Setialaksana, W. (2023). Andragogy, Peeragogy, Heutagogy and Cybergogy Contribution on SelfRegulated Learning: A Structural Equation Model Approach. *International Journal of Instruction*, *16*(3), 551–572. DOI: 10.29333/iji.2023.16330a

Baker, R. S., & Inventado, P. S. (2016). Educational data mining and learning analytics: Potentials and possibilities for online education. *Emergence and innovation in digital learning: Foundations and applications*, 83-98.

Baker, R., & Siemens, G. (2014). Learning analytics and educational data mining. *Cambridge handbook of the leaning sciences*, 253-272.

Baker, R. S., & Inventado, P. S. (2014). Educational data mining and learning analytics. In Larusson, J. A., & White, B. (Eds.), *Learning Analytics* (Vol. 7, pp. 61–75)., DOI: 10.1007/978-1-4614-3305-7_4

Baltezarević, R., & Baltezarević, I. (2024). Students' attitudes on the role of artificial intelligence (AI) in personalized learning. *International Journal of Cognitive Research in Science. Engineering and Education*, *12*(2), 387–397.

Ban, Y., Qi, Y., & He, J. (2024). Neural contextual bandits for personalized recommendation. In WWW 2024 Companion - Companion Proceedings of the ACM Web Conference (pp. 1246–1249). Association for Computing Machinery. https://doi.org/DOI: 10.1145/3589335.3641241

Bandi, A., Kongari, B., Naguru, R., Pasnoor, S., & Vilipala, S. V. (2025). The rise of agentic ai: A review of definitions, frameworks, architectures, applications, evaluation metrics, and challenges. *Future Internet*, *17*(9), 404. DOI: 10.3390/fi17090404

Bandura, A. (2001). Social cognitive theory: An agentic perspective. *Annual Review of Psychology*, *52*(1), 1–26. DOI: 10.1146/annurev.psych.52.1.1 PMID: 11148297

Banerjee, A., Lamrani, I., Hossain, S., Paudyal, P., & Gupta, S. K. S. (2020). *AI Enabled Tutor for Accessible Training*. DOI: 10.1007/978-3-030-52237-7_3

Banerjee, R., Trappel, J., & Van Audenhove, L. (2024). Evaluating 'Meaningful Connectivity': Digital Literacy and Women in West Bengal, India. *Palgrave Studies in Digital Inequalities*, (Part F4289), 225–248. DOI: 10.1007/978-3-031-28930-9_11

Banerjie, S., Zhu, Y., Freeman, I., Machado, J. V., Ahmed, A., Sarker, A., & Al-Garadi, M. (2025). Agentic AI in Healthcare: A Comprehensive Survey of Foundations, Taxonomy, and Applications. *Authorea Preprints*. DOI: 10.36227/techrxiv.176238073.31262603/v1

Banihashem, S. K., Noroozi, O., van Ginkel, S., Macfadyen, L. P., & Biemans, H. J. A. (2022). A systematic review of the role of learning analytics in enhancing feedback practices in higher education. *Educational Research Review*, *37*, 100489. DOI: 10.1016/j.edurev.2022.100489

Bapna, R., Bapna, S., Kumar, P., Pamuru, V., Umyarov, A., & Yang, M. (2025). Agentic AI and Managers' Analytics Capabilities: An Exploration. *Available at SSRN* 5293722. DOI: 10.2139/ssrn.5293722

Barnes, E., & Hutson, J. (2024). Navigating the ethical terrain of AI in higher education: Strategies for mitigating bias and promoting fairness. *Forum for Education Studies*, *2*(2), 1–29. DOI: 10.59400/fes.v2i2.1229

Barua, L., & Lockee, B. B. (2024). A review of strategies to incorporate flexibility in higher education course designs. *Discover Education*, *3*(1), 127. DOI: 10.1007/s44217-024-00213-8

Bayram-Jacobs, D., Henze, I., Evagorou, M., Shwartz, Y., Aschim, E. L., Alcaraz-Dominguez, S., Barajas, M., & Dagan, E. (2019). Science teachers' pedagogical content knowledge development during enactment of socioscientific curriculum materials. *Journal of Research in Science Teaching*, *56*(9), 1207–1233. DOI: 10.1002/tea.21550

Behnagh, R. F., & Yasrebi, S. (2020). An examination of constructivist educational technologies: Key affordances and conditions. *British Journal of Educational Technology*, *51*(6), 1907–1919. DOI: 10.1111/bjet.13036

Bekteshi, L. (2025). Education in the era of AI and immersive technologies: A systematic review. *Journal of Research in Engineering and Computer Sciences*, *3*(1), 1–14. DOI: 10.63002/jrecs.31.779

Bender, E. M., Gebru, T., McMillan-Major, A., & Shmitchell, S. (2021). On the dangers of stochastic parrots: Can language models be too big? In Irani, L., Kannan, S., Mitchell, M., & Robinson, D. (Eds.), *Proceedings of the 2021 ACM conference on fairness, accountability, and transparency* (pp. 610–623). Association for Computing Machinery, New York, NY, United States. DOI: 10.1145/3442188.3445922

Bender, S. M. (2024). Awareness of artificial intelligence as an essential digital literacy: ChatGPT and Gen-AI in the classroom. *Changing English, 31*(2), 161–174. DOI: 10.1080/1358684X.2024.2309995

Bennett, R. E. (2011). Formative assessment: A critical review. *Assessment in Education: Principles, Policy & Practice, 18*(1), 5–25. DOI: 10.1080/0969594X.2010.513678

Bernstein, M. H., Atalay, M. K., Dibble, E. H., Maxwell, A. W. P., Karam, A. R., Agarwal, S., Ward, R. C., Healey, T. T., & Baird, G. L. (2023). Can incorrect artificial intelligence (AI) results impact radiologists, and if so, what can we do about it? A multi-reader pilot study of lung cancer detection with chest radiography. *European Radiology, 33*(11), 8263–8269. DOI: 10.1007/s00330-023-09747-1 PMID: 37266657

Bettahi, A., Beloudha, F.-Z., & Harroud, H. (2025). Continuous-Time Modeling in Educational Data Mining and Learning Analytics: A Literature Review on Methods, Ethics, and Emerging AI Trends. *IEEE Access : Practical Innovations, Open Solutions, 13*, 181443–181464. DOI: 10.1109/ACCESS.2025.3622103

Bhagwanrao, N. N., & Tiwari, B. B. (2025). Optimizing Investment Approaches using AI-Driven Predictive Analysis and Cloud Analysis. *2025 World Skills Conference on Universal Data Analytics and Sciences (WorldSUAS)*, 1–6. DOI: 10.1109/WorldSUAS66815.2025.11199193

Bhardwaj, V., Zhang, S., Tan, Y. Q., & Pandey, V. (2025). Redefining learning: Student-centered strategies for academic and personal growth. *Frontiers in Education, 10*, 1518602. Advance online publication. DOI: 10.3389/feduc.2025.1518602

Biesta, G. J. J. (2010). *Good education in an age of measurement: Ethics, politics, democracy.* Taylor & Francis.

Bilotti, U., Di Dario, D., Palomba, F., Gravino, C., & Sibilio, M. (2023). Machine learning for educational metaverse: How far are we? *In Proceedings of the 2023 IEEE International Conference on Consumer Electronics (ICCE)* (pp. 1-2). Berlin, Germany: IEEE. DOI: 10.1109/ICCE56470.2023.10043465

Bilý, J., & Miština, J. (2023). Using an interactive whiteboard to increase the effectiveness of teaching at secondary schools. *Resource*, •••, 38–49. DOI: 10.53349/resource.2023.is1.a1189

Biswas, A., & Talukdar, W. (2025). *Building Agentic AI Systems: Create intelligent, autonomous AI agents that can reason, plan, and adapt.* Packt Publishing Ltd.

Black, P., & Wiliam, D. (1998). Assessment and classroom learning. *Assessment in Education: Principles, Policy & Practice, 5*(1), 7–74. DOI: 10.1080/0969595980050102

Blog.Khanacademy (2025). *Explore AI in Your Teaching: A One-Hour PD Experience with Khan Academy.* Blog.Khanacademy.Org. https://blog.khanacademy.org/explore-ai-in-your-teaching-a-one-hour-pd-experience-with-khan-academy/

Boateng, O., & Boateng, B. (2025). Algorithmic bias in educational systems: Examining the impact of AI-driven decision making in modern education. *World Journal of Advanced Research and Reviews, 25*(1), 2012–2017. DOI: 10.30574/wjarr.2025.25.1.0253

Bonilla-Priego, M. J., García-Sánchez, I.-M., & Pérez-Bueno, J.-C. (2024). Evaluating the success of a learning management system used in a supplemental learning model. *Innovations in Education and Teaching International*. Advance online publication. DOI: 10.1080/09639284.2024.2424269

Booth, B. M., Bosch, N., & D'Mello, S. K. (2023). Engagement Detection and its Applications in Learning: A tutorial and selective review. *Proceedings of the IEEE, 111*(10), 1398–1422. DOI: 10.1109/JPROC.2023.3309560

Borghoff, U. M., Bottoni, P., & Pareschi, R. (2025). Human-artificial interaction in the age of agentic AI: A system-theoretical approach. *Frontiers in Human Dynamics, 7*, 1579166. DOI: 10.3389/fhumd.2025.1579166

Borrella, I., & Ponce-Cueto, E. (2025). Design principles and impact of a learning analytics dashboard: Evidence from a randomized MOOC experiment. *Applied Sciences (Basel, Switzerland), 15*(21), 11493. DOI: 10.3390/app152111493

Boskabadi, M. R., Cao, Y., Khadem, B., Clements, W., Gerek, Z. N., Reuthe, E., & Mansouri, S. S. (2025). Industrial Agentic AI and generative modeling in complex systems. *Current Opinion in Chemical Engineering, 48*, 101150. DOI: 10.1016/j.coche.2025.101150

Bouchareb, A., & Ghedir, H. (2024). Harnessing artificial intelligence for educational innovation: Enhancing learning outcomes and teaching practices. *African Transactions on Research in Education, 5*(3), 414–431. DOI: 10.70091/atras/AI.26

Bouchrika, I. (2026). 2026 Are Online Education Degrees Respected by Employers? In *Research.com*. https://research.com/advice/are-online-education-degrees-respected-by-**employers**

Boud, D., & Molloy, E. (2013). Rethinking models of feedback for learning: The challenge of design. *Assessment & Evaluation in Higher Education, 38*(6), 698–712. DOI: 10.1080/02602938.2012.691462

Bourbour, M. (2023). Using digital technology in early education teaching: Learning from teachers' teaching practice with interactive whiteboard. *International Journal of Early Years Education, 31*(1), 269–286. DOI: 10.1080/09669760.2020.1848523

Bouzidi, R., De Nicola, A., Nader, F., & Chalal, R. (2019). A systematic literature review of gamification design. In *Proceedings of the 20th Annual Simulation and AI in Games Conference (GAME-ON 2019) (Breda, The Netherlands). EUROSIS, Ostend, Belgium.*

Bozkurt, A. (2023). Generative artificial intelligence (AI) powered conversational educational agents: The inevitable paradigm shift. *Asian Journal of Distance Education, 18*(1), 198–204. http://www.asianjde.com/ojs/index.php/AsianJDE/article/view/718

Brookhart, S. M. (2001). Successful students' formative and summative uses of assessment information. *Assessment in Education: Principles, Policy & Practice, 8*(2), 153–169. DOI: 10.1080/09695940123775

Brunetti, R., Ferrante, S., Avella, A. M., Indraccolo, A., & Del Gatto, C. (2024). Turning stories into learning journeys: The principles and methods of immersive education. *Frontiers in Psychology, 15*, 1471459. DOI: 10.3389/fpsyg.2024.1471459 PMID: 39712545

Bryce, T. G. K., & Blown, E. J. (2024). Ausubel's meaningful learning re-visited. *Current Psychology (New Brunswick, N.J.), 43*(5), 4579–4598. DOI: 10.1007/s12144-023-04440-4

Buckreus, K., & Ally, M. (2020). "Smart" practices: Machine intelligence for transforming pedagogy and learning. In *Bridging human and machine: Future education with intelligence* (pp. 53–73). Springer. DOI: 10.1007/978-981-15-0618-5_4

Bukar, U. A., Sayeed, M. S., Razak, S. F. A., Yogarayan, S., & Sneesl, R. (2024). Decision-making framework for the utilization of generative artificial intelligence in education: A case study of ChatGPT. *IEEE Access : Practical Innovations, Open Solutions, 12*, 95368–95389. DOI: 10.1109/ACCESS.2024.3425172

Bulathwela, S., Pérez-Ortiz, M., Holloway, C., Cukurova, M., & Shawe-Taylor, J. (2024). Artificial intelligence alone will not democratise education: On educational inequality, techno-solutionism and inclusive tools. *Sustainability (Basel), 16*(2), 781. DOI: 10.3390/su16020781

Bulut, O., Beiting-Parrish, M., Casabianca, J. M., Slater, S. C., Jiao, H., Song, D., . . . Morilova, P. (2024). The rise of artificial intelligence in educational measurement: Opportunities and ethical challenges. *arXiv preprint arXiv:2406.18900.*

Bulut, O., Beiting-Parrish, M., Casabianca, J. M., Slater, S. C., Jiao, H., Song, D., & Morilova, P. (2024). The Rise of Artificial Intelligence in Educational Measurement: Opportunities and Ethical Challenges. *Chinese/English Journal of Educational Measurement and Evaluation, 5*(3). Advance online publication. DOI: 10.59863/MIQL7785

C2PA. (2018). C2PA Technical Specification: C2PA Specifications. In *C2pa.org*. https://spec.c2pa.org/specifications/specifications/1.0/specs/C2PA_Specification.html

C2PA. (2019). *C2PA Implementation Guidance: C2PA Specifications.* In *C2pa.org*. https://spec.c2pa.org/specifications/specifications/1.0/guidance/Guidance.html

C2PA. (2024). *Content Credentials C2PA Technical Specification*. https://spec.c2pa.org/specifications/specifications/2.1/specs/_attachments/C2PA_Specification.pdf

C2PA. (2024). Content Credentials: C2PA Technical Specification: C2PA Specifications. In *C2pa.org*. https://spec.c2pa.org/specifications/specifications/2.2/specs/C2PA_Specification.html

C2PA. (2025). C2PA and Content Credentials Explainer: C2PA Specifications. In *C2pa.org*. https://spec.c2pa.org/specifications/specifications/2.2/explainer/Explainer.html

C2PA. (n.d.). *C2PA Technical Specification*. Retrieved July 23, 2026, from https://spec.c2pa.org/specifications/specifications/1.3/specs/_attachments/C2PA_Specification.pdf

C2PA. (n.d.). Overview. In *c2pa.org*. Retrieved July 23, 2026, from https://c2pa.org/

Cabrera, U. O. I., Vilca, J. S., Oliva, E. G. C., García, K. R. S., Rojas, R. G., & Casaverde, M. H. (2024). *Artificial intelligence in the ethics of education*. Editorial Macro., DOI: 10.70288/emc.9789915970646

Çağlar-Özhan, Ş., Tekeli, P., & Arkün-Kocadere, S. (2025). Comparison of AI-Generated and instructor feedback: No significant difference in perceived feedback quality and neither on performance. *Journal of Computer Assisted Learning*, *41*(5), e70134. Advance online publication. DOI: 10.1111/jcal.70134

Cai, Z., Mao, P., Wang, D., He, J., Chen, X., & Fan, X. (2022). Effects of scaffolding in digital game-based learning on student's achievement: A three-level meta-analysis. *Educational Psychology Review*, *34*(2), 537–574. DOI: 10.1007/s10648-021-09655-0

Campos, D. G., & Scherer, R. (2023). Digital gender gaps in Students' knowledge, attitudes and skills: an integrative data analysis across 32 Countries. *Education and Information Technologies 2023 29:1*, *29*(1), 655–693. DOI: 10.1007/s10639-023-12272-9

Candy, P. C. (1991). *Self-direction for lifelong learning. A comprehensive guide to theory and practice*. ERIC.

Çapuk, S. (2015). ICT Integration models into middle and high school curriculum in the USA. *Procedia: Social and Behavioral Sciences*, *191*, 1218–1224. DOI: 10.1016/j.sbspro.2015.04.409

Carless, D., & Boud, D. (2018). The development of student feedback literacy: Enabling uptake of feedback. *Assessment & Evaluation in Higher Education*, *43*(8), 1315–1325. DOI: 10.1080/02602938.2018.1463354

Carless, D., Salter, D., Yang, M., & Lam, J. (2011). Developing sustainable feedback practices. *Studies in Higher Education*, *36*(4), 395–407. DOI: 10.1080/03075071003642449

Carlo Giovine and Roger Roberts. (2024). *Building AI trust: The key role of explainability*. McKinsey & Company. https://www.mckinsey.com/capabilities/quantumblack/our-insights/building-ai-trust-the-key-role-of-explainability

Carr, N. (2020). *The shallows: What the Internet is doing to our brains*. WW Norton & Company.

CAST. (2024). Universal Design for Learning Guidelines version 3.0. CAST. https://udlguidelines.cast.org/

Catalan, B. I., & Martinez, E. (2020). Understanding applicants'reactions to gamified recruitment. *Journal of Business Research*, *110*, 41–50. DOI: 10.1016/j.jbusres.2019.12.041

Cebolla, A., Herrero, R., Ventura, S., Miragall, M., Bellosta-Batalla, M., Llorens, R., & Banos, R. M. (2019). Putting oneself in the body of others: A pilot study on the efficacy of an embodied virtual reality system to generate self-compassion. *Frontiers in Psychology*, *10*, 1–10. DOI: 10.3389/fpsyg.2019.01521 PMID: 31338048

Celik, I., Dindar, M., Muukkonen, H., & Järvelä, S. (2022). The promises and challenges of artificial intelligence for teachers: A systematic review of research. *TechTrends*, *66*(4), 616–630. DOI: 10.1007/s11528-022-00715-y

Celik, I., Gedrimiene, E., Siklander, S., & Muukkonen, H. (2024). The affordances of artificial intelligence-based tools for supporting 21st-century skills: A systematic review of empirical research in higher education. *Australasian Journal of Educational Technology*, *40*(3), 19–38. DOI: 10.14742/ajet.9069

Cetinguc, B., & Calik, E. (2025). Navigating Innovation Process With Integration Of Artificial Intelligence. *IEEE Engineering Management Review*, •••, 1–27. DOI: 10.1109/EMR.2025.3624362

Chaaban, Y., Qadhi, S., Chen, J., & Du, X. (2024). *education sciences Understanding Researchers ' AI Readiness in a Higher Education Context : Q Methodology Research.*

Charokar, K., & Dulloo, P. (2022). Self-directed Learning Theory to Practice: A Footstep towards the Path of being a Life-long Learner. In *Journal of Advances in Medical Education and Professionalism* (Vol. 10, Issue 3). DOI: 10.30476/jamp.2022.94833.1609

Chaudhry, M. A., Cukurova, M., & Luckin, R. (2022). A transparency index framework for AI in education. *arXiv*. /arXiv.2206.03220DOI: 10.1007/978-3-031-11647-6_33

Chawla, C., Chatterjee, S., Gadadinni, S. S., Verma, P., & Banerjee, S. (2024). Agentic AI: The building blocks of sophisticated AI business applications. *Journal of AI. Robotics & Workplace Automation*, *3*(3), 1–15. DOI: 10.69554/XEHZ1946

Cheah, Y. H., Lu, J., & Kim, J. (2025). Integrating generative artificial intelligence in K-12 education: Examining teachers' preparedness, practices, and barriers. *Computers and Education: Artificial Intelligence*, *8*, 100363. DOI: 10.1016/j.caeai.2025.100363

Chekour, M., Laafou, M., & Janati-Idrissi, R. (2018). What are the adequate pedagogical approaches for teaching scientific disciplines? Physics as a case study. *Journal of Educational and Social Research*, *8*(2), 141–148. DOI: 10.2478/jesr-2018-0025

Chen, H. (2024). The ethical challenges of educational artificial intelligence and coping measures: A discussion in the context of the 2024 World Digital Education Conference. *Science Insights Education Frontiers, 20*(2), 3263-3281.

Chen, X., Xie, H., Zou, D., & Hwang, G. J. (2020). Application and theory gaps during the rise of artificial intelligence in education. *Computers and Education: Artificial Intelligence*, *1*, 100002. DOI: 10.1016/j.caeai.2020.100002

Chergui, M., Nagano, A., & Ammoumou, A. (2024). Toward an adaptive learning system by managing pedagogical knowledge in a smart way. *Multimedia Tools and Applications*, *84*(24), 27777–27793. DOI: 10.1007/s11042-024-20207-w

Cheung, L. H., Wang, L., & Lei, D. (2025). Conversational, agentic AI-enhanced architectural design process: Three approaches to multimodal AI-enhanced early-stage performative design exploration. *Architectural Intelligence*, *4*(1), 1–25. DOI: 10.1007/s44223-025-00092-5

Chew, N. (2025, September 25). *Digital Identity in an AI-Agent Economy: Rethinking Authentication.* Medium; MITB For All. https://medium.com/mitb-for-all/digital-identity-in-an-ai-agent-economy-rethinking-authentication-13da94cce035

Chheang, V., Sharmin, S., Marquez-Hernandez, R., Patel, M., Rajasekaran, D., Caulfied, G., . . . Barmaki, R. L. (2024). Towards anatomy education with generative AI-based virtual assistants in immersive virtual reality environments. *arXiv, 2306*(17278), 1-11. /arXiv.2306.17278DOI: 10.1109/AIxVR59861.2024.00011

Chigamba, T. (2021). Exploring the pedagogical value of using Smartboards and Tablets in high school physical science classrooms. (Project: MEd course work). University of the Witwatersrand.

Chiu, T. K., Falloon, G., Song, Y., & Vincent, W. L. (2024). A self-determination theory approach to teacher digital competence development. *Computers & Education, 214*, 105017. DOI: 10.1016/j.compedu.2024.105017

Chiu, T. K., Xia, Q., Zhou, X., Chai, C. S., & Cheng, M. (2023). Systematic literature review on opportunities, challenges, and future research recommendations of artificial intelligence in education. *Computers and Education: Artificial Intelligence, 4*, 100118. Advance online publication. DOI: 10.1016/j.caeai.2022.100118

Choi, J. I., Yang, E., & Goo, E. H. (2024). The effects of an ethics education program on artificial intelligence among middle school students: Analysis of perception and attitude changes. *Applied Sciences (Basel, Switzerland), 14*(4), 1588. DOI: 10.3390/app14041588

Claassen, J. (2025). *Assessing the Relationship Between School-Based Assessment and Matric Performance in Mathematics: A Quantitative Analysis of Poor Schools in Limpopo.* Stellenbosch University. Retrieved from https://resep.sun.ac.za/wp-content/uploads/2024/12/WP04_25-Assessing-the-relationship-between-school-based-assessment-and-matric-performance-Janke-Claasen.pdf

Clark, A., & Chalmers, D. (1998). The extended mind. *analysis, 58*(1), 7–19. https://www.jstor.org/stable/3328150

Clark, R. (2010). Evidence-based training methods: A guide for training professionals. American Society for Training and Development. https://archive.org/details/evidencebasedtra0000clar

Cloud Security Alliance. (2024). *Leveraging Zero-Knowledge Proofs in Machine Learning and LLMs: Enhancing Privacy and Security*. Cloudsa. https://cloudsecurityalliance.org/blog/2024/09/20/leveraging-zero-knowledge-proofs-in-machine-learning-and-llms-enhancing-privacy-and-security

Constantinescu, G.-G., Silion, D., & Iftene, A. (2024). Using artificial intelligence and mixed realities to create educational applications of the future. *Procedia Computer Science, 246*, 3313–3332. DOI: 10.1016/j.procs.2024.09.308

Content Authenticity Imitative. (2021). Getting started with Content Credentials | Open-source tools for content authenticity and provenance. In *Contentauthenticity.org*. https://opensource.contentauthenticity.org/docs/getting-started/

contentauth. (2023). *c2pa-cpp/examples/training.cpp at main · contentauth/c2pa-cpp*. GitHub. https://github.com/contentauth/c2pa-cpp/blob/main/examples/training.cpp

Contrino, M. F., Reyes-Millán, M., Vázquez-Villegas, P., & Membrillo-Hernández, J. (2024). Using an adaptive learning tool to improve student performance and satisfaction in online and face-to-face education for a more personalized approach. *Smart Learning Environments, 11*(1), 6. DOI: 10.1186/s40561-024-00292-y

Cordero, J., Torres-Zambrano, J., & Cordero-Castillo, A. (2024). Integration of generative artificial intelligence in higher education: Best practices. *Education Sciences, 15*(1), 32. DOI: 10.3390/educsci15010032

Córdova-Esparza, D. M. (2025). AI-powered educational agents: Opportunities, innovations, and ethical challenges. *Information (Basel), 16*(6), 469. DOI: 10.3390/info16060469

Crawford, K. (2021). *Atlas of AI: Power, politics, and the planetary costs of artificial intelligence*. Yale University Press.

Credential Engine. (2025, June 29). *Powering Skills-Based Hiring Through Better Data | Credential Engine*. Credential Engine. https://credentialengine.org/resources/powering-skills-based-hiring-through-better-data/

Cukurova, M. (2024). The interplay of learning, analytics, and artificial intelligence in education: A vision for hybrid intelligence. *British Journal of Educational Technology, 56*(2), 469–488. DOI: 10.1111/bjet.13514

D'Mello, S., & Graesser, A. (2015). Feeling, thinking, and computing with affect-aware learning. In Calvo, R., D'Mello, S., Gratch, J., & Kappas, A. (Eds.), *The Oxford handbook of affective computing* (pp. 419–434). Oxford University Press., DOI: 10.1093/oxfordhb/9780199942237.013.032

Dadhich, A., Yadav, R., Yadav, M., Huzooree, G., & Dewasiri, N. J. (2025). Teacher–AI collaboration and the future of the educator's role. In *Advances in computational intelligence and robotics* (pp. 355–378). IGI Global. DOI: 10.4018/979-8-3693-8744-3.ch013

Dai, C.-P., Ke, F., Pan, Y., & Liu, Y. (2023). Exploring students' learning support use in digital-game-based math learning: A mixed-methods approach using machine learning and multi-case study. *Computers & Education, 194*, 104698. DOI: 10.1016/j.compedu.2022.104698

Dai, C.-P., Ke, F., Zhang, N., Barrett, A., West, L., Bhowmik, S., & Yuan, X. (2024). Designing conversational agents to support student teacher learning in virtual reality simulation: A case study. *In Proceedings of the CHI Conference on Human Factors in Computing Systems* (pp. 1-8). Honolulu, USA: ACM. DOI: 10.1145/3613905.3637145

Dai, K., & Liu, Q. (2024). Leveraging artificial intelligence (AI) in English as a foreign language (EFL) classes: Challenges and opportunities in the spotlight. *Computers in Human Behavior, 159*, 108354. DOI: 10.1016/j.chb.2024.108354

Dang, T., Liu, C., & Peng, M. (2023). Low-latency mobile virtual reality content delivery for unmanned aerial vehicle-enabled wireless networks with energy constraints. *IEEE Transactions on Vehicular Technology, 72*(2), 2189–2201. DOI: 10.1109/TVT.2022.3212868

Darling-Hammond, L., Flook, L., Cook-Harvey, C., Barron, B., & Osher, D. (2019). Implications for educational practice of the science of learning and development. *Applied Developmental Science, 24*(2), 97–140. DOI: 10.1080/10888691.2018.1537791

Dash, S., & Bhoi, C. (2024). Exploring the intersection of education and artificial intelligence: A comprehensive review. *International Journal of Multidisciplinary Approach Research and Science, 2*(2), 601–610. DOI: 10.59653/ijmars.v2i02.637

Davis, C., Bush, T., & Wood, S. (2024). Artificial intelligence in education: Enhancing learning experiences through personalized adaptation. *International Journal of Cyber and IT Service Management, 4*(1), 26–32. DOI: 10.34306/ijcitsm.v4i1.146

De Souza Zanirato Maia, J., Bueno, A. P. A., & Sato, J. R. (2023). Applications of Artificial intelligence models in educational analytics and decision making: A Systematic review. *WORLD (Oakland, Calif.)*, *4*(2), 288–313. DOI: 10.3390/world4020019

de Souza, A. P., Conceição, C. de J., Pancoto, M. A., Cecote, N. Q. B., Pedra, R. R., Oliveira, R. M. da S., Pinão, V. R. Z., & Gomes, W. T. (2024). Personalização da aprendizagem com inteligência artificial: Como a IA está transformando o ensino e o currículo. *Aracê*, *6*(3), 5816–5831. DOI: 10.56238/arev6n3-092

de Vreugd, L., van Leeuwen, A., Jansen, R., & van der Schaaf, M. (2024). Learning analytics dashboard design and evaluation to support student self-regulation of study behaviour. *Journal of Learning Analytics*, *11*(3), 249–262. DOI: 10.18608/jla.2024.8529

Deci, E. L., & Ryan, R. M. (2000). The" what" and" why" of goal pursuits: Human needs and the self-determination of behavior. *Psychological Inquiry*, *11*(4), 227–268. DOI: 10.1207/S15327965PLI1104_01

Deci, E. L., & Ryan, R. M. (2008). Facilitating optimal motivation and psychological well-being across life's domains. *Canadian Psychology*, *49*(1), 14–23. DOI: 10.1037/0708-5591.49.1.14

Deci, E. L., & Ryan, R. M. (2012). Self-determination theory. In Paul, A. M. V. L., Kruglanski, A. W., & Higgins, E. T. (Eds.), *Handbook of theories of social psychology* (Vol. 1, pp. 416–436). SAGE. DOI: 10.4135/9781446249215.n21

Deckker, D., Sumanasekara, S., & Fakhrou, A. (2025). AI-powered personalised learning: Promise and pitfalls. *World Journal of Advanced Research and Reviews*, *26*(3), 2081–2095. DOI: 10.30574/wjarr.2025.26.3.2425

Del Rosario Navas Bonilla, C., Carrasco, L. M. V., Pupiales, J. C. G., & Noriega, D. E. M. (2025). The Future of Education: A Systematic Literature Review of Self-Directed Learning with AI. *Future Internet*, *17*(8), 366. DOI: 10.3390/fi17080366

Delello, J. A., Watters, J. B., & Garcia-Lopez, A. (2024). Artificial intelligence in education. In *Advances in business information systems and analytics* (pp. 1–26). IGI Global. DOI: 10.4018/979-8-3693-3003-6.ch001

Delgado-von-Eitzen, C., Anido-Rifón, L., Fernández-Iglesias, M. J., & Ruiz-Molina, M. (2025). Qualitative Analysis of a Blockchain-Based System Adoption for Academic Credentials Verification That Complies with the GDPR: GAVIN Project. *Applied Sciences (Basel, Switzerland)*, *15*(22), 11958. DOI: 10.3390/app152211958

Department of Basic Education (DBE). (2017). *Professional development framework for digital learning*. DBE.

Department of Basic Education. (2011). *Curriculum and Assessment Policy Statement Physical Sciences Further Education and Training Phase Grades 10-12*. Government Printing Works.

Department of Basic Education. (2014). *Physical Sciences School-based assessment exemplars- CAPS Grade 12 Teacher Guide.* Retrieved from https://www.education.gov.za/SchoolBasedAssessmentTasks2014/tabid/611/Default.aspx

Department of Basic Education. (2024). *Naional Senior Certificate School Subject Report.* Retrieved from https://www.ecexams.co.za/2024_NSC_Exam_Results/2024 NSC School Subject Report.pdf

Department of Economics and Statistics. G. of T. N. (2020). *Tamilnadu COVID Pulse Survey.* https://des.tn.gov.in/en/node/344

Department of Education. (2004, September 2). White Paper on e-Education: Transforming Learning and Teaching through Information and Communication Technologies (ICTs). *Government Gazette* (26734), pp. 3 - 46.

Depietro-Covey, K. E. (2023). *Northeast Pennsylvania Teachers' Self-Reported Adoption of Technology Integration: A Qualitative Comparative Case Study. (DEd thesis).* Northcentral University.

Deterding, S., Dixon, D., Khaled, R., & Nacke, L. (2011). From Game Design Elements to Gamefulness: Defining Gamification. *Proceedings of the 15th International Academic MindTrek Conference: Envisioning Future Media Environments, MindTrek 2011.* 11. 9-15. DOI: 10.1145/2181037.2181040

Devaki, V., Suresh, C., & Boopathi, L. (2025). Building Teacher Skills for Effective Integration of Technology in the Classroom. Https://Services.Igi-Global.Com/Resolvedoi/Resolve.Aspx?Doi=10.4018/979-8-3373-0771-8.Ch012, 269–302. DOI: 10.4018/979-8-3373-0771-8.ch012

Devaki, V., Suresh, C., & Sunkesula, M. A. (2025). Multicultural Diversity in Perspective Views on Pluralism. Https://Services.Igi-Global.Com/Resolvedoi/Resolve.Aspx?Doi=10.4018/979-8-3693-8196-0.Ch001, 1–34. DOI: 10.4018/979-8-3693-8196-0.ch001

Dhal, S., Samantaray, S., & Satapathy, S. C. (2022, February). From chalk boards to smart boards: An integration of IoT into educational environment during Covid-19 pandemic. *Intelligent Data Engineering and Analytics: Proceedings of the 9th International Conference on Frontiers in Intelligent Computing: Theory and Applications (FICTA 2021)* (pp. 301-309). Singapore: Springer Nature.

Díaz, B., & Nussbaum, M. (2024). Artificial intelligence for teaching and learning in schools: The need for pedagogical intelligence. *Computers & Education*, *217*, 105071. DOI: 10.1016/j.compedu.2024.105071

Dieterle, E., Dede, C., & Walker, M. (2024). The cyclical ethical effects of using artificial intelligence in education. *AI & Society*, *39*(2), 633–643. DOI: 10.1007/s00146-022-01497-w PMID: 36185064

DIF. (n.d.). *DIF FAQ.* In *identity.foundation.* Retrieved July 23, 2026, from https://identity.foundation/faq

Dlamini, R. (2022). Digital equity in schools: A multilevel analysis of in-service teachers' technological knowledge competencies. *Journal of Educational Studies*, *21*(2), 40–60.

Dobrescu, P., Durach, F., & Vladu, L. (2025). AI USE IN EDUCATION: INSIGHTS FOR THE MITIGATION OF RISKS. *INTED Proceedings*, *1*, 4124–4130. DOI: 10.21125/inted.2025.1045

Doğan, S., Betin-Can, A., & Garousi, V. (2014). Web application testing: A systematic literature review. *Journal of Systems and Software*, *91*, 174–201. DOI: 10.1016/j.jss.2014.01.010

DoraHacks. (2019). *KYA-Passport - Know Your Agent Passport | Buidls | DoraHacks.* DoraHacks. https://dorahacks.io/buidl/26333

Dorri, A., Kanhere, S. S., & Jurdak, R. (2018). Multi-agent systems: A survey. *IEEE Access : Practical Innovations, Open Solutions*, *6*, 28573–28593. DOI: 10.1109/ACCESS.2018.2831228

Dron, J., & Anderson, T. (2014). *Teaching crowds: Learning and social media.* Athabasca University Press.

Du Plooy, E., Casteleijn, D., & Franzsen, D. (2024). Personalized adaptive learning in higher education: A scoping review of key characteristics and impact on academic performance and engagement. *Heliyon*, *10*(21), e39630. DOI: 10.1016/j.heliyon.2024.e39630

Dube-Xaba, Z. (2024). School-Based Assessment as a Driver of Self-Regulated Learning: Experiences of Tourism Learners. *40th AAEA Conference Proceedings*, (pp. 46-60). DOI: 10.38140/obp2-2024-04

Duong, N. T., Thi, T. D., & Pham, V. K. (2025). A comparative study on AI-based learning behaviors: Evidence from Vietnam. *International Journal of Human-Computer Interaction*, *41*(16), 10007–10023. DOI: 10.1080/10447318.2024.2430433

Dutta, A., & Chauhan, S. (2025). Artificial Intelligence in Student Privacy and Data Security. *International Journal of Advanced Research in Computer Science*, *16*(3), 146–151. DOI: 10.26483/ijarcs.v16i3.7261

Dweck, C. S., & Yeager, D. S. (2019). Mindsets: A View From Two Eras. *Perspectives on Psychological Science*, *14*(3), 481–496. DOI: 10.1177/1745691618804166 PMID: 30707853

Dwivedi, Y. K., Helal, M. Y. I., Elgendy, I. A., Albashrawi, M. A., Hughes, L., Shawosh, M., & Jeon, I. (2025). Artificial intelligence agents and agentic systems in hospitality and tourism: Challenges, opportunities and research agenda. *International Journal of Contemporary Hospitality Management.*

Dwyer, N., Harrison, M., O'Mara, B., & Harley, K. (2024). Inclusive gaming through AI: A perspective for identifying opportunities and obstacles through co-design with people living with MND. *Frontiers of Computer Science*, *6*, 1379559. Advance online publication. DOI: 10.3389/fcomp.2024.1379559

Dyulicheva, Y. Y., & Glazieva, A. O. (2021). Game based learning with artificial intelligence and immersive technologies: an overview. *In Proceedings of the 4th Workshop for Young Scientists in Computer Science & Software Engineering* (pp. 146-159). Kryvyi, Rih, Ukraine: CEUR Workshop Proceedings. Retrieved from chrome-extension://efaidnbmnnnibpcajpcglclefindmkaj/https://ceur-ws.org/Vol-3077/paper05.pdf

Earl, L. (2003). *Assessment as learning: Using classroom assessment to maximize student learning*. Corwin.

Edwards-Fapohunda, M. O., & Adediji, M. A. (2024). Sustainable development of distance learning in continuing adult education: The impact of artificial intelligence. *Iconic Research and Engineering Journals*, *8*(1), 113–114.

Elmasri, R., & Navathe, S. (2016). Fundamentals of Database Systems. Pearson eLibrary. https://elibrary.pearson.de/book/99.150005/9781292097626

Elnaffar, S., Rashidi, F., & Abualkishik, A. Z. (2025). Teaching with AI: a systematic review of chatbots, generative tools, and tutoring systems in programming education. *arXiv preprint arXiv:2510.03884.*

Elting, J., & Desio, M. G. (2024). AI prompts for nursing students to support independent learning. *Nurse Educator*, *49*(5), E243–E243. DOI: 10.1097/NNE.0000000000001633 PMID: 38502639

Elvis, M. (2025). Reframing AI in education: A Vygotskian perspective on proximal development. *International Journal of Arts, Humanities &. Social Science*, *6*(Special Issue), 7–13. DOI: 10.56734/ijahss.v6nSa2

Engenes, I., & Gamlem, S. M. (2025). Exploring AI-driven feedback as a cultural tool: A cultural-historical perspective on design of AI environments to support students' writing process. *Integrative Psychological & Behavioral Science*, *59*(1), 23. Advance online publication. DOI: 10.1007/s12124-025-09894-8

Entrust Cybersecurity Insitute. (n.d.). *2025 Identity Fraud Report ENTRUST CYBERSECURITY INSTITUTE PRESENTS*. Retrieved July 23, 2026, from https://www.entrust.com/sites/default/files/documentation/reports/2025-identity-fraud-report.pdf

Equality, L. (2023). *Kolibri Platform*. https://learningequality.org/kolibri/about-kolibri/

Erawati, N. K., & Adnyana, P. B. (2024). Implementation of Jean Piaget's theory of contructivism in learning: A literature review. *Indonesian Journal of Educational Development*, *5*(3), 394–401. DOI: 10.59672/ijed.v5i3.4148

Erduran, S., & Levrini, O. (2024). The impact of artificial intelligence on scientific practices: An emergent area of research for science education. *International Journal of Science Education*, *46*(18), 1982–1989. DOI: 10.1080/09500693.2024.2306604

Essa, S. G., Celik, T., & Human-Hendricks, N. E. (2023). Personalized Adaptive Learning Technologies Based on Machine Learning Techniques to Identify Learning Styles: A Systematic Literature Review. *IEEE Access : Practical Innovations, Open Solutions*, *11*, 48392–48409. DOI: 10.1109/ACCESS.2023.3276439

Ethics Guidelines for Trustworthy AI. (2019). *High-level expert group on artificial intelligence*. European Commission. https://digital-strategy.ec.europa.eu/en/library/ethics-guidelines-trustworthy-ai

Evans, C. (2013). Making sense of assessment feedback in higher education. *Review of Educational Research*, *83*(1), 70–120. DOI: 10.3102/0034654312474350

Ezeoguine, E. P., & Eteng-Uket, S. (2024). Artificial intelligence tools and higher education student's engagement. *Edukasiana: Jurnal Inovasi Pendidikan*, *3*(3), 300–312. DOI: 10.56916/ejip.v3i3.733

Fadlelmula, F. K., & Qadhi, S. M. (2024). A systematic review of research on artificial intelligence in higher education: Practice, gaps, and future directions in the GCC. *Journal of University Teaching & Learning Practice*, *21*(6), 146–173. DOI: 10.53761/pswgbw82

Famaye, T., Bailey, C. S., Adisa, I., & Irgens, G. A. (2024). What Makes ChatGPT Dangerous Is Also What Makes It Special": High-School Student Perspectives on the Integration or Ban of Artificial Intelligence in Educational Contexts. *International Journal of Technology in Education*, *7*(2), 174–199. DOI: 10.46328/ijte.651

Farahani, M. S., & Ghasmi, G. (2024, July). Artificial intelligence in education: A comprehensive study. In *Forum for Education Studies* (Vol. 2, No. 3, pp. 1379-1379). DOI: 10.59400/fes.v2i3.1379

Faridi, B., & Shaheen, S. S. (2024). From chalkboards to digital boards: The evolution of educational apps in India through digital transformation. *International Journal of Multidisciplinary Trends*, *6*(9), 42–52. DOI: 10.22271/multi.2024.v6.i9a.481

Farooqi, S. A. (2025). Ethical framework for AI in education. In *Advances in computational intelligence and robotics* (pp. 153–188). IGI Global. DOI: 10.4018/979-8-3373-5550-4.ch007

Farooqi, M. T. K., Amanat, I., & Awan, S. M. (2024). Ethical considerations and challenges in the integration of artificial intelligence in education: A systematic review. *Journal of Excellence in Management Sciences*, *3*(4), 35–50. DOI: 10.69565/jems.v3i4.314

Fatima, A., Shaheen, A., Ahmed, S., Fazal, B., Ahmad, F., Liew, T. W., & Ahmed, Z. (2024). Exploring the use of gamification in human-centered agile-based requirements engineering. *Frontiers of Computer Science*, *6*, 1–16. DOI: 10.3389/fcomp.2024.1442081

Favero, L., Pérez-Ortiz, J., Käser, T., & Oliver, N. (2025). Do AI tutors empower or enslave learners? Toward a critical use of AI in education. *arXiv*. /arXiv.2507.06878DOI: 10.48550

Fedorov, V. A. (2021). SCIENTIFIC INFORMATION ABOUT THE INTERNATIONAL SCIENTIFIC-PRACTICAL CONFERENCE «Linguistic picture of the world under the conditions of multilingualism and multiculturalism: Translational, linguistic and didactic aspects». *Scientific Journal Modern Linguistic and Methodical-and-Didactic Researches*, (1), 94–95. DOI: 10.36622/MLMDR.2021.32.1.010

Fenwick, T., Edwards, R., & Sawchuk, P. (2012). *Emerging approaches to educational research: Tracing the sociomaterial*. Routledge.

Ferreira, H. R., & Santos, A. M. P. (2022). A review of strategies for implementing learning technologies in organizations. *2022 17th Iberian Conference on Information Systems and Technologies (CISTI)*, 1–6. DOI: 10.23919/CISTI54924.2022.9820254

Filgueiras, F. (2024). Artificial intelligence and education governance. *Education, Citizenship and Social Justice*, *19*(3), 349–361. DOI: 10.1177/17461979231160674

Fink, M. C., Robinson, S. A., & Ertl, B. (2024). AI-based avatars are changing the way we learn and teach: Benefits and challenges. *Frontiers in Education*, *9*, 1–8. DOI: 10.3389/feduc.2024.1416307

Fitrianto, I., Setyawan, C. E., & Saleh, M. (2024). Utilizing Artificial Intelligence for Personalized Arabic Language Learning Plans. *International Journal of Post Axial: Futuristic Teaching and Learning*, 30-40.

Fleckenstein, J., Liebenow, L. W., & Meyer, J. (2023). Automated feedback and writing: A multi-level meta-analysis of effects on students' performance. *Frontiers in Artificial Intelligence*, *6*, 1162454. Advance online publication. DOI: 10.3389/frai.2023.1162454

Floridi, L., Cowls, J., Beltrametti, M., Chatila, R., Chazerand, P., Dignum, V., Luetge, C., Madelin, R., Pagallo, U., Rossi, F., Schafer, B., Valcke, P., & Vayena, E. (2018). AI4People—An ethical framework for a good AI society: Opportunities, risks, principles, and recommendations. *Minds and Machines*, *28*(4), 689–707. DOI: 10.1007/s11023-018-9482-5 PMID: 30930541

Fook, C. Y., & Sidhu, G. K. (2011). School based assessment among ESL teachers in Malaysian secondary schools. *Journal of the Malaysian Education Dean's Council*, *9*, 75–87.

Foong, Y. P., Pidani, R., Sithira Vadivel, V., & Dongyue, Y. (2024). Singapore smart nation: Journey into a new digital landscape for higher education. In Kwok, A. O. J., & Teh, P.-L. (Eds.), *Emerging technologies in business: innovation strategies for competitive advantage* (pp. 281–304). Springer., DOI: 10.1007/978-981-97-2211-2_13

Forero-Corba, W., & Bennasar, F. N. (2024). Techniques and applications of Machine Learning and Artificial Intelligence in education: a systematic review. *RIED-Revista Iberoamericana de Educación a Distancia, 27*(1).

Franco D'Souza, R., Mathew, M., Mishra, V., & Surapaneni, K. M. (2024). Twelve tips for addressing ethical concerns in the implementation of artificial intelligence in medical education. *Medical Education Online*, *29*(1), 2330250. DOI: 10.1080/10872981.2024.2330250 PMID: 38566608

Freitas, K. (2022). Low-stakes writing in an active-learning classroom needs focus and feedback to be effective. *The Journal of Economic Education*, *54*(3), 243–255. DOI: 10.1080/00220485.2022.2075505

Fryer, L., & Carpenter, R. (2006). Bots as language learning tools. *Language Learning & Technology, 10*(3), 8–14. DOI: 10.64152/10125/44068

Fu, J. S. (2013). Complexity of ICT in education: A critical literature review and its implications. *International Journal of Education and Development using ICT, 9*(1), 112-125.

Fullan, M., Azorín, C., Harris, A., & Jones, M. (2024). Artificial intelligence and school leadership: Challenges, opportunities and implications. *School Leadership & Management*, *44*(4), 339–346. DOI: 10.1080/13632434.2023.2246856

Fundi, M., Sanusi, I. T., Oyelere, S. S., & Ayere, M. (2024). Advancing AI education: Assessing Kenyan in-service teachers' preparedness for integrating artificial intelligence in competence-based curriculum. *Computers in Human Behavior Reports*, *14*, 100412. DOI: 10.1016/j.chbr.2024.100412

Fung, K. K., Lai, C. Y., Hung, S. L., Yu, Y., & He, L. (2025). A Systematic Review of the Digital Divide Experienced by Migrant Women. *Journal of International Migration and Integration*, *26*(2), 1177–1204. DOI: 10.1007/s12134-024-01222-0

Gadbois, S., & Haverstock, N. (2009). Using SMART Board Technology to Teach Grade 6 Science: Teachers' Experiences with and Perceptions of Its Use. In *Manitoba Education Research Network (MERN) Research Forum on Science, Mathematics, Technology, Teaching and Learning*. Winnipeg, Manitoba.

Gajdamaschko, N. (2015). Vygotsky's sociocultural theory. In *International encyclopedia of the social & behavioral sciences* (pp. 329–334). Elsevier., DOI: 10.1016/B978-0-08-097086-8.23203-0

Galindo-Domínguez, H., Delgado, N., Campo, L., & Losada, D. (2024). Relationship between teachers' digital competence and attitudes towards artificial intelligence in education. *International Journal of Educational Research, 126*, 102381. DOI: 10.1016/j.ijer.2024.102381

Galindo-Domínguez, H., Delgado, N., Losada, D., & Etxabe, J. M. (2024). An analysis of the use of artificial intelligence in education in Spain: The in-service teacher's perspective. *Journal of Digital Learning in Teacher Education*, *40*(1), 41–56. DOI: 10.1080/21532974.2023.2284726

Galitsky, B., Chernyavskiy, A., & Ilvovsky, D. (2024). Truth-o-Meter: Handling multiple inconsistent source repairing LLM hallucinations. *In Proceedings of the 47th International ACM SIGIR Conference on Research and Development in Information Retrieval* (pp. 2817-2821). Washington DC, USA: ACM. DOI: 10.1145/3626772.3657679

Galvin, B. (2025). The role of foresight in public policy: Lessons from deliberative democracy and perspectival realism. *European Journal of Futures Research, 13*(1), 1. Advance online publication. DOI: 10.1186/s40309-024-00246-0

García-López, I. M., & Trujillo-Liñán, L. (2025). Ethical and regulatory challenges of Generative AI in education: A systematic review. *Frontiers in Education, 10*, 1565938. DOI: 10.3389/feduc.2025.1565938

García-Méndez, S., De Arriba-Pérez, F., & Del Carmen Somoza-López, M. (2024). A review on the use of large language models as virtual tutors. *Science & Education, 34*(2), 877–892. DOI: 10.1007/s11191-024-00530-2

Garg, V. (2025). Designing the Mind: How Agentic Frameworks Are Shaping the Future of AI Behavior. *Journal of Computer Science and Technology Studies, 7*(5), 182–193. DOI: 10.32996/jcsts.2025.7.5.24

Garzón, J., Patiño, E., & Marulanda, C. (2025). Systematic review of artificial intelligence in education: Trends, benefits, and challenges. *Multimodal Technologies and Interaction, 9*(8), 84. DOI: 10.3390/mti9080084

Gašević, D., Dawson, S., & Siemens, G. (2014). Let's not forget: Learning analytics are about learning. *TechTrends, 59*(1), 64–71. DOI: 10.1007/s11528-014-0822-x

Gaynes, R. (2017). The discovery of penicillin—New insights after more than 75 years of clinical use. *Emerging Infectious Diseases, 23*(5), 849–853. https://pmc.ncbi.nlm.nih.gov/articles/PMC5403050/. DOI: 10.3201/eid2305.161556

Gbordzekpor, S. H., Kwakye, D. O., & Aggrey, J. (2023). Multimedia Resources Available in Senior High Schools and Mathematics Teachers' Perceived Ability to use them in Teaching Due to their Gender. *Journal of Education and Teaching Methods, 2*(1), 23–43. DOI: 10.58425/jetm.v2i1.118

Gebhard, S. (2008). Vygotsky and the zone of proximal development. In *Encyclopedia of information communication technologies* (pp. 948–950). IGI Global., DOI: 10.4018/978-1-59904-881-9.ch148

Gebru, T., Morgenstern, J., Vecchione, B., Vaughan, J. W., Wallach, H., Daumé, H.III, & Crawford, K. (2021). Datasheets for datasets. *Communications of the ACM, 64*(12), 86–92. DOI: 10.1145/3458723

Geo-JaJa, M. A. (2013). Education localization for optimizing globalization's opportunities and challenges in Africa. In S. Majhanovich & M. A. Geo-JaJa (Eds.), *Economics, aid and education: Implications for development* (pp. 159–181). Sense Publishers, Rotterdam. DOI: 10.1007/978-94-6209-365-2_11

Geyser, H. (2025). Decoloniality, digital-coloniality and computer programming education. *ACM Transactions on Computing Education, 24*(4), 1–30. DOI: 10.1145/3702332

Ghosh, R. K., Çela, E., Chakraborty, S., Gupta, B., Dutta, G., Chakraborty, S., & Roy, S. (2025a). Ethical artificial intelligence and machine learning in Self-Service technologies. In IGI Global eBooks (pp. 155–204). https://doi.org/DOI: 10.4018/979-8-3373-1295-8.ch007

Ghosh, R. K., Chakraborty, S., & Dutta, G. (2025b). AI in Enhancing Bilingual Proficiency. In Advances in computational intelligence and robotics book series (pp. 141–176). https://doi.org/DOI: 10.4018/979-8-3373-0275-1.ch005

Giannikas, C. N. (2021). Interactive whiteboards in EFL from the Teachers' and students' perspective. *Research Papers in Language Teaching & Learning*, *11*(1), 203–219.

Gibson, D., Kovanovic, V., Ifenthaler, D., Dexter, S., & Feng, S. (2023). Learning theories for artificial intelligence promoting learning processes. *British Journal of Educational Technology*, *54*(5), 1125–1146. DOI: 10.1111/bjet.13341

Gipps, C. (1994). *Beyond testing: Towards a theory of educational assessment*. Routledge.

Giray, L. (2024). AI Shaming: The Silent Stigma among Academic Writers and Researchers. *Annals of Biomedical Engineering*, *52*(9), 2319–2324. DOI: 10.1007/s10439-024-03582-1 PMID: 38977530

Gkintoni, E., Antonopoulou, H., Sortwell, A., & Halkiopoulos, C. (2025). Challenging cognitive load theory: The role of educational neuroscience and artificial intelligence in redefining learning efficacy. *Brain Sciences*, *15*(2), 203. DOI: 10.3390/brainsci15020203 PMID: 40002535

Glassner, A., & Back, S. (2020). Connectivism: Networks, knowledge, and learning. In *Exploring heutagogy in higher education* (pp. 45–63). Springer. DOI: 10.1007/978-981-15-4144-5_3

Gligorea, I., Cioca, M., Oancea, R., Gorski, A., Gorski, H., & Tudorache, P. (2023). Adaptive learning using artificial intelligence in e-learning: A literature review. *Education Sciences*, *13*(12), 1216. DOI: 10.3390/educsci13121216

Godyn, M., Kedziora, M., Ren, Y., Liu, Y., & Song, H. H. (2022). Analysis of solutions for a blockchain compliance with GDPR. *Scientific Reports*, *12*(1), 15021. DOI: 10.1038/s41598-022-19341-y PMID: 36056166

Goel, A. K., & Polepeddi, L. (2018). Jill Watson: A virtual teaching assistant for online education. In *Learning engineering for online education* (pp. 120-143). Routledge.

Goger, A. (2025). There's more to skills-based hiring than just removing degree requirements. In *Brookings*. https://www.brookings.edu/articles/theres-more-to-skills-based-hiring-than-just-removing-degree-requirements/

Gökçearslan, S., Tosun, C., & Erdemir, Z. G. (2024). Benefits, challenges, and methods of artificial intelligence (AI) chatbots in education: A systematic literature review. *International Journal of Technology in Education*, *7*(1), 19–39. DOI: 10.46328/ijte.600

Goktas, P., & Grzybowski, A. (2025). Shaping the Future of Healthcare: Ethical Clinical Challenges and Pathways to Trustworthy AI. *Journal of Clinical Medicine*, *14*(5), 1605. DOI: 10.3390/jcm14051605 PMID: 40095575

González-Calatayud, V., Prendes-Espinosa, P., & Roig-Vila, R. (2021). Artificial intelligence for student assessment: A systematic review. *Applied Sciences (Basel, Switzerland)*, *11*(12), 5467. Advance online publication. DOI: 10.3390/app11125467

Goodfellow, I., Bengio, Y., & Courville, A. (2016). Deep Learning. MIT Press. https://mitpress.mit.edu/9780262035613/deep-learning/

Goodier, M. (2025). Revealed: Thousands of UK university students caught cheating using AI. In *the Guardian*. The Guardian. https://www.theguardian.com/education/2025/jun/15/thousands-of-uk-university-students-caught-cheating-using-ai-artificial-intelligence-survey

Goosen, L., & Koekemoer, A. (2011). Pre-Service Teachers' Attitudes Towards Effective Teaching And Meaningful Learning In Technology Education. In Mogari, D., Mji, A., & Ogbonnaya, U. I. (Eds.), *Proceedings of the ISTE International Conference* (pp. 382–394). Unisa Press., Retrieved from http://uir.unisa.ac.za/bitstream/handle/10500/22467/L.%20Goosen%20&%20%20A.%20Koekemoer.pdf?seque

Gourlay, L., Rodríguez-Illera, J. L., Barberà, E., Bali, M., Gachago, D., Pallitt, N., Jones, C., Bayne, S., Hansen, S. B., Hrastinski, S., Jaldemark, J., Themelis, C., Pischetola, M., Dirckinck-Holmfeld, L., Matthews, A., Gulson, K. N., Lee, K., Bligh, B., Thibaut, P., & Knox, J. (2021). Networked Learning in 2021: A Community Definition. *Postdigital Science and Education*, *3*(2), 326–369. DOI: 10.1007/s42438-021-00222-y PMID: 40477233

Gouseti, A., James, F., Fallin, L., & Burden, K. (2024). The ethics of using AI in K-12 education: A systematic literature review. *Technology, Pedagogy and Education*, *34*(2), 161–182. DOI: 10.1080/1475939X.2024.2428601

Goyal, S. (2025). A Critical Review of Agentic AI: Core Technologies, Applications, Ethical Implications, and Future Research Directions. *Jurnal Masyarakat Informatika*, *16*(2), 268–283. DOI: 10.14710/jmasif.16.2.77084

Graesser, A. C., Conley, M. W., & Olney, A. (2012). Intelligent tutoring systems. In Harris, K. R., Graham, S., Urdan, T., Bus, A. G., Major, S., & Swanson, H. L. (Eds.), APA educational psychology handbook: Vol. 3. *Application to learning and teaching* (pp. 451–473). American Psychological Association., DOI: 10.1037/13275-018

Graesser, A., Chipman, P., Haynes, B., & Olney, A. (2005). AutoTutor: An intelligent tutoring system with Mixed-Initiative dialogue. *IEEE Transactions on Education*, *48*(4), 612–618. DOI: 10.1109/TE.2005.856149

Grájeda, A., Burgos, J., Córdova, P., & Sanjinés, A. (2024). Assessing student-perceived impact of using artificial intelligence tools: Construction of a synthetic index of application in higher education. *Cogent Education*, *11*(1), 2287917. DOI: 10.1080/2331186X.2023.2287917

Grubaugh, S., Levitt, G., & Deever, D. (2023). Harnessing AI to power constructivist learning: An evolution in educational methodologies. *EIKI Journal of Effective Teaching Methods*, *1*(3). Advance online publication. DOI: 10.59652/jetm.v1i3.43

GSMA. (2023a). *The Mobile Gender Gap Report*. https://www.gsma.com/r/gender-gap/

GSMA. (2023b). *The State of Mobile Internet Connectivity 2023*. www.gsmaintelligence.com

Gudipati, M. R. (2025, November). Agentic AI: A Tool-Guided Approach to Achieving Precision in Engineering Numerical Operations. In *Abu Dhabi International Petroleum Exhibition and Conference* (p. D021S081R007). SPE. DOI: 10.2118/229446-MS

Gudyanga, R. (2020). Probing physical sciences teachers' chemical laboratory safety awareness in some South African high schools. *African Journal of Research in Mathematics. Science and Technology Education*, *24*(3), 423–434.

Guettala, M., Bourekkache, S., Kazar, O., & Harous, S. (2024). Generative artificial intelligence in education: Advancing adaptive and personalized learning. *Acta Informatica Pragensia*, *13*(3), 460–489. DOI: 10.18267/j.aip.235

Guo, S., Zheng, Y., & Zhai, X. (2024). Artificial intelligence in education research during 2013–2023: A review based on bibliometric analysis. *Education and Information Technologies*, *29*(13), 16387–16409. DOI: 10.1007/s10639-024-12491-8

Gupta, D., & Benila, S. (2025). Attention-Guided U-Net With Grad-CAM for Explainable Polyp Segmentation in Colonoscopy Images. *IEEE Access : Practical Innovations, Open Solutions*, *13*, 185125–185136. DOI: 10.1109/ACCESS.2025.3626159

Gutierrez, S. S. M., Pérez, S. L., & Munguía, M. G. (2022). Artificial Intelligence in e-Learning Plausible Scenarios in Latin America and New Graduation Competencies. *IEEE Revista Iberoamericana de Technologias del Aprendizaje*, *17*(1), 31–40. DOI: 10.1109/RITA.2022.3149833

Hadi Mogavi, R., Deng, C., Juho Kim, J., Zhou, P., & Kwon, D., Y., Hosny Saleh Metwally, A., Tlili, A., Bassanelli, S., Bucchiarone, A., Gujar, S., Nacke, L. E., & Hui, P. (. (2024). ChatGPT in education: A blessing or a curse? A qualitative study exploring early adopters' utilization and perceptions. *Computers in Human Behavior: Artificial Humans*, *2*(1), 100027. DOI: 10.1016/j.chbah.2023.100027

Hadick, M. (n.d.). *Scaffolding Autonomy: Designing for Trust and Learning in AI-Supported Autodidactic Environments.*

Halagatti, M., Gadag, S., Mahantshetti, S., Hiremath, C. V., Tharkude, D., & Banakar, V. (2023). Artificial intelligence: the new tool of disruption in educational performance assessment. In *Smart analytics, artificial intelligence and sustainable performance management in a global digitalised economy* (Vol. 110, pp. 261–287). Emerald Publishing Limited., Retrieved from https://www.emerald.com/books/edited-volume/15334/chapter-abstract/86524842/Artificial-Intelligence-The-New-Tool-of-Disruption?redirectedFrom=fulltext DOI: 10.1108/S1569-37592023000110A014

Han, P.-C. (2025). Artificial intelligence in education. In *Advances in computational intelligence and robotics* (pp. 387–408). IGI Global. DOI: 10.4018/979-8-3373-5102-5.ch014

Handley, H. (2023). Best practices for using online interactive whiteboards. *The journal of applied instructional design, 12*(4), 57-73.

Hariyanto, H., Studi Pendidikan Profesi Guru, P., Dharmacarya, J., Tinggi Agama Buddha Negeri Raden Wijaya Wonogiri, S., Bahasa dan Seni, F., Studi Pendidikan Seni Musik, P., Negeri Sunan Kudus, I., Xaveria Diah Kristianingsih, F., & Maharani, R. (2025). Artificial intelligence in adaptive education: a systematic review of techniques for personalized learning. *Discover Education 2025 4:1, 4*(1), 458-. DOI: 10.1007/s44217-025-00908-6

Hashim, A. S., Awadh, W. A., & Hamoud, A. K. (2020). Student Performance Prediction Model based on Supervised Machine Learning Algorithms. *IOP Conference Series. Materials Science and Engineering, 928*(3), 032019. DOI: 10.1088/1757-899X/928/3/032019

Hattie, J., & Timperley, H. (2007). The power of feedback. *Review of Educational Research, 77*(1), 81–112. DOI: 10.3102/003465430298487

Hawkinson, E. (2025). Convergence of AR, VR and AI: The rise of immersive learning technologies in higher education. *Extended Reality, AI, and Discursive Formations, 21*, 21–34. DOI: 10.1145/3371647.3371667

Heasman, B., Williams, G., Charura, D., Hamilton, L. G., Milton, D., & Murray, F. (2024). Towards autistic flow theory: A non-pathologising conceptual approach. *Journal for the Theory of Social Behaviour, 54*(4), 469–497. DOI: 10.1111/jtsb.12427

Heffernan, N. T., & Heffernan, C. L. (2014). The Assessments Ecosystem: Building a Platform that Brings Scientists and Teachers Together for Minimally Invasive Research on Human Learning and Teaching. *International Journal of Artificial Intelligence in Education, 24*(4), 470–497. DOI: 10.1007/s40593-014-0024-x

Heinrich, E. (2025). A Systematic-Narrative Review of Online Proctoring Systems and a Case for Open Standards. *Open Praxis, 17*(3). Advance online publication. DOI: 10.55982/openpraxis.17.3.836

Hemmler, Y. M., & Ifenthaler, D. (2024). Self-regulated learning strategies in continuing education: A systematic review and meta-analysis. *Educational Research Review, 45*, 100629. DOI: 10.1016/j.edurev.2024.100629

Heritage, M. (2010). *Formative assessment: Making it happen in the classroom.* Corwin.

Herrera-Ramírez, J. A., Treviño-Villalobos, M., & Víquez-Acuña, L. (2021). Hybrid storage engine for geospatial data using NoSQL and SQL paradigms. *Tecnología en Marcha, 34*(1), 40–54. DOI: 10.18845/tm.v34i1.4822

He, W. (2024). Application and development trends of artificial intelligence in education. *Journal of Education and Educational Research, 10*(1), 157–160. DOI: 10.54097/bf5qzn92

Hoidn, S. (2016). Constructivist foundations and common design principles of student-centered learning environments. In *The pedagogy of higher education* (pp. 23–103). Palgrave Macmillan., DOI: 10.1057/978-1-349-94941-0_2

Ho, K. H., Hou, Y., Chu, C. C., Chan, C. K., Pan, H., & Chan, T. T. (2023). Work in progress: An AI-assisted metaverse for computer science education. *In Proceedings of the 2023 IEEE World Engineering Education Conference* (pp. 12-15). Bogota, Colombia: IEEE. DOI: 10.1109/EDUNINE57531.2023.10102819

Holmberg, J. (2017). Applying a conceptual design framework to study teachers' use of educational technology. *Education and Information Technologies*, *22*(5), 2333–2349. DOI: 10.1007/s10639-016-9536-3

Holmes, W., Bialik, M., & Fadel, C. (2019). Artificial Intelligence in Education: Promises and Implications for Teaching and Learning. Center for Curriculum Redesign. https://discovery.ucl.ac.uk/id/eprint/10139722/

Holmes, W., Bialik, M., & Fadel, C. (2019). *Artificial intelligence in education promises and implications for teaching and learning*. Center for Curriculum Redesign.

Holmes, W., Porayska-Pomsta, K., Holstein, K., Sutherland, E., Baker, T., Shum, S. B., Santos, O. C., Rodrigo, M. T., Cukurova, M., Bittencourt, I. I., & Koedinger, K. R. (2022). Ethics of AI in Education: Towards a Community-Wide Framework. *International Journal of Artificial Intelligence in Education*, *32*(3), 504–526. DOI: 10.1007/s40593-021-00239-1

Holstein, K., Aleven, V., & Rummel, N. (2020). A conceptual framework for human–AI hybrid adaptivity in education. In *Lecture notes in computer science* (pp. 240–254). Springer. DOI: 10.1007/978-3-030-52237-7_20

Hoque, M. R. (2020). The impact of the ICT4D project on sustainable rural development using a capability approach: Evidence from Bangladesh. *Technology in Society*, *61*, 101254. DOI: 10.1016/j.techsoc.2020.101254

Horvat, S., Horvat, T., Havaš, L., & Crčič, D. (2025). AI-powered chatbots for enhancing accessibility in higher education - design and implementation. *Elektrotehniski Vestnik, 92*(1/2), 61-67. https://go.openathens.net/redirector/liberty.edu?url=https://www.proquest.com/scholarly-journals/ai-powered-chatbots-enhancing-accessibility/docview/3203965895/se-2

Hosseini, S., & Seilani, H. (2025). The role of agentic ai in shaping a smart future: A systematic review. *Array (New York, N.Y.)*, *26*, 100399. DOI: 10.1016/j.array.2025.100399

Hu, C., Zhang, L., Lim, Y., Wadhwani, A., Peters, A., & Kang, D. (2025, July). REPRO-BENCH: Can Agentic AI Systems Assess the Reproducibility of Social Science Research? In *Findings of the Association for Computational Linguistics: ACL 2025* (pp. 23616-23626).

Huang, R., Spector, J. M., & Yang, J. (2019). Educational technology. In Lecture notes in educational technology. https://doi.org/DOI: 10.1007/978-981-13-6643-7

Huang, C., Zhang, Z., Mao, B., & Yao, X. (2023). An Overview of Artificial Intelligence Ethics. *IEEE Transactions on Artificial Intelligence*, *4*(4), 799–819. DOI: 10.1109/TAI.2022.3194503

Huang, K. (2025). The Genesis and Evolution of AI Agents. In Agentic, A. I. (Ed.), *Theories and Practices* (pp. 1–22). Springer Nature Switzerland. DOI: 10.1007/978-3-031-90026-6_1

Huang, L., & Wang, Y. (2023). From engagement to immersion: A self-determination theory and approach to gamified cultural tourism. *Emerging Technologies and Future of Work*, *117*, 277–288. DOI: 10.54941/ahfe1004428

Huang, S., Lai, X., Ke, L., Li, Y., Wang, H., Zhao, X., Dai, X., & Wang, Y. (2024). AI Technology panic—Is AI Dependence Bad for Mental Health? A Cross-Lagged Panel Model and the Mediating Roles of Motivations for AI Use Among Adolescents. *Psychology Research and Behavior Management, 17*(0), 1087–1102. DOI: 10.2147/PRBM.S440889 PMID: 38495087

Hughes, L., Dwivedi, Y. K., Li, K., Appanderanda, M., Al-Bashrawi, M. A., & Chae, I. (2025). AI Agents and Agentic Systems: Redefining Global it Management. *Journal of Global Information Technology Management, 28*(3), 1–11. DOI: 10.1080/1097198X.2025.2524286

Hughes, L., Dwivedi, Y. K., Malik, T., Shawosh, M., Albashrawi, M. A., Jeon, I., Dutot, V., Appanderanda, M., Crick, T., De', R., Fenwick, M., Gunaratnege, S. M., Jurcys, P., Kar, A. K., Kshetri, N., Li, K., Mutasa, S., Samothrakis, S., Wade, M., & Walton, P. (2025). AI agents and agentic systems: A multi-expert analysis. *Journal of Computer Information Systems, 65*(4), 1–29. DOI: 10.1080/08874417.2025.2483832

Hung, W. (2014). Intrinsic and extrinsic intentional learning: The difference made by self-determination. *Australian Journal of Education, 58*(1), 50–58. DOI: 10.1177/0004944113517832

Huot, S., & Loch, S. (2025a). Digital practices in Cambodian EFL classrooms: Teacher narratives from remote learning. In K. Khette & Tayade (Eds.), *Proceeding of one day national conference on English language, literature, cultural studies and media studies* (Vol. 2, pp. 19–31). Centre for Learning, Research and Development, Savda, Maharashtra. DOI: 10.5281/zenodo.16921807

Huot, S., & Loch, S. (2025b). From rote to reflective: Integrating ChatGPT to transform learning outcomes in Cambodian education. *International Journal of Language and Literary Studies, 7*(4), 1–15. DOI: 10.36892/ijlls.v7i4.2188

Huot, S., Loch, S., Nget, R., & Em, S. (2025). Exploring multiliteracies in the digital era: A framework for 21st-century learning. [CJESS]. *Cambodian Journal of Educational and Social Sciences, 2*(1), 7–27. DOI: 10.69496/cjess.v2i1.50

Huot, S., & Such, C. (2025). Leveraging social media for language learning: Opportunities and challenges. [JEILT]. *Journal of Education Innovation and Language Teaching, 1*(2), 10–29. DOI: 10.63381/jeilt.v1i2.56

Huot, S., & Tep, P. (2025). Advancing ChatGPT for pedagogical innovation in Cambodia: Insight from global evidence and local implications. *The Context: Journal of English Studies, 12*(4), 115–135. DOI: 10.5281/zenodo.15806972

Huo, W., Yuan, X., Li, X., Luo, W., Xie, J., & Shi, B. (2023). Increasing acceptance of medical AI: The role of medical staff participation in AI development. *International Journal of Medical Informatics, 175*, 105073. DOI: 10.1016/j.ijmedinf.2023.105073 PMID: 37119693

Hussein, H. A., Ahmed, A. M., Shawkat, S. A., & Kamil, R. A. (2022, November). The effect of using smart board technology on the educational process in the colleges of education in terms of features and challenges. *AIP Conference Proceedings. 2394.* AIP Publishing LLC. DOI: 10.1063/5.0122282

Hwang, G. J., & Chang, C. C. (2024). A self-determination theory-based digital gaming approach to enhancing EFL learners' competence in applying professional English. *Educational Technology Research and Development, 73*(2), 1205–1223. DOI: 10.1007/s11423-024-10445-y

IEEE. (2019). *Ethically aligned design: A vision for prioritizing human well-being with autonomous and intelligent systems*. IEEE Global Initiative on Ethics of Autonomous and Intelligent Systems. https://standards.ieee.org/wp-content/uploads/import/documents/other/ead1e.pdf

Ifenthaler, D. (2025). Information processing re-visited: Reciprocal perspectives on artificial intelligence and human-centered systems. *AI-Enhanced Learning*, *1*(1), 229–243. DOI: 10.70725/465418kgasdx

Ifenthaler, D., Gibson, D., Prasse, D., Shimada, A., & Yamada, M. (2020). Putting learning back into learning analytics: Actions for policy makers, researchers, and practitioners. *Educational Technology Research and Development*, *69*(4), 2131–2150. DOI: 10.1007/s11423-020-09909-8

Ifenthaler, D., Majumdar, R., Gorissen, P., Judge, M., Mishra, S., Raffaghelli, J., & Shimada, A. (2024). Artificial intelligence in education: Implications for policymakers, researchers, and practitioners. *Technology. Knowledge and Learning*, *29*(4), 1693–1710. DOI: 10.1007/s10758-024-09747-0

Igboanugo, B. I., Egolum, E. O., & Igboegwu, E. N. (2021, November). Reducing The Abstract Nature Of Chemistry Through Science-Technology-Society Instructional Approach. *South Africa International Conference on Education Proceedings* (pp. 57-64). African Academic Research Forum.

Illi, C., & Elhassouny, A. (2025). Edu-Metaverse: A comprehensive review of virtual learning environments. *IEEE Access : Practical Innovations, Open Solutions*, *13*, 30186–30210. DOI: 10.1109/ACCESS.2025.3540944

Imran, M., Almusharraf, N., Abdellatif, M. S., & Abbasova, M. Y. (2024). Artificial intelligence in higher education: Enhancing learning systems and transforming educational paradigms. *International Journal of Interactive Mobile Technologies*, *18*(18), 34–48. DOI: 10.3991/ijim.v18i18.49143

International Education Accreditation Council. (2025). Examining the Effect of Accreditation Challenges on Educational Quality and Global Recognition. In *Ieac.org.uk*. https://www.ieac.org.uk/53-Examining-the-Effect-of-Accreditation-Challenges-on-Educational-Quality-and-Global-Recognition-blog.php

Ion, T., & Popescu, E. (2024). An innovative distance learning platform for mathematics education in secondary schools: Design, development and preliminary studies. *Education and Information Technologies*, *30*(5), 5529–5560. DOI: 10.1007/s10639-024-13040-z

Iqbal, M., Khan, N. U., & Imran, M. (2024). The role of artificial intelligence (AI) in transforming educational practices: Opportunities, challenges, and implications. *Qlantic Journal of Social Sciences*, *5*(2), 348–359. DOI: 10.55737/qjss.349319430

Istrate, O. (2024). AI agents in education: An early systematic review of emerging roles, potential, and limitations. *Revista de Pedagogie Digitală*, *3*(1), 24–30. DOI: 10.61071/RPD.2496

Ivanashko, O., Kozak, A., Knysh, T., & Honchar, K. (2024). The role of artificial intelligence in shaping the future of education: Opportunities and challenges. *Futurity Education*, *4*(1), 126–146.

Jaaska, E., Lehtinen, J., Kujala, J., & Kauppila, O. (2022). Game-based learning and students' motivation in project management education. *Project Leadership and Society*, *3*, 100055. DOI: 10.1016/j.plas.2022.100055

Jafari, F., & Keykha, A. (2024). Identifying the opportunities and challenges of artificial intelligence in higher education: A qualitative study. *Journal of Applied Research in Higher Education*, *16*(4), 1228–1245. DOI: 10.1108/JARHE-09-2023-0426

Jagatheesaperumal, S. K., Ahmad, K., Al-Fuqaha, A., & Qadir, J. (2024). Advancing education through extended reality and internet of everything enabled metaverse: Applications, challenges, and open issues. *IEEE Transactions on Learning Technologies*, *17*, 1120–1139. DOI: 10.1109/TLT.2024.3358859

Jaggavarapu, M. K. R. (2025). The evolution of agentic ai: Architecture and workflows for autonomous systems. *Journal Of Multidisciplinary*, *5*(7), 418–427.

Jammeh, A. L., Karegeya, C., & Ladage, S. (2022). The Smartboard in Chemistry Classrooms: What is Its Effect on Chemistry Teaching and Learning in Selected Topics in Grade 11? *International Journal of Learning. Teaching and Educational Research*, *21*(9), 217–231.

Jang, E. E., & Sawaki, Y. (2025). Advancing language assessment for teaching and learning in the era of the artificial intelligence revolution: Promises and challenges. *Language Testing*, *42*(4), 02655322251348685. DOI: 10.1177/02655322251348685

Jang, Y., Choi, S., Jung, H., & Kim, H. (2022). Practical early prediction of students' performance using machine learning and eXplainable AI. *Education and Information Technologies*, *34*(9), 274–300. DOI: 10.1007/s10639-022-11120-6

Jaradeh, M. Y., & Auer, S. (2025). Deep Research in the Era of Agentic AI: Requirements and Limitations for Scholarly Research. In *CEUR Workshop Proceedings* (Vol. 4065).

Jatileni, C. N., Sanusi, I. T., Olaleye, S. A., Ayanwale, M. A., Agbo, F. J., & Oyelere, P. B. (2024). Artificial intelligence in compulsory level of education: Perspectives from Namibian in-service teachers. *Education and Information Technologies*, *29*(10), 12569–12596. DOI: 10.1007/s10639-023-12341-z

Jeong, H. (2025). From curriculum to strategy: Tracing shifts in AI Education policy in South Korea through keyword and topic analysis. *Asia Pacific Journal of Education*, •••, 1–30. DOI: 10.1080/02188791.2025.2580988

Jeong, Y., Lee, Y., Bryun, G., & Moon, J. (2024). Navigating the creation of immersive learning environments in Roblox: Integrating generative AI for enhanced simulation-based learning. *In Proceedings of the 10th International Conference of the Immersive Learning Research Network* (pp. 1-4). Glasgow, United Kingdom: iLRN. DOI: 10.56198/5M1RHT9ZJ

Jho, H. (2024). Learning beyond boundaries: Addressing the transformative and challenging impacts of artificial intelligence on education. *Preprints*. DOI: 10.20944/preprints202408.1788.v1

Jiang, Y. H., Li, R., Zhou, Y., Qi, C., Hu, H., Wei, Y., . . . Wu, Y. (2024). Ai agent for education: von neumann multi-agent system framework. *arXiv preprint arXiv:2501.00083*.

Jiang, Y. (2025). Interaction and dialogue: Integration and application of artificial intelligence in blended mode writing feedback. *The Internet and Higher Education*, *64*, 100975. Advance online publication. DOI: 10.1016/j.iheduc.2024.100975

Jie, Z., & Sunze, Y. (2023). Investigating pedagogical challenges of mobile technology to English teaching. *Interactive Learning Environments*, *31*(5), 2767–2779. DOI: 10.1080/10494820.2021.1903933

Jin, W., Du, H., Zhao, B., Tian, X., Shi, B., & Yang, G. (2025). A comprehensive survey on multi-agent cooperative decision-making: Scenarios, approaches, challenges and perspectives. *arXiv preprint arXiv:2503.13415*. DOI: 10.2139/ssrn.5106265

Jin, F. J., Yan, L., Martinez-Maldonado, R., Gašević, D., Chan, P. W. K., & Tsai, Y. (2025). Latent classes of self-reported feedback experiences: Exploring students' challenges, motivations, and action-taking behaviours in feedback processes. *Instructional Science*, *53*(6), 1395–1427. DOI: 10.1007/s11251-025-09744-5

Joel Augustus, D., Asiegbu Victor, I., & Obinna, E. (2025). Leveraging artificial intelligence (AI) for educational development in Nigeria: Examining the challenges and opportunities. *Journal of Social Sciences*, *2*(2).

Johannes Cronje. (n.d.). *Exploring_the_Role_of_ChatGPT*.

Johnson, L. S, A. B., Estrada, V., & Freeman, A. (2016). The NMC Horizon Report: 2015 Higher Education Edition. https://eric.ed.gov/?id=ED559357

Joshi, A. (2021). Understanding '5 Gogy': Pedagogy, Andragogy, Peeragogy, Heutagogy, and Cybergogy. *Cummins College Digest of Engineering Education*(2). Retrieved from https://cumminscollege.org/wp-content/uploads/2023/04/2.-CCDEE_Issue-2-2021.pdf#page=7

Juan, H., & Nagappan, R. (2025). A comprehensive literature review on AI-enhanced autonomous learning mechanisms in vocational education. *Malaysian Journal of Social Sciences and Humanities*, *10*(3), e002958. DOI: 10.47405/mjssh.v10i3.2958

Jung, I. (2019). Connectivism and networked learning. In *Springer briefs in education* (pp. 47–55). Springer., DOI: 10.1007/978-981-13-7740-2_6

Jung, L. A., & Guskey, T. R. (2007). Standards-based grading and reporting: A model for special education. *Teaching Exceptional Children*, *40*(2), 48–53. https://eric.ed.gov/?id=EJ849801 and https://eric.ed.gov/?id=EJ849801. DOI: 10.1177/004005990704000206

Júnior, J. F. C., Lins, P. P. M., de Oliveira, A. P. S., Ruas, G. C. R., Neto, R. A. D. R., Moraes, L. S., de Barros, M. J., Martins, P. C. M., Lopes, L. C. L., Schimidt, M. Q., Giese, W., & Santos, I. B. D. (2025). Algorithms vs. autonomy: The risks of dependence on AI in the critical training of students. In *Seven Editora eBooks*. DOI: 10.56238/sevened2025.026-014

Kahn, P., Carrigan, M., Smith, P., Murtagh, L., Liu, R., & Song, F. (2025). Teacher agency and generative artificial intelligence: Teaching in higher education as a responsive, cultural activity. *Learning, Media and Technology*, •••, 1–12. DOI: 10.1080/17439884.2025.2575993

Kalim, U., Kanwar, A., Sha, J., & Huang, R. (2025). Barriers to AI adoption for women in higher education: a systematic review of the Asian context. *Smart Learning Environments 2025 12:1*, *12*(1), 38-. DOI: 10.1186/s40561-025-00390-5

Kambala, Y. J., & Mathe, R. (2022). Importance of smart classroom: A study. *Journal of Multidisciplinary Research, 2*(1), 25–35. DOI: 10.37022/tjmdr.v1i2.280

Kanumolu, G., Urlana, A., Charaka, V. K., & Garlapati, B. M. (2025). Agent ideate: A framework for product idea generation from patents using agentic ai. In *Proceedings of the 2nd Workshop on Agent AI for Scenario Planning* (pp. 50-57).

Karakose, T., & Tülübas, T. (2024). School Leadership and Management in the Age of Artificial Intelligence (AI): Recent Developments and Future Prospects. *Educational Process: International Journal, 13*(1), 7–14. DOI: 10.22521/edupij.2024.131.1

Karataş, F., Eriçok, B., & Tanrikulu, L. (2025). Reshaping curriculum adaptation in the age of artificial intelligence: Mapping teachers' AI-driven curriculum adaptation patterns. *British Educational Research Journal, 51*(1), 154–180. DOI: 10.1002/berj.4068

Kar, S. K., Bansal, T., Modi, S., & Singh, A. (2024). How Sensitive Are the Free AI-detector Tools in Detecting AI-generated Texts? A Comparison of Popular AI-detector Tools. *Indian Journal of Psychological Medicine, 47*(3), 275–278. DOI: 10.1177/02537176241247934 PMID: 39564235

Karunanayake, N. (2025). Next-generation agentic AI for transforming healthcare. *Informatics and Health, 2*(2), 73–83. DOI: 10.1016/j.infoh.2025.03.001

Kasneci, E., Seßler, K., Küchemann, S., Bannert, M., Dementieva, D., Fischer, F., Gasser, U., Groh, G., Günnemann, S., Hüllermeier, E., Krusche, S., Kutyniok, G., Michaeli, T., Nerdel, C., Pfeffer, J., Poquet, O., Sailer, M., Schmidt, A., Seidel, T., & Kasneci, G. (2023). ChatGPT for good? On opportunities and challenges of large language models for education. *Learning and Individual Differences, 103*, 1–9. DOI: 10.1016/j.lindif.2023.102274

Katsamakas, E., & Pavlov, O. V. (2024). *Artificial Intelligence and the Transformation of Higher Education Institutions : A Systems Approach*. 1–21.

Katsamakas, E., Pavlov, O. V., & Saklad, R. (2024). Artificial intelligence and the transformation of higher education institutions: A systems approach. *Sustainability (Basel), 16*(14), 6118. DOI: 10.3390/su16146118

Katsenou, R., & Deliyannis, I. (2025). PROGRAMMING AS PLAY: A COLLABORATIVE AUTOETHNOGRAPHY ON AI LITERACY IN EDUCATION. *INTED Proceedings, 1*, 5661–5671. DOI: 10.21125/inted.2025.1448

Kaushal, V., Singh, B., & Devi, S. (2023). *Digital Literacy In India: Benefits and Challenges*. http://cok.pratibha-spandan.org

Kayyali, M. (2024). The future of AI in education. In *Advances in educational technologies and instructional design* (pp. 367–406). IGI Global. DOI: 10.4018/979-8-3693-7220-3.ch013

Kayyali, M. (2025). Generative AI and education. In *Advances in computational intelligence and robotics* (pp. 25–52). IGI Global. DOI: 10.4018/979-8-3693-8332-2.ch002

Kazanidis, I., & Pellas, N. (2024). Harnessing generative artificial intelligence for digital literacy innovation: A comparative study between early childhood education and computer science undergraduates. *AI*, *5*(3), 1427–1445. DOI: 10.3390/ai5030068

Kennedy, A. I., Mejía-Rodríguez, A. M., & Strello, A. (2022a). Inequality in remote learning quality during COVID-19: Student perspectives and mitigating factors. *Large-Scale Assessments in Education*, *10*(1), 1–31. DOI: 10.1186/s40536-022-00143-7 PMID: 36590105

Kennedy, I., & Cronjé, J. (2023). The dynamics of access to ICT and technology practices of secondary school teachers. *Electronic Journal of e-Learning*, *21*(3), 200–210. DOI: 10.34190/ejel.21.3.2999

Kestin, G., Miller, K., Klales, A., Milbourne, T., & Ponti, G. (2025). AI tutoring outperforms in-class active learning: An RCT introducing a novel research-based design in an authentic educational setting. *Scientific Reports*, *15*(1), 17458. DOI: 10.1038/s41598-025-97652-6

Khairnar, C. M. (2015). Advance pedagogy: Innovative methods of teaching and learning. *International Journal of Information and Education Technology (IJIET)*, *5*(11), 869–872. DOI: 10.7763/IJIET.2015.V5.629

Khan Academy. (n.d.-a). *Khanmigo for learners: Always-available tutor, powered by AI.* Https://Www.Khanmigo.Ai/. Retrieved December 9, 2025, from https://www.khanmigo.ai/learners

Khan Academy. (n.d.-b). *Meet Khanmigo: Khan Academy's AI-powered teaching and learning companion*. Khanmigo.Ai. Retrieved December 9, 2025, from https://www.khanmigo.ai/

Khan, B. F., & Ahmed, S. (2025). An agile approach for collaborative inquiry-based learning in ubiquitous environment. *International Journal of Advanced Computer Science and Applications*, *16*(1), 323–333. DOI: 10.14569/IJACSA.2025.0160132

Khan, W., Kumar, T., Zhang, C., Raj, K., Roy, A. M., & Luo, B. (2023). SQL and NoSQL database software architecture performance analysis and assessments—A systematic literature review. *Big Data and Cognitive Computing*, *7*(2), 97. DOI: 10.3390/bdcc7020097

Khatibi, M., & Fouladchang, M. (2015). Connectivism: A review. *International Journal of Indian Psychology*, *2*(4). Advance online publication. DOI: 10.25215/0204.049

Khlaif, Z. N., Salha, S., & Kouraichi, B. (2021). Emergency remote learning during COVID-19 crisis: Students' engagement. *Education and Information Technologies*, *26*(6), 7033–7055. DOI: 10.1007/s10639-021-10566-4

Khodadad, D. (2023). Creating a supportive and effective learning environment for engineering students. [iJEP]. *International Journal of Engineering Pedagogy*, *13*(8), 33–50. DOI: 10.3991/ijep.v13i8.41755

Khosravi, H., Buckingham Shum, S., Chen, G., Conati, C., Tsai, Y.-S., Kay, J., Knight, S., Martínez-Maldonado, R., Sadiq, S., & Gašević, D. (2022). Explainable artificial intelligence in education. *Computers & Education: Artificial Intelligence*, *3*, 100074. Advance online publication. DOI: 10.1016/j.caeai.2022.100074

Khosrawi-Rad, B., Grogorick, L., Janson, A., Keller, P., Benner, D., & Robra-Bissantz, S. (2025). Let's play with AI! A 2x2 experiment on collaborative vs. competitive game elements for pedagogical conversational agents. In *Proceedings of the SIGSVC Pre-ICIS Workshop 2024. 4* (pp. 1–14). ACM., Retrieved from https://aisel.aisnet.org/sprouts_proceedings_sigsvc_2024/4/

Khreisat, M. N., Khilani, D., Rusho, M. A., Karkkulainen, E. A., Tabuena, A. C., & Uberas, A. D. (2024). Ethical implications of AI integration in educational decision making: Systematic review. *Educational Administration: Theory and Practice*, *30*(5), 8521–8527.

Khun, J. (2026). *Color-coded conceptual framework for AI-enabled gamified independent learning* [Figure 2]. In *Customizing playful education through gamification: AR/VR and immersive agents to enhance learning* (book proposal). National University.

Khurana, A., Gawshinde, S., & Shaheen, M. (2025). The Intersection of Neuromarketing and Ethical Consumerism in Sustainable Finance. In *Strategic Blueprints for AI-Driven Marketing in the Digital Era* (pp. 461–494). IGI Global Scientific Publishing. DOI: 10.4018/979-8-3373-3897-2.ch014

Kim, B.-J., Jeong, S., Cho, B.-K., & Chung, J.-B. (2025). AI Governance in the Context of the EU AI Act. *IEEE Access : Practical Innovations, Open Solutions*, *13*, 144126–144142. DOI: 10.1109/ACCESS.2025.3598023

Kim, H., Han, B., Kim, J., Lubis, M. F. S., Kim, G. J., & Hwang, J.-I. (2024). Engaged and affective virtual agents: Their impact on social presence, trustworthiness, and decision-making in the group discussion. In Mueller, F. F., Kyburz, P., Williamson, J. R., Sas, C., Wilson, M. L., Dugas, P. T., & Shklovski, I. (Eds.), *Proceedings of the 2024 CHI conference on human factors in computing systems* (pp. 1–17). Association for Computing Machinery, New York, NY, United States. DOI: 10.1145/3613904.3642917

Kim, Y., & Baylor, A. L. (2006). A social-cognitive framework for pedagogical agents as learning companions. *Educational Technology Research and Development*, *54*(6), 569–596. DOI: 10.1007/s11423-006-0637-3

Kiškis, M. (2023). Legal framework for the coexistence of humans and conscious AI. *Frontiers in Artificial Intelligence*, *6*, 1205465. DOI: 10.3389/frai.2023.1205465 PMID: 37808620

Kizil, V. (2019). Peer assessment in EFL writing classes. *The Journal of International Lingual Social and Educational Sciences*, *5*(1), 101–111. DOI: 10.34137/jilses.560099

Klinck-Van der Merwe, R., & Goosen, L. (2024). A Framework for Online Learning Analytics in K-12 Classrooms as a Precursor for Personalized Learning: Emergent Practices in Schools. In *Emergent Practices of Learning Analytics in K-12 Classrooms* (pp. 115–141). IGI Global., DOI: 10.4018/979-8-3693-0066-4.ch0067

Klinck-van der Merwe, R., & Goosen, L. (2025). Artificial Intelligence Algorithms as a Precursor for Personalized Learning and Education: Real-World Applications of Innovation. In Mallik, S., Mathivanan, S., Sangeetha, S., & Soufiene, B. (Eds.), *Real-World Applications of AI Innovation* (pp. 175–198). IGI Global Scientific Publishing., DOI: 10.4018/979-8-3693-4252-7.ch009

Knowles, M. S. (1975). *Self-directed learning* (Vol. 291). Association Press New York.

Knox, J. (2025). Educational development in the postdigital era. In Peters, M. A., Green, B. J., Kamenarac, O., Jandrić, P., & Besley, T. (Eds.), *The geopolitics of postdigital educational development* (pp. 21–40). Springer., DOI: 10.1007/978-3-031-99378-7_2

Köbis, L., & Mehner, C. (2021). Ethical Questions Raised by AI-Supported Mentoring in Higher Education. *Frontiers in Artificial Intelligence*, *4*, 624050. Advance online publication. DOI: 10.3389/frai.2021.624050 PMID: 33997774

Komaragiri, V. B. (2025). Agentic AI for Autonomous Network Orchestration: A New Frontier in Telecommunications. *EKSPLORIUM-BULETIN PUSAT TEKNOLOGI BAHAN GALIAN NUKLIR*, *46*(1), 221–241.

Kong, S. C., Korte, S. M., Burton, S., Keskitalo, P., Turunen, T., Smith, D., Wang, L., Lee, J. C.-K., & Beaton, M. C. (2025). Artificial Intelligence (AI) literacy–an argument for AI literacy in education. *Innovations in Education and Teaching International*, *62*(2), 477–483. DOI: 10.1080/14703297.2024.2332744

Kong, S. C., & Yang, Y. (2024). A human-centered learning and teaching framework using generative artificial intelligence for self-regulated learning development through domain knowledge learning in K–12 settings. *IEEE Transactions on Learning Technologies*, *17*, 1562–1573. DOI: 10.1109/TLT.2024.3392830

Kortemeyer, G. (2022). Self-Sovereign Identity User Scenarios in the Educational Domain. In er.educause.edu. Retrieved July 23, 2026, from https://er.educause.edu/articles/2022/4/self-sovereign-identity-user-scenarios-in-the-educational-domain

Kostopoulos, G., Gkamas, V., Rigou, M., & Kotsiantis, S. (2025). Agentic AI in Education: State of the Art and Future Directions. *IEEE Access : Practical Innovations, Open Solutions*, *13*, 177467–177491. DOI: 10.1109/ACCESS.2025.3620473

Kotlyar, I., & Krasman, J. (2025). Student reactions to AI versus human feedback in teamwork skills assessment. *International Journal of Educational Technology in Higher Education*, *22*(1), 57. Advance online publication. DOI: 10.1186/s41239-025-00555-9

Koutra, D., Huang, L., Kulkarni, A., Prioleau, T., Soh, B. W. Y., Wu, Q., . . . Zou, J. (2025). Towards Agentic AI for Science: Hypothesis Generation, Comprehension, Quantification, and Validation. In *ICLR 2025 Workshop Proposals*.

Kowald, D., Yang, D., & Lacic, E. (2024). Editorial: Reviews in recommender systems: 2022. *Frontiers in Big Data*, *7*, 1384460. DOI: 10.3389/fdata.2024.1384460

Kronenberg, F., & Poole, F. (2022). *From buzzword to the classroom – exploring VR gaming for language learning*. The FLTMAG., DOI: 10.69732/DHUI4343

Kshetri, N. (2025). Revolutionizing Higher Education: The Impact of Artificial Intelligence Agents and Agentic Artificial Intelligence on Teaching and Operations. *IT Professional*, *27*(2), 12–16. DOI: 10.1109/MITP.2025.3550697

Kucirkova, N. (2019). The learning value of personalization in children's reading recommendation systems: What can we learn from constructionism? *International Journal of Mobile and Blended Learning*, *11*(4), 1–15. DOI: 10.4018/IJMBL.2019100106

Kuhn, C., Khoo, S. M., Czerniewicz, L., Lilley, W., Bute, S., Crean, A., Abegglen, S., Burns, T., Sinfield, S., Jandrić, P., Knox, J., & MacKenzie, A. (2023). Understanding Digital Inequality: A Theoretical Kaleidoscope. *Postdigital Science and Education*, *5*(3), 894–932. DOI: 10.1007/s42438-023-00395-8 PMID: 40479087

Kuklick, L. (2025). Effects of learner choice over automated, immediate feedback. *Learning and Instruction*, *96*, 102065. DOI: 10.1016/j.learninstruc.2024.102065

Kumar, P., Mazrouei, B. S. A., Fayyaz, M. F., Jan, S. A., & Maysari, J. A. (2025, November). Realizing the Need for Agentic AI for Subsurface Data and Workflows. In *Abu Dhabi International Petroleum Exhibition and Conference* (p. D021S069R003). SPE. DOI: 10.2118/229586-MS

Kumar, S., Rao, P., Singhania, S., Verma, S., & Kheterpal, M. (2024). Will artificial intelligence drive the advancements in higher education? A tri-phased exploration. *Technological Forecasting and Social Change*, *201*, 123258. DOI: 10.1016/j.techfore.2024.123258

Kundu, A., & Bej, T. (2021). Ingestion and integration of ICTs for pedagogy in Indian private schools. *E-Learning and Digital Media*, *18*(2), 163–184. DOI: 10.1177/2042753020957493

Kyrlitsias, C., & Michael-Grigoriou, D. (2022). Social interaction with agents and avatars in immersive virtual environments: A survey. *Frontiers in Virtual Reality*, *2*, 1–13. DOI: 10.3389/frvir.2021.786665

Laine, T., & Lindberg, R. (2020). Designing engaging games for education: A systematic literature review on game motivators and design principles. *IEEE Transactions on Learning Technologies*, *13*(4), 804–821. DOI: 10.1109/TLT.2020.3018503

Lameras, P. (2022). A vision of teaching and learning with AI. In *Proceedings of the 2022 IEEE Global Engineering Education Conference (EDUCON)* (pp. 1796–1803). IEEE. DOI: 10.1109/EDUCON52537.2022.9766718

Lampropoulos, G. (2025). Combining artificial intelligence with augmented reality and virtual reality in education: Current trends and future perspectives. *Multimodal Technologies and Interaction*, *9*(11), 1–28. DOI: 10.3390/mti9020011

Lan, M., & Zhou, X. (2025). A qualitative systematic review on AI empowered self-regulated learning in higher education. npj Science of Learning, 10, 21. https://doi.org/DOI: 10.1038/s41539-025-00319-0

Lan, Y. (2024). Through tensions to identity-based motivations: Exploring teacher professional identity in Artificial Intelligence-enhanced teacher training. *Teaching and Teacher Education*, *151*, 104736. DOI: 10.1016/j.tate.2024.104736

Learn & Work Ecosystem Library. (2024). Fraudulent Credentials. In *Learn & Work Ecosystem Library*. https://learnworkecosystemlibrary.com/topics/fraudulent-credentials/

Lee, I.-J. (2021). Kinect-for-windows with augmented reality in an interactive roleplay system for children with an autism spectrum disorder. *Interactive Learning Environments*, *29*(4), 688–704. DOI: 10.1080/10494820.2019.1710851

Lee, Y. J., Davis, R. O., & Ryu, J. (2024). Korean in-service teachers' perceptions of implementing artificial intelligence (AI) education for teaching in schools and their AI teacher training programs. *International Journal of Information and Education Technology (IJIET)*, *14*(2), 214–219. DOI: 10.18178/ijiet.2024.14.2.2042

Lehrer, K., Mawoyo, M., & Mbaye, S. (2017). *The impacts of interactive smartboards on learning achievement in Senegalese primary schools, 3ie Grantee Final Report.* New Delhi: International Initiative for Impact Evaluation (3ie). Retrieved from https://www.3ieimpact.org/sites/default/files/2019-01/GFR-PW2.14-NEPAD-Senegal-e-school.pdf

Leong, W. Y., Leong, Y. Z., & San Leong, W. (2024, October). Artificial Intelligence in education. In *IET International Conference on Engineering Technologies and Applications (ICETA 2024)* (Vol. 2024, pp. 183-184). IET.

Lérias, E., Guerra, C., & Ferreira, P. (2024). Literacy in artificial intelligence as a challenge for teaching in higher education: A case study at portalegre polytechnic university. *Information (Basel)*, *15*(4), 205. DOI: 10.3390/info15040205

Lestari, D. P., Supahar, , Paidi, , Suwarjo, , & Herianto, . (2023). Effect of science virtual laboratory combination with demonstration methods on lower-secondary school students' scientific literacy ability in a science course. *Education and Information Technologies*, *28*(12), 16153–16175. DOI: 10.1007/s10639-023-11857-8

Leta, F. M., & Vancea, D. P. C. (2023). Ethics in education: Exploring the ethical implications of artificial intelligence implementation. *Ovidius University Annals. Economic Sciences Series*, *23*(1), 413–421. DOI: 10.61801/OUAESS.2023.1.54

Létourneau, A., Deslandes Martineau, M., Charland, P., Karran, J. A., Boasen, J., & Léger, P. M. (2025). A systematic review of AI-driven intelligent tutoring systems (ITS) in K-12 education. npj Science of Learning, 10, 29. https://doi.org/DOI: 10.1038/s41539-025-00320-7

Leu, S., & Lee, J. (2025). *Verifiable Credentials Wallets in a Skills-First Talent Marketplace. Jobs for the Future*. JFF.

Levin, I., Semenov, A., & Gorsky, M. (2025). Papert's vision realized: Constructionism and generative AI. In *Constructionism conference proceedings* (Vol. 8, pp. 419–426). DOI: 10.21240/constr/2025/36.X

Libertson, F. (2023). Inner transitions in higher education in Sweden: Incorporating intra-personal skills in education for sustainable development. *International Journal of Sustainability in Higher Education*, *24*(9), 213–230. DOI: 10.1108/IJSHE-12-2022-0395

Li, J., Zheng, Z., Chai, Y., Li, X., & Wei, X. (2023). FaceMe: An agent-based social game using augmented reality for the emotional development of children with autism spectrum disorder. *International Journal of Human-Computer Studies*, *175*, 103032. DOI: 10.1016/j.ijhcs.2023.103032

Li, M. (2025). Integrating artificial intelligence in primary mathematics education: Investigating internal and external influences on teacher adoption. *International Journal of Science and Mathematics Education*, *23*(5), 1283–1308. DOI: 10.1007/s10763-024-10515-w

Li, M. D., & Little, B. P. (2023). Appropriate Reliance on Artificial Intelligence in Radiology Education. *Journal of the American College of Radiology*, *20*(11), 1126–1130. DOI: 10.1016/j.jacr.2023.04.019 PMID: 37392983

Lim, E. M. (2024). Metaphor analysis on pre-service early childhood teachers' conception of AI (Artificial Intelligence) education for young children. *Thinking Skills and Creativity*, *51*, 101455. DOI: 10.1016/j.tsc.2023.101455

Linderoth, C., Hultén, M., & Stenliden, L. (2024). Competing visions of artificial intelligence in education—A heuristic analysis on sociotechnical imaginaries and problematizations in policy guidelines. *Policy Futures in Education*, *22*(8), 1662–1678. DOI: 10.1177/14782103241228900

Lin, H., & Chen, Q. (2024). Artificial intelligence (AI)-integrated educational applications and college students' creativity and academic emotions: Students and teachers' perceptions and attitudes. *BMC Psychology*, *12*(1), 487. DOI: 10.1186/s40359-024-01979-0 PMID: 39285268

Lin, H., Wan, S., Gan, W., Chen, J., & Chao, H.-C. (2022). Metaverse in Education: Vision, opportunities and challenges. *Computer Science*, *14951*, 1–10. DOI: 10.1109/BigData55660.2022.10021004

Liu, X. (2025). Reconceptualizing foreign language learning through artificial intelligence within the framework of the zone of proximal development. *GBP Proceedings Series, 8*, 9–15. DOI: 10.70088/790gnb90

Liu, H., Zhang, T., Li, F., Yu, M., & Yu, G. (2024). A probabilistic generative model for tracking multi-knowledge concept mastery probability. *Frontiers of Computer Science*, *18*(3), 183602. Advance online publication. DOI: 10.1007/s11704-023-3008-x

Liu, R., Zenke, C., Liu, C., Holmes, A., Thornton, P., & Malan, D. J. (2024, March). Teaching CS50 with AI: leveraging generative artificial intelligence in computer science education. In *Proceedings of the 55th ACM technical symposium on computer science education* V. 1 (pp. 750-756).

Liu, T., Liu, Z., Zhu, F., & Mao, Z. (2023). Dual Parallel-PMSM System Using Single PMSM Control Hardware: A PLL-Integrated UIO Approach. *IEEE Transactions on Power Electronics*, *38*(12), 15300–15313. DOI: 10.1109/TPEL.2023.3309901

Liu, Z., Guo, T., Liang, Q., Hou, M., Zhan, B., Tang, J., Luo, W., & Weng, J. (2025). Deep learning based knowledge tracing: A review, a tool and empirical studies. *IEEE Transactions on Knowledge and Data Engineering*, *37*(8), 4512–4536. DOI: 10.1109/TKDE.2025.3552759

Li, Z. (2024). The shadow of the algorithm: The ethical blind spot of artificial intelligence education. *Journal of Education. Humanities and Social Sciences*, *26*, 1146–1152. DOI: 10.54097/pk0ajq60

Lodge, J. M., De Barba, P., & Broadbent, J. (2024). Learning with generative artificial intelligence within a network of co-regulation. *Journal of University Teaching & Learning Practice*, *20*(7). Advance online publication. DOI: 10.53761/1.20.7.02

Lo, N., Chan, S., & Wong, A. (2025). Evaluating teacher, AI, and hybrid feedback in English language learning: Impact on student motivation, quality, and performance in Hong Kong. *SAGE Open*, *15*(3), 21582440251352907. Advance online publication. DOI: 10.1177/21582440251352907

Loos, E., Gröpler, J., & Goudeau, M.-L. S. (2023). Using ChatGPT in Education: Human Reflection on ChatGPT's Self-Reflection. *Societies (Basel, Switzerland)*, *13*(8), 196. DOI: 10.3390/soc13080196

Luarn, P., Chen, C.-C., & Chiu, Y.-P. (2023). Enhancing intrinsic learning motivation through gamification: A self-determination theory perspective. *International Journal of Informaton and Learning Technology*, *40*(5), 413–424. DOI: 10.1108/IJILT-07-2022-0145

Luckin, R. (2018). *Machine learning and human intelligence. The future of education for the 21st century*. UCL institute of education press.

Luckin, R. (2023b, July 14). Yes, AI could profoundly disrupt education. But maybe that's not a bad thing. *The Guardian*. Retrieved from https://www.theguardian.com/commentisfree/2023/jul/14/ai-artificial-intelligence-disrupt-education-creativity-critical-thinking

Luckin, R., & Holmes, W. (2016). *Intelligence unleashed: An argument for AI in education*. Pearson. https://www.pearson.com/content/dam/corporate/glob

Luckin, R., Holmes, W., Griffiths, M., & Forcier, L. B. (2016). Intelligence Unleashed: An Argument for AI in Education. Pearson. https://www.scirp.org/reference/referencespapers?referenceid=3391328

Luckin, R., Holmes, W., Griffiths, M., & Forcier, L. B. (2023). *AI and education: Guidance for policy makers (No. 253). OECD Education Working Papers*. UNESCO.

Luckin, R. (2023a). The ethics of AI in education: Self-regulation, autonomy, and the human factor. *AI & Society*, *38*(2), 211–228.

Luckin, R., George, K., & Cukurova, M. (2022). *AI for school teachers* (2nd ed.). CRC Press. DOI: 10.1201/9781003193173

Luckin, R., Holmes, W., Griffiths, M., & Forcier, L. B. (2016). *Intelligence unleashed: An argument for AI in education*. Pearson Education.

Luo, Y., Lai, J., Shi, S., Chen, C., Qi, S., Zhang, J., & Wang, Q. (2025). Castor: Optimizing Deep Learning Job Scheduling in Multi-Tenant GPU Clusters via Intelligent Colocation. *IEEE Transactions on Cloud Computing*, •••, 1–18. DOI: 10.1109/TCC.2025.3624752

Luo, Z., Tan, X., He, M., & Wu, X. (2023). The seewo interactive whiteboard (IWB) for ESL teaching: How useful it is? *Heliyon*, *9*(10), e20424. Advance online publication. DOI: 10.1016/j.heliyon.2023.e20424

Lye, C. Y., & Lim, L. (2024). Generative artificial intelligence in tertiary education: Assessment redesign principles and considerations. *Education Sciences*, *14*(6), 569. DOI: 10.3390/educsci14060569

Ma, X., & Wang, J. (2024, October). WIP: Active Learning through Prompt Engineering and Agentic AI Simulation-A Pilot Project in Computer Networks Education. In *2024 IEEE Frontiers in Education Conference (FIE)* (pp. 1-5). IEEE.

Machajewski, S. (2024). *AI instructional framework*. Open Science Framework. DOI: 10.35542/osf.io/j8ct9

Ma, D., Akram, H., & Chen, I. H. (2024). Artificial intelligence in higher education: A cross-cultural examination of students' behavioral intentions and attitudes. *International Review of Research in Open and Distance Learning*, *25*(3), 134–157. DOI: 10.19173/irrodl.v25i3.7703

Maghsudi, S., Lan, A., Xu, J., & Van der Schaar, M. (2021). Personalized education in the artificial intelligence era: What to expect next. *IEEE Signal Processing Magazine*, *38*(3), 37–50. DOI: 10.1109/MSP.2021.3055032

Mah, D. K., & Groß, N. (2024). Artificial intelligence in higher education: Exploring faculty use, self-efficacy, distinct profiles, and professional development needs. *International Journal of Educational Technology in Higher Education*, *21*(1), 58. DOI: 10.1186/s41239-024-00490-1

Mahmoud, C. F., & Sørensen, J. T. (2024). Artificial intelligence in personalized learning with a focus on current developments and future prospects. *Research and Advances in Education*, *3*(8), 25–31. DOI: 10.56397/RAE.2024.08.04

Mahmoudi-Dehaki, M., & Nasr-Esfahani, N. (2025). Enhancing engagement and equity in personalized learning through adaptive systems. In *IGI Global eBooks* (pp. 219–246). IGI Global., DOI: 10.4018/979-8-3373-0740-4.ch009

Mahrishi, M., Abbas, A., & Siddiqui, M. K. (2024). Global initiatives towards regulatory frameworks for artificial intelligence in higher education. *Digital Government: Research and Practice*, *6*(2), 1–9. DOI: 10.1145/3672462

Malhotra, C. (2024). *Digital India: Past, Present and Future*. 325–345. DOI: 10.1007/978-3-658-43014-6_19

Mansour, N., Aras, C., Staarman, J. K., & Alotaibi, S. B. M. (2024). Embodied learning of science concepts through augmented reality technology. *Education and Information Technologies 2024 30:6, 30*(6), 8245–8275. DOI: 10.1007/s10639-024-13120-0

Mao, J., Chen, B., & Liu, J. C. (2024). Generative artificial intelligence in education and its implications for assessment. *TechTrends*, *68*(1), 58–66. DOI: 10.1007/s11528-023-00911-4

Marais, E., Marais-Botha, R., & Coertzen, F. (2024). Constructing an artificial intelligence higher education environment: Guidelines for the future. In *Helsinki University Press eBooks* (pp. 173–192). Helsinki University Press., DOI: 10.33134/HUP-25-9

Marengo, A., Pagano, A., Pange, J., & Soomro, K. A. (2024). The educational value of artificial intelligence in higher education: A 10-year systematic literature review. *Interactive Technology and Smart Education*, *21*(4), 625–644. DOI: 10.1108/ITSE-11-2023-0218

Marginson, S. (2010). Higher education in the global knowledge economy. *Procedia: Social and Behavioral Sciences*, *2*(5), 6962–6980. DOI: 10.1016/j.sbspro.2010.05.049

Marina Harvey. (2024, January 3). *The role of reflection for learning and metacognitive development*. Improvewithmetacognition.Com. https://www.improvewithmetacognition.com/reflection-for-learning-and-metacognitive-development/

Marquardson, J. (2024). Embracing Artificial Intelligence to Improve Self-Directed Learning: A Cybersecurity Classroom Study. *Information Systems Education Journal*, *22*(1), 4–13. DOI: 10.62273/WZBY3952

Martin, G., & Olszewska, J. (2025). Automation Testing Framework for Reliable Autonomous Agentic AI. *2025 IEEE Engineering Reliable Autonomous Systems (ERAS)*, 1-8.

Martin, F., Zhuang, M., & Schaefer, D. (2024). Systematic review of research on artificial intelligence in K-12 education (2017–2022). *Computers and Education: Artificial Intelligence*, *6*, 100195. DOI: 10.1016/j.caeai.2023.100195

Ma, S., & Lei, L. (2024). The factors influencing teacher education students' willingness to adopt artificial intelligence technology for information-based teaching. *Asia Pacific Journal of Education*, *44*(1), 94–111. DOI: 10.1080/02188791.2024.2305155

Mateer, S. (2020). *The Effects of Graphic Novels on the Affective Domain in Elementary Boys: A Case Study of a 4th Grade Boys Book Club.* (DEd dissertation). Indiana University of Pennsylvania.

Mattar, J., Santos, C. C., & Cuque, L. M. (2022). Analysis and comparison of international digital competence frameworks for education. *Education Sciences*, *12*(12), 932. Advance online publication. DOI: 10.3390/educsci12120932

MATTR. (2026, May 15). *Decentralized Identifiers (DIDs)*. MATTR Learn; MATTR. https://learn.mattr.global/docs/concepts/dids

Mazzocca, C., Acar, A., Uluagac, S., Montanari, R., Bellavista, P., & Conti, M. (2025). A survey on decentralized identifiers and verifiable credentials. *IEEE Communications Surveys and Tutorials*, *27*(6), 3641–3671. DOI: 10.1109/COMST.2025.3543197

McComas, W. F. (2013). Constructivist teaching practices. In *Science education research and practice in Europe* (p. 23). Sense Publishers., DOI: 10.1007/978-94-6209-497-0_20

McLeod, G. A., Barr, J., & Welch, A. (2015). Best Practice for Teaching and Learning Strategies to Facilitate Student Reflection in Pre-Registration Health Professional Education: An Integrative Review. *Creative Education*, *06*(04), 440–454. DOI: 10.4236/ce.2015.64044

Mehboob, K., Kamran, F., & Ain, Q. U. (2024). From chalkboards to digital platforms: The impact of media on modern education. *Gomal University Journal of Research*, *40*(4), 411–424. DOI: 10.51380/gujr-40-04-02

Mellado-Moreno, P. C., Sánchez-Antolín, P., & Blanco-García, M. (2021). Trends in formative and summative student assessment in Web of Sciences. *Alteridad*, *16*(2), 166–179.

Melo-López, V. A., Basantes-Andrade, A., Gudiño-Mejía, C. B., & Hernández-Martínez, E. (2025). The Impact of Artificial Intelligence on Inclusive Education: A Systematic Review. *Education Sciences 2025, Vol. 15, Page 539, 15*(5), 539. DOI: 10.3390/educsci15050539

Memarian, B., & Doleck, T. (2024). A review of assessment for learning with artificial intelligence. *Computers in Human Behaviour: Artificial Humans*, *2*(1), 100040. DOI: 10.1016/j.chbah.2023.100040

Memarian, B., & Doleck, T. (2024). Human-in-the-loop in artificial intelligence in education: A review and entity-relationship (ER) analysis. *Computers in Human Behavior: Artificial Humans*, *2*(1), 100053. DOI: 10.1016/j.chbah.2024.100053

Meng, Y., Xu, W., Liu, Z., & Yu, Z. G. (2024). Scientometric analyses of digital inequity in education: problems and solutions. *Humanities and Social Sciences Communications 2024 11:1, 11*(1), 1052-. DOI: 10.1057/s41599-024-03480-w

Merchán Sánchez-Jara, J. F., González Gutiérrez, S., Cruz Rodríguez, J., & Syroyid Syroyid, B. (2024). Artificial intelligence-assisted music education: A critical synthesis of challenges and opportunities. *Education Sciences, 14*(11), 1171. DOI: 10.3390/educsci14111171

Merino-Campos, C. (2025). The impact of artificial intelligence on personalized learning in higher education: A systematic review. *Trends in Higher Education, 4*(2), 17. DOI: 10.3390/higheredu4020017

Merkebu, J., Veen, M., Hosseini, S., & Varpio, L. (2024). The case for metacognitive reflection: A theory integrative review with implications for medical education. *Advances in Health Sciences Education : Theory and Practice, 29*(4), 1481–1500. DOI: 10.1007/s10459-023-10310-2 PMID: 38345690

Merriam, S. B. (2001). Andragogy and Self-Directed Learning: Pillars of Adult Learning Theory. *New Directions for Adult and Continuing Education, 2001*(89), 3–14. DOI: 10.1002/ace.3

Meyer, J., Jansen, T., & Fleckenstein, J. (2025). Nonengagement and unsuccessful engagement with feedback in lower secondary education: The role of student characteristics. *Contemporary Educational Psychology, 81*, 102363. DOI: 10.1016/j.cedpsych.2025.102363

Mezirow, J. (1991). *Transformative dimensions of adult learning*. Jossey-Bass.

Miao, F., & Holmes, W. (2023). Guidance for generative AI in education and research. UNESCO. https://www.unesco.org/en/articles/guidance-generative-ai-education-and-research

Miao, F., Holmes, W., Huang, R., & Zhang, H. (2021). AI and education: Guidance for policy-makers. UNESCO. https://unesdoc.unesco.org/ark:/48223/pf0000376709

Miao, J., Thongprayoon, C., Suppadungsuk, S., Garcia Valencia, O. A., Qureshi, F., & Cheungpasitporn, W. (2024). Ethical Dilemmas in Using AI for Academic Writing and an Example Framework for Peer Review in Nephrology Academia: A Narrative Review. *Clinics and Practice, 14*(1), 89–105. DOI: 10.3390/clinpract14010008 PMID: 38248432

Miglani, P. (2025, May 6). *Invisible Chains: caste, religious, nationalism, and the struggle for freedom to innovate in India*. https://openresearch.ocadu.ca/id/eprint/4722

Mikeladze, T., Meijer, P. C., & Verhoeff, R. P. (2024). A comprehensive exploration of artificial intelligence competence frameworks for educators: A critical review. *European Journal of Education, 59*(3), e12663. DOI: 10.1111/ejed.12663

Mikros, G. (2025). Large Language Models and Forensic Linguistics: Navigating Opportunities and Threats in the Age of Generative AI. *arXiv preprint arXiv:2512.06922.*

Milgram, P., & Kishino, F. (1994). A taxonomy of mixed reality visual displays. *IEICE Transactions on Information and Systems, E77-D*(12), 1321–1329. 10.1.1.102.4646

Mimoudi, A. (2024). AI, personalized education, and challenges. In *Proceedings of the International Conference on AI Research* (Vol. 4, No. 1, pp. 271–280). DOI: 10.34190/icair.4.1.3133

Ministry of Health & Family Welfare. (2019). *National Family Health Survey (NFHS-5) (2019-21).*

Ministry of Statistics and Programme Implementation. (2018). *India - Household Social Consumption: Health, NSS 75th Round Schedule-25.0 :July 2017-June 2018.* https://microdata.gov.in/NADA/index.php/catalog/152

Min, K., & Siegel, C. (2011). Integration of SMART board technology and effective teaching. *Imanager's Journal on School Educational Technology*, *7*(1), 38–47. DOI: 10.26634/jsch.7.1.1518

Minn, S. (2022). AI-assisted knowledge assessment techniques for adaptive learning environments. *Computers and Education: Artificial Intelligence*, *3*, 100050. DOI: 10.1016/j.caeai.2022.100050

Mishara, P. (2024). The ethical implications of AI in education: Privacy, bias, and accountability. *Journal of Informatics Education and Research*, *4*(2). Advance online publication. DOI: 10.52783/jier.v4i2.1827

Mishra, P., & Koehler, M. J. (2006). Technology pedagogical content knowledge: A framework for teacher knowledge. *Teachers College Record*, *108*(6), 1017–1054. DOI: 10.1111/j.1467-9620.2006.00684.x

Mishra, R. A., Bhaskar, P., & Khan, M. (2025). An integrated blockchain architecturefor sustainable higher education administration. *On the Horizon. The International Journal of Learning Futures*, *33*(4), 460–474.

Misra, P., & Srivastava, R. (2024). Digital Divide and Sustainable Development. *World Sustainability Series*, (Part F3420), 451–472. DOI: 10.1007/978-3-031-68427-2_23

Mizumoto, A., & Eguchi, M. (2023). Exploring the potential of using an AI language model for automated essay scoring. *Research Methods in Applied Linguistics*, *2*(2), 100050. Advance online publication. DOI: 10.1016/j.rmal.2023.100050

Mkpae, S. G., & Obowu-Adutchay, V. (2017). School-based assessment: Benefit and teachers' perception in Nigerian secondary schools. *International Journal of Education and Evaluation*, *3*(2), 19–27.

Mogboh, V. E., & Okoye, A. C. (2019). Formative and summative assessment: Trends and practices in basic education. *Journal of Education and Practice*, *10*(27), 39–45.

Mogoale, P., Pretorius, A., Mogase, R., & Segooa, M. (2025). Ethical considerations in artificial intelligence-driven environments for higher education. *South African Journal of Information Management*, *27*(1), a2007. Advance online publication. DOI: 10.4102/sajim.v27i1.2007

Mohan, R. (2023). *Measurement, evaluation and assessment in education*. PHI Learning Pvt. Ltd.

Mökander, J., & Axente, M. (2021). Ethics-based auditing of automated decision-making systems: Intervention points and policy implications. *AI & Society*, *38*(1), 153–171. DOI: 10.1007/s00146-021-01286-x

Molotsi, A. R. (2014, November). *Secondary-school teachers' information communication technology competencies in classroom practices*. Pretoria: University of South Africa. Retrieved from http://hdl.handle.net/10500/18586

Moosa, S., & Ramnarain, U. (2023, July). The impact of an empowerment evaluation professional development program on physical sciences teachers' attitudes, beliefs and behavioral intentions to integrate ICT into their science lessons. *Frontiers in Education, 8*, 1159373. Advance online publication. DOI: 10.3389/feduc.2023.1159373

Mørch, A. I., & Andersen, R. (2023). Human-centred AI in education in the age of generative AI tools. In *CEUR Workshop Proceedings* (Vol. 3408). https://ceur-ws.org/Vol-3408/short-s2-08.pdf

Morris, T. H. (2019). Self-directed learning: A fundamental competence in a rapidly changing world', International Review of Education. *International Review of Education, 65*(4), 633–653. DOI: 10.1007/s11159-019-09793-2

Motamary, S. (2025). Empowering Retail Oss/Bss Platforms With Agentic Ai And Scalable Data Engineering. *Metallurgical and Materials Engineering*, 1361-1380.

Mouta, A., Pinto-Llorente, A. M., & Torrecilla-Sánchez, E. M. (2024). Uncovering blind spots in education ethics: Insights from a systematic literature review on artificial intelligence in education. *International Journal of Artificial Intelligence in Education, 34*(3), 1166–1205. DOI: 10.1007/s40593-023-00384-9

Mouta, A., Torrecilla-Sánchez, E. M., & Pinto-Llorente, A. M. (2024). Design of a future scenarios toolkit for an ethical implementation of artificial intelligence in education. *Education and Information Technologies, 29*(9), 10473–10498. DOI: 10.1007/s10639-023-12229-y

Msafiri, M. M., Kangwa, D., & Cai, L. (2023). A systematic literature review of ICT integration in secondary education: What works, what does not, and what next? *Discover Education, 2*(44), 44. Advance online publication. DOI: 10.1007/s44217-023-00070-x

Muawanah, U., Marini, A., & Sarifah, I. (2024). The interconnection between digital literacy, artificial intelligence, and the use of E-learning applications in enhancing the sustainability of Regional Languages: Evidence from Indonesia. *Social Sciences & Humanities Open, 10*, 101169. DOI: 10.1016/j.ssaho.2024.101169

Muralidharan, K., Singh, A., & Ganimian, A. J. (2019). Disrupting Education? Experimental Evidence on Technology-Aided Instruction in India. *The American Economic Review, 109*(4), 1426–1460. DOI: 10.1257/aer.20171112

Murdan, A. P., & Halkhoree, R. (2024, June). Integration of Artificial Intelligence for educational excellence and innovation in higher education institutions. In *2024 1st International Conference on Smart Energy Systems and Artificial Intelligence (SESAI)* (pp. 1-6). IEEE. DOI: 10.1109/SESAI61023.2024.10599402

Murugesan, S. (2025). The rise of agentic AI: Implications, concerns, and the path forward. *IEEE Intelligent Systems, 40*(2), 8–14. DOI: 10.1109/MIS.2025.3544940

Musolin, M. H., Ismail, M. H., Farhan, M., Rois, N., Ismail, A., Huda, M., & Rohim, M. A. (2024, February). Understanding of artificial intelligence for Islamic education support and service: insights from empirical literature review. In *International Congress on Information and Communication Technology* (pp. 27-43). Singapore: Springer Nature Singapore.

Mustafa, M. Y., Tlili, A., Lampropoulos, G., Huang, R., Jandrić, P., Zhao, J., Salha, S., Xu, L., Panda, S., Kinshuk, , López-Pernas, S., & Saqr, M. (2024). A systematic review of literature reviews on artificial intelligence in education (AIED): A roadmap to a future research agenda. *Smart Learning Environments, 11*(1), 59. DOI: 10.1186/s40561-024-00350-5

Mustafaraj, E. (2025, May). Dreams in Hypertext: Berners-Lee, Agentic AI, and the Next Web Frontier. In *Companion Publication of the 17th ACM Web Science Conference 2025* (pp. 19-21).

Mwansa, G., Ngandu, M. R., & Mkwambi, Z. (2025). Bridging the digital divide: exploring the challenges and solutions for digital exclusion in rural South Africa. *Discover Global Society 2025 3:1, 3*(1), 54-. DOI: 10.1007/s44282-025-00189-2

Myers, G. J., Sandler, C., & Badgett, T. (2011). *The Art of Software Testing* (3rd ed.). Wiley., https://www.oreilly.com/library/view/the-art-of/9781118133156/

Mzekandaba, S. (2016, July 14). *Gauteng gets more tech into classrooms*. Retrieved November 22, 2022, from ITWeb: https://www.itweb.co.za/content/okYbe97XVlRqAWpG

Nair, G. K., Setia, R., Samad, N. Z., Zahri, R. N., Luqman, A., Vadeveloo, T., & Ngah, H. C. (2014). Teachers' knowledge and issues in the implementation of school-based assessment: A case of schools in Terengganu. *Asian Social Science, 10*(3), 186–194.

Naixin, Z., Wai Yie, L., Tong, Z., & Changqing, W. (2024). Artificial Intelligence in Engineering Education: A Review of Pedagogical Innovations. *INTI JOURNAL, 2024*(46), 1–10.

Nancy, W., Parimala, A., & Livingston, L. M. (2020). Advanced teaching pedagogy as innovative approach in modern education system. *Procedia Computer Science, 172*, 382–388. DOI: 10.1016/j.procs.2020.05.059

Naseer, F., Khan, M. N., Tahir, M., Addas, A., & Aejaz, S. M. H. (2024). Integrating deep learning techniques for personalized learning pathways in higher education. *Heliyon, 10*(11), e32628. DOI: 10.1016/j.heliyon.2024.e32628 PMID: 38961899

National Cyber Security Centre. (2025). *Content Credentials: Strengthening Multimedia Integrity in the Generative AI Era* - DoD, accessed on December 22, 2025, https://media.defense.gov/2025/Jan/29/2003634788/-1/-1/0/CSI-CONTENT-CREDENTIALS.PDF

Nazaretsky, T., Mejia-Domenzain, P., Swamy, V., Frej, J., & Käser, T. (2025). The critical role of trust in adopting AI-powered educational technology for learning: An instrument for measuring student perceptions. *Computers and Education: Artificial Intelligence, 8*, 100368. Advance online publication. DOI: 10.1016/j.caeai.2025.100368

Ndwandwe, K. P., Ramaligela, S. M., & Mtshali, T. I. (2024). The effectiveness of smartboards in enhancing technology teachers' creativity. *African Perspectives of Research in Teaching and Learning, 8*(1), 1-9. Retrieved from https://search.proquest.com/openview/23f638fecb3234a7a0c6df7f7ee5a357/1?pq-origsite=gscholar&cbl=5126680

Nedungadi, P., Tang, K. Y., & Raman, R. (2024). The transformative power of generative artificial intelligence for achieving the sustainable development goal of quality education. *Sustainability (Basel), 16*(22), 9779. DOI: 10.3390/su16229779

Neelu, A., Pramod, J. P., & Lahari, A. (2025). Optimizing Networks Using AI and Machine Learning: The Role of Agentic AI in Transforming Network Management. In *The Power of Agentic AI: Redefining Human Life and Decision-Making: In Industry 6.0* (pp. 229–254). Springer Nature Switzerland. DOI: 10.1007/978-3-031-89424-4_16

Neumann, A. T., Arndt, T., Köbis, L., Meissner, R., Martin, A., de Lange, P., Pengel, N., Klamma, R., & Wollersheim, H.-W. (2021). Chatbots as a Tool to Scale Mentoring Processes: Individually Supporting Self-Study in Higher Education. *Frontiers in Artificial Intelligence, 4*, 668220. Advance online publication. DOI: 10.3389/frai.2021.668220 PMID: 34337393

Newman-Griffis, D. (2025). AI Thinking: A framework for rethinking artificial intelligence in practice. *Royal Society Open Science, 12*(1), 241482. DOI: 10.1098/rsos.241482 PMID: 39780964

Ng, D. T. K., Chan, E. K. C., & Lo, C. K. (2025). Opportunities, challenges and school strategies for integrating generative AI in education. *Computers and Education: Artificial Intelligence*, 100373.

Ng, D. T. K., Su, J., Leung, J. K. L., & Chu, S. K. W. (2024). Artificial intelligence (AI) literacy education in secondary schools: A review. *Interactive Learning Environments, 32*(10), 6204–6224. DOI: 10.1080/10494820.2023.2255228

Ng, D. T., Xinyu, C., Leung, J. K., & Chu, S. K. (2024). Fostering students' AI literacy development through educational games: AI knowledge, affective and cognitive engagement. *Journal of Computer Assisted Learning, 40*(5), 2049–2064. DOI: 10.1111/jcal.13009

Nguyen, A., Gul, F., Dang, B., Huynh, L., & Tuunanen, T. (2025). Designing embodied generative artificial intelligence in mixed reality for active learning in higher education. *Innovations in Education and Teaching International, 62*(5), 1632–1647. DOI: 10.1080/14703297.2025.2499177

Nguyen, A., Kremantzis, M., Essien, A., Petrounias, I., & Hosseini, S. (2024). Enhancing student engagement through artificial intelligence (AI): Understanding the basics, opportunities, and challenges. *Journal of University Teaching & Learning Practice, 21*(6), 1–13. DOI: 10.53761/caraaq92

Nguyen, A., Ngo, H. N., Hong, Y., Dang, B., & Nguyen, B. P. T. (2023). Ethical principles for artificial intelligence in education. *Education and Information Technologies, 28*(4), 4221–4241. DOI: 10.1007/s10639-022-11316-w PMID: 36254344

Nguyen, N. D. (2023). Exploring the role of AI in education. *London Journal of Social Sciences, 6*(6), 84–95. DOI: 10.31039/ljss.2023.6.108

Nicol, D. J., & Macfarlane-Dick, D. (2006). Formative assessment and self-regulated learning: A model and seven principles of good feedback practice. *Studies in Higher Education, 31*(2), 199–218. DOI: 10.1080/03075070600572090

Nicoletti, B., & Appolloni, A. (2025). A digital twin framework for enhancing human–agentic AI–machine collaboration. *Journal of Intelligent Manufacturing*, •••, 1–17.

Niemi, H. (2021). AI in learning. *Journal of Pacific Rim Psychology, 15*, e34. DOI: 10.1177/18344909211038105

Nikolopoulou, K. (2024). Generative artificial intelligence in higher education: Exploring ways of harnessing pedagogical practices with the assistance of ChatGPT. *International Journal of Changes in Education, 1*(2), 103–111. DOI: 10.47852/bonviewIJCE42022489

Ninaus, M., & Sailer, M. (2022). Closing the loop – The human role in artificial intelligence for education. *Frontiers in Psychology, 13*, 956798. DOI: 10.3389/fpsyg.2022.956798 PMID: 36092115

Ninaus, M., & Sailer, M. (2022). The human role in artificial intelligence for education: A systematic review. *Computers and Education: Artificial Intelligence, 3*, 100083. DOI: 10.1016/j.caeai.2022.100083

NIST. (n.d.). *NIST AI 100-4 Reducing Risks Posed by 5 Synthetic Content 6*. Retrieved July 23, 2026, from https://airc.nist.gov/docs/NIST.AI.100-4.SyntheticContent.ipd.pdf

Noothigattu, R., Bouneffouf, D., Mattei, N., Chandra, R., Madan, P., Varshney, K. R., Campbell, M., Singh, M., & Rossi, F. (2019). Teaching AI agents ethical values using reinforcement learning and policy orchestration. *IBM Journal of Research and Development, 63*(4/5), 2:1–2:9. https://www.cs.cmu.edu/~rnoothig/papers/policy_orchestration.pdf. DOI: 10.1147/JRD.2019.2940428

Nopas, D. (2025). Algorithmic learning or learner autonomy? Rethinking AI's role in digital education. *Qualitative Research Journal*. Advance online publication. DOI: 10.1108/QRJ-11-2024-0282

Nowak, K. L., Fox, J., & Fox, J. (2018). Avatars and computer-mediated communication: A review of the definition, uses and effects of digital representations on communication. *6*, 30-53. Retrieved from https://nbn-resolving.org/urn:nbn:de:0168-ssoar-55777-7

NSCBlog. (2025). Addressing credential fraud in higher education. In *Clearinghouse Today Blog*. https://www.studentclearinghouse.org/nscblog/addressing-credential-fraud-in-higher-ed/

Nuci, K. P., Tahir, R., Wang, A. I., & Imran, A. S. (2021). Game-based digital quiz as a tool for improving students' engagement and learning in online lectures. *IEEE Access : Practical Innovations, Open Solutions, 9*, 91220–91234. DOI: 10.1109/ACCESS.2021.3088583

Nvidia DLSS. NVIDIA Developer. (n.d.). https://developer.nvidia.com/rtx/dlss?sortBy=developer_learning_library%2Fsort%2Ffeatured%3Adesc%2Ctitle%3Aasc

O'Connell, C. (2018). Learning as a shared process: Vygotsky and the socio-cultural theories of learning. In *Vygotsky and sociocultural approaches to teaching and learning* (pp. 161–176). Routledge., DOI: 10.4324/9781315299358-10

Obaid, S. (2022). The effect of smart board on students' engagement in English. *International Journal of Research in Social Sciences & Humanities, 12*(3), 52–64. DOI: 10.37648/ijrssh.v12i03.004

Obenza, B. N., Salvahan, A., Rios, A. N., Solo, A., Alburo, R. A., & Gabila, R. J. (2024). University students' perception and use of ChatGPT: Generative artificial intelligence (AI) in higher education. *International Journal of Human-Computer Studies, 5*(12), 5–18.

Obidovna, D. Z. (2024). The pedagogical-psychological aspects of artificial intelligence technologies in integrative education. *International Journal Of Literature And Languages*, *4*(03), 13–19. DOI: 10.37547/ijll/Volume04Issue03-03

Odri, G. A., & Ji Yun Yoon, D. (2023). Detecting generative artificial intelligence in scientific articles: Evasion techniques and implications for scientific integrity. *Orthopaedics & Traumatology: Surgery & Research*, *109*(8), 103706. DOI: 10.1016/j.otsr.2023.103706 PMID: 37838021

OECD. (2019). *OECD Principles on Artificial Intelligence*. Paris: Organisation for Economic Co-operation and Development. https://oecd.ai/en/ai-principles

OECD. (2023). AI and the Future of Skills, Volume 2: Methods for evaluating AI capabilities. OECD Publishing. https://doi.org/DOI: 10.1787/a9fe53cb-en

OECD. (2023). *Artificial intelligence in education: Challenges and opportunities*. OECD Publishing.

OECD. (2024). *AI in Education: Accreditation and Quality Frameworks*. OECD Education Directorate.

Ogegbo, A. A., & Ramnarain, U. (2022, August 6). Teaching and learning Physics using interactive simulation: A guided inquiry practice. *South African Journal of Education*, *42*(1), 1997. Advance online publication. DOI: 10.15700/saje.v42n1a1997

Oguguo, B. E., & Ocheni, C. A. (2023). Cybersecurity: a tool for curbing examination breaches and improvement of quality of large-scale educational assessments. *Information Security Journal: A Global Perspective, 33*(2), 1-15. DOI: 10.1080/19393555.2023.2284761

Oguguo, B. C., David, N. A., Uwake, S. I., Omeke, F. C., Ugorji, C. O., Ngwu, A. N., & Okebanama, C. I. (2023). Influence of internet of things cybersecurity (IoTCS) on educational assessment practices in university learning spaces in Nigeria. *Journal of E-Learning and Knowledge Society*, *20*(2), 55–66. DOI: 10.20368/1971-8829/1135973

Olawade, D. B., Weerasinghe, K., Teke, J., Msiska, M., Boussios, S., & Hatzidimitriadou, E. (2025). Evaluating AI adoption in healthcare: Insights from the information governance professionals in the United Kingdom. *International Journal of Medical Informatics*, *199*, 105909. DOI: 10.1016/j.ijmedinf.2025.105909 PMID: 40198930

Oleet, J. B., & Yu, C. (2025). AI and the future of education. In *Advances in computational intelligence and robotics* (pp. 407–440). IGI Global. DOI: 10.4018/979-8-3693-7873-1.ch015

Olojo, O. J., Akinwumi, I. O., & Olofin, S. O. (2022). Comparative analysis of secondary school students' performance in science subjects in Ekiti State, Nigeria. *Brock Journal of Education*, *10*(3), 73–84. DOI: 10.37745/bje.2013/vol10no3pp.73-84

Olujimi, P. A., Owolawi, P. A., Mogase, R. C., & Wyk, E. V. (2025). Agentic AI frameworks in SMMEs: A systematic literature review of ecosystemic interconnected agents. *AI*, *6*(6), 123. DOI: 10.3390/ai6060123

Omodan, B. I. (2025). Redefining the role of supervisors in the era of artificial intelligence: Implications for hybrid postgraduate research governance. *Cogent Education*, *12*(1), 2536534. Advance online publication. DOI: 10.1080/2331186X.2025.2536534

Opesemowo, O. A. G., & Adekomaya, V. (2024). Harnessing artificial intelligence for advancing sustainable development goals in South Africa's higher education system: A qualitative study. *International Journal of Learning. Teaching and Educational Research*, *23*(3), 67–86. DOI: 10.26803/ijlter.23.3.4

Opesemowo, O. A., & Ndlovu, M. (2024). Artificial intelligence in mathematics education: The good, the bad, and the ugly. *Journal of Pedagogical Research*, *8*(3), 333–346. DOI: 10.33902/JPR.202426428

Organisation for Economic Co-operation and Development (OECD). (2023). Opportunities, Guidelines and Guardrails for Effective and Equitable Use of AI in Education. In *OECD Digital Education Outlook 2023: Towards an Effective Digital Education Ecosystem*. OECD Publishing., DOI: 10.1787/2b39e98b-

Orsmond, P., & Merry, S. (2011). Feedback alignment: Effective and ineffective links between tutors' and students' understanding of coursework feedback. *Assessment & Evaluation in Higher Education*, *36*(2), 125–136. DOI: 10.1080/02602930903201651

Orsmond, P., Merry, S., & Callaghan, A. (2004). Implementation of a formative assessment model incorporating peer and self-assessment. *Innovations in Education and Teaching International*, *41*(3), 273–290. DOI: 10.1080/14703290410001733294

Osher, D., Cantor, P., Berg, J., Steyer, L., & Rose, T. (2018). Drivers of human development: How relationships and context shape learning and development1. *Applied Developmental Science*, *24*(1), 6–36. DOI: 10.1080/10888691.2017.1398650

Ouariach, S., Ouariach, F. Z., & Khaldi, M. (2025). Artificial intelligence as a harbinger of engagement and collaboration. In *Advances in educational technologies and instructional design* (pp. 147–180). IGI Global. DOI: 10.4018/979-8-3373-2262-9.ch006

Outay, F., Jabeur, N., Bellalouna, F., & Hamzi, T. A. (2024). Multi-agent system-based framework for an intelligent management of competency building. *Smart Learning Environments*, *11*(1), 41. Advance online publication. DOI: 10.1186/s40561-024-00328-3

Ouyang, F., & Jiao, P. (2021). Artificial intelligence in education: The three paradigms. *Computers & Education: Artificial Intelligence*, *2*, 100020. DOI: 10.1016/j.caeai.2021.100020

Owan, V. J., Abang, K. B., Idika, D. O., Etta, E. O., & Bassey, B. A. (2023). Exploring the potential of artificial intelligence tools in educational measurement and assessment. *Eurasia Journal of Mathematics, Science and Technology Education*, *19*(8), em2307. Advance online publication. DOI: 10.29333/ejmste/13428

Owens, C., & Wu, T. (2025). Passkeys and Verifiable Digital Credentials: A Harmonized Path to Secure Digital Identity | FIDO Alliance. In *FIDO Alliance*. https://fidoalliance.org/passkeys-and-verifiable-digital-credentials-a-harmonized-path-to-secure-digital-identity/

Özer, M. (2024). Potential Benefits and Risks of Artificial Intelligence in Education. *Bartin University Journal of Faculty of Education, 13*(2).

Ozodakhon, K. (2024). The benefits and drawbacks of using artificial intelligence (ChatGPT) in education. *University Research Base*, 805-808.

Pack, A., & Maloney, J. (2024). Using artificial intelligence in TESOL: Some ethical and pedagogical considerations. *TESOL Quarterly*, *58*(2), 1007–1018. DOI: 10.1002/tesq.3320

Packer, M. J., & Goicoechea, J. (2000). Sociocultural and constructivist theories of learning: Ontology, not just epistemology. *Educational Psychologist*, *35*(4), 227–241. DOI: 10.1207/S15326985EP3504_02

Paduraru, C., Paduraru, M., & Stefanescu, A. (2025, June). Enhancing Game AI Behaviors with Large Language Models and Agentic AI. In *Proceedings of the 33rd ACM International Conference on the Foundations of Software Engineering* (pp. 286-296). DOI: 10.1145/3696630.3728553

Pagliara, S. M., Bonavolontà, G., Pia, M., Falchi, S., Zurru, A. L., Fenu, G., & Mura, A. (2024). The Integration of Artificial Intelligence in Inclusive Education: A Scoping Review. *Information 2024, Vol. 15, Page 774, 15*(12), 774. DOI: 10.3390/info15120774

Paige, K., & Lloyd, D. (2012). Pedagogical Practices and Science Learning with a Focus on Educating for Sustainability for Pre-service Primary and Middle Years Educators. In Tan, K., & Kim, M. (Eds.), *Issues and Challenges in Science Education Research* (pp. 191–207). Springer., DOI: 10.1007/978-94-007-3980-2_13

Paige, K., & Lloyd, D. (2016). Use of future scenarios as a pedagogical approach for science teacher education. *Research in Science Education*, *46*(2), 263–285. DOI: 10.1007/s11165-015-9505-7

Palanisamy, P. (2018). *Hands-On Intelligent Agents with OpenAI Gym: Your guide to developing AI agents using deep reinforcement learning*. Packt Publishing Ltd. Retrieved from https://dl.acm.org/doi/abs/10.5555/3285236

Pamisetty, A. (2024). Application of agentic artificial intelligence in autonomous decision making across food supply chains. *Available at SSRN* 5231360.

Panadero, E. (2017). A review of self-regulated learning: Six models and four directions for research. *Frontiers in Psychology*, *8*, 422. Advance online publication. DOI: 10.3389/fpsyg.2017.00422

Panait, L., & Luke, S. (2005). Cooperative multi-agent learning: The state of the art. *Autonomous Agents and Multi-Agent Systems*, *11*(3), 387–434. DOI: 10.1007/s10458-005-2631-2

Pandey, R. (2025). The Rise of Agentic AI: Redefining Human–Machine Collaboration. [IJARCST]. *International Journal of Advanced Research in Computer Science & Technology*, *8*(5), 12794–12801. DOI: 10.15662/IJARCST.2025.0805005

Papert, S. (1980). *Mindstorms: Children, computers, and powerful ideas*. Basic Books., DOI: 10.5555/1095592.C1104753

Pardo, A., Han, F., & Ellis, R. A. (2016). Combining University Student Self-Regulated Learning Indicators and Engagement with Online Learning Events to Predict Academic Performance. *IEEE Transactions on Learning Technologies*, *10*(1), 82–92. DOI: 10.1109/TLT.2016.2639508

Pardo, A., & Siemens, G. (2014). Ethical and privacy principles for learning analytics. *British Journal of Educational Technology*, *45*(3), 438–450. DOI: 10.1111/bjet.12152

Pargmann, J., Berding, F., Rebmann, K., & Riebenbauer, E. (2025). How AI feedback supports lesson planning in vocational teacher education: A longitudinal intervention study using an analytical AI platform. *Empirical Research in Vocational Education and Training, 17*(1), 26. Advance online publication. DOI: 10.1186/s40461-025-00202-7

Parikh, N. A. (2026). Agentic AI in Product Management: A Co-Evolutionary Model. In *High Performance Leadership for Organizational Excellence: Innovation, Technology, and Resilience* (pp. 1-36). IGI Global Scientific Publishing.

Paris, S. G., & Paris, A. H. (2003). Classroom applications of research on self-regulated learning. In Good, T. L., & Levin, J. R. (Eds.), *Educational Psychology* (pp. 89–101). Routledge., DOI: 10.4324/9781410608130

Park, W., & Kwon, H. (2024). Implementing artificial intelligence education for middle school technology education in Republic of Korea. *International Journal of Technology and Design Education, 34*(1), 109–135. DOI: 10.1007/s10798-023-09812-2 PMID: 36844448

Passey, D., Ntebutse, J. G., Ahmad, M. Y. A., Cochrane, J., Collin, S., Ganayem, A., Langran, E., Mulla, S., Rodrigo, M. M., Saito, T., Shonfeld, M., & Somasi, S. (2024). Populations Digitally Excluded from Education: Issues, Factors, Contributions and Actions for Policy, Practice and Research in a Post-Pandemic Era. *Technology, Knowledge and Learning 2024 29:4, 29*(4), 1733–1750. DOI: 10.1007/s10758-024-09767-w

Patel, C., Suthar, F., & Patel, S. (2025). AI agents in education: Transforming learning through intelligent systems. *Preprints.* DOI: 10.20944/preprints202506.1870.v1

Patel, K. (2024). Agentic AI for Self-Healing Production Lines: Autonomous Root Cause Analysis & Correction. *Journal of Information Systems Engineering & Management, 9*, 124–135.

Paulsen, L., & Lindsay, E. (2024). Learning analytics dashboards are increasingly becoming about learning and not just analytics: A systematic review. *Education and Information Technologies, 29*(11), 14279–14308. DOI: 10.1007/s10639-023-12401-4

Pawar, M., & Rai, R. D. (2023). Ethical challenges of artificial intelligence in education: Achieving learner centricity with respect to learner autonomy. In *Proceedings of the International Conference on Computers in Education.* DOI: 10.58459/icce.2023.1437

Peddi, S., & Manoharan, G. (2025). Ethical guidelines for the thoughtful implementation of AI in higher education. *EthAIca, 5*, 409. DOI: 10.56294/ai2026409

Pedersen, I., & Duin, A. (2022). AI agents, humans and untangling the marketing of artificial intelligence in learning environments. *55th Annual Hawaii International Conference on System Sciences (HICSS)* (pp. 4-13). IEEE Computer Society. DOI: 10.24251/HICSS.2022.002

Pellas, N. (2024). Comparing quality and autonomous learning of teacher professional development programs in MOOCs and LMS. *Education and Information Technologies, 30*(7), 9005–9039. DOI: 10.1007/s10639-024-13154-4

Perez, J., Castro, M., & Lopez, G. (2023). Serious games and AI: Challenges and opportunities for computational social science. *IEEE Access : Practical Innovations, Open Solutions, 11*, 62051–62061. DOI: 10.1109/ACCESS.2023.3286695

Perin, A. J. (2025, July 29). *So...What are these Decentralized Identifiers?* DEV Community. https://dev.to/joojscript/sowhat-are-these-decentralized-identifiers-130l

Perkins, M., Furze, L., Roe, J., & MacVaugh, J. (2024). The Artificial Intelligence Assessment Scale (AIAS): A framework for ethical integration of generative AI in educational assessment. *Journal of University Teaching & Learning Practice, 21*(6), 49–66. DOI: 10.53761/q3azde36

Petrov, I., Chikurtev, D., & Krusteva, A. (2025). Artificial Intelligence and Cyber Security in Education: Bibliographic Mapping and Entropy Analysis of Science Research (SCOPUS, 2015-2024). *2025 19th Conference on Electrical Machines, Drives and Power Systems (ELMA)*, 1–8. DOI: 10.1109/ELMA65795.2025.11083516

Petrus, I. (2019). SMITHGROUP-AI: THE FUTURE OF BUILDING CONTROLS: SMITHGROUP-AI would be an independent, multifunctional reinforcement learning software agent responsible for the monitoring and control of all agents that control all building systems. *Engineered Systems, 36*(4), 32-36. Retrieved from https://go.gale.com/ps/i.do?id=GALE%7CA584177473&sid=googleScholar&v=2.1&it=r&linkaccess=abs&issn=08919976&p=AONE&sw=w

Piaget, J. (1972). The Psychology of the Child. Basic Books. https://archive.org/details/psychologyofchil00piag_0

Piaget, J. (1952). *The origins of intelligence in children.* International Universities Press. DOI: 10.1037/11494-000

Piaget, J. (1964). Part I: Cognitive development in children: Piaget development and learning. *Journal of Research in Science Teaching, 2*(3), 176–186. DOI: 10.1002/tea.3660020306

Ponnusamy, P., Ghias, A., Yi, Y., Yao, B., Guo, C., & Sarikaya, R. (2022). Feedback-based self-learning in large-scale conversational ai agents. *AI Magazine, 42*(4), 43–56. DOI: 10.1609/aimag.v42i4.15102

Pop, M. V., Ton , G., Flonta, F. V., & Flore, M. (2025). Agentic AI in STEM Education: Enhancing Cognitive Flexibility and Workforce Readiness. *BRAIN. Broad Research in Artificial Intelligence and Neuroscience, 16*(1 Sup1), 239-249.

Popenici, S. A. D., & Kerr, S. (2017). Exploring the impact of artificial intelligence on teaching and learning in higher education. *Research and Practice in Technology Enhanced Learning, 12*(1), 22. DOI: 10.1186/s41039-017-0062-8 PMID: 30595727

Porter, Z., Calinescu, R., Lim, E., Hodge, V., Ryan, P., Burton, S., Habli, I., Lawton, T., McDermid, J., Molloy, J., Monkhouse, H., Morgan, P., Noordhof, P., Paterson, C., Standen, I., & Zou, J. (2025). INSYTE: A classification framework for traditional to agentic AI systems. *ACM Transactions on Autonomous and Adaptive Systems, 20*(3), 1–39. DOI: 10.1145/3760424

Portugal, I. D. S., Alencar, P., & Cowan, D. (2024, December). An agentic AI-based multi-agent framework for recommender systems. In *2024 IEEE International Conference on Big Data (BigData)* (pp. 5375-5382). IEEE. DOI: 10.1109/BigData62323.2024.10825765

Poupard, M., Larrue, F., Sauzéon, H., & Tricot, A. (2025). A systematic review of immersive technologies for education: Effects of cognitive load and curiosity state on learning performance. *British Journal of Educational Technology*, *56*(1), 5–41. DOI: 10.1111/bjet.13503

Pratham. (2025). *"PadhAI": Transforming literacy with AI-powered reading assessments | Pratham UK.* https://pratham.org.uk/pratham-launches-padhai-transforming-literacy-with-ai-powered-reading-assessments/

Preetha, B., Venkataraman, G., Hariharan, G. N., & Prabavathy, V. R. (2022). The "Every Child A Scientist" program: Using digital technologies to enhance science learning among middle grade students from corporation schools in Chennai. *CSI Transactions on ICT*, *10*(3), 237–244. DOI: 10.1007/s40012-022-00368-5

Pressman, R. S. (2020). *Software Engineering: A Practitioner's Approach* (9th ed.). McGraw-Hill Education.

Pushparani, R. (2025). Review on collaboration intelligence in education. *International Research Journal on Advanced Engineering Hub*, *3*(9), 3606–3611. DOI: 10.47392/IRJAEH.2025.0526

Qu, M. (2025). Future of language learning: Unveiling the power of AI-Driven adaptive platforms to tailor language learning based on learners' needs, proficiency and learning styles. *European Journal of Education*, *60*(2), e70116. Advance online publication. DOI: 10.1111/ejed.70116

Qureshi, F., Khan, M., Jabeen, S., & Shah, S. (2025). Exploring blockchain transaction patterns using graph-based visualization. In *Cybersecurity, Cybercrimes, and Smart Emerging Technologies* (pp. 155-166). CRC Press. Retrieved from https://www.taylorfrancis.com/chapters/edit/10.1201/9781003614197-16/exploring-blockchain-transaction-patterns-using-graph-based-visualization-fahad-qureshi-maqbool-khan-saima-jabeen-sajid-shah

Rabiatu, M. M., & Shehu, S. A. (2024). Adopting artificial intelligence (AI) in education: Challenges & possibilities. *Asian Journal of Advanced Research and Reports*, *18*(2), 106–111. DOI: 10.9734/ajarr/2024/v18i2608

Rahayu, M. A., & Makmur, A. (2024). The effectiveness of using smartboard interactive toward learning innovation in schools. *JIV-Jurnal Ilmiah Visi*, *19*(1), 23–31. DOI: 10.21009/JIV.1901.3

Raheem, T., & Hossain, G. (2025, May). Agentic AI Systems: Opportunities, Challenges, and Trustworthiness. In *2025 IEEE International Conference on Electro Information Technology (eIT)* (pp. 618-624). IEEE. DOI: 10.1109/eIT64391.2025.11103638

Rahiman, H. U., & Kodikal, R. (2024). Revolutionizing education: Artificial intelligence empowered learning in higher education. *Cogent Education*, *11*(1), 2293431. DOI: 10.1080/2331186X.2023.2293431

Rahimi, A. R., & Tafazoli, D. (2022). The role of university teachers' 21st-century digital competence in their attitudes toward ICT integration in higher education: Extending the theory of planned behavior. *The JALT CALL Journal, 18*(2), 238–263. DOI: 10.29140/jaltcall.v18n2.632

Rahman, A., Arabi, S., Rab, R., Rahman, A., Arabi, S., & Rab, R. (2021). Feasibility and Challenges of 5G Network Deployment in Least Developed Countries (LDC). *Wireless Sensor Network, 13*(1), 1–16. DOI: 10.4236/wsn.2021.131001

Raihan, M. M. H., Subroto, S., Chowdhury, N., Koch, K., Ruttan, E., & Turin, T. C. (2025). Dimensions and barriers for digital (in)equity and digital divide: A systematic integrative review. *Digital Transformation and Society, 4*(2), 111–127. DOI: 10.1108/DTS-04-2024-0054

Raji, I. D., Smart, A., White, R. N., Mitchell, M., Gebru, T., Hutchinson, B., Smith-Loud, J., Theron, D., & Barnes, P. (2020). Closing the AI accountability gap: Defining an end-to-end framework for internal algorithmic auditing. In *Proceedings of the 2020 Conference on Fairness, Accountability, and Transparency* (pp. 33–44). Association for Computing Machinery. https://doi.org/DOI: 10.1145/3351095.3372873

Ramasamy, J. V., Md Yunus, M., & Hanim Ismail, H. (2025).. . *Effectiveness of Google Read-Along Application in Improving Reading Skills of Rural Area Upper Primary ESL Classroom INTERNATIONAL JOURNAL OF ACADEMIC RESEARCH IN PROGRESSIVE EDUCATION AND DEVELOPMENT,* (14). Advance online publication. DOI: 10.6007/IJARPED/v14-i1/24948

Ramirez, E. A. B., & Esparrell, J. A. F. (2024). Artificial Intelligence (AI) in Education: Unlocking the Perfect Synergy for Learning. *Educational Process: International Journal, 13*(1), 35–51.

Ramsden, P. (2019). *Successful Teaching and Learning in Grade 10 - 12 Subjects.* Department of Basic Education. Retrieved from https://www.eccurriculum.co.za/Circulars/2022-Circulars/04%20FET%20%20Successful%20Teaching%20and%20Learning%20Framework-2019%20FINAL%20DOCUMENT.pdf

Rane, N. (2024). Enhancing the quality of teaching and learning through Gemini, ChatGPT, and similar generative Artificial Intelligence: Challenges, future prospects, and ethical considerations in education. *TESOL and Technology Studies, 5*(1), 1–6. DOI: 10.48185/tts.v5i1.1000

Rannisto, A., & Vainionpää, F. (2025). Trust-Affording Action: Citizens' Everyday Relations With Algorithmized Public Services. *Social Inclusion (Lisboa), 13*, 10001. Advance online publication. DOI: 10.17645/si.10001

Rapaka, A., Dharmadhikari, S. C., Kasat, K., Mohan, C. R., Chouhan, K., & Gupta, M. (2025). Revolutionizing learning - A journey into educational games with immersive and AI technologies. *Entertainment Computing, 52*, 1–8. DOI: 10.1016/j.entcom.2024.100809

Rasa. (n.d.). *Build AI Agents you can trust to handle real world complexity.* Rasa.Com. Retrieved December 9, 2025, from https://rasa.com/

Raslan, G. (2024). The impact of the zone of proximal development concept (scaffolding) on the students problem solving skills and learning outcomes. In BUiD Doctoral Research Conference 2023 (LNCE, Vol. 473, pp. 59–66). Springer. https://doi.org/DOI: 10.1007/978-3-031-56121-4_6

Raza, S., Sapkota, R., Karkee, M., & Emmanouilidis, C. (2025). Responsible Agentic Reasoning and AI Agents: A Critical Survey: Proposal for Safe Agentic AI via Responsible Reasoning AI Agents (R2A2). *SuperIntelligence-Robotics-Safety & Alignment, 2*(6).

Raza, A., Ahmed, U., Saleem, K., Sarwar, M., Shaheen, M., & Farooq, M. S. (2025). Employing Natural Language Processing Techniques for the Development of a Voting-Based POS Tagger in the Urdu Language. In *Innovations in Optimization and Machine Learning* (pp. 23–46). IGI Global Scientific Publishing. DOI: 10.4018/979-8-3693-5231-1.ch002

Redecker, C. (2017). *European framework for the digital competence of educators: DigCompEdu*. Publications Office of the European Union. https://joint-research-centre.ec.europa.eu/system/files/2018-11/digcompeduorg-en-2018-11_a4new.pdf

Renkema, M., & Tursunbayeva, A. (2024). The future of work of academics in the age of Artificial Intelligence: State-of-the-art and a research roadmap. *Futures, 163*, 103453. DOI: 10.1016/j.futures.2024.103453

Ren, X. (2025). Policy, pedagogy, and technological disruption: Teacher agency in AI-integrated educational ecosystems. *Business and Social Sciences Proceedings*, *2*, 31–37. DOI: 10.71222/azryt912

Riedl, M. O. (2019). Human-centered artificial intelligence and machine learning. *Human Behavior and Emerging Technologies*, *1*(1), 33–36. DOI: 10.1002/hbe2.117

Rigopouli, K., Kotsifakos, D., & Psaromiligkos, Y. (2025). Vygotsky's creativity options and ideas in 21st-century technology-enhanced learning design. *Education Sciences*, *15*(2), 257. DOI: 10.3390/educsci15020257

Rink, J. E. (2012). Instruction from a learning perspective. In *Teaching physical education for learning* (pp. 157–176). Routledge., DOI: 10.4324/9780203487150-16

Robert, A., Potter, K., & Frank, L. (2024). The impact of artificial intelligence on students' learning experience. *Wiley Interdisciplinary Reviews: Computational Statistics*, *2*(01), 75–84.

Rokhsaritalemi, S., Niaraki, A. S., & Choi, S. M. (2021). A review on mixed reality: Current trends, challenges and prospects. *Applied Sciences (Basel, Switzerland)*, *10*(2), 636–662. DOI: 10.3390/app10020636

Roll, I., & Wylie, R. (2016). Evolution and revolution in artificial intelligence in education. *International Journal of Artificial Intelligence in Education*, *26*(2), 582–599. DOI: 10.1007/s40593-016-0110-3

Romero, C., & Ventura, S. (2010). Educational Data Mining: A Review of the state of the art. *IEEE Transactions on Systems, Man, and Cybernetics. Part C, Applications and Reviews*, *40*(6), 601–618. DOI: 10.1109/TSMCC.2010.2053532

Roshanaei, M. (2024). Towards best practices for mitigating artificial intelligence implicit bias in shaping diversity, inclusion and equity in higher education. *Education and Information Technologies*, *29*(14), 18959–18984. DOI: 10.1007/s10639-024-12605-2

Rossi, I., Lima, J., Sabatke, B., Nunes, M., Ramirez, G., & Ramirez, M. (2021). Active learning tools improve the learning outcomes, scientific attitude, and critical thinking in higher education: Experiences in an online course during the COVID-19 pandemic. *Biochemistry and Molecular Biology Education*, *49*(6), 888–903. DOI: 10.1002/bmb.21574 PMID: 34652877

Rotondi, V., Kashyap, R., Pesando, L. M., Spinelli, S., & Billari, F. C. (2025). Leveraging mobile phones to attain sustainable development. *Proceedings of the National Academy of Sciences of the United States of America, 117*(24), 13413–13420. DOI: 10.1073/pnas.1909326117 PMID: 32482867

Ruangpattanakul, K. (2025). Enhancing English Writing Competence and Self-Correction Awareness through the RADAR Process in Argumentative Writing. *Journal of English Language and Linguistics, 6*(2), 220–238. DOI: 10.62819/jel.2025.1171

Ruano, I., Estévez, E., Gámez, J., & Gómez, J. (2023). Standards for the integration of online laboratories with learning management systems. *IEEE Access : Practical Innovations, Open Solutions, 11*, 125267–125290. DOI: 10.1109/ACCESS.2023.3330666

Ruiz-Rojas, L. I., Salvador-Ullauri, L., & Acosta-Vargas, P. (2024). Collaborative working and critical thinking: Adoption of generative artificial intelligence tools in higher education. *Sustainability (Basel), 16*(13), 5367. DOI: 10.3390/su16135367

Russell, S. J., & Norvig, P. (2020). *Artificial intelligence: A modern approach* (4th ed.). Pearson.

Rusum, G. P., & Anasuri, S. (2025). Agentic AI: Building Self-Directed Software Agents with Multimodal Reasoning. *American International Journal of Computer Science and Technology, 7*(1), 1–14. DOI: 10.63282/3117-5481/AIJCST-V7I1P101

Ryan, R. M., & Deci, E. L. (2020). Intrinsic and extrinsic motivation from a self-determination theory perspective: Definitions, theory, practices, and future directions. *Contemporary Educational Psychology, 61*, 101860. DOI: 10.1016/j.cedpsych.2020.101860

Sadler, D. R. (1989). Formative assessment and the design of instructional systems. *Instructional Science, 18*(2), 119–144. DOI: 10.1007/BF00117714

Sağın, F. G., Özkaya, A. B., Tengiz, F., Geyik, Ö. G., & Geyik, C. (2024). Current evaluation and recommendations for the use of artificial intelligence tools in education. *Türk Biyokimya Dergisi, 48*(6), 620–625. DOI: 10.1515/tjb-2023-0254

Şahin, M. (2012). Pros and cons of connectivism as a learning theory. *International Journal of Physical and Social Sciences, 2*(4), 437–454.

Saidin, N., Kamarozaman, N. F. H., Roslan, F. S., Ralib, A. A. M., & Sing, L. K. (2021). Graphene-oxide Coated on Fiber Bragg Grating for Temperature Sensor. *2021 8th International Conference on Computer and Communication Engineering (ICCCE)*, 269–273. DOI: 10.1109/ICCCE50029.2021.9467205

Salameh, W. A. K.Waleed Abdullatif Khader Salameh. (2024). The dual role of AI in personalized learning: Enhancements and hindrances for diverse learners. *International Journal of Science and Research Archive, 13*(2), 62–67. DOI: 10.30574/ijsra.2024.13.2.2057

Säljö, R. (2022). Learning from a sociocultural perspective. In *International encyclopedia of education* (pp. 36–43). Elsevier., DOI: 10.1016/B978-0-12-818630-5.14006-0

Salloum, S. A. (2024). AI perils in education: Exploring ethical concerns. *Artificial intelligence in education: The power and dangers of ChatGPT in the classroom*, 669-675.

Salloum, S. A., Salloum, A., & Alfaisal, R. (2024). Objectives and Obstacles of Artificial Intelligence in Education. *Artificial Intelligence in Education: The Power and Dangers of ChatGPT in the Classroom*, 605-614.

Salloum, S. A. (2024). AI perils in education: Exploring ethical concerns. In *Studies in big data* (pp. 669–675). Springer., DOI: 10.1007/978-3-031-52280-2_43

Samala, A. D., Rawas, S., Wang, T., Reed, J. M., Kim, J., Howard, N. J., & Ertz, M. (2025). Unveiling the landscape of generative artificial intelligence in education: A comprehensive taxonomy of applications, challenges, and future prospects. *Education and Information Technologies*, *30*(3), 3239–3278. DOI: 10.1007/s10639-024-12936-0

Sămărescu, N., Bumbac, R., Zamfiroiu, A., & Iorgulescu, M. C. (2024). Artificial intelligence in education: Next-gen teacher perspectives. *Amfiteatru Economic*, *26*(65), 145–161. DOI: 10.24818/EA/2024/65/145

Samudra, A. (2022). Gendering the Digital Divide in India. SSRN *Electronic Journal.* https://doi.org/ DOI: 10.2139/SSRN.4112879

Samuel, Y., Brennan-Tonetta, M., Samuel, J., Kashyap, R., Kumar, V., Krishna Kaashyap, S., Chidipothu, N., Anand, I., & Jain, P. (2023). Cultivation of human centered artificial intelligence: Culturally adaptive thinking in education (CATE) for AI. *Frontiers in Artificial Intelligence*, *6*, 1198180. DOI: 10.3389/frai.2023.1198180 PMID: 38106981

Sana, E., Fitriani, A., Soetarno, D., & Yusuf, M. (2024). Analysis of user perceptions on interactive learning platforms based on artificial intelligence. *Journal of Computer Science and Technology Application*, *1*(1), 26–32. DOI: 10.33050/corisinta.v1i1.12

Sanchez, D. R., Langer, M., & Kaur, R. (2020). Gamification in the classroom: Examining the impact of gamified quizzes on student learning. *Computers & Education*, *144*, 1036–1066. DOI: 10.1016/j.compedu.2019.103666

Santamaría, J. S. (2025). *A pedagogical sense of artificial intelligence in education.* Open Science Framework. DOI: 10.31219/osf.io/z4bg6_v1

Sanusi, I. T., Agbo, F. J., Dada, O. A., Yunusa, A. A., Aruleba, K. D., Obaido, G., Olawumi, O., & Oyelere, S. S.Centre for Multidisciplinary Research and Innovation (CEMRI). (2024). Stakeholders' insights on artificial intelligence education: Perspectives of teachers, students, and policymakers. *Computers and Education Open*, *7*, 100212. DOI: 10.1016/j.caeo.2024.100212

Sanusi, I. T., Ayanwale, M. A., & Chiu, T. K. (2024). Investigating the moderating effects of social good and confidence on teachers' intention to prepare school students for artificial intelligence education. *Education and Information Technologies*, *29*(1), 273–295. DOI: 10.1007/s10639-023-12250-1

Sanusi, I. T., Ayanwale, M. A., & Tolorunleke, A. E. (2024). Investigating pre-service teachers' artificial intelligence perception from the perspective of planned behavior theory. *Computers and Education: Artificial Intelligence*, *6*, 100202. DOI: 10.1016/j.caeai.2024.100202

Saputra, I., Kurniawan, A., Yanita, M., Putri, E. Y., & Mahniza, M. (2024). The evolution of educational assessment: How artificial intelligence is shaping the trends and future of learning evaluation. *Indonesian Journal of Computer Science, 13*(6). Advance online publication. DOI: 10.33022/ijcs.v13i6.4465

Sarıdaş, G. (2025). The use of artificial intelligence agents in education. *International Society That Learn Journal, 2*(1). Advance online publication. DOI: 10.64782/istlj22286172

Sarwari, A. Q., Javed, M. N., Mohd Adnan, H., & Abdul Wahab, M. N. (2024). Assessment of the impacts of artificial intelligence (AI) on intercultural communication among postgraduate students in a multicultural university environment. *Scientific Reports, 14*(1), 13849. DOI: 10.1038/s41598-024-63276-5 PMID: 38879546

Sarwar, M. A., & Ms Saima, A. G. (2024). The role of artificial intelligence in shaping the future of education at higher secondary level. *Journal of Education and Social Studies, 5*(1), 34–45. DOI: 10.52223/jess.2024.5104

Sasikala, P., & Ravichandran, R. (2024). Journal of Digital Learning and Education. *Journal of Digital Learning and Education, 4*(2), 145–155. DOI: 10.52562/jdle.v4i2.1234

Satav, A. (2025). Enterprise API & Platform Strategy in the era of Agentic AI. *Journal of Computer Science and Technology Studies, 7*(1), 380–385. DOI: 10.32996/jcsts.2025.7.1.28

Sato, E., Shyyan, V., Chauhan, S., & Christensen, L. (2024). Putting AI in fair: A framework for equity in AI-driven learner models and inclusive assessments. *Egitimde ve Psikolojide Ölçme ve Degerlendirme Dergisi, 15*, 263–281. DOI: 10.21031/epod.1526527

Scardamalia, M., & Bereiter, C. (2014). Smart technology for self-organizing processes. *Smart Learning Environments, 1*(1), 1. Advance online publication. DOI: 10.1186/s40561-014-0001-8

Schiff, D. (2022). Education for AI, not AI for education: The role of education and ethics in national AI policy strategies. *International Journal of Artificial Intelligence in Education, 32*(3), 527–563. DOI: 10.1007/s40593-021-00270-2

Schneider, D., Biener, V., Otte, A., Gesslein, T., Gagel, P., Campos, C., & Grubert, J. (2021). Accuracy evaluation of touch tasks in commodity virtual and augmented reality head-mounted displays. *In Proceedings of the 2021 ACM Symposium on Spatial User Interaction* (pp. 3485279-3485283). New York, USA: ACM. DOI: 10.1145/3485279.3485283

Schwaber, K., & Sutherland, J. (2017). *The Scrum Guide*. Scrum Alliance.

Selwyn, N. (2024). On the limits of artificial intelligence (AI) in education. *Nordisk tidsskrift for pedagogikk og kritikk, 10*(1), 3-14.

Selwyn, N. (2019). *Should robots replace teachers?: AI and the future of education.* John Wiley & Sons.

Selwyn, N. (2019). What's the problem with learning analytics? *Journal of Learning Analytics, 6*(3). Advance online publication. DOI: 10.18608/jla.2019.63.3

Selwyn, N. (2021). *Education and technology: Key issues and debates.* Bloomsbury Publishing.

Serban, A., Poll, E., & Visser, J. (2020). A standard driven software architecture for fully autonomous vehicles. *Journal of Automotive Software Engineering, 1*(1), 20. DOI: 10.2991/jase.d.200212.001

Shabani, K., Khatib, M., Tabataba'i Uinversity, A., & Ebadi, S. (2010). Vygotsky's Zone of Proximal Development: Instructional Implications and Teachers' []. www.ccsenet.org/elt]. *Professional Development (Philadelphia, Pa.), 3*(4), •••.

Shailendra, S., Kadel, R., & Sharma, A. (2024). Framework for adoption of generative artificial intelligence (GenAI) in education. *IEEE Transactions on Education, 67*(5), 777–785. DOI: 10.1109/TE.2024.3432101

Shalwa. (2025). AI Plagiarism Statistics 2025: Transforming Academic Integrity. In *Artsmart.ai*. https://artsmart.ai/blog/ai-plagiarism-statistics/

Shamsuddinova, S., Heryani, P., & Naval, M. A. (2024). Evolution to revolution: Critical exploration of educators' perceptions of the impact of Artificial Intelligence (AI) on the teaching and learning process in the GCC region. *International Journal of Educational Research, 125*, 102326. DOI: 10.1016/j.ijer.2024.102326

Shamszare, H., & Choudhury, A. (2023). Clinicians' Perceptions of Artificial Intelligence: Focus on Workload, Risk, Trust, Clinical Decision Making, and Clinical Integration. *Healthcare (Basel), 11*(16), 2308. DOI: 10.3390/healthcare11162308 PMID: 37628506

Shankar, B., Jyothi, P., & Bhattacharyya, P. (2024). In-context Mixing (ICM): Code-mixed Prompts for Multilingual LLMs. *Proceedings of the Annual Meeting of the Association for Computational Linguistics, 1*, 4162–4176. DOI: 10.18653/v1/2024.acl-long.228

Sharif, H., Atif, A., & Nagra, A. A. (2025). Deepfake-Style AI Tutors in Higher Education: A Mixed-Methods Review and Governance Framework for Sustainable Digital Education. *Sustainability (Basel), 17*(21), 9793. DOI: 10.3390/su17219793

Sharma, A., & Chaturvedi, S. (2025). Agentic AI with Model Context Protocol. *ICT Systems and Sustainability: Proceedings of ICT4SD 2025, Volume 2, 2*, 433.

Sharma, M. S., & Bansal, D. (2017). Constructivism as paradigm for teaching and learning. *International Journal of Physical Education. Sports Health, 4*, 209–212.

Sharma, S., Singh, G., Sharma, C. S., & Kapoor, S. (2024). Artificial intelligence in Indian higher education institutions: A quantitative study on adoption and perceptions. *International Journal of System Assurance Engineering and Management*, •••, 1–17. DOI: 10.1007/s13198-023-02193-8

Sharples, M. (2023). Towards social generative AI for education: Theory, practices and ethics. *Learning. Research and Practice, 9*(2), 159–167. DOI: 10.1080/23735082.2023.2261131

Sheelam, G. K. (2024). Towards Autonomic Wireless Systems: Integrating Agentic AI with Advanced Semiconductor Technologies in Telecommunications. *American Online Journal of Science and Engineering (AOJSE), 2*(1).

Sheelam, G. K., & Komaragiri, V. B. (2025). Self-Adaptive Wireless Communication: Leveraging ML And Agentic AI In Smart Telecommunication Networks. *Metallurgical and Materials Engineering*, 1381-1401.

Sheelam, G. K. (2025). Architecting Agentic AI for Real-Time Autonomous Edge Systems in Next-Gen Mobile Devices. *Advances in Consumer Research. Association for Consumer Research (U. S.)*, *2*(3).

Shepard, L. A. (2000). The role of assessment in a learning culture. *Educational Researcher*, *29*(7), 4–14. DOI: 10.3102/0013189X029007004

Sholeh, M. I. (2025). Educational transformation through artificial intelligence. In *Advances in computational intelligence and robotics* (pp. 25–40). IGI Global. DOI: 10.4018/979-8-3693-7260-9.ch002

Shtayyat, A., Gawanmeh, A., & Mashaleh, A. (2025). Risk analysis of AI integration in educational systems. In *Advances in computational intelligence and robotics* (pp. 401–428). IGI Global. DOI: 10.4018/979-8-3373-0832-6.ch017

Shute, V. J., & Zapata-Rivera, D. (2012). Adaptive Educational Systems. In P. J. Durlach & A. M. Lesgold (Eds.), Adaptive Technologies for Training and Education (pp. 7–27). chapter, Cambridge: Cambridge University Press. https://doi.org/DOI: 10.1017/CBO9781139049580.004

Shute, V. J. (2008). Focus on formative feedback. *Review of Educational Research*, *78*(1), 153–189. DOI: 10.3102/0034654307313795

Siemens, G. (2005). Connectivism: A learning theory for the digital age. *International Journal of Instructional Technology and Distance Learning*, *2*, 3–10. http://www.itdl.org/Journal/Jan_05/article01.htm

Siemens, G., Marmolejo-Ramos, F., Gabriel, F., Medeiros, K., Marrone, R., Joksimovic, S., & De Laat, M. (2022). Human and artificial cognition. *Computers & Education: Artificial Intelligence*, *3*, 100107. DOI: 10.1016/j.caeai.2022.100107

Si, J. (2025). Exploring AI literacy, attitudes toward AI, and intentions to use AI in clinical contexts among healthcare students in Korea: A cross-sectional study. *BMC Medical Education*, *25*(1), 1233. DOI: 10.1186/s12909-025-07766-8 PMID: 40885994

Simons, A., Wohlgenannt, I., Zelt, S., Weinmann, M., Schneider, J., & Brocke, J. V. (2023). Intelligence at play: Game-based assessment using virtual-reality application. *Virtual Reality (Waltham Cross)*, *27*(3), 1827–1843. DOI: 10.1007/s10055-023-00752-9

Sindakis, S., & Showkat, G. (2024). The digital revolution in India: Bridging the gap in rural technology adoption. *Journal of Innovation and Entrepreneurship*, *13*(1), 1–28. DOI: 10.1186/s13731-024-00380-w

Singer, J., Marx, R. W., Krajcik, J., & Chambers, J. C. (2000). Constructing Extended inquiry Projects: Curriculum materials for science Education Reform. *Educational Psychologist*, *35*(3), 165–178. DOI: 10.1207/S15326985EP3503_3

Singh, G., & Thakur, A. (2024). AI in education. In *Advances in computational intelligence and robotics* (pp. 18–38). IGI Global. DOI: 10.4018/979-8-3693-2964-1.ch002

Singha, S., & Singha, R. (2024). The application of artificial intelligence in education: Opportunities and challenges. *Educational perspectives on digital technologies in modeling and management*, 282-292.

Singh, S. (2017). Bridging the gender digital divide in developing countries. *Journal of Children and Media*, *11*(2), 245–247. DOI: 10.1080/17482798.2017.1305604

Singh, S., Pandey, J. K., Rai, M., & Saxena, A. K. (2024). Advancements in Facial Expression Recognition Using Machine and Deep Learning Techniques. In *Machine and Deep Learning Techniques for Emotion Detection* (pp. 149–166). IGI Global. DOI: 10.4018/979-8-3693-4143-8.ch007

Skedsmo, G., & Huber, S. G. (2025). Beyond the score: Validity, equity, and interpretation in diverse assessment contexts. *Educational Assessment, Evaluation and Accountability*, *37*(2), 163–169. DOI: 10.1007/s11092-025-09459-8

Slade, S., & Prinsloo, P. (2023). Learning analytics, ethics, and student data: A systematic review. *British Journal of Educational Technology*, *54*(1), 1–17. DOI: 10.1111/bjet.13271

SMART Technologies ULC. (2025). *SMART Support*. Retrieved from How can we help you?: https://support.smarttech.com/

Smith, T. S., Holland, A. C., White, T., Combs, B., Watts, P., & Moss, J. (2021). A Distance Accessible Education Model: Teaching Skills to Nurse Practitioners. *The Journal for Nurse Practitioners*, *17*(8), 999–1003. DOI: 10.1016/j.nurpra.2021.05.018 PMID: 35165528

Sommer, D., Schmidbauer, L., & Wahl, F. (2024). Nurses' perceptions, experience and knowledge regarding artificial intelligence: Results from a cross-sectional online survey in Germany. *BMC Nursing*, *23*(1), 205. DOI: 10.1186/s12912-024-01884-2 PMID: 38539169

Song, Y., Wu, K., & Ding, J. (2024). Developing an immersive game-based learning platform with generative artificial intelligence and virtual reality technologies - "LearningverseVR". *Computers & Education: X Reality, 4*, 1-7. DOI: 10.1016/j.cexr.2024.100069

Sonntag, M., Mehmann, S., Mehmann, J., & Teuteberg, F. (2024). Development and Evaluation of a Maturity Model for AI Deployment Capability of Manufacturing Companies. *Information Systems Management*, *42*(1), 37–67. DOI: 10.1080/10580530.2024.2319041

Sorensen, S. (2025). The Great Reimagining: A Bridge & Blueprint for Jobs, Flourishing, and a New Human Era in the Age of AI. In *ResearchGate*. Independently published.

Sova, R., Tudor, C., Tartavulea, C. V., & Dieaconescu, R. I. (2024). Artificial intelligence tool adoption in higher education: A structural equation modeling approach to understanding impact factors among economics students. *Electronics (Basel), 13*(18), 3632. DOI: 10.3390/electronics13183632

Sperling, K., Stenberg, C. J., McGrath, C., Åkerfeldt, A., Heintz, F., & Stenliden, L. (2024). In search of artificial intelligence (AI) literacy in teacher education: A scoping review. *Computers and Education Open*, *6*, 100169. DOI: 10.1016/j.caeo.2024.100169

Spinelli, C. G. (2008). Introduction: The benefits, uses, and practical application of informal assessment procedures. *Reading & Writing Quarterly*, *24*(1), 1–6. DOI: 10.1080/10573560701753005

Squires, D., & Preece, J. (1999). Predicting Quality in Educational software. *Interacting with Computers*, *11*(5), 467–483. https://doi.org/. DOI: 10.1016/S0953-5438(98)00063-0

Staberg, R. L., Febri, M. I., Gjøvik, Ø., Sikko, S. A., & Pepin, B. (2023). Science teachers' interactions with resources for formative assessment purposes. *Educational Assessment, Evaluation and Accountability*, *35*(1), 5–35. DOI: 10.1007/s11092-022-09401-2

Steiss, J., Tate, T., Graham, S., Cruz, J., Hebert, M., Wang, J., Moon, Y., Tseng, W., Warschauer, M., & Olson, C. B. (2024). Comparing the quality of human and ChatGPT feedback on students' writing. *Learning and Instruction, 91*, 101894. Advance online publication. DOI: 10.1016/j.learninstruc.2024.101894

Stelea, G., Robu, D., & Sandu, F. (2025). AccessiLearnAI: An accessibility-first, AI-powered E-learning platform for inclusive education. *Education Sciences, 15*(9), 1125. DOI: 10.3390/educsci15091125

Stevens, A. F., & Stetson, P. (2023). Theory of trust and acceptance of artificial intelligence technology (TrAAIT): An instrument to assess clinician trust and acceptance of artificial intelligence. *Journal of Biomedical Informatics, 148*, 104550. DOI: 10.1016/j.jbi.2023.104550 PMID: 37981107

Stolpe, K., & Hallström, J. (2024). Artificial intelligence literacy for technology education. *Computers and Education Open, 6*, 100159. DOI: 10.1016/j.caeo.2024.100159

Storey, V. A., & Wagner, A. (2024). Integrating artificial intelligence (ai) into adult education: Opportunities, challenges, and future directions. [IJAET]. *International Journal of Adult Education and Technology, 15*(1), 1–15. DOI: 10.4018/IJAET.345921

Storozhyk, M. (2024). Philosophy of future: Analytical overview of interaction between education, science, and artificial intelligence in the context of contemporary challenges. *Futurity Philosophy, 3*(1), 23–47.

Strielkowski, W., Grebennikova, V., Lisovskiy, A., Rakhimova, G., & Vasileva, T. (2024). AI-driven adaptive learning for sustainable educational transformation. *Sustainable Development (Bradford), 33*(2), 1921–1947. DOI: 10.1002/sd.3221

Sulistiyono, M., Hasyim, J. W., Bernadhed, B., Liantoni, F., & Sidauruk, A. (2024). Comparative study of marker-based and markerless tracking in augmented reality under variable environmental conditions. *Journal of Soft Computing Exploration, 5*(4), 413–422. DOI: 10.52465/joscex.v5i4.503

Sun, J., Gan, W., Chao, H.-C., Yu, P. S., & Ding, W. (2023). Internet of Behaviors: A survey. *IEEE Internet of Things Journal, 10*(13), 11117–11134. DOI: 10.1109/JIOT.2023.3247594

Suresh, C., Ali, S. M., & Devaki, V. (2025). Perception About Usage of GAI Tools in Teaching and Research by Teachers and Students in Higher Education Institutions. Https://Services.Igi-Global.Com/Resolvedoi/Resolve.Aspx?Doi=10.4018/979-8-3693-8191-5.Ch015, 381–412. DOI: 10.4018/979-8-3693-8191-5.ch015

Suresh, A., Jacobs, J., Clevenger, C., Lai, V., Tan, C., Martin, J., & Sumner, T. (2024). Using AI to promote equitable classroom discussions: The TalkMoves application. In Zhai, X., & Krajcik, J. (Eds.), *Uses of artificial intelligence in STEM education* (pp. 371–398). Oxford University Press., DOI: 10.1093/oso/9780198882077.003.0017

Suryanarayana, K. S., Kandi, V. P., Pavani, G., Rao, A. S., Rout, S., & Krishna, T. S. R. (2024). Artificial intelligence enhanced digital learning for the sustainability of education management system. *The Journal of High Technology Management Research, 35*(2), 100495. DOI: 10.1016/j.hitech.2024.100495

Sutton, P. (2012). Conceptualizing feedback literacy: Knowing, being, and acting. *Innovations in Education and Teaching International, 49*(1), 31–40. DOI: 10.1080/14703297.2012.647781

Suura, S. R. (2024). Agentic artificial intelligence systems for dynamic health management and real-time genomic data analysis. [EJAAI]. *European Journal of Analytics and Artificial Intelligence*, *2*(1).

Sysoieva, I., Pukas, A., Dobizha, N., Pohrishchuk, B., Pohrishchuk, O., & Nadvynychnyy, S. (2025). Synergy of Information Technology and Management: Digital Strategies for Improving Management Efficiency. *2025 15th International Conference on Advanced Computer Information Technologies (ACIT)*, 287–292. DOI: 10.1109/ACIT65614.2025.11185822

Sywelem, M. M. G., & Mahklouf, A. M. E.-S. (2024). Ethical considerations in the integration of artificial intelligence in education: An overview. [CSIT]. *Computer Science and Information Technology*, *14*, 201–216. DOI: 10.5121/csit.2024.141201

Taber, K. S. (2024). Educational constructivism. *Encyclopedia*, *4*(4), 1534–1552. DOI: 10.3390/encyclopedia4040100

Tabor, J. (2025). Cognitivism, constructivism, and the classroom. In *Advances in computational intelligence and robotics* (pp. 211–240). IGI Global. DOI: 10.4018/979-8-3373-6007-2.ch007

Tahir, M., Hassan, F. D., & Shagoo, M. R. (2024). Role of artificial intelligence in education: A conceptual review. *World Journal of Advanced Research and Reviews*, *22*(1), 1469–1475. DOI: 10.30574/wjarr.2024.22.1.1217

Tal, M., Herscovitz, O., & Dori, Y. J. (2021). Assessing teachers' knowledge: Incorporating context-based learning in chemistry. *Chemistry Education Research and Practice*, *22*(4), 1003–1019. DOI: 10.1039/D0RP00359J

Tan, X., Cheng, G., & Ling, M. H. (2024). Artificial intelligence in teaching and teacher professional development: A systematic review. *Computers and Education: Artificial Intelligence*, 100355.

Tanaka, S. (2025). *Beyond the algorithm: Reimagining education in the age of AI personalization*. Open Science Framework. DOI: 10.31235/osf.io/rdvwg_v1

Tandon, N., & Shaheen, M. (2024). AI-driven innovations for environmental sustainability across sectors. In *Maintaining a sustainable world in the nexus of environmental science and AI* (pp. 429–454). IGI Global. DOI: 10.4018/979-8-3693-6336-2.ch017

Tang, K. H. D. (2024). Implications of artificial intelligence for teaching and learning. *Acta Pedagogia Asiana*, *3*(2), 65–79. DOI: 10.53623/apga.v3i2.404

Tanksley, T. C. (2024). "We're changing the system with this one": Black students using critical race algorithmic literacies to subvert and survive AI-mediated racism in school. *English Teaching*, *23*(1), 36–56. DOI: 10.1108/ETPC-08-2023-0102

Tan, L. Y., Hu, S., Yeo, D. J., & Cheong, K. H. (2025). Artificial intelligence-enabled adaptive learning platforms: A review. *Computers and Education Artificial Intelligence*, *9*, 100429. Advance online publication. DOI: 10.1016/j.caeai.2025.100429

Tan, X., Cheng, G., & Ling, M. H. (2025). Artificial intelligence in teaching and teacher professional development: A systematic review. *Computers and Education: Artificial Intelligence*, *8*, 100355. DOI: 10.1016/j.caeai.2024.100355

Tao, Y., Zhang, G., Zhang, D., Wang, F., Zhou, Y., & Xu, T. (2022). Exploring persona characteristics in learning: A review study of pedagogical agents. *Procedia Computer Science*, *201*, 87–94. DOI: 10.1016/j.procs.2022.03.014

Tariq, M. U. (2024). Navigating the personalization pathway. In *Advances in educational technologies and instructional design book series* (pp. 265–291). https://doi.org/DOI: 10.4018/979-8-3693-3641-0.ch012

Tashtoush, M. A., Wardat, Y., Ali, R. A., & Saleh, S. (2024). Artificial intelligence in education: Mathematics teachers' perspectives, practices and challenges. *Iraqi Journal for Computer Science and Mathematics*, *5*(1), 20. DOI: 10.52866/ijcsm.2024.05.01.004

Tassoti, S. (2024). Assessment of students use of generative artificial intelligence: Prompting strategies and prompt engineering in chemistry education. *Journal of Chemical Education*, *101*(6), 2475–2482. DOI: 10.1021/acs.jchemed.4c00212

Taufikin, M. S. I., Supaat, S., Azifah, N., Nikmah, F., & Kuanr, J., & Parminder. (2024). The impact of AI on teacher roles and pedagogy in the 21st century classroom. In *2024 International Conference on Knowledge Engineering and Communication Systems (ICKECS)* (pp. 1–5). IEEE. DOI: 10.1109/ICKECS61492.2024.10617236

Tawil, S., & Miao, F. (2024). Steering the Digital Transformation of Education: UNESCO's Human-Centered Approach. *Frontiers of Digital Education 2024 1:1*, *1*(1), 51–58. DOI: 10.1007/s44366-024-0020-0

Teane, F. M. (2024). Technological literacy and its influence on teachers' adoption of a blended learning approach. *Reading & Writing-Journal of the Reading Association of South Africa*, *15*(1). Retrieved from https://hdl.handle.net/10520/ejc-reading_v15_n1_a426

Tefo, R. M., & Goosen, L. (2024b). Exploring Transdisciplinary Approaches to Teaching Physical Sciences in Gauteng, South Africa: The Pedagogy of Using Smartboard Technologies. In R. Kumar, E. Ong, S. Anggoro, & T. Toh (Eds.), *Transdisciplinary Approaches to Learning Outcomes in Higher Education* (pp. 327-346). IGI Global. DOI: 10.4018/979-8-3693-3699-1.ch010

Tefo, R. M. (2021). *The influence of smartboards on the teaching and learning of grade 12 Physical Sciences in Tshwane District*. University of South Africa.

Tefo, R. M., & Goosen, L. (2024a). Fostering Pedagogical Innovation Through the Effective Smartboard Instruction of Physical Sciences: Technologies in Gauteng Schools, South Africa. In Khaldi, M. (Ed.), *Fostering Pedagogical Innovation Through Effective Instructional Design* (pp. 287–307). IGI Global., DOI: 10.4018/979-8-3693-1206-3.ch013

Teng, M. (2024). Metacognition and autonomy in building a community for language learning through VR digital gaming. *Computers & Education: X Reality*, *4*, 100060. DOI: 10.1016/j.cexr.2024.100060

Tenzin, S., Tendar, P., & Zangmo, N. (2022). Enhancing Students' Understanding of Abstract Concepts in Physics by Integrating ICT in Teaching-Learning Process. *Asian Journal of Education and Social Studies*, *26*, 68–80. DOI: 10.9734/ajess/2022/v26i230624

Teresa4Now, T. E. (2024, August 11). *The Power of Self-Reflection in an AI-Driven World*. ServiceNow. https://www.servicenow.com/community/intelligence-ml-blog/the-power-of-self-reflection-in-an-ai-driven-world/ba-p/3100439

The Center for Global Enterprise. (n.d.). *The Right to be Forgotten Meets the Immutable A Practical Guide to GDPR-Compliant Blockchain Solutions*. Retrieved July 23, 2026, from https://www.cravath.com/a/web/636/3898415_1.pdf

Thompson, S. J., & Dowd, C. (2023). *The evolution of compliance for state authorization of distance education*. State Authorization Network.

Thorat, S. H. (2025). Agentic AI for Customer Service and Contact Center Solutions. *Journal of Computer Science and Technology Studies*, *7*(8), 444–451.

Thorat, V., Rao, P., Joshi, N., Talreja, P., & Shetty, A. R. (2024). Role of artificial intelligence (AI) in patient education and communication in dentistry. *Cureus*, *16*(5). Advance online publication. DOI: 10.7759/cureus.59799 PMID: 38846249

Tigere, M. T., & Netshitangani, T. (2022). School management teams' perceptions of ICT integration in township and rural secondary schools of KwaZulu-Natal, South Africa: Infrastructure challenges. *Gender & Behaviour*, *20*(3), 20022–20041.

Tilepbergenovna, U. A. (2024). The role of artificial intelligence in education. *International Journal of Pedagogics*, *4*(10), 184–187. DOI: 10.37547/ijp/Volume04Issue10-32

Tiwari, A. (2025). Beyond Automation: The Emergence of Agentic Urban AI. *Automation*, *6*(3), 29. DOI: 10.3390/automation6030029

Tiwari, A. (2025). Conceptualising the emergence of Agentic Urban AI: From automation to agency. *Urban Informatics*, *4*(1), 13. DOI: 10.1007/s44212-025-00079-7

Tlili, A., Shehata, B., Adarkwah, M. A., Bozkurt, A., Hickey, D. T., Huang, R., & Agyemang, B. (2023). What if the devil is my guardian angel: ChatGPT as a case study of using chatbots in education. *Smart Learning Environments*, *10*(1), 15. DOI: 10.1186/s40561-023-00237-x

Topali, P., Haelermans, C., Molenaar, I., & Segers, E. (2025). Pedagogical considerations in the automation era: A systematic literature review of AIEd in K-12 authentic settings. *British Educational Research Journal*, *51*(6), 2777–2809. DOI: 10.1002/berj.4200

Topali, P., Ortega-Arranz, A., Rodríguez-Triana, M. J., Er, E., Khalil, M., & Akçapınar, G. (2025). Designing human-centered learning analytics and artificial intelligence in education solutions: A systematic literature review. *Behaviour & Information Technology*, *44*(5), 1071–1098. DOI: 10.1080/0144929X.2024.2345295

Topaz, M., Peltonen, L. M., Michalowski, M., Stiglic, G., Ronquillo, C., Pruinelli, L., Song, J., O'Connor, S., Miyagawa, S., & Fukahori, H. (2025). The ChatGPT effect: Nursing education and generative artificial intelligence. *The Journal of Nursing Education*, *64*(6), e40–e43. DOI: 10.3928/01484834-20240126-01 PMID: 38302101

Tran, T. T. T. (2025). Enhancing EFL writing revision practices: The impact of AI- and teacher-generated feedback and their sequences. *Education Sciences*, *15*(2), 232. Advance online publication. DOI: 10.3390/educsci15020232

Triantafyllou, S. A., & Sapounidis, T. (2023, March). Game-based Learning approach and Serious Games to learn while you play. *World Engineering Education Conference (EDUNINE)* (pp. 1-6). IEEE. DOI: 10.1109/EDUNINE57531.2023.10102872

Tripathi, S. (2024). Exploring the Differences: Private Blockchain vs Public Blockchain. In *Spydra.app*. https://www.spydra.app/blog/exploring-the-differences-private-blockchain-vs-public-blockchain

Trust Over, I. P. (2025, September 24). *Working Groups.* Trust Over IP. https://trustoverip.org/get-involved/working-groups/

Trust Over, I. P. (n.d.). *Defining a complete architecture for Internet-scale digital trust.* In *Trust Over IP*. Retrieved July 23, 2026, from https://trustoverip.org/

Trust Over, I. P. Foundation. (2020). *Introducing the.* Retrieved July 23, 2026, from https://trustoverip.org/wp-content/uploads/2020/05/toip_introduction_050520.pdf

Trust Over, I. P. Foundation. (2021). *Introduction to Trust Over IP.* https://trustoverip.org/wp-content/uploads/Introduction-to-ToIP-V2.0-2021-11-17.pdf

Trust Over, I. P. Foundation. (2022, November 15). *Learn & Work Ecosystem Library.* Learn & Work Ecosystem Library. https://learnworkecosystemlibrary.com/organizations/trust-over-ip-toip/

Trusts, T. A. T. A. (2023). *Learning fillip.* https://horizons.tatatrusts.org/2025/april/tata-trusts-horizons-learning-fillip.html

Truvera. (2026). Verifiable Credentials: The Ultimate Guide 2023. In www.dock.io. Retrieved July 23, 2026, from https://www.dock.io/post/verifiable-credentials

Tsakeni, M. (2023). Primary preservice science teachers' perceptions of practical work in remote learning environments. *Journal of Curriculum Studies Research*, *5*(1), 44–62. DOI: 10.46303/jcsr.2023.5

Tsayang, G., Batane, T., & Majuta, A. (2020). The Impact of Interactive Smart Boards on Students' Learning in Secondary Schools in Botswana: A Students' Perspective. *International Journal of Education and Development Using Information and Communication Technology*, *16*(2), 22–39.

Tumanggor, A. M., & Supahar, S. (2020). The development of diagnostic test instrument for mathematical representation ability (PhysDTRA) in high school physics learning. *Journal for the Education of Gifted Young Scientists*, *8*(4), 1439–1455. DOI: 10.17478/jegys.777425

Tzirides, A. O. O., Zapata, G., Kastania, N. P., Saini, A. K., Castro, V., Ismael, S. A., You, Y., Santos, T. A., Searsmith, D., O'Brien, C., Cope, B., & Kalantzis, M. (2024). Combining human and artificial intelligence for enhanced AI literacy in higher education. *Computers and Education Open*, *6*, 100184. DOI: 10.1016/j.caeo.2024.100184

Uddin, M. R. (2024). The role of the digital economy in Bangladesh's economic development. *Sustainable Technology and Entrepreneurship*, *3*(1), 100054. DOI: 10.1016/j.stae.2023.100054

Uden, L., & Ching, G. S. (2024). Activity theory-based ecosystem for artificial intelligence in education (AIED). *International Journal of Research Studies in Education, 13*(5). Advance online publication. DOI: 10.5861/ijrse.2024.24000

Umar, U., & Purwanto, M. B. (2025). AI and decision assistance for enhancing self-directed learning. [English Teaching Journal]. *ETERNAL, 16*(2), 457–465. DOI: 10.26877/eternal.v16i2.1524

UNESCO. (2021). *AI and education: Guidance for policy-makers.* UNESCO., DOI: 10.54675/PCSP7350

UNESCO. (2021). *Recommendation on the ethics of artificial intelligence.* UNESCO Publishing.

UNESCO. (2021a). *AI and education: Guidance for policy-makers.* UNESCO. https://unesdoc.unesco.org/ark:/48223/pf0000376709

UNESCO. (2021b). *Recommendation on the ethics of artificial intelligence.* Paris: UNESCO. https://unesdoc.unesco.org/ark:/48223/pf0000381137

UNESCO. (2023). *Guidance for generative AI in education and research.* UNESCO.

UNESCO. (2023). *Report on the results of the Working Group concerning a sensitization strategy to reinforce public awareness.* https://unesdoc.unesco.org/ark:/48223/pf0000385421

UNESCO. (2023a, July). *Generative AI and the future of education.* Retrieved from https://unesdoc.unesco.org/ark:/48223/pf0000385877

UNESCO. (2023b, September 6). *UNESCO survey: Less than 10% of schools and universities have formal guidance on AI.* Retrieved from https://www.unesco.org/en/articles/unesco-survey-less-10-schools-and-universities-have-formal-guidance-ai

UNESCO. (2023c, September 8). *Guidance for generative AI in education and research.* Retrieved from https://unesdoc.unesco.org/ark:/48223/pf0000386693

UNESCO. (2023d, November 30). *How generative AI is reshaping education in Asia-Pacific.* Retrieved from https://www.unesco.org/en/articles/how-generative-ai-reshaping-education-asia-pacific

UNESCO. (2024). *AI literacy and the new digital divide: A global call to action.* https://www.unesco.org/ethics-ai/en/articles/ai-literacy-and-new-digital-divide-global-call-action. Accessed April 5, 2026.

UNESCO. (2024, April). *Draft AI competency frameworks for teachers and for school students.* Retrieved from https://www.unesco.org/sites/default/files/medias/fichiers/2024/04/UNESCO-Draft-AI-competency-frameworks-for-teachers-and-school-students.pdf

UNHCR. (2023). *Digital Literacy and Skills.* https://www.unhcr.org/innovation/wp-content/uploads/2023/11/DigitalLiteracy_ConceptNote_UNHCR.pdf

UNHCR. (2024). *Evaluation of UNHCR's Support to Refugee Health, Education and Economic Inclusion in West and Central Africa.* https://www.unhcr.org/sites/default/files/2024-07/Evaluation%20of%20UNHCR%27s%20Support%20to%20Health%2C%20Education%2C%20and%20Economic%20Inclusion%20in%20West%20and%20Central%20Africa.pdf

United Nations Industrial Development Organization. (2023). Annual Report 2023. In *Webpage*. https://www.unido.org/annual-report-2023

Usak, M., Ozden, M., & Eilks, I. (2011). A case study of beginning science teachers' subject matter (SMK) and pedagogical content knowledge (PCK) of teaching chemical reaction in Turkey. *European Journal of Teacher Education*, *34*(4), 407–429. DOI: 10.1080/02619768.2011.592977

Utrecht University. (2025, July 31). *High-risk AI*. Utrecht University. https://www.uu.nl/en/organisation/ai-policy/teachers/ai-compliance/high-risk-ai

Uunona, G. N., & Goosen, L. (2023). Leveraging Ethical Standards in Artificial Intelligence Technologies: A Guideline for Responsible Teaching and Learning Applications. In Garcia, M., Lopez Cabrera, M., & de Almeida, R. (Eds.), *Handbook of Research on Instructional Technologies in Health Education and Allied Disciplines* (pp. 310–330). IGI Global., DOI: 10.4018/978-1-6684-7164-7.ch014

Uunona, G. N., & Goosen, L. (2024). Leveraging Ethics in Artificial Intelligence Technologies and Applications: E-Learning Management Systems in Namibia. In Ortiz-Rodriguez, F., Leyva-Mederos, A., Tiwari, S., Hernandez-Quintana, A., & Martinez-Rodriguez, J. (Eds.), *Semantic Web Technologies and Applications in Artificial Intelligence of Things* (pp. 173–185). IGI Global., DOI: 10.4018/979-8-3693-1487-6.ch008

Uunona, G. N., & Goosen, L. (2025a). Leveraging Ethics for Supporting Students' Artificial Intelligence Skills Development in Namibia. In Khaldi, M. (Ed.), *Supporting Personalized Learning and Students' Skill Development With AI* (pp. 203–230). IGI Global. DOI: 10.4018/979-8-3693-8965-2.ch011

Uunona, G. N., & Goosen, L. (2025b). Navigating Ethical Consideration of Artificial Intelligence and the Metaverse in Scientific Research. In Al Aqad, M., Sorayyaei Azar, A., Albattat, A., & Singh, A. (Eds.), *Navigating AI and the Metaverse in Scientific Research* (pp. 213–236). IGI Global Scientific Publishing., DOI: 10.4018/979-8-3373-0340-6.ch011

Uygun, D. (2024). Teachers' perspectives on artificial intelligence in education. *Advances in Mobile Learning Educational Research*, *4*(1), 931–939. DOI: 10.25082/AMLER.2024.01.005

VanLehn, K. (2006). The Behavior of Tutoring Systems. *International Journal of Artificial Intelligence in Education*, *16*(3), 227–265. DOI: 10.3233/IRG-2006-16(3)02

VanLehn, K. (2011). The relative effectiveness of human tutoring, intelligent tutoring systems, and other tutoring systems. *Educational Psychologist*, *46*(4), 197–221. DOI: 10.1080/00461520.2011.611369

Varanasi, R. A., Dell, N., & Vashistha, A. (2024). Saharaline: A Collective Social Support Intervention for Teachers in Low-Income Indian Schools. *Conference on Human Factors in Computing Systems - Proceedings*, (24). DOI: 10.1145/3613904.3642617

Varsik, S., & Vosberg, L. (2024a). The potential impact of Artificial Intelligence on equity and inclusion in education. *OECD Artificial Intelligence Papers, OECD Artificial Intelligence Papers, 23*. DOI: 10.1787/dee339a8-en

Vella, S. (2023, October 12). *The consequences of ignoring AI in schools: A missed opportunity*. 3CL Foundation. https://www.3cl.org/the-consequences-of-ignoring-ai-in-schools-a-missed-opportunity/

Venkatesh, A. N., & Jayavardhan, G. V. (2025). Future of Work: Managing Ethical Challenges of Agentic AI and Super Intelligence in Organizations. *Advances in Consumer Research. Association for Consumer Research (U. S.), 2*, 5277–5284.

VerifyEd. (2025). *Badge and Wallet Solutions: 5 Essential Digital Credential Tools 2025*. Verifyed.Io. https://www.verifyed.io/blog/badge-wallet-solutions

VerifyEd. (2025). Examples of Digital Identities: 5 Essential Types for 2025. In *Verifyed.io*. https://www.verifyed.io/blog/digital-identity-examples

Vesna, L., Sawale, P. S., Kaul, P., Pal, S., Snv, B., & Murthy, R. (2025). Digital Divide in AI-Powered Education: Challenges and Solutions for Equitable Learning. *Journal of Information Systems Engineering & Management, 10*(21s), 300–308. DOI: 10.52783/jisem.v10i21s.3327

Vieriu, A. M., & Petrea, G. (2025). The impact of artificial intelligence (AI) on students' academic development. *Education Sciences, 15*(3), 343. DOI: 10.3390/educsci15030343

Vistorte, A. O. R., Deroncele-Acosta, A., Ayala, J. L. M., Barrasa, A., López-Granero, C., & Martí-González, M. (2024). Integrating artificial intelligence to assess emotions in learning environments: A systematic literature review. *Frontiers in Psychology, 15*, 1387089. DOI: 10.3389/fpsyg.2024.1387089 PMID: 38966729

Viswanathan, P. S. (2025). Agentic AI: A comprehensive framework for autonomous decision-making systems in artificial intelligence. *International Journal of Computer Engineering and Technology, 16*(1), 862–880. DOI: 10.34218/IJCET_16_01_069

Vorobyeva, K. I., Belous, S., Savchenko, N. V., Smirnova, L. M., Nikitina, S. A., & Zhdanov, S. P. (2025). Personalized Learning through AI: Pedagogical Approaches and Critical Insights. *Contemporary Educational Technology, 17*(2), ep574. DOI: 10.30935/cedtech/16108

Vygotsky, L. S. (1978). *Mind in society: The development of higher psychological processes*. Harvard University Press.

Vygotsky, L. S. (1978). *Mind in Society: The Development of Higher Psychological Processes*. Harvard University Press., DOI: 10.2307/j.ctvjf9vz4

W3C. (2021). *Credentials Community Group*. Github.Io. https://w3c-ccg.github.io/meetings/2021-09-13-vc-education/

W3C. (2025). *Verifiable Credentials Overview*. In *W3.org*. https://www.w3.org/TR/vc-overview/

W3C. (n.d.). Verifiable Credentials Data Model v2.0. In www.w3.org. Retrieved July 23, 2026, from https://www.w3.org/TR/vc-data-model-2.0/

Wadesango, N. (2021). Challenges of teaching large classes. *African Perspectives of Research in Teaching and Learning, 5*(2), 127–135.

Waghale, A., Potdukhe, N., & Rewarkar, R. (2024). AI in gaming: From simple algorithms to complex agents. *In Proceedings of the 2nd DMIHER International Conference on Artificial Intelligence in Healthcare, Education and Industry* (pp. 1-5). Wardha, India: IEEE. DOI: 10.1109/IDICAIEI61867.2024.10842756

Walt.id. (2025). Verifiable Credentials: A Simple Guide to How They Work. In *Walt.id*. https://docs.walt.id/concepts/digital-credentials/verifiable-credentials-w3c

Walter, Y. (2024). Embracing the future of Artificial Intelligence in the classroom: The relevance of AI literacy, prompt engineering, and critical thinking in modern education. *International Journal of Educational Technology in Higher Education*, *21*(1), 15. DOI: 10.1186/s41239-024-00448-3

Wang, J., & Fan, W. (2025). The effect of ChatGPT on students' learning performance, learning perception, and higher-order thinking: insights from a meta-analysis. In *Humanities and Social Sciences Communications* (Vol. 12, Issue 1). DOI: 10.1057/s41599-025-04787-y

Wang, C. (2024). Using design thinking for interdisciplinary curriculum design and teaching: A case study in higher education. *Humanities & Social Sciences Communications*, *11*(1), 307. Advance online publication. DOI: 10.1057/s41599-024-02813-z

Wang, C., Wang, H., Li, Y., Dai, J., Gu, X., & Yu, T. (2025). Factors influencing university students' behavioral intention to use generative artificial intelligence: Integrating the theory of planned behavior and AI literacy. *International Journal of Human-Computer Interaction*, *41*(11), 6649–6671. DOI: 10.1080/10447318.2024.2383033

Wang, H., Luo, W., Xie, X., Zheng, P., Huang, W., & Huang, J. (2025). Adv-Inversion: Stealthy Adversarial Attacks via GAN-Inversion for Facial Privacy Protection. *IEEE Transactions on Information Forensics and Security*, *20*, 11892–11906. DOI: 10.1109/TIFS.2025.3625635

Wang, J., & Li, J. (2024). Artificial intelligence empowering public health education: Prospects and challenges. *Frontiers in Public Health*, *12*, 1389026. DOI: 10.3389/fpubh.2024.1389026 PMID: 39022411

Wang, J., Tang, Y., Hare, R., & Wang, F.-Y. (2024). Parallel intelligent education with chatgpt. *Frontiers of Information Technology & Electronic Engineering*, *25*(1), 12–18. DOI: 10.1631/FITEE.2300166

Wang, R. E., Ribeiro, A. T., Robinson, C. D., Loeb, S., & Demszky, D. (2025). Tutor CoPilot: A human-AI approach for scaling real-time expertise (EdWorkingPaper No. 24-1056). Annenberg Institute at Brown University. https://doi.org/DOI: 10.26300/81nh-8262

Wang, S., Christensen, C., Cui, W., Tong, R., Yarnall, L., Shear, L., & Feng, M. (2023). When adaptive learning is effective learning: Comparison of an adaptive learning system to teacher-led instruction. *Interactive Learning Environments*, *31*(2), 793–803. DOI: 10.1080/10494820.2020.1808794

Wang, S., Huang, S., Chien, Y., Ren, D., Li, H., Gao, Z., & Shidujaman, M. (2025). Enhancing student engagement through AI-driven embodied pedagogical agents: A comparative study informed by self-determination theory. In Kurosu, M., & Hashizume, A. (Eds.), Lecture Notes in Computer Science: Vol. 15769. *Human-Computer Interaction HCII 2025*. Springer., DOI: 10.1007/978-3-031-93861-0_13

Wang, S., Wang, F., Zhu, Z., Wang, J., Tran, T., & Du, Z. (2024). Artificial intelligence in education: A systematic literature review. *Expert Systems with Applications*, *252*, 124167. DOI: 10.1016/j.eswa.2024.124167

Wang, T., Zheng, P., Li, S., & Wang, L. (2023). Multimodal Human–Robot Interaction for Human-Centric Smart Manufacturing: A survey. *Advanced Intelligent Systems*, *6*(3), 2300359. Advance online publication. DOI: 10.1002/aisy.202300359

Wang, X., Wu, Y. C., Ji, X., & Fu, H. (2024). Algorithmic discrimination: Examining its types and regulatory measures with emphasis on US legal practices. *Frontiers in Artificial Intelligence*, *7*, 1320277. DOI: 10.3389/frai.2024.1320277 PMID: 38836021

Wang, Y. (2024). Integration of AI technology and ZPD: Pinpointing the zone of student development to promote educational innovation and efficiency improvement. *Journal of Education. Humanities and Social Sciences*, *38*, 99–104. DOI: 10.54097/wws14m21

Warrier, A. (2025). Collaborative Agentic AI for Personalized Treatment Protocol Optimization: Autonomous Clinical Decision Networks. *International Journal of Emerging Trends in Computer Science and Information Technology*, 154-164.

Webb, C., Luckin, R., & Ecoff, E. (2023). Ethical principles for the development and application of artificial intelligence in K-12 education. In *International Handbook on Education Development in the Asia-Pacific* (pp. 2501–2519). Springer Nature Singapore. DOI: 10.1007/978-981-19-6887-7_120

Wedlake, S., Iribe Ramirez, Y., Carson, K., Jowaisas, C., Keyes, D., & Houghton, M. (2021). Creating a Digital Bridge: Lessons and Policy Implications from a Technology Access and Distribution Program for Low-income Job Seekers. SSRN *Electronic Journal*. https://doi.org/DOI: 10.2139/SSRN.3898330

Wei, X., & Liu, X. (2023). Bipartite Synchronization of Multiplex Networks With Cooperative-Antagonistic Interactions. *2023 China Automation Congress (CAC)*, 7308–7312. DOI: 10.1109/CAC59555.2023.10451543

Weidener, L., & Fischer, M. (2024). Artificial intelligence in medicine: Cross-sectional study among medical students on application, education, and ethical aspects. *JMIR Medical Education*, *10*(1), e51247. DOI: 10.2196/51247 PMID: 38180787

Weidlich, J., Fink, A., Frey, A., Jivet, I., Gombert, S., Menzel, L., Giorgashvili, T., Yau, J., & Drachsler, H. (2025). Highly informative feedback using learning analytics: How feedback literacy moderates student perceptions of feedback. *International Journal of Educational Technology in Higher Education*, *22*(1), 43. DOI: 10.1186/s41239-025-00539-9

Weitekamp, D., & Koedinger, K. (2023). Computational models of learning: Deepening care and carefulness in AI in education. In *Communications in computer and information science* (pp. 13–25). Springer., DOI: 10.1007/978-3-031-36336-8_2

Wen, C. K. (2023). Creating a Trustworthy AI Tutor: A Challenge Worth Embracing or a Bite Too Big? In *Medium*. https://puddles-of-water.medium.com/creating-a-trustworthy-ai-tutor-a-challenge-worth-embracing-or-a-bite-too-big-3815f5c82de0

Westera, W., Prada, R., Mascarenhas, S., Santos, P., Dias, J., Guimarães, M., Georgiadis, K., Nyamsuren, E., Bahreini, K., Yumak, Z., Christyowidiasmoro, C., Dascalu, M., Gutu-Robu, G., & Ruseti, S. (2020). Artificial intelligence moving serious gaming: Presenting reusable game AI components. *Education and Information Technologies*, *25*(1), 351–380. DOI: 10.1007/s10639-019-09968-2

Widad, J. (2025). The Evolution of Autonomy: From Reactive AI to Agentic AI. *The Power of Agentic AI: Redefining Human Life and Decision-Making: In Industry 6.0*, 1-9.

Wijaya, T. T., Yu, Q., Cao, Y., He, Y., & Leung, F. K. S. (2024). Latent Profile Analysis of AI Literacy and Trust in Mathematics Teachers and Their Relations with AI Dependency and 21st-Century Skills. *Behavioral Sciences (Basel, Switzerland)*, *14*(11), 1008. DOI: 10.3390/bs14111008 PMID: 39594308

Wilbraham, S. J., Jones, E., Brewster, L., Priestley, M., Broglia, E., Hughes, G., & Spanner, L. (2024). Inclusion or isolation? Differential student experiences of independent learning and wellbeing in higher education. *Education Sciences*, *14*(3), 285. DOI: 10.3390/educsci14030285

Wiliam, D. (2011). *Embedded formative assessment*. Solution Tree.

Williamson, B. (2017). Who owns educational theory? Big data, algorithms and the expert power of education data science. *E-Learning and Digital Media*, *14*(3), 105–122. DOI: 10.1177/2042753017731238

Williamson, B. (2024). The social life of AI in education. *International Journal of Artificial Intelligence in Education*, *34*(1), 97–104. DOI: 10.1007/s40593-023-00342-5

Williamson, B., Macgilchrist, F., & Potter, J. (2023). Re-examining AI, automation and datafication in education. *Learning, Media and Technology*, *48*(1), 1–5. DOI: 10.1080/17439884.2023.2167830

Williamson, T. (2021). *The philosophy of philosophy*. John Wiley & Sons.

Williams, P. (2025). *Human–AI learning: Architecture of a human-agentic AI learning system*. *Preprints.org*. DOI: 10.20944/preprints202508.1351.v1

Winstone, N., & Carless, D. (2020). *Designing effective feedback processes in higher education: A learning-focused approach*. Routledge.

Wissuchek, C., & Zschech, P. (2025, June). Challenges in Managing the Relationship Between Agentic AI Systems and Humans in Organizations. In *International Conference on Business Information Systems* (pp. 3-17). Cham: Springer Nature Switzerland. DOI: 10.1007/978-3-031-94193-1_1

Woolf, B. P. (2010). *Building Intelligent Interactive Tutors: Student-centered Strategies for Revolutionizing E-learning*. Morgan Kaufmann.

World Bank. (2023). *Digital development overview: Expanding connectivity and digital access*. https://www.worldbank.org/en/topic/digitaldevelopment. Accessed April 5, 2026.

World Bank. (2023a). *Digital Progress and Trends Report*. https://www.worldbank.org/en/publication/digital-progress-and-trends-report

World Bank. (2023b). *Digital Progress and Trends Report*. https://www.worldbank.org/en/publication/digital-progress-and-trends-report

Wu, J. X., Wu, Y., Chen, K. Y., & Hua, L. (2023). Building socially intelligent AI systems: Evidence from the trust game using artificial agents with deep learning. *Management Science*, *69*(12), 7236–7252. DOI: 10.1287/mnsc.2023.4782

Wu, X. Y. (2024). Artificial Intelligence in L2 learning: A meta-analysis of contextual, instructional, and social-emotional moderators. *System*, *126*, 103498. DOI: 10.1016/j.system.2024.103498

Wu, Y., Cao, J., & Xu, G. (2023). Fairness in recommender systems: Evaluation approaches and assurance strategies. *ACM Transactions on Knowledge Discovery from Data*, *18*(1), 10. Advance online publication. DOI: 10.1145/3604558

Xiaohong, B. (2024). Transforming University Research and Education: Unleashing the Potential of Immersive Multimedia and AI-Assisted Blended Learning Through Online Gaming. *Computer-Aided Design and Applications*, *21*, 106–119. DOI: 10.14733/cadaps.2024.S5.106-119

Xia, Q., Weng, X., Ouyang, F., Lin, T. J., & Chiu, T. K. (2024). A scoping review on how generative artificial intelligence transforms assessment in higher education. *International Journal of Educational Technology in Higher Education*, *21*(1), 40. DOI: 10.1186/s41239-024-00468-z

Xia, Y., Shin, S. Y., & Lee, H. A. (2024). Adaptive learning in AI agents for the metaverse: The ALMAA framework. *Applied Sciences (Basel, Switzerland)*, *14*(23), 11410. Advance online publication. DOI: 10.3390/app142311410

Xu, A., Du, M., Yu, T., Puvvadi, M., Yu, T., Guo, Y., & Gottschlich, J. G. (2025, August). Agentic AI for Enterprise: Emerging Applications and Real-world Challenges. In *Proceedings of the 31st ACM SIGKDD Conference on Knowledge Discovery and Data Mining* V. 2 (pp. 6300-6301). DOI: 10.1145/3711896.3737871

Xu, W., & Ouyang, F. (2021). A systematic review of AI role in the educational system based on a proposed conceptual framework. *Education and Information Technologies*, *27*(3), 4195–4223. DOI: 10.1007/s10639-021-10774-y

Yadav, R., Huzooree, G., Yadav, M., & Gangodawilage, D. S. K. (2025). Generative AI for personalized learning content creation. In *Advances in computational intelligence and robotics* (pp. 107–130). IGI Global. DOI: 10.4018/979-8-3693-8744-3.ch005

Yadav, S. (2024). Artificial Intelligence (AI) Integration in Higher Education: Navigating Opportunities and Ethical Frontiers in Education with Advanced Technologies. In *Impact of artificial intelligence on society* (pp. 43-59). Chapman and Hall/CRC.

Yadav, U., & Shrawankar, U. (2025). Artificial intelligence across industries: A comprehensive review with a focus on education. *AI applications and strategies in teacher education*, 275-320.

Yagyaeva, E., Turobova, M., Nazirova, R., Daminova, Y., Merganova, N., & Oripova, N. (2024). A Layout of Bridging Learning Process to fill the Gaps Through AI to make the Technical Education for Better Access. *2024 4th International Conference on Advance Computing and Innovative Technologies in Engineering (ICACITE)*, 612–616. DOI: 10.1109/ICACITE60783.2024.10617424

Yambal, S., & Waykar, Y. A. (2025). Future of education using adaptive AI, intelligent systems, and ethical challenges. In *Advances in educational technologies and instructional design book series* (pp. 171–202). https://doi.org/DOI: 10.4018/979-8-3693-6527-4.ch006

Yang, A. (2024). Challenges and opportunities for foreign language teachers in the era of artificial intelligence. *International Journal of Education and Humanities*, *4*(1), 39–50. DOI: 10.58557/(ijeh).v4i1.202

Yang, C., Wang, T., & Xiu, Q. (2025). Towards a Sustainable Future in Education: A Systematic Review and Framework for Inclusive Education. *Sustainability (Basel)*, *17*(9), 3837. DOI: 10.3390/su17093837

Yang, H., Hu, J., Hu, S., Xu, Z., Ou, X., Geng, J., Tang, L., & Huang, T. (2026). A survey of deep learning based knowledge tracing from cognitive processing perspective. *Neurocomputing*, *660*, 131879. DOI: 10.1016/j.neucom.2025.131879

Yang, W., Hu, X., Yeter, I. H., Su, J., Yang, Y., & Lee, J. C. K. (2024). Artificial intelligence education for young children: A case study of technology-enhanced embodied learning. *Journal of Computer Assisted Learning*, *40*(2), 465–477. DOI: 10.1111/jcal.12892

Yang, W., Li, H., & Lee, J. C. (2025). Tailoring AI agents for early learning: The creative project approach. *Computers and Education: Artificial Intelligence*, *9*, 100473. Advance online publication. DOI: 10.1016/j.caeai.2025.100473

Yang, X. (2023). A historical review of collaborative learning and cooperative learning. *TechTrends*, *67*(4), 718–728. DOI: 10.1007/s11528-022-00823-9

Yang, Y., Chen, L., He, W., Sun, D., & Salas-Pilco, S. Z. (2024). Artificial intelligence for enhancing special education for K-12: A decade of trends, themes, and global insights (2013–2023). *International Journal of Artificial Intelligence in Education*, •••, 1–49.

Yannier, N., Hudson, S. E., Chang, H., & Koedinger, K. R. (2024). AI adaptivity in a mixed-reality system improves learning. *International Journal of Artificial Intelligence in Education*, *34*(4), 1541–1558. DOI: 10.1007/s40593-023-00388-5

Yellanki, S. K., Kummari, D. N., Sheelam, G. K., Kannan, S., & Chakilam, C. (2025). Synthetic Cognition Meets Data Deluge: Architecting Agentic AI Models for Self-Regulating Knowledge Graphs in Heterogeneous Data Warehousing. *Metallurgical and Materials Engineering*, *31*(4), 569–586. DOI: 10.63278/1487

Yelne, S., Chaudhary, M., Dod, K., Sayyad, A., & Sharma, R. (2023). Harnessing the Power of AI: A Comprehensive Review of Its Impact and Challenges in Nursing Science and Healthcare. *Cureus*, *15*(11), e49252. DOI: 10.7759/cureus.49252 PMID: 38143615

Yenduri, G., Kaluri, R., Rajput, D. S., Lakshmanna, K., Gadekallu, T. R., Mahmud, M., & Brown, D. J. (2023). From assistive technology to metaverse - technologies in inclusive higher education for students with specific learning difficulties: A review. *IEEE Access : Practical Innovations, Open Solutions*, *11*, 64907–64927. DOI: 10.1109/ACCESS.2023.3289496

Yılmaz, Ö. (2024). Personalised learning and artificial intelligence in science education: Current state and future perspectives. *Educational Technology Quarterly*, *2024*(3), 255–274. DOI: 10.55056/etq.744

Yim, I. H. Y. (2024). A critical review of teaching and learning artificial intelligence (AI) literacy: Developing an intelligence-based AI literacy framework for primary school education. *Computers and Education: Artificial Intelligence*, *7*, 100319. DOI: 10.1016/j.caeai.2024.100319

Yim, I. H. Y., & Su, J. (2025). Artificial intelligence (AI) learning tools in K-12 education: A scoping review. *Journal of Computers in Education, 12*(1), 93–131.

Yin, J., Zhu, Y., Goh, T.-T., Wu, W., & Hu, Y. (2024). Using Educational Chatbots with Metacognitive Feedback to Improve Science Learning. *Applied Sciences (Basel, Switzerland), 14*(20), 9345. DOI: 10.3390/app14209345

Yin, Q.-Y., Yang, J., Huang, K.-Q., Zhao, M.-J., Ni, W.-C., Liang, B., Huang, Y., Wu, S., & Wang, L. (2023). AI in Human-computer Gaming: Techniques, Challenges and Opportunities. *Machine Intelligence Research, 20*(3), 299–317. DOI: 10.1007/s11633-022-1384-6

Young, J. (2024). The rise of artificial intelligence in education. *International Journal of Innovative Research and Development, 13*(2). Advance online publication. DOI: 10.24940/ijird/2024/v13/i2/FEB24019

You, S. (2024). A qualitative case study on the implementation experience of curriculum using generative AI. *Korean Educational Research Association Journal, 62*(4), 1–26. DOI: 10.30916/KERA.62.4.1

Yuan, L., & Liu, X. (2025). The effect of artificial intelligence tools on EFL learners' engagement, enjoyment, and motivation. *Computers in Human Behavior, 162*, 108474. DOI: 10.1016/j.chb.2024.108474

Yue, B., & Li, H. (2023). The impact of human-AI collaboration types on consumer evaluation and usage intention: A perspective of responsibility attribution. *Frontiers in Psychology, 14*, 1277861. DOI: 10.3389/fpsyg.2023.1277861 PMID: 38022995

Yue, M., Jong, M. S. Y., & Ng, D. T. K. (2024). Understanding K–12 teachers' technological pedagogical content knowledge readiness and attitudes toward artificial intelligence education. *Education and Information Technologies, 29*(15), 19505–19536. DOI: 10.1007/s10639-024-12621-2

Yu, L., Li, Y., & Fan, F. (2023). Employees' Appraisals and Trust of Artificial Intelligences' Transparency and Opacity. *Behavioral Sciences (Basel, Switzerland), 13*(4), 344. DOI: 10.3390/bs13040344 PMID: 37102857

Zadorina, O., Hurskaya, V., Sobolyeva, S., Grekova, L., & Vasylyuk-Zaitseva, S. (2024). The role of artificial intelligence in creation of future education: Possibilities and challenges. *Futurity Education, 4*(2), 163–185.

Zahedi, M. H., Farahani, E., & Peymani, K. (2023). A virtual e-Learning environment model based on metaverse. *In Proceedings of the 10th International and the 16th National Conference on E-Learning and E-Teaching*, (pp. 1-7). Tehran, Iran. DOI: 10.1109/ICeLeT58996.2023.10139894

Zarei, M., Mamaghani, H. E., Abbasi, A., & Hosseini, M. S. (2024). Application of artificial intelligence in medical education: A review of benefits, challenges, and solutions. *Medicina Clínica Práctica, 7*(2), 100422. DOI: 10.1016/j.mcpsp.2023.100422

Zawacki-Richter, O., Marín, V. I., Bond, M., & Gouverneur, F. (2019). Systematic review of research on artificial intelligence applications in higher education–where are the educators? *International Journal of Educational Technology in Higher Education, 16*(1), 1–27. DOI: 10.1186/s41239-019-0171-0

Zenda, R. (2024). The importance of teaching resources on physical sciences learners' academic achievement in rural schools: A case of South Africa. *Social Education Research*, *5*(2), 407–420. DOI: 10.37256/ser.5220244624

Zhang, W., Majumdar, A., & Yadav, A. (2024). *CHAI for LLMs: Improving Code-Mixed Translation in Large Language Models through Reinforcement Learning with AI Feedback*. https://arxiv.org/pdf/2411.09073

Zhang, H., Perry, A., & Lee, I. (2025). Developing and validating the artificial intelligence literacy concept inventory: An instrument to assess artificial intelligence literacy among middle school students. *International Journal of Artificial Intelligence in Education*, *35*(1), 398–438. DOI: 10.1007/s40593-024-00398-x

Zhang, K., & Aslan, A. B. (2021). AI technologies for education: Recent research and future directions. *Computers & Education: Artificial Intelligence*, *2*, 100025. DOI: 10.1016/j.caeai.2021.100025

Zhang, Q. (2023). Secure preschool education using machine learning and metaverse technologies. *Applied Artificial Intelligence*, *37*(1), 1–25. DOI: 10.1080/08839514.2023.2222496

Zhang, S., Wang, H., & Yi, X. (2025). Exploring Collaboration Patterns and Strategies in Human-AI Co-creation through the Lens of Agency: A Scoping Review of the Top-tier HCI Literature. *Proceedings of the ACM on Human-Computer Interaction*, *9*(7), 1–43. DOI: 10.1145/3757594 PMID: 41869684

Zhang, Y., & Zhang, X. (2024). The impact of online interaction and information technology accessibility on academic engagement among international undergraduate students in chinese universities: The mediating effect of learning interest. *Acta Psychologica*, *249*, 104478. DOI: 10.1016/j.actpsy.2024.104478 PMID: 39217769

Zhao, C. (2024). AI-assisted assessment in higher education: A systematic review. *Journal of Educational Technology and Innovation*, *6*(4). Advance online publication. DOI: 10.61414/jeti.v6i4.209

Zhao, H., Chen, Y., & Liu, W. (2023). Socially responsible human resource management and employee moral voice: Based on the self-determination theory. *Journal of Business Ethics*, *183*(3), 929–946. DOI: 10.1007/s10551-022-05082-5

Zhao, Y., Zhao, M., & Shi, F. (2023). Integrating Moral Education and Educational Information Technology: A Strategic approach to enhance rural teacher training in Universities. *Journal of the Knowledge Economy*, *15*(3), 15053–15093. DOI: 10.1007/s13132-023-01693-z

Zhao, Y., & Zhong, R. (2024). Paradigm Shifts in Education: An Ecological analysis. *ECNU Review of Education*, *8*(1), 21–40. DOI: 10.1177/20965311241296162

Zheng, L., Niu, J., Zhong, L., & Yang, T. (2022). Effects of a learning analytics-based real-time feedback approach on knowledge elaboration, knowledge convergence, interactive relationships and group performance in CSCL. *British Journal of Educational Technology*, *53*(6), 1617–1637. DOI: 10.1111/bjet.13156

Zhou, R., Poechmueller, P., & Wang, Y. (2022). An Analog Circuit Design and Optimization System With Rule-Guided Genetic Algorithm. *IEEE Transactions on Computer-Aided Design of Integrated Circuits and Systems*, *41*(12), 5182–5192. DOI: 10.1109/TCAD.2022.3166637

Zhou, X., Zhang, J., & Chan, C. (2024). Unveiling students' experiences and perceptions of artificial intelligence usage in higher education. *Journal of University Teaching & Learning Practice, 21*(6), 126–145. DOI: 10.53761/xzjprb23

Zhu, H., Sun, Y., & Yang, J. (2025). Towards responsible artificial intelligence in education: a systematic review on identifying and mitigating ethical risks. *Humanities and Social Sciences Communications 2025 12:1, 12*(1), 1111-. DOI: 10.1057/s41599-025-05252-6

Zhu, C., Hsia, S.-K., Hu, X., Liu, Z., Shi, J., & Ramani, K. (2025). agentAR: Creating augmented reality applications with tool-augmented LLM-based autonomous agents. *In Proceedings of the ACM Symposium on User Interface Software and Technology* (pp. 1-23). Busan, South Korea: ACM. DOI: 10.1145/3746059.3747676

Zimmerman, B. J. (2000). Attaining self-regulation: A social cognitive perspective. In Boekaerts, M., Pintrich, P. R., & Zeidner, M. (Eds.), *Handbook of self-regulation* (pp. 13–39). Elsevier., DOI: 10.1016/B978-012109890-2/50031-7

Zimmerman, M. (2018). *Teaching AI: Exploring new frontiers for learning*. ASCD.

Zohuri, B., & Mossavar-Rahmani, F. (2024). Revolutionizing education: The dynamic synergy of personalized learning and artificial intelligence. *International Journal of Advanced Engineering and Management Research, 9*(1), 143–153. DOI: 10.51505/ijaemr.2024.9111

Zuberi, A. (2025, December 15). *How Decentralized Identifiers (DIDs) Will Transform Online Identity*. Digitap. https://digitap.app/news/guide/how-decentralized-identifiers-dids-will-transform-online-identity

Zumbach, J., Rammerstorfer, L., & Deibl, I. (2020). Cognitive and metacognitive support in learning with a serious game about demographic change. *Computers in Human Behavior, 103*, 120–129. DOI: 10.1016/j.chb.2019.09.026

About the Contributors

Momina Shaheen is an academic and researcher in computer science with over 8 years of experience in teaching and research. She currently serves as a Lecturer in Computing and Programme Leader at the University of Roehampton London. Her work focuses on edge computing, the Internet of Things, federated learning, and cybersecurity, with applications across smart cities, healthcare, finance, and education. Shaheen holds a B.Sc. in Information Technology, an M.Eng. in Software Engineering, and defended her Ph.D. in Computer Science, focusing on improving deep learning performance in federated machine learning. Her academic contributions include over 46 peer-reviewed publications in Q1 journals, multiple book chapters, and editorial work, earning her an h-index of 9 and over 400 citations. She has taught a wide range of undergraduate and postgraduate modules, including algorithms, software development, artificial intelligence, and data visualization. In addition to her teaching, she leads international collaborations and actively contributes to curriculum design, grant writing, and supervision of research projects. She also served as a reviewer for prominent journals such as Nature (under Early Career Reviewer Program), MDPI Electronics, IEEE Access, IET Information Security, Springer Scientific Reports, PLOS ONE, and ACM Transactions, and has chaired international conferences. Shaheen is committed to fostering innovation in computing education, and intelligent systems.

Jay Kumar Pandey is currently working as an Assistant Professor in the Department of Electrical & Electronics Engineering at Shri Ramswaroop Memorial University, Barabanki (U.P.) India. Dr. Pandey has completed his Ph.D. and has done his M.Tech. with specialization in Power Control (Instrumentation) and also done his MBA from Finance and Marketing. His subjects of interest are related to Artificial Intelligence, Biomedical & Healthcare, Image Processing, Machine Learning and Renewable energy. He has 15 years of teaching and research experience has published more than 30 research papers in National and International journals /conferences & Book Chapters in CRC, NOVA, Taylor & Francis, Springer and IGI Publisher. Dr. Pandey is an editor of books (edited) published by reputed publishers Apple Academy Press, IGI, Elsevier, Wiley-IEEE, NOVA, Bentham Science, IAP, Emerald Publication, Taylor & Francis & Cambridge Scholar .Dr. Pandey is also Editor of Journal of Technology Innovations and Energy United States. Dr. Pandey having reviewer in different conference/Journal/Book Chapters like (The Journal of Supercomputing in Springer Nature, IGI publishing, Journal of Security and Communication Networks Hindawi, Journal of Biomimetics, Biomaterials and Biomedical Engineering (JBBBE) Scientific Net, Switzerland, Advanced Engineering Forum (AEF) Scientific Net, Switzerland)

Faizan Ahmad is a recognized leader in the field of Computer Science, specializing in Human-computing interaction who previously led a Research Center for Human-Computer Interaction in his previous role for 5 years and published 20 high-quality research articles with in prestigious journals and conferences such as Smart Learning Environments (SMLE)(Q1), Interactive Learning

Environments (NILE)(Q1), Multimedia Tools and Applications (MTAP)(Q1), ACM PRICAI, and ACM OzCHI. He is academic editor in two Q1 journals. Currently, he is serving a research and teaching leadership role at Cardiff Metropolitan University Wales, UK. He lead research on Human-computer Interaction. He has led an international research collaboration, currently leading MoUs signing with international research institutions.

Jawad Rasheed received a B.S. degree in telecommunication engineering from the National University of Computer and Emerging Sciences, Pakistan. He then moved to Turkey, earning an M.S. degree in electrical and electronics engineering and a Ph.D. in computer engineering. He was a gold medalist and was awarded the Academic Excellence Award for securing straight A's in O' Level exams held by Cambridge University. Later, he also received a prestigious Doctorate and Research Scholarship for his Ph.D. studies (for three years). Dr. Rasheed is currently working as an Associate Professor at the Department of Computer Engineering at Istanbul Sabahattin Zaim University, Turkey. He is the author/co-author of over 60 articles published in well-reputed journals and highly-ranked conferences. He serves as editor of several reputed journals including PLoS ONE, International Journal of Computational Intelligence Systems, PLoS Digital Health, and Current Medical Imaging. He was guest/lead guest/topic editor for special issues at the Symmetry, Mathematics, Healthcare, Applied Sciences, Electronics, and Journal of Sensor and Actuator Networks. Recently, he served as a book editor for Springer Lecture Notes on Data Engineering and Communications Technologies (Forthcoming Networks and Sustainability in the IoT Era) and Lecture Notes on Network Systems (Forthcoming Networks and Sustainability in the IoT Era). In addition, he is the general chair of IEEE ICAIoT and IEEE/Springer FoNeS-AIoT and chairs the technical program committee of Springer FoNeS-IoT 2021. His research interests include artificial intelligence and image processing. pattern recognition, IoT, LLM, and data analytics.

Maqbool Khan is an Associate Professor at the American University of Bahrain (AUBH). Previously, he served as a Post-Doctoral Researcher at the Software Competence Center Hagenberg (SCCH), Austria, and as an Associate Professor at Pak-Austria Fachhochschule: Institute of Applied Sciences and Technology (PAF-IAST), Pakistan. Dr. Khan received fully funded scholarships for his MS studies at Huazhong University of Science and Technology (HUST) and PhD studies at Nanjing University in 2011 and 2013, respectively, funded by the China Scholarship Council (CSC), China. He has multidisciplinary expertise and professional experience in Big Data Analytics, Cloud Computing, Predictive Maintenance, Data Science, Artificial Intelligence, and Machine Learning. With more than 15 years of experience in both academia and industry, he has worked with multinational companies including Siemens and Atos. He is also a certified Google Cloud Professional Cloud Architect. Dr. Khan is an active researcher involved in several funded research projects with international collaborators and has contributed to research in AI-driven systems, cloud technologies, and data-intensive apps.

***

Mohammad Abu Kausar Currently serving as the Associate Professor of the Department of Information Systems and holding the vital role of College Academic Advising Officer and Media Officer, Dr. Mohammad Abu Kausar brings a wealth of experience and dedication to the academic arena. His journey at the University of Nizwa began in 2016 when he joined the College of Economics, Management, and Information Systems, leaving an indelible mark on the institution. Before assuming his current esteemed position, Dr. Mohammad Abu Kausar demonstrated versatility by working as both an Assistant Professor and a Software Engineer. This dual role showcases his comprehensive understanding of academia and practical applications in the realm of Information Systems. Dr. Mohammad Abu Kausar`s research pursuits delve into the realms of Information Retrieval, Web applications, Programming Languages, and Databases. His scholarly endeavors contribute significantly to the ever-evolving landscape of these domains. Beyond his academic endeavors, Dr. Mohammad Abu Kausar actively participates in numerous professional associations, underscoring his commitment to staying at the forefront of technological adv

Jaime Aguilar-Ortiz holds a Ph.D. in Mathematics and is a recognized researcher with an extensive academic and scientific trajectory, currently a member of Mexico's National System of Researchers. His scholarly output includes over 40 peer-reviewed research and dissemination articles, complemented by the authorship and co-authorship of more than 40 educational and scientific books across mathematics, financial education, programming, artificial intelligence, and applied technologies. He has also contributed to the creation of digital and educational resources, including academic portals, videogames, and over 100 educational films, always combining rigorous mathematical foundations with innovative applications of artificial intelligence. His current research focuses on deep tabular learning, fuzzy logic, reinforcement learning, natural language processing, and neural networks, seeking to apply cutting-edge AI methodologies to address social problems and foster technological development, while strengthening postgraduate education and research in Mexico and beyond.

Adnan Ahmad holds a BS (Hons) and MS in Computer Science from GCU and LUMS, Pakistan, respectively. He also acquired PhD in Computer Science from Massey University, Auckland, New Zealand and Post-Doc from Saint Louis University, Madrid, Spain. He has around eighteen years of teaching and research experience at various educational and research institutes. More than 67 peer-reviewed articles in renowned conferences and journals are on his credit including Trustcom, Computers & Security, ACM transactions, and IEEE Communication Magazine. He is an associate editor of 5 international journals, a reviewer of various IEEE, Elsevier, IET, and springer journals, and part of TPC of several prestigious conferences. He is also an external evaluator for National Ignite R&D fund, PITB research fund, DICE-IET, and many other international funding agencies. Moreover, he has organized multiple international workshops in Belgium, Kazakhstan, Pakistan, Portugal, and Spain. He has supervised 14 PhD, 26 MS thesis students, and several startup projects. He has also co-authored two books on emerging technologies in distributed systems. He is the founding in-charge of Center of Advance Research in Distributed Systems and Security (CARDS) research group & Cybersecurity Research Group (CSRG) at COMSATS University Islamabad, Pakistan. His research interests include Cyber Security, Digital Forensics, Penetration Testing, Distributed Systems, and Internet of things (IoT). Currently, he is performing his duties as Tenured Associate Professor at COMSATS University Islamabad, Lahore Campus, Pakistan.

Faizan Ahmad is an esteemed Senior Lecturer at the University of East London. He has been internationally recognized for his exceptional scientific achievements, holding the prestigious titles of UK's Global Talent, endorsed by The Royal Society, and UK's Academic Fellow, awarded by The Higher Education Academy. His research is driven by a passion for creating the next generation of Human-Centered AI (HCAI) systems and intelligent immersive learning technologies. His work lies at the intersection of AI, education, and human experience, where he designs personalized learning solutions that adapt intelligently to learners' needs. He has made significant contributions to developing and applying these systems in high-engagement immersive environments such as interactive Virtual Reality (VR) classrooms, Augmented Reality (AR) frameworks, and gamified learning platforms. With 10 years of overseas academic experience, his prolific research efforts have resulted in 45 research articles, with 22 published in prestigious Q1 journals. He also holds key leadership roles, including serving on the editorial boards of high-impact journals like Scientific Reports (Nature Portfolio) and Humanities & Social Sciences Communications (Springer Nature). Furthermore, he is co-editing forthcoming volumes with major publishers, including Elsevier, Springer, and Cambridge University Press.

Sohaib Ahmed is working as a Senior Lecturer in the School of Computer Science, Faculty of Innovation and Technology, Taylor's University, Malaysia. He received PhD degree from Massey University, New Zealand. In addition, he also received his PGD degree from Massey University, New Zealand with distinction. Earlier, he graduated as BS in Computer Engineering from Sir Syed University of Engineering & Technology, Karachi, Pakistan. Dr Ahmed has around 17 years of teaching and research experience. He has published more than 40 peer-reviewed articles in high-quality journals and conferences. He also voluntarily provides editorial services to various high-impact factor journals. He supervised a PhD and 14 MS students and successfully completed a couple of funded projects. He is also Certified Scrum Master (CSM). His research interests include AI in education, educational technology, AI in software engineering, gamification, and agile software development.

Vinsens is an emerging researcher affiliated with the Department of Computer Science, Esa Unggul University. His academic interests include Artificial Intelligence, Business Information Systems, Human-Technology Interaction, Social Networking, and Risk Management. Despite being an undergraduate student, he has actively engaged in collaborative research, academic writing, and scientific discussions in technology-related disciplines. He is passionate about bridging the gap between digital innovation and human behavior in organizational and societal contexts. His goal is to contribute to impactful, interdisciplinary knowledge through research and academic publishing.

Ashraf Alam is an Assistant Professor in the Department of Education at NIT Calicut, Kerala, India. He has been recognised among the *World's Top 2% Scientists* by Stanford University and Elsevier. He earned his Ph.D. from IIT Kharagpur, where his research engaged with foundational concerns in educational policy, curriculum design, educational technology, philosophy of education, innovation in education, educational administration, governance, and pedagogical transformation. His academic contributions include more than 100 Scopus-indexed publications and over 100 conference presentations delivered at national and international academic forums. His work has appeared in reputed research publication platforms including Elsevier, Springer, Taylor & Francis, CRC Press, Routledge, Atlantis Press, Springer Nature, Palgrave Macmillan, and IEEE. His work is grounded in a transdisciplinary orientation that draws from educational sciences, digital pedagogy, curriculum theory, learning analytics, sustainability education, instructional design, artificial intelligence, ethics of technology, and socio-technical studies. Dr. Ashraf's scholarship strives to interrogate and expand the boundaries of educational thought by examining the epistemological, ethical, and social dimensions of digital and post-digital pedagogies. His work critically engages with the changing nature of knowledge production, learner agency, pedagogical mediation, and institutional transformation in technologically saturated educational environments. He is particularly invested in advancing inclusive digital learning, gamified instructional strategies, AI-mediated educational ecosystems, and ethically governed technology integration in education. His research agenda is animated by the pursuit of design-oriented, ethically attuned, and contextually responsive frameworks that can support meaningful educational reform. Through his work, he seeks to contribute to the development of pedagogical models that are not only technologically innovative but also socially just, epistemically inclusive, developmentally sensitive, and aligned with the broader goals of sustainable and human-centred education.

Daniel Amoah-Oppong is a physical education teacher and researcher with over 19 years of professional experience. He is currently pursuing a PhD in physical education at the University of Cape Coast, with a specialisation in curriculum and pedagogy. He earned his master's degree in physical education from the same institution in 2022. He holds a bachelor's degree in physical education from the University of Education, Winneba (2013), and a Teacher's Certificate "A" from Enchi College of Education (2005). Professionally, he teaches physical education at Jukwa Senior High Technical School and serves as a coordinating supervisor for teaching practice at the University of Cape Coast. His work in sport also includes roles as a football referee and sports trainer. His research focuses on physical education, sports administration, and referee development. His publications examine psychological resilience among football referees and violence against second-division referees in the Central Region, including the drivers of abuse from fans, players, and coaches. He has also investigated broader social issues, such as the effects of illegal mining on sport participation and social welfare in Ghana. In addition, he co-authored Effective data visualisation for researchers: principles, tools, and applications.

Nizirwan Anwar, MT, IPM, ASEAN.Eng, APEC.Eng is a Lecturer in the Department of Informatics Engineering, Faculty of Computer Science, Universitas Esa Unggul, under the auspices of the Kemala Bangsa Education Foundation (YPKB). The author was born in the city of Bandung on July 24 1964, completed his bachelor's degree from the Physics Study Program, Faculty of Mathematics and Natural Sciences, Padjadjaran University, Bandung in 1989 and continued the Electrical Engineering Study Program, Faculty of Engineering (dh. Postgraduate Study Program) University of Indonesia, Jakarta, completing his studies in 1995, obtaining a Bachelor of Engineering Intermediate Professional (IPM) and ASEAN Engineer (ASEAN.Eng). Alhamdulillah has produced several reputable and indexed published scientific papers at national and international levels (research categories: Internet of Things, Cryptography, Bibliometrics and Data Science). To date, he is registered as active in several professional organisations, National Lecturer BKD assessor (NIRA), as a reviewer in Arjuna accredited journals (Kemendikbud Saintek), Scientific Committee, Central Executive of the Vocational Agency BKI PII,

Arockiasamy is currently an Associate Professor in Information Systems and Assistant Dean of College of Economics Management and Information Systems, University of Nizwa, Sultanate of Oman. He has 35 years of experience in Teaching, Research, and Community Services including 7 years of experience as a Dean of College of Economics Management and Information Systems, University of Nizwa, Sultanate of Oman. Dr. Arockiasamy obtained his MPhil and PhD in Computer Science from Bharathiar University, Coimbatore, INDIA. Prior to that, he obtained an MSc. in Computer Science from Bharathidasan University, Tiruchirappalli, INDIA. His main expertise and research interests are in the field of image processing, Blockchain technology, and data mining. He is also involved in various funded research projects inside and outside Oman. He has published over 70 research papers in international journals and conferences and also published three booklets on Information Technology and published four book chapters as well. He has been invited as a Keynote Speaker in the number of

International and NationalConferences in India and abroad. He is a recognized 'PhD. Research Supervisor' from universities in India and abroad. Four Research Scholars have already completed their PhD. in Computer Science under his supervision. He has been acting as an external examiner to evaluate the PhD. thesis of many Universities from India. Dr. Arockiasamy was serving as an external reviewer of various National / InternationalJournals. He is also serving as an External Advisory Committee member for many international conferences organized in India and Oman. Dr. Arockiasamy was a popular writer in a well-established Tamil Newspaper "Daily Thanthi" for more than 7 years and published more than 400 articles from March 2004 to December 2010. Dr. Arockiasamy joined the faculty of Information Systems at the University of Nizwa in 2007. Prior to his current position, he worked at a college affiliated to Bharathiar University since 1990. He was a Professor and Director, Department of Computer Science and Applications for 17 years in a reputed institution in India.

Murathoti Rajendra Nath babu, holds a Post Graduate degrees in Mathematics, Sociology, Psychology, English and Education (M.Ed.-University 1st Rank), M. Phil. and obtained Ph.D. in Education from Sri Venkateswara University. Presently he is working as an Associate Professor in the Department of Education, Nagaland University (A Central University). He has 15 years research and teaching experience at B.Ed., M.Ed., M.A.(Education), Ph.D. levels. He has successfully guided 60 M.Ed./M.A. degree dissertations, 2 M.Phil. Degrees and 4 Ph.D. Degrees and at present 6 Ph.D. Scholars working under his guidance. He has presented more than 70 papers at national and international seminars, conferences and workshops. For his credit, from 2015, he has published 26 articles in various national and international journals including UGC Care Listed, Scopus & Web of Sciences, 9 books, 11 book chapters. He has cleared UGC NET with JRF Education in 2009 Teacher Eligibility Test (APTET) Paper-I & Paper-II in July 2011 & January 2012, AP DSC (District Selection Committee)-TRT (Teacher Recruitment) Mathematics for the Post of School Assistant in mathematics post (2nd Rank) in 2012 and also Departmental Tests Accounts Tests like Executive Officers (141), Gazetted Officers of Education Department (88,97) in 2013. He got Junior Research Fellow (UGC) award in 2009, senior research Fellow (UGC) in 2012 and in 2012 DSC. Having Administrative Experience as Teacher-in-charge, Department of Teacher Education, Warden, Ramei Men's Hostel, Convener, Nagaland State Education Common Entrance Test (NSEDCET)-2019 & 2020. He has Completed 2 Research Projects funded by PMMMNMTT(MHRD) Scheme, Ministry of Education, New Delhi, Nagaland Education Mission Society, Government of Nagaland & 1 Research Project ongoing funded by ICSSR, New Delhi.

Bartholomeus Dimanche Carl Beth is a computer science enthusiast with a strong interest in research and academic writing. His expertise lies in writing scientific journals and exploring topics related to technology, data systems, and innovation in computing. With a passion for continuous learning, he aims to contribute to the advancement of knowledge in the field of computer science through high-quality research and publications.

Sandip Chakraborty is an Assistant Professor in the Department of Computational Sciences at Brainware University, Kolkata, India. His teaching and research interests span artificial intelligence and machine learning, human–computer interaction, self-service technologies, AI-driven wellness technologies, web accessibility, and the use of natural language processing for sustainability and corporate governance. He actively mentors student projects in IoT and data-driven applications and contributes book chapters and journal articles in these domains.

Sovannaroth Chheang earned her bachelor's degree in English from Build Bright University, Phnom Penh, in 2016, where she built a solid foundation in language studies, communication, and pedagogy. She began her teaching career in 2013 as a Tutor at the Kindergarten Association, conducting both part-time and full-time English programs. Since 2018, she has served as a Teacher of English and General Assistant at Sovanna Elton Foreign Language School. Through these roles, she has developed broad expertise in classroom management, language instruction, curriculum design, and student engagement, supporting the school's mission of advancing foreign language learning. Ms. Chheang's academic interests center on pursuing a master's degree in English education or related fields within the humanities and social sciences. Passionate about integrating global research methodologies into her practice, she aims to enhance pedagogy, foster classroom innovation, and promote effective, research-informed teaching. Her commitment lies in bridging academic research with real-world practice to advance English education in Cambodia and beyond.

Devaki V serves as an Assistant Professor at the Department of Education (SASHE), SASTRA Deemed to be University, Thanjavur. She holds a Master of Science in Physics from Alagappa University, Karaikudi, graduating with the distinction of second rank in the university. Additionally, she completed her Master of Education at Sri Sarada College of Education, Salem, Tamil Nadu. She qualified for the position of Assistant Professor in Physics and Education, having successfully cleared the Tamil Nadu State Eligibility Test and also passed the Central Teacher Eligibility Test. She has completed her doctoral studies in the Department of Education at Bharathidasan University, Tiruchirappalli. Her research interests encompass metacognition, neurocognition, the pedagogy of science, and experiential learning.

Ocotlán Diaz-Parra is a Professor and Researcher at Universidad Politécnica de Pachuca (UPP), a National Researcher under the Secretaria de Ciencia, Humanidades, Tecnología e Innovación program, and an Adjunct Researcher at the National Laboratory of Autonomous Vehicles and Exoskeletons (LANAVEX). His research interests include Smart Cities, Smart Water, Smart Education, Smart Government, Smart Healthcare, Smart Farming, Smart Energy, Smart Sports, Smart Food, Smart Tourism, Algorithmic Finance, Algorithmic Portfolio Management, Applications and Theory of Algorithms, Bio-inspired Algorithms, Combinatorial Optimization Problems, Compilers, Computational Intelligence, Computational Complexity Theory, Computational Financial Intelligence, Complexity of Algorithms, Complexity of Instances, Computational Statistics, Computer Networks, Computer Science Security, Cybercrimes, Data Mining, Education, Evolutionary Computation, Heuristic Optimization Techniques in Bioinformatics, Hybrid Evolutionary Algorithms, Hybrid Optimization Algorithms, Machine Learning, Meta-heuristics, Operations Research, Operations Management, Parallel & Distributed Computing, Production Planning and Logistics Optimization, Project Scheduling Problems, Software Engineering, and Transgenic Algorithms.

Carlos R. Domínguez-Mayorga holds a Ph.D. in Sciences specializing in Artificial Intelligence, with a foundational background in Physics and Mathematics. His research focuses on Deep Learning, NLP, neural networks, and the development of predictive models. He has an extensive track record in scientific publications and graduate program management, applying cutting-edge data science techniques to engineering and sustainability projects.

Gourab Dutta has done BTech and MTech in computer science. He has a long experiences of teaching in several colleges . He has also published many articles and book chapters in different reputed publications.He is currently working as assistant professor in department of Computational; Sciences, Brainware University,

Sallam Osman Fageeri is an Associate Professor at the College of Economics, Management & Information Systems (CEMIS) at University of Nizwa. he obtained his M.sc and PhD in information technology from Sikkim Manipal University India and Universiti Teknologi PETRONAS Malaysia respectively. he is an Associate Professor and former Dean of Faculty of Computer Science and Information Technology, Al-zaiem Alazhari University, Khartoum, Sudan. His main research interests are on Computational Intelligence, machine learning and mobile computing.

Kaneez Fatima Sadriwala Associate Professor in Accounting, A/Head Department of Accounting, College of Economics Management and Information Systems, University of Nizwa Dr. Kaneez Fatima works in the field of Accounting, Business Statistics and Marketing, Her research span is multidisciplinary, spreading from - Financial Analysis, Accounting for SMEs, Artificial Intelligence,E-Learning, Entrepreneurship, student's learning process and measurement of learning outcome to Accounting Ontology, Bibliometic Analysis by Vosviewer etc. She, along with her student team won TRC (The Research Council, Oman) awards twice for best research project, one in year 2015, followed by another in year 2018. She has published two books, 'Marketing Management' and 'Mall Management' from Himalaya Publishers, with several research papers on national and international platforms. She is a renowned orator and has represented the university on various international platforms. Dr. Kaneez Fatima received her Master's in Commerce (Accounting and Business Statistics) in 1991 and Ph.D. degree in Commerce from Mohanlal Sukhadia university, Udaipur, India in 2004, and FDP from Indian Institute of Management (IIMA), India in 2009 and served as Professor cum Director at Aravali Institute of Management, Udaipur, India prior to joining University of Nizwa in February 2010.

Rahul Kumar Ghosh is an esteemed academic and assistant professor at Brainware University, Kolkata. With a rich history in computer science and education, he holds a Master of Science (M.Sc.) in Applied Statistics and Analytics from Maulana Abul Kalam Azad University of Technology, West Bengal, another Master's degree in Information Technology and a Doctor of Philosophy (Ph.D.) from Seacom Skills University, West Bengal. His thesis, titled "Digitalization of Education Credentials Using PERMANENT EDUCATION NUMBER: An Empirical Approach Towards Greener Environment" reflects his interests in the intersection of education, technology, and environmental sustainability. He has also qualified for NET-UGC in the subject of computer science and application, earning the Junior Research Fellowship (JRF) position. Dr. Ghosh is a Microsoft Certified Technology Specialist (Database Administrator) and has completed various courses in database management systems and programming. His dedication to research and academia is reflected in his numerous publications in esteemed journals and conferences. He has presented research papers on various topics, including knowledge management, digital

Leila Goosen is a full professor in the Department of Science and Technology Education of the University of South Africa. She holds a C2 rating via the South African National Research Foundation. Prof. Goosen was an Associate Professor in the School of Computing, and the module leader and head designer of the fully online signature module for the College for Science, Engineering and Technology, rolled out to over 92,000 registered students since the first semester of 2013. She usually supervises around ten Masters and Doctoral students, and has successfully completed supervision of 43 students at postgraduate level. Previously, she was a Deputy Director at the South African national Department of Education. In this capacity, she was required to develop ICT strategies for implementation. Before that, she had been a lecturer of Information Technology (IT) in the Department for Science, Mathematics and Technology Education in the Faculty of Education of the University of Pretoria. Her research interests have included cooperative work in IT, effective teaching and learning of programming and teacher professional development.

Hind Hammouch holds a Ph.D. in Economics and Management from the Faculty of Legal, Economic, and Social Sciences (FSJES) at Sidi Mohamed Ben Abdellah University in Fez, Morocco. She currently serves as a Professor at the Institute for Training in Offshoring Professions in ICT and Audiovisual Sectors (IFMOTICA) in Fez and as a lecturer at FSJES Fez, where she teaches undergraduate and graduate-level courses. Her research interests span corporate social responsibility (CSR), (Environmental, Social, and Governance) ESG, management control systems, organizational and financial performance, as well as the integration of artificial intelligence in sustainable development. Dr. Hammouch has authored and co-authored numerous peer-reviewed articles published in Scopus-indexed journals, as well as scholarly book chapters with IGI Global and other international academic publishers. Her academic contributions also include editorial board memberships and peer-review engagements with several reputable international journals and conferences. With a multidisciplinary background and a strong commitment to applied research, Dr. Hammouch's work contributes to bridging the gap between theory and practice in emerging areas of management, sustainability, and digital innovation.

Sovanna HUOT is a scholar, currently pursuing a Ph.D. in Political Science at the University of Delhi, India, under a prestigious ICCR scholarship (2022). He serves as the Vice Principal of a government-recognized high school in Cambodia, where he actively leads academic innovation and institutional development. Sovanna's academic journey reflects a breadth of interdisciplinary expertise. He completed a two-year teacher training program (2010–2012) and holds bachelor's degrees in English and Educational Administration. His postgraduate achievements include master's degrees in law and TEFL, both earned through competitive scholarship programs, and a Master of Education in School Leadership with a specialization in Upper Secondary School Principalship from the National Institute of Education, Phnom Penh (2021). His research centers on educational reform, digital pedagogy, and the intersection of policy and practice in glonacal (global–national–local) contexts. With a growing portfolio of peer-reviewed publications, he contributes actively to the fields of political science and education. His scholarly work is indexed in Scopus (Author ID: 59316244400).

Jennie Lee Khun is an adjunct professor for Purdue Global University and National University. Prior to completing her Doctorate in Strategic Leadership she worked for Shepherd University as an IT Business Analyst and later IT Operations and Project Manager. Jennie received her MBA from Shepherd and her undergraduate IT degree from Kaplan University. She currently works as the NIH OD CIO with the United States Federal government and holds industry certifications including CISSP, PMP, PMI-ACP, and ITILv4. Jennie grew up a military brat and cites that upbringing for her love of travel. She enjoys swimming, baking, and playing board games.

Ryan Putra Laksana is a lecturer at the Faculty of Computer Science, Universitas Esa Unggul, Indonesia. He has extensive experience in teaching and research related to Information Technology, with a particular focus on the Internet of Things (IoT), project management, and other IT-related subjects. His academic interests include the development of intelligent systems, the integration of IoT in modern infrastructures, and the application of agile methodologies in IT project management. Ryan actively engages in research and collaborative projects aimed at advancing digital innovation and technology adoption in education and industry. His dedication to fostering technological literacy and developing practical IT solutions reflects his commitment to bridging the gap between academic research and real-world implementation.

Mahammad Ali Sunkesula is a PGT-Physics at AP Model School and Jr. College, Amarapuram, Sri Sathya Sai District, Andhra Pradesh. He holds multiple Master's degrees in Philosophy, Physics, Telugu, and Education from various universities in Andhra Pradesh. He earned his Master of Philosophy in Education from Periyar University, Salem, Tamil Nadu, and his Doctoral research degree in Philosophy of Education from Dravidian University, Kuppam, under the expert guidance of Prof. Balaganapathi Devarakonda. Dr. Mahammad Ali has a rich and diverse experience in academic writing, teaching, translation, statistical analysis, and research. He has worked as a Junior Linguist and Project Fellow in notable projects such as ILCI and UGC. This experience has enabled him to author, co-author, and edit 17 books/reference materials and 10 research papers. He also completed Post-Doctoral research at Dr. BR Ambedkar Open University, Hyderabad, Telangana, under the guidance of Prof. MTV Nagaraju. Prior to his current role, he served as an Assistant Professor and Principal in various education colleges across five Indian states.

Muhammad Faraz Manzoor is an Assistant Professor in the Department of Artificial Intelligence at the University of Management and Technology. He holds a Ph.D. in Computer Science and conducts research in machine learning, deep learning, and natural language processing. His work focuses on developing advanced computational models and algorithms that address real-world challenges in artificial intelligence, combining theoretical rigor with practical applications to enhance both academic understanding and technological innovation.

Muhammad Virga Mulia is a Software Engineer specializing in the development of reliable, efficient, and scalable software solutions. He possesses strong technical expertise in Java, JavaFX, Laravel, MySQL, and Node-RED, with practical experience in IoT-based systems and data warehouse design. His work emphasizes secure communication, system optimization, and architectural precision. With a commitment to continuous learning and innovation, he aims to contribute to the advancement of technology through high-quality engineering and data-driven development

Mohammad Nasar is an Assistant Professor and Head of the Department of Computer Science at Mazoon College, Oman, affiliated with Missouri University of Science and Technology, USA. With over 15 years of teaching and research experience, his areas of expertise include artificial intelligence, machine learning, deep learning, and data analytics. He has published extensively in Scopus- and IEEE-indexed journals and conferences, authored a book, filed a patent, and received national-level research funding. He also serves as a reviewer and advisory board member for various international journals.

Junaid Nasir Qureshi is an impact-driven technologist and academic leader whose career spans over 17 years, sharply divided between significant contributions to the software industry and advanced academic research. Holding a Ph.D. in Computer Science from the University of Management and Technology, Lahore, Pakistan, he possesses a rare and powerful combination of 10 years of intensive industry experience and over 7 years of dedicated service in academia. Currently, Dr. Qureshi is a dynamic Assistant Professor in the Department of Computer Science at Bahria University, Lahore Campus (BULC). In this role, he is not only shaping the next generation of computing professionals through rigorous teaching and mentorship but is also aggressively pursuing cutting-edge research to advance the field. His career is defined by his proven ability to seamlessly translate theoretical knowledge into real-world applications, effectively closing the gap between the classroom and the computing frontier. His diverse and high-impact research portfolio is focused on the most critical emerging technologies, including: • Blockchain Technology: Pioneering the exploration of decentralized applications

Rabie A. Ramadan is a Full Professor at the University of Nizwa, Oman, and is affiliated with the Computer Engineering Department at Cairo University, Egypt. He holds a Ph.D. in Computer Science and Engineering from Southern Methodist University (SMU), USA. His research interests include IoT, Security, Wireless Sensor Networks, Computational Intelligence, and Brain–Computer Interfaces, with over 140 publications in leading journals and conferences. Prof. Ramadan has led major funded projects, including collaborations with CERN, FP7, and ITEA, and has founded several advanced research labs. He also serves as a reviewer for top agencies such as the EU Research Council and NSF.

Osama Rehman is a Senior Lecturer at School of Computer Science, Taylor's University, Malaysia. He received his B.S. in Computer Engineering and M.S. in Network Engineering, both from Sir Syed University of Engineering and Technology, Pakistan, followed by his Ph.D. in Electrical & Computer Engineering from Sultan Qaboos University, Oman. He served as a faculty member and Head of Department at the Department of Software Engineering, Bahria University, Pakistan. Prior to that, he worked as a Postdoctoral Researcher and as a Research Assistant, both at Sultan Qaboos University – Oman. Dr. Rehman has 40+ research publications, and his current research interests are mainly related to AI in Cybersecurity, Internet of Things, and Connected Vehicles. Dr. Rehman supervised and produced several research scholars and has worked on several funded research projects pertaining to cybersecurity for cyber-physical systems, vehicular networks and EM radiations measurement and analysis. Dr. Rehman also possesses expertise in accreditation processes for computing programs, academic administration and mentorship skills of junior academicians. Dr. Rehman has also got elevated to the rank of senior member IEEE and is a lifetime member of the Pakistan Engineering Council.

Jorge A. Ruiz-Vanoye is a Professor and Researcher at Universidad Politécnica de Pachuca (UPP), a National Researcher under the Secretaria de Ciencia, Humanidades, Tecnología e Innovación program, and an Adjunct Researcher at the National Laboratory of Autonomous Vehicles and Exoskeletons (LANAVEX). Additionally, he holds the title of Lecturer-level Researcher for the Agency for the Quality of the University System of Catalonia (Generalitat de Catalunya). His research interests include Smart Cities, Smart Water, Smart Education, Smart Government, Smart Healthcare, Smart Farming, Smart Energy, Smart Sports, Smart Food, Smart Tourism, Algorithmic Finance, Algorithmic Portfolio Management, Applications and Theory of Algorithms, Bio-inspired Algorithms, Combinatorial Optimization Problems, Compilers, Computational Intelligence, Computational Complexity Theory, Computational Financial

Intelligence, Complexity of Algorithms, Complexity of Instances, Computational Statistics, Computer Networks, Computer Science Security, Cybercrimes, Data Mining, Education, Evolutionary Computation, Heuristic Optimization Techniques in Bioinformatics, Hybrid Evolutionary Algorithms, Hybrid Optimization Algorithms, Machine Learning, Meta-heuristics, Operations Research, Operations Management, Parallel & Distributed Computing, Production Planning and Logistics Optimization, Project Scheduling Problems, Software Engineering, and Transgenic Algorithms.

Ratan Sarkar is an Assistant Professor in the Department of Education, Tezpur University (A Central University), Assam, India. Previously, he served nearly seven years as Assistant Professor in the Department of Teachers' Training (B.Ed.), Prabhat Kumar College, Contai (Vidyasagar University), and as Guest Faculty at National Institute for Empowerment of Persons with Intellectual Disabilities, Regional Centre, Kolkata. He holds a Ph.D. in Education from Pondicherry University, an M.Ed. and M.Phil. in Special Education from Ramakrishna Mission Vivekananda Educational and Research Institute, Belur Math, and an M.A. in Education and Technology from Tata Institute of Social Sciences, Mumbai. He began his academic journey with a B.Ed. in Special Education (Jadavpur University) and a B.A. in English (Hons) from Siliguri College (University of North Bengal), Darjeeling. Dr. Sarkar has published extensively in leading journals (SAGE, Springer, Routledge, Wiley), authored books, chapters, and reviews, and led projects under the Ministry of Education, Govt. of India. His works on inclusive education, EdTech, disability studies, policy advocacy to advance equitable learning ecosystems.

Chinna Suresh is an Assistant Professor in the Department of Education at the School of Arts, Sciences, Humanities, and Education (SASHE), SASTRA Deemed to be University, Thanjavur, Tamil Nadu, India. He earned his Ph.D. in Education from Sri Venkateswara University, Tirupati, Andhra Pradesh, in 2018, and his M.Sc. in Mathematics from Sri Krishnadevaraya University, Anantapur, Andhra Pradesh, in 2010. His research interests include ICT in Education, Mathematics Pedagogy, Gender Studies, and Teaching Strategies.

Francisco Rafael Trejo-Macotela received the PhD degree in Electronics from the National Institute of Astrophysics, Optics and Electronics (INAOE), Puebla, Mexico. He is a Certified LabVIEW Associate Developer (CLAD) accredited by National Instruments and holds professional competence certifications in the EC0477 and EC0217 standards issued by the National Council for Standardisation and Certification of Competencies (CONOCER). He is currently Professor and Researcher in the Master's programmes in Mechatronics and Information and Communication Technologies, and the PhD programme in Advanced Science and Technology, at the Polytechnic University of Pachuca (UPP), Mexico. During his academic career at UPP, he has held several leadership positions, including Director of Mechatronics Engineering (2007–2009), Director of Research, Innovation and Postgraduate Studies (2015–2023), and Coordinator of the Master's Programme in Information and Communication Technologies (2023–2024). He also served as Professor and Researcher in the Departments of Mechatronics (2006–2007) and Telematics (2009–2015). He has contributed to numerous research and innovation projects and has participated in more than eight evaluation processes for master's and doctoral programmes within the National Postgraduate System (SNP) of the Secretariat of Science, Humanities, Technology and Innovation (SECIHTI). He is an Adjunct Researcher at the SECIHTI National Laboratory for Autonomous Vehicles and Exoskeletons (LANAVEX). He currently serves as an evaluator for the Interinstitutional Committees for the Evaluation of Higher Education (CIEES), the Engineering Education Accreditation Council

(CACEI–COPAES), and the Higher Education Evaluation and Accreditation System (SEAES) through the Peer Registry for Diagnostic and Formative Evaluation (REPEV) of the Mexican Ministry of Public Education (SEP). In 2019, he served as an External Peer Evaluator for the accreditation of Ecuadorian universities and polytechnic institutions under the Higher Education Quality Assurance Council (CACES). He has also acted as a peer evaluator for postgraduate programmes within the National Postgraduate System (SNP) and as a project evaluator for the Innovation Incentives Programme (PEI) of SECIHTI. He is currently a Level 1 member of the National System of Researchers (SNI) of SECIHTI. His research interests include Integrated Circuit Design, Analogue and Digital Electronics, Automation, Embedded Systems, Cyber-physical Systems, Internet of Things, Telecommunications, Smart Cities, Smart Water, Precision Agriculture, Educational Technology, Artificial Intelligence, Machine Learning, Autonomous Navigation, and Optimisation.

Index

A

B

C

D

E

F

G

H

I

L

M

O

P

R

S

T

V

www.ingramcontent.com/pod-product-compliance
Lightning Source LLC
LaVergne TN
LVHW060252011026
849161LV00011B/2702